THE DIARIES OF AUGUSTUS GRIFFIN

Diary, Vol. I, index
Diary, Vol. I, page 218
Two pages from the original manuscript of the Diaries, both from Volume I. Augustus Griffin often made his own index (above), and he frequently augmented entries, sometimes years later, offering additional information and commentary (below).
Courtesy of The Brooklyn Historical Society.

Augustus Griffin
Lithograph by Savony, Major & Knapp, NY, 1857 (facing).

THE DIARIES OF
Augustus Griffin

~

1792–1852

Edited, with an introduction by

FREDRICA WACHSBERGER

Foreword by Natalie A. Naylor

OYSTERPONDS HISTORICAL SOCIETY
Orient, New York

Grateful acknowledgment is made to the following organizations whose
generous support made this publication possible: InterAmericas®/Society of
Arts and Letters of the Americas, a program of The Reed Foundation,
and Furthermore: a program of the J. M. Kaplan Fund.

The Diaries of Augustus Griffin, 1792-1852 is published in paperback
and in a deluxe hardcover edition limited to 150 numbered copies.

OYSTERPONDS HISTORICAL SOCIETY
P.O. Box 70
Orient, New York 11957

Library of Congress Control Number: 2009924382

ISBN: 978-0-9785247-3-9, deluxe hardcover
ISBN: 978-0-9785247-4-6, paperback

Designed and typeset in Minion by Rita Lascaro
Printed on acid-free paper by Maple-Vail Book Manufacturing, York, Pennsylvania

First Edition

CONTENTS

VOLUME II

ILLUSTRATIONS

FOREWORD

AUGUSTUS GRIFFIN is the preeminent historian of Oysterponds—today's Orient and East Marion. Griffin was born in Southold in 1767 and lived in Orient most of his ninety-nine years. Since it was published in 1857, Augustus Griffin's *Journal* has been an important record of the history and family genealogies of Long Island's North Fork. This *Diaries of Augustus Griffin, 1792-1852* provides Griffin's original diaries and includes excerpts from a diary he prepared for his daughter Cleora in 1850 in Appendix A. The manuscripts of the handwritten diaries have been meticulously transcribed and edited by Fredrica Wachsberger.

Griffin's *Diaries* provide a unique insight into his life, his community, and his times. Diaries are an important primary source for historians, recording first-hand observations and descriptions of people and events. A number of Long Island manuscript diaries have been preserved. The largest number is in East Hampton Library's Pennypacker Long Island collection; public libraries on the North Fork also own some. None covers as long a period as Augustus Griffin's, which spans sixty years. In addition, his "Diary for Cleora" includes some of his memories of earlier years. Diaries today are most often associated with women. Indeed, the other Long Island diaries that have been published are by a grandmother in Oyster Bay (*The Diary of Mary Cooper: Life on a Long Island Farm, 1768-1773*, 1981) and a young girl in Center Moriches (*Nettie's Diary: The 1880s Diary of Nettie Ketcham*, 1995).

Augustus Griffin married Lucretia Tuthill (probably in 1791, though in none of these diaries does he mention their wedding or anniversary). The Griffins enjoyed a long and happy marriage. They had seven children, six of whom survived to adulthood (Appendix C has information on their children). Lucretia is not prominent in the *Diaries*, however, except when they are apart, as sometimes when he is teaching, or when she is away. Then he writes how much he misses her. He refers to her as Mrs. G. and does mention her when she is ill, gives birth, or accompanies him on a visit. Doubtless, however, Lucretia Griffin was a full partner in the operation of their inn, cooking, cleaning, laundering, and providing other aspects of housekeeping for guests and boarders. (Mary Cooper had so many visitors that her diary gives a glimpse of what Lucretia

Griffin experienced with paying guests decades later. See also Wendy Gamber's *The Boardinghouse in Nineteenth-Century America* for the exhausting work involved.) The only mention of hired help is in 1846 when "Miss Jane Terry" was engaged "to assist us in housework" (II: 339 [310]). After his wife dies in 1849 at the age of eighty, Griffin pours out his grief in the *Diaries*. He does not attempt to continue operating the inn after her death.

Griffin recounts his family's experiences during the American Revolution in his "Diary for Cleora." He also recounts the heroism of Long Island women during the Revolution in his published *Journal*.

It is useful background to the *Diaries* to quote here two descriptions of Orient by outsiders, which are included in my book, *Journeys on Old Long Island* (2002). The first is by Timothy Dwight, president of Yale College, who passed through Orient on a journey to Long Island in 1804 and described the community:

> The parish of Oysterponds . . . is only one mile in breadth, but is populous. The land is good, and the people are industrious and thrifty. A considerable number of the inhabitants are fishermen. The agriculture has lately been much improved, but the people suffer not a little from ecclesiastical contentions. It contains a Presbyterian church and has a settled minister, but there are many sectaries [sectarians or religious dissenters]. The houses are about as numerous as in Southold and of as good an appearance (*Journeys*, p. 77).

The second reference occurs in *Historical Collections of the State of New York* (1842), by John W. Barber and Henry Howe, in which the authors devote only one sentence to Orient: "The peninsula of Oyster Ponds is the eastern extremity of the island; the village, now called Orient, contains two churches, two docks or wharves, and upwards of 500 inhabitants" (*Journeys*, p. 187; Barber and Howe devote greater attention to Greenport, which had grown rapidly to become the largest community in the Town of Southold).

Griffin begins his *Diaries* when he is twenty-six years old, married with a young daughter, and teaching school in Blooming Grove in Orange County, New York. Many relatives and friends from Oysterponds had settled in the area. Griffin's most frequent comments are on the weather, whether rain or snow, cold or hot, windy or pleasant. On many days, his entry is limited to a report on the weather. He also records births, deaths, and marriages. Visiting people was one of the most popular leisure-time activities of the day, and Griffin frequently describes visits to and from acquaintances.

Griffin's *Diaries* provide insight into teaching and schooling in the years before New York State mandated tax-supported schools in 1812. Families in Blooming Grove and the other communities where he taught joined to hire a teacher. As was fairly typical at that time, Griffin taught in a number of different locations. Teachers were usually engaged for quarter sessions of three months. At the end of the quarter, Griffin settled accounts with the parents of his students. The schoolhouses where he taught, like most in rural areas, were one room, and students of varying ages were enrolled. When he had in his class "large boys" in their early twenties, it was unusual enough for him to note in his diary (I: 5 [6]).

One might wish for details about his "keeping school," but Griffin seldom reports more than the number of scholars—at times forty or fifty—or that his school was "crowded." At the end of a session, schools often had an exhibition for parents when students would recite poems and demonstrate what they had learned. Griffin does occasionally mention an exhibition. Schoolmasters needed to be able to make quill pens, using a (pen) knife. Handwriting was an important skill, and Griffin's manuscript is evidence of the quality of his cursive writing (see sample pages from his *Diaries* on p. 408).

Teaching at that time was rarely a life-long career. Griffin taught off and on for twenty years of his early adulthood, but during most of that time he also farmed, kept animals, clammed, and even operated a store in Orient. Eventually he concentrated on running an inn but probably continued some farming and fishing.

Religion is a pervasive aspect of life during Griffin's time, and the *Diaries* reflect Griffin's strong religious views. Many of his diary entries indicate that he is very familiar with the Bible. In the list of his reading in 1844 and 1845 (included here in Appendix B-II), Griffin indicates that he read the Bible through twice in those two years. Many religious books are in the 1839 inventory of his library (included in Appendix B-I), and they predominate in his reading in 1844–1845.

Interestingly, in the early part of the *Diaries,* he does not often mention attending church. When he was in Orange County, he may have lived at a distance from a church. In 1796, he mentions the three and one-half mile distance to the church in Goshen as "a good excuse of [not] attending meeting." He added, "However if we improve our time as we ought, it matters not much where we are on the Sabbath" (I: 35 [84]). On some Sundays, he mentions reading Jonathan Edwards's *History of Redemption* or other religious works. In later years in Orient, where the church was close, he attended religious services more often. Griffin takes note of religious revivals and religious camp meetings (outdoor revival services) nearby in Jamesport.

Many Long Islanders in the late eighteenth and nineteenth centuries moved west to less settled land upstate, in New Jersey, or other areas further west. Some from Oysterponds and the eastern end of the island settled in Orange County. Griffin built one house there and bought another, but he did not stay, despite having relatives and friends in the area.

In the early years of the *Diaries,* while living in Orange County, Griffin makes a number of trips back to Long Island. After settling in Orient, though living more than a hundred miles from New York City, he is not isolated and travels to the city fairly often, sometimes seeking better economic opportunities. When Griffin is operating his store or inn, he is literally at the center of local village life. Community celebrations on the Fourth of July and Washington's Birthday are often at the inn. When in 1844 the Long Island Railroad reaches Greenport (ten miles west of Orient), it greatly facilitates travel, shortening the time to New York City from several days to a few hours. (The railroad was built to be a short cut to Boston, via a steamer to Connecticut, when it seemed that a railroad could not transverse the many hills and rivers in Connecticut.) Griffin takes advantage of the railroad to travel to New York City, and to visit his daughter and her family in Williamsburgh. He is even able to go to Hempstead and return the same day.

Twenty-first-century readers can identify with Griffin's concern about growth and change in Orient and nearby Greenport. He notes that what had been a five-hundred-acre farm in Orient has eleven or twelve families living there in 1845. (See also the selection in Appendix A on Greenport's growth.)

Griffin's *Diaries* provides detailed information on life in rural New York in the early national and antebellum years. Whether in Orange County in the 1790s or in Orient in the nineteenth century, the social life and customs he describes are typical of much of upstate New York and Long Island through the first half of the nineteenth century. The Oysterponds Historical Society is to be congratulated for publishing *The Diaries of Augustus Griffin.* Long Island historians and others interested in local history will benefit from this primary source.

Poet John Orville Terry of Oysterponds composed a poem in the late 1840s entitled "Augustus Griffin, Esq." (p. xxiv). It begins, "I know an old gentleman, fully fourscore, / Who yet seems among us as young as of yore—" and includes among its lines, "his friends are delighted to sit, / To feast on his lore and regale on his wit." Readers today can "feast on his lore" and will delight in making the acquaintance of this interesting man, his family, neighbors, and community through his *Diaries.*

Natalie A. Naylor
Long Island Historian
Professor Emerita, Hofstra University

ACKNOWLEDGMENTS

THE OYSTERPONDS HISTORICAL SOCIETY (OHS) is grateful to Deborah Schwartz and the Brooklyn Historical Society for permission to publish *The Diaries of Augustus Griffin, 1792-1852* and to the institutions whose generous financial support made this publication possible: InterAmericas®/Society of Arts and Letters of the Americas, a program of The Reed Foundation, and Furthermore: a program of the J. M. Kaplan Fund. We are grateful to Susan B. Gardner and Martha B. Cassidy and to Ruth and Reginald Tuthill for additional funding.

The project would never have materialized without the generosity of former OHS Trustee Elizabeth Gilpin, who funded the creation of a digital copy of the original manuscript by the Northeast Document Conservation Center. This provided an enormous aid to transcription, as well as a permanent copy for the OHS archives.

My thanks go to Dr. Natalie Naylor for writing the foreword and for sharing her formidable knowledge and patient editorial skills, and to Keri Christ for her research and her contribution to the transcription. For their encouragement and enthusiasm for the project, I thank Jacquetta Haley; James G. Basker, president of the Gilder Lehrman Institute of American History; Joshua M. Ruff, F. Henry Berlin History Curator, The Long Island Museum of American Art, History, and Carriages at Stony Brook, Long Island; and Antonia Booth, Southold town historian. For their invaluable knowledge, insights, and perspective, I am grateful to Elinor Williams and Donald Boerum, former presidents of OHS. OHS archivist Amy Kasuga Folk, former director William McNaught, and director Ellen Cone Busch have been enormously helpful. Sara Garretson and Ann ffolliott were instrumental in obtaining foundation support.

Karen Braziller, Chairman of the OHS Publication Committee, oversaw every step of bringing the transcribed manuscript to publication. Her expertise and dedicated attention were invaluable. I thank Rita Lascaro, designer; Enid Stubin, proofreader; and Laura Ogar, indexer; their professional high standards and generosity are much appreciated. And I thank Sylvia Newman for her patience and support.

Fredrica Wachsberger

INTRODUCTION

THE DIARIES OF AUGUSTUS GRIFFIN cover an unusually long time—sixty years—from 1792 to 1852, and are uniquely significant for the history of Orient and East Marion, and for the North Fork of Long Island. Griffin creates a bridge from the past to the present; many of the homes that were familiar to Griffin still stand in the Orient Historic District, and he tells us who built them, and who built his own chimney and dug his own well, and how much he paid for them. He also gives us great detail about his own time. He tells us which sloops were taking produce to New York, how much the farmers were paid for a bushel of potatoes, and how many thousands of boney fish were hauled in by the seines. He reports which texts were chosen for sermons on the Sabbath. He describes extreme weather and dramatic shipwrecks. He also remarks on his many friends and his family members, their achievements and their travails. But the diaries also offer a personal perspective on larger challenges faced by the emerging Republic and, particularly, faced by its citizens. They form, finally, an American document, a record of an individual life that is both unique and in many ways typical of the lives of Americans in small rural communities during the first century of the Republic. The diaries, bound in two volumes, are in the collections of the Brooklyn (formerly the Long Island) Historical Society, which has permitted the Oysterponds Historical Society (OHS) to transcribe and publish them. Thanks to a generous contribution from a former trustee, OHS has had the manuscript digitally copied to make it accessible to scholars.

Augustus Griffin (or Griffing, which he uses throughout these diaries) was born in 1767, before the American Revolution, and died in 1866, after the end of the Civil War. Considered Orient's historian, he is best known for having published his *Journal* in 1857, in his ninetieth year. It is primarily a history of the founding of Southold, genealogies of the first families of Oysterponds (now Orient and East Marion), and a history of local churches and ministers. He had access to the family records of his relatives and neighbors and also consulted his own earlier writings—incidents published in the *Journal* appear earlier in two manuscripts that are in the Oysterponds Historical Society collections.

The diaries differ from his published *Journal.* For some of the years, they are an almost daily record of events both large and small in his life and the lives of the members of his community. While Griffin spent the first seven years recorded in the diaries teaching school upstate in Orange County, New York, in 1798 he built a house in Oysterponds and from 1800 spent the rest of his long life there. He operated the house as a tavern and inn. Expanded by later owners, the Vails, to become a boarding house, known as Village House, it is the most important historic structure of the Oysterponds Historical Society and stands on its original site on Village Lane in the Orient Historic District.

Griffin's diaries are a record of an attempt to invent a life and a moral way to live it, contemporaneous with the self-invention of "these United States," as he calls the new Republic. At the same time, it is a record of the growth of a small rural community of farmers and fishermen, remotely situated at the eastern edge of the country, yet in constant communication with New York City and, through seafaring, with New England, the Caribbean, and the larger world.

> In the year 1750 It is said there was in the (then Oysterponds) now Orient about forty dwelling houses, and from 40 to 50 families—In 1780 somewhere about fifty dwellings—Now in 1844 there is about one hundred or a trifle over—and four stores, two or three shoe factories and that number of Joiner's shops. The farms are of course small, but the owners of them very industrious, and their yield is truly astonishing ...   (II: 248 [44])

Griffin's great-great-grandfather, Jasper Griffing, had emigrated from Wales around 1675 and settled in Southold. Griffin's paternal grandfather, Samuel, married Martha Vail; his father, James, married Deziah Terry; and his own wife, Lucretia, was a Tuthill. Griffin was related by blood or marriage to most of the Oysterponds families. This was to be both a comfort and a challenge for a man who found himself in constant competition for limited opportunities in a very small village. Having lost an effort to obtain the position of postmaster in January of 1821—"as It is, Joseph Terry, and his friends, have by unfair means, cheated me out of it"—he was so upset that he returned to the incident in his diary two months later:

> Here, we see, that the low darstedly, envious workings of some, have succeeded in their nefarious aims, and now chuckle at getting the game, although they feel to know they obtained it by dishonor & cheating—   (I: 109 [283])

This sort of outburst is infrequent for Griffin. More commonly he says, as he does in 1828, "submission, is the most proper, when to oppose is useless," or, more frequently, "If you are angry, count 1000 before you speak."

The second son of a large family, Griffin was forced to find his own way. Self-described (in a "Diary" in the OHS archive, written in 1827–30 and dedicated to his daughter, Cleora, in 1850, Appendix A) as having had a "slender" constitution, and finding himself unfit for ship carpentry, seamanship, tanning, or any of the few available trades, Griffin in 1789 walked to New York and traveled on to Orange County, where relatives had settled, and taught himself arithmetic in order to become a schoolmaster. This was to become a constant fallback position in difficult times, although he was twice relieved of his position. With a wife and small child, he returned to Oysterponds and, having built a house, endeavored to improve his family's situation by taking in guests, getting a tavern license, and, inspired by a meeting with an apparently successful merchant, becoming a shopkeeper. This last effort did not go smoothly for the inexperienced Griffin, who frequently questioned his own judgment. In 1815 his affairs began to "look lowry," and in 1816, in the famous year of "a frost every month in the spring & summer," he began to face real disaster. In March, he went to New York and

> laid in a pretty handsome assortment of dry goods & groceries—Goods, at this time, were very high—a risk (I fear) In the purchase . . . June, July, & August, European goods fell amazingly, and I found (alas to my sorrow) my fears in March last were well founded—The whistle was too dearly purchased—Its musick was harsh, and Its expense grieveous—   (I: 85 [218])

He was subsequently threatened with prison and forced to sell everything he owned (except his house) to pay his debtors. In the *Diaries*, he only alludes to this crisis; in the "Diary for Cleora," he describes his humiliation (Appendix A).

Griffin applied for his first tavern license in 1809 and kept an inn until the death of Lucretia, his wife of almost sixty years, in May of 1849. Village House, as it was probably already known, became a center of community life, hosting elections, tax collections, and other civic events, as well as Washington's Birthday celebrations. For many years it was the final stop of the mail stage. With it, Griffin earned the respect of the community, and he was ultimately appointed Commissioner of Deeds, auctioneer, and Commissioner of Schools. Even the tavern, however, was not without anxieties for its owner, since from the beginning he suffered a moral conflict over the sale of alcohol.

> This year, in May, for the first time in my life, I took out a Tavern
> License—An honorable calling, no doubt, but a very delicate
> one in dealing out Spiritual Liquors to those whom we are well
> persuaded will use It to the hurt of themselves, and families—
>
> (I: 77 [197])

Within two years of his enlarging his "Bar Room" in 1837, Temperance had swept into Orient, and Griffin, hoping "the Father of unbounded Mercies will vouchsafe me forgiveness," gave up the sale of spirits and became a supporter. His daughter Honora had married William Wilcox, who became an ardent proselytizer and traveling lecturer, and in 1844 opened a Temperance hotel "on the Te[e]total system" at the wharf. By 1846, Griffin writes: "The no license ticket has prevailed in every Town in the county of Suffolk except one, and that is Huntington—I am sorry for the families of that town—" (II: 330[293]). In three-quarters of a century, Prohibition would become the law of the land.

While Griffin's day-to-day interest was in the events of his own life and the lives of his family and community, he was witness to and impacted by national struggles and technological revolutions. Oysterponds was occupied by the British during the Revolution and blockaded during the War of 1812. In the "Diary for Cleora," Griffin tells the story, later repeated in his published *Journal,* of his father's escape from the British by jumping out the window. (In the "Diary," the story is different, and more colorful in the telling. See Appendix A.) During the War of 1812, he served commanders of the British fleet in his tavern, and he recounts the abduction by the British of the young Joshua Penny. The blockade severely disrupted travel and trade by water, and Griffin complains about being forced to travel overland to New York for supplies.

Griffin and his family traveled a surprising amount—for business and to visit friends and relatives in New York, Orange County, and Connecticut. It is in following his travels that we experience with him the technological transformation of America. He made frequent trips to New York by a succession of means—from foot, horse, coach, and sloop to steamboat and railroad. In the summer of 1837, with his wife, he took a trip of nineteen days to New York, Orange County, and Albany, in which they covered seven hundred miles by foot, carriage, sloop, stagecoach, and steamboat.

The railroad reached Greenport in 1844. In 1847, Griffin rode "the cars" to New York for the first time and listed every stop. From the city, he rode by horse or carriage out to Harlem to see the Coffer dam, and "took an interesting view of the two reservoirs—The stupendous bridge, over which is to pass the pipes for leading the Croton water to supply the City." He was well aware of the transformative importance of the great technological advances of the nineteenth century. In 1846, the results of a state election were reported by telegraph:

> The votes were perhaps finished canvasing by 10 or 11 OClock P.M. The result was known in N.York by the Telegraph this morn from almost all the small Towns from Buffalo to Brooklyn, and It reached Greenport by 1 OClock P.M. to day—Who could have believed such a discovery 20 years ago, would have even been made! What next!! The question is does mankind gain on the great whole by inventions more than they lose
>
> (II: 340–41 [312–13])

Four days after his wife's funeral on the twenty-first of May in 1849—"Alas with her has gone all my Earthly rational enjoyments"—Griffin, then eighty-two years old, took an extended trip of mourning to New York and Orange County to weep with his children and his extended family; he traveled for eight weeks.

Mortality was constantly on Griffin's mind. His diary records the births, marriages, and deaths of family members and members of the community, and thereby the ravages of smallpox, dysentery, yellow fever, and consumption, the infant deaths and deaths in childbirth, and the dreadful losses at sea.

> In June this year 1826 my Brother James lost four sons by drowning, all in one day—Daniel, Joseph, David, & Benjamin—the eldest 24—the youngest 14 years—with them was lost at the same time James Beebe, & son—Joel King & Horace Clark—
>
> (I: 125 [319])

Beginning about 1818, Griffin's brief obituaries contain assurances that the deceased "died the death of the Righteous." As his mother is dying, he writes that "these tattered garments of mortality, these habiliments of dying flesh and pain, will be exchanged for the spotless robe of Christ's Rightiousness and the mantle of Eternal Youth—"

Griffin belonged to the (Calvinist) Congregational Church, but he also attended Quaker meetings in Westchester, invited Methodists to preach in his house, and, on one of his trips, attended, in one day, four churches of four different denominations. Primarily, Griffin looked to the gospels and to eighteenth-century British writers and theologians like John Wesley, Isaac Watts, Laurence Sterne, and Edward Young, not only for solace but also for guidance in the morality of day-to-day existence. As he aged, he became increasingly pessimistic about his fellow man, and he frequently quotes Young: "Man to Man, is the sorest, surest Ill." But in the same entry he reveals an enduring hopefulness:

> I would that Mankind would so conduct, and act, in their every intercourse with each other, that another Doct. Young might find urgent reasons to publish to the world, that Man to Man, (in the now 19th Century) is the safest, surest good—May we not Hope, that such an Effulgent season is fast approaching— such a Mellenium of peace, & serenity, unspeakable, is now at our doors—   (II: 297 [217])

The Manuscript and Editing Procedures

The diary is in two volumes of approximately the same length, but while Volume I covers a period of fifty-two years, from 1792 to 1843, Volume II covers only eight, from 1844 to 1852, when Griffin, in his late seventies and eighties, wrote almost daily. Bound at the end of Volume II are twenty-three pages of poems, musings, and thoughts of his late wife, which have not been included in the transcription. Originally, there were three diaries which Griffin reports having taken to his son Sidney in Hempstead, Long Island. They were bound during his lifetime into two volumes, and the pages were renumbered by Griffin in pencil. He also added an index to each volume, which, together with some of the entries, makes it clear that Griffin, an innate historian, expected the diary to be read by others, if only friends and relatives. The indexed references are here included in the general index.

Volume I is particularly problematic; some years have only two or three entries, and it is often clear that Griffin is later adding from other notes or journals, and sometimes perhaps rewriting to make a fine copy. Over the years, he frequently reviewed the entries and added, in the margins, notes on the later lives of the people he mentions. Marginalia is sometimes keyed to the text by an asterisk, sometimes not, following Griffin's original. In this transcription, Griffin's page numbers are presented in brackets []. Griffin's occasionally archaic spelling (for example, *buisness, aimable, voyge, untill*) is retained; clarifications are provided in brackets. Also retained are his arbitrary capitalization, lack of apostrophes, and use of dashes instead of periods; some of these practices changed over the years. The underlining is his. Where Griffin made later corrections or superscript additions to clarify the text, they are included without notation. Marginalia are rendered in the margins, in smaller type.

The Notes are intended to clarify some of Griffin's references and are cited using the page number of the present edition along with the page number of the original diary in brackets. In Appendix A are excerpts from Griffin's unpublished "Diary for Cleora" (in the Oysterponds Historical Society archive), which relate some of his experiences prior to 1792. While parts of these were repeated in the published *Journal* (1857), they are fresher and livelier here. There is also a detailed description of his bankruptcy in 1817. In Appendix B is a list of books that he notes owning or having read. The genealogy, Appendix C, is meant as an aid to readers to identify some of Griffin's relatives.

It is hoped that Griffin's unique voice will continue to speak on the page and charm the reader as it has charmed the transcriber.

Fredrica Wachsberger
Orient, New York, 2009

AUGUSTUS GRIFFIN, ESQ.

by John Orville Terry

I know an old gentleman, fully fourscore,
Who yet seems among us as young as of yore—
He's always at home, conversational, free,
And a courteous old gentleman always is he.

He walks down the street with his cane in his hand,
With a step of importance, an air of command,
And if a good story he chanced to begin,
He first shoves his handkerchief up to his chin.

Though his stature be small, 'tis surrounded with grace,
And his heart, I am certain, is in the right place,
For mirth and good nature sit perched on his brow,
Tho' time has run over it oft with his plough.

His words are well chosen, his language refined,
And his visage reflects an intelligent mind;
An eye for the beauties of nature betrays
That the fire of the poet continues to blaze.

His mind is a record of ages and dates,
And his knowledge to others with pride he relates—
Grand-fathers, grand-mothers, great-uncles and aunts,
All start into life from his memory's haunts.

He dresses with taste, and is cheerful and gay,
And looks like a prince in his best holiday,
Tho' stern o'er his features impressed is the sage,
The signet of virtue, the wisdom of age.

In a moss-covered cottage, alone and retired,
Lives this worthy old patriarch, loved and admired,
Where often his friends are delighted to sit,
To feast on his lore and regale on his wit.

And long may he live in his pleasant abode,
And flowers spring up to the end of the road—
And when with life's journey his struggles shall cease,
May his sun set in brightness, his eyes close in peace.

From *The Poems of J.O.T., consisting of Songs, Satires and Pastoral Descriptions, chiefly depicting the scenery, and illustrating the manners and customs of the ancient and present inhabitants of Long-Island,* by John Orville Terry (New York: George F. Nesbitt, Printer, 1850).

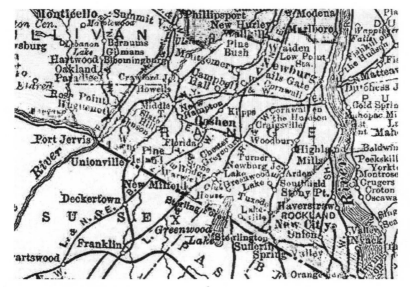

**Village House,
as it is today**
*Augustus Griffin's
original house, built
in 1798, was 20 by 27
feet. The present
building reflects the
Vail expansion and
renovation of the
1860s and 1880s
(facing).*

Orange County, 1875
F.W. Beers, Atlas of Orange County, New York *(Chicago: Andreas, Baskin and
Burr, 1875); detail. The North, or Hudson River is on the right. From 1791 to 1797,
Griffin was a schoolmaster in Blooming Grove, about eight miles east of Goshen.*

Southold Town, 1873
F.W. Beers, Atlas of Long Island, New York *(New York: Beers, Comstock and Cline, 1873).*

VOLUME I

East Marion

1858 Chace map of East Marion; detail. J. Chace, Map of Suffolk County, L.I., New York *(Philadelphia: John Douglass, 1858).*

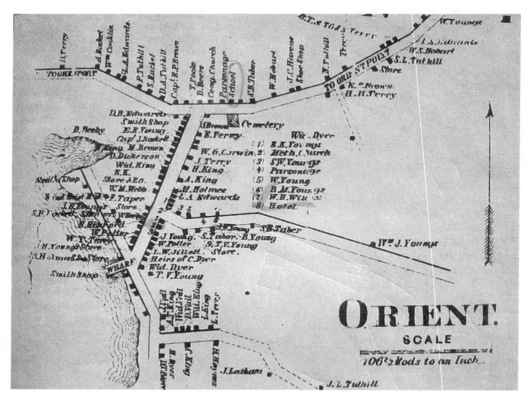

Orient

1858 Chace map of the present-day Orient Historic District; detail. At the time this map was drawn, Griffin had already sold Village House to Samuel Gelston Vail. It is identified on the map as (8) Hotel.

1792

[1] June 25th 1792—We have a few days since commenced keeping house, or becoming what is called a family—There is three of us—viz. myself, my wife Lucretia, and daughter Harriet Lucretia—We have a room in the house of a Mr. Asael Coleman, in a small village called Colemantown, so designated from having a number of families of that name in the place—the Town of which this district forms a part is Blooming-Grove, in the County of Orange, State of New York—I have taught a school in this vicinity since May 1791

December 2nd 1792 The smallpox by inoculation is now much in this part of the country—Our physician, or the one in the most practice (Doct. Anthony Davis) has as it is said 600 patients under his care at this time—

3rd December—As there is such a tide of smallpox, I think my school [2] must be discontinued a few days—

Tuesday 4th Decem. 1792 Considerable commotion in the neighbour-hood about the smallpox—some censure, and reflections—

Wednesday 5th Novem. warm for the season of the year—Mrs. Griffing & daughter Harriet visited Mr. William Hudson Senior, a man of marked virtue, and sterling honesty—Aged about 75 years. Messrs Caleb and Abner Colemans families are being inoculated this day—

Thursday 6th—A pleasent day—P.M. the Doctor A. Davis innoculated my little family—Mrs. G- & Harriet

Friday 7th A snowstorm

Saturday 8th Our Friend Silas Vail visited us—he is now teaching school about two mile from my school house—his wife to whom he was lately married is yet with her [3] Father, Judge Thomas Youngs, of Southold, Longisland—

Sabbath 9th My family is yet at Mr. Hudsons—

Monday 10th Took my family home—she Mrs. G has been absent 5 days—My truly pleasant host or landlord, Asael Coleman, has his family inoculated this day—

Tuesday 11th Stoped or discontinued my school of the present on the account of the multiplicity of smallpox—

Wednesday 12th cold weather—

Thursday 13th Died this Morn Miss Mehitable Coleman, the very aimable, and affectionate daughter of Caleb and Thezia Coleman—She was 16 years of age—a victim of consumption—

Friday 14th Attended the funeral of Miss C—

Saturday 15th—Winter, with its frosts—

[4] Sabbath 16th December 1792—Doct. Davis's hundreds of patients are now feeling the effects of well meaning attentions for their future welfare—

Monday 17th My dear little family are beginning to be down with the disorder—

Tuesday 18th—Smallpox appears to be the order of the day—

Wednesday 19th We now and need resignation and patience—

Thursday 20th Moderate weather

Friday 21st- What is called fair weather—not very cold—Friend S. Vail stoped with us an hour or so—

Saturday 22nd Snow storm

Sabbath 23rd Pleasent—some of my scholars are quite sick with the smallpox—viz. Amina Tuthill and Saml Bartlett in particular—Mrs. G. rode out this day—

Monday 24th Rain—

Tuesday Our dear Brother Elisha, immediately from Longisland, the [5] land of my Father & Mother visited us this day—Our joys were <u>felt</u> on our receiving him to our humble abode—our Sister, Lucinda, has been in the country with us some months—and is now undergoing the effects of innoculation

Tuesday 25th Thanksgiving with us in this region—

Wednesday 26th Commenced School, after a vacation of two weeks—

Thursday 27th Was visited by Msrs. Samuel Racket & Matthew Tuthill—The latter a resident of Oysterponds, Longisland, the former a respectable farmer of Oxford, Orange County N.Y.—

Friday 28th Some of my scholars are 24 & 26 years

Saturday 29th—not any school—

Sabbath 30th Friend S. Vail with us—

*See page 579
Monday 31st Evening* Anselm Helms Esq., Benj.Tuthill with friend Vail was with us

1793

Tuesday 1st January 1793—Brother Elisha goes home with uncle Noah Terry

[6] 1793 1st January Brother James's birthday—He, brother James, was

my Mothers first child—her first son—born on the first month in the year,
and the first day of the month—

Wednesday 2nd Jan. 1793—The ground is now clothed with a heavy coat
of Snow—

Thursday 3rd Very cold weather—

Friday 4th A cold rain storm—

Saturday 5th mild, and warm—

Sabbath 6th continues moderate—

Monday 7th A full School—many of them large boys, or young Men of
24 and 26 years of age—

Tuesday 8th Warm & pleasant for January

Wednesday 9th Not any frost last night—Brother Elisha left us for
Longisland last night—

Thursday 10th Continues pleasant—Brother Elisha returned to us this
Morn—the river was too full of ice to admit its navigation—

Friday 11th Squally, and it looks like cold near

Saturday 12th Very cold—A Mr. Charles Hewlett, assists me in School as
scholars are plenty

Sabbath 13th High Wind N-W- & cold—

[7] Monday 14th yesterday departed this life Francis Horton, daughter of
Jeremiah Horton Esq.—She was aged 6 years—an interesting child—

        Nipt in the bud—e'er yet in early bloom
        Your called to live beyond the dreary tomb

Tuesday 15th Pleasant—

Wednesday 16th N-W—rain storm—My scholars generally about 40
daily—

Thursday 17th Storm of rain continues, until 2 P.M. when it commenced
snowing until eve, it ceased—

Friday 18th considerable moderate—Friend Silas Vail visited us this eve—

Saturday 19th continued moderate

Sabbath 20th Friend S. Vail stoped with us this day—brought his diaries with
him—he mentions a circumstance of January 1793 which I was pleased with—
Doct. David M. Arnell, now a student of Physic, with Doct. Jonathan Swezey of
Goshen visited us this day—He is a young man, I believe of much promise

Monday 21st Warm for winter—about 50 scholars—

[8] Tuesday 22 January 1793 High wind N.W.—An ellection this day—I
attended—

Wednesday 23rd cold—

Thursday 24th A cold blustering day—

Friday 25th Am now attending a night school—that with the day keeps me busy

Saturday 26th Getting me home some wood

Sabbath 27th Mr. James Vail, brother to Silas visits us—an aimable, well informed young man—His very excellent Father Peter and Mother Patty Vail died about the year 1776 nearly at the same time, with the smallpox at Aquebogue—our Cousin Phineas Terry called on us this day—a truly likely young man

Monday 28th Cold—

Tuesday 29th Forgot to take my dinner with me, of counsel parted, not of choice—

Wednesday 30th P.M. snowstorm

Thursday 31st Visited Uncle Saml. Racket, who has just come from Longisland—

Friday 1st Feb. 1793 At Uncle Saml. yet—Visited Mr. Silas Young Senior, he came to this country with his 3 brothers, Henry, Abimel, [9] Ruben, in 1734 or 5 now near 60 years of age—Himself & Ruben are still living—aged men I should think 80.

Saturday 2nd The anniversary of my birth—26 years of my little point have gone with the years beyond the flood—The tale of mortal life—Alas, how soon It's told!

Monday 4th Snow—it's now good sleighing which is much improved here—

Tuesday 5th Rainstorm—Wind W—

Wednesday 6th Our Friend Samuel Tuthill, with his aimable Wife, paid us a sociable visit this day—he is the 2nd son of the late Major Barnabas Tuthill, of Southold, L.Island—

Thursday 7th Clear & cold—

Friday 8th Wind S—It is said the N. [Hudson] River is now pretty clear of ice

Saturday 9th—pleasant and quite warm—Friend Vail with us some time—We attended to the Marriage of a Mr. Jonathan Corey to Mrs. Ama Curtis—[10] Died this Saturday 9th Feb. 1793—a young Man by the name of Curtis, son to a widow Curtis

Sabbath 10th cold wind N.W—

Monday 11th High N. wind & cold

Tuesday 12th A snow storm—so severe, I shall not go my mile to the schoolhouse

Wednesday 13th Snow still continues to fall

Thursday 14th—Toiled hard to get home some wood—

Friday 15th A deep snow on the ground

Saturday 16th Cold & calm—good sleighing—

Sabbath A rain storm—wind S.

Monday 18th Very bad traveling in consequence of slops & mud

Tuesday 19th some rain—

Wednesday 20th A rainy night

Thursday 21st A squally day—Brother Elisha goes to New Windsor

Friday 22nd Elisha returned

Saturday 23rd Some snow—

[11] Sabbath 24th A moderate storm—wrote to my Friend Doct. Thomas Vail—

Monday 25th Brother Silas leaves for Long Island this day—the dear land of nativity

Tuesday 26th A.M.—a hailstorm—P.M. Rain—

Wednesday 27th Warm with showers of rain—very bad traveling—mud & mire—

Thursday 28th Cold—High wind N.W.—Visited Mr. Richard Goldsmith, myself, wife, and little Harriet—Stoped with them the night—Mr. G—is a prominent wealthy Farmer in this district, and a Man of veracity—Has an excellent, aimable wife—[Note added in 1848] see page 579

Friday 1st March 1793—Weather mild—Captn. David Hawkins,* living near Goshen, broke his leg by falling from his horse   *See page 585

Saturday 2nd Continues pleasant—visited, with my family, Mr. Samuel Moffatt—An excellent, useful Man

[12] Sabbath 3rd March 1793—Pleasant—Friend Vail with us—

Monday 4th Something like spring

Tuesday 5th Moderate weather, as several days past—Evening, rain and squally—

6th Clear & pleasant- My school is yet large—Mr. Hezekiah Howel's (late Sherief Howel) coloured servant, was found dead in her bed this morn—It is supposed she died in a fit

Thursday 7th Pleasant—Thus far the winter has not been a hard one—Last Tuesday eve, Mr. Samuel Gregg was married to Miss Polly Hobwit, both of Wallkill, Orange County N-Y—

Friday 8th A warm rain storm—My invaluable Friends, Asael Colemans Joiner shop, which was just by his Grist mill, took fire this morn, which was got under by the neighbours with much exertion

[13] Saturday 9th High N.W. wind and cooler—wrote this day to my very dear Mother & Father—Friend Vail, & his brother James, are the bearers of our package of letters to Long Island friends—

Sabbath 10th The two friend Vails are with us this day—

Monday 11th A moderate rainstorm

Tuesday 12th The two Messrs Vail leave for Long Island this morn—Friend Silas Vail has taught School this winter in Blaggs Clove, within a mile of where I reside—

Wednesday 13th A hard snowstorm—

Thursday 14th so pleasant and mild that the snow goes off in haste

Friday 15th pleasant—the traveling a mile 5 days in the week with wet feet, in consequence of sloppy weather, affects, I find, my health—

Died this past winter with the smallpox Mrs. Sally Dolittle (formerly Solomon) from Long Island—She was an aimable peace-[14]able woman, but unfortunately united in marriage to a jealous, miserable wretch of a Man whose narrow soul was incapable of appreciating the society of an excellent woman—

Saturday 16th A Springlike day—

Sabbath 17th March, 1793 pleasant—My good Landlord, Asael Coleman, one of Popes "noblest works of God" rode out a few miles to the residence of Doct. Davis—while there, a Man came hastily in to the Doct. saying his assistance was needed immediately, as a boy just by had his hand cut off a few minutes before—

Monday 18th Mild weather—Our landlady, Mrs. Esther Coleman, is a woman of great value to her family & neighbors—As a nurse and Midwife, her attentions are deserving of great consideration—To me & mine, she has proved a friend indeed and in need—

Friday 19th A rain & hail storm—Rode out to Uncle Saml. Racket at Oxford—By many he [?] island justly stiled a friend to [page trimmed]

[15] He is a Man, friendly, kind, sociable, generous, and proverbially hospitable to his numerous acquaintance and connections—

Wednesday 20th Wind South, of course warm—

Thursday 21st A snowstorm, 1 P.M. it clears off with wind N-W—

Friday 22nd High wind N-N-W- Cool—

Saturday 23rd Moderate, but cool

Sabbath 24th—Hard frost last night—Mrs. Griffing and myself walked to our neighbors Benjamin Tuthills—Mrs. Tuthills' grandfather was from Oysterponds, Long Island—He, Mr. Tuthill, with his very kindhearted wife have been to my family everything that is calculated to impress our gratitude and acknowledgements—

Monday 25th Clear & pleasant—Had a letter from friend S. Vail, dated 14th Inst.

Tuesday 26th Wind S-E—P.M. a rain storm

Wednesday 27th N-W- wind & cool—Had another letter from my friend S.Vail

Thursday 28th cool wind N-W—Abner Coleman raised a house for his brother Obed, a young married man

[16] Friday 29th March 1793 A brisk wind W—Our neighbour William Hudson Jun. raised a waggon house—This Young Gentleman, aged about 25 years, is an Only Son—an open hearted, sociable, rather forward, not prepossessing companion—has had some good chance for improvement, but by indulgence has in some measure missed the right mark—Probably from knowing his Father had a handsome property which in time would become his to do with as he should in that event please—At the age about twenty, in a freak of youthful inconsideration, he left the society of a doting Mother and too fond Father, and proceeded to New York—Shipped on board a Vessel for the West Indies—After a boistrous voyge, of some months in which the Vessel was cast away—he finally reached his Fathers fine side, completely cured of all roving propensities—He is now a good neighbour, kind husband, but still [17] a little too fond of what is called jovial company—We are pleased to notice that in him, in his pious Father, and his charitable Mother, we have found friends, always just in time—

Saturday 30th Cold N-E- wind—

Sabbath 31st pleasent

April 1st 1793—mild—Some call this April Fool day—Who but trifles now and then—

Tuesday 2nd Attended Town meeting, which was held at the house of Mr. John Brewster near Blooming Grove meeting House—A large collection of Men & boys, with much excitement, and needless noise—Alas! Where will the larger part of this motly group be 50 years hence—Ah, where? [later added in pencil]

Wednesday 3rd Warm, for April—

Thursday 4th As mild as yesterday—Uncle Noah Terry called on me a few minutes at my Schoolhouse—

Friday 5th Dry weather for April—

Saturday 6th A few sprinkles of rain—

Sabbath 7th Wind N.W. Cooler than days last—Am just informed that Joseph King & family has moved into this region, near Blooming Grove—

[18] Monday 8th Aunt Sally, (wife to uncle Noah Terry) with her son, Jasper, paid us a visit this day—

Tuesday 9th Wind S.W.—Pleasant

Wednesday 10th High wind S—rain A.M.—P.M. a gale of wind N-W-

Thursday 11th More moderate

Friday 12th Wind S-W- with some rain

Saturday 13th Clear, yet cool—To measure Time, assuredly requires a good Moral reflecting Mathematician—

Sabbath 14th Read considerable in [Jonathan] Edwards history of redemption—Our Clergy generally pronouce it a good work—

Monday 15th Cold & uncomfortable, moreso as we have had several pleasent days of the last week—

Tuesday 16th Weather more mild

Wednesday 17th Pleasent—P.M. a letter from our friend James Vail—

Thursday 18th Pleasent

Friday 19th Some rain last night—

[19] Saturday 20th April A cold N-E- wind, with some rain—Called on Messrs. Saml Moffatt, Richard Goldsmith and Jeremiah Horton and made a settlement with them for the tuition of their children the past Winter—

At my return home, met our friend James Vail—He informs me that Joseph King and family are now at the house of George Brown, Esq., in Smiths Clove, stoping there a few days until he can purchase a place near or in Blooming Grove—

Heard the Death this day of Judge Thomas Youngs, Father of my friend Silas Vails wife—He was assuredly a valuable member of Society, and a wise councilor, and the poor Mans & orphans friend—He was aged 75 years—

Sabbath 21st Was visited by our Cousin Phineas Terry—

Monday 22nd Pleasent

Tuesday Fine weather—Started for N.York with James Vail & Charles Hewlett

[20] At New Windsor, I dined with Mr. Benjamin Havens family—about 5 OClock P.M. went on board the Packet, and set sail for N.York—in getting aboard, in the mail boat, we had a rough time and got wet Jackets—

Wednesday 24th Pleasent—at anchor off West Point celebrated in our Revolutionary war—Here our Washington—[Henry] Knox—[Nathaniel]

Green & [Thaddeus] Cosciusco [Kosciusko], with many other Master Spirits, spent many important hours—Here it was that [Benedict] Arnold plotted the destruction of the country—and the accomplished but unfortunate Andre paid the forfeit of his life in consequence of Arnold's treason

Thursday 25th—Arrived in New York about 3 p.m. where I was so happy to meet with my brother Moses and my much esteemed friend John King. [21] In the year 1787 Mr. King just mentioned was one of my most intimate associates—Much of our leisure times was spent together—in sentiment and amusements we were one, and the same—indeed, I felt to hold him as a deserving young man, truly worthy of my best respects, and highest consideration- since that eventual time, the buisness of life has called us into different parts of the country, and we have met but seldom to interchange civilities, and mutual good will—yet we both believe our friendship formed at that period is now as bright and fresh as ever, and will continue so while conversant with sublinary things—

Friday 26th Met this day our Friend Silas Vail and wife—stoped the night, with Deacon Richard Smith

[22] Saturday 27th April 1793 A rainstorm, with a high N-E- wind—Amid the gale and storm, called on Friend Vail & wife—lodged this night on board Sloop Minerva—

Sabbath 28th Wind continues brisk N-E- Spent some time this day with my Brothers, Elisha & Moses—My Brothers—O, the sacred appellation— What obligations we are continually under, to cherish the holy ties of true brotherhood, and a divine unity—

Monday 29th Pleasent—

Tuesday 30th Mild weather—Spent some time with S. Vail & wife—His brother James entered as a Clerk with Mr. Samuel Terry, dry goods Merchant, in Maidenlane—

As I was just leaving for home I met my good Father, after receiving his blessing I set sail for home—went [23] on board—after sailing about 5 miles cast anchor for the night—

May 1st 1793 Under sail with wind S-W- and at 7 P.M. landed at New Windsor, immediately set off on foot for ColemanTown, about 10 or 12 miles—David Cook & Charles Hewlett was my company

Thursday 2nd 1 A.M. arrived at our humble dwelling—found my family well

Friday 3rd Cloudy—Visited Joseph King & family, who now live in the upper part of Blooming Grove—

Saturday 4th Again with my wife visited King & wife—Tarry with them the night—

Sabbath 5th Returned home this morn

Monday 6th Rode out as far as Goshen, stoped the night with my old and esteemed Landlord, with whom I made my agreable home in the summer & autumn of 1789 & 90—Joshua Brown

[24] Tuesday 7th May 1793—Rode out to what is called Empting Town, a small village near Goshen—called on Mr. Thomas Payne, son of the late Reverend Mr.*Payne of Cutchogue, Southold, Long Island—With Mr. Payne, I rode out to Wisners Bridge—returned and stoped the night with Mr. Payne, whose wife & family are very agreeable. Ever since I arrived in the Goshen country, I have received the most marked civilities from Mr. Payne. His attentions, assuredly, give him a just claim to my particular esteem—I trust it will endure all my life—

*Rev. Mr. Payne died in 1766 at Cutchogue

Wednesday 8th Pleasent—On my way home called on my former school-mate and friend, Phineas Payne, who was my playmate, at Southold in 1781-2- & 3—Our meeting [25] was truly agreable—He has been teaching school in this country some months, and is now about returning home to his dear Southold—by him I write to my Longisland friends—

Thursday 9th Good weather—

Friday 19th Pleasent—

Saturday 11th Dry weather—

Sabbath 12th Read Edwards on redemption

Monday 13th Pleasent but dry—commenced School, it being the 7th quarter in this district-

Tuesday 14th warm—

Wednesday 15th Cooler than some days back—We ought to acknowledge at all times our daily mercies, and tremble to think of our poor returns, and Ingrattitude

Thursday 16th continues dry—Mrs. Griffing, my sister Lucinda & myself spent the evening at Mr. Henry Greggs—

Friday 17th begins to be very dry

Saturday 18th Pleasent—

[26] Sabbath 19th May 1793—Some rain this morn. Attend Meeting at Blooming Grove—Preacher Mr. Bennoni Bradner—

Mrs. Field arrived at our residence this evening—the sisters were joyful in salutations, such as becomes a family of love—Mrs. F brought us a letter from James Vail, and of the return of my brother James from a Voyge at Sea, he having been absent from his home twelve months—

Monday 20th Warm weather—Rec'd letter from Friend S. Vail, and another from my dear sister Deziah—She affectionately says Our best of Mothers, says I must read the following lines, viz;

> Peace is the blessing that I seek
> How lovely are its charms
> I am for peace, but when I speak
> They all declare for [arms?]

Tuesday 21st A clear day—Visited Mr. Benj. Brewster—He is a Man of sterling integrity—sound sense, and an honest Man—

[27] Wednesday 22nd—a refreshing shower- Bought 13 acres of land of Mr. David Corwin, this day, for which I paid him in full 50 Doll[ar]s—it is the first foot of land I ever could call my own—

Thursday 23rd Pleasent—rather cool—

Friday 24th Fine weather—

Saturday 25th Weather as yesterday—Am now cutting timber for a home which I propose to build, one & ½ stories, 26 by 22 feet—to stand on the main road leading from New Windsor to Blooming Grove

Sabbath 26th At home reading

Monday 27th Dismissed my school, altogether, this summer, in order to attend to the building my house—We hope it will be for the best—Perhaps too hasty—

Tuesday 18th Uncomfortable, damp and misty wet—cut more timber this day

Wednesday 29th Some rain

Thursday 30th Cloudy—Mr. Abner Coleman assisted me in drawing my timber for my house—

Friday Thick, hazy weather—

[28] Saturday 1st June 1793 A rain storm—Bargained with Mr. Daniel Tuthill, (Brother to the Benjamin Tuthill, before mentioned) to frame my House by the job & find himself with board—

Sabbath 2nd Occasionally showers—The late dry ground is now wet—

Monday 3rd Rode out to Major Thomas Moffatts, and purchased of him a quantity quarter stuff boards—Mr. Moffatt has been a conspicuous County Clerk, in Goshen, for 20 years—He served with honor in the Army of Washington, in our Revolutionary struggle for the glorious Independence, which we now enjoy—Rec'd a letter from Mr. James Vail—

Tuesday 4th some rain—

Wednesday 5th Assisted the Carpenters

Thursday 6th Rain—yet in the midst, I rode to Oxford some 5 miles, from which I returned wet & weary—

[29] Friday 7th Pleasant—

Saturday 8th what is termed "good weather"—Rode to Newburgh, bought 6000 Shingles—

Sabbath 9th Tarried at home—Some such the Bible says "divided the spoil"—

Monday 10th Pleasant—Went with Mr. Hugh Turner and his Horse team after my Shingles at Newburgh—as the wagon broke, after getting the Shingles onto it, we had to leave them—

Tuesday 11th Pleasant

Wednesday 12th Fair weather

Thursday 13th Squally weather

Friday 14th mild day—Saturday 15th Fair weather—Visited Goshen, with Mrs. Field, my wife's sister—we staid the night with Mr. Nathaniel Tuthill, whose attentive wife was Patty Wickham,* of Southold Long Island—We were treated with much civility by Mr. Tuthill & wife—

Sabbath 16th Attended meeting at Goshen, Mrs. Field with Mrs. Tustin, Widow of the late Col Benjamin Tustin

[30] Monday 17th June 1793 A squally day—Spent it with my old agreable landlord, Capt. Joshua Brown, and his obligeing good Mother*—Her kindnesses to me, when a lone stranger, in her family 1789 & 90 has left an impression of regard for her and her Husband, Uncle Josh, (as they call him) that must remain bright while I shall continue to be blessed with recollections of favours conferred—Her Husband has been for many years one of the most respectable Farmers in this County—a very pious Charitable man—greatly beloved, but for some years past his mind appears to be confused, and his buisness, and farm, is conducted by his son Capt. Brown—Yet deranged as he is he shows great kindness to me, and his friends, who visit him.—Returned home this eve—

Tuesday 18th Fair weather—

Wednesday 19th Pleasant—

[31] Thursday 20th June 1793 Pleasant—

Friday 21st A rain storm—Rode out to Blooming Grove, to John Chandler, Merchant—Returned wet as a drowned rat, as it is often said of those wet—

Saturday 22nd Clear day—

Sabbath 23rd Fair day—Attended Blooming Grove meeting

Monday 24th Cool

*Mrs. Tuthills youngest son Oliver visited me at my House in Orient on the 24th of October 1861 which was 48 years after my visit to his fathers in Goshen*see page 588

*She is a Woman of 75 years—as straight and active as a woman of 25—aimable and agreeable in conversation—I have found her always kind

Tuesday 25th Raised my House partly in a rain storm, which commenced about 4 P.M.—

Wednesday 26th clear—Rode out to New Windsor with Brother Richard S. Hubbard—he goes to Troy—

Thursday 27th Mild day—

Friday 28th Howed out my corn, near an acre

Saturday 29th Pleasant

Sabbath 30th Read much in Edwards on redemption

Monday 1st July 1793 Fine weather—How important is our every moment! Yet how astonishingly vain is Man in his improvement of them—

Tuesday 2nd Pleasant—

Wednesday 3rd Fair weather—

Thursday 4th Wind W-S-W- & clear—<u>Independence</u>

[32] Friday 5th July 1793- Rain—Spent a part of the day at Mr. Joshua Curtis's, an industrious, kind, benevolent man—To me, his expressions of charity have been such as to merit my disinterest goodwill towards him and his attentive family—

Saturday 6th Weather very warm

Sabbath 7th Pleasant—Rec'd a letter from my friend Silas Vail—its contents were pleasing—

Monday 8th A fair day—Rode out with Brother R.S. Hubbard—

Tuesday 9th Rain this Morn—This day, My dear Lucretia, our little Harriet, with my sister Lucinda and Sister Hannah Field, set off for Longisland—Sister Betsey King, and myself, accompany them as far as New Windsor—About 6 P.M. while at New Windsor, we had a severe rain & thunder storm—The rain rendered the roads so bad that we had to leave the wagon [33] a ½ mile from my residence—Am fearful my house, now only in frame, has sustained damage—

Wednesday 10th Arose early and repaired to my house (1½ miles) found it all in good order—

Thursday 11th Assisted Wm. Hudson Jr. in his harvest—

Friday 12th—Assisted Benjamin Tuthill in his harvest—

Saturday 13th Went to Mr. Chandlers—Our cousin Sally Terry visited us this day—She is aimable, beautiful, & accomplished—She was much disappointed in learning of my dear wife's absence from home—

Sabbath 14th Pleasant—waited on our cousin Sally to Blooming Grove Meeting—Evening she returned to her home, <u>Me, to mine</u>, which begins to be lonesome in consequence of its chief ornaments absence—

Monday 15th Fair day—

Tuesday 16th Pleasant—

Wednesday 17th Pleasant—

[34] Thursday 18th July 1793—Fine Harvest weather

Friday 19th some rain—Rode out to Little Britain, about 4 miles—

Saturday 20th Pleasant—

Sabbath 21st—Warm, and clear—

Monday 22nd—Time rools on—But will it forever rool!!—

Tuesday 23rd Its summer & warm—

Wednesday 24th Very warm—Rode out to Newburgh to see a Schooner launched—after which I went on board the Packet Sloop Maria, Capt. John Anderson, and sailed for N.York—

Thursday 25th arrived at N.York, and then walked up to Mr. Saml. Terrys, Merchant, in Maidenlane, where I met my friend James Vail, in good spirits and glad to see me—

Friday 26th This morn I met with great joy my Brother James, whom I have not seen this more than 16 months—by James I heard of my dear wife, and our (35) little Harriet—Likewise met with my early friend John King—his Brother Frederick, Sam'l Brown, an early playmate of mine—with this goodly number of my early associates was my cousins Jonathan Terry & Noah Beebe—all of which I am pleased to believe were heartily glad to see me, as I was them. We when children, used to be much together—now grown to manhood, our different callings render It necessary to be scattered in different parts of the country, and some of us (a solemn thought) perhaps now meet for the last time—

Took lodging this night on board Capt. Benjamin Bailys Vesel, with my friend John King—This juvenile friend of mine, is possessed of one of the pleasentest, mildest dispositions. No one to become acquainted with him but must be prepossessed in his favour—He acknowledges now, as he has done this some years, that he cherishes the most respectful consideration of me, as I do certainly of him, but [?] we must now meet but seldom [page trimmed]

[36] Saturday 27th July 1793—Met this day with my Brothers Elisha & Moses—By them I wrote to my dear wife—to Silas Vail—Took leave of my Brothers, repaired on board of the Maria, Capt. Anderson, and set sail for Blooming Grove, by the way of Newburgh—Mr. James Vail accompanied me—

Sabbath 28th 5 A.M. arrived at Newburgh—Immediately after landing, left for Coleman Town, where we arrived 2 P.M.—

Monday 29th Pleasant—

Tuesday 30th Fair weather—

Wednesday 31st A moderate rain—

•

Thursday 1st August—Pleasant—James Vail with me—

Friday 2nd With Mr. James Vail, rode out to Uncle Noah Terrys—

Saturday 3rd Set off for home but with such a pain in my head, was obliged to stop, and stay the night with Mrs. Tustin & her two kind sons— James & Thomas—

[37] Sabbath 4th Feel so much better, that P.M. I leave for home—

Monday 5th Quite well—

Tuesday 6th Squally—James Vail is yet with me—

Wednesday 7th Pleasant—

Thursday 8th Fine weather—

Friday 9th Rain—Mr. James Vail leaves for LongIsland, he takes letters to my dear wife—and Brother James & friend Silas Vail

Saturday 10th Pleasant—

Sabbath 11th Visited this day by Absalom Racket, Nephew of Friend Silas Vails wife—An excellent young Man—

Monday 12th Pleasant—

Tuesday 13th—Good weather—

Wednesday 14th Rain—

Thursday 15th Pleasant—

Friday 16th Fine day—

Saturday 17th Quite warm—rode out to Goshen—

Sabbath 18th Rain—Read in Youngs Night Thoughts

[38] August 19th 1793 Rec'd a letter from my dear Lucretia, informing me that she and our little Harriet are now at New Windsor, waiting for me to come, and assist them home—Of course I was, as soon as possible, with them—we all arrived at our humble abode about 6 P.M.—

Tuesday 20th Pleasant—rec'd Letters from friend S. Vail etc-etc—He writes his wifes dowry, by her Father, is from one to two thousand Dollars— May it prove a convenience, although it often does not—See page 275—

Wednesday 21st Pleasant—

Thursday 22nd Attended at my new house building the chimney—

Friday 23rd—Good weather for our Carpenters & Masons—

Saturday 24th Pleasant

Sabbath 25th Some rain—

Monday 26th Good day—

Tuesday 27th Pleasant—the cattle of my [page trimmed]

[39] Wednesday 28th August 1793—Pleasant—sold my horse to a Mr. Cunningham, of Oxford, where I tarried the night—

Thursday 29th It was today I sold my Horse etc—etc—
Friday 30th Returned home from Oxford
Saturay 31st Pleasent—

Sabbath 1st September 1793—
Monday 2nd Pleasent—
Tuesday 3rd Fine weather—
Wednesday 4th Something unwell this day or two—
Thursday 5th Fair weather—at my building
Friday 6th Some rain—
Saturday 7th Pleasent—Rode out to Newburgh
Sabbath 8th Our little Harriet unwell
Monday 9th Harriet continues ill—
Tuesday 19th Some rain—Mrs. Esther Coleman, our good landlady, sets off for Longisland this day—She takes letters to our friends in that region—
Wednesday 11th Harriet continues sick
Thursday 12th Pleasent
Friday 13th Mrs. Susannah Bartlet leaves for Long [40]—Island to see her friends in that quarter—She is now a widow, poor, and truly acquainted with misfortunes, and the treachery and disappointments incident to a dependence on a heartless world—
Saturday 14th Septemb. 1793 Pleasent—
Sabbath 15th A cloudy day—
Monday 16th Rains—
Tuesday 17th Our little Harriet has been unwell this some time, is now much better
Wednesday 18th Good weather—
Thursday 19th Pleasent—
Friday 20th—visited by Mr. James Vail, just from Long Island—by him I rec'd letters
Saturday 21st Walked out to my new house with friend J. Vail—
Sabbath 22nd Pleasent—
Monday 23rd Weather as yesterday—
Tuesday 24th A cloudy day—
Wednesday 25th Fair weather
[41] Friday 27th Sept. 1793—Clear weather—
Saturday 28th Pleasent
Sabbath 29th As yesterday—weather
Monday 30th Doing not much—

•

Tuesday 1st Oct. 1793—

Wednesday 2nd Carpenters endeavoring to get my house as to admit of our moving into it soon—

Tuesday [sic] 3rd Attended to my house—

Friday 4th—

Saturday 5th Pleasent—

Sabbath 6th Clear & cool—Our Friend Noah Tuthill, from LongIsland, visited us this day—He purposes to move his family into these parts—at Deerpark—

Monday 7th Pleasent—

Tuesday 7th [8th] and Wednesday 9th Fixing to move into our new habitation—Thursday took possession of our new tenement—We confess, we have left as pleasent, as accommodating, and oblidging Landlord, and Landlady, as this, or any other country [page trimmed]

[42] Friday 11th Oct. 1793 Mrs. Esther, & Desire Coleman, arrived home from LongIsland—They brought us letters from friends in that favoured land—

Saturday 12th Assisted in putting things to rights in our new abode—

Sabbath 13th Cool—

Monday 14th & Tuesday 15th with the carpenters etc—etc—

Wednesday 15th—Thursday 16th- & Friday 17th not much doing of use—Am just informed that 4000 people have died the past summer of the Yellow Fever—

Saturday 19th at home

Sabbath 20th Attended Blooming Grove meeting with Mrs. G—

Monday 21st cool—

Tuesday 22nd Have just heard of the Marriage of Mr. Silas Howel, to our Sister Hannah Field—They were married in Connecticut State—

Wednesday 23rd—Cool—

Thursday—Do[ditto]—

[43] Friday 25th Mrs. G—at Joseph Kings—

Sabbath 27th Mrs. G- returned home

Monday 28th & Tuesday 29th [Museing?] off my little point

Thursday 31st Was Married this day Mr. William Corwin, with Miss Rebecka Drake—A good young Man, & an aimable young Woman—

Friday 1st & Sat. 2nd November, buisy in preparing to commence a School, in my old place of tuition—

Sabbath 3rd Attended meeting—A Mr. Halsey was the Speaker—

Monday 4th & Tuesday 5th Dark & Cloudy; commenced school

Wednesday 6th Some rain—Our Harriet unwell—

Thursday 7th Pleasent—

Friday 8th Weather as yesterday—

Saturday 9th—

Sabbath 10th Good weather—Our young Friend Absalom Racket called on us this day—

Monday 11th A high wind N-W-

[44] Tuesday 12th November 1793—Pleasent

Wednesday 13th A Snow storm

Friday 15th Clear & Pleasent—Absalom Racket called on us this day, he is now going to NewYork—

Saturday 16th This day Abner Tuthill, son of Benjamin Tuthill (our friend) aged 6 years died after an illness of a few days—

Sabbath 17th cloudy—

Monday 18th A rain storm

Tuesday 19th Buisy in my school—

Wednesday 20th It has been thus far a cold November—Wind, to day N—Was visited this day by a Methodist Preacher, by name Pelham—He appeared to be truly pious—Stoped with us the night—

Thursday 21st—A damp snow—The Preacher left us after breakfast this morn

Friday 22nd Pleasent—

Saturday 23rd Our very dear Brother Moses came to us this day from LongIsland—left our good parents well—good news—

[45] Sabbath 24th cool—

Monday 25th- Tuesday 26th & Wednesday 27th—In School, with about 40 large & small children

Thursday 28th A moderate Snow Storm—Rode out to Oxford with Jonathan Racket of Rocky Point Longisland—He is a laborious, peaceable, honest young Man—Has resided in this country several years, at farming labour by the year—

Satur 30th Purchased me a horse—I fear its not a wise move, as I am confined to a school and have little to do for a horse—Time will explain—

Sabbath 1st Decem. 1793 P.M. Squally with hail & rain

Monday 2nd Tuesday 3rd & Wenesday 4th A heavy snow storm this 4th

Tuesday 5th & 6th Clear weather—killed my pork [hog] this 6th

Saturday 7th A warm rain storm, which takes off the snow visibly—

[46] Sabbath 8th Decem. 1793 Cold, and blustering—Rain fell in torrents last night

Monday 9th Almost a hurricane of wind N-W—

Tuesday 10th Very cold—Miss Abigail Wickham from LongIsland, visited us this day—She is Sister to the Mrs. Patty Tuthill mentioned sometime back—

Wednesday 11th Pleasent—Visited this morn, my invaluable Friend Asael Coleman

Thursday 12 & Friday 13th Assisted Joseph King, who is fixing our front room, for winter—

Saturday 14th A squally day—

Sabbath 15th more mild weather

Monday 16th Hazy—

Tuesday 17th Pleasent—

Wednesday 18th Snow & rain—

Thursday 19th Pleasent weather—School very full—

[47] Friday 20th & Saturday 21st Cold days

Sabbath 22nd Continues very cold—

Monday 23rd A large school, and dark weather

Tuesday 24th A moderate rain—

Wednesday 25th Provided a Christmas Supper for a number of young couples this evening—It came off midling well, all things considered—Some of them a little too much excited—There was not any doubt but some imprudence was with us, but not much true wisdom—

Thursday 26th A cold day, and high wind—

Friday 27th & Saturday 28th cold, winter weather—

Sabbath 29th Read John Westleys [Wesley's] life—He was a wonderfully industrious, persevering man—

Monday 30th Cold—Cold—

Tuesday 31st It thus ends the year 1793—Forever—What a word!!—

1794

[48] January 1st 1794—A new Year! This day my Brother James is 29 years old—His prudence in all his actions, and converse, from his youth up has been conspicuous—He certainly has many marks of one of the Sons of Peace—And who are they? The Bible says they shall be called the children of God—

Thursday 2nd Clear & cold—Lucretia, my wife, is not well—

Friday 3rd Mrs. Griffing still unwell—

Saturday 4th More mild & warmer than days past—Messrs Thomas V. & Absalom Racket from LongIsland visited us this day—The former purposes to board with us sometime—

[49] Sabbath 5th High wind—

Monday 6th Wrote to my friend Silas Vail this day—

Tuesday 7th Winter in the brightest colours—School very full—too much so to do them justice—I will try—

Wednesday 8th More with School much crowded—

Thursday 9th Warm

Friday 10th Very warm for Jan. People appear to say it is uncommon

Saturday 11th Very muddy walking in consequence of the grounds thawing—

Sabbath High wind this 12th N-W—

Monday 13th Snow squalls A.M.—P.M. Steady Snow—Last evening was married Richard Goldsmith Junr. to Miss Martha Coleman, daughter of our friends Asael & Esther Coleman—

Tuesday 14th Snow storm—

Wednesday 15th Cool, good sleighing—

[50] Thursday 16th Jan. 1794 The sleighs fly by—

Friday 17 Pleasent & clear—

Saturday 18th Fine Winter weather

Sabbath 19th Weather as yesterday

Monday 20th The snow is pretty much disappeared—

Tuesday 21st rain—Wednesday 2nd warm—Not comfortable overhead, and intollerable overhead [underfoot]—

Thursday 23rd A hard Snow Storm—

Friday 24th high wind N-W—Our friend Samuel Tuthill, formerly from LongIsland, visited us. He is now from Tioga, where he has moved his family, sometime since—He bids fair to become a Man of property—

Saturday 25th Cold wind, and high N-W—

Sabbath 26th Weather more calm—

Monday 27th Very cold—

Tuesday 28th A cloudy day

[51] Wednesday 29th Jan. 1794—A Snowstorm

Thurday 30th Sleighing very good, and is much improved, as people are now convey their produce to Market, and their wheat to the Mills to be manufactured into flour—

Thursday 31st Winter in earnest, the Horses feel It in being continually on the go with the music of many bells—

Saturday 1st Feb. 1794 Wind N-W- and very cold—

Sabbath 2nd 27 years since I became an inhabitant of this uncertain World—I have been protected through seen and unseen dangers, May my many mercies be sanctified, in time, and beyond its transient limits.

Monday 3rd Pleasant—our friend Absalom Racket, commences board with us this day—He is ciphering [doing arithmetic] and writing etc—etc—

[52] Tuesday 4th Feb. 1794 Weather moderate—

Wednesday 5th More cold—Mrs. Griffing & myself rode out to Oxford, to Uncle Samuel Rackets, where we met George Brown Esq. and wife, & Joseph King & wife—It was an agreable interview, as we considered our meeting was conducted on social good feelings, and a hearty welcome of our kind host, & his tender wifes good cheer well served us in the nicest order—

Thursday 6th A very sharp cold day—Returned home this morn.

Friday 7th Snow goes off pretty fast, as it is warmer than yesterday

Saturday 8th With Mrs. G- visited Uncle Saml. Racket, tarried with him the night—

[53] Sabbath 9th with Uncle Saml. Racket, and Mrs. Griffing, rode to Uncle Noah Terrys about 12 miles

Monday 10th Some rain—At Uncle Terrys

Tuesday 11th Rode home, where we arrived about sun down—left Mrs. Griffing at Joseph Kings—

Wednesday 12th warm—Lucretia returned home this Eve—

Thurday 13th & Friday 14th Cloudy, and unpleasant—

Saturday 15th & Sabbath 16th—Weather pleasant for the season—

Monday 17th Pleasant—

Tuesday 18th Cloudy day—

Wednesday 19th- Day as yesterday

Thursday 20th High wind N-W- and cold—

Friday 21st Continues cold—

Saturday 22nd Mild weather

[54] Sabbath 23rd Feb. 1794 Snow storm

Monday 24th Clears up this morn, but remains very cold—

Tuesday 25th cold, and good sleighing—I think there is 100 sleds & sleighs passes my door, with produce and pleasure parties each day, at this time

Wednesday 26th Weather extreme cold—

Thursday 27th—Steady cold
Friday 28th More mild—

March 1st 1794 Weather as yesterday—Waited on Friend Thomas V. Racket, out to Squire Whites, Father of Judge Nathan H. White—To John Moffatts—and to my good friends Asael Colemans—At our [55] return, in the eve, found our little Harriet had [scalded?] herself—

Heard this evening of the death of the friend of my youth, with whom I have spent some years of great intimacy, John King—He died on the island of Jamaica—He was 28 years of age—To me, he was an associate beyond expressible, pleasant, prepossessing, and agreable—But death pays no attention to Earthly ties, but severs the silver cords of the most sacred Friendship! The pitcher of human Joys will, and must be broken at the Fountain—Our last meeting was on the Morning of July 16th 1793

[56] Sabbath March 2nd 1794 Quite a thaw—
Monday 3rd Some rain
Tuesday 4th High wind—
Wednesday 5th Cold, much so—
Thursday 6th S-E- Snowstorm
Friday 7th A rain storm—traveling very unpleasent—
Saturday 8th At School—
Sabbath 9th Attended meeting—on my return called in at Mr. John Brewsters, a Man some advanced in life, and appears to be a Man who does not any buisness, as to labouring with his hands—I think from what I have seen of him, that he spends the larger part of his hours each day in sitting at his front door, on a seat, in his piazza [porch]—In warm weather I have seldom seem him in any other place—and I often pass his residence

[57] While at Brewsters, was highly entertained by the conversation of Messrs David Denison, and Nathaniel H.Howel, on the commotions in France & Europe in general—

A stormy time in France in these days—
Monday 10th Pleasant—
Tuesday 11th Dismissed my School—Its very probable, for the last time, in this District—There is something solemn, and pensive, in such an emphatic expression—O this chequered shadow life—
Wednesday 12th Purchased a cow of a Mr. Jeremiah Williams—
Thursday 13th Pleasant—
Friday 14th Rode out to Little Britain, to a Vendue—I find It bad trav-

illing, especially with a poor horse—Met at said Vendue, My friends with whom I spent the winter of 89 & 1790—viz. James & Thomas Tustin—

Saturday, & Sabbath 15th & 16th Pleasent weather—

Monday 17th Pleasent, Rode out about 6 miles to Smiths Clove—Stoped the night with Mr. Gilbert King, who was formerly from LongIsland—

[58] Tuesday 18th March 1794 Warm—visited George Brown Esq., this A.M.—Returned home this eve—

Am informed that friend Silas Vail is sick with the pleurisy at his residence, Sterling [Greenport], LongIsland—

Wednesday 19th Thursday 20th Friday 21st and Saturday 22nd Moderate days, or weather, as we say—Wisdom, we are told from a divine source, is the principle thing, yet how few there are who obtain it, but by sad experience and when the chance for improving by its invaluable use has passed away—This letting go a certainty for an uncertainty is a sad bargain—Esau found It so when he sought carefully with tears, what he had foolishly parted with for a trifle—a momentary gratification—

Sabbath 23rd—Fair weather—The above observations were suggested on remarks being made in my leaving my school altogether—

[59] Monday 24th & Tuesday 25th Wind N-W—Nothing of note—

Wednesday 26th Our Friends, Thomas V- & Absalom Racket, who have been stoping with us sometime, leave this day for LongIsland—Two excellent young Men, Grandsons of the late Judge Thomas Youngs of Sterling, LongIsland, N.Y.—

Thursday 27th & Friday 28th- Fair weather—Mr. James Vail visited us—

Saturday 29th Rain

Sabbath 30th Attended meeting

Monday 31st Rain—Called on Mr. Asael Coleman, and John Benjamin—This Benjamin has been a good employer of mine since I have located in this place, which is now near 3 years—He says he was on duty as a soldier, at the execution of the unfortunate Andre—A more prepossessing, finished Gentleman and sensible address, and deportment, he, Benjamin, says he never saw in any of the sons of [page trimmed]

[60] Tuesday 1st April 1794 High wind N-W—Attended Town Meeting at the House of John Brewster—A large company, and much Rum—I fear not much Wisdom—

Wednesday 2nd Light wind N—

Thursday 3rd Rain, with Thunder—Am settling up my School bills, with those who have put their children under my care since 1791—except for a short time—As its likely this is my last accounts with them in this way, I feel affected at the solemn consideration—They, as Fathers of a united district, have merited and have my most respectful consideration— I shall, while life continues, remember, with grateful emotions, of hearty good will, the civilities of Samuel Moffatt—Richard Goldsmith, Hugh Turner—Abner Coleman—John Booth[?]—Jonathan Brooks—William Hudson—Caleb Coleman—John Benjamin—Benjamin Tuthill [61] Asael Coleman—Anselm Helm—Benjamin Brewster—Jeremiah Horton, & Joshua Curtis—All—all, deserve and have merited my best respects, and cherished remembrance—

*This beautiful and bright young Man was lost at sea in Novemb. 1796

Friday 4th—Pleasant—My Brother Moses* sets off this day for the Land of our Fathers—Longisland—He has been near us since Novem. 23rd last— has taught a School in the lower part of East division, about 3½ miles from us for the last 3 months—We have had the satisfaction of his visits, often through the past winter—He now leaves this county, perhaps forever—Not a thought to be made light of—

Saturday 5th A chilly, raw day—Had an agreable visit this day from my honest friend Thomas Tustin—I found him all I could wish to solace, amuse, and do me good, in the dreary winter, and spring of 1790, while I boarded with his good [page trimmed]

[62] An elderly gentleman, by the name of Clark, called on us this day, he was amongst the early settlers of this Goshen Country—He is a pious Man, over 80 years of age—

From Sabbath 6th to Tuesday 8th Chilly kind of weather—

Wednesday 9th Rec'd a letter from Thomas V. Racket, in which he says himself & Brother A. had an excellent time home, where they found them all well, and glad to see them—

Thursday 10th Cool—

Friday 11th Wind N-E- and cool—

From Saturday 12th to Tuesday 15th weather Springlike—This last date was visited by our Friend Silas Vail—It was a pleasing interview—

Wednesday 16th Friend leaves in view of looking for a place, to purchase in some of our near districts

Thursday 17th Mr. Richard S. Hubbard, immediately from LongIsland, called on us, [63] says his family, with Mother Tuthill, are now at NewWindsor, waiting to get conveyence up to this place—8 P.M. Mother Tuthill arrived at my house—That excellent goodhearted Man, Mr. Jonas Seely, of Oxford, brought her up, without fee, or reward—It was a joyful meeting, with my wife and the Mother—

Saturday 19th Assisted Brother Hubbard in moving his family and affects into a House he hires of Abner Coleman—

Sabbath 20th Warm—

Monday 21st Wind high S-W—

Tuesday 22nd A rain storm—Noah Tuthill, our cousin, visited us— He is just now from Longisland—by him received a letter from Doct. Thomas Vail—

Wednesday 23rd This day Friend Silas Vail leaves us for Longisland, having not found any place to locate in this region to suit him

[64] Thursday 24th Apl. 1794 Rain, with squalls

Friday 25th—

Saturday 26th Blustering

Sabbath 27th Wind high W—Mr. Bradners text was this day Isaiah 61st 1st—

Monday 28th Rain

Tuesday 29th Pleasent—Attended Ellection at Mr. John Brewsters, the house where I find the Town Meetings are at present held, although Its but a private house—There is not any good Public Hotels, in this vicinity, suitable for Public meetings—The great and Patriotic Washington, is yet our President—no perfection here—

Wednesday 30th Wind high N-W—Our neighbour, Daniel Corwin, raised his house this day—This is the Man, [from whom] I purchased my land, on which I built my present Tenement—[65] His house stands about 20 rods west of mine- and mine about a mile east of Blooming Grove Meetinghouse, or Church—

Thursday the 1st May 1794 & Friday 2nd—Fair days—Planted some in my garden, for the first this season, and the first I ever planted on my own soil—

Saturday 3rd Warm—Settled accounts with Mr. E. Cutter, a Blacksmith near us—

Sabbath 4th Attended meeting—Mr. Bradners Text was Matthew 11—28th

Monday 5th Tuesday 6th Wednesday 7th & Thursday 8th were what we call Fair days, as to the weather—

Friday 9th Cloudy—A coloured Man called Cuffee is assisting me in making Stone fence—Rather more heavy lifting than teaching A-B-C—

Saturday 10th Quite warm—Our friend Absalom Racket visited us this day, He is immediately from LongIsland—Not any letters by him—Rather a disappointment—

[66] Sabbath 11th- Monday 12th- Tuesday 13th May 1794 Good weather—Wrote letters to our LongIsland Friends, sent them by Miss Mehitable King, a resident of O-ponds [Oysterponds, now Orient and East Marion] L. Island—

Wednesday 14th Some rain—Mrs. G unwell, the Doct. Visited her—

Thursday 15th Pleasent—

Friday 16th As yesterday

Saturday 17th Rode out to Mr. Jonathan [Broadis's?]—and Samuel McConns—The first is a large Farmer, the 2nd an extensive Merchant, a Manufacturer of flour etc etc—He purchases thousands of bushels of wheat—

Sabbath 18th Cool for May

Monday 19th Tuesday 20th & Wednesday 21st It is growing dry—on the 21st our dear Harriet had a convulsion fit—such illness alarmed and affected us—

[67] Friday 23rd—our Harriet had another ill turn similar to the other of the 21st—

Saturday 24th A rain storm—It is much needed, as its getting dry—On June 8th 1794, Mrs. Griffing was confined with a Son—on Friday 13th June the little Infant died, having appeared to suffer much ever since its birth—

July 17th Mrs. Griffing continues very unwell—In this month, Doctor Thomas Vail, who had been to Albany, and was returning to Long Island, put on shore at New Windsor, a handsome Horse, which he sent to me by our friend James Vail, with written directions to sell it the best I could—

September—1794 Mrs. G. continues unwell but not so low as she has been—a distressing ague follows her up, which keeps her very weak—

Sold Vail's horse this month, repaired to Long Island, to Plumisland, found my parents well and glad to [68] see me—While with my parents, two or three days I had a severe fit of the ague—

After calling on my Uncles, Aunts, and friend Silas Vail, and paying Doc. Vail for his horse, I returned home with my eldest Sister Deziah with me—found my dear wife yet very feeble—Doctor Davis, and Miller, who[']ve attended her in my absence, say her raging fever was very similar to the Yellow Fever, which proved so fatal to hundreds in New York sometimes since—I admonish myself very much to blame in leaving home as I have done in this case, although at the time of leaving I felt to believe Mrs. Griffing slowly getting better—To my sorrow it has proved far otherwise—I now lament the imprudent step, and hope the Sin will be forgiven—"to err is human, to forgive is divine"—

20th Septem. 1794 [69] Mrs.Griffing is getting so much better, as to set up considerable—

28th Sept. 1794 Sold my place and premises to Mr. Daniel Corwin, the Gentleman of whom I purchased the land of in May 1793—I gave him at the time 50 Dollars for the 13 acres, on which I built a house and partly finished it. It has altogether probably cost me 250 Dollars—perhaps more—As it is, I have sold for about 400 Doll[ar]s—

October 1794 I moved my family and effects to Bethelem [Bethlehem], within about four miles of New Windsor, to a room I rented of a Mr. Deniston—My intention was to keep School in the district, as there appears to be an opening for one, and the people were encouraging me to take one—Well, I leave Coleman Town with a notion of peculiar respect, for all my friends in the vicinity—A more interesting, friendly neighbourhood and society I never shall know, as each individual, with whom I have been engaged [70] in buisness within this three years past, I have at all times found full of kindness, accommodation, and good will towards me, who had came a stranger among them—To name one, whose expressions of marked kindnesses to me, and mine, at all times, and especially in time of actually need, I must name all—

In the winter of 1791 & 92 while teaching school in this District, I had for a pupil, a young Man by name Josiah Smith, a very aimable, agreable young Man, of the most agreable address, and prepossessing conversation—About 20 years of age—His time in School was writing, drawing Bills & etc etc He intends, he says, to go to Philadelphia in the Spring and if possible get a clerkship in some place where by strict attention, and correct conduct, he can rise to some eminence, as a Clerk in some respectful situation—I parted with this interesting young Man in March 1792. In the summer ensuing that date, I received a letter from him, informing me he [71] got a handsome clerks birth in a conspicuous Lumber yard, at a handsome salary—In the Autumn of 1793 I received another Letter from him, stating the awful ravages of the Yellow Fever in the City of Philadelphia. He says it took off 4000 in a short time—He never never left the city but stuck close to his buisness and escaped the fever! He was now a clerk in one of the Banks, in that City—Should I again hear from him I shall notice it—

October 1794 As before observed, I am at Bethelem—The last of this month I rode out [to] Goshen, where there I met a Mr. John Hudson, who told me he had a small place of about 10 acres of land, with a house & barn on it which he would sell immediately, with possession—I returned home

to consider of it until tomorrow, which would be Saturday 25th—It came—
I went and closed the bargain for about 300 Dolls—on 27th & 28th I moved
my family [72] and effects to my new situation, which is in the East division
of Goshen, within 2½ miles of the Court house—

Novem.—My dear Wife still continues to droop with the Ague, although
betwixt the ill turns she walks about house—

December—Absalom Racket is with us—

1795

January 1795 A cold month this the first winter I have undertook to pass
without teaching a school since 1790—this month Mrs. G- appears to be
gaining her health—Our sister Deziah, who came with me to this part of the
country in September last left us for LongIsland, about the middle of
Novem. Past—We have just heard, this first January 1795—that this truly
affectionately kind, invaluable daughter, and Sister, while on her way home
in NewYork took the small pox, and within 15 days of her arrival home,
died—She was 24 years of age—but few leave so large a circle of sentimental
friends as she has [73] to mourn her untimely exit from all terrestrial
things—She was assuredly an interesting, agreable, edifying warm friend,
and companion—But she is gone, & we must follow, and know where to
find her—

Feb. 1795 Is an open, rather thawing month—Brother Hubbard & Silas
Howel live within 2 and 3 miles of us—Joseph King within 4 miles—Uncle
Sam'l Racket about 4½ miles—We see them often this winter—

March comes in cold—on the 15th we had a severe Easterly Snow storm—
A thick wet snow, occasioned by the dampness, at falling, and then freezing
so as to nearly bear a Man when walking, makes travilling a caution—

April—Spring opens pretty Fair—The last of this month, Capt. Phineas
Rumsey, our neighbour, a Man not much over sixty years, died with the 3rd
stroke of the palsy—
Attended Town Meeting, on the 1st Tuesday [74] of this month, which
was held at Goshen Courthouse—Our neighbour, John Vail, a Man near 60
years, was voted in Supervisor—

•

May 1795 Planted about one acre of corn ground—I have a garden of about 30 rods of ground—

June 1795—Built some castles in the air this month, but as they have not much foundation they, I justly fear cannot amount to much—

July 1795 Was visited by my own very dear Father and Mother—After staying with us a day or two, they went to Uncle Noah Terrys, near Minnisink—After a sociable visit to my Uncles, and other friends in these parts they returned to LongIsland—This was to me, to us, and I hope to them a useful, seasonable, and satisfactory visit—
About the 10th of this month last Mrs. Sibil Terry, Wife of Mr. Constant Terry, died very sudden—She was [75] one of the excellent of the earth— In works of Charity, kindness, and affectionate good deeds, she had no superior—

August 1795 was a warm month—Friend A. Racket bought a noble cow for me to keep for the milk etc etc—

Septemb. My Acre of Corn, which bid fair for a plentiful yield, is destroyed by my neighbours cattle! Thus it was at Coleman Town—Tis too bad—Is this to be the affects of my Farming? If so, what will it amount to but a nothing—

October 1795—We have plenty of peaches—some bushels—and a good garden—But my corn—Yes the corn—gone—

November 1795 Thomas V Racket is now studying Physick [medicine], at the House of Mr. Jonath Brooks, with Doct. A. Davis—We have several agreable visits from our good friend Doct. David B. Arnel, now of Deerpark—

[76] December 1795 The first of this month I visited Doct. Arnel, stoped with him two days—Bought Halls juvenile Essays of him—
Our Friend A Racket takes the school at Deerpark [in western Orange County, 14 miles from Goshen] this Winter—And I commence the School at Greycourt near Major Thomas Moffatts—about a good round mile from my house, over hills & dales—

In the spring of this year, 1795, Mrs. Bull, a Widow Lady, living within 2½ miles of us, died aged 102 or 3 years of age—she was the first white person or Woman that took lodging in Goshen—the place where she lodged was beside a brook near where afterwards stood the house of [?]

1796

1796 Jan 1st Have a pretty good school—As I carry my dinner, Mrs. G-
leads rather a lonesome life, not often she says having a visitor during the
day—My only track through my gate, on the snow in the morning, as I pass
out, remain unbroken when I return at night—However—She, and our little Harriet appear to enjoy themselves, in expecting our return—

[77] February 2nd 1796 A cloudy day—The anniversary of my birth—
This day, 29 years ago, I, as my parents inform me, made the first step on the
treacherous bridge of this uncertain, certain state of a shadowy existence—
It is full of meaning, and full of accountability—God grant me a consideration adequate to my responsibility, and immortality—

Wednesday 3rd A Snow storm—

Thursday 4th It ceased to storm, yet it may justly be called a cloudy,
dark day—

Friday 5th Was visited this day by my friend Absalom Racket—He carries
with his every association and intercourse with me, and mine, emphatical
expressions of genuine good will and a real interest in our every comfort—

Saturday 6th A small snow storm—Friend Racket left us this P.M. for his
School, at Deerpark—

Sabbath 7th Winter, and cloudy

[78] Monday 8th Feb. 1796—A pleasant morn—This noon spell, as we
say, I walked over to Mr. John Hudsons, a distance of ⅓ mile—He sends
two interesting children to my school—A girl, Ila, and son, Horace—
Mr. Hudson was from Longisland, and in his younger years spent some
time on the Seas—He is a well read and very sensible prepossessing
Man—Full of fascinating conversation, intermixed with the convivial
and well timed anecdotes—An agreeable companion, and associate, Mr
Hudson has but few superiors—Farther than morality, as to Church fel-
lowship, he honestly makes not any profession—Of course he is no hypocrite—Such I find Mr. John Hudson, who is now about 36 years of
age—a Man of good face, good figure, stands about 5 feet 7½ inches and
of dignified move & deportment—Of this gentleman I bought the place
I now live on—

[79] Tuesday 9th Pleasant weather—

Wednesday 10th Snow Storm—

Thursday 11th A rain Storm this morn—Foggy, and thick through the day—

Friday 12th A cold N-W- wind, which blows furiously—

Saturday 13th Cloudy—It has been excellent Sleighing this time, and the Horses appear to show that their owners improve it

Sabbath 14th St. Valentine's day—Birds, it is said, chuse their mates this day, and we never know but they make a wise choice—Why is it that reasonable creatures are less fortunate, (often) in a selection for life?

Monday 15th High wind, and very cold

Tuesday 16th Wind continues blustering, N-W- Capt. David Sweezey, a Man of 47 years, a pleasent, no buisness man, often calls in, and sees us— We are pleased with his friendly calls—His Brother is Doct. Jonathan Sweezey, an eminent Physician of Goshen, A Man really beloved and of high consideration—

[80] Wednesday 17th Feb. 1796 A cloudy day—

Thursday 18th A snow storm—

Friday 19th A pleasent—

Saturday 20th What is pronounced good weather—

Sabbath 21st Very cold—Sleighing has been good this 7 weeks—distressing to some Horses, as they abundantly show its truth—Rum, & Gin, give more speed, than corn & oats to the hungry, weary old Roans, and Dobbins—

Monday 22nd A light Snow—

Tuesday 23rd High wind, with a smothering drift of the new fallen snow

Wednesday 24th A cold time—

Thursday 25th More mild—

Friday 26th A small rain, yet not so as to spoil the sleding—

Saturday 27th calm day—

Sabbath 28th Not pleasent overhead, and as to travilling, it is intollerable—

[81] Monday 29th Feb. 1796—Leap year—

Tuesday 1st March—Good sleding continues—

Wednesday 2nd A snow storm—its toilsome to tru[d]ge the snowbanks a mile over hills of no small magnitude, adjoining deep hollows—

Thursday 3rd It snows

Friday 4th high wind, and the snow flies

Saturday 5th Mild, which is agreable after such stormy weather—

Sabbath 6th Pleasent—it has now been pretty good sleighing since 10th Jan. near 8 weeks—

Monday 7th A cloudy day—

Tuesday 8th Snow squalls—

Wednesday 9th Very cold—

Thursday 10th Pleasent—

Friday 11th As yesterday—

Saturday 12th Was visited this day by our substantial friend Absalom Racket just from Deerpark, where is yet engaged in teaching School

A Miss Maria H. Smith is assisting Mrs. Griffing who is now unwell—

[82] Sabbath 13th March 1796 Pleasent—walked out to Greycourt with Absalom Racket—

Monday 14th Fair weather—

Tuesday 15th Some rain, and a dense fog—This morn, Mrs. Griffing was confined with a daughter—a beautiful, and as it was said of the infant Moses, previous to his being put into the Ark of bulrushes, "It was a goodly child"—We name it Deziah Narcissa—

Wednesday 16th Rain, with Thunder, this morn—P.M. Squally

Thursday 17th A high wind—and pretty cold

Friday 18th About 10 A.M. it commenced snowing, which subsides in a Squall—

Saturday 19th—It clears off cold

Sabbath 20th To speak loud, and with earnestness to those whom we know are not deaf, denotes imprudence, and lack of judgement at the time—"Soft words turn away wrath"

[83] Monday 21st March 1796 A cloudy atmosphere—This day our Friend A. Racket closes his School, at Deerpark, where he has now taught one quarter—

At this time an old Gentleman, by name John Sybolt (I believe from Germany) is residing at Deerpark, a farmer—Many years ago (perhaps more than 35) he lived on Shelter Island (Longisland) I expect then, a poor, and single man—I believe he worked at the time for Mr. Thomas Deering [Dering], who was quite a landed man, on said S-Island—Sybolt is now possessor of a handsome estate—has two respectable Sons, well to live— one of them a useful Justice of the Peace—The Father is now a venerable and aged man—

Wednesday 23rd Friend A. Racket arrived at our house—Tarried with us the night—

Thursday 24th A blustering day, as to wind—Friend Racket with me in School—

Friday 25th Cold morn, not much warm through the day—

[84] Saturday 26th March 1796—Major Henry Brewster has within a week or two past lost two very interesting, promising daughters, by Death— The eldest about 11 years old—

Sabbath 27th The Goshen Church is about 3½ miles from us, and not having any horse, a good excuse for [not?] attending meeting—However, if we improve our time as we ought, it matters not much where we are on the Sabbath—I say if we are right, we cannot be wrong at the same time—

Monday 28th A moderate rainstorm

Tuesday 29th Hazy weather—

Wednesday 30th A pleasant day—

Thursday 31st A beautiful, clear sun—Friend A. Racket with us—This evening my Friend Constant Terry whose timely civilities I greatly realized in bygone days, spent the evening with us—[85] His expressions of kindness, united with those of his invaluable Wife, when I first arrived in this country, in 1789, will make the most lasting impression of gratitude, in my breast, while my heart is continued to beat in that seat of life—She was a Dorcas in deeds and acts of charity—He was generous, and accommodating to a Proverb—

Friday 1st Apl 1796—Pleasant—My quarter School is out this day—Have a small exhibition of my Scholars—A number of spectators, with the parents of the children, all which appeared well pleased, and satisfied with the improvement of my charges—

Saturday 2nd April Pleasant weather—Attended a Vendue at Abraham Vails—A young married man, not more than 20 years of age, the son of Mr. John Vail, our present Supervisor of this Town—This evening attended a debating meeting, at Chester, 2½ miles from us—the question was, "Is slavery just, or not"—I was on the negative—There was much said and wrote—Not as I [?] grammatically flowery—[page trimmed]

[86] Sabbath 3rd April 1796—Good weather—A. Racket, with us and his society is always in time—

Monday 4th—The weather is fair—

Made several calls with Friend Racket—

Tuesday 5th Wind brisk N.W.—of course cool—Attended Town meeing at Goshen Courthouse—A. Racket with me, on our way home, stoped at Mr. John Vails, whom we had been ellecting into the office of Supervisor—

Wednesday 6th cool—A. Racket is yet with us

Thursday 7th Thick smoky air—Attended a Vendue at Abraham Townsends—

Friday 8th With Friend Racket went to Warrick [Warwick], about 12 miles, on our way stoped at a Mr. Barnabas Hortons, an excellent good man, and greatly possessed of that which is greater than Faith and Hope—Charity. I believe he is a descendant of Barnabas Horton, the first of the name, who landed at Southold in 1640—

[87] Was hospitably entertained the night at a Mr. Nobles—who appeared, and no doubt is, a Man of strict veracity and actual benevolence—

Saturday 9th Returned home, well pleased with our excursion, and the acquaintance we had formed—While out on our walk, we called at the house of Robert Ludow [Ludlow?] Esq., who was formerly from Sagharbour, where he married his wife, who is a most aimable and accomplished woman—Mr. Ludow was not at home, but his wife was all attention to make our short stop comfortable, and refreshing—Mr. Ludow has two spritely, promising boys,* James & Augustus—What other children they have I know not—At any rate, the family appeared, with the Mother, to be what we call "a likely family"

Saturday 23rd Quite dry—April—There is at this time, in this neighbourhood, 3 or 4 young men, if they ought to be called men, who appear to make it their buisness to prowl around this, and other adjacent neighbourhoods, and under [88] cover of a dark night, a just semblance of their deeds mutilate and materially injure their neighbours goods and chattels—They appear to select victims to vent their spleen and malice upon whose innocence and civility would warrant them better treatment from any beings, but monsters of meanness & rascality—One of these and the most forward is Selah Smith* whose name in this region needs only to be mentioned to be detested—I may be hasty, in handing his name to those of afteryears, yet my reasons for doing so is sufficient in my humble opinion—I have not seen Smith, but a few times since I have located in his neighborhood, but when I have come in contact with him, his looks, demeanor, eyes, and actions bespeak him to possess a heart as black as Egyptian Darklings—The private injuries inflicted on my property, by this midnight walker, and his mise-[89]rable associates, constrains me to speak this freely (perhaps a little more softly would be more prudent) of a man, whom I may forgive, but ought not to forget, without some consessions—I now leave him—If I shall live some years to come, I may notice this unpleasent circumstance, and his whereabouts*

Monday 2nd May 1796—Pleasant Springlike weather—My Friend A. Racket has taken the Blooming Grove School, at the Church, at least the schoolhouse is just by the meeting house—

Tuesday 3rd White frost this morn

*These young men became officers in the Navy in the [?]

*This same Selah Smith died at Sagharbour on Longisland, about 1847 or 8, while on a visit to his daughter, who had married a Mr. [Friend?] of that village—50 years after, no doubt, but he had seen the evil of [?]deeds and repented of such early [?]

Wednesday 4th Visited Brother S. Hubbards family—While there I met my wifes Mother, whom I have not seen this 12 months past—

Thursday 5th Attended the exhibition of the Scholars of a Mr. Tupper, whose School is at Chester—They performed very well—

Friday 6th Read, when I can, in Rollins Ancient History

[90] Saturday 7th May 1796—A fine, or good rain

Monday 9th A rain storm

Tuesday 10th A.M. Rain—P.M. Clears off pleasent

Wednesday 11th Rain this morn—Evening clears up Pleasent—

Thursday 12th Thunder—Shower last night—Pleasent this morn—

Friday 13th—A mild morn—Dined with Mr. John Hudson—

Saturday 14th—fair weather

Thursday 19th—Clear—

Monday 21st Some rain this day, and then some shines—

Saturday 28th Rain—Our dear young friend A. Racket, is taken quite ill—

June 4th visited friend Racket, [91] who lies very sick at the house of John Chandler, Merchant, Blooming Grove—He, in my opinion, is a dangerously sick man, but manifests much patience, and resignation—I could wish he had a more suitable place, as the room in which he is confined is adjoining the Store, where there is much talk, and noise, especially by those who purchase Rum, as many do in these parts just now—I left him after being with him not an hour—His fever was high, and at times his reason much impaired—

Monday 7th June 1796 This day departed this life our dear, and invaluable Friend, Absalom Racket, aged about 26 years—In him, we have a loss, which it is not in the power of mortals to repair—He was the constant, undeviating, kind, interesting, sentimental Friend, and the Man, (if there ever was one) without deceit, and guile—He has thus [page trimmed] left us to contemplate his numerous virtues

[92] June 19th 1796 Warm, and what is called growing weather

Monday 20th & 21st great dews this some mornings—We greatly miss the agreable visits we were lately want to have from the late dear Absalom R—His conversation, and society always, and at all times rendered our situation tolerable, even when writhing under the discouraging evils and private injuries inflicted on me, noticed April last [Selah Smith, pp. 87–88]—His cheerful aid to lighten my drooping spirits were always in time, and successful—But alas!—that crystal fountain is now dried up, and that stream of consolation to me, and mine, is now dried up—

Friday 24th Saturday 25th—Some Thunder, but its getting something dry—Am preparing my Scholars to have a small exhibition at the end of the present quarter—

[93] Sabbath 26th June 1796 Uncle Noah Terry and Capt. Rufus Tuthill visited us—Tuthill is from LongIsland, and stays with us the night—Uncle Terry leaves this eve for his home, over to the Drowned Lands, about 10 or 12 miles from Goshen Court house—

Monday 27th Capt. Tuthill leaves for LongIsland this morn—P.M. Received a letter from Brother James Griffing, and one from Doct. Thomas Vail, who has some time since moved his family to Vermont—Says in his communicaton he has lost his daughter (a pretty girl) of 10 years of age, named Sophia—

Tuesday 28th Not a clear day—yet not any rain—

Wednesday 29th Warm & dry—

Thursday 30th High wind ends this month—I have, pretty attentively, read [Charles] Rollins 8 volumes of Ancient History through, and not, I hope neglected my school charges, and interesting family—This I have done within 13 weeks past—

[94] July 1st & Saturday 2nd Hot weather—but dry—Visited Mr. J. Hudsons, these noon spells—

Monday 4th Received a letter from Mrs. Maria Gregg, conceived in expressions of much tenderness, respecting the death of our late friend Absalom—In the letter is these lines—viz.

> The Birds, the Groves, the flowers remain—
> But Damon, still I seek in vain.

Mrs Gregg is a Widow Lady of about 24 years of age, an accomplished and well informed Woman, with one child by her husband, with whom she lived but a short time—Death making the separation—Our friend, of whom she so tenderly mentions, has often told me that his impressions in her favour were (he believed) reciprocal, and that she was his friend—they had [95] occasionally met, and that such interviews were strengthening the cords of a sentimental Friendship—But alas! The uncertainty of all sublinary [mortal] things!—

Friday 8th General Training at Goshen—I had formerly belonged to the troop of Horse—but now, at this time a spectator only—

Saturd. 9th Betwixt school, noonspell visited Major Thomas Moffatt, a Gentleman, very deservedly respected—noticed before in this journal—

Tuesday 12th Fair day—our little Harriet quite ill—

Read some in the writings of the eccentric [Laurence] Sterne—He says, and justly," My hair grew grey, while I am comeing [combing] it"—

I am now, and have been this some months past, holding a correspondence with Doct. David R. Arnell of Deerpark—

[96] Friday 15th July 1796—Rain, which is much needed—

Monday 18th this noonspell, visited John Hudsons

Tuesday 19th Mrs. G- & myself visited Joseph Kings—Tarried with them the night—

August 23rd Nothing of any particular note for the last 30 days—

In said time, I have been engaged in my School—Once, in said time, I have been witness of an occurrence, which might not be out of place to notice to the peaceable quiet friend, who shall, or may chance to read my observations of the weather, and my whereabouts, at this period of my uninteresting little point—Well—in the said 30 days, past, that is, in, or on one of them, as I was taking some refreshment [97] with a young Married couple whose honeymoon was scarcely passed away—At my first setting down to the Table, I observed the Lady, to look the picture of melancholy and the gentleman (who was all politeness, and attention to me) looked unutterable things at his wife—She soon broke silence by asking him, how he could reconcile his conduct in staying out so late the past night. Such late hours would soon destroy her. He replied sharply, that he should do as he pleased, and her prudence would show itself in her immediate silence. She answered with dignity, sobs, and tears, that such a command bespoke the Tyrant, not the gentleman, much less the tender confiding Husband—He turned and with apparent (great) wrath said, if she made another single observation, he would horsewhip her. With self-respect she replied that his words, and threats [98] of that outlandish, and savage cast, were in perfect keeping with the lowest vestiges of mortality, and the sooner she was rid of a disgrace to humanity, the better—At this he arose from the Table (she being already up about the room), seized his silver mounted riding whip, which he applied with much seeming carelessness around the lower parts of her flowing dress, where I presume not one stroke touched any portion of her body—of course, there was not any wound from this astonishing application but wounded feelings—The Gentleman after this ungenteel act mounted his horse and rode off—She, drowned in tears and sighs—turned to me, and observed with emphasis, "Mr. Griffing, you have seen an act [99] committed, which must only be seen to be believed—She immediately set about packing up her articles for a move (as she said) forthwith, from the house—But behold the mutability of sublinary resolves! In the brief space of about two days after this

[top of page, in pencil] see Griffins Journal page 264 printed

strange adventure, I was so happy as to meet them in the successful tide of conjugal love—She was arrayed with taste in a new and elegant silk dress, with every other costly appendage, calculated to make her look as he always viewed her when he kept rational hours, and discarded the contents of the accursed cup—The above Gentleman is about 25 years of age—As handsome, well informed a gentleman as the country affords, and at this time possessed of a handsome property, lately left him by his late too fond and, (I fear) indulgent Father—[page trimmed]The cup will yet ruin him

[100] Thursday 25th August 1796 Am just informed of the death of Thomas Tustin, whom I have often before mentioned, in my Journal—He was a young Man, of sterling merit, upright, courteous, affable, and accommodating in all his intercourse with his fellow Man—A dutiful son, and loving, and affectionate Brother, and a confidential Friend—He has this some time past been engaged in carrying the Mail, from Goshen to New York—While on his way from N. York to Goshen (about ten days since) he was taken with a fever, which terminated in his early dissolution—He leaves a Mother, who has drunk deep at the fount of affliction, to again renew the garb of mourning—She is the widow of the late Col Benjamin Tustin, who was killed at the battle of Minisink [1779]—In the winter of 1789 & 90, I boarded with [101] her and her two sons James & Thomas, from all of which I received the most interesting, and hearty expressions of esteem and goodwill—His age about 24 years—Thus it is within two short months, I have lost by death two sincere and disinterested friends—A treasure invaluable to our existence, yet without which, the wealthiest mortal is assuredly poor, and wretched—The names of Absalom Racket, and Thomas Tustin, will have a conspicuous place in my memory, while its Tablet shall hold a place on the shores of mortality—

The following lines, I wrote for Absalom Racket, a few months before he died—It was on Friendships being renewed in a future state—

> There Jonathan has his David met,
> And Watts, his Gunston too—
> And O, my valued pleasent friend,
> May I there meet with you—

[102] From Friday 26th to Wednesday 31st 1796 not anything of interest occurred—Only one small rain, in said time—My school occupied the chief of my attention—

Noon spells, often visit Mr. John Hudson, whose manner, conversation, and ingenuity in relating incidents and well timed anecdotes are assuredly engaging—He is a man of much reading, of some considerable in his younger years, and <u>now</u> of close observation—His society is much courted by the neighbouring Physicians, Lawyers, and sociable men of the world— Our Priests respect and often converse with him, but appear to think, without apprizing him of it, that Mr. Hudson is, with his prepossessing acquirements, tinctured largely with Skepticism—We believe him to be no hypocrite—A truly honest man in his principles, and as to his knowledge of the Christian dispensation, we may pray he may yet be enlightened in his understanding for substantial joys beyond time [page trimmed]

[103] Mr. Hudson has two aimable children, a daughter and a Son—The former about 9 years old—the latter 7—The Girl Ila—the boy Horace

Friday 2nd Septem 1796—A rain storm—

Saturday 3rd Storm continues—

Sabbath 4th Walked to Goshen—

Wednesday 14th Rec'd a letter from Edward C. King of Acquebogue LongIsland—He and Absalom Racket were Juvenile Friends—He speaks very feelingly of his Friends Death—

Thursday 15th Answered E. C. Kings letter

Sabbath 18th wrote to my Brother James, and another to <u>John Wiggins</u>, a man if its possible to be such a one as Nathaniel, in St John was called, so is our <u>John Wiggins</u>, a Man in whom appears to be no guile—

Wednesday 12th October 1796—One of my little scholars—an interesting girl of 6 years, is at this time very sick—

On the 16th of this Month, my Sister Lucinda was married to Rufus Tuthill Jr. of Oysterponds

[104] Monday 24th October 1796 I am making calculations to sell my place, which is a pleasent one, and located in a neighborhood, of many excellent kind hearted, very obliging Men, with their hospitable families— From them, myself & family have in every emergency received every civility we could wish, and certainly their names, by us, will always, and wherever located, be held in grateful remembrance—

November 1st 1796 Yesterday departed this life, John Chatfield, a young man of aimable manners and industrious habits—He was about 25 years of age, and Grandson to Squire John Chatfield, now of Easthampton, Longisland—This Squire Chatfield, was many years since in England, and while there heard the good, and celebrated Doct. Isaac Watts preach—Says he well recollects his venerable and debilitated appearance, and his solemn, and pathetic mode of address

[105] November 9th 1796 Sold my place to a Mr. John Thompson, for the sum of 500 Dollars, near 100 of it is owing to the loan office—Mr. Thompson, with his family moves into one of the rooms immediately, although I retain a right to occupy a part of the house until May ensuing— A Mr. Peter Snider (brotherinlaw to Thompson) with his wife and his one child, likewise moved into the kitchen of said house—So, there is now three families in the house, which we hope will make old saying good, viz. "better off have one house full than two spoilt"

Sabbath 4th Decem. 1796 On the morning of this day departed this life our youngest daughter Deziah Narcissa, aged 8 month & 20 days—A more promising, goodly, and interesting child seldom blesses the embraces of the Tenderest of Parents- And weep in Fathers [page trimmed]

[106] In Decem. Of this year 1796 I made a Vendue [auction], and sold off about 70 Dollars worth of such things, as we thought it would not be needful to carry with us to New York—Gave 3 months credit—I presume not a wise move—

1797

January, 1797 Did little, or nothing of consequence—We are making arrangements for a move in the ensuing Spring.

February, commenced small School in our kitchen, but as things turned, I quit It in the course of a week—

On the 7th March, I set off for New York—Took the packet from NewWindsor—Had a tedious unpleasent passage, which, with being quite unwell, rendered my situation, and time gloomy, and anything but comfortable—We arrived in Town on the 10th and took lodgings at the House of Mr. Richard Smith, at 4 dollars per Week—With Mr. Smith, I stoped until the 1st [107] of April—While in Town, I wrote about a week in the office of Francis Lynch Esq., attorney at Law—Mr. Lynch had with him as a student, a young aquaintance, and friend of mine, from Oysterponds, Longisland— by name Elisha W. King—This very aimable, and wellinformed young man appeared to interest himself very much in getting a situation suitable for myself, and family—

Early, on a Sabbath Morning, feeling anxious to hear from my family, I walked to the Slip near the Battery, to one of the New Windsor Packets, on which I, in attempting to step on board, my foot slip[p]ed, and fell 5 or 6 feet across the gunwale of the Vessel, on my breast, which at the time nearly deprived me of consciousness—It was a serious blow from the effects of which (from my internal feelings) I much feared would prove mortal—A painful, and restless night followed the accident—early next morning, I made shift to get on board the Packet, and in 36 hours [108] I was with my family, and had a Doct. whose prescriptions were blessed, and I was soon about—but an awful soreness is left, and whether I shall ever again be as sound, as before, <u>time</u>, the great explainer of the dreaded future, will tell—

The last of this present Month April 1797 I again left my family in the Goshen stage for N.York—I think I am now quitting this part of the country <u>forever</u>, as we are disposing our affairs so as my family can come to me in May—As many of my neighbors, and those in this quarter, with whom I have done buisness, have my respectful consideration, I take pleasure to just mention their names, as deserving a particular place in the record of those well meriting my future agreeable recollection—John Hudson—Henry Youngs—David Swezey—Phineas Ramsey & excellent Mother—Scudder Newman—Joseph Conkling—Jesse Carpenter—Isaac Youngs—with others, and their good families, all share our best wishes—

[109] Mr. Jesse Carpenter has now living with him his venerable Father & Mother, near 90 years of age each—Have lived together near 78 years—and to appearance in love and unity—I deem them to be the oldest couple, as Man & wife, I ever knew—

The men of note in Goshen at this time 1797 are Genl. Moses Hatfield, a Revolutionary soldier—Capt. John Wood, was taken at the battle of Minisink, and the only one who was captured, but what was instantly put to death—He was permitted to return home about two years after his captivity—There is Col. Jesse Woodhull,* John Hathorne, now a Member of Congress, with others etc etc—

Our ride in the Stage took 4 [hours]—was pleasent—Mr. John Hudson was with me—There was a French Lady, very amusing, as well as pretty sensibly loquatious and full of Politics—She displayed an elegant Gold watch, a rich dress, and a handsome person—In about thirty hours we arrived in the City—I put up to my old place, Deacon Richard Smith—Brother to General Woodhull [page trimmed]

[110] On the first of May, I commenced writing in the office of William

*Col Woodhull is brother to General N[athaniel] Woodhull was killed on Longisland in the War of the Revolution

L. Rose, Attorney at Law, No. 100 John St., for a small compensation—I left Mr. Rose about the 12th—

On the 20th My Wife & little Harriet arrived in Town, we immediately moved into the house I had engaged for us, No. 52 Division Street—

On the 30th I engaged myself to Mr. Robert Bogardus, a conspicuous Lawyer, in Cherry Street—With this Gentleman, I continued until the 17 August, well satisfied with my situation, the family, and compensation—

On the day that John Young was hung for the murder of Robert Berwick, Deputy Sherief, moved out of N.York—Arrived at Oysterponds, we took a room of Daniel T. Terry Esquire—

Commenced keeping the O-ponds School, on the 26th Sept. My engagement is for one year—

In October 1797 moved my family into a part of Capt. Henry Kings house, within 15 rods of the Schoolhouse—[111] Mrs. Griffing was confined with a daughter, on the 5th Sept. 1797—and my sister Lucinda, on the 6th with a daughter—

1798

In January 1798 my Scholars daily were nearly 50—Feb. & January of this year have been very moderate months—Had an Exhibition in the Meeting house in March—Pretty good satisfaction—April I commence my 3rd quarter—

In May I hired the whole of the House of Capt. H. King—As I have took no note of the State of the weather for some time past, I will best now correct that neglect—

Monday 28th, Tuesday 29th Wednesday 30th & Thursday 31st we had copious rains, with High wind a part of the time on each day from S-E- & E—

Friday 1st June, Showers A.M.—This evening My Dear Wife and little daughter leave for Goshen—And may our Father in Heaven protect and prosper her journey, and in his own good time return her home to our Society, which at all times, assuredly [Page trimmed]

[112] A young man by name Caleb Dyer at this time (June 1798) rents a

shop adjoining my house, for which he occupies in manufacturing Shoes—
This, rather an engaging young man, it somehow strikes me, ought to receive
a passing notice in my journal, which may accidentally amuse someone who
may know his after history should he live a half century after this date—
Master Dyer (for so I must now call him, he being only 17 years of age)
informs me that his father was Caleb Dyer, Esquire, who was sailing master
of the American frigate Shelalah, of 36 guns, and 400 men—She sailed from
Philadelphia in 1782, and after leaving the coast, never was heard from
since—Young Dyer, being at the time about 6 months old, with an only sister
and a disconsolate Mother, was now left to buffet the waves and Storms, of
a [113] conflicting, and uncertain World—the Widow, in the course of a few
years married a Mr. Asa Smith, whom when young Dyer became of sufficient
age taught him the shoemakers trade—Dyer soon showed his Fatherinlaw
his quickness to learn, and his uncommon proficiency in making two pairs
of good shoes to his bosses one—At this time as before observed, being 17
years old he has bought his time, for a certain amount of money, which when
he accumulates, and hands to his Father, he is to be his own man—We think
him a forward, ingenious, calculating youth—He says his opportunities for
improvement in reading, and writing have been very limited, yet, his ideas of
buisness and buisnessmen, certainly show there is Tallents somewhere about
the young fellow, if improved aright warrant future notice.

[114] Now, from day to day he sits, to appearances full of glee and good
nature, in the shop, whistling, singing, and hammering, while (in my opinion) looking forward to manhood, buisness, consequence, and property-
Just to see him as he sits all attention to his Sole, Last, End- and Awl—

Saturday 2nd June, Sabbath 3rd & Monday 4th all were pleasent—In the
time I visited Longbeach, had 14 Gulls eggs—Visited Sterling at my Brother
James's, who now lives with his family in a room of Henry Beebe's house—
Our Friend Edward C King is now with me in my dear wifes absence—

Tuesday 5th considerable rain—

Thursday 7th Some little rain in the morn—Went to Gardners Island—
point—and gathered 24 Gulls eggs—

Friday 8th Saturday 9th Sabbath 10th and Monday 11th with the exception of the 8th were pleasently cool days with wind E- and S-E—

[115] 1798 Tuesday 12th Wednesday 13th Thursday 14th and Friday 15th
In said time we had some good Showers of rain, followed with a pleasant
Sun, and refreshing breezes—

I have been taking the cold bathe, these several mornings, by plunging
into the waters of the Sound—naked—

Saturday 16th Wind N-E—Visited Shelterisland

Sabbath 17th Wrote two Letters, one to E.W. King, Student at Law, in N.York—the other to our cousin Lydia Terry, near Goshen, 2nd daughter of our Uncle Noah Terry of Orange County N.Y.

Monday 18th Wind S-W—This day, Noah Tuthill, wife, Polly, and Sister Hannah, with Mr. Charles Durling, and his wife (Lydia Terry, that was) all left for Goshen, their now residence—

Tuesday 19th Wednesday 20th Thursday 21st and Friday 22nd All fine pleasant days, except the last, which was a little Foggy—On this day I was quite ill—could barely manage to attend my School—

Saturday 23rd Early repaired to the Spacious Sound and took a leap into the bosom of agitated [page trimmed]

[116] Sabbath 24th June 1798 A fine morn, made more delightful by the melody of the joyous linnet, Redbreast, & mounting Lark—

Monday 25th Tuesday 26th and Wednesday 27th—In this time, some rain, with High wind S-W—Almost too ill to be at School—

Thursday 28th Was visited by our Friend Edward C. King—Likewise was the joyful recipient of a communication from my dear and absent Wife, who left on the first of the month—

Friday 29th Showers with Thunder—

Saturday 30th With Edward C. King, I visited Sterling, Stoped there the night—

Sabbath 1st July—Pleasant Morn—Returned home, which I find lonesome, and uncongenial to my feelings, as the social, and endearing ornament of my humble abode is away—Hope keeps the heart whole—

My very dear Mother and Father called on me this day—their value I am unable to truly appreciate—I humbly acknowlege—while my duties to them [page trimmed]

[117] Monday 2nd July & Tuesday 3rd on the 3rd my Brother Elisha visited me—on the 2nd Showers & Thunder—E.C. King with me

Wednesday 4th Independence, Forever—The morning opens with the roar of cannon from the adjacent towns, announcing in reverberating acclamations the return of that auspicious day, on which those sterling Patriots of the Revolution put their hands in bold relief to the Sacred Instrument drawn up by the Sage Jefferson, which forever severed the cord, which bound these united colonists to old Mother Britain—

This evening, myself, with several others, repaired to Pasture, or as some call it Prospect Hill, on the top of which we raised a pole, not 30 feet high—

on said pole we put a Tar barrel, with a quantity of pitch in it, to which we set fire, which made a famous show for many miles around—with a number of smart discharges from the musketry, of the young men, with us, around the pole, while it sent forth its brilliant contents we closed the conspicuous day—

[118] Jared Gardner was one of said company. This young gentleman is brother to Doc. John Gardner, our most respectable physician in this region—He, Jared, possesses great personal <u>attractions</u>, with a complete figure, suavity of manner, a winning, prepossessing address, united with a genteel Academical education—and is a first-rate preceptor in our english Schools—But with all these gifts, and natures highly polish, he is fast verging to the precipice of ruin—Dissipation, with her lurid, fake glare is leading him, those haunts of vice, where the noblest of human fabrics will soon be exchanged for deformity, wretchedness, pain, and a premature dissolution—

Thursday 5th Visited Adjutant Daniel Tuthill—stoped with him the night—

Friday 6th—Saturday 7th & Sabbath 8th—With this last date, ends my 3rd quarter of my year teaching or engagement in this place—These days the weather was good

[119] Monday 9th July 1798—My very dear and kind Lucretia, and our little Deziah arrived home this day—No doubt there are many who know how to appreciate such interviews—the cold, icy, calculating, spleenenic piece of humanity stiled <u>Bachelor</u>, to the contrary notwithstanding—

July 25th Edward C. King is with us, he is visiting Pasture Hill, on which he is exercising his muse, in a piece of poetry on the prospect from the hill—

This month I purchased me a building lot near the harbor at Oysterponds Harbor, of Capt. Jeremiah Youngs, ½ acre for $50—

August 1798—Bought of Squire Thomas Youngs timber for building me a house on my land, which I purchased a short time since—My neighbors with their teams collected and drawed it home for me without fee or reward, for which I tend them my hearty thanks.

[120] Septem. 1798 Engaged Mr. Beriah M. Cleeve and his brother Isaac, to Frame my house, and enclose it, this ensuing Autumn—On the last of this month, the Mssrs. Cleeve commenced on the house ([pencil] see page 329)

October—my house was raised—It is of one story, and 27 by 22 feet—

•

November—Built my chimney with two fireplaces—the Mason was a
Mr. Baker, from Sagharbour, a man over 60 yrs of age—While at work on
the chimney, Mr. Ephraim King called at the house, and spent some half
hour time in cheerful, and pertinent remarks on his travils by sea, and the
incidents common to West India voyges—He was now bound on a voyge to
some foreign land, but observed he had objects here of such interest to him
that he should go with buoyant hopes of returning in the spring.

[121] November 6th 1798—Left for New York on board Capt. Jonathan
Terry, I had for my fellow passenger our young friend Elisha W. King—two
sicker men, from the rolling of a Vessel, I doubt whether there ever was—
Two days, and as many nights I never took a particle of substance—At the
commencement of the third day, the Capt. out of pure commiseration
landed us at Blackrock, where by kind nursing and a good nights lodging,
we were so far refreshed as to leave for New York where we arrived on the
9th—

The Yellow Fever, which has proved so fatal the last summer, has almost
subsided—It is said it has swept off 2000 of the inhabitants—

The last of the month returned to my family—Weather cool—

1799

January 1799—Was a very cold

[122] January 1799—As before noticed was a hard winter month—Joseph
King, the husband of my dear wife's sister Betsey, is with us just now—he
is from some cause, disposition, temper, want of judgement or something,
an unhappy, turbulent tyrant in his family—Of course his industrious, virtuous wife has very little domestic comfort—They appear to be like Doc.
Watts unhappy matches, "chained to wretchedness, and strife"—

February 1799—This month was severely tedious until the 20th when It
softened down to a more thawing point—

The last of this month I, with Mr. Ezekial Glover, went to Sagharbour
and got me a lot of boards—Had a [?] time [page trimmed]

[123] On the 7th of March I moved with my family into my new House,
It being the second house, which I had ever built, and the third one I had
owned—I built my first one in 1793—Sold it in 1794—Bought my next one
in 1794—sold it in 1796—

Hay is now 20 Dolls per Ton—I have a cow, but not any hay but what we buy at the above rate—

I, at this time owned ½ of the Oysterponds Wind Mill, which I had bought last autumn—Sold her this spring

I relinquished my School this May—1799—

Mr. John Tuthill, son to old uncle John, called Hollow John, from his living in a hollow and who died in 1795—The above said John, the Son, moved from this, his mother's place, where he has possessed a handsome property, to the State of Vermont—He has been a restless, uneasy man, and a sore trial to his good old Father—He moves in August [page trimmed]

[124] 1799 I forgot to mention last Novem. 1798 that Mr. Christopher Tuthill senior died aged about 73 years—Integrity, industry, & economy, and honesty were conspicuous in all his intercourse with his fellow Man—By his first, and only wife, he had six sons, and six daughters, all of which lived to arrive to middle age, that is the youngest died more than thirty years of age—

In August 12th 1799 I commenced keeping a school in Sterling, in their new School House, which stands on the main road, on the west part or side of Squire Thomas Young's Farm, on the north side of the road, and about ½ mile from the old mansion house of the late Judge Youngs—

That good old colored man, known as Jack Conklin, or Longhouse Jack, died about the first of this August—A more pious Man we seldom shall [page trimmed] [125] Jack was an African, brought into this country about 55 years ago, all of which time he has lived in bondage, except the last 5 or 6 years of his life—In these last years, his infirmities and age, rendered him unable to do but little towards his maintenance—His friends built him a small, very plain low cottage in which himself, his aged Wife Doll, lived, perhaps with more real comfort, contentment, and true Joy than is ever known in the most splendid, and decorated Mansions—Jack was proverbial for his honesty, and faithfulness in every trust, committed to his core without one deviation, for his whole time of servitude, and to the day of his dismission from the scene of sorrow, pain and toil—His profession in the Christian Faith, and his unwavering belief in his Salvation, by his Lord, and Savior Jesus Christ for near 60 years, astonished the learned Divine, rejoiced the Fathers, and Mothers in Isarel [Israel] and shook the sandy foundations on which the Skeptic builds his falacious hopes—

[126] John <u>Tatoo</u>, another African about Jack's age, and died about the same time, was honest faithful and trusty, and a good upright man—He talked much plainer English than <u>Jack</u>, whose pronunciation was much broken—

Tuesday 13 August 1799, Wednesday 14th and Thursday 15th were pleasent, but the weather is dry—

This 15th, Mr. James Baily died—He had commenced building a Grist Mill, at what is called the Dam on the beach near Rockypoint—His Wife, whom he had lately married, was Betsey, the daughter of Mr. Thomas Moore, of near Sterling—

Friday 16th Visited my family this eve—Rec'd a letter from S. Vail

Saturday 17th Considerable rain—Wind S-E- from which quarter It has come this 4 days

Sabbath 18th Rain—

Monday 19th & Tuesday 20th High wind E—

[127] Wednesday 21st August 1799 cool E- wind—visited my family this eve—

Thursday 22nd Wind E—

Friday 23rd Wind S—warmer—Yellow Fever rages in and is very fatal in NY and people are moving out by the hundreds—

Saturday 24th Visited my dear family this eve—

Sabbath 25th Very warm—

Monday 26th Took passage, with Mr. Frederick Taber Jr. to Rockypoint in his ships boat, but as the tide was ahead of us, we toiled hard at the oars, which with much fatigue, we got to Rockypoint about 3/4 after 8 A.M.—Hardly reached my School by time—9 O Clock—

A Mr. Ker, from N.York died last night on board of a Sloop bound to Sterling, where they arrived this morn—He was Fatherinlaw to Samuel Terry, Son of the late Col. Thomas Terry

Tuesday 27th—Fine weather—This noonspell called on Uncle Jonathan Tuthill, with E.W. King—On my way to School, stoped into Capt. Silas Webb—

Visited my family this eve—

[128] Wednesday 28th August 1799—On my way to Sterling School this morn, stoped at Mr. Daniel Moores, & took breakfast—

At my school, I met Mr. John Wiggins, as honest, peaceable, upright, useful (in his sphere) as we can find among the children of Men.

Noonspell, at Mr. Jekiel Wheatons, who with his excellent wife, are an interestingly valuable, exemplary, aged couple—

Thursday 29th High S. wind—Stoped this night with Mr. Daniel Moore, whose mild placid, hospitable Wife is full of the milk of human kindness— my Bedfellow was the quiet charitable Mr. John Wiggins—

Friday 30th Wind W—

Saturday 31st—Wind W—Myself, Mrs. Griffing, Frederick Taber & wife, Joseph Terry Esq. & wife, Capt. Frederick King & wife, together took a sail to East Hampton, that is to the Landing, at the North side of that Town, to the house of Mr. Jeremiah Terry, where we were furnished with plenty of watermellons, and other refreshments to our satisfaction, after which [129] [we] left for home, where we arrived in good health about midnight—

Sabbath 1st Septem. Some rain—Wind S—

Tuesday 3rd Wind E—cool—E.W. King, with a Mr. John Billons, just from N.York, confirm the fatal effects of the Yellow [fever] in that City—

Wednesday 4th Wind E- with some rain—

Heard this day of the death of Reverend Isaac Overton* who was originally of Southold, but for a number of years past a preacher of the Gospel, of the Presbyterian Church—He has some two or three years since left Oysterponds, where he laboured in the Gospel field, some months—We believe him to have been a sincere well-minded Man, and as a Preacher, improving in that sacred, holy calling—I should suppose his age a little turned of forty—

*Brother to Gen. Seth Overton, formerly of Southold, but now of Portland Connecticut— In August 1852 Gen. Overton died aged 93 years

Thursday 5th Some rain—Wind E—

Friday 6th & Saturday 7th It rains some on both of these days, with wind E—This 7th visited my home—

Sabbath 8th Wind E—dark weather—Wrote to Doc. Thomas Vail, of Vermont

[130] Monday, 9th September 1799—Wind E—Had an interview with cousin Jasper Terry, Uncle Noah Terry's son—

Tuesday 10th Rain—with my family this eve—E.C. King called at the school house a few minutes—he is just from N.York

Thursday 12th Wind S—Friend S. Vail just called on me—

Friday 13th Wind S—

Saturday 14th A squally day, with Thunder & rain—At home this eve- I ought to have observed, that I went to Shelterlisland, and got home some wood—Mrs. Griffing went with me as far as Rockypoint—

Monday 16th This eve visited Widow Elizabeth Booth, she was the Wife of the late Capt. Joseph Booth—took tea with E.C. King & E.W. King at Mrs. Booths—

Friday [Tuesday] 17th visited Uncle Thomas Terry at Southold- stoped with him the night—

Wednesday 18th Wind E—Cool—With my family this eve

[131] Thursday 19th Friday 20th Saturday 21st & Sabbath 22nd Some cooler, with wind E—

Monday 23rd Tuesday 24th & Wednesday 25th—Cooler than a week or two past—Wind N-W—Rec'd a letter from Friend S. Vail, who informs me of his intention of going soon to Palmertown, where he had lived with his family some time after 1794—up to 1798—

Thursday 26th Friday 27th & Saturday 28th—Continues more cool & pleasant—Wrote to my affectionate & tender Mother now at Plumisland— At home this eve—

Sabbath 29th Squally—John Billons, A would be quaker, spoke this eve at Mr. Jeremiah Kings—I have not faith for his sincerity—But—stop- what is my Faith!—

Monday 30th High wind N-W- and very low tide—

Tuesday 1st October 1799 Wind N-W—Our friend S. Vail called on me this noon—

[132] Wednesday 2nd October 1799—considerable frost to be seen this morn—P.M.—Capt. Frederick King and David King, in a carriage; Mr. John Jay on horseback (Mr. Samel Hobart's son in law), Capt. David Webb, and Silas Webb, in another carriage, and passed the School house, in high spirits, Their drive was equal in speed, and certainly as furiously as the famous Jehu of ancient, holy writ—Those recreations and amusements, which yield a satisfaction in retrospect, are rational as well as respectable—

Thursday 3rd and Friday 4th were thick and hazy, with wind from the Easterly board—

Saturday 5th Wind S—With Mr. Ezikial Glover, I went to Sagharbour— while there I visited Mrs. Lucretia Howel, a cousin of Mrs. Griffing—Miss H. is in a law [page trimmed]

[133] October 1799 Sabbath 6th High wind N-W—

Monday 7th at my School—noonspell, visited Uncle Jonathan Tuthill, his Wife, my Aunt Mehitable, Sister to my Mother—This aunt is such a one as the wise man says is "a crown to her husband"—

Tuesday 8th—Some rain—with winds S- E—This eve, visited Benjamin Moore, Son to our present Supervisor, Mr. Thomas Moore, one of our most respectable Townsmen—Benjamin is now a Married Man—and the most respectable, accommodating and valuable of neighbors—I believe he is at this time a Militia Capt.

Wednesday, 9th—Wind N-W- & cool—Feel the effects, in my breast, of the accident, which I experienced on the 1st of April 1797—This Morn, E.C. King called on me a few minutes—

Thursday 10th A severe rainstorm, yet amidst copious Floods I walked to my school about 4½ miles—wet as a drowned rat—

[134] Thursday 10 October 1799 A severe rainstorm—Amid the copious flood I walked to my school house, 4½ miles, where I arrived as wet as a soaked sponge—

Friday 11th Wind E- & cool—E.C. King took me to my family this eve in a carriage, in <u>which</u> he was going to O-ponds—

Saturday 12th Wind E- & cool weather—Mr. King, again, took me on my way to my School this morn—

Sabbath 13th October 1799- Wind N-E- & thick weather—our Venerable Father took dinner with us this day—P.M., I, with my Father, visited our Uncle Daniel T. Terry, where I met my affectionate Mother, whose health, at best, is poor, but her resignation, and acquiescence to the intire will of her Heavenly Father, is truly a partern [pattern] to all who profess to love the Lord Jesus Christ—The eve, had at my house the company of Miss Hannah Tuthill and Mr. Edward C. King—

[135] Monday 14th Wind N-E—This P.M. it rains—

Tuesday 15th Clear and cold—was visited this eve at my Schoolhouse by Friend Silas Vail

Wednesday 16th A cool N-W- wind—

Thursday 17th A rainstorm—P-M- wind shifted to the N-W- & blows a gale—

Friday 18th Very cool, with plenty of ice this morn—Samuel Hobart Jr. has his large Smack, drove on shore on the sound side, near Squire Thomas Youngs land, and It probably will be lost—

Saturday 19th continues cool, yet this morn calm—A Mr. John C. Rudd,* *see page 580 a School Teacher, on Shelterisland, visited us this day, at my house—Stoped with us the night—

Sabbath 20th Some rain—Wind S—Rudd leaves this P.M. for the Island—He appears to be determined to improve in Education

[136] Monday 21st October 1799 & Tuesday 22nd Fair weather, wind S— shifted to N-W—

Wednesday 23—Caleb Dyer, mentioned June 1798* is now working in a *see page 112 shop of mine at 12 ½ cents per week—

Tuesday 24th Wind N-W—cold, freezing weather—I might have observed (as it is a fact) that I walked to my house at Oysterponds from my Schoolhouse, which stands on the west side of Squire Thomas Youngs's Farm, about 4½ miles, in 51 minutes—

Friday 25th Wind S-W—Brother Elisha visited me—

Saturday 26th Southerly weather—

Sabbath 27th—Died, on Sabbath last, about 2 P.M. Jonathan N. Havens Esquire, a Representative in the Congress of these United States—Said to be a very valuable member of that body, and truly a Man greatly beloved—

[137] Monday 28th A storm of Wind & rain, yet amidst its drenching, soaking waters, I walked to my School, for which imprudence I received a severe headache—Rec'd a letter from Mr. J.C. Rudd—

Tuesday 29 A light wind N—

Wednesday 30th Killed me a Beef this, which I had off West Neck Shelterisland, a lot of Land owned by our Mother Tuthill—

Thursday 31st Wind S-W—conversed a minute or two with Mrs. Deborah Tuthill, Widow, of Mr. John Tuthill (commonly called Hollow John). She is rising 80 years of age—

November 1st 1799 Wind brisk W-N-W—Bought a watch of brother Elisha for 22 dollars—

Saturday 2nd This morn, brother Elisha, Luther Tuthill, our Excellent John Wiggins, and Capt. Samuel Hobart, all leave for Charlestown, South Carolina on a fishing voyge—Capt. David King, Passenger—Likewise, Capt. Frederick King, as far as N. York—

Sabbath 3rd Very cool wind N-W—

Tuesday 5th from Shelterisland [page trimmed]

[138] Wednesday 6th Novem 1799 Wind W—

Friday 8th A rain Storm—

Saturday 9th Wind N-W—Got my wood home—A good job towards the comforts of coming Winter—

Sabbath 10th Our O-ponds people have been engaging a Priest as their pastor—a Mr. Emerson Foster—

Monday 11th Closed my first quarters School in this place—Rec'd a letter from my Friend and early preceptor Doct Thomas Vail, now of Vermont—

Tuesday 12th Pleasent—engaged myself this day to teach the School, in this place (Sterling) for the ensuing six months—

Departed this life last evening Mrs. Lucretia Lester, a widow of three and more score years—Her death was sudden, and with very little pain—She appeared to be well, and was in good spirits about the house, the day previous to her death—A more useful woman, as nurse, doctress, and [139] midwife, is seldom to be found—perhaps, in those honorable stations, she never had her superior—Her mild, well-timed expressions of tenderness, and manner of waiting on the hypocondriac, the fidgety splenetic, and all those who were often applying to her for advice, and relief from complaints, which she knew was nothing but conceit—and a shaded fancy that something horrible had got hold of them—To such applicants, she was of more value than a cartload of quacks—To the actually sick, and afflicted, she was at all times an Angel of Mercy, and an invaluable Mother in Israel—We understand that rising 1200 women have been confined under her care, as a Midwife, and she has never lost but one of said number—

Wednesday 13th Wind N- & high—

Thursday 14th My Father visited us this day

Friday 15th the wind S—I visited Plum Island where, at present my parents reside

Saturday 16th Returned home—Brother Warren home with us—

[140] Monday 18th November 1799—High wind W—Went to Shelterisland with brother Warren, and got three Sheep, in a small boat—had a rough and, I think, a rather dangerous time—howsomever we arrived home safe, and much wearied—

Tuesday 19th A fresh N- wester—

Wednesday 20th Pleasent—Agreed with Francis W. Clark, to build me a well, for 12 dollars—

Saturday 23rd Some rain—

Monday 25th Commenced my 2nd quarters School, at Sterling

Tuesday Novem 26th Wind N- and cool—Board with Widow Elizabeth Booth—Relic of the late Capt. Joseph Booth, who died about the year 1794 or 5—A worthy, valuable member of Society—

Wednesday 27th high wind N-W—Built a fire in my front room, in the house I now live in, and which I built in 1798 and 9—today for the first time—

[141] Thursday 28th Novem. 1799 Wind S-E- and rain—

Friday 29th Wind S-W- & squally—Sterne observes in his usual, rather light, yet striking manner, "See! While I am writing my hair grows grey!"

Saturday 30th Wind N-W—

December 1st Wind W-N-W—Brother James took dinner with us-

Monday 2nd A raw South wind—Friend Silas Vail begins School at Oysterponds this day—

Tuesday 3rd Easterly weather—

Wednesday 4th Wind N-W—

Thursday 5th Wind E- with Snow until 3 P.M. when it commenced a rain storm—

Friday 6th Wind N- very light—The Snow which fell yesterday, It appears had fled, not being able to stand before a warm rain—Wrote to my Cousin Amon T. Griffing—

[142] Saturday 7th Decem 1799 An E- Wind with a rain storm—

Sabbath 8th Fair weather—Mr. Rufus King & wife visited us this Eve—

Monday 9th It blows a gale N-W An airy cold walk to my School this morn of near 5 miles—Joshua Racket and Victor Booth commenced attending my School this day—Joshua is the brother of late friend Absalom Racket of endearing memory—Mr. V. Booth is son to Mr. E. Booth, with whom I now board—he is a kind hearted, pleasent, agreable young man—

Tuesday 10th—Pleasent, yet chilly cold—

Wednesday 11th—A South west rainstorm—

Thursday 12th cold—put a bucket to my well for the first time since it was dug and became a Well of water—

It's Thanksgiving Day—John Adams is our President—took dinner with my wife at our friends, Adj. Daniel Tuthills—his [143] wife, who assuredly ranks high amongst Ledyards extraordinary Women, was all attention to our comforts—

This evening sold my shop to Caleb Dyer, the young Shoemaker noticed in June 1798 in this journal—Mark, this is the first building, or tenement he ever owned—It is 7 by 8 feet—

Friday 13th Wind E—with Snow—We just hear, through brother James, of the safe arrival of brother Elisha, and those who left with him, arrival in Charlestown- SC—Elisha writes that John Hobart is dead, died some short time since at Sea, or in some foreign port, we know not which, as he does not mention the circumstances of his death—He was a likely young man—Attended my school last winter—about 18 years of age—The son of Mr. Samuel Hobart, and his wife Jerusha, who mourn the premature loss of a beloved Son—

Saturday 14th—Fair weather—Good sleding—

Sabbath 15th Pleasent—

[144] Monday 16th December 1799—Pleasent—P.M. a damp Snow, which dissolves near as fast as It falls—

Tuesday 17th A North E- Snowstorm—this is the 4th Snow this winter—Visited Capt Austin Booth this eve*—he entertained me with an interesting

*this valuable member of society died the September 1849 aged 74 years

account of his late visit to the State of Vermont—Gave minute particulars of his <u>time</u>, <u>attention</u>, and the civilities shown him, while among that hospitable people of the Green Mountain—His journey to and from that State—The recital, and his manner of communicating the excursion, was <u>to me</u> very agreable—An Evening to be recollected with the pleasent ones—Wednesday 18th Fair weather—Am now keeping a small evening school—

Thursday 19th A Snowstorm until P-M- It commenced raining

Friday 20th Clear—light wind N-W-

[145] Saturday 21st A-M- Mild—P-M- Snows

Sabbath 22nd Pleasant—Wind W—

Monday 23rd South Wind, and pleasant—We have just got the news of the death of George Washington, a Man who stands with the first on the rolls of fame as a benefactor, and a blessing to the human family—No doubt, while virtue and civilization pervade these United States, he, Washington, will have the judicious name of "Saviour of his Country"—He died, on the 14th Inst, after about 24 hours illness—

Tuesday 24th Pleasant—

Wednesday 25th N-W- wind & cool—Took dinner, a Christmas one, at Capt. David Webb's—I learn my dear Mother is quite ill—

Thursday 26th Fine pleasant weather—Mr. David Wiggins launched a handsome schooner this day, called the David—I attended—They did not float her—

[146] Friday 27th Decemb. 1799—Pleasant—Wind S—

Saturday 28th Beautiful weather—

Sabbath 29th Pleasant—Mrs. G- was confined this morn, with a daughter whom we shall name Cleora—

Monday 30th A rainstorm, with wind E—Visited at my School by Mr. John C. Rudd—the Shelterisland Teacher—

Tuesday 31st What is called good weather—this day ends the Century! What a sublime thought—Who is there among the millions now on Earth that saw the commencement of 1700! Yes, and who is there now born that will see the ushering in of 1900!!—

1800

Wedneday 1st Jan. 1800—Pleasant—

Thursday 2nd Fair day—

Friday 3rd Pleasant—

Saturday 4th Pleasent weather—Mrs. G- continues not very well—

Sabbath 5th Blustering weather—

[147] Monday 6th January 1800—fine day—wrote to E.W. King—had a line from Mr. J.C. Rudd—with verses on our little infant Cleora—

Thursday 7th Cold N-W- wind—Wrote to E.C. King NY—he is now a clerk in some establishment in that city—

Wednesday 8th wind N-W—wrote to Mr. J.C. Rudd—He intends by dint of study and perseverence, he says, to become well versed in every science and useful acquirements and requisite for the Orator, Statesman or Preacher*—He certainly shows great perseverance and unwearied diligence in trying to make a self taught Man, or Scholar—time, if he lives 30 years will tell what will be his success, and what follows this, and what he will be then—He has our best wishes, for his success in all his lawful endeavors—

[148] Thursday 9th January 1800—light N-W- wind—Died, yesterday, very suddenly, Mrs. Zipporah Brown, wife of Capt. John Brown of Ham Island—She was an excellent woman, all such as one as Solomon says is a crown to her husband—She was about 40 years of age—has been the affectionate Mother of ten children, nearly all of which are left to mourn her irreparable loss—

Friday 10th moderate N-W- wind—Capt. Frederick King just passed the schoolhouse on his way to N-York, from which he is bound on a Sea voyge—

Saturday 11th Wind E—& cloudy—

Sabbath 12th A South light wind—

Monday 13th A fair day—Yesterday morning Christopher Brown Jr.'s wife was confined with a Son, which they call Christopher, which will be the 3rd now living in succession of the family—The Mother is the daughter of Mr. Thomas Terry, the son of the late Col. Thomas Terry, of this place—

[149] Tuesday 14th January 1800—Fine weather—Rec'd a long letter from Mr. J.C. Rudd—lodged this night with Mr. Benjamin Moore of Cutchogue—A man greatly admired for his strict piety, and seasonable addresses to all his associates, and acquaintance, to [make?] the gospel rule the unalterable standard of their life—We believe him to be a candid, sincerely good man, as we may call those whose life corresponds with their profession—

Wednesday 15th Warm, & clear weather—

Thursday 16th Mild, and Pleasent—Have a school of about 50 scholars—

Friday 17th- continues very mild—This morn, now mid winter, saw two musquitos, briskly flying about the window as they do in the month of

*In 1805 or 6 he was admitted and licensed to preach as an Episcopalian! Under the invitation of Bishop Moore—N.Y. From 1808 to about 1848 Mr. Rudd was an Episcopalian preacher in good standing—he died in 1848 See the notice of Mr. Rudd's death in Griffin's Journal

August—As they are a hot weather insect, it looks like the singular to see them enjoying themselves in the dead of Winter—Something like a frost in harvest, or a swallow in a snowstorm—

[150] Saturday 18th Jan. 1800—Wind S. with rain—Visited Adj. Daniel Tuthills—

Monday 20th A cool N.W. wind—

Tuesday 21st Clear & pleasant—

Wednesday 22nd What is called open weather—Rec'd a letter from J.C. Rudd—

Thursday 23rd N.W. wind cool—

Friday, 24th- A pleasant day—Mrs. Polly Youngs, Wife to Mr. Daniel Youngs, was confined with a son, whom they name James—Mrs. Youngs, when a girl, was Polly Glover, the daughter of the late Ezekial Glover, whose wife was Mary Terry—

Saturday 25th A snowstorm—

Sabbath 26th Wind very high & cold from N-W—

Monday 27th More mild wind, light N-W—Eve some snow—

Wednesday 28th Pretty cold this morn—Wind N-W—

Thursday 30th Very cold—with wind N-W—

Friday 31st Wind E-N-E—

[151] Friday 1st February 1800 Snow squalls—

Saturday [2nd], extremely cold—N-W- wind—My birth was this day 33 years ago—Alas! Where are they?

Monday 3rd Easterly wind—

Tuesday 4th A severe E- rain storm with wind very high

Wednesday 5th Wind light W-N-W—

Thursday 6th Pleasent—

Friday 7th A Northerly cold wind, as the wind from that corner generally is, even if its August—Mr. Rudd visited us—was in buoyant spirits—

Saturday 8th Wind N—but light—

Sabbath 9th A snowstorm with wind N-E—

Monday 10th A cold Northerly wind—

Tuesday 11th A blustering N-W- cold time

Wednesday 12th Cold, with wind as yesterday

Thursday 13th Feb. A real blow of N-W- wind—Visited Joseph Webb & Daniel Harris, and Henry Beebe

[152] Friday 14th Feb. 1800 It blows hard from N-W—A.M. It snows considerable—P.M. A rain storm—

Saturday 15th A gale of wind W-N-W—

Sabbath 16th Wind tedious as yesterday

Monday, 17th Cold N-W- weather—Mrs. Polly Youngs, the wife of Mr. Daniel Youngs, died last night, she has suffered greatly since the birth of her infant son on the 24th last month—

Mr. Rudd visited us this eve at my place of board—

Tuesday 18th Wind N-W-1/2 W—

Wednesday 19th A cold W- wind—

Thursday 20th—Rec'd a letter from Mr. Amon Taber—A [?]

Friday 21st At Mr. Booths—Mr. Rudd was with us the night—

Saturday 22nd A windy month take it altogether thus far, my 2nd quarters School ends this day—

Sabbath 23rd Not a clear day—Rather what we call a flattering one

[153] Tuesday 25th February 1800—a pleasent day, and very suitable for an exhibition of my scholars, which we had—a number of spectators, from Shelterisland, Southold and west of that attended, and say they were well pleased with the performances—Messrs. Joshua Racket, J.C. Rudd, Victor Booth and Augustus G Brown were amongst the speakers—

Wednesday 26th—High wind N-W—

Thursday 27th—wind W-N-W—Visited my dear Parents at Plumb Island—My dear and best of mothers' health is very delicate—

Friday 28th Wind E—

Saturday 1st March wind E-N-E—A snowstorm—

Sabbath 2nd Clears up with a moderate wind N.W.—Returned home from the Island—

Monday calm & pleasent

Tuesday 4th Commenced my 3rd quarters school—

[154] Wednesday 5th March 1800 A S-W- wind—

Thursday 6th Snow squalls—N-W- wind—

Friday 7th A cold N.Wester—

Saturday 8th A cold blustering evening—returned home to my family—

Sabbath 9th A Snowstorm—

Monday 10th Good sleighing this morn—

Tuesday 11th A calm day—Sleds are moving in prime motion—And the way that Bill and Jo carry the girls, a sleigh riding, is a caution to old roan— Took a ride this eve with Messrs. Hazard, & Joshua Racket, Messrs. Thomas and Joshua Youngs—& Mr. Wines Osborne, as far as Mattituck, in a sleigh—returned rather too late—

Wednesday 12th Wind N-W- by W—rather warmer—The snow shows it—Thursday 13th A West wind—

Friday 14th Quite mild—

Saturday 15th An Easterly wind—Rode to my family with Mr. Hazard Racket who was born in O-ponds in [page trimmed]

[155] Sabbath 16th March 1800 Clear, with a Westerly wind—

Monday 17th P.M. Wind E—

Tuesday 18th Wind E—Thunder & rain this eve—

Wednesday 19th Blustering wind W-N-W-

Thursday 20th A severe gale S-W-

Friday 21st Pleasant morn—P-M—A rain—

Saturday 22nd A North East Rain—

Sabbath 23rd A cold North wester—

Monday 24th Pleasent—

Tuesday 25th Fair, clear sky—Rec'd a letter from E.W. King of NY-

This evening, Joshua Racket and myself visited Mr. Rudd at Genl. Dering's, stoped with him the night—took breakfast at the Generals—

This morn 26th Wednesday John Martin, a Young Man, who sometime since stoped with me at Oysterponds, a fine young man, died in N.York, a few days since, says E.W. King in his letter—

Thursday 27th Warm & Pleasant—

[156] Friday 28th March 1800—Pleasant—

Saturday 29th Wind E—with a rain storm

Sabbath 30th Wind continues E- & N-E—

Monday 31st More mild, wind W—Victor Booth left yesterday for NewYork, to spend the Summer as a Clerk, in a China Store.

Tuesday 1st April 1800—A very high wind W—Was visited by Mr. John C. Rudd—He stoped with us the night.

Wednesday 2nd Wind continues to blow hard from the Western board—Mr. Rudd left us for his home, Shelterisland—

Thursday 3rd A South wind—

Friday 4th A North E. Rainstorm—

Saturday 5th The storm continues—

Sabbath 6th It has cleared off—pleasant—Wrote to my Friend Doc. Thomas Vail, now of Vermont—

Monday 7th A fine day, as we pronounce it when it suits our turn—

Tuesday 8th Pleasant—This evening, Rev'd Daniel Youngs of Acquebogue preached at my Schoolhouse—He is a gifted [page trimmed]

[157] Wednesday 9th April 1800—A gale of wind, N—

Thursday 10th A South warm wind—

Friday 11th Wind, as yesterday—Rec'd a letter from Victor Booth, now of N.York—Have news from Brother Elisha, who is now in Charlestown S.C.

Saturday 12th Some rain with a South Wind

Sabbath 13th Wind S.W. with a little rain

Monday 14th An Easterly moderate rain—

Tuesday 15th A fresh, stiff wind W—

Wednesday 16th A West N.W. wind—

Thursday 17th Dismissed my school, altogether, with the intention of going to New York, to if possible to get into some better, or more profitable, buisness—

Saturday 19th Pleasant—

Sabbath 20th, Monday 21st, Tuesday 22nd, & Wednesday, 23rd—Weather, these days, variable—With the wind in said time almost from every point in the compass—Mr. Joshua Racket with us—fixing to go to N.York—

[158] April 29th 1800 Took passage, at Oysterponds point, on board of a Cutchogue Sloop, for NewYork, in company with our friend Joshua Racket—one of the passengers on board with us was a young Mr. Benjamin Case, who informed me he was going to NewYork, to lay in a small stock of dry goods and groceries, having very recently commenced dealing in those articles—Although Mr. Case lives only 12 or 14 miles west of me, I do not recollect of any acquaintance or previous knowledge of him—As I found, and conversed with him, I felt much impressed to suppose that his future course and life might prove of some note, and consequence, to his town, perhaps Country—He is now not over 22 years of age—Should he live to see 60, then it will be known what his course has been—And the scenes which has opened on our country, in the course of that eventual period of its history—

[159] May 1, 1800—Arrived in NewYork, took lodging at a house near Peckslip—in the same room, in which we lodged, was Capt. Caleb Brewster of the Revenue Cutter—He was a Revolutionary character of some respectable note—We found him a sociable, communicative, agreable gentleman—While in NewYork, up to the 14th I visited Flatbush and Westchester—

On the 15th I set off for Oysterponds to my family where I arrived on the 16th—

On 22nd June I left home again for N-Y- where I found myself safely landed on the 25th—

Sabbath 29th repaired to Westchester—

Monday 30th Engaged myself to teach at the school at this place 3 months, for 70 dollars & board found—Committee were John White, Bazil I. Bartow & Benjamin Ferris—

Thursday 3rd July 1800 Visited NewYork—

Friday 4th In Town, amidst noise & confusion—wrote to my dear wife— called on my good friend John [page trimmed] Vessel in which he [trimmed]

[160] Saturday 5th returned to Westchester—

Monday 6th Commenced my School—Do not feel as much at home as at Sterling—I think Its probable I shall find I have gone from home, but so It is—Bought wit is best, if not paid too highly for—

8th 9th 10th & 11th Not any thing of note occurred—At my School, which is a full one—

12th Friday—It is said here that the present hot weather is as warm as any previous warm weather this 7 years past—

Sabbath 13th—Walked over Throgsneck—took a look at the splendid seat of Hon. John Sloss Hobart, the companion of Washington, in judicial affairs, though not a soldier—

Monday 14th Very hard Thunder—I think this place, situated about where the Tides meet, occasions severe squalls of rain & Thunder—

[161] Tuesday 15th July 1800—Wednesday 16th—Easterly weather

Thursday 17th The trustees visited the school

Friday 18th & Saturday 19th—weather fine—

Sabbath 20th Attended the friends meeting, which was held, with not a word spoken—My employers are most of them of that persuasion—

Rec'd a letter this day from my dear Lucretia—Full of the spirit of divine love, and the most salutary admonition—

Rec'd a letter from John C. Rudd—P.M. attended the Episcopalian Church—The Preacher, a Mr. Williams—A venerable, I hope a good man, as he is a good speaker—Text Prov. 12—26th—Thunder, & rain this eve—

Monday 21st—A notice, in my wife's letter, from my tenderest of mothers, to read the 4 chapters of proverbs—

Tuesday 22nd A rain storm—wrote to Mr. Rudd

[162] Wednesday 23rd July 1800—A fair day—wrote to Mrs. Griffing—

Thursday 24th Very pleasent, just cool enough to enjoy a short walk— This place appears to be very fertile in yielding Paddy's fresh from Cork— On the Sabbath or on a hollowday [holiday], the street is pregnant with groups of those characters, throwing quoits and other amusements, inter-spersed with horid oaths, and convulsive roars of laughter—These men appear from their brogue, and manner to have just come over, and engaged themselves to the rich Farmers in these parts, of which there is a number—

Friday 25th—it is very warm—sent on my letters, to NewYork, from which they go to my family—

Saturday 26th Warm & its getting dry—

[163] Sabbath 27th July 1800—A pleasent day—After attending the Episcopal church, at noon, dined with a Widow Lawrence, a respectable lady of about 50 years—she has two likely sons, and an aimable, dutiful daughter—

Monday 28th An Easterly wind—As I have not mentioned my place of board, I will now correct that neglect—I stop with a Mr. (as he professes to be a quaker) I ought to say with Daniel Billens—He is a corpulent chubby looking Man of 60 years, of warm temperament, hasty, ignorant, and conceited—Is a quaker, in earnest, by profession, but in heart, those who winter and summer with him, must have a peculiar mind, not to doubt that his sincerity goes any deeper than the surface—His wife is (I think older than himself) all the domestic, quiet, industrious, and frugal helpmeet—She is certainly a worthy woman, well deserving of a man of sterling integrity, and genuine sensibility—They have two sons and a daughter—this last is the youngest—

[164] Tuesday 29th July 1800—Wednesday 30th & Thursday 31st were warm and dry, with but little wind—

Thursday [Friday] 1st August 1800—Wind E—

Saturday 2nd continues dry—Wrote to my family and friends, on Longisland—P.M. Assisted my Landlord, Mr. Billems, in some buisness

Sabbath 3rd Was visited this day, by Messrs. Joshua Racket, William Hall, Samuel Cowdry, Peter Maverick, and John Billings Junr.—they were from New York (their place of residence) in a Hacking Coach—Our host and hostess, was all attention to their comforts and refreshments—They left about 4 P.M.—

Towards evening, took a walk on Throgsneck, with the Widow Lawrence's son William, a young man, in whose favor, I feel strongly prepossessed—He is about 20 years of age—a comfort, and a solace to his Mother—

Monday 4th—Clear, and Pleasent—[165] P.M. As the avocations of the day, I walked near two miles in pursuit of Apples—Obtained but a very few fit to eat, they being not ripe—

Tuesday 5th A light N-W- wind—more comfortable

Wednesday 6th A cooler morn than any this 30 days—

Thursday 7th Pleasant—Very dry—

Friday 8th A Thunder Shower this morn, but it soon clears off warm—

Saturday 9th Some fine Showers this day with Thunder—

Sabbath 10th Showers this A.M.—P.M. Attended the Episcopalian Church—dined with Widow Lawrence—

Monday 11th North West wind, Wrote to Joshua Racket, by Mr. Billens the Landlord—

Tuesday 12th Wind very light N-W- A.M.—P.M. South—

Wednesday 13th A.M. Rain, with Thunder—P.M. clears off cool, light wind N-W—

[166] Thursday 14th August 1800—A Pleasent day, not uncomfortable warm—

Friday 15th—More warm—A light breeze W- by N—

My school, take it altogether, has been a very full one—The larger part of my Scholars are the children of strict quakers—Of course they are not to put Sin to their yes or no—It requires some tact to suit all around—However I am led to believe, I have in general given satisfaction thus far—

Saturday 16th Pleasant—Not any school—Visited Benjamin Ferris, and Bazil J. Bartow—Two of the committee of my School—

Sabbath 17th An Easterly rain storm—

Monday 18th It has cleared off with a refreshing N-W- breeze—Took Tea with Mr. Thomas Robertson, an Innkeeper, in this Village—His children attend my school—

Wednesday 20th Comfortable, as to warmth

Thursday 21st Pleasant—P.M. caught some [page trimmed]

[167] Friday 22nd August 1800—Warm—

Saturday 23rd Company training in this place—Rum showed Its power, in a too free use of it—by many of the trainers, and some quarreling was the consequence—One sword was broken and one Man slightly wounded—

Rec'd 4 letters this morn—from J.C. Rudd, Silas Vail—Samuel Cowdry & Joshua Racket—had the joy of hearing from my dear family.

Sabbath 24th—a cool E- wind—Attended Friends Meeting, was pleased with a good discourse, and a moving prayer—

Visited a Mr. L.A. Hunt, a respectable Farmer Bachelor of 40—he treated us with good fruit—and delicious apricots—A young man, Mr. Pell, a clerk to Benjamin Ferris, was with us—

Monday 25th Sultry hot—Answered some of my Letters, rec'd the other day—

Tuesday 26th Pleasant

Wednesday 27th As warm as Yesterday—Took tea at Widow Lawrences—Thunder this eve

Thursday 28th Some rain—Rec'd a letter from [page trimmed]

[168] Friday 29th August 1800 Very warm, sultry weather—Wrote to my Friend Silas Vail, in answer from one of his, rec'd a few days since—

Saturday 30th Rec'd this morn two letters from my Wife—They were a refreshing cordial, in time, and when needed—

Sabbath 31st A pleasant—I have formed a very agreable acquaintance, since I have resided in this Village—with Mr. Jonathan Randell, a gentleman formerly of Fishers Island—Mr. Randell is now owner of a beautiful Farm on Throgsneck, with a handsome Mansion thereon—He has a very pleasent and interesting family, from which I have, and do, receive the most marked civilities—took tea, at Mr. Randell's this Eve—

Monday 1st September 1800 Pleasant—Sent a packet of letters to LongIsland this morn—

Tuesday 2nd Spent some time this eve with John White, a respectable member of the Society of Friends—One of our committee—He and family treat me with much respect—

[169] Thursday 4th Sept. 1800—An agreeable N-W- wind—

Friday 5th Clear & Pleasant—

Saturday 6th Rec'd 3 letters—viz. from Brother James—J.C. Rudd—& E.W. King—this last was a censorious communication—Shall not answer it—

Sabbath 7th Attended church—John Billems visited his Father this day, from N.Y.—

Monday 8th Wrote two Wills today, for some of my quaker friends—It is their creed not to live without a Will—

Tuesday 9th Very warm—

Wednesday 10th Wind, E- by N—

Thursday 11th Took a cold bath this morn—

The trustees say, as my health appears to be poor, they will let me off, although they affirm that they are well satisfied with attention to their children, and the improvement made—

I commenced the School July 7th of course I have taught two months & 4 days, making my dues about 50 Dolls, at the rate of 70 dolls per quarter—

Friday 12th & Saturday 13th—Settled up my bills—And Sabbath 14th repaired to N.York—From which I shall soon leave for LongIsland—

[170] Having now taken my leave of this district, as a Schoolmaster, very likely for the last time, I will just notice this place, the committee & etc etc— The Village of Westchester is about 14 miles East from N.York City—It has two Churches, viz. Episcopalian, and a Friends—a good School-house, a Dock, one handsome flouring mill—these with about 15 or 20 dwelling houses, and stores, form the principle part of the place or village—Two Packet boats ply to and from NewYork about every other day—These boats are about 30 Tons each—

A number of the Inhabitants (near the village) are men, some advanced in life, having been in the mercantile buisness, in NewYork, for the last 25 or 30 years, in which time their 100 Talents have gained them thousands— They have now retired to this place, built themselves spacious county seats, in which to spend the close[ing] scenes of their eventual, we hope a satisfactory, Life—How much real satisfaction, and [171] domestic joy they will take in this their evening of days, a few more fleeting weeks of time will tell in language all can well understand—

Two Brothers, by name Haviland, betwixt 60 and 70 years of age, of the sect friends, have just built them each beautiful county seats, with every convenience attached to them—John White (a Friend), one of the Trustees is a Man of strict veracity, kind, sociable, and a truly benevolent Man—His attention to my comforts has made the most pleasent impressions in his well doing, here and hereafter—

Benjamin Ferris, another trustee was all toward my convenience, I could wish, or desire—Bazil I. Bartow, the 3rd trustee, was all the gentleman, and the neighbor to me, while in his vicinity, and his children under my care— John White is about 60—Benjamin Ferris about 36—& Bazil I. Bartow about 25 years—

*[pencil]these three men now [?] all [page trimmed]

Col. Hamond has a superb seat at Throgs Point—

Westchester is very fertile in corn, which they cultivate, at much expense, in consequence of trying to see who can raise the best crops

[172] Inquiries may be attoned for, and forgiven,

> While <u>insults</u> admit of none, on this side Heaven
> The mind they do degrade in the Esteem—
> And naught on Earth, an Insult can redeem.
>   From Junius's prose

He who can order his <u>speech</u>, at all times, and In all places, in Wisdom, adorned with prudence, is certainly not inferior to the celebrated Athenian philospher—viz. Socrates

Sabbath 14th Septemb. 1800 Evening arrived in New York—15th & 16th in Town—17th sailed for the home of my youth, the land of my Fathers—

[173] I have observed in the opposite page (which comes down to September 14th, 1800), at which time I was in New York, that I closed my School in Westchester—as noticed—

On the 17th September I left New York for my home at Oysterponds, where I arrived on the 20th Sept—Found my wife, and little ones, all well—As I deemed It for the best, I thought I would make another attempt to obtain some kind of clerkship livelihood in New York. I again left my family, on the 12th of October, 1800, and arrived in Town, on the 14th—This, to me, was the most unpleasent parting from my wife, and children, that I had ever experienced—My doubts of taking this step, at this time, and the requests of my children not to go, and especially my Daughter, Deziah, of three years, quite upset me—She followed my to the door, with her Angel voice, crying "Papa don't stay, Papa don't stay"—

[174)] On my first arrival in N.York I received encouragement of employment as a copyist, in the offices of Frances Lynch Esq. Howsomever, disappointment proved my lot, and the better way I conceive is a calm, if not a cheerful submission to the methods of a just and wise providence—It is very probable that I lost this, above said situation through the treachery of John Billens, who had taken my good friend Joshua Racket into partnership in his buisness as a Grocer etc.etc. through my recommendation*—Racket and Billens, having quarreled, and dissolved partnership just before my arrival in Town—In their parting assunder, Billens, who was one of the most imprudentest of Men, and the sole transgressor—There we will leave him, having become my enemy, for having provided him a good, honest man, for a partner—

*7 or 8 months since

[175] I observed I would leave him (Billens), but first must observe that after his dissolution with Racket he broke to pieces, as they call it, failed, and took to School Keeping—Racket lost by Billens about 500 dollars

On the 26th October, the present month, I was offered a school at Bloomingdale, about six miles out of town, at sixteen dollars per month and board—My employer was a Mr. Thomas Adderly,—He was quite a blustering, forward, at the same time well-informed man—Conceited to the brim—My Scholars were very young, but of the higher sort of families—The Bownes, DePysters,* Olive, Strikers etc etc—General A. Hamilton is residing, at his seat, within a short distance of my schoolhouse (he calls

*a french gentleman, with his family, who repaired to our Country, to get clear of the troubles now raging in France—

his place Grange.) I board with a Mr. James Striker, whose hospitable Mansion stands within a few rods of the Hudson River—Mr. Striker appears to be one of the pleasentest and agreablest of men—his address at Morn, [176] noon, and evening, always with a pleasant smile, is such as to make you feel happy, and at home—His frugal, industrious, aimable wife is much the counterpart of her invaluable husband—Their eldest son* Garrit is about thirteen years old—he with his two younger brothers, and three fine Sisters, in Obedience, good behavior, and useful improvement, are an ornament to this excellent family—Their marked kindness to me (a lone stranger) made an impression of gratitude, not to be obliterated, but with my existence—

*This boy, at that time 1800 is now 1845 a Militia Brigadier General in New York

On the 2nd November I walked to the City—met there with my wife's Sister, Hannah, wife to Mr. Silas Howel of Newburgh—I returned home to my livelihood at Bloomingdale, as they call the place, on the 3rd.

Saturday 15th Walked to the City, and at Mr. Samuel Harper's I received two letters, from my Long Island home- one from my [177] dear wife, and the other from my friend Silas Vail—My wife's communication awakened in my throbbing breast all of the inexplicable emotions of the Father, and the would be tenderest, and the most affectionate of Husbands—I fear this absence, and effort, to advance the comforts, and necessaries for my dear family, is going to prove a failure—Well, I meant It for good—should It prove otherwise, I hope a becoming resignation will show me my future course—

November 21 1800 we had a snowstorm—

22nd and 23rd the Sleighs pass the Schoolhouse, some of their inmates, from their movement, and motions, appear to be in high glee—Not so with me, who am experiencing all the unpleasent sensations reasonably accrueing in an absence from a companion, & pledges, as dear as this Earth can give.

[178] A day or two ago I see pass my Schoolhouse on foot Jared Landon Esq., with one or two other Gentlemen, on their way to NewYork, they having landed just above, on the wind and tides preventing the Vessels headway—These men were the Suffolk County Legislature—had been to Albany to vote for a President of these United States—

On the 1st December the time for which I engaged at this place is up—

2nd repaired to N-York—

3rd received letters from home, with one from my Sentimental Friend Silas Vail—

On the 8th settled up my affairs at Bloomingdale, came back to NewYork—Made earnest attempts to get buisness in NewYork for the winter, but could not succeed to any kind of advantage—On the 21st [179] I called on Mr.William Hubbard, a Gentleman formerly from Southold L.I— Staid with him some hours—At this time he was a Clerk to a Mr. C__Ville— Mr. H. is a pious, and in every sense of the word a good Man—He is now near 50 years of age, was a Son to the late William Hubbard, Merchant at Southold—Long Island (1770 and on)—

My Friend Joshua Y. Racket sails for Savannah, in Georgia, next week on a trading voyge—

On the 22nd December 1800 I took passage for my home on board of a Sagharbour sloop—Capt. Crowel—One of our passengers was Mr. John Foster, formerly of Sagharbour, but had been living in other parts for many past years—He was now considerable over Eighty years of age—On board our Vessel, as passengers, were several old sea Captains and others, heads of families—We had a sociable, and an agreable time—all being cheerful, communicative, and disposed to make the passage pleasent—[180] Capt Hubbard Latham observed to us that he had lived in the Married state about thirty years, and in said time, himself, and Wife, had never exchanged one solitary word of censure, no, not one Syllable of fault, or blame—Our married men, on board were happy to acknowledge themselves very pleasently situated with companions of their choice, yet to go as far as Capt Latham had they could not, and keep truth on their side—Capt. Latham was a man of strict veracity, Industry, and economy—Of course we had not any reason to disbelieve his extraordinary course in the connubial state for thirty odd years—

Arrived home on the 24th by the way of Sagharbour—Took with me a barrel of Oranges, belonging to the [181] before mentioned Mr. John Foster—Sold them on commission—This, Mr. Foster was many years since the Owner of the house called Udall House, at that time, and many years afterwards, the largest house in Sagharbour—

The oranges I took of Mr. Foster sold off in quick time—Mrs. Ruth Tuthill (wife to Adjutant Daniel Tuthill) purchased a number of them, for her family, and for the poor, of her neighborhood—her charity and attention to the poor is not exceeded by anyone of her sex in the Town—Her expressions of tenderness, kindness, and affectionate hospitality is proverbial, as far as she is known, and will be greatefully remembered, and spoken of, long after she has left these mortal shores—Her benevolent Husband is a man of wealth, and she, with the heart of a Deborah, knows how to do good, and make glad her indigent neighbors with [page trimmed]

[182] All who know Mrs. Tuthill know as well as myself that her value in society cannot be too highly appreciated—such then will cheerfully indulge this notice by <u>one</u> to whom she has been all the <u>Mother</u> and <u>Friend</u>—

1801

Up to the 14th Jan. 1801 It has been mild and warm for Winter—This evening, visited my dear Parents at Rocky Point, and attended a Methodist meeting at Uncle Stephen Vails—The preacher was a young man named <u>Merwin</u>, an ingenious speaker aged 22 years—That Man of God called Uncle Peter Vail was there, whose prayer was powerful & truly affecting—The text was Proverbs 4th "Wisdom is the principle thing, therefore get Wisdom"—Tarried the night with my friend Silas Vail—

15th Thunder at a distance this morn—About 11 A.M. It commenced a smart shower, attended with a very sharp lightning, [183] and heavy thunder—I do not remember of hearing and seeing such a storm in any January before—Evening returned home—

17th wrote to our Mother Tuthill (my wife's mother) who is at present with her Brother Doct. Jonathan Havens of Hogneck, near Sagharbour—

18th January 1801 Joseph King (whose wife is Betsey, my wife's Sister) arrived at our house—His residence, or home, is in Goshen (Orange County). By him we received letters from our friends and connections in that region—Their favours informed us of their being in the enjoyment of good health—refreshing news—to all—

February 2nd A fine day—I went to Sagharbour—

This day is the aniversary of my birth—34 years is gone since I landed on this shore of eventual mortality—Alas! How have I improved my time (in which I have known good, and evil) Has it been in a preparation for those blissful regions where sorrow can never come—

[184] All this month (Feb. 1801) has been what is called very moderately cold—viz. not a cold month. March comes in quite mild—I had not any steady, nor profitable, buisness to attend to this past winter—I have spent more time in <u>eeling</u>, and <u>clamming</u>, the last two months than any two previous months this twenty years past—I believe I have not passed a winter without being in a school, as an instructor, this eight or nine years before—This month (April) I exchanged my <u>house</u>, and lot, at the landing (Oysterponds harbour) with Capt. Johathan Terry, for the house & lot formerly belonging to the late Capt. Henry King—The said Capt. King died in Philadelphia, about a year since—His frugality, industry, and strict econ-

omy, had procured him, with a blessing, a handsome property—say 9 or 10,000 Dollars, which he willed to his young Widow, who was Polly Terry, before her marriage—daughter of my Uncle Jonathan Terry.

[185] Moved into my bargained habitation in a day or two after the exchange—

The wind has been E- and somewhere towards that point, near twenty days in this month—

The last of this month, departed this life Doct. Jonathan Havens—In all that endears the name of Father, he shown in the fairest light—as a husband, he was affectionate and tender—as a neighbor, generous, charitable, and full of kindness—A friend & benefactor to the poor, and an Invaluable cit-izen—To his surviving Sister Mary, he was always (in all her many trials) all—all the anxious, and endearing Brother—He has left a handsome prop-erty, in personal and <u>real</u> estate, to his eight surviving children—four sons & four daughters—A fertile farm of four hundred acres, within about two miles of the flourishing village of Sagharbour—his age about 67.

[186] May 11 1801- I commenced school in this place (Oysterponds)—I had taught here before a number of quarters—say from 1797 Sept. to March 1799. Since this last date, I have taught School (as before noticed) at Sterling, Southold, Westchester and <u>Bloomingdale</u>, in the neighborhood of New York—Now, I am satisfied, It would have been much better for <u>me</u>, and <u>mine</u>, had I continued in the old place, where, It has pleased my friends to call me to preside again—I have fully realized Doct. Franklin's excellent observation, where he says, "I never see an oft removed tree thrive so well as those that settled be"—

June of this year has been (the first part of it) very promising for Hay, and early Vegetables—The last of it grows dry—dry—

July—it continues to grow very dry—The people have called a feast, although in the midst of Harvest—it was not well-attended—

[187] On the 20th July 1801 we had an excellent rain, which was a feast to our parched corn fields—

August proves to be a wet month—the last of this month, the eastern part of this place, called Oysterponds lower neck, was visited with that dire-ful malady, called Dysentary—

On the 6th Benjamin K. Hobart lost his only child, an Infant daughter, aged 2 months—

I received a letter from Elisha W. King, in answer to one I wrote him 12 months since, acknowledging his fault, in lending an ear to a slanderer, respecting me, at that time (I was then in Westchester)—

September—A warm month—the sickness in the lower neck increases— Two of my scholars, Thomas Vail & Henry Youngs, died on the 20th & 21st— two fine, promising, and very Interesting boys—

October—on the first of this month another of my scholars died, a daughter of Eliphalet & Ruth Beebe—
[188] Seventh this month (October 1801) Benjamin King Hobart moved his family to Sagharbour—Mr. Hobart had been teaching the school in this place—He has now engaged a good school at Sagharbour, where we hope he will do well—

November 1801 Very dry, until the 17th when we had an excellent rain—
On the 12th of this month, ended my 2nd quarter of this season— Commenced my 3rd quarter on the 16th—
On the 21st we had a small snowstorm—the first snow this autumn—
The last of this month commenced selling groceries, on a commission, for my cousin Amon T. Griffing—
In this (Nov) month died Mr. Thomas Vail, of this place, in the lower neck—his age near 60 years—He was called, and we suppose justly, a man of sound sense, strong [189] mind, and good reasoning powers—well versed in the scriptures, and we believe, as others do, he was spiritually taught—As a mechanick, house joiner, he was an excellent workman—An honest man—

1802

1802—I now have a considerable stock of groceries, owned by John T. Havens, his brother Capt. Gabriel, and Amon T. Griffing, in company—I sell (as before observed) on a Commission—

In the October of this year, that blessing to the poor of her neighborhood & friends, departed this life, after a distressing illness of six months, Mrs. Ruth Tuthill,* particularly noticed in page 181—
Mrs. Griffing was confined the 1st of November of this year with our fifth daughter, whose name we call Narcissa Lee—

In the autumn of this year 1802 a preacher of the Methodist order by name of John Finigan, a man of talents and sound piety, came to my house once a fortnight during the winter and preached the evening of each visit, with much good—He may be said to be the finest of the sect, known much in the place

*Mrs Ruth Tuthill is noticed on page 181—& her Husband Daniel Tuthill—

1803

1803 In April of this year I visited Goshen, Orange County See, and conversed with many of my former acquaintances in that region, where I [190] spent a number of the years of my chequered, and may I not say, eventual life—from 1789– to 1797—

On the 16th this April 1803 departed this life Jemima Terry, wife to my uncle Jonathan Terry—All that was aimable, prudent, and virtuous in woman, was conspicuous in her, as a wife, mother, sister, & neighbor—She was about 50 years of age

Built me a store this season 19 by 15 feet—

[in pencil] Rev. Emerson Tuthill is now 1803 the preacher in Oysterponds—he preached this Polly Tuthills funeral

Died on the 2nd or third of September 1803 Mrs. Polly Tuthill, the very aimable and truly endearing wife of Mr. Noah Tuthill, and the [page trimmed]

1804

In 1804 I gave up my school, in consequence of having to attend to my store rather too much for my school employers—At least they thought my tradeing, as I now did considerable, would engross too much of that attention, which the scholars ought to receive a larger share of—

This Autumn, I went to N.York and purchased for my owners a stock of goods—

[191] 1804 Rode through the Island for the first time on horseback—I had once before passed through the Island but It was on foot, in the year 1789—

I built me a Barn, in the fall of this year (1804) on the south side of the road, opposite my House, on a lot of about four Acres of Land, I bought just before, of Amon T. Griffing—

On the 4th of June this year, 1804, Mrs. Griffing was confined with a daughter, we name Honora Seward—

In the summer of 1803 our daughter Harriet attended the school of Mrs. M. Palmer of N.York one quarter—Her schooling was 8 dollars & 93 cents separate from board—

1805

1805—this Spring, I again went to N.York and laid in goods, for my owners—In N-Y- I contracted an agreable aquaintance with a Mr. Samuel Bartlet—A young man of Sterling virtues—His prepossessing manner, address, and generous deportment made impressions in his favour, that cannot be effaced but with my existence—

July the 8th Captain Joseph Webb, David King, and Mr. Thomas Terry were all three [192] drowned while attempting to cross from Sagharbour to Sterling—the boat filled with water, and sunk, about two miles from Sagharbour—Only one of their bodies were found, viz. Mr. Terrys—He was Grandson to the late Col. Thomas Terry, who died about year 1776 or 7

Capt. Orange Webb, of Sterling (called by many Uncle Short) died in the August 16th of this year—1805—near 80 years of age—

Visited N.York this fall—buisness as in the Spring—

August 4th about midnight, Mrs. Griffing was confined with a son, whom we call Sidney Lorenzo

1806

1806—Spring—went to NewYork on buisness as heretofore—

Deacon Azariah Tuthill died this year aged 82 or 3 years—Born about 1724—A Man much gifted in prayer, and was a staunch keeper up of the meetings in the Oysterponds Church for about 20 years, a great part of which time they were without any settled Minister—it is probable, that in faithfulness, as a deacon, [193] and in improving his gifts in keeping up meetings, by prayer, and reading Sermons, he has rarely been exceeded—his gifts in addresses to the throne of Grace were admirable, affecting, and sensibly impressive—His figure in, and out of the Desk, especially when in devotional exercise, reminded us of the deeds of Nehemiah of the Scriptures—The Deacon was in indigent circumstances at the time of his death—No doubt he was too much neglected by the Church, of which he had been so very faithful, and attentive a Member—

In March 14th of this year (1806) Christopher Brown Jr. died aged 30 years—

It was in the spring of this year I purchased of my Wife's Mother (Mary Tuthill) a piece of land on ShelterIsland, what has been called and yet is called "a Westneck right"—The said piece of land contains about 60 acres—

On the 7th October 1806 I went to NewYork with Doctor Seth H. Tuthill, in my carriage, drawn by his horse—We had a pleasent visit of a week or 10 days—stoped at [Vogas's?] about 10 miles west of Riverhead

1807

[194] 1807—At NewYork, in the Spring, laid in a stock of goods as usual—

This summer bought out Amon T. Griffing's part of the goods, viz. his third, of the stock—I gave him 400 Dolls—the Mssrs. Havers would not sell at that rate—But to get the buisness into my own hands, I very imprudently consented to give my obligation for near three times that amount— This was <u>one</u> of the marked unreasonable actions of my life—

In the autumn of this year, 1807, I exchanged my place for the one I had given for my present one in the spring of 1801—Am to take possession in the ensuing Spring—of 1808.

Visited NewYork this fall, after goods as heretofore—Likewise went to NewLondon, from which I rode to Guildford, to see my daughter Deziah— [195] She was living with my aunt Mary Stone—That is with Uncle Meadad, & Mary Stone

My friend Joseph Moore (of Rockypoint) went with me to Guildford— We had a good Carriage, with a spirited horse, for about six dollars—The ride is about forty miles—This was late in December 1807—At NewLondon, purchased a H.H.'d [hogshead] of rum, Ao [another] of molasses—and a barrel of sugar—

In October of this year died Stephen Vail, the husband of my Aunt Ruth—He was a man of most tender feelings, and could not see his fellow mortals in distress without using every laudable effort to relieve them—His age about 66 years—

1808

1808- In March, I think about the 7th, moved to my new place, although (as before noticed) It was the one I had owned, about seven years before— Took with me my Store house & corn crib—

This Spring built or added to my house about 11 feet on the east end— making a room & bedroom—

[196] Built this Summer. a picket fence around my Garden, dooryard & etc- etc—Set out six handsome English Cherry trees—

Captain Jeremiah Youngs and myself purchased each of us a wooden Clock for the sum of twenty dollars each. We believe they were the first of the kind ever known in this Town, and very likely in the County—

My much esteemed young friend Nathaniel T. Hubbard was with us several weeks this summer, and handsomely posted up my books—

Built me a snug Barn this year—1808—

Capt. Jonathan Tuthill died this season—Was Husband to my affectionate Aunt Mehitable—He was a kind husband, tender Father, and a valuable neighbor—His age about 66 years—

1809

[197] 1809—Continued to sell goods, at pretty quick sales—but prone to give too much credit, as I fear It will prove in the sequel—Well, time explains such traffick—

A long embargo at this time—It raises the price of goods, and that occasions buisness with us rather dull—

This year, like the years past, glides swiftly, unheeded away. Fast, very fast, I am advancing to that precipice from which I must leap into that world where change shall be no more—This is a truth, if properly considered might yield us a harvest of incalculable usefulness—

This year, in May, for the first time in my life, I took out a Tavern License—An honorable calling, no doubt, but a very delicate one in dealing out Spiritual Liquors to those whom we are well persuaded will use It to the hurt of themselves, and families—

1810

[198] 1810 This year commences (in this place) with considerable of a Religious revival—A number of our neighbors appear to believe they have found a peace that the world can neither give nor take away—A tranquility to be experienced, but not to be expressed—

A Mr. Ezra Haines is the preacher at this time, In this place (Oysterponds)—About 20 members have been added to the church—The fruit they are to bring forth, time will fully make known—To myself, I may well say—Adam, where art thou!—

In the summer of this year, I took Mrs. Griffing with me to NewYork— We went by land, in our own carriage—returned in about two weeks— brought with us a stock of goods—if good they prove to be.

In July 1810 I gave Caleb Dyer 83 dollars & 33 cents for 1/6th of a smack called the Industry—

1811

[199] 1811—Buisness with me this Spring much as heretofore—On some accounts, rather duller—

This summer took my daughter Harriet to New York with me by land—I took her to that extraordinary man called the rainwater doctor—Thousands were flocking to him daily, with every complaint humanity is heir to—from the boy, to the aged, and decriped [sic] old Man—from the little girl, to the Matron of fourscore—His office was thronged to an overflow—Our daughter's complaint was in her eyes—We put up a few days at our cousins—A.T. Griffing, New Town [today Elmhurst]—This phenomenon, in the physical world, of a healer of the distresses incident to mortals, kept his house in Brooklyn—

In December went to New York with Capt. Jonathan Terry, his vessel the Romana, a small sloop—

On the 20th August 1811 Deacon Peter Brown's wife was confined with a daughter—Aug 35th 1811 I went with Mrs. Griffing to Aquebogue to hear Rev. Daniel Youngs preach. Mr. Charles Vail was married to Polly Richmond Sept. 4 1811. Capt. Seldom Dayton, his wife—Jernet Wilke, Olive Hubbard, all with us 11 September.

Mr. Samuel Philips, brother to Mrs. William H. Helms, boarded with us this summer, at least to October

[200] After laying in a stock of winter goods, we set sail for Oysterponds on the 22nd December 1811—On the 24th about 11 A.M. we met two sloops, near Fortunes Island, opposite Old Guilford, on their way to New York—At the time, the weather was very mild, wind light S—and cloudy—One of said vessels was a new and completely built sloop, owned in part, and commanded by Davis Conkling, of Easthampton—He was much of a buisness man, great flow of spirits, prepossessing in his manners, and greatly respected by a huge circle of connections, friends, and acquaintance—The other Vessel was from Cutchogue, commanded by a Mr. Wells. E'er the next morning, before sunrise, this last Vessel was lost with every person on board—two of the passengers were [201] Samuel Davids, and Samuel Paine—Both of them keeping store in Cutchogue—two much respected Men, and very useful neighbors, and affectionate Fathers, and heads of families—A Mr. Jonas Wicks, of Southold, was on board—an Industrious likely man—He has left an interesting family—

Capt. Conkling, after his vessel was cast on shore, he with two or three others attempted to find some house, yet before reaching one, he became too much exhausted to proceed. The others leaving him under a small bush soon found one, and sent and took Capt Conkling to the house, at which they conveyed him to appearance in the last stages of life—and thus It was. He only lived but a few minutes after his arrival there—

Two of the passengers, a Brother and Sister, were found next morning on the deck of said Vessel frozen to death—another Man dead on the shore—the Vessel was [202] full of water, and ice—We, In the Roman (Capt. J. Terry) arrived home, and got on shore to our families, just before 12 o'clock, Midnight, on the 24th

About ½ past 12 A.M. on the 25th it commenced snowing, blowing, and freezing, equal, if not superior, in violence, to any storm within the last 100 years—Frederick Taber, in the sloop Seaflower, of our place, came into our harbor about 20 minutes after us, but the storm was beginning—They cast out their Anchors—the windlass tore away—the vessel drifted on to RamIsland [on Shelter Island]—And Taber, with his crew, and passengers, much exhausted, and near perishing with cold, reached the hospitable abode of Mr. Thomas Tuthill, where they were kindly attended to and made comfortable—

[203] Our Vessel was drove before next morn on shore, on Long Beach, full of water, and soon covered with Ice—Of course, all the goods that water would damage were pretty well lost—Well, our property was lost, and for some purpose, we hope for our final good, we were at this time preserved—The calamity was an awful one, and will long be remembered, as a singular providence—

Jeremiah Y. Tuthill (husband to my Aunt Patience) found next morning, after the storm, 6 or 7 of his yearlings & two years old cattle frozen to death in one of his fields—It was certainly the coldest, and distructive storm, that I ever knew—and very likely that ever was known. It came so unexpected, and so sudden, that many—very many, who do buisness on the water were caught, as it were at unawares, and not ever supposing destruction was at the door.

1812

[204] 1812. January has been a very cold, and blustering month—

On the 19th departed this life Capt. Matthew Tuthill, aged about 40 years—As Master of one of our handsome coasting Vessels, the was one of the most industrious, active, prudent and honestest of Men—His integrity, and accommodateing expressions to all with whom he had to do, was unsurpassed, and as he went weekly, with the produce of this place, to NewYork, his buisness was with almost the whole Town—He has left a wife

*named Howel
and Phebe

and two young children (*a son & daughter) to mourn the loss of one of the most affectionate of Husbands and Fathers—

Our country appears, from what the newspapers inform us, and other sources, to be on the eve of a great Calamity—a War—And who ever knew of a good war?

[205] In June of this year War was declared betwixt this country and great Britain—We think they are the sole agressors—It is a sore scourge, and we must submit to it with a becoming humility—hopeing good will come, yet, to us, as a nation—

In July, Mrs. Griffing, with me, rode through the Island to New York—from thence, after one nights stay in town, through York Island, over Kingsbridge, to Yonkers, where we put up at a Mr. Odell's—Mr.O- was an aged man, of 80 odd years—Had kept an Inn for many years, but <u>now</u> had given it up, yet condescended to entertain us—which he did very much to our satisfaction—Said his house had been the stopping place, for many years past, of our prominent publick Men—Col. A[aron]Burr, and his accomplished Daughter, always made [206] It their home when they travilled that way—Mr. Odell highly entertained us through the evening with instructive stories, and amusing anecdotes, of revolutionary and olden time—He observed feelingly that he thinks he never knew a more accomplished young woman than was Miss Theodicia[Theodisia] Burr—

The next night we put up to an Inn, about ten miles this side of Fishkill. The 3rd night from N.York, we arrived at Fishkill, and stoped a day or two with Benjamin Brown, whose aimable wife, Hannah, is Mrs. Griffing's niece—From B. Browns, we went over the River to Newburgh, and stoped with Mr. Silas Howel, whose well informed wife was Mrs. G's Sister Hannah—After stoping with them several [207] days, we started for home—We stoped at Capt. Wm. Hudsons, In the east part of Blooming grove. Mr. Hudson lives near the Old Stone School House in which I had taught school in the years 1791-2-3 & part of 1794—In that time, I received the most affectionate kindness, and attention from Capt. Hudson, and his very pious and prudent Father, and tender Mother—Then, they were venerable for <u>goodness</u> & <u>years</u>—Now they are gone to the reward of a well spent life—

From Mr. Hudsons we proceeded to Oxford, and stopped for the night with Mr. Samuel Racket—A very hospitable, sociable, open hearted Man—He was in early life from Long Island, but was now a Man with a family,

well settled, and in handsome circumstances—Travillers, into the country
(where he resides), who are from Southold, or Acquebogue, by calling on
him, receive every expression, and [208] accommodation, calculated for the
comfort and satisfaction of those who for the time are absent from their
natal spot—

From Mr. Rackets next morning, we left for New York—Passed
Townends iron works, at a mountainous place called Sterling—passed those
extensive Nail Factories called Piersons's—Tarried the night, not far from
Hackensack, at a Mr. Odell's Inn—Was well entertained—next day proceed
on to the Hobocken Ferry, which we crossed over in a small Steamboat—
Found our friends in Town well—Staid with them one night—Proceeded
home, on the South road—Arrived to our residence after an absence of
about 18 days, having traviled near 500 miles, and in said time enjoyed ourselves, as well as could be expected—

[209] In rideing through Tarry Town (on our way to Fishkill) I stoped
my horse at the very place where the tree had stood, under which the men
were reclining who captured Major [John] Andre—There, I observed to
Mrs. Griffing, is the spot where 32 years ago the blooming, accomplished,
but unfortunate Andre found all his hopes and expectations blasted forever—"Honors lost," himself doomed to an ignominious death—His fate
certainly appears to be a hard and very curious one—especially when we
believe hm to have been a finished gentleman, and an honest man—
However he was no better than Capt. Nathan Hale, whose execution was
similar, yet much more aggravating, and much less mercy shown him by
his hartless captors—

The coincidence of Arnold's Death, and the distruction of that tree,
under which Andre was taken, is surely worthy of notice—[210] On the very
day the news of Arnolds death reached Tarry Town, a flash of lighting from
a terrific black cloud shivered that noble tree into many pieces—

1813

1813. We now are in the midst of a bloody and unreasonable War, with
what we have been taught to call our Mother Country—The British Ships
of War are now In Gardners Bay, the Sound, and off NewLondon daily—
two or three 74's & frigates—Comodores Hardy and Capel—with Captains
Burdett & Coote etc etc——They often land, and come to my house—are
civil & respectful—

Hardy's Lieut., with a barge crew, came to my house a day or two after

*it was on the 21st August, the day after Penny was taken, that the Lieutenant and 4 men with him were at my house

they had taken off Joshua Penny*—The officer spiritedly observed, that they had got him, and no doubt as circum[stances] [211] were, although Penny's Father was an aged Man, he, the Father, would no doubt outlive his Son—

In August of this year 1813 died my much and deservedly esteemed Friend, Capt. Nathaniel King, aged 51 years—As a Son, Husband, Father, neighbor, and Citizen, he was in every sense of the word Invaluable—

In consequence of the Sounds being infested with novascotia privateers, I hired a two horse Wagon, to go by land to NewYork, after goods—My friend Wm. Conkling went as driver—In the end, I find it has cost more than It came to—The expenses exceeded the profit—Of course, It was an imprudent Step—A step that gave a bad complection to my Winters buisness—

In Novem 15th we had a great, and I might say, heavy Snowstorm—

1814

In June 1814 my dear Mother Griffing was with us one night.— our Mother Tuthill, and sister Polly Hubbard, was likewise with us—This was the last visit from our precious Mother Griffing, in which she staid all night with us

In summer this year, the British with their barges took a handsome sloop near Shelter Island belonging to Capt Trip of New Bedford— Capt. Trip with his crew escaped in his long boat, but the vessel & a full [cargo?] he lost— I think his name was Lemuel Trip—

1814 This Spring took my daughter Cleora with me by land to New York— At Patchogue changed away my Carriage for one of a different construction— [212] I gave in exchange one hundred Dollars—which I paid in Shoes—In this traffick, I believe I gave too much—Not a profitable trade with me—But Its done, and cannot (like the laws of the Medes & Persians) be altered—What is more proper than to carefully look before we leap—especially If Its a ditch we are going to jump over in a dark night, amidst hail and rain—

While in N.Y. I purchased about 800 Dolls. worth of Goods, half of which I sent on by Water, the remainder I took on with me by land—Those by water were taken by the Novascotia refugees and, to me, nearly all lost— The Vessel, which took them, was commanded by one Seely, a connection of the families of that name In Goshen, Orange County, N.York—

I left Cleora at Brooklyn, with the Miss Halls, [213] to learn the millinary trade, for which I gave the Miss Halls Forty dollars—

The beforesaid misfortune, or we feel previledged to say, robbery, spoilt this summers buisness with me—

This Fall took with me, in my carriage to N.York, Capt. Charles Noyes—He, Noyes, is now (1814) living at Sterling, in Southold, in consequence of the war, which when its over, he intends to move to his old home, NewYork, and resume his former livelyhood as commander of a ship in the European Trade—He, Noyes, is a connection of Capt. Hardin, of Revolutionary memory—

Cleora returned home with me, having been at Brooklyn six months— A small company, calling themselves Videtts, were this season quartered at Southold—They were ordered to ride (one or two of them) to Oysterponds every day on the lookout—feed their horse or horses, take dinner etc etc at my house, and return to their Station at Southold the same evening—This they were to continue to do until further orders—

[214] On the 8th day of November 1814 my Beloved Mother Deziah Griffing took her final farewell of this world (with all its productive poisons, the fruits of sin, and mans disobedience) and entered Triumphant in the Chariot of her Redeemers love into that Glorious City spoken of in Revelations 21st 3 & 4th verses—

Capt. Mayhoe in a fine sloop loaded with flour was in company with Trip but escaped—see pages 212 & 213—

this year 1814 was drowned in Plum Gut Noah Beebe a man of sound Piety and great Faith of a Happy immortality—he was son to Silas Beebe mentioned in page 143 in first journal—

1815

In February 1815 the Joyful news of peace saluted our ears—It was good news from a far country, or cool water to a thirsty famished soul—The Videtts now left us, without paying more than half of my just and moderately charged bill—Another bad business!

In July, I went to N.York, bought a small lot of goods—my <u>means</u> prevented a larger purchase—Affairs began to look lowry—It is hard to make brick without straw—Where there is no wood therefore the fire goeth out

[215] August 12th (1815) an Easterly storm—13th 14th 15th 16th 17th very sultry, hot, with wind S by E—& foggy weather—It continues extremely warm up to the 22nd—Finally It has been a very warm sultry month—

Mr. Dickerson has preached with us occasionally, this past season—A plain, <u>good</u>, sincere, wellminded, honest, unlettered Man—And yet well versed in that love to God which passeth all human knowledge. Not to be taught but by the Holy Spirit, that is in the School of Christ—

My wife, with me visited Acquebogue Sept 2, tarried there two nights, and one night at* Mr. William Hubbards, Southold—A hospitable, kindhearted, pious Man—His excellent pleasent Wife was the daughter of Judge Jared Landon of Cutchogue—returned home on the 5th—up to the 12th very warm.

*Squire Jared Landons Son in law

On the 23rd a severe Easterly rainstorm, up to the 11 A.M. when it blew a hurricane, unroofing some houses & barns [216] in this, and other places—The tide rose, as high, perhaps higher, than it has within the last fifty years—It covered a part of my garden—Mrs. Hetty Hobart, wife to Mr. Joshua Hobart, was landed from a boat, at the foot of my garden, to the northend of Thom. V. Youngs house—About 12 at noon, the wind changed to S-W-, takeing In Its tremendous course, in this and other places 20 miles around, thousands of trees up by the roots, and prostrating many beautiful Orchards—

From the 24th September to the 6th of October 1815 it was very moderate, and warm weather—I forgot to observe that in the 30th of September Capt. Grant B. Racket was Married to Miss Ziporah T. Brown—

Considerable of the Dysentery in our neighborhood—An aimable little girl from New York, Betsey Dunning, died with said disorder in this month (October)—

> Sweet babe—so soon escaped the ills of life
> And landed safe, beyond the reach of strife,
> [217]Oh happy Child! So soon to you 'twas given
> To quit dull Earth, for all the Joys of Heaven—
> Babes wash'd in Jesus precious blood do prove.
> Sweet little Cherubs, in the realms of love—

30th October 1815 departed this life, after a long and distressing illness, Mr. Gideon Y. King—

> Farewell, my friend, you've left a world of pain,
> For that, I trust, where joys forever reign—
> From cares, from grief, from wretched doubts & strife,
> The Saint, through death, emerges into life—
> Eternal Peace, and beatific love
> Awaits the pious in their last remove

In December of this year, Sidney, our son, broke his thigh—Doct. S.H. Tuthill set It very handsomely, and in the course of sixty days, in part of which time he suffered much, he was able to walk—

1816

I taught the Oysterponds school, 2nd district, one quarter—continued my School through January 1816 & February, and then gave it up to my old friend Doct. Thomas Vail, who has just come to the place from Vermont after 20 years absence—

.

[218] March 1816—Went to NewYork—laid in a pretty handsome assortment of dry goods & groceries—Goods, at this time, were very high—a risk (I fear) In the purchase—

The 16th of this March we had an uncommon storm—

June, July, & August, European goods fell amazingly, and I found (alas to my sorrow) my fears in March last were well founded—The whistle was too dearly purchased—Its musick was harsh, and Its expense grieveous—

In Feb. 7 our harbor is shut up with ice—people cross to Rocky Point [East Marion]—

In March 7th of this year (1816) Mrs. Submit Petty, wife to Mr. Joseph Petty, died, a few hours after the birth of an Infant Son—They name it Joseph—Mrs. Petty was an excellent woman—and the life of the vocal singing worship in the Church—This notice ought to have been inserted in page 184 of the Diary-

1816 November 23rd Mr. Joseph Petty died, aged about 50—He was a peaceable quiet, good neighbor, husband and Father—

[219] On the 26th November Capt. John King died aged about 62—Capt. King was very retired in his habits—Seldom going beyond the precincts of the Town in which he and his ancestors for three or four generations claimed as their Earthly residence—the Capt. had a peculiar way, and mode, of action, in performing his buisness, and doings with his neighbors, peculiar to himself—It was not his natural trait to be prepossessing in his every days address—But we have no doubt of the goodness of his heart, and that his aims, in all his intercourse with men, were just, and honorable—His feelings were tender, easily wrought upon, as was his constitution, feeble, and health never good—To us he was ever the undeviating friend—He has left no children—a wife survives him—as kind, as tender, and as affectionate a woman as ever adorned her Sex—He died in full hopes of a happy immortality—

1817

[220] 1817 January was a very cold month—Feb. continues extreme cold—Our harbor froze pretty much over—people cross from us to Rocky

January 1816 died Mary Brown, daughter of the late Benjamin Brown Esq. She was a maiden lady of 75 years, full of good works, an excellent woman—long known by the name of Aunt Molly—In March died Hannah Tuthill, daughter of Adjutant Daniel and Ruth Tuthill. She was beloved and an endearing, affectionate child—Died the same day Thomas Terry

I think it was in this year 1816 we had a frost every month in the spring & summer—it pretty much ruined the corn

In September 1816 Sylvanus Mulford, son to Mr. Elisha Mulford took his portion 1000 Dollars which his father gave him and took his disparture for a small village in Pennsylvania called Montrose where commenced keeping [?] now in 1847 he is rich, respectable—

In September 1817
my friend, and the
friend of the
widow &
fatherless,
departed this life
in the 36th year of
his age Thomas S.
Lester Esq.

Point on the Ice—This makes two winters in course, that it has been shut with Ice—

This month, a Mr. Potter, a Ventriloquist, stoped with us a few nights— Performed some of his extraordinary feats etc etc

A Mr. Levi Hathaway was with us some days—Preached two or three times in our meeting house—was of the denomination of <u>Christians</u>, as they stile themselves—He was certainly an ingenious explainer of the Scriptures, and appeared to be a pious Man—God knows the heart—What a solemn, important, and alarming truth—

The young and aimable wife of Joshua Tuthill died this year—Clarisa Harlow, aged about 20 years—

1818

1818- May 3rd Died Mr. David Petty, aged about 50 years—He was industrious, and indefatigable in [221] laboring to procure property, and get his affairs (Tenements—Farm, and stock) suitable to his, as his movements may have shown, very <u>anxious</u> mind—This anxiety might be his fault—yet in his dealings with all with whom he had to do, always displayed the honest, and nicest punctuality—

April 25th Mrs. Sibil Taber, wife to Mr. Amon Taber, departed this life— In every sense of the word she was the pleasent wife and affectionate Mother—she was about 70 years of age—

In June, <u>Mr. Silas Howel</u>, and wife Hannah, Mrs. Griffings sister from Orange County, paid us a visit—Mr. Howel was a native of Long Island, about 50 odd years ago—He met one of his old neighbors, and kinsmen, that he had not seen over 50 years—It was an interesting meeting, at my house, and full of incident to the curious in such as think more of their relatives than a calf does of his grandfather—The gentleman whom he met was Capt. Stephen Howel of Sagharbour—Our brother Howel & his Industrious wife stoped with us a few days, then returned to their home—

Pecuniary embarrassments rendered absolutely necessary to quit store-keeping for the present—[see page 312]

[222] Received this May 1818 of Asa Adams, of Boston, a quantity of Crockery, and Cordage, by the hands of Caleb Dyer—These Articles was sent

with a verbal order to me, for to sell on a commission—The Crockery was in Crates, as It came from Europe—of course, we could not tell how much the brokage was until opened—And the rolls of cordage appeared to have been broke, and part of them gone—In short Adams proved to be a knave enough to ship them In this way—Dyer, double dealing sufficient to deliver what he pleased of the ropes, and call It the whole, and I the greatest dupe, to receive them, and be liable to account for them all, as these two deceivers should say—Altogether, it was to me, and mine, a very troublesome, unpleasant buisness—How careful we ought to be in buisness of consequence, about trusting to the fair speeches of strangers—yes, often of our own acquaintance—

[223] This year 1818 June 1st Capt. David Webb died, aged about 52 years—Capt. Webb had commanded several handsome Ships in the European trade—Was a Man universally esteemed for his social and agreable qualities—Just in his dealings and accommodating almost to a fault—Preposessing and kind to all around him—He was handsome in person and figure, benevolent, Manly, generous, charitable, and we believe him sincerely virtuous—And to sum it all up, though last, not least, he died the death of the Righteous—"Blessed are the dead who die in the Lord"

Having but little buisness of consequence to attend to, aside from waiting on travillers as an Inn Keeper—It was deemed advisable to commence a School in one of my rooms—I began that livlihood in Nov. with considerable encouragement from my immediate neighbours, whose countenance bespoke friendship—Prosperity gains friends, adversity tries them—Capt Jeremiah Youngs—Elisha Racket, and Mr. Ezekial Glover, and others, were my very agreable employers—and their children [224] of the first order, In attention, and obedience—Without partiality, I could not but notice with marked precision, John, Elisha Racket's oldest son. I observe, he displays something peculiarly interesting in his manner, movements, and observations at play with his juvenile companions—To an open, frank, earnest avowal of his every little remark, in the sports of vacation, he displays a decision and magnanimity of mind, rarely (in my view) to be met with in a boy of his age—viz. 7 or 8 years—He appears to have formed the Idea of Mankind, that, no kind of deception, duplicity, or deceit was, or ever could be known, or indulged among them—What a noble conception of his fellow species—yet, alas, how falacious, my young friend, will find them in the future intercourse, you may have with the inhabitants of this mundane sphere—

[225] John has two brothers younger than himself—Fine, industrious,

August 8th 1818 Died this day Mrs. Rebecca Terry, wife of Capt. Jonathan Terry, a truly excellent woman

attentive boys, and should they live to act upon the Theatre of buisy life, from their movements and displays in school, I should hope that respectability, integrity, honor and intrinsic worth would adorn them through all the meanders of their future walks in this chequered life—These brothers names are Elisha Sherry & Sidney Philander—

1819

It is generally said that the Cat species will live about 14 or 16 years only—in February of this year our old domestic cat, which we raised from a kitten, which was given us in March 1798, died—she must have been 21 years, as this is now 1819

July 22 1819 died Capt. Thomas Webb of Cutchogue—Capt Webb was for 20 years a seafaring man, and much of that time commanded a Vessel—he died, we believe, a Christian—Died January 8 this year Jeremiah King, generally called Uncle Long, aged 81 years

1819—much of this year was made very unpleasant with the buisness of Asa Adams—In April, I rented my store to Adams, for one year, for thirty dollars, In which he put a Mr. William F. Clark, with a store of goods—they obligated to sell no liquors to be drank in said store, as that privilege was mine, as a Tavern—In this they forfeited their word, honor, & obligation— In the end it was a troublesome, perplexing concern, and caused me and mine inconceivable uneasiness and anxiety—

[226] 1819—In July (having but little to attend to in my Tavern,) I engaged myself to teach the district school at Sterling, for one quarter—On beginning my school, I was much impressed with my present situation, and that of twenty years ago—In the ensuing August, It will be 20 years since I engaged to teach in this same place—I taught then two quarters, and the parents, who now employ me, were (some of them,) then, my Scholars—And the scenes, and changes, I have passed through since that eventual period, in retrospect, tends to deep thought and profound contemplation—"How solid all where change shall be no more" And to that unknown region we must all soon—ah, very soon, arrive—It is a truth, let It be uttered as It may, or considered in what light It will—Divine inspiration says "there is no discharge in that war"

[227] The winter of 1819 & 20 I spent chiefly in my bar room—Too much neighbour custom, I fear, for good morals—The children of Jonadab was, no doubt wiser, better, and truely happier, than the men of the present generation.

The Mr. Clark, mentioned on page 57 lived in the house opposite, owned and built some years since by Capt. Frederick King—Mr. Clark is a Man whose suavity of manners, and every days deportment gave him much respect with all with whom he had to do—As a merchant, he was deservedly preposessing—

1820

May 2nd 1820—Rode to Southold, took my wife with me—we took dinner with our dutiful daughter Harriet—that is with our soninlaw Abner Wells—

Took out my 11th Tavern license this day—having taken out my first in 1809—

3rd Wednesday—Capt. Lyndes King ploughed my corn ground—and carted out the manure.

[228] Thursday 4th May 1820 Dry for the time of year

Friday 5th Planted my corn—Some of it 16 inches apart,with one kernel in a hill—An experiment—

Saturday 6th—Up to this date, the O-ponds Seine has caught only about 13,000 bunkers [menhaden].

Sabbath 7th Wrote to our Mother Tuthill, who is near Newburgh, confined to her room, in consequence of a fall some four years ago—She has been a woman of sorrow, affliction and much disappointment, for many of the last years of her life—In 1768 she lost her husband, Nathaniel Tuthill—He was a Man of superior excellence—and, from what we have heard of him, we should not think It improper, to say in him there dwelt no guile—It appears that with the termination of his life, a seal was set on all her earthly comforts—

[229] Wrote to James Preston, and our daughter Deziah, at Ashford Connecticut—

Monday 8th Foggy—Wind E—where it has been this some days—

Tuesday 9th wind E—Capt. G.B. Racket sails for N.Y. in the Schooner Enterprise—

Wednesday 10th—A calm day—

Thursday 11th—Wind S—and a very dry May—And a sign of but little Hay—

My Uncle Thomas Terry stoped with us some short time, this day—In charity, benevolence, and disinterested affection he stands in the first ramk of the noblest of his fellows—

Saturday 13th Strong S-W- wind—within the last three days the seine has took 200,000 bunkers—

Departed this life on Thursday last Benjamin Coleman Esquire, of Southold—In mechanicks he was a very ingenious artist—

[230] My neighbor, Capt. Jeremiah Youngs, has caught in his set nets over 10,000 bunkers up to this date, this season—

Sabbath 14th May—Wind W- & cool—P.M. Went to RockyPoint—Stoped some time with my lonely, and venerable, Father, who is now in his eighty-first year—See, and conversed with Capt. Stephen Randell, a sincere good hearted, prepossessing Man—He has lately become a resident in Rockypoint—Owns the farm of the late Mr. John Moore—

In April of this year 1820 my friend and preceptor Doct. Thomas Vail departed this life aged 60 years—A more particular notice of this gentleman is in my Journal p. 104

Monday 15th A calm, warm day—We just learn, by the papers, that DeWitt Clinton has the majority of votes for governor over Mr. Tompkins—

Our Mr. Wm. Clark (mentioned a few pages back) has this day purchased 40 barrels of codfish at ¾ of a cent per H [hogshead?]—

Tuesday 16th about 7 A.M. it commenced and continued to rain all day

[231] 17th Wind E-S-E—Our cousin Russell Terry weeding his corn—its early as I ever knew weeding corn before—

18th A.M. calm P.M. a breeze E-S-E-

Capt. Frederick King gone to the Sagharbour today

19th Wind E-S-E- Cloudy & cool—11 A.M. it began to rain, which it continued to do through the day—The seine has caught, within two or three days past near 60,000 fish—

20th High wind N-N-W—until 10 A.M. when it hauled to S- with squalls—Seine took this day about 12,000 fish—Some Men from Lyme with us—Cool evening—

21st A.M. cool—wind E-S-E—Cloudy with a light rain—called this day on my cousin Capt. Jonathan Terry, who is sick—

22nd A rain Storm—Wind E—I enjoyed a little inward tranquility this morn—none can bestow it but HIM who sits enthroned in light eternal & unchainable—To him be all the Glory, for every favour & mercy, we find new every morning fresh every [morn?]

[232] May 23rd, 1820. High wind S-W—The sloop Young Romp, Wm. S. Hobart, Master, arrived home from Charlestown this morn—She has been absent 7 months—

John Tillinghast Jr. Studying Arithmetic with us just now—A Mr. Mackie, and two other Gentlemen with us boarding from beyond Albany—

24th Morning high wind W-S-W—12 at noon It dies away—P.M. some showers—Doctor Gardner with us an hour or so—

25th Wind high N-N-W—Just at night calm—the seine took 14,000 fish—The sloop Fanny, Daniel Beebe, sails for N.York—

26th—A hard E—rain storm

27th—cool—it clears up this A.M.—Capt. S. Randell & wife visited us— Mrs. Griffing and myself, with them, called on Mr. Samuel Hobart Sr., [233] who is very sick—Mr. Randell prayed with him, too, I trust to Mr. Hobart's comfort—

Visited deacon Peter Brown's wife, Mr. Randell prayed with her—She is sick—

28th Clear & pleasent—Took Narcissa & Honora with me to Southold— Found our daughter Harriet & Family well—

At the Methodist meeting, Mrs. Lydia Payne gave us a Solemn and an affectionate exhortation—She appears to enjoy some of the consolations, which rejoiced good old Jacob's heart when he was informed that Joseph was yet alive, and saw the waggons, which were sent to convey him to his long lost child, now, Lord over all the land of Egypt—

The seine caught this day 10,000 fish—

29th Wind strong from S-W—Walked to Adjutant Tuthills, with my boarders—Mssrs. Mackie, Lomis & _____

30th Wind as yesterday—Walked to Capt. Rufus Tuthill Sr., My boarders with me—

[234] May 31 1820—A N-E- rainstorm, through and cool—

June 1st Wind light S-W—Messrs. Mackie and my other boarders left this day for their home in Washing[ton] County, N.Y.—

A Mr. _____ Deverell, an Englishman, has been our preacher, this year past—He is a man of good natural abilities, yet not sufficiently watchful (In my opinion) to take the pastoral charge of a congregation—hastiness, united with imprudence, are very unfit attendance on a preacher of the Gospel—While we believe him sincere, we greatly regret his unguarded movements, words, and actions—Mr. Deverell says he served some time in the british fleet, as a Lieutenant—

The seine caught 60,000 fish this evening.

6th June, our neighbor Capt. Jeremiah Youngs [235] took his wife and our daughter Cleora in a sail boat to Southold this day—Capt. Youngs is very much out of health—has been perceptibly failing since June 1816—

8th Wind fresh S-W½ W—rode to Cutchogue—stopped at Col. Benj. Case's—

If we feel to have Jacobs God for our God, we have a sure foundation

9th Wind N-E-by N—

10th Wind E-S-E—Rode out with Mrs. Griffing to Col. Jeremiah Moore's—Stoped a short time with my venerable but lonely Father—found him, all things considered, comfortable—In the course of the day, we called on Mrs. Elizabeth Webb, the aimable and bereaved Widow of Capt. David Webb—Called on David Wiggins Jr. & our sister Lucretia—David has been unable to help himself since 18th—An afflicted family—Called on our esteemed Aunt Hetty Tuthill—On Brother James—Took tea with Mr. & Mrs. Randell—returned home at sunset—

11th June, was visited this day by Mr. Elam Conkling, a pious, sincere and truly good Man, [236] his life, dealings, conversation and manners, united with his prayers, warrant the belief of his deserving the sublime appellation of a Man of God—A name rather to be chosen than great riches—

12th Friend Elam left after breakfast—

13th thick & drizzly weather A.M., wind E-S-E-, P.M. W-S-W—Attended as assistant auctioneer a Vendue in Southold—Selling the goods & chattels of the late Benj. Coleman Esq—

14th Our dear daughter Harriet, with Benj. Wells' wife, visited us this day—rain this eve

15th Very pleasant—A Mr. Dan'l Mandeville Chisey, a Silver Smith, with us from New Haven—

Within a day or two the seine has took 40,000 fish—

17th Very high wind E-S-E—Several riverhead Sloops, in our harbour, wait for weather suitable to waft themselves to RhodeIsland—Mr. Chisey left this day—

18th—Sabbath—Mr. Ezra King preached with us this day—

[237] We are informed that the Reverend Elisha Gillett died a few days since, at or near Patchogue—he was about 87 years old—had been a Baptist preacher about 40 years—He was faithful, diligent, upright, and conciencious in his divine vocation—Although his gifts in communication were small, his ardor, and zeal in religious instruction was worthy of his calling—He died with unshaken confidence in the love, faith, and assurance of a Joyful immortality—We are informed the following were his last words—viz.

> My willing soul would stay
> In such a frame as this
> And sit and sing herself away
> To everlasting bliss—

23rd Went to longbeach, got 72 gulls eggs—

24th Captain Stephen Randell and wife stoped with us a short time today—Wind S-S-E—

25th Sabbath—Wind W-S-W—

26th Wind E-N-E—Mrs. Griffing unwell this eve—

Capt. Jonathan Terry very unwell, It is thought dangerous—

[238] 27th June 1820. The Rev. Moses Swezy and wife with us—Mr. Swezey, as a watchman on the walls of Zion, agreable to his situation, and abilities, I doubt if he has his superior—Religion, pure and undefiled reli-

gion, and the field of the gospel, is his element, and chief delight—He is assuredly a Son of great consolation to his church and people—and Joy and rejoicing to all believers wherever he is called to deliver his messages of love, reproof, and affectionate and endearing exortations to make sure of the pearl of great price—The Joys of Eternal life—

28th Mr. Swezey left this eve—Four of those people, called Quakers, stoped with us this eve—

29th This morn, at 9, they, the friends, hold a meeting at the church— One of the women (there was two of them) the Eldest preached an [239] Interesting discourse—I think her name is Phebe—This evening they left, going west—

30th Wind W-S-W—

July 1st 1820—Rode to Aquebogue with Mrs. Griffing. Stoped the night with Bartlett Griffing—

July 2nd Sabbath—Attending Meeting—Sacrement, administered— Stoped the night with Mr. Swezey—

3rd This morn, after purchasing 33 quarts of cherries for 100 cents- returned to our home

4th Independence—

5th Wind W-S-W- dry weather—

6th Wind as yesterday—Hot, and dry—

7th Rode to Aquebogue with my Friend Peleg C. King, after cherries— Returned this eve—

At this Time, The Schooner Enterprise Grant B. Racket, and the Sloop Experiment, Caleb Dyer, Sail, and follow the Boston trade pretty steady through the Season—

12th July, went to Shelterisland, and gathered a quantity of English cherries of General Dering—

[240] July 13th 1820. Wind S-W—Capt. Frederick King reaping his small Field of wheat—A reverse of fortune—perhaps imprudence had astonishingly changed this Man's position—He has now scarce the means to procure the necessaries of a comfortable subsistence—A few years ago, he commanded, (with respect, and ability) a Ship of more than 1000 Tons—has commanded several from two to 500 Tons—This appears to be a freak of fickle Fortuna—

17th Monday—rode down the neck with Mr. John Hart—

18th It is at this time very dry—

19th Rode down the neck with some of the Rockypoint young men viz.

two of my nephews Moses & Milton Griffin, and our enlivening young Friend, Joel King—

21st A refreshing rain—

[241] 22nd Rode to Town, found Harriet (our daughter) comfortable with an Infant two or 3 days old—It was new, and grateful to us, to find her so well—

Departed this life, this day, 2 o'clock P.M., my early and constant friend, and juvenile associate, Capt. Jonathan Terry, aged 50 years—Capt. Terry has followed the coasting buisness, from this to New York, for the last twenty-five years—as Master of a good, safe Vessel—His attention, carefulness, prudence, and aims to benefit his customers, has justly procured him their lasting goodwill—He has died, greatly lamented by a large circle of connections & friends—

24th Went to Shelterisland—Took dinner with Mr. Samuel B. Nicoll—On my return stoped a short time with Thomas Tuthill, at Ramisland

Tuesday 25th died this evening Jonathan Youngs, a Son of Mr. Lemuel Youngs—He died with the lock jaw—occasioned by running a fishbone in his foot—He was a very promising boy of about 11 years old.

[242] Thursday 27th July 1820 Rain—Received a letter from Doct. Nicol Dering—respecting the Widow Abigail Sawyers needing assistance from her friends in this quarter—

A Mr. Dunning, SonInlaw to Mr. Sam'l C. Hobart—He is a Butcher—undertook to show us how to dress a calf in stile—which we think he performed to satisfaction—

28, Got me home 3 cords of wood, from Shelterisland—A refreshing rain this eve—

29th Some fine showers—Wind S- & high—

Sabbath 30th Showers—

31st G. B. Racket & Dyer sailed for Boston—

Got home 6 cords of wood, from Shelterisland

Wednesday 2nd August 1820 Died this day Sally, the daughter of Mr. Rufus & Sally King, aged about 16 years—A child that lay very near her parents heart, but she is taken, no doubt for the best, and from the evil to come—

3rd Received a communication from our children at Ashford—Preston & Deziah

[243] August 5th 1820 Showers—Wind S-S-W—

6th Wind E-S-E—

Monday 7th Our BrotherInlaw, Richard S. Hubbard, & Polly, his wife, came from N.York, on a visit to us—Mr. Hubbard is a very worthy Deacon of one of the Presbyterian Churches in N-Y—He is a Man of sound Faith, great patience, true humility, and unrelenting Industry—A kind husband, tender Father, obliging neighbour, and a valuable citizen—Mrs. Hubbard comes assuredly near, very near, of being one in whom dwells no deceit.

On the 8th in company with our Visitors, called on several of our neighbors—

Wednesday 9th A Mr. Foulk, with his Family, five in number, came to stop with us a few days—Mr. F is owner of much property in the west Indias—likewise a large ship owner—Our eccentrick neighbor, Capt. John Brown, has and does command some of his Vessels—Much, I understand, to Mr. Foulk's satisfaction—and Brown's profit.

[244] Sabbath 13th August 1820 Died this morning Mr. Samuel Hobart Sr—aged about 74 years—Mr. Hobart married in this place (Oysterponds) Jerusha, the daughter of Mr. Benjamin King, known for many years as Uncle Ben—Soon after Mr. Hobart's marriage, which was about 45 years since, he moved into Goshen, Orange County, where he staid a few years—he then moved into Lyme, Connecticut—from there, about 1793, he moved his family, wife and seven children, to this place, where years before he had married his wife—

Here, he opened a small store—and with strict attention, and economy, soon accumulated property, so as to purchase land, and build him a house, and barn, which he as now possessed near thirty years—In many respects, he has been useful in his day, and [245] generation, expecially as a house carpenter, and house joiner—

As a Tavern Keeper, with all the rest of that vocation, he has no doubt sold to those who distressed their families with their drams—It has been too long the custom for neighbors to frequent dramshops. Of course the vender, and the purchaser, both err—Aside from this, we hope Mr. Hobart dealt honorably, and have reason to believe he died in the Christian faith—

15th Wind E-N-E—

16th quite cool—Wind E—Ten couple, young men & women, took tea with us this evening—they stop with us to night—

17th This morn 18 of them took breakfast with us—they were from Connecticut—P.M. rode to Sterling with Mr. Foulk & family

18th Mr. Foulk, with his family, left us for N.Y.

20th Brother James stoped with us an hour or so this day—Mr. Nicol sent me 6½ cords today

[246] Tuesday 22nd August 1820 Rec'd 7½ cords of Mr. Nicoll this day to sell for him.

6 couple of young men & women stoped with us a short time, this morn, from Mattituck.

He that builds his immortal interest on the Rock of ages, shall never be moved—The Earth, with its brightest productions, can have no charms for him—He knows the fact, that there is nothing below the Sun but <u>vanity</u>, & vexation of Spirit—

25th Started for Newburgh

26th about 8 P.M. arrived within about 2 miles of N.York—

27th arrived in Town [NYC], about sunrise, found Friends all well—Fore noon, attended meeting at the Rutgers Church—P.M. went on board of the line of Battleship Franklin—She was the largest ship I had ever visited—On board, everything appeared in its place—And all her equipment in the nicest precision. [247] This noble Ship was named after a Man, who was once a runaway boy, strolling the streets of Philadelphia in a shabby dress, eating his rool of cake, while looking forlorn & forsaken—stoped the night with our friend Capt. James Wilkie—

28th Rode out to Manhattanville with Capt. Wilkie, and returned by the way of Harlem—Took dinner with Friend N.T. Hubbard—at 8 P.M. set off for N.Burgh In a Sloop—

29th Off against <u>Tappan</u>, a place become famous, and interesting, as the last <u>acts</u>, and <u>scenes</u>, of the accomplished, but unfortunate [John] Andre—

The highlands—the <u>palisaidoes</u> [*sic*], or <u>rocks</u>, on the margin of the Hudson, which rise in sublime grandeur, hundreds of feet perpendicular, strike the eye of the attentive observer, with sensations of awe and admiration for <u>their</u> Omnipotent Author—

Arrived at Newburgh 9 P.M. Stoped the night at a Mr. French's

30th took breakfast with my Friend and former pupil Thom. Helms

[248] 30th August 1820 Attended camp Meeting about 3 miles above Newburgh, on the Hudson River. At 1 P.M. Started in a waggon for Silas Howel's, where I arrived ½ past 3—Found them all well except our venerable Mother Tuthill—She remains very feeble—

31st Spent much of the day with our afflicted but blessed Mother—blessed she assuredly is, with an unshaken confidence, and faith, that her Heavenly Father, who is about to release her, shortly, from <u>sin</u>, and all its consequences, and give her an abundant entrance into his beatific presence, where all is praise, glory, and endless adoration—Where, these tattered garments of mortality, these habiliments of dying flesh and pain, will be exchanged for the spotless robe of Christ's <u>Righteousness</u> and the <u>mantle</u> of Eternal Youth—Triumphing in these assured prospects, she sits calmly waiting her Father's will.

[249] This evening rode out to Montgomery, 7 miles, to see my friend Joshua Y. Racket—found him and family well—

September 1st 1820. Rode out with Friend Racket to Washington Ville— This <u>place</u>, now quite a number of houses—a large store or two—was, in 1793 & 4, without a house (except a tumbling down loghouse)—a forest— I, at that <u>time</u>, taught School within a mile of It—now, I find, within the time, since I was here, everything greatly changed—and, alas, many with whom I was agreeably familiar have gone the way of all the earth—Stoped this night with Uncle S. Racket—

2nd Saturday, called on Sister Betsey, Mrs. Griffing's sister—She has drunk deep of affliction's bitter cup—The products of worldly expectations—

Left Uncle S. Racket 10 A.M. for Goshen, where I met my long and much esteemed friend, Doct. David R. Arnold—It is now 18 years since we have had the satisfaction of an Interview—It was to me a season of refreshing, & no doubt to him

[250] 1 P.M. with Mr. Joshua Racket and friend Arnell, visited Chechunk Springs, situated about 3 miles North of Goshen—they are a new discovery, and begin to be much frequented for the salutary and medicinal qualities of their waters—A committee of medical Gentlemen have reported favourably of those Springs, as published in the Orange County Doct. Society, for 1820—

While at Goshen called on my brother Samuel C., who is keeping school in the vicinity—Dined with the Doct.—<u>then</u> we left, he, the Doctor, accompanying us about 5 miles on our way—stoped this night with Friend Racket—

Sabbath 3rd—At 1 P.M. took leave of Friend Racket, and his accomplished wife and interesting family, and traveled to Brother Howels, where I arrived at 3 P.M.

[251] September 4th 1820 At Mr. Howel's this day Benjamin Brown, and his wife, Hannah, Mrs. Griffing's niece, and Fanny, Mr. Howel's daughter, now married to a Mr. Oliver, who was likewise with them, all on a visit—Spent most of the day in the room, with our afflicted Mother Tuthill—

5th ½ past 3 P.M. took an affectionate leave of our aged Mother, Mr. &

Mrs. Howel, & family—and proceeded to New Windsor—While at New Windsor, called on Mrs. Mitta Havens, Widow of the late Benjamin Havens, who was originally from Moriches, on Longisland—Mr. Havens was well known, and celebrated, for his agility and great strength, often shown to conspicuous and publick Character, in, and around Orange County—On the whole he was in his daily avocations a mild and peaceable Man—At the same time, his known powers of body often led him into unpleasent situations—It would be more proper to say he was enticed into company, such as does not reflect comfort or profit.

[252] At ½ past 6 P.M. I went on board of the packet sloop Tombolin, Saml. Logan, Master—

I forgot to observe, that, while at New Windsor, I called on Seth Brown, with whose pleasent family I took tea—Mrs. Brown is an excellent woman, full of the most aimable traits, and qualities which render the Wife and Mother an invaluable blessing to the family, over which she is called to preside—

On the 7th After a pleasent passage, with very sociable and good company, we arrived in N.York—here, I met, with much satisfaction, my Brother James, with whom, on board his Vessel, I took breakfast—Spent the day with our friends N.T. Hubbard & James Wilkie. With those two gentlemen I took a supper of Oysters, at the famous Washington Hall—

8th Took passage for home on board Brother James's Vessel—Stoped, (on account of the head tide) an hour or so at NewTown creek, and called on our [253] agreeable cousin, Amon Taber Griffin's widow, with her three children—She is an affectionate woman, of many trials and much sorrow— Her husband, an interprizing, buisness, careful, industrious, and useful man, died, in the meridian of life about two years ago. He was the fourth Son of Peter Griffin, who died (as I have before observed) on board the prisonship, in 1781 or two—

Came to an anchor, this evening, near Westchester, at Isaac Clauson's landing—Took lodging on shore, at a Mr. Scofields—

Capt. Wilkie's two daughters, are with me—are going to board with us the ensueing Winter—Jennet, and Louisa, the two eldest children—

9th Visited, with the little girls, the late Mr. Clausons spacious Mansion, near the landing where our Vessel lays—The house has an imposing appearance, as you sail up and down the east River—It is at this time uninhabited, except by rats, and spiders. We walked over its stylishly finished rooms, which [254] appeared like the former receptacles of depart[ed]magnificence—Here, a short time since, the ambitious owner of this splendid seat,

entertained his numerous visitors and dignified guests, with the richest lux-
uries, and <u>wines</u>, of <u>our</u>, and other lands—Musick, good cheer, and the convivial board, resounded their echos through these spacious halls and
ornamented apartments—It was here that Mr. Clauson showed his marked
civilities, to the notorious, and the daring Capt. Stepthon Haley (now an
officer in France)

Alas, the mutability of the brightest, and most permanent of all sublinary
things! <u>These painted rooms</u>, and those delighted walks, will be known no
more to their buisy proprietor forever! Mr. Clauson, and his wife, have
exchanged these mortal goods for the coffin & winding sheet, and his family,
scattered up and down the world—What a lesson for human grandeur.
What is human greatness?

[255] Sabbath 10th September 1820—Set sail early this morn for O-ponds
(our home) where we arrived safe & sound about 4 P.M. found my family
well, and in good spirits—

11th High wind S-W—Unwell, with a bad cold, attended with a cough—

12th Wind W-N-W—more cool, than some days past—

13th Weather as yesterday—some better of my cold—

14th Wind E-S-E—Brother R. S. Hubbard with us, with his daughter,
Mrs. Wilkie—Mrs. Griffin unwell—

15th Brother Hubbard returned to Mattituck—

Mr. Ebenezer Hedges of Easthampton took dinner with us on the 10th.
A man of sound piety and truly possessed of Abraham's faith—A goodly
Man, and a Christian—

16th & 17th- Wind W-S-W—& 18th—Attended the Vendue of Mr.
Deverell, as Auctioneer—[256] This Mr. James Deverell has been the
Preacher, in this place something over a year—is now about to remove into
Connecticut, at a place called Miltown, as their preacher in that parish—I
have noticed this teacher in divine things in Page 234

19th Wind E- and rain storm

20th Cool wind N-W-

21st Wind E-S-E Our Deziah, and her husband came to us this eve, from
their residence Ashford C-T-

22nd Died this morning Mrs. Ketiviah Randell, the very kind, tender,
pious, and truly affectionate wife of Mr. Stephen Randel, of Rockypoint—

23rd Wind W-S-W-

Sabbath 24th A pleasent, calm day. J.H. Preston left for N.York—took
passage with Capt. Wm. S. Hobart in the Sloop, Young Romp

25th Wind West—cool—

[257] Thursday 26th Septem. 1820 Wind E-N-E—

27th Weather as yesterday

28th D[itt]o—D[itt]o—

29th A calm day

30th Westerly weather

Oct. 1st Wind E-N-E—

2nd Rode to Southold—Stoped the night with my long respected associate and friend Zacheus Goldsmith—With him I spent one of my most agreable evenings—His conversation and company yields me much improvement and permanent satisfaction—I hold him as deserving a distinguished place amid the circle of my disinterested friends—

3rd An Easterly rain storm—Repaired home to my family this evening—

4th Wind High E—

5th A calm, serene, and what is called a pleasent day

6th Wind E- with rain—

7th Wind E-N-E—considerable cool—

Sabbath E-S-E wind—

(258) Monday 9th Octr 1820. High wind E-N-E- with rain—

10th E-N-E- Wind Sidney & Preston, took a sail to Sagharbor—

11th A fresh S-Wester—Preston & Sidney returned from S.Harbor—

12th—It blows hard from W-N-W—Rode to Sterling to see Mrs. Elizabeth Webb. She is thought to be dangerous Ill—Mr. Deverell (the late preacher with us) moves off this day—

13th James H. Preston, his wife (our daughter) and Cleora left us this eve, for Ashford in Connecticut—

14th Wind W-S-W—Unwell this eve—How weak, how frail is poor human nature!

15th Hard wind E-S-E- with a rain storm

16th Wind N-W-

17th A high N-Wester

18th N-E- wind and cool—

[259] Thursday 19th Fixt a part of my Store room for a School, the ensuing winter, for a few select Scholars—Wilkies two little girls stop with us this coming winter

21st 22nd & 23rd Variable weather—Wind mostly N-N-E-

24th Wind W-N-W- and it blows high—

25th hired out my waggon to Asa Patrige Esq. to convey him to NewYork—Mr. Patrige* is a conspicuous Merchant, at Sagharbour, of some

*Mr. Patrige died in N.York 1854 aged 90 years— His wife a week before

time standing—He was a Schoolteacher of much credit for 10 or 12 years, previous to his present mercantile livelihood—

26th & 27th cool weather—

28th moderate N-W- wind—

Sabbath 29th Ezra Youngs preached with us this day—Mr. Youngs is a descendant of the Reverend Joshua Youngs, who was the first preacher in Southold.

30th I commenced school in a part of my storeroom.

Does permanent peace grow in natures best cultivated gardens? I wot not—Not any soil short of the shores of immortality can produce such effulgent fruit

[260] 31st Octo'r 1820 Wind S-S-W—very light

November 1st mild weather

2nd Wind E-S-E—Attended the auction of the personal Estate of the late Mrs. Elizabeth Webb, as Auctioneer—Mrs. Webb died about ten days ago, in the triumphs of that love which is stronger than Death—As a Wife, Mother, and neighbour she was invaluable—As a Christian, she was an ornament to the profession, and the glory of her sex—In 1818, as noticed in 55 page, Mrs. Webb lost her Husband. He was the husband of her early, and sentimental love—from this severe stroke, she never recovered, but for two years, has been a humble, resigned, and devoted pious mourner—They are now united—Sanctified—Where parting is no more—

30th Wind N-W- by W—

[261] 4th Wind & weather as yesterday—

Sabbath 5th November 1820—Mr. Jonathan Hunting preached with us— Mr. H. is a grandson of a Mr. Hunting, formerly a preacher in EastHampton for more than fifty years—from 1696 to 1752 or 3—

6th High wind N-W—A Mr. Pierpont, from near NewHaven, with articles to sell—There is something peculiar in Mr. Pierponts manner, address, and commonplace chat, to induce one to rather like his company, and wish to remember him—I should suppose him turned of fifty—

7th Mr. Pierpont left for Litchfield, Connecticut. We made a Hogshead of Beer, agreeable to a receipt of Mr. Pierpont—

8th 9th & 10th Some frost about these days with N- winds—Time—O, fleeting time! What courser can keep pace with thy onward course?

11th Slaughtered my old Cow, which was disagreable, as she had been to us a useful, kind, and docile, orderly Animal—yielding us butter & milk—

[262] Sabbath 12th Novem 1820 It has been a severe snowstorm all the past night, and this morn It commences a heavy rain—Wind high E-N-E—

13th Wind as yesterday, and a cold snow storm—The trees are loaded, and clothed with the crystal garb of Ice—It appears rather early in the season to have such a profusion of Ice & snow—The wind has been so powerful that from Its effects several Vessels are on shore—Two, we understand, on Shelterisland—

14th Moderate, Wind W-S-W—Never perhaps colder in Novem.—

15th After a storm, It is said, comes a calm. The late cold storm has so chilled the little chub mackerel that they are driving up on our Shores by hundreds, with some remains of life in them—at least many of them—

16th continues calm—

[263] 17th & 18th Two calm days, added to 2 or 3 past ones

19th Wind very light S.W.—Rode out to Lathams & took dinner with him—

20th Wind light S-W—Rec'd two barrels of apples from N-Y—with flour & butter etc-etc-

21st & 22nd Wind more brisk S-W- & N-W-

23rd Killed my hog—Wt. 260 [Lbs?]

24th & 25th Damp weather, Wind S-W-

Honora & Sidney went to Southold—Found our dear daughter Harriet & family well—

26th Sabbath Wind N-W—Mr. Ezra Youngs preached with us—

28th & 29th—Cool N-W- Wind

30th A heavy frost—N-N-W- wind—

Decem. 1st N-W- cold wind

2nd & 3rd Wind fresh N-W- Some signs of a storm

4th A rainy day

5th Moderate weather—Died this day Mr. Samuel Youngs, aged 42 years—Mr. Youngs was a peaceable, quiet, & a good neighbour—one of those few that never would hurt anyone.

[264] Wednesday 6th Decem. 1820—Thanksgiving day through the State—Mrs. Griffing rode out to Southold—Received a letter from our children, at Ashford—they were well, yet a perusal of It affected us as parents—

7th—Wind W-N-W—

8th—Died this day Mrs. Mariann Cleaveland, the very aimable and endearing Wife of Doct. Henry H. Cleaveland—aged 21 years—She was the eldest daughter, and child, of my late deservedly esteemed Friend Capt.

Jonathan Terry—Was married to Mr. Cleaveland, about 16 months since, with every prospect (as much as health & youth can promise) of all the domestic Joys, and pleasures which the connubial state is capable of yielding the virtuously united, in its silken bands—But, alas, the cord is cut asunder, and the bridel enjoyments are exchanged for the Coffin, and the winding Sheet—the utmost bounds of all human devices

[265] 9th High wind N-W—Mrs. Griffing is yet at Southold, where she went on the 6th

11th weather as yesterday—

12th Wind N—Mrs. Griffin returned home from Southold.

13th, 14th,& 15th Weather more moderate than some days past—We have had blustering, cold and rough weather, almost continually for 3 or four weeks past—

16th, 17th & 18th—Some cool days—with high N-W- winds—Wilkie's two eldest daughters with us boarding & Schooling—

19th A rain Storm—

20th & 21st Wind N- & N-W-

22nd Some Snow this morn—soon clears off with wind N-W-

23rd & 24th—What we call flattering weather, which ends in a rainstorm—

25th 1820 ago the Angels came down to our benighted Earth, and sang "Glory to God on high, peace on Earth, and good will towards Man"

[266] 26th Decem. 1820 A blustering day, with some snow

27th Very cold, Wind N-E-N—

28th N-E- wind—some snow—ends in a rainstorm

29th Continues to rain, but the ground is to hard with frost to take It in—of course it is almost a flood—

30th Wind W-N-W—Dan'l Bebee is at this time our main coasting master in the [Fanny?] sloop vessel to N.Y.—C. Dyer, in the Sloop Experiment, goes mostly to Boston—

31st—Wind as yesterday—

1821

January 1, 1821—A new year—O may It prove to me & mine a permanent good year

2nd Wind high—Cold weather—In Temperence, and Spiritual things, It is assuredly much like this frosty weather—As It is a cold dull time—

3rd & 4th our harbour froze out perhaps 3 or 400 rods—

[267] 5th, 6th, & 7th Winter clouds, wind & weather. My unshaken friend, Ithuel Hill, with us—some snow—

8th Wind N-N-W—The snow drives into large banks

9th Wind S-W-—Our friend, Hill left us—

10th & 11th Some time high wind N-W—then it becomes moderate with a light Snow—

12th I have a school, In the North part of my store of about 30 Scholars—rather crowded for a room 13 ft by 12—

13th & 14th Snows hours, then It clears off with high wind N-N-W—

15th D[itt]o—D[itt]o—

16th Was this day visited by our Friends James Wilkie & Nathaniel T. Hubbard of and from N-Y—

17th A severe snow storm, Wind E-N-E—Rode out with Capt. Wilkie and his two children as far as Capt. Rufus Tuthills—the banks of Snow rendered the roads almost unpassible—Of course our ride was unpleasent

[268] 18th January 1821 Very cold weather—

19th The extreme cold has froze our harbour over—to do that, we call It cold weather. Our friends N.T. Hubbard & James Wilkie left this day for N-Y—In their sleigh

20th 21 & 22nd Extreme cold, as It has been this 3 weeks—Perhaps, as cold as any 3 weeks within 5 years—

Wm. F. Clark went off—or moved off this day—to Boston—

23rd Snow, about 4 inches deep—A Mr. Whitney, a Gunsmith, has been, with his wife, living with Mr. & Mrs. F. Clark, this sometime past. He, Whitney, is going to move to Newburgh, to set up his trade—

About this time, I have much anxiety, in consequence of Crockery, Cordage, and 'tubs, sent on by Caleb Dyer, from Asa Adams of Boston—never received any of the 'tubs, and only a part of the Cordage—and a part of the Crockery was broke—All was charged to [269] me, although I never bought a particle of It—All that I did receive, I accounted justly for—In the sequal I was used (in words & threats) very unhandsome, about the buisness, and I have no doubt all in consequence of Dyers duplicity—[This incident was already described on page 222 as taking place in May 1818]

The words in 2nd Kings 19 Chap & 6th & 7th verses were a comfort, & a permanent consolation to me—They were with me, some time before I arose, in the Morn—and [k]new not at first where to find them—

24th Snow squalls—our daughter Harriet is with us—

25th Wind N-N-W—Extreme Cold—Snow is in high banks—more so than this some years past—

26th Our harbour froze so that people cross over to Rocky point—

27th Plenty of ice in the Sound—It is said they cross It at Huntington—

[270] Sabbath 28th January 1821—Received a Letter, yesterday, from Mr. Baily, Post Master, in NewYork, respecting my getting the appointment as Post Master, in this place (Oysterponds)—It appears, if I had wrote him sooner, I should have got the appointment, but as It is, Joseph Terry, and his friends, have by unfair means, cheated me out of It—Capt. Daniel Beebee, and many others, will testify, to the correctness of my observations on the subject—

29th Our harbour is froze as hard as it has been, perhaps this Ten years past—I acknowledge myself too inattentive, and cold towards those important realities, which ought at all times and in all places, ingross our most lively attention—A wise Man will build his house on the rock—yes, the Rock of ages never moves—

30th & 31st—Young men, and boys, are using their skates with toil and great glee on our harbour—

[271] They are hireing out the seats in our meeting house for the first time, in this place, I believe—It is much disapproved of by some of our aged people—

February 1st 1821—A Southerly Storm of rain

2nd The aniversary of my birth 54 years this day since I commenced my entrance of the treacherous bridge of life—

3rd Considerable of a thaw—very muddy underfoot—Jennet Wilkie, our little boarder, is quite unwell—

4th & 5th Rainy weather, with some snow—Jennet some better—

6th 7th & 8th Snow rain & calm—unsettled weather

9th Some white frost—with wind S—

10th Visited my Venerable Father, who, considering his age, enjoys a tolerable share of health—He is now over 82 years of age—Likewas called on Mr. Truman & wife—an aged couple—he is near 80 years—They resemble Zachariah & Elizabeth, walking in the ordinances of the Lord blameless

[272] 11th & 12th Feb. 1821 Some rain—Some thick foggy weather—

13th Wind N-N-W—

14th A snow storm Wrote this day to Capt. G.B. Racket, who is now at CharlesTown S.C.

15th & 16th Snow storm, for several hours

17th Snow drives furiously into lofty banks, which to mount is high glee for the boys—

18th & 19th Wind N-W- & cold—but clear—Doct. John Gardner called on us yesterday

21st fine weather

22nd It snows 23rd It rains

24th Rec'd two Letters, one from our Children at Ashford—the other from N.T. Hubbard N-Y—Preston writes that our daughter Deziah is confined with a daughter—Our sensations on the news are such as parents know—

25th A cold day—Dyer sails for Boston with produce—

[273] 26th It snows—Wrote to my friend N.T. Hubbard

27th My kinsman Daniel T. Terry Esq. brought me a quantity of English Hay—This uncle of mine is assuredly one of the most valuable members of society—A peacemaker, and a wise Councilor—

My neighbor and open hearted friend sailed for N.York in the Smack Java—

28th A snow & rain storm—

March 1st 1821 A Mr. John Rogers of Mattituck staid with us last night—

2nd Very high wind N-W—

3rd Went to Rockypoint on official business—Some snow—Wind E-N-E—

Sabbath 4th Went to Capt. Tuthills Sr. He and Capt. Stephen Randell held a meeting at Capt.T—at least at the lower School house—

5th & 6th Very cold—Capt. Elias Terry sails for Sandyhook, on a fishing voyge

[274] 7th & 8th March 1821 Wind high N-W- and cold weather for March—At this time, & for a year past, I have held the office (from the honorable the Council of appointment) viz. Commissioner of Deeds, Judgement Bonds etc etc—Auctioneer, and commissioner of Schools—

9th & 10th Doct. Tuthill and others of Southold folks called on us—Ellectioneering for Town officers—

Sabbath 11th Our friend Elam Conkling attended meeting with us at the School House—Mr. Conkling is truly a Godly Man—Appears to possess a large portion of that blessed Spirit of humility, and pureness of heart, spoken of in Matthew 5th Chap & 8th verse—We have known him for some years, in all of which time, he has acted, conducted and lived the Christian—

[275] Was this day informed of the death of my long, and much esteemed, and truly invaluable Friend, Silas Vail—This dear man is often

mentioned in the years 1792—3 & 4 of my Diary. Previous to those years, we had commenced a correspondence by letters, and pretty strictly continued it, until within a short time before his death—I have many letters* from him wrote in a feeling, and an affectionate style—all breathing the effusions of piety, morality, and warm desires for that holiness of heart, which constitutes the faithful believer, in the sublime truths of the everlasting Gospel—For the last 30 years, he has been a great reader of theological works—The Bible, he often observed, was to him, the book of books—Its soul cheering precepts, he esteemed as the pearl of great price, and his daily prayer was that its sublime mysteries, and Heavenly beauties might be satisfactory understood, and made plain to his understanding—Truth, appeared to be the object of his anxious pursuit, and we believe he attained it in all the sweet foretastes of a happy immortality.

*A number of them are in the hands of his son, Franklin S. Vail

[276] For more than 30 years, his buisness has been teaching School— The arduous duties of that honorable but unthankful profession, he performed with credit to himself, advantage to his scholars, and satisfaction to his employers—In the war of the revolution, when about sixteen years of age, he was taken prisoner, carried into New York, and imprisoned some time, I have been told in the old sugar house!—kept on short allowance, and otherwise hardly dealt with—that calamity, united with a severe attack of the bilious colic, so impaired his constitution that he never fully recovered it afterwards—

About the year 1794 he married Betsey, the fourth daughter of Judge Thomas Youngs, of Southold—By this Lady, he had two aimable Children, a Son, and Daughter—After his marriage, he removed to PalmerTown, near Saratoga, entered into partnership with Doct. Gamaliel Vail (a connection of his) and commenced store keeping—but alas, this buisness, [277] as it was conducted, very contrary to his mind, proved altogether a failure—This misfortune & grievous disappointment, friend Vail fully attributes to the extravagence of the Doct.—And from other sources of information, we suppose there is no doubt of It—This sad catastrophe, brought on some domestic disquiet, which with a shattered, broken down constitution, made the last ten years of his eventual life very unpleasent—But in the midst of all these complicated difficulties, he ever made the glories of true and undefiled religion his constant, and uppermost study—Always appearing anxious to be found in the straight and narrow road, which leads to life eternal, and regions of Glory—

It is now about one & ½ years since he left this place, for the residence of his Brother James, a Merchant, at Saratoga—Our parting was, to me, and no doubt so to <u>him</u>, very affecting, made more so by his observing, empathet-ically, that he did not think he should ever return here more!—Yet he hoped, if that was his lot, we should meet again, and renew our <u>friendship</u>, among the sanctified, in loves unbounded regions

[280] [*sic*] After residing with his brother (where he received every civility and kindness) about 15 months, his health, which was poor before, began visibly and rapidly to decline—He now saw, and was satisfied that the time of his final dissolution was at hand—his chequered, and eventual life was soon to close, and with a Christian, humble submission he calmly awaited the important moment—Bourne up by the consciousness of his sins having been done away, through the attoning blood of his Saviour Jesus Christ, he calmly fell asleep in the Arms of sovereign Mercy—In Feb. 1821. He was born, I have understood, in 1759—

Is not friendship, like the immortality of soul, too good to <u>be believed</u>?

<u>In Heaven</u>
There Jonathan has his David found!
And Watts, his Gunston too!
And O, my dear and valued friend
May <u>there</u> I meet with <u>you</u>—

[281] Monday 12th March 1821—Wind S-W- by W—

13th Was visited by our pious friends Elam Conkling, and our aimable, and truly religious Cousin Parnol Wiggins—They appeared to be on the Mount of redeeming Grace, and dying love—Strong in the Lord, Strong in the God of their Salvation—

14th Some rain A.M.—P.M. It ceased to rain, but remained cloudy—Visited Major Nathaniel King—an aged man, born in 1730—I think he tells me he held a military commission under George the second, in 1756 or 8—

15th 16th 17th & 18th Cold N-W- weather, with some snow—

19th & 20th uncommon cold, and blustering wind E-S-E- with some snow—Wm. F. Clark moves this day for NewBurgh—

Lean not on <u>Earth</u>, it has a barbed dart
To wound afresh thy palpitating heart—
On its sharp point, thy peace, it bleeds—it hies
And hope—sweet hope—Alas! expires & dies—

[282] March 21st 1821 A hard storm of rain, wind, S—A Gentleman

Musician with us this morn, Mr. Selden—We were highly entertained with his gifted performances—He left us this evening—

22nd We lately had a large parish meeting for the purpose of getting the minds of the people, where the post office should be located and who should be postmaster, providing we can get the mail rout extended to our place. It now comes no nearer to us than Southold village. As there was two candidates, myself and Joseph Terry, the votes were taken by Ballot—On counting the votes, It appears 55 were for Augustus Griffing & 35 for Joseph Terry—Yet by a neglect of my friends, and Especially my confidential advisor, and sincere wellwisher, who was too honest to suspect, the opposite party, capable of that duplicity, and meanness, which they have (as we hear), practiced to carry their points, and obtain the object—Daniel T. Terry, Esq is my friend, referred to above—He was so sanguine that [283] if justice was done him, and me, I should have received the appointment—his confidence in the minority was such, that from their fair speeches, he delayed to send on the meeting and Its decision—they took advantage of this dilatoriness—sent on one, or two, of these wary double dealers, to the Post Master at Southold—Informing him that the people here wished an office at Oysterponds, and that he would take the trouble to write on to Washington, on the subject,—and get Joseph Terry appointed Postmaster—Thus he has done, as rumor says—he not knowing that there was any other Man, in the place, thought of, for the situation, or that wished It—Here, we see, that the low darstedly, envious workings of some, have succeeded in their nefarious aims, and now chuckle at getting the game, although they feel to know they obtained it by dishonor & cheating—[see p. 270, Jan. 1821]

23rd Rode to Southold—On my way called on Col. Jeremiah Moore, Aunt Mehitable Tuthill, Mr. John Payne, Doct. John Gardner, and Phineas Payne—[284] Stoped the night with my daughter Harriet and her husband, Abner Wells—

24th March 1821—Showers this morn—After It cleared off 10 A-M—Walked to Judge Case's—Rev'nd Mr. Huntings, Squire Moses Clevelands with whom I took dinner—Came back to our children, took my horse & rode home, where I arrived about sunset—

25th & 26th Squally weather—dismissed my School, which I have attended in a part of my storeroom since last November—

Nathaniel Hubbard of Mattituck, a worthy, honest industrious and useful man, stoped with us the night—Mr. Hubbard is one of the deacons of his parish Church—

27th Snows two several times this day—Rev. Moses Swezy, and Deacon Daniel Terry stoped with us the night—Preached with us in the evening

28th Wind high N-W- & cold—Rode to Rockypoint & Sterling, at this latter place, Mr. Swezy preached—I took dinner with Mr. Jerome—

[285] 29th Doct. Henry H. Cleveland commenced School in this district—

30th 31st Moderate weather—A Mr. Hallet preached with us—we believe a <u>good</u>, at the same time <u>he is</u> truly an unlettered man—

Sabbath 1st April 1821 A pleasant day

2nd Some Snow squalls—

Departed this life, this morn, Capt. Jeremiah Youngs, one of my intimate Juvenile companions—his age 54 years—About one month my senior—Our intimacy began very early in life, being of the same age, and our parents living within 25 rods of each other—His manner, movements, and disposition was always such that his company was a solace, in all the situations allotted me in his immediate neighbourhood—As a companion, he was pleasing and confiding—As a friend true & magnanimous—As a neighbour, and associate, he was affectionate and accomidating, almost to a fault—The <u>Widow</u>, and the <u>Fatherless</u> all testify to his ready, and seasonable relief—

[286] Capt. Jeremiah Youngs was the favourite nephew of the late Messrs. William & Samuel Youngs—They both died without children, neither of them having ever been Married—Wm. Died about 1774 and Samuel 1776, leaving their intire estate to Jeremiah, their esteemed and adopted Child, who was then about nine years of age—At the age of about twenty three, he married Lydia, the third daughter of Mr. Stephen Vail, of Rockypoint. By this virtuous aimable, and industrious Woman, he has had Seven likely Sons, and three agreably accomplished Daughters—

While Comodore Decatur, In the Ship United States, lay at anchor, in the Sound, opposite Oysterponds beach, near Browns Hills, Capt. Youngs visited his Ship, took with him a fat Sheep, which he handsomely presented to the Comodore, who invited him into the cabin, and treated him with the most marked respect and consideration—[287] The Comodore told him his present was duly and feelingly appreciated, and he hoped from certain considerations he should see him (Youngs) another day—But so it is, they, <u>here</u>, have never met more—

Capt. Youngs enjoyed tolerable health until June 1816, when he took a sudden, great cold, which brought on a severe sickness, from which in a

number of weeks, he partially recovered—A distressed cough set in, which
continued to affect his lungs, and finally proved fatal as first observed—

He was certainly susceptible of the most tenderest emotions, at the distress or affliction of his fellow mortals—A tale of woe always melted his
generous soul, and if he had any enemies, they must actually have been of
a species much lower than the famed Hamans fourth Cousins—that is, they
must be the last & most degraded of our race—

[288] 3rd April 1821 Blustering, cold, for April—

4th This day the mortal remains of our friend Capt. J.Y. was committed
to the dust—

> "O Death, all eloquent, thou only prove
> What dust we doat[dote] on when 'tis man we love"

5th Our Soninlaw, A. Wells, visited us, an hour or so—

6th Wind E-S-E—Sowed some parsnip seeds in my garden—

7th Rode to Southold—Returned in the eve—

8th 9th & 10th Very moderate weather—Moved my horse shed to the
road, at least to the street, N. of my house—

11th Went down neck, and took the acknowledgement of a Deed, to N.G.
Beebe, from Daniel Beebee, and Esther, his wife—Some snow this day—

12th 13th & 14th Some part of the time a severe rain & wind storm—
Clears off wind W-S-W—

S.B. Nicoll, a Lawyer, stoped with us an hour or so—

15th & 16th Some part of the time squally, then calm—then wind E—
appears to be a gathering storm

17th Rain, hail, and finally a Snowstorm—Wind E-N-E and severe gale—

[289] 18th Wind N.W. Sleighs fly by merrily, with Bells, and glee—A little
uncommon so late in April

19th 20th & 21st Very rough, blustering weather for so late in season—

Sabbath 22nd Weather more mild—Mr. Richard Floyd Nicoll preached
with us—I think him a gifted man, and well versed in the Scriptures—He
is now about 35 years of age—Was born heir to a large estate on
Shelterisland—say 3000 acres of land—to be his after his Father's decease—
Whether he will yet possess it, as yet, we know not—His worthy Father yet
lives—He, Richard, has spent the first 25 years of his life, quite imprudently,
and with much extravagance—About 8 or 9 years ago there appeared to be
a great change wrought in him—The whole man appeared to be turned
quite about—The world, and his friends saw the alteration for the better,

and rejoiced wondering. His desires became so strong to warn his fellow mortals to shun the course which had nearly ruined him that he deemed it his bounden duty to step into the field of the gospel, and proclaim its alarming truths—

[290] 23rd & 24th April 1821st Weather more mild

25th Ellection at our house—

26th High wind E-S-E—Was visited by Mr. Franklin Vail, son to my late dear friend Silas Vail—He appears to be a very promising young Man—Is I understand, studying for the Ministry—He has my best wishes, that he may prove worthy of being the son of Silas & Betsey Vail, and the grandson of that worthy, good, and venerable Man, Judge Thomas Youngs, late of our Town of Southold—

27th & 28th Wind E-S-E—Henry S. Hobart arrived from Charlestown S.C. where he had been doing buisness through the past winter—

29th Harriet, our dear daughter, with her Husband & children, with us this day—

30th A rain storm—A Mr. Billings and Capt. Maxwell Griffing stoped with us the night—

[291] May 1st 1821 Some rain—P-M- pleasant

2nd Wind E-S-E—Took Harriet to her home yesterday and dined at Mr. [Crowels?]—

3rd Rode out to Southold—Dined with Lieutenant Benjamin Hallock— Stoped the night with my worthy Uncle Thomas Terry—

5th Very blustering—Wind E- by N—Rec'd letters from our Children at Ashford, informing of the death of Deziah's first child—

6th & 7th Blustering weather—

8th 9th & 10th A part of the time calm & some part blustering—A Mr. Hallet (mentioned before) preached with us—

11th & 12th Sidney started to go to Jamaica, Queens County to stop with Mr. Sleight, a printer, awhile

13th Mr. Ezra Youngs preached with us—

14th 15th 16th & 17th The seines have taken about 50,000 Boney fish—

18th 19th & 20th Received a letter at Mr. Sleights 15th from Sidney who is now Mr. Sleights at Jamaica—Sidney arrived—

Moderate weather these days—

21st 22nd & 23 Some rain—Honora took with her to New York Wilkie's two girls

[290][*sic*] 24th May 1821 Some rain—

25th Attended the Vendue of Widow Jerusha Hobart as Auctioneer

26th Some rain—

27th Wind S-W—cool—

28th mild weather—

29th Weather as yesterday—

30th & 31st Thunder & rain—

1st June 1821 A rain storm—

2nd Some rain—

3rd Rode with my wife to Southold—I attended meeting—Mrs. Griffing staid with our daughter Harriet—Evening we rode home—

4th Received a letter, from Sidney

5th & 6th Rode to Southold—Was disappointed this day—Well, such experience is to be expected here, and he that bears up under them best shows most of the Man—

7 8 & 9th Fine Spring like weather—

10th Visited an Island surrounded pretty much by salt meadow, in our place, called GidionsIsland, having [291] been in the possession of Gidion Youngs & his descendants for a Century or more—Our venerable Friend Mr. Ezekial Glover accompanied me—There is on said Island the remains of Fortifications, and erections by the natives, well worth the attention of the curious—On the mounds thrown up by those sons of the Forest, has been trees, standing, perhaps two or three hundred years old—the oldest of them have been cut down this 50 years since—Those works of the tribes of our once American wilderness are well worth a particular jaunt to said Island. Our naturally Philosophic Moralist, Mr. Glover, viewed these relics of the tawny race of ancient days, with profound observations, and curiously worded remarks—To the northward and westward of this Island, about two hundred rods, on the farm to which It belongs, is oyster & clam shells almost covering acres of ground—In some places, they lay on, and in the soil 10 or 12 inches thick—They are in a crumblein state—hardly any of them intire as when caught, perhaps by hands, which have been mouldered into dust this 500 years—

[292] 11th 12th 13th & 14th June 1821—Rain twice in these days—Variable winds from S-W—E- & N-E—

15th Visited Longbeach—got 30 Gulls Eggs—

16th Our Seine caught a draught of fish, say 100,000—Wilkie's two girls returned with Honora—

18th & 19th Rode to Southold—Unwell with a head ache—

20th June—Ellection held at my house—of course considerable Company with us, and much talks—perhaps <u>little</u> of it to the purpose—

21st Col Watrous Beckwith called on us, with his daughter (who pays fillial attention to him.) He is much out of health—He has been an active buisness and considerable of a publick Man, in his County, for 25 years past—A <u>Sherief</u>—<u>Trustee</u> &c&c—Owned and carried on a large Cloth, and weaving factory—Was much, and we believe deservedly respected, by all with whom his buisness called him to act—His residence is [293] in Lyme, State of Connecticut—

22nd A Mr. (Some say he is a Colonel) Hull, from Stonington is with us—He is buying Stock—Appears to be full of life, and Ideas of shewing his buisness habits to the best advantage—However for our hospitalities the night, we received the civilities of a gentleman—

23rd Purchased two lambs, of about a week old, in order to raise them by hand, for to be around the house & yard—I purchased them of my Uncle Daniel T. Terry for 1 dollar—

Sabbath 24th Narcissa & Honora rode out to Southold—

25th very warm—sultry—hot—

26th Our friend, Capt. Grant B. Racket, arrived home from Charlestown, South Carolina, having been absent nine months—All well—A Mr. Mott, from upper Canada, came to stop with us awhile—he is in feeble health—

Our nephews Moses & Milton Griffin called on us from a whaleing Voyge, of 12 or 16 months—

28th & 29th Squally weather, with some rain—Our daughter Cleora arrived home from Ashford having been away 9 months—30th Hot & calm weather—

[294] July 1 Sabbath 1821—Mr. Ezra Youngs preached with us—

2nd Pleasent—Rode out to Sterling with Mr Mott—while at my Brother James, where we had stoped, I received, from his son Moses, a very neatly wrought whale bone cane, as a present—I highly appreciate the expression of his friendly consideration, and intend to have the year of its presentation, with my name, engraved on It in Silver—It was worked in 1820, and presented me, as above said 1821—

It rained some this eve—

3rd High wind W-N-W—

4th July—Cool—Independence—45 years since its August declaration—Some considerable company—more in consequence of Its being the birth day of our nation—

5th 6th & 7th Wind Easterly—Went to Longbeach, and picked up 77 gulls Eggs—

8th Unwell—To the keen observer it is <u>plain</u> that the Man [295] or woman of property is altogether more noticed, and flattered, than those are who have not where to lay their head—There may be some so sufficiently virtuous as to have not [illegible; in pencil] for gold & silver, but such wise and benevolent characters are, in this adultrious age, are a phenomenon amongst their fellows—

9th 10th & 11th Summer like weather—Winds E- & S—

12th Capt. Frederick Lee, at my house—he is all the gentleman, in movements, manners, and conversation—commands the Revenue Cutter

13th went to Sagharbour—returned in the Eve—

14th & 15th Cherries are now plenty and good—

On the Sabbath, Mr. Ezra Youngs preached with us—

16th & 17th Very warm about these days—some rain—

18th Rode out to Lathams

19- 20 & 21st Some rain with wind E—some calm—& hot weather

22nd Mr John Rogers of Mattituck, a travelling trader, with us—A bright, preposessing young man—

[296] 24th 25th & 26th July 1821—Good weather, and pleasent for July— A little sprinkle of rain, yet not enough to wet the ground, which is now getting dry—

27th & 28th some few drops of wet—

29th Mr. Jonathan Hunting preached with us—

30th Made us a HHd[hogshead] of Beer, to sell to the seiners, and others—quick sale at 3 Cts per quart—

31st John C. Hill (son to my much esteemed friend Ithuel Hill) stoped with us the night—

August 1st 2nd & 3rd Moderate, and dry weather—

4th Last Thursday evening, a Mr. Denison preached with us, he was accompanied by Mr. Peter Vail of Southold—Mr. Vail is a pious, good man, and as upright in his walk, dealings with those with whom he has buisness, and conversation, as any one Man, we know of in <u>this</u>, or any other country—His exhortations, and prayers, are truly affecting and edifying—

[297] Take him all in all, he is, and has been this many years, an ornament to society, to the Church, and to the Christian community—

Our daughter Harriet is with us—

5th Mrs. Griffing tried the cold bath—being out of health—

6th & 7th Some sprinkle of rain—

9th Messrs. Thompson & Hunting, Cutchogue & Southold Priests, preached with us this day, It being a Fast—

10th Very—very dry weather—

11th August 1821. A Gentleman (I believe a Lawyer) from Georgia, with his Wife, Sister, Nephew, & three Children, took lodging with us—

12th This morn, the above said family left us for NewYork—

13th My wife set off for Ashford, Connecticut to see our daughter Deziah and family—I forgot to observe that Mr. Hildreth, whose Sloop was wrecked on Truman's Beach on the first of this month, boarded with us about this time—His Vessel was almost a total loss—

[298] 14th 15th & 16th August 1821 Dry weather—corn & other things suffer—

17th Wind this some days E- by S—

Wrote this day to my early, and constant, and very dear Friend, Doct. David R. Arnoll—Our acquaintance and correspondance began about the year 1795—at that time he was studying Physick, was[with] Doct. Jonathan Swezy, near Goshen, Orange County, New York—I was living in said county—At this time, he is practicing in Goshen, and I am a resident of Southold, in Suffolk County on Longisland—

I have received a letter from Mrs. Griffing, dated the next day after she left—

18th A fine shower, the first sufficient to wet the parched ground this some weeks—

19th A Mr. Luce, from Acquebogue, preached with us—

20th 21st &22nd—Very sultry, hot, and in said days much Thunder & lightning—when It clears up cool N-W- wind—

[299] 23rd Still cool—wind N-W—Were we more attentive to our duty, in reflecting on our situation, as to the all important affair of our eternal concerns, we should discover more prudence, and wisdom to obtain the one thing needful—We know that the most permanent productions of Earth is altogether Vanity—yet our eager persuit of them is as astonishing as It is vain & foolish—A competency is necessary to the prudent—But a flood of wealth drowns every vestige of comfort to the possessor. The larger his possessions, the larger his wretchedness—"Lean not on Earth, 'twill pierce thee to the heart"—

24th & 25th Variable weather—

26th Maria Nicoll and Fanny Strong, both from Shelterisland, stoped with us the night—

27th Visible eclipse of the Sun—Wind N-E-

28th Wind N- E-

29–30 & 31st Wind as Yesterday—Mr. John Rogers of Mattituck with us—As before observed, an active traveling Merchant—

[300] September 1st 1821- Squally weather, with wind S-W-

2nd Some rain—

3rd Squally, wind S-S-W—At 6 P.M. It commenced blowing a gale E-S-E- and by 9 o'clock It blew a complete hurricane. A more severe gale of wind, which continued 7 or 8 hours, has not been experienced this Nine years past— Several Vessels, were in the Sound, from Boston, ladened with Ashes—one [of] them, the Antelope, foundered, and sunk—every soul on board perished—Caleb Dyer, sailing at the same time, barely escaped sinking—The preservation of his Vessel, himself, passengers, and crew, is said (and probably true) to be oweing to that cool, calculating, veteran sailor, David Pool—He, calm, with mind unmoved, using all his nautical skill, through one of the most tempestuous nights, and apaling dangers, rarely known in our waters—

[301] 4th & 5th Still midling blustering winds S-W- by W—

6th Messrs Hildreth, and George Raymond left us for their residence, Sagharbour—

Mr. Mott left this day for his home in upper Canada—He has been with us since 22nd June—We have realized in him the prepossessing agreable and very aimable young man—His conversation and agreable manners have made impressions on our minds, lasting, and truly pleasent—Squire Mott (that is name) leaves us with our united prayers, for his health, comfort, & happiness, in all places where ever his destiny may lead him—He is about 27 years of age—

Mrs. Griffing returned, this eve, with our Son in law, James A. Preston—

7th 8th & 9th Capt. James Glover, plies, as a coaster, betwixt this and Boston, about these days—We believe him to be a confiding, industrious, open hearted buisness like young Man—About 12 years ago, he was an active boy, living with us—His manners, and movements, at that time ago of errand boy, gave me much promise that his Manhood would produce some useful fruit—

[302] Monday 10th September 1821 - Wind high E-S-E—

11th Capt. Samuel Hobart, launched his Sloop—She was built near where our Windmill has stood near 50 years—She is now taken down, and another erected, in 1810, on the road, or lane, leading from the Oysterponds harbour to the main road—Hobart's Vessel is called the Young Romp—

12th 13th & 14th Some rain—Winds from S-W—N-N-W- to N-E—

15th Wind N-N-E—Major Nathaniel King, who is over 90 years of age, called on us—travels smart on foot, and appears in general in good Spirits—

16th 17th & 18th James H. Preston arrived from N.York—

19th Preston went to Sagharbor, returned in the evening—

20th Wind S-W- G.B. Racket sailed for Charlestown on 18th—

[303] 21st Wind S-W-

22nd Our Soninlaw, James H. Preston, with our Children, Cleora & Son Sidney, set off this day for Ashford—

23rd Mr. Ezra Youngs preached with us—

24th & 25th Visited Mr. Nicoll, at Shelterisland—

26th Capt. Henry Hobart sailed for South Carolina—Charlestown—

27th 28th & 29th Flattering weather, and variable—

30th High wind E-S-E—

October 1st 1821—Rain

2nd Clears off wind W-S-W

5th 6th 7th & 8th Some moderate—Some high wind—from the points W- to E-N-E—

9- 10- & 11th much such weather as days past—A Mrs. Green with us some days—A fine, good circumspect old Lady—A connection of the patriot American General of that name [Nathaniel Green]—

13th Mrs. Green left us for Boston—

14th & 15th Cool—16th more moderate—

[304] 17th October 1821—high wind N-W- & so it is this 18th—

19th Mrs. Griffing rode to Southold—

20th moderate, mild weather—

21st Sabbath, Mr. Lee, from Lyme, preached with us—An independent congregational—

22nd 23rd & 24th—cool N-W- weather—

25th Our venerable and very dear Father Griffing, at our house, some time today—He is 82 years old this month—his Spirits, and health, is as good as can be expected, at his time of life—especially considering his lonely situation, having lost one of the most agreable, pious, and virtuous wives that ever was bestowed on mortal Man—My Father & Mother lived together fifty years—

26th Mrs. Deziah Racket with us, as Tayloress—She is the widow of our friend Daniel Havens Racket—a kind, benevolent, worthy member of Society—A tender Father and an affectionate Husband—He died in June 1815—June

[305] 27th Wind S-W—

28th & 29th Weather & wind as some days past—
30th Evening, I set off for N.York—
31st arrived in town this eve—

November, the first of it spent in NewYork—returned home about as wise as when I left, and as satisfied, that unmingled comforts are not to be obtained from a World which cannot produce an unchangeing materiel— Its numerous and highest productions are all mixed up with pain, sorrow, grief, wretchedness and tears—

My passage from NewYork home was a tedious one of three days—

This month (November) I let out my storeroom to a Mr. John Downs, a conspicuous merchant of Riverhead, for Eighteen Shillings per week, and board for his Clerk, who is to take charge of the store—Mr. John Rogers (mentioned before as a travelling trader) is said clerk, and super-intends the Store—

1822

In January 1822 Mr. Downs, owner of the goods, died very sudden, of course the store was immediately shut up, by order of the executors of Mr. Downs's will—

[306] 1822 I was taken quite ill on the first of January, and continued so pretty much all the month—

In Feb. the Executors of Mr. Downs came down from Acquebogue, Sold off a part of the goods to Mr. John Rogers, who concluded to take the Store, and commence tradeing on his own concern—

In May I took the district School, for one quarter—

A Mr. Horace Beebe, a Young Man from Vermont, boarded with us this Summer—He is much out of health—He appears, and no doubt is, a valu-able, well-informed young man—To us he is a stranger, but the brief acquaintance we have been so happy as to form with him has given us impressions in his favour, of such good will as not to be erased, while we possess the pleasing recollections of an acquaintance with Horace Beebe— March 14th H. Josiah Albertson was married to our cousin Esther Terry, daughter of A. T. Terry

The Autumn of this year brought with it to our sequestered village much

On the 7th March of this year (1822) my venerable Father visited us, took dinner, after which he walked home to Rockypoint from whence he had come—[page trimmed]

On the 10th of March (1822) our dear, venerable Father was at our house some hours—

Died on 22nd March Orin Tuthill, son to Noah and Polly Tuthill. He [page trimmed] since of the word, worthy[?]

sickness, and a number of deaths. In September died Major Nathaniel King [307] aged 91 years—he was born in May 1731. Of course he was at the time of his death in his 92nd year—He held a commission, I think, of Lieutenant or Capt. under George the 2nd—He was a very sociable, generous, kind-hearted, pleasing old gentleman—at all times, especially when in company that suited him, he was full of life and chat, moral & entertaining—this course he enjoyed nearly to the close of a long life. He died professing the faith which works by love & purifies the heart—

Major King was in the old French [and Indian] war, with my uncle Daniel Griffing. At that time 1758 they contracted a friendship which was very warm, and continued, with patriotic brightness through a long life, my uncle, dying at the age of 86 soon after the Major's death—about a year.

In October died John Tillinghast Junior aged about 21—He was a young man of much promise—much beloved and much to be depended on by his aged and mourning good Father—

A young Lady, Betsey Ryon, aged about 17, died this month—the only daughter of her Widowed Mother—She was aimable, and an affectionate child.

[308] In November died our much and deservedly esteemed friend, Elisha Racket—He was a man of the strictest veracity, punctual in all his dealings to a proverb—A worthy member of the community, shunning as a deadly poison every semblance of baseness and duplicity—The truth he would speak, and maintain, (as to what I have seen, and believe) as the pearl of his life—

In 1814 we, jointly, owned a small Sloop, which was taken by the british off New London—I wrote a letter to the Comodore, which Capt. Racket undertook to carry on board his Majesty ship of 74 guns. With truly a noble daring, he set off by the way of Plumisland, in a small skiff, with a strong Southwest wind—he succeeded, amidst a tremendous sea, to reach the Ship, off New London—handed the Letter to the stern and haughtly Comodore, Capel, who read in It that the bearer was a worthy, honest, industrious, good, but poor Man, depending much on his vessel [309] for the support of his family—should consider having his Vessel restored to him, a favour which himself, his family, and neighbours would highly and duly appreci-ate—The request was granted—Friend Racket returned with his Vessel, in pretty good Spirits, much fatigued—

This month died our boarder, and particularly agreable associate for the year past, John Rogers—He had took the store, as before observed, of Mr.

Downs's Executor, and commenced tradeing, under very favourable aus-
pices—did a handsome buisness—was much approved of, and greatly
beloved by his numerous customers, and the community at large, yet alas,
the uncertaintly of all things in this uncertain state! In the Sunshine, and
brightness of all his expectations, his schemes of earthly bliss is blasted,
and himself a victim to disease and Death—Well, we think we have fully
proved him an upright, honest, benevolent, kind hearted young Man—A
sympathising brother and an endearing tender affectionate son, to his
Widowed Mother.

[310] Mr. Rogers leaves an only Sister, the wife of Mr. Irad Reeve of
Mattituck—He has left a large circle of friends, and respectable acquaintance who mourn (and justly) the early exit of so much comliness, worth,
and usefulness, from our midst—To a comly person, he united the sweetest
disposition, and the most agreable manners—In a word, we only need to
know him to love him—His age about 25 years—his death 14th November.

Likewise, died this month, at Rockypoint, Mr. Isaiah King, aged about
30 years, a respectable, industrious, useful, good neighbour, husband,
Father, & friend—

Last year, 1821, died Mr. Ithuel Hill, of Sagharbour—Mr. Hill was an
industrious, accommodating, truly upright, consistant man, in all his dealings with his fellow man—Any, and every thing, like meaness and duplicity,
he would shun, as baneful in his view, as the Bohontipas of Java—I knew
him by a long and agreable acquaintance—[311] He moved into Sagharbour
about 35 years ago—carried on the Stone Cutting and marble Sculpter buisness—Was the Architecture of the Monuments, over the graves of the hon.
Ezra L'Hommedieu, Thomas S. Lester Esq., John Gardiner Esq. of Gardiners
Island—and others. Under his direction and superintendence, the bones of
Mssrs. Sylvester,* and Dering, and their Wives, were taken up from the family burying ground, near the old Sylvestor Mansion house, at the head of
Derings Harbour, and reenterred at the meeting house on the Island—The
tables neatly placed over them, as before—some of them had been buried
70 years or more—

*Mr. Sylvester &
wife was buried
about 70 years
ago. Mr. Dering &
wife about 20 &
30

Mr. Hill cut the first grave stones that were set up in the burying ground
at this place, which is near our Congregational meeting house, Oysterponds,
about 1791—While Mr. Hill was on a visit to the East, the vessel stoped at
Tarpolen Cove [Massachusetts], a short time—while there, he was taken
violently ill, which terminated his life in a few hours. He was buried at the
cove, where there is a suitable pair of grave stones, to mark the spot where
reposes the ashes of (I trust) an honest man

[312] In March 22nd & April of this year, 1822, I visited Ashford to see my children, Deziah, Sidney, and Cleora—found them well, with our good Soninlaw, James H. Preston—Attended their Town Meeting—formed some agreable acquaintances with Mr. Works, (Grandfather of James H. Preston) with Capt. David Kyes—his Brother, Squire Kyes—and a goodly number of others whose memory I shall fondly cherish, as Its very probable I shall never see them more—distance, and my time of life reasonably forbid such an expectation—

Returned home in about 3 weeks, with Cleora—

1823

1823* In the Spring of this year, bought of Mr. John Hubbard of Matittuck (Administrator of the Personal estate of our friend the late John Rogers) the intire lot of goods and fixtures for the sum of near 800 Doll[ar]s—with which, by making some addition, I opened a pretty good store*—Soon found trade brisk, and customers favourably disposed. It was now near five years since I had ceased to keep a store on my own account—

*In July 1817 I gave up storekeeping altogether in consequence of great embarassments—A change has now taken place, and I now [page trimmed] keeping again, after a lapse of 5 years—1823

9th March my Father James Griffing was with us

[313] About the 25th of October this year (1823) died Doct. John Gardner, of Southold—As a Physician, and Surgeon, with us, in this Town, he was universally esteemed, approved, and successful. His suavity of manners, and well told and timed anecdotes, were generally efficacious to those patients, who were more hypochondriack than sick—His practice was about 20 miles west of him, and the same easterly, by taking in Plumisland, which he attended—

In the War of the Revolution, he was some time Surgeons Mate, on board one of the American Frigates. He commenced practice in Southold in about 1782 or 3—Married Miss Abigail Worth, one of the most aimable, pious, and beautiful of women. She died ten, or twelve years since, in the triumphs of great faith—He married a second wife, Peggy, the eldest daughter of Major Calvin Moore—A fine, good, discreet, prudent woman. The large Marble Stone, at the head of the Doctors Grave, paints the Man in true, good and agreable character for 40 years of his life—It's well worth a perusal.

[314] May 2nd 1823. Was visited this day by my venerable Father—Wisdom directs us to revere, honor, and administer all the comfort to

him, in our power—This is my bounded duty—"He that know his Masters will, and does it not, shall be beaten with many stripes" Says divine inspiration—

Usher N. Moore, with Chancy (his Son) was at our house on the 15th & 16th January 1823.

Gelston Vails Wife was confined with a Son 2nd November 1823—they name David—

Luther Topliff at my house 26th November 1823. I notice this because Mr. Topliff had been sometime concerned in buisness, with our Soninlaw, James H. Preston—

Our Faithful and steady Friend, Christopher Tuthill, died Novem. 26th 1823, aged about 63 years, born in 1760—Industry, economy, and kindness, was conspicuous traits in his useful and laborious life—At the age of 17 he enlisted into the army of the revolution—was at the battle on the west end of Longisland [Battle of Long Island, August 1776].

[315] As a soldier, he was resolute, calm, and justly daring—As a Husband, Father, friend and neighbour he was all and in each, and every station, the good and the upright—An honest man is the noblest work of God—

Rensaler King, (Son of the late Mr. Joel King,) was drowned in Plumbgut, Decem. 4th of this year—He was a fine agreable and much beloved young Man—he leaves a Wife & two pretty children to mourn his early, and untimely exit—

Mr. Lemuel Youngs's Son, George, died Novem. 15th at the South—A very bright, industrious, promising young Man, the hopes and expectations of his aged, and dependent Father, and the Filial son of his tender Mother— he was aged about 17—

Henry Harris of Sagharbour, and formerly a very agreable boarder of ours, was drowned on 27th Novem. of this year—Take Mr. Harris, all in all, he was a fine, deserving, good hearted young man of about 23 years—

Sidney, our Son, kept a school at Cutchogue, commenced this Nov. 1823 and continued until March 1824.

On the 8th November 1823 died Peggy, the very pleasant, prudent, aimable and affectionate wife of the late Doct. John Gardner of Southold. She was his second wife—Saturday 10th May our son Sidney sailed for Boston as cook on board Schooner Enterprize, Grant B. Racket Master

Henrietta, (daughter of our Brother Elisha and Hannah Griffing) was married to Hewlett Smith of New York this July 1823

George S. Conkling (son of Samuel Conkling) boarded with us this summer, his business shoemaking—In 1842 he was a professed dentist

1824

[316] On the 16th June 1824 was drowned at the harbour in Oysterponds, near the shore, Capt. Frederick King, aged about 53 years— Capt. King had been for more than thirty years a Seafaring Man—For

about 26 years of said time, had been commander of many different Vessels—Some of them noble, and fine Ships, viz. The Ship <u>Rose</u>—The <u>American Eagle</u> (of over 1000 Tons)—The <u>John Drew</u>, to London—The <u>Northern Liberties</u>, a letter of Marque, of 16 Guns—In the late war he commanded for about three months a privateer—I think her name was the Jehu—He was a noble looking, handsome, and powerful Man—rather hasty—much fire, not always too attentive to his better judgement—He had a benevolent heart, tender and feeling to those who were indigent, and poor in circumstances—Whenever he was <u>stern</u>, and harsh, he was not himself—he was not <u>Frederick King</u>! Such <u>seasons</u> we have known him to experience, but there was a cause—An <u>indulgence</u>, which in his proper moments he despised.

Mrs. Cynthia King, Wife of Capt. F. King, died September 29th aged 78. She was a worthy, good & virtuous Woman—

[317] George Champlin, a young man from Lyme, Connecticut, commenced board with us this July 13th 1824—An active buisnesslike youngster, of 20 years of age—He appears (although an entire stranger) from his movements, observations, and suavity of address, to promise to be of some use, benefit, and satisfaction to the community of his fellow Men—May God favour him with prosperity, health, and Wisdom in all his future course, is our undisembled wish and prayer—

Capt. Christopher Brown died on the 19th July of this year 1824 aged 79 years—Capt. Brown suffered much in the War of the revolution—Was imprisoned in NewYork—Suffered there with the Smallpox—and privations—Capt. Rufus Tuthill, Judge Thomas Youngs, & Judge Jared Landon were his fellow prisoners—Through a long life he sustained the good name of a quiet and peaceable man—Indulgent as a husband and affectionate as a Father, and permanent as a friend—

[318] Died December 10th of this year, 1824, Our Father, James Griffing—In his 86th year. The kind, the accommodating, and best of Fathers, husbands, neighbours and Friends—Many of the incidents of his eventual life I have noticed in another Diary, or Journal—

Capt. John Brown Sen. died this year, with the cancer—He had been a very useful, active, interprising man—Sometime a soldier, in our Revolutionary War—At the battle on Long Island, he behaved with courage, and decision—We think, from a long and early acquaintance with him, that he had a heart succeptable of the tenderest and best religious emotions—

Leveret Reeve, who was sometime our Militia Captain, moved himself &

family to Patchogue this year—He had made a member of my family, for some years before he was married—Say from 1808 to 1813—Take him as we found him, he was an obliging, clever man—

1825

In 1825 I found trade very brisk—went to New York twice this year, and laid goods to a pretty large amount—

[319] In the summer of this year, June 1825, Doct. George O. Sumner of Connecticut commenced board with us & began to <u>practice</u> as a Doctor in this place—Likewise, another young man from the same State commenced board with us by name Marvin Holms—They appear to be men of good moral deportment, with Temperence habits and principle. The Doctor, a Baptist by profession—

Mr. Holms is out of <u>health</u>—In hopes to obtain this <u>jewel</u>, he comes to this our sequestered part of this Island—May he realize his most sanguine hopes as to better health, and goodness, and mercies follow him through all this future course—

This year Narcissa very unwell—

1826

In 1826 Mrs. Abigail Tuthill, wife to our friend Noah Tuthill,* died, after a long, painful and distressing malady—She was all that is good, kind & benevolent in woman, crown immortal to her husband.

On the 7th of August, this year 1826, died Mr. Richard Brown, aged 63 years—Naturally, a kind, feeling, very well behaved Man—Aimable in his address, mild and forbearing in his conversation, and prepossessing in manners to all classes—

[320] This year 1826th My buisness was some affected by Calvin King and Orville Terry opening a store at the landing, at the harbour—

1827

1827—This Summer, I bought Calvin Kings & Orville Terrys intire store, goods, fixtures, and all, for a given price, at three different payments—I met them punctual, and promptly—Did buisness rather too premature, and not

*this excellent woman was the playful infant in Mrs. Terry's arms, mentioned in my journal page 88

In June this year 1826 my Brother James lost four sons by drowning, all in one day—Daniel, Joseph, David, & Benjamin—the eldest 24—the youngest 14 years—with them was lost at the same time James Beebe, & son—Joel King & Horace Clark

In the summer of the year 1825 my very inestimable, good, and permanent friend Dr.David R. Arnell was with us

Mehitable Racket, Widow of the late Mr. John Racket of Rockypoint, died on the 19th August 1826. She was a Woman, full of kindness, and sound piety Samuel Benjamin Nicol, of Shelterisland, died September of this year aged 65 years. His Father owned ten miles square, near [Shoreham?]

to advantage—Attempted to open a second store, at the landing, and carried it on some weeks, but I soon found it an injudicious procedure, and backed out as soon as possible—

Capt. Rufus Tuthill Sen. Lost his excellent, kind and endearing wife Mary this October 11th 1827—

1828

1828—George Champlin, who is now and has been one of my family, this some years, is commencing store keeping, just below me, betwixt us and the harbour landing—This, of course, will not facilitate my trade, but submission, is the most proper, when to oppose is useless—

Mr. Amon Taber died this 12th March 1828—He had been an active, industrious, ingenious, well informed Man, through a long life—He was well versed in the Mathematicks—He married in early life Sibil the eldest daughter of Colonel Thomas Terry—Mr. Tabor was 84 years at the time of his death—

[321] 1828 In September 21 Died Lydia, the very worthy and prudent wife of Capt. Elias Terry—All the qualities calculated to render a wife aimable and invaluable to her Husband & family, was richly centered in our friend Mrs. Lydia Terry—Mrs. Terry was born in 1786 & Capt. Elias Terry was born in 1784—

Daniel Russel Terry died, this 28th Decem. 1828—A young man, at his first setting out, gave great promise, of present, and future usefulness—But the spoiler came, and blasts all our expectations—and this promising, fascinating youth in his forenoon of life, falls, and is consigned to an early grave—

Died this August 1828 Mr. Elisha Mulford, aged 78—Mr. Mulford came to Orient 1805 in the Spring—He was a substantial, worthy, good Man, formerly from Easthampton—having removed to this place about 23 or 4 years since and purchased the farm once belonging to Col Thomas Terry—An excellent situation—Mr. Mulford was, for many years, a member of the late Doct. Samuel Buells Church [in Easthampton]—We believe Mr. M. fulfilled, in all his walks, his profession, as an honest Man and a Christian—

•

[322] 1825 Our Soninlaw, James H. Preston, moved his family,and effects into the House, formerly owned, and built by Capt. F. King—

Mrs. Polly Hubbard, my wifes sister, with us this August

My Sister, Lucretia's Husband, David Wiggins Jr., died this [blank] 1826— After a long & distressing illness which he bore with Christian fortitude and with out a murmur—

In June 1827 G. Champlin and myself went to Riverhead—was at the trial of Charles Youngs, he was sentenced to the State Prison 3 years—

Abner Wells's Sister, Polly, died 29th May 1827—An excellent Mother, wife, daughter & Christian—

In August 1827 I waited on James H Prestons Father, Mr. John Preston, to Riverhead—returned on the next day

Jeremiah Beebe, Son to the late Samuel Beebe & Milla Beebe, died Apl 2nd 1828—A pretty, active boy—

September 1828* Thomas Perry, Married Jerusha, daughter of Joshua & Mehitable Hobart—Likewise Thomas S. Youngs to Miss Hannah King—

1829

August 1829 Caleb Dyer began to build a wharf at the landing at the foot of the lane, or road leading to the Oysterponds harbour—the beach on which the wharf is commenced belongs to the house of our friend Capt Jeremiah Youngs—

[323] This February 4th 1829 Died Mr. David Tuthill, aged about 66 years—Mr. Tuthill was the 3rd son of Mr. Christopher Tuthill, who is particularly noticed in my Diary of November 1798—Mr. David Tuthill was a retired, peaceable, industrious, consciencious neighbor—Morally attentive to his own Interest, and the comforts and the present and future wellbeing of his family—He was one of the twelve children which his Father had by his only wife

Edward H. Griffin & wife with us September 1829

In August 6th 1829 Died, with the lockjaw, Edward, Son of Frederick & Polly Taber—An industrious young man, and of much hopes, and expectations to his Fathers family, and his own young wife & infant child—He was aged about 24 years—

1827 Novem. 21 died William Conkling, son of Mr. Jonathan & & Parnol Conkling of Hashamomaque— Mr. Conkling was an industrious, inoffensive, honest Man—[?] Man of a good flow of spirits, and pleasingly lively as a [?]—his road through life [page trimmed]

*Our Cousin Peter W. Tuthill was married to Laura, daughter of Daniel T. & [Melinda?] Terry Apl 2nd 1828

Sidneys first child, a boy, Chatham Augustus, born 14th March 1829

Preston & J. Took a sail, with Capt. Frederick Lee, in the Revenue Cutter to Shelterisland May 1829—This year wrote to my estimable friend Daniel Tuthill in Vermont—

John Luck Jr., a preposessing, talented, and exemplary priest of the Methodist order, was often at my house this year—a good useful Man—

1830

In 1830 Greenport (to which a road had been laid out, about 1827) began to have the appearance of doing something in Seawise & coast wise buisness—They have now two stores—a small wharf, and one or two Whaling ships—

This year Dec. 12th 1830 Mr. Daniel Youngs died, aged 74 years—Mr. Youngs was when young, some time in the Army of the United States in 1776—When he returned [324] home, after serving faithfully his time, for which he entered the service—Laboured, by days work and otherwise, In jobs etc etc—And by dint of indefatigable industry, and prudence, laid by sufficient to purchase a piece of land, and build himself a comfortable tenement about 1786 or 7—He was at the time of his death possessed of lands & tenements worth from 2 to 3000 Doll[ar]s, all the fruits of prudence and industry—He was an obliging neighbour, and uncommon ingenious, and handy with carpenters, Masons, & Joiners tools—and we hope an honest Man—

In this year, 1830, My very early, and much esteemed Friend, Edward C. King, died—He was greatly respected by a large circle of connections and literary friends—At the time of his Death, his family was living at Newburn [New Bern], North Carolina—himself, had left them but a few days before, for NewYork, where he died a day or two after his arrival—He wrote respectable poety and [325] his *Grindstone** (founded on an amusing, but real fact was not without merit)—It was well known to many in Oysterponds & Sterling, in 1818 & 20—

He was the eldest of the only two children of Capt. Benjamin King, an accomplished and much respected Gentleman, who died about the close of the American Revolution—He, Edward, was sometime an assistant Justice, in Newburne—and it is said did honor to the office—

In August of the year 1830 (or near that time) Mrs. Harriet Petty (wife to Orange Petty) was confined with three children, at a birth—two Girls & a Boy—They survived but a day or two—

Adl. Daniel Tuthill died July 17th 1830; was born March 13th 1747—

1831

In 1831 two more Ships, are now added to the two first purchased, at Greenport, making four—The place has the appearance of growing—

Sabbath evening 31st October 1830 Our very dutiful daughter, Cleora, was married to James Hemel McNeill— Decem. 3rd 1830 A court at my House—Pettiah Fordham prosecuted [bottom page trimmed]

Our Soninlaw James H. Preston moved his family to Ashford Connecticut the 9th December 1830 to take charge of the factory in which he is concerned

A Doctor [?], boarder with us this month—a likely Man

*Mrs. Betsey Conkling (widow of the late Wm. Conkling) had those verses, at this time 1830—

Died Mary King Terry, the filial & aimable daughter of Elias & Lydia Terry in the 9th Decemb. 1830—Mr. Preston built his house at the head of the street, or lane, leading to Orient harbour, in the Summer of 1830 [page trimmed]

3rd February 1831 My Friend, and the friend of mankind, Jesse Terry, died at Southold, greatly lamented by all who were so happy as to truely know him, and his ability, and success as a Peace Maker—and a son of kindness—[326] Mr. Terry was united with his brother Jonathan in the coast wise buisness, for more than twenty years—In all said time they were greatly beloved, respected, and prosperous—They lived, acted, and loved as brothers indeed, & truth— To me, and mine, he was ever the constant, undeviating, hospitable friend, in time of need—At such a time, I have realized the lasting benefit of his cool, wise, and well timed Council—His memory to us, will be dear, while we are endowed with precious recollections.—He was in the sixtieth year of his age—

In April of this year 1831 Dolly Vail, wife to Mr. Henry Vail, was confined with three children at one birth, one boy & two girls—they all died within two or three days—

1832

1832 In Novem. 1832 died at Charleston South Carolina, Capt. Grant B. Racket, aged about 35 years—He was truly a valuable Man, invaluable as Master of a Vessel, as a friend—neighbor—citizen—associate—husband— Father and Son—A man of agreable address, and truly pleasing manners- [327] When about twenty years of age, he commanded a Smack, owned by Capt. Jeremiah Youngs—His success, prudence, and energy was such as to secure the highest goodwill, of his owner, who realized a handsome income from a stock, managed by such a skillful, persevering, trusty, young Man— Thus early, and through his brief life, we can unhesitatingly affirm that the utmost confidence could be reposed at all times in Grant B. Racket—"An honest Man is the noblest work of God"

His remains were brought home in the Spring of 1833 and interred in the buriel ground of this place, where a Stone marks the spot where reposes his ashes—

In the Spring of this year 1832, I put a second story on my house— Matthew Orsborn, Jr., was the Carpenter—A very prudent, peaceable, industrious, agreable young Man—We were well satisfied with his work, and with him, and his good dispositioned Apprentice, Edward Prince—

[328] In this year 1832, one of the Whale Ships, of Greenport, was lost— Crew & part of the oil saved—

Capt. Daniel Beebe, moved his family & affects to Hogneck the 20th March of this year—

1833

There is now at Greenport, 1833, five stores, and one at Rockypoint—
And at our O-ponds, <u>three</u>, such as they are—

12th April 1833 Departed this life James H. Preston, aged about 33 years—
As a Soninlaw he was invaluable—As a husband, Father, Brother, neighbour,
Son, & friend, none ever surpassed him in all those tender and noble relations of life—To the Church he was an ornament—To the Christian Faith,
the brightest example, and to the World, a blessing—

1834

This Spring 1834 James McNeil, our Soninlaw, moved his Family to
NewYork, from Southold—
　　Rather an unpleasent April—
　　7th May 1834 A hard rain storm—
　　8th Received a store of Groceries, from N-Y—
　　9th Honora arrived home from N-York—
　　[329] 10th May 1834 Cool, with some rain—P.M. planted corn & potatoes—
　　11th Sabbath A Mr. James, a Baptist, preached with us—Mr. James was
the very prominent means of getting the handsome Baptist Church built at
Greenport, which when completed (much through his strenuous exertions)
they, his people, over which he had satisfactorily presided, as a faithful
watchman & pastor, dismissed him—much to his sorrow, and I, with many
others, believe unjustly—Ingrattitude, what is its effects?
　　Some thunder & rain this eve—
　　12th & 13th Cool N-W- wind—& blustering
　　14th Very cool, backward weather—
　　15th Indeed, <u>this</u>, thus far, may be set down as cold for this time in the
Season—
　　Our Grandson John A. Preston arrived from Ashford—
　　16th Rather more mild—Wind S-W—
　　17th Cold again—N-W- wind—
　　[330] 18th May 1834—Mr. J. Hunting preached with us—Wind S-W—
　　19th Mrs. Griffing & myself rode out to Greenport—brought home 500
shingles—
　　20th more mild—Some dry, or it begins to be

21st Rode out to Riverhead—took with me our late soninlaw (James H. Preston's) Brother John A. Preston—

22nd We returned home, Deziah very ill—

23rd Mrs. Griffing, and our grandson John A. Preston Rode out to Southold—to Abner Wells—Returned this eve—Wind E—

24th Wind E—one of our Seines took this day about 400,000 little shad—

25th Wind as yesterday, with some rain which is much needed—

I ought to have noticed that on Friday the 23rd John A. & Harriet M. Preston (our grandchildren) set off for Ashford, Connecticut [331] with their uncle John H. Preston—

26th & 27th Some rain & some pleasant—This day our Daughter Harriet was confined with a Son, they call It after Abner—

29th Cool, for the time of year—& some wet—

30th Some cool—

31st Pleasant—

June 1st Came in with some rain—

2nd It blows heavy from W-S-W-

3rd Cool northwester—

4th Wednesday, Mrs. Griffing & myself rode to Riverhead, to visit our Son Sidney & family

5th rain—wind E—

6th Returned home—high East Wind—

7th warm—very much so—

8th Sabbath, Mr. Hunting preached with us—

9th As warm a day as we have known this summer—Received a Letter from our very affectionate child Cleora, who now with her family is living in NewYork

[332] 10th June 1834 Thick, and Foggy—

11th Very warm—Wind S—Some rain, with Thunder this eve—

12th More cool—Wind N-W—

As a Commissioner of Schools, I officiated at Hazard L. Moores this day, with my colleagues—

13th Friday, Some rain—Capt. John Terry (Grandson to the late Col. Thomas Terry) now commands a handsome Schooner, near 100 Tons—His Nautical skill, in my opinion, well entitles him to such a situation—

14th Capt. Terry sails for Bangor, for the Messrs Holms, to obtain a cargo of Lumber etc—May success attend in the voyge, and all hands—

15th Cool wind N-E—Received a letter from Sidney, our Son, at Riverhead—Wrote to John H. Preston—Ashford—

[333] 16th June 1834 Died this morning Elisha Sisson, aged about 49 years—He had been an active, industrious Man, whose buisness centered on the water, where he spent the larger part of his time, from early boyhood, to his sudden death—As a Smack Master, for many years, he had been successful—He was at times eccentric, and in some buisness transactions, odd, and to his damage, in his worldly goods—Yet, we believe him to have always conducted his affairs upon the sound principles of right—professing strong faith in the Gospel, of our Lord Jesus Christ—He was a Member of good standing in the Church of Upper Acquebogue—His death was occasioned by a stick of timber, falling against his bowels—

This life, what is it? A maze, a dream! An anxious moment of disappointments, and Its gone—Like the dashing of a mighty wave, on the sandy shore—Its murmurs die away, & Its soon forgot amid succeeding [woes?]

[334] Tuesday 17th June 1834 The warmest day, of any one this season, thus far—It certainly has been a very cold spring—

18th A hard rain last night, and this morn, with Thunder—Wind E—

19th & 20th What is called fine, and good weather—Wind W—

21st Attended, with and as a Commissioner, at H.L. Moores—on School business—

22nd & 23rd Clear & pleasant—

24th Wind S- by W—

25—Very warm—Wrote to John A. Preston—

26th Wind S-W—

27th Wind High S—

Revenue Cutter in our harbour—Lieutenant visited us—Rain, & Thunder this eve—

28th cool W- wind—

Sabbath 29th A wet night, and it continues to rain this morn—30th Little shad are now taken very plenty, with us—Politics run high—look at our journals of that time—

[335] July 1st 1834 A cloudy morn—wind N—

2nd Weather, much as yesterday

3 & 4th Still dark & Cloudy—

This 4th a large party dined with us—100 or more set down, to a table, prepared under my trees—A noisy day—Independence & etc etc

Speaking of Mr. Amon Taber Junr., in page 152 & 320—his family informs me that in early life from the age of 18 to 25, he made several voyges to the Westindias, and other parts, of our Tarraquous Globe—He once was shipwrecked on one of the Westindia Islands, and suffered much from starvation, and other privations—

On one of his voyges, when bound home, they fell in company with a Ship, with which they kept near aboard, one intire day, which was a pleasent one—The ships company appeared very merry, and happy, with musick, and dancing on board—Night came, and with it a heavy Thunder storm, a flash of lightning struck the Ship, set her on fire—destroyed her, and every person on board perished—They, the vessel [336] in which Mr. Taber was in, could render no assistance, although near them, at the awful moment— She burnt, with a tremendous solemn sight, made more so, Mr. Taber supposes, by the cargo of Rum, Brandy, Gin, and Wine with which she was deeply freighted—What an awful lesson to teach us the uncertainty of all sublinary things—

Mr. Taber was born about the year 1745. Built the house, which is now (1845) owned and occupied by his daughter Betsey (now the Widow Conkling), and her only child, and son, William T. Conkling—Mr. Taber had by his wife, Sibil (who is mentioned in page 152) seven Children—6 daughters, and one Son—This Son, Pardon T. Taber, was a respectable and valuable member of Society—He died, at his residence in Sagharbour, aged ___ years—much lamented—As a Captain of the Artillery, in Sagharbour, he was conspicuously honourable—

[337] Amon Taber Junr. joined the American Army, and was in the campaign on Longisland, in 1776, when General Washington showed the British legions the most consummate skill, and Wisdom, in leading, directing, and governing the undisciplined troops of his beloved country, to the eventual (he greatly believed) final conquest of their enemies—

Mr. Taber returned to his young and interesting family, early in 1777— Attended strickly to his buisness, as a house Joiner, and Carpenter—For more than 30 years, he occasionally, winter evenings, taught the Mathematicks to young men, who desired the art of Navigation, Surveying etc etc—He understood the Logarithms well—And his instruction was the good & sure old way—They now work on a new and different scale altogether—

Mr. Amon Taber was the son of Amon Tabor Sen. who came from New London about the year 1732 and married Molly Brown, the daughter of Samuel Brown, about the year 1740, by whom he had one daughter, Patience, and two sons, Amon & Frederick—She, Molly Brown, was the grand daugh-

ter of Samuel and Rebecca Beebe of Plumisland—This elder A. Taber, on his
first coming to this place, was called [?] in house architecture—He built the
famous Meeting House at Southold in 1733, and finished off the pews in
high stile, in their [?][page trimmed]

for a more full
notice of Amon
Taber and family
see my 1st journal
p. 309

[338] 5th July 1834—Had the satisfaction this day of welcoming to our
humble Mansion Benjamin Brown, and his aimable Wife Hannah—from
Goshen, Orange County—Mrs B- is niece to Mrs. Griffing—Mr. Brown is
Grandson to the late Benjamin Brown Esq. Who died about 1774—In
those days he was known, and called (always by his neighbours and
acquaintance) "Justice Brown"—I knew him and remember his being a
large, grave looking man; and at Church, (where I generally saw him,) he
always sat in the desk, with the Deacon—At his death, I was about seven
years old—

The 6—7—8 & 9th July 1834 It was extreme warm—Some foggy
weather—

10th & 11th—It was rather more comfortably cool—

12th Mr. Benjamin B. & his pleasant wife left us for their home—Orange
County

[339] Sabbath 13th July 1834—A rain storm—It is certainly a copious
rain—and it comes in good time—

14th Sultry hot—wind S-W—

15th & 16th A Mr. Hall, Merchant, from N.York with his accomplished
Wife, came to stop with us a few days—

17 & 18th Pleasant, growing weather—Some N-E- wind—A sprinkle of
rain—

19th & 20th purchased 50 Albany boards at 18 Cts a piece—

Rode to Greenport, where I spent an hour this A-M- Heard a person
speak much this day, in strains of considerable eloquence, of his honesty,
and good deeds—The only difference in the address, of the person today,
and the Pharisee in the Scriptures, was, the first was to his fellow Men, the
latter to his Maker, who knew all the secrets of his heart, and every movement, and action of his selfish life—No doubt, our honest neighbours know
our characters, without our assistance to portray It—

[340] 20th July 1834 Rode to Southold, with Mr. Hall, It being Sabbath,
we attended meeting—A Mr. Cook, the Preacher—A moderate Speaker—
Stoped sometime with our dear Eldest daughter Harriet, now the wife of
Abner Wells—We esteem him, as a worthy, and good soninlaw—

Weather more cool—

21st A mild day—Evening, a hard Thunder, and rainstorm—Very sharp lightning—

22nd Fine sweet air this morn—Mr. Hall caught near 100 black fish this day & yesterday—

23rd—Warm & Calm—

24th Conveyed Mr. & Mrs Hall to Capt. Lathams this morning early—While at Capt. L-s I met for the first time Councillor Sampson, one of the Irish patriots, associated with the Celebrated and [341] unfortunate Robert Emmet, and his Brother, Thomas Adis Emmet—After the condemnation, and execution, of Robert, Messrs Sampson, T.A. Emmet, and others, fled to this Country, where they found a comfortable asylum, from British deception, and Lordly Tyrany—

25th July—Bought 3 loads of English hay of James H. Brown, who is about to leave this, his natal place, and migrate, with his family to NewYork—

26th Warmer than we have had in any time this season—

On the broad map of mortality, stand these important truths in character, ledgible in all Tongues, and Languages—"There is no discharge in that war" "No exemption from Death"

27th continues very warm—With Mrs. Griffing, visited our children at Southold—

28th & 29th Some cooler in consequence of wind N—

[342] Wednesday 30th July 1834 continues comfortably cool—Hewlet Smith and wife called on us—She is the only child, by my Brother Elisha's first wife Hannah, who was the daughter of Major Nathaniel King—She was a very aimable, and truly an excellent woman—

Narcissa, and Honora, went to Southold, to see the wild Beasts—

31st Honora went to Riverhead to see the Man who is to be hung this day, for the murder of his wife—Wrote to my friend Zacheus Goldsmith, yesterday—

Friday 1st August 1834—Wind light from N—The man, at Riverhead, to be hung, was respited for the present—

2nd & 3rd Wind N.—Cloudy—Our daughter Cleora, and child, with us just from N.Y.—

4th It is very warm, again—

5th Wind light N-W—comfortably wet—It is growing dry—

[343] 6th August—Warm & dry—Light wind W-S-W—

7th Some suppose this <u>day</u> as warm, as any <u>one</u>, this seven years past-Other 30 years!

8th After a sultry hot night, we have this morn a delightful cool breeze N- E—

9th Wind, N-N-E—& very dry—

10th Wind E-S-E—It being Sabbath, A Mr. Porter preached with us— Received a friendly, and an affectionate Letter, from Zacheus Goldsmith Esq last evening—This Gentleman has been an undeviating friend of mine for the last forty years—In said time, we have had many seasons of very agreable interchange of civilities, and such intercourse as is only known to disinterested associates—I could once name a goodly number of such friends, but alas, they have nearly all disappeared, and gone to that "bourne whence no traviller returns"—

11th Wind E-S-E—A small Sprinkle of rain—not sufficient to wet the ground which is very dry—

[344] 12th August 1834 wind W-S-W—Warm

13th Sultry warm—Rode to Lathams—His boarders are quite numerous, and of all sizes and characters—

Our Son Sidney and family with us this evening

14th Wind S & foggy—Sidney & family left this Morn—Cleora, left, for Southold—

15th A refreshing breeze N-W by N—

How important, how Sacred, are those words of our Saviour, to his Disciples, viz. "What I say unto one, I say unto all, Watch"—A solemn, and strict attention to those injunctions, will always, and at all times, insure a sure safety from those scenes of sorrow, and bitter reflections, which are ever attendant, on the careless and unwatchful—

16th Wind N-N-W—cooler

17th Sabbath—Some light showers—which were greatly needed—

[345] 18th Wind W-N-W—Some sprinkle of rain, but not as yet sufficient to wet the Earth, which is now very dry—The corn suffers—

19th Wind, as yesterday

20th Weather as yesterday—

21st Wind W—Mr. Baldin Gardner, Merchant of NewYork, stoped with us last night—He is a polished gentleman, of welltimed suavity of address—

22nd Rode to Riverhead, this afternoon—Took with me in my carriage, a travilling gentleman, for which conveyence, he gave me five Dollars—

Our Son, Sidney, lost an infant Son this day, aged nine months—He was a beautiful and an interesting child—"And weeping Fathers and Mothers build their Childrens Tomb"—The sweet little Innocence was named Sidney—

23rd After attending the funeral of our grand child, I returned home, where I arrived about 9 OClock P.M—

Sabbath 24th Wind W—Not any rain to wet the ground since July 21st

[344] [*sic*] 25th August 1834 Wind W—

26th Wind E-S-E—

27th Wind E—About as much rain as a good large dew—

28th A calm day—and very dry—

29th—much such a still day as yesterday—

30th Fresh breeze E-S-E—

Sabbath 31st Wind light E-N-E—Very sickly in N-Y—and quite mortal

Monday 1st Septem. 1834—A refreshing rain—

2nd A calm day—

3rd A cloudy day—

4th Wind W-S-W—and very warm—

5th Copious Showers—Almost a flood

6th Wind W—clear weather—Rode to Riverhead with Mrs. Griffing—

7th Sabbath, Attended meeting at upper Acquebogue—Evening, attended the commencement of a campmeeting at JamesPort—

[345] [*sic*] Mr. Tribbet gave us a very ingenious and, we hope, a Spiritual discourse—He is called an excellent preacher, of the denomination of Methodist—

Stoped the night with our hospitable Friend, Mr. Daniel Downs, whom I have long since deemed a sound, upright, Industrious, honest, and useful Man—

8th On our way home this morn, stoped at Mr. John Wells's, Cutchogue, with whom we took breakfast—This excellent Friend of ours was Grandson to the late Timothy Wells, who was son to the Reverend Timothy Wells, that was pastor, over the Church, at upper Acquebogue, from about 1760 to 1781—This above said John was the son of the late John Wells, who was son to the above said Timothy, first mentioned, who died about 1794 or 5—

9th Sidney, and his wife, whom we found, at our house on our return from Riverhead, we took with us to Capt. Rufus Tuthills, after spending the day very agreably returned home in the eve—

[346] Wednesday 10th Septem. 1834—Rode out to Greenport—cool—Narcissa and Honora gone to Jamesport to Camp Meeting—

11th Wind N-W- & cool—The girls returned home this eve—

12th Continues comfortably cool—Wind N-W—

13th Wind W—Rode with Mrs. Griffing to see our daughter Harriet & family, at Southold—Attended, officially, my buisness, as Commmissioner of Schools—Returned home this eve—

Sabbath 14th A Mr. Newel, at our house, a profile Taker [silhouette maker?]—does his buisness pretty snug—

15th Fine weather—

16th Rode out to Greenport—

17th A cloudy, S-W- windy day—

18th Calm—& warm—

19th Cleora, set off for NewYork—

[347] 21st Sabbath—A warm, sultry day—

22nd A calm day—Was visited today by Silas Webb, & wife, now living in N.York—Capt. Webb was the youngest son of the late Mr. Orange Webb, Inn Keeper, for many years, at Sterling, Southold—Capt. Silas has been, from this his native Town, abroad, for near thirty years—Much of said time he has been commander of a number of fine or noble Ships, on the European trade. He has often, with his Wife, spent several months together in, and about London, viewing the magnificence, and curiosities of this, one of the most popular cities in our Universe—

When he left this place more than 25 years ago, his Brothers, Sisters, connections, and neighbours, were all living in, and about the place of his birth, and boyhood—The land, on which the growing village of Greenport now stands, was a farm owned by his Brother David—On the present site there was neither a road, wharf, nor House, nor anything relating to its ever becoming [348] a port for Ships, and merchandise—The change so forcibly struck Capt. Webb on his visiting his Father's old mansion (just east of Greenport) that it is said he wept, and observed to those with him that it was too much for him, he wished to return to N.Y. as soon as possible—"What the eye don't see, the heart don't greive at"—

From 23rd Sept. to the 30th, very warm—except the last eve, It was cold even to a White frost—

Oct. 1st Warm & calm

Up to the 9th very light winds, and those S—

10th A fine copious rain—

11th Clears off with high wind N-W—

13th & 14th cool—Some white & black frost—

17th & 18th Wind fresh S-W—

30th Wind N-W—cool—
[349] 31 Oct. An Easterly Storm, clears off cold—

Novem. From 1st to 18th High winds, and colder than generally so
early—I might have mentioned a severe rain & hail storm on the 16th &
17th
Finally November has been a blustering month—

Decem. has been marked with much rain, high winds, and rather a cold
month—

1835

Jan. 1835 Commenced with very cold, windy weather—Indeed It has
been so from the 12th of Decem. up to the middle of this month—for 30
of the last days, it has been a freezing time with wind from the N- course—
People have been crossing on the Ice, from Greenport to Shelter Island,
this some time—

Febr. 1835 continues cold—Our harbour frozen almost over to the
Island—People are passing, repassing from Rocky Point and Greenport to
the Shelterisland daily—

March 1835 continues to hold severely cold—Our harbour shut with ice
sufficiently strong to walk on it with safety up to the 6 or 8th, which is
uncommon for so late in the season—

[350] April 1st 1835 From the first to the 9th cold, sour, rainy weather,
with wind on the S & Easterly course—
A full Town meeting on the 7th—Spent an hour or two in conversation, at the above meeting, with my friend Zacheus Goldsmith—Our
interviews (although not often) were always in time, and sentimentally
agreable to each other—In this, our meeting, he observed with solemnity
that he of late experienced sensations of sudden acute distresses, and ill
turns, which led him to believe he should probably suddenly be called to
that "bourne, whence no traviller returns"—Today, he observed, I feel
pretty well, but of late I certainly am subject to allarming poor turns, and
what is to be the consequences, we are yet to learn—I, (says he), feel to
calmly wait for whatever is to be my future lot here, trusting to the Mercy

of our heavenly Father for time & Eternity—[351] This friend returned home that evening—

Next day, he was out, and around as usual through the day—In the evening, some of his neighbours called in and spent an hour or two with him in pleasent and enlivening converse—they left him to all appearance in comfortable health. About 10 OClock, he complained to his family of feeling ill, and took immediately to his bed—grew suddenly alarmingly worse, and in a few minutes expired—Aged about 70 years—His faith in the promises of God, as portrayed in the Gospel, was, and has been strong, & unshaken for many years—His life, as a farmer, and much worldly buisness entrusted to his hands, has been, we believe without reproach—

April 14th Very cold—Ice this morn an inch thick in our troughs, and tubs etc

16th A hard snowstorm—

17th It holds cold, with plenty of snow & frost

18th High winds N-N-W—Ice of sufficient thickness to bear a Man—

[352] April 24th 1835 A cold northwester—

25th Some Snowing this Morn—

May 3rd Rode to Riverhead,with Mrs. Griffing

5th Returned home—Weather, as it has been, all this Spring, uncommon cold & blustering—

June 3rd 1835—Set off this day, with Mrs. Griffing, for NewYork, by land—Stoped the night with our Son at Riverhead—

4th Rode to Patchogue, stoped the night with our friend Capt. Gano Gillett—Was agreeably, and sumptuously entertained—Capt. Gillet was a pupil at my school in about 1802—A bright boy—

5th We rode to Jamaica, where we stoped the night—On our way, we stoped at Hempsted, and took a late dinner, at Conklings Inn—

6th Rode to N-Y- by the way Williamsburgh Ferry, where we crossed early—took breakfast with Rogers Williams, corner of Grand Street & the Bowery

[353] On the 8th took passage in the Steamboat, for Newburgh, where we arrived at about 11 A.M—At 4 P.M. Mrs. G & myself took passage for Hamptonburgh, in a large farmers wagon, of the coursest sort—after a severe, and truly painful jolting, pounding, & thumping, of two or more hours we arrived to our friend Benjamin Brown Esq., where we were joyfully & cordially received—

Mrs. Griffins Sister, Hannah Howel, is at Mr. Browns—It appeared to be an affectionate and tender meeting—We tarried two nights at Browns—In said time, I visited Goshen, and the surburbs [sic]—To me the visit brought many solemn impressions, and vivid recollections, of nights & days, and seasons past, and gone forever—The tenements, Stores, and places, where in my juvenile glee, I use to daily frequent, alas! How changed! Their occupants all gone! Their aspect changed, and a new generation arose, which we know not—40 years has thus effaced, the glowing picture, which so pleased me in 1790—1—2—3—4—5 & 6—Now in 1835 its beauty obliterated—

[354] Major James Tusten & General Abraham Vail, of that generation, and at time my sociable inmates, are yet living, and like myself advancing in the wane of life—We met—shook heartily the hands, and talked seriously of Aul Lang Syne—

11th June, repaired to Newburgh—Stoped the night with our sincerely good Brother Samuel Caddle Griffing—On the 12th took passage for NewYork, where we arrived on the 13th—Arrived to our natal spot about the 20th, where I found Narcissa very unwell—Mrs. G- stoped at Riverhead with Sidney whose wife is confined with twin girls—

June has been a very dry month—It continued so until the 28th July, on which day we had some rain—

August 4th & 5th 1835 two very cool nights for the season—
6th Wind E-S-E—
About 18th our friend N.T. Hubbard, and his good Wife, & 3 children, paid us a very agreable visit—It was our satisfaction to have [355] their cheering, enlivening, animating company, and conversation 3 or 4 days—To us, this visit was a treat in season, and regular time—For It he has our hearty & unfeigned thanks—On the 23rd They left for their residence, N-Y—

27th we had a copious rain, It is the first sufficient to wet the ground, as it needed, since the 1st of June—

This day 28th Nathaniel T. Hubbards two children, Walter O. & Susan, with a Mr. Ketcham, came to stop with us a few days—

From the 1st Septem. To the 30th there was hardly a drop of rain fell—It has been a dry, dry season—A pretty cool Septem. with one or two frosts—

October 11th Narcissa, & Honora set off for N.York & Newburgh—To defray their expences I gave them Eleven dollars—

•

They returned on the first of Novem. having been gone 3 weeks—Novem. has been a moderate month—still dry—Some rain the last of the month and high wind—

[356] December 1835 was a cold month, especially about the middle of It, when we had 3 or 4 as cold days, probably as has been experienced in any Decem. within 20 years past—

Our harbour shut with ice thick enough to bear walking on a mile or so from the shore—

1836

January 1836 First part of quite moderate—the rest of this month, extreme cold—Our harbour & bays all shut up—Plenty of snow, and ditto of sleighing, which is much improved—

Feb. 1836 Continues severely Frigid—People cross the harbour, from Rockypoint to longbeach point—from Greenport to Shelterisland, and from Dyers Wharf to any part of longbeach, and Rockypoint, with sleigh & horse—

29th (It being Leapyear) our harbour still closed with Ice—This eve, Jasper Y. Tuthill crossed to Rockypoint, with horse & sleigh—

March 1st a great rain, which continued to pour down for near 24 hours, that with the snow caused almost a flood—

[357] March 3rd Our harbour continues shut with ice as It has been since about the 15th of Decem. last—A thing very uncommon for the last 30 years—

7th people are crossing to & from Rockypoint with horses—Brother James, & Jasper Y. Tuthill has crossed this day—Late indeed for such a travel, on a bridge, without sleepers—

Quite a religious revival in our vilage, at this time—

April 1836 At this time, my wife caught the measles, at one of the afternoon Meetings—After suffering greatly with It some weeks, she recovered—but as It left her eyes very weak, I much fear Its final effects—

I ought to have observed, that the Ice, moved off out of the harbour about the 18th of March or 19th, on which day before its removal, our brother Warren crossed from Rocky point to longbeach—such an instance is rarely known—I think he crossed the 17th

In April of this year, Mrs. Mulford, Widow of the late Mr. Elisha Mulford, died aged 89 years—She was altogether a fine, discreet, valuable woman—

[358] On the 5th April 1836, I shook hands with a* Widow Penny, aged 101 years, if she was born in 1735 as she is pretty positive she was—She says nineteen years old in 1754—She is the oldest person I ever see—She has a dignified expression of countenance—is sociable, intelligent, and free, and pleasently communicates interesting circumstances which came under her observation 80 or 90 years ago—Her features are so marked with precision, and traits of correctness, that we must conclude she once possessed an agreable pleasing face, united to a handsome person—But Time, the conkering hand of time, has made its ravages, and inrodes, on what was once known and admired as well proportioned clay—

*Mrs. Penny died in 1838 in her hundred and 3rd year—

13th April We have a hard S-E- Snowstorm—It has finally been a cold, freezing April—

May 3rd & 4th two whale Ships of Greenport arrived—The Delta, with 1800 barrels, & Triade 1500—

[359] 7th A rain storm—Our two seins have caught about 6000 shad—

9th Joseph McNeill, has been with us 2 weeks or more—left us this day—Mrs. Griffings measles leaves her very feeble—

15th & 16th rather dry—High winds—generally S-S-W—

Last week, at the courthouse at Riverhead, A Man was pronounced guilty of Murder, and condemned to be hung on the 2nd of July ensuing—those who advocate takeing life, except in self defence, would do well to read with candor, Doctor [Benjamin] Rush's essays on that important subject—

Our Son, Sidney (we understand) spoke feelingly in court, on the trial—

After court, Sidney, and wife, visited us—

An india rubber pedlar stoped with us on the 17th and on the morning of the 18th It is supposed he stole Ezekial N. Glovers watch, a good one worth about 15 or 20 Dollars—

A Mr. Josiah Knight is now, and has been stoping with us this 10 days—He is putting up hay scales for Dyer & others in O-

[360]18th 19th & 20th May 1836 we entertained 10 men & 2 boys to one or more meals victuals a piece—Some of them were surveying the roads through the Town—Their names were, some of them, Sidell, Craton, Peters, Wm. A. Overton, Capt. David London, & two boys—

21st John Hart & Son, and Mr. Samuel Terry, Merchant with us—The two former left this eve—Mr. Terry stops the night—

From the 24th to the 31st the wind was generally Easterly—Some times pretty high—some rain, and cool—Mr. Terry stoped with us until the 28th—

29th A Mr. Seymour, Merchant from N.York, stoped with us the night—

June 1st 1836 A Man from Boston took Dinner with us—

[361] 3 & 4 June Wind E—& some rain—We have had a long time Easterly weather—

On the 3rd day of this month June 1836 the corner stone of the first Methodist church, in our Village (Orient) was laid by the Reverend Samuel King—He is Soninlaw to Mr. Thomas V. Youngs, of the same place—

It stands about 35 rods from Orient landing, or from the wharf, at the harbour—called <u>now</u> Dyers wharf

Without <u>charity</u>, Man is as sounding brass & a tinkling symbol—A sound without a substance—A profession without possession! Alas, who are those priviledged souls, possessed with that Heavenly <u>jewel</u>, that pearl of great price? I would ask with all humility, who are those highly favoured ones? The great apostle to the Gentiles has answered the important question—The possessor of Charity! Those who are endowed, and abound in that Heavenly grace, have immortal riches—A house not made with hands, immortal in the Heavens—

[362] From the 5th to the 7th June 1836 It was much of the time Easterly, Northerly & Southerly weather—some rain in said time

From the 24th of last May, up to the present 8th June, it has been almost constant succession of Easterly winds—

To view Man, in a religious light—To view him in a philosophic light—To view him as he is altogether vanity, the creature of a bustling moment—What is the result of such an astonishing view? Why, It is sufficient to stain the pride of all earthly glory, and restless ambition—

Well might Mrs. Rowe exclaim, in the immediate prospect of the dissolution of the body, "What a dream, is mortal life!"

He became a judge of the court some time before his death

*Capt. Gano Gillet, and wife, with us on a visit this 8th

9th As pleasant as any day this 25 days—

11th & 12th Rather cool—Wind N.E—

[363] 14th Wind N-E- It has been somewhere near that point, except now & then a day or two since the 23rd May—A thing, as to weather, scarce known by our eldest Men—About 22 or 24 days

15 June the Union Seine took this morn about 130000—The Jackson Seine about 200000 of little shad, or boney fish—

Yesterday, the <u>Universal Meeting house</u>, at Southold, was dedicated— 18th Wind, warm from S-W- by S—

Wheat turns out very poor this year, in this place—Capt. Rufus Tuthill will not, it is thought, realize his seed off of 12 acres—

20 A smart thunder Shower with plenty of rain—

21st High wind E—Some rain again this morn—

22 continues much rain through the night

23 rains moderately all day—Wind cool E—

24th Wind E—cool—

[364] 25th June 1836 Cool, E- wind—A melancholy time as to wheat in this place—It is nearly all cut off—Corn looks poor, and the weather has been such as to retard the growth of hay—

George Champlin raised his store, just below me on this road—

26th Wet, drizzly, uncomfortable weather—

27th A great rain—Wind yet E—as it has been much of the time for this 35 days—

28th Wind S-W—Rode to Greenport early

29th Some rain—wind E—Warm

30th Warm, and close weather—

July 1st 1836—Cloudy—Wind S—Our country is getting full of Societies—It would take time and paper to enumerate them all—Such as <u>Tract- Dorcas- Benevolent- Washington- Fayett- Jackson</u>, and a lot of others—they may yield some good I hope—

[365] Some suppose their number serves rather to divide, rather than to unite—Those resting on the broad basis of Charity must, we believe, produce the peaceable fruits of Righteousness—Human nature is human nature, and we must go beyond <u>that</u>, if we do not show some partiality for our own society, in preference to others—This is nature—

July 2nd Calm & moderate—We have considerable company, especially this eve—

3rd The late rain alters much the face of things—Vegetation appears to brighten up, and recruit—

July 4th An era important in the History of our Republic—A national Jubilee—which will be revered, and kept as such, we hope, while this country sustains a name amongst the nations of the Earth—60 years, this day since the inhabitants of this conspicuous land declared themselves Free &

Independent—The <u>hands</u> that wielded the distinguished quill, in signing the bold Declaration, are now all mouldering in the dust—But the names of those patriots will stand in bold relief, while Liberty has an Asylum on this mundane Sphere—

[366] Tuesday 5th July 1836 Warm S- wind—The Ship Triade sailed this day on a Whaling Voyge—A Mr. Losper [?] I believe is her commander

Wednes 6th Wind S-W- & warm—

7th Weather, and wind, as yesterday—

Life, how short!—how treacherous! How full of incident!—Even if extended to 60 or 70 years, It passes as a tale that is soon told—In fleetness It resembles the weavers shuttle, 'tis here!—'tis gone—gone forever—

8th Four road Surveyors with us—

What a lesson of humility, Our Saviour taught his disciples, and left the important precept for all professors of Christianity—"What I say unto <u>one</u>, I say unto <u>all</u>, Watch"—"First cast out the Beam, out of thine own Eye, and then thou shall see clearly to take out the mote out of thy neighbours, or Brothers Eye—"

[367] 9th July 1836 Fair weather—Wind S- by W—

10th Wind E- by S—

Company from Greenport—Considerable rain—A French gentleman with us—came yesterday—

11th Rain—Wind E-N-E—

12th What we call fine rain, wets rather more than a large Fog—Continues through the day, and evening—

13th Thick drizzly weather—Mssrs. Bledenburgs & Co left us this day—they have been surveying the road through the Town—

14th Wind S—A company of whalemen at our house—They were <u>unwise</u>, and <u>noisy</u>—uncongenial to my, or to our feelings—

We can swallow somethings at 20 years of age, that will not go comfortably down at 75—

15th Wind E—The French Gentleman, Mr. D. Anteroches, left us, this day, having stoped with me since the 9th—

[368] 16th July 1836 Wind as it has been all the week E—It has blown more from that quarter, since the 1st of May last, (I think) than any seventy five days in succession, for many years agone—perhaps we might say with safety, Fifty!—

17th Cool wind from N-E- Our Son, Sidney, and family, who have been with us a few days, left for their residence—Riverhead—They came on the 13th—

18th Wind cool N-W—Mr. Andrew J. Cunningham,with his good, and cheerful wife, formerly Louisa Withie, came (to stop with us sometime) last Saturday evening—

19th Warm & pleasant—

A large, and rude company, from Greenport this day stoped the night— 5 of them took breakfast, 16 of them eat Supper—

Mrs. Griffing set out for Riverhead, to visit Sidney & Family—

20th Wind S-W—

[369] 21st July 1836 Rode out to Greenport this morn with Mr. Cunningham—The Ship Delta of Greenport sailed this day on a Whaling voyge—

22nd Hot calm weather—

23rd Wind N—of course cool—

As we descend the vale of life, a shaded horizon appears to be gathering just before us—we begin to lose the elastic step, which was wont to mark our up and down movements—Our Spirits flag, while that vivid fire, which illumined our juvenile course is perceived to burn lower and lower—A solemn prelude to the final extinction—An important, yet serious Truth—

24th & 25th Warm S-E- wind—

26th A rain Storm—

27th Wind E-S-E—Hiram Tuthill, (son of my late very dear friend, Noah Tuthill,) set off this day for Michigan, where he proposes to settle himself for life—He is young, perhaps 2 or 3 & twenty years of age—

[370] 28th July 1836 Warm wind S. by W—

29th Wind S—Cloudy—

30th Some considerable rain through the night—this morn clears up Wind S-S-W—

31st Mrs. Griffin returned from Riverhead where she has been since the 19th—

Mr. Cunningham & wife left this morn for N-Y—

Monday 1st August 1836 Wind W—

2nd Some rain last night—A cool morn Wind N—Faith in the goodness of our Heavenly Father, is inexpressibly sweet to the possessor, and full of Glory when we feel to stand upon the threshold of Eternity—

3rd Pleasant Westerly weather, rode out to Latham's with my dear, feeble, and Widowed daughter, Deziah Preston—

She has experienced the loss, of as kind, affectionate, tender, and valuable a husband, as ever died—With Doct. Watts, she can say justly,

"This soul of mine that dreadful wound has bourn
Off from its side, Its dearest half is torn—
The rest lies bleeding & but lives to mourn—"

[371] 4th August—Our daughter, Cleora, arrived from N.Y. on a visit to us—

5th Wind N- & cool—Cloudy—

6th Wind E-S-E—Some rain—

Sabbath 7th Fine pleasent weather—Wind S-W—

8th Wind W—Our late rains, with some S- winds appears to have helped the corn, and the other summer crops, so that they look promising—Wheat as before observed is much cut off—

9th commences with an Easterly rain storm—Cleora & Husband rode out to Southold—

10th Cool N- wind—

5 of the railroad Surveyors took dinner with us yesterday—

11th Our Friend Doct. Henry A. Cleveland called on us this day—He is now in handsome practice in the State of Massachusetts—

Wm. H. Ellis, Collector, of the port of New Haven, & family, took dinner with us Yesterday—[372] Mr. Ellis is much of the gentleman, and very pre-posessing in his address and conversation—Mrs. Ellis is all the Lady, and full of tender benevolence—

Samuel H. Landon, & wife called on us—He is Grand Son to the late Judge Jared Landon—

12th cool N-W- wind—

13th Wind N—Northern lights bright this eve—

14th Morn Wind N-W- Eve it died away calm—

15th Wind N—cool—Camp meeting commences at JamesPort this day—

16th Wind light N—Rode to Southold with Mrs. Griffing—Stoped the night with our child Harriet, and Husband—She is very unwell—

17th Returned home this eve by the way of Greenport—

[373] 18th Wind N-E- & cool—Mr. R. Williams, Sidneys Wifes Father, came to our house from N-York—

19th Wind S- & rain all the forenoon—

20th Wind N-W—cool for August—Rode to the O- Point, with Mr. Williams—Took dinner with Cousin David Terry—We made several calls—Returned home about 4 P.M—

21st quite cool—pretty near cold enough for a frost—Mr. Williams left for N.Y—his home—

22nd Still holds cool—

23rd Weather as yester, and several days past cool—wind N-W—

24th Wind E—It argues something in the Man, if he is sane, to be com-posed, calm, and collected, in the midst of a storm of wind, thunder, or words—

25th Wind W—

[374] 26th 1836 August—Warm, & pleasant

27th What people are in the habit of calling good weather—But the question is, (perhaps it is a proper one,) whether there is such a thing as bad weather! If we are right, and possess that spirit and temper of the Gospel, in which we can say "Its all yea, and Amen" then we can say with the Shunamite Woman, whose only child and son lay dead in her house, "It is well"—

Sabbath 28th Mild, and pleasant—

29th Wind S-W- by S—Cleora and her children left this day for N-Y—

30th Rained some fine Showers last night—Wind high this morn, W-S-W—

Blackberries plenty at Shelterisland, about these days—Honora & Narcissa, gone after them, this day—Our youngest Brother, Samuel C. is now with us on a visit—He lives at Newburgh

[375] 31st Wind cool N-W—It resembles Autumn

September 1st 1836—Wind high from S-W-

The Summer now closing for 1836 has been a cold one—Wheat with us has been pretty much cut off—

2nd Wind, this morn N-W—There was some rain last night—The late rains gives the farmers in our region plenty of pasture—A satisfaction to better manufacturing Brunetts—

3rd Some rain—What a Solemn, important, and Soul rejoicing Truth is this "that Gods tender mercies are over all his works"—

Wind S-E—

4th A cloudy day—Ezekial N. Glovers youngest child died last night—Its name Lewis—

5th Some rain, by short intervals through the day—company training at our house—

6th Cool wind E-N-E-

[376] 7th Septem 1836—Wind E—cool—

8th Wind E-N-E- A cloudy, dark, day—It looks much like a storm near—

9th Wind E—cool—

Some considerable company with us—Are any of them, or me—Wise?—
11th Wind E—cloud, It has been some days past—
12th Wind as yesterday—
Tuesday 13th At 9 this A-M- I left for N.York—Went on board the sloop Liberator, David T. Glover, Master—Weighed anchor, about 10 with a fair, light wind, steared our course for N-Y—At sun set, off Wading River—

14th Slept but little last night—troubled with the nightmare—an oppression on the seat of life—an inexpressible, and alarming sensation, while asleep—As we are sailing, our onward course for NewYork, It brings on the most solemn reflections of the many [377] passages I have took with my two very dear Friends (now no more) Jonathan & Jesse Terry—With these two greatly esteemed, and Juvenile associates, I have took passage for N-Y- and other places, occasionally for 20 years—And with them, I always felt myself at home, receiving the most affectionate civilities—Their expressions of long and continued kindnesses, have left impressions, which can only be erased when time with me shall be no more—

We met this day I should judge 2 or 300 vessels

15th This morn, calm, came to off Hart Island—We have had a dark, foggy night—The Steam boats, with a multiplicity of passengers, passed us in the gloom of night—

Arrived at the Dock at Peck slip about noon—Found our daughter Cleora & Family well—Stoped with them the night—

16th Cleora walked out with me shoping—purchased two silk dresses, one of them for my dear wife, if It had been a diadem, set in diamonds [378] she would well become It, as she has richly merited that, and more—Narcissa had the other—they cost about Eight dollars—

17th Visited our former pupil (when I taught school at O-Ponds in 1802 or 3) John King—He is now doing a handsome and I presume a profitable buisness—Has a great flow of spirits, pleasing in his conversation and address, united with many expressions of <u>civilities</u>, in their proper time & place—Visited my <u>Friend</u>, and the worlds friend, N.T. Hubbard—called on one of our former boarders, A Mr. Jennings—Met today my two nieces, from O-Ponds, Caroline & Lucinda Wiggins—

Evening got my goods on board, and set sail for our residence—E- end L. Island—

18th On our way Eastward—

19th At 8 A.M. arrived at the dwelling of my dear family, well, and to add to such a Joy, found my beloved daughter, Harriet, with us—

[379] 20th Wind light, S & warm—very much so—

21st A warm Septem. thus far—

22nd Light S- by E—

23rd Some little rain—P.M- calm—

Our kind endearing daughter left us this day with her Husband, Abner Wells—A fine, pleasant, good Soninlaw—and an attentive, pleasant Husband—

24th Considerable rain—Wind light E by S—

Narcissa took 2 Men passengers to Riverhead today in my Carriage for 4½ Dollars—

25th Sept 1836 Cool, high wind N-N-W—

16th Much such weather as yesterday—

Our small orchard gives us plenty of apples [this] year—Are we possessed with hearts of gratitude for the innumerable mercies which flow into us continually?—

27th A squally, windy day—Wind S-S-W—

28—Weather, as yesterday

29th Continues blustering

[380] Friday 30th September 1836 A mild day—Calm through the intire day—

October 1st—Wind light from S- by E

2nd Cloudy & windy—S-S-W—

Died this day, about 10 A.M., my Aunt Ruth Vail (widow of the late Stephen Vail) aged 92 years wanting about 30 days—She was, and invariably has ever been one of those women whose price is above Rubies—

3rd Wind S-W—

4th Strong wind E—Attended the funeral of my venerable Aunt Ruth

5th It blew a severe gale last night E—Considerable rain—Tide very full—Squally through the day—

6th the gale continues Wind N-W—

7th Wind moderates down—

8th Wind light E—Worked on our dooryard fence—

[381] 9th A pleasant day—

10th Cool N-E- Wind—Widening the road, opposite my house and land—

11th Wind strong E—Northern lights bright last eve—

12th A hard Easterly Storm of wind, rain & a very high tide—

13th A mild day succeeds the storm—

14th finished moving my fence, in widening the road—

15th Wind light W—Honora, set off for N.Y. last Thursday—Had a present of a hat, from my pleasent daughter Cleora, this day

Sabbath 16th Wind E—Some showers of rain—Rode to Southold, to see our daughter & dear family—

17th High Wind W—Caleb Dyer, commenced building a store, on the end, or near his wharf—

18th Wind W-N-W—The railroad surveyors, Eight of them, took supper with us—

[382] Wednesday 19th Oct. 1836 Wind S-W- & Cloudy

20th Wind powerful from S-W- by S—Some rain—It blew, for a short time today, near a hurricane—

Sidell, and his surveying Company, left us this noon, and proceeded to Lathams, to stop with him, a few days—

21st Wind strong N-N-W—Snow squalls—

22nd Cool—some frost—Wind N-W—

23rd Cool—

24th A mild day—Wind light W—Capt. Rufus Tuthill visited us, came part of the way on foot—He is 90 years old wanting about 60 days—He sung us the 99th Hymn 2nd Book of Ruth—

25th Wind N-N-W & cool—It has froze ice, in our troughs, and 'tubs, standing in the shade, throughout the day, rather uncommon for October—

[383] 26th Wind N-N-W- Yet not so cold as yesterday—

27th Wind, W-N-W—1/2 W—Hazy—

28th Blustering—Wind N- by W—Honora arrived home from N-Y—

29th Very squally—Wind W-S-W—

30th Quite cool—Rode to Lathams—A hard frost this eve—Bids fair to be a cold night—

31st A.M. Wind N-N-W—P.M. E- by N—

Novem. 1st 1836 A white frost this morn—Wind light—Evening calm—

2nd High wind S—It commenced about noon a severe rain Storm—

3rd A blustering N-W-Wind—and freezing cold—

4th A chilly, almost calm day—Sister Lucretia with us, on a visit—

5th Scarce any wind, yet a cloudy day—Six railroad Surveyors stoped with us last night—[384] These rail road Surveyors have stoped with us occasionally since 18th last May—

6th Oct. 1836 Sabbath—Cold, raw weather—Wind N-W—

Monday 7th Ellections, held at my house—[Martin] Vanburen, Democratic Candidate—[Benjamin] Harrison, Whig C[andidate]—

Tuesday 7th I was taken very ill,with an acute pain in the upper part of my hip—So distressing was the pain, that I was unable to set up more than a few minutes at a time, for near twenty days—The Doct. said It was the Sciatica—

November 1836 has been a blustering cold, windy month—Wind, much of the time N-W- & S-W- with some hard storms, in all the month—

Decem. comes in with cold N-W- winds—About 10 & 12th the weather was mild—the 21st a hard rain storm—

1837

January 1837—comes in very cold—our O-Ponds harbour froze out, so as to bear walking on It quite a distance out from the shore—perhaps 2/3rds of a mile—

On the 10th we had good Sleighing—

On the 21st Died, our Worthy Friend Col. Jeremiah Moore—aged about 50 years—Mr. Moore was a Worthy, useful, kind, and benevolent citizen, neighbour, & member of Society—Much beloved—An affectionate Father, and tender Husband—

22nd A rain Storm, of 16 hours, when It commenced Snowing, which It continued to do for several hours—Finally, January has been a tight winter month—

Feb. 1837 Continues severely cold—

On the 2nd It moderated down to "pleasant" point—

9th & 10th a cold rain storm—

[386] 20th Febr 1837 A rainstorm—as It was on the 15th & 16th

23rd We had a hard storm of Snow—Narcissa left for Southold & Riverhead—

P.M—A heavy rain set in—That, with the melting of the snow, makes almost a flood—The weather in Feb. through has been very changeable cold & warm—Wet & dry—Wind high & low—

March began with cold—on the 7th we think the ground has as much frost in It as It has had in any winter this 8 winters past—[when?] it is froze from 10 to 15 inches deep—

Our friend Capt. R. Tuthill passed here on his way to Greenport, in a Carriage—He is in his 91st year—

On the 9th It rained steady near 17 hours
From 10th to 22nd It was cold piercing E- & N- Wind—

[387] April 1837 Comes in with a severe rain Storm—Wind high E—
There has been a frost about every night of this month up to the 14th and
this day is a squally one—The remaining part of this month was more like
Spring approaching—

May 1837 on its first was a hard frost—on the 17th—18th & 19th It rained
in abundance—
I forgot to notice that on the 10th we had copious hail storm—Some of
the hail stones were much noticed, as uncommon large—It is said they
measured 3 or 4 inches in circumference—Considerable damage was done
to Glass windows—If the wind had been high at the time, there would
have been much more distruction amid the vegetable, and animal
Kingdoms
[388] May 1837 Take It altogether, has been a wet, cool, & windy
month—It has passed off, and gone with the years beyond the flood—The
anxious moments, and inexpressible sensations, incident to reasonable, or
rational beings, which occupied our days of May 1837, have gone, gone,
forever—

June comes in raining—From the 1st to the 10th the wind was generally
Easterly—10th it rained & hailed—
Altered our Barr Room, and put, or made a part of my store room into a
rum vending place—is it right to sell, intoxicating drinks?—This is an
important question!—I begin to think it is a question which ought to be
asked every day to us, who deal in It—And our answers ought to be slow,
considerate, and when we feel our accountablility to our Father, in Heaven—
[389] 13–21 & 22nd June, we had rainstorms—June goes out with thick
Smoky weather—
A Col Peck stoped with us some time in this month—He is Grand Son
to the late Benjamin King, of this place, who was better known by all the
young people of 1777 to 1791 by the name of Uncle Ben—at the time over 60
years—A house Carpenter—He died over 70 years of age—
On the 27th June, died Capt. Samuel Hobart, aged about 64 years—Capt.
Hobart had followed the Sea for a livelihood for many years—perhaps 45
years—about 20 of them he commanded some fine vessels—He was industrious, frugal & of good Judgement—Sound and wise in council, towards

undertaking buisness for advantage—We hope he always kept an inward Eye on securing a place beyond this veil of Sorrow, as he said his Faith was unshaken in the merits of our Lord & Saviour Jesus Christ—

[390] July 1st 1837 With Mrs. Griffing, visit our children at Southold & Riverhead—returned home, on the 3rd, amid small rain Showers—I might observe the 1st day was a very warm one—

July 6th Left, with Mrs. Griffing, for Greenport, from which we went on board the Sloop Prudence, Capt. Wm. Booth, and left the dock for New York—

7th Some rain—came to anchor, at Rikers Island about 10 P.M.—

8th Saturday we arrived in N. York about 11 A.M.—Walked to Ms. McNeills, found our daughter Cleora, and family well, and glad to see us— To meet our children, after many days of Sepparation, and find them in health, is a satisfaction known only to parents, who love, and are beloved by their pledges of a virtuous, and sanctified union—

[391] Sabbath 9th July 1837 Attended meeting fore, and afternoon—

10th Took passage in the Steamboat Rochester for Newburgh, 7 A.M.- Our Friend N. T. Hubbard took us to the Steamboat, in his coach, near two miles—This expression of kindness to us is only one of a thousand, he has indulged me, and mine. The impression these civilities make on our sensibility, are only to be arrased [erased] by the corroding hand of old time—

We arrived at Newburgh 11 A.M., found our youngest Brother Samuel C. Griffin & family well, and they cordially welcomed us to their pleasent abode—Stoped with them untill the evening of the 11th when, with our Brother, we left for Albany, in the Steamboat (I forgot her name)—We arrive at A[lban]y at 8 A.M. on the 12th—We then took another small Steamboat for Troy, where soon arrived—We then took the stage and rode to Lansingburgh—While at this place we took dinner—walked around the Town [392] with which we were very well pleased—At this place, I have had a Cousin, by name Joshua Griffing, live for a number of years past—was much disappointed to learn that he, and family, had moved further back into the country—having left this Town some months since—

After two or three hours stay here, we rode to Troy, spent an hour or two in viewing this beautiful situation, and in the Stage rode to Albany, and stoped the night at Clinton Hotell—

Thursday 13 July 1837—Spent the day in walking over this old dutch City (Albany)—Some few of the old houses, built of the bricks, brought from Holland, more than one hundred years ago, are yet standing, as monuments of what was doing in bygone days—Days when the war whoop, and Indian dance, were common in our now poppulated and highly favoured land—

[393] We observed one house, whose iron figures told It to have been built in 1729. That is 100 years ago—The city now has many splendid and well finished buildings—in a stile, to give It quite an imposing appearance—The Capitol, being situated on a beautiful and commanding eminence, shows to much advantage—In front of said Capitol, is a handsome park, nicely enclosed with neat and substantial Iron railing—

When we were ascending the stone steps, and entering the spacious hall of said house, Mrs. Griffing observed with emotion, "Here" says she, once sat (for many days) our very kind, and affectionate—yes invaluable friends, to us, now all gone to that bourne whence none return—We mentioned names with feelings of true sensibility—Daniel T. Terry—Ezra Lhomadieu, Jared Landon & Thomas S. Lester—True patriots as representatives in the Councils of our State, and nation—

[394] On the 13th P.M. We went over to Greenbush, and stoped the night with our Cousin Phineas Terry's daughter—An excellent, kind, hospitable woman—She is married to a fine Man, by name Green—Here we were treated with marked attention, and respect—

On the 14th we passed over to Albany, and took dinner with a Widow Henry, a Lady of near 70 years, a descendant of the first dutch settlers, of this ancient City—This woman, although an intire Stranger, appeared to use every means in her power to make our time with her pass off with satisfaction and comfort—Assuredly her civilities to us demands our gratitude, and sweetest remembrance, while we shall sojourn, as strangers & pilgrims on Earth—

5 OClock P.M. we went on board the Ohio, Steamboat, for Newburgh, where we arrived [395] about 12 midnight—Walked up to Brother Samuels & took lodging for the night—

15th Hired a carriage & horse to convey us out five miles to our Nephews, Charles & Rensaler Howells—Stoped the night with Rensaler—

Sabbath 16th Rode out to Benjamin Brown Esq.—Found him, his good family, and Mrs. Griffings Sister Hannah Howel, all in good health, and to appearance very glad to see us—and we have not a doubt but they were so—

Evening returned to Charles Howells, with whom we stoped the night—the ride is about 9 miles out, and the same in—

17th Rode to my Brother Samuels Newburgh—At 5 P.M. took passage on board the Steamboat for N.York, where we arrived on the 18th about 8 A.M.—took a carriage, and rode to Mr. Neills—Our daughters—found them all well—

19th Walked over the Town, made several calls

[396] Tuesday 20th July 1837—Rode out with our Friend N.T. Hubbard, and his aimable wife—We visited the Tunnel, at Harlem, through the solid rock—It is, or was a Herculean task to accomplish the stupendous work— After viewing for some time this modern wonder, we returned to friend Hubbards—In the evening, we, at least, myself, with friend Hubbard, attended a musical concert, of some of the most talented Musicians—

21st Purchased some Groceries, and Sundries, and made preparation to leave on the Morrow—

22nd took leave of our friends, went on board Capt. Wm. Booth, of the Sloop Prudence, and sailed towards home—

At 2 P.M. anchored off Hallets cove [west of Astoria]—Visited the quite celebrated Grant Thurborns Garden*—Was introduced to the [397] little gentleman and he shook me heartily by the hand, with which I was well pleased—If small, and eccentric, he appears to have a great heart & a noble mind—

*Mr. Thurburn died Feb. 1863 in his 90th year of age—

23rd On our passage home—

24th arrived home to our family, and was gratified to find them all well— Our absence had been 19 days, and our travil had been, by water and land, 700 miles—I might have observed that on the 17th, while at our kinsmans, Charles Howells, he took me in his carriage (about 7 A.M.) out about four miles to the ancient residence of the once Governor Cadwal[la]der Colden— He held that office in this State about 1764—about 1766 he purchased a large tract of land, in this region, and built the <u>mansion</u> which we are now visiting—The hand of time has made visible inrode on all its former magnificence—It appears to be fast tumbling into ruins, and It is probable It will soon be said, "this is the place where Governor Coldens house stood"—

[398] The property, at the time of its purchase, was somewhere about 2000 acres of handsomely situated land—It has now nearly all gone out of the name—The old Mansion house* is now occupied by other names, of no connection—It looks like a deserted castle—But alas! What is that to Its once dignified possessor! He with a numerous family, of three generations, now rest in a selected and reserved spot, enclosed with stone fence, within a short distance of the old castle, of gothic structure—

*It was taken intirely down about 1844—And governor Coldens tract of land has nearly, or quite gone out of the name—1849

I would have willingly visited the Cemetery, and read the inscriptions on the monuments of the illustrious dead, but the morning was attended with a heavy dew, and our friend Charles much out of health, It was deemed prudent to deny myself of that satisfaction—

The Seraphic Hervey says "Here lies the great"

False Marble, tell me where—Nothing but poor & sordid dust lies here"

*Stoped with us, for a few days in this month, a Mr. Parshel, of New York City—

[399] *August 10th & 12th 1837 Wind E- and rain—In noting the weather, occasionally, for forty years past, I have noticed that there has been but a few Augusts that have passed without a considerable of an Easterly storm—Some of them have lasted with wind Easterly from 2 to 8 days—

A Mr. Glean staid with us about a week at this time—He says, he owns much property in the West Indies—

16th The wind is still E- & continues to rain some today, and It has done so, a little every day for ten days past—

18th It showers copiously this morn, as it rained some yesterday—

21st Wind continues E- It is now about 15 days since it has blown from that direction—

The Ship Franklin, Charles Griffin Master, has been detained from putting to Sea, in consequence of the E- Wind & Storm—She is bound on a Whaling Voyge—

[400] 22nd August 1837—A Thunder Shower this morn—Franklin Ship sailed—

23rd Cold weather for August—Wind N-W-

24th Wind S- and rain—

28th Two Friends, or Quakers, with us viz. James Sleeper, and William Hancock—They appear to be men of strict piety, and good intentions—

30th Thunder shower, this evening—

September 1st Cool morn—Sidney (our Son) & wife with us last night—they left this noon for residence Riverhead—

7th It appears to be getting rather dry—Ten couple, of young people, stoped with us yesterday, a short time—they were in light Carriages—Pleasure, and satisfactory amusement was the object of anxious persuit—How much they obtained, and how agreeable their reflections, were in after retrospect, each one best can know, and does know—

[401] 9th September 1837 A shower this morn

15th High wind E-N-E—Dyer has just finished his house at the landing facing his wharf—

Lewis A. Edwards has opened a tavern, or Inn, in said house—Rent 200 dollars a year—An extravagant rent—In the end, we believe It will prove one of Mr. Edwards's bad bargains—probably Its his first—and certainly we hope he will never make a second one, that will give him a pang—He is, or appears to be, a worthy, respectable, well minded man—

From the 9th to the 26th we have had not any rain—Of course its getting quite dry—Very high wind this 26th S-S-W—

This month died Mrs. Zipporah, widow, of the late Capt. Grant B. Racket—She was aimable, affectionate, kind, and tender in all the relations of wife, mother, neighbour, and friend—

28th Wind E—Continues dry—

[402] Oct. 1837 from the 3rd to the 5th I am at Riverhead—Court time— Wind E—with rain on the 5th—Orin O. Wickham stoped with us the night—

6th A cloudy day—Reason, and my own judgement tell me, the important truth, that I am fast descending the gloomy vale of years—and that vale assuredly terminates in the final dissolution of these mortal remains of ours—"There is no discharge in that war" Bible

12th McNeill, with our very filial and truly affectionate daughter, Cleora, & family, left us for NewYork and took their passage on board the Sloop Prudence, Capt. Booth—

Friday 13th A hard N-E- rain Storm—It clears up this P.M—Cold—

To speak safe, It is thought best to say but little

[403] Sabbath 22nd Octo. 1837—Rode to Riverhead,with Mrs. Griffing— We attended meeting at upper Acquebogue, fore and afternoon—Stoped the night with our Son Sidney—

Monday 23rd Returned as far as Abner Wells, Southold—Found endearing and loveing daughter Harriet, & family, comfortable, and as we always have found her, glad to see us—In that sweetest dispositioned child, we are almost at times constrained [to] say of her, "she is a daughter in whom there is no guile"—Assuredly to us, now in the decline of life, she is a comfort indeed—We appreciate it and with Doct. Watts, can feel & say, "Children and friends are blessings, too, when God our sovereign makes them so"—

24th Arrived home—

26th High E- Wind—with rain—

27th Continues to rain—October goes out, with very blustering weather—

[404] Nov. 6 1837 Ellection at my house—With us, it has been held, now, 30 times in the last 20 years, in which the whole time I have kept Tavern, and in which buisness (or calling if you please) I have waded through waves of sorrow, sin, and woe—Where I have erred, (and no doubt I often have) I

hope the Father of unbounded Mercies will vouchsafe me forgiveness—"To err is human, to forgive is divine"—

My prayer, daily is, <u>O may It become a prayer of Faith</u>, that I may <u>loath</u>, and <u>hate</u> sin, as a deadly poison, and shun it in its every shape & form—To be a recipient of Love, which is stronger than Death, and that <u>garb of humility</u>, which will wear brighter and brighter round Eternity is all of my prayer, my desire, and hope, which May God grant for the Mediators sake, Amen & Amen—

[405] 14th Novem. 1837—A Snow storm—8 P.M. It clears off—Cold N-W- wind follows the closeing of the storm—

15th Sleighs with their many bells, fly merrily with their tinkling music—P.M. Sun affects the white coat which covers the Earth—

25th Commences with a severe Snow Storm—Not any mail, in consequence of the Storm—the Snow drives much

26 & 27—Weather very cold for the season—Took our daughter Harriet to her home, at Southold—Found our Son & his wife there—brought them home with me—

28th Mild weather—

29th Much as yesterday—

30th Continues moderate—November goes out, as the saying is like a lamb

[406] December 1837 Comes in mild & pleasant—From the 1st to the 16th we had two or three small snows—

On the 17th It snowed through the day, with cold tedious weather—

18th A hard rainstorm

21st A.M. considerable snow fell—P.M. It melts, or with the warm wind, It pretty much all dissolves, and disappears—

22nd Our Son, Sidney, sent his two Sons, Chatham Augustus and Augustus Rogers, to board with us, a number of weeks—He purposes to spend the Winter in Albany, as he is a Representative in the Assembly of this State (N.York)—

29th A pleasant, mild day—This year is on threshold of leaving us forever—Soon, very soon, it will be said that 1837 is numbered with the years beyond the flood—

1838

[407] January 1st 1838 was a moderate & pleasant day—

5th Very warm—the ground is settled, and is suitable order for ploughing—

12th It grows cold—& blustering—

13th Cold winter weather—

14th Winter in its icy colours—

15th More mild—

16th Pleasant, & warm enough to be comfortable

17th weather much as It has been this three days past—

Capt. Rufus Tuthill called on us this day—His birthday this—being born in the year of our Lord 1747—Of course he is ninety one years of age this day—He can walk off two or three miles, without seeming fatigue

21st Continues moderate—

22nd Ditto—ditto—

23rd Pleasant—

24th As yesterday—We understand the North River is open

[408] 26th January 1838—It is said that the North, or Hudson river, is open, and free from Ice, to Albany—Not a common thing so late in January—Some Showers—similar to those we have in Apr.

29th Squally, and it begins to look dreary in the Northern board—

30th Very high wind from N-N-W—

31st What is called, and justly, very cold weather—

Feb. 1st Continues to increase in cold—

6th It freezes our harbour rapidly—

16 & 17th—Our harbour shut up with ice

18th Cold extremely so—

19th Good Sleighing, having had plenty of that necessary article for sliding, fall on the 16th & 17th

I forgot to notice that we had considerable thunder and lightning on the 15th

February 15th on this day our daughter Honora was confined with a son, which they name William Augustus Goodridge

[409] From 20th Feb. to 28th It was very severely cold, our harbour, pretty much froze over—Wind for 10 or 12 days steady N-W & N—

March 1st Continues cold—wind Northerly, as It has been this 14 days past—

6th Wind partially subsides—

7th Calm, and mild—Ice drove in huge piles on longbeach point—Perhaps some of the piles are 15 or 18 feet high—

A revival of Religion In this place (Oysterponds)—Many (and some of them, of late great opposers) now appear to have found the pearl of great price, and boldly go from house to house and proclaim a free, and glorious Salvation, through the attoning blood of Jesus Christ, our Lord—

From the 8th to the 17th it was mild, pleasant weather—

18th It was a severe Snow Storm—A driving, Easterly high wind—

27th It snowed so as to clothe the ground about 4 or 6 inches—

[410] 29th March 1838—A Snow storm

Cousin Peter W. Tuthill moved his house about 100 rods, nearer his Fathers—

Apl. 1st Cold—

6th Still holds chilly, raw weather, Wind N-W—

There is much Scarlet Fever, at this time, in this place—mostly among Children—A number of deaths with It, at Riverhead—Greenport & Rockypoint—Assuredly there is no discharge in that war—

9th Wind E—

10th As yesterday—Some white frost this morn—

23rd Wilcox & Honora commenced keeping house, at David Beebes— May the blessing of Heaven rest upon them, at all times, untill they are permitted to become members of its blessed family

[411] 26th Apl. A rainy day—

May 4th—A visit from our Son Sidney & his affectionate Wife—He is not very well, as to health—

5th A Storm of rain—Wind E-S-E—

8th A.M. pleasant—P.M. cloudy & chilly—Wind E-S-E—Narcissa set off for N.Y.—Sidney & wife left for Riverhead—

10th Squally with Hail & rain—On this day, one year ago—we had hail & rain

19th up to this date, this month we have had 4 rain storms

23rd It rains—

24th It rains copiously—Bought me two pigs 6 weeks old—

Five facts—1 A Firm Faith is the best Divinity—

2nd A good life, is the best Philosophy—

3rd A clear conscience, the law—

4th Honesty, the best Policity[policy]—

5th Temperence, the best Physic—

[412] May 26th 1838 Wind E—with rain—Very high winds this five or 6 days past—A part of the time It blew a gale from S-S-W & S—A heavy Fog—

May goes out Cool, and midling wet—

•

June 1st up to the 4th warm—

5th A refreshing shower—Wind E-S-E—

14th Very warm, as It has been this some days—

The Saviour of our wicked, and sinful World, told his beloved John, and Faithful James, at a certain time, when they indulged in an unreasonable, or improper request, "You (says he to these two faithful disciples) know not what manner of spirit you are of—"

If this was the case, of these two eminent Servants of Christ, how stands it with us, who are full of depravity, and Stupidity—"to obey is better than Sacrifice, and to harken that [than?] the fat of Rams—"

[413] June 18th 1838—High wind, from N-N-E—It is growing rather dry—

23rd Continues to grow dry—

25th Warm—very warm—Wind S-W—Rains this evening—How can we expect safety, and security, when we sleep at our post—

28th A little rain—not enough to wet the ground, which is dry—

July 2nd Intensely warm—

3rd As yesterday—

4th Ditto Ditto—

5th As warm, or hot as it is generally known in any Summer month—

9th Continues dry & warm—

10th As close as days past—

11th Very—very warm nights—Son Sidney & wife stoped with us on the 9th & 10th—

13th A small shower—It is certainly dry

[414] July 18th 1838 It rained a few minutes—It sweetened the air, and revived, for the moment the drooping plants—

20th A smart rain, of some hours, attended with sharp thunder & lightning—

Nathaniel Boiseau, of Southold, had his barn burned, with lightning a day or two since—Grain & Hay in it—

21st High wind N-W—

25th A copious rain this morn—It ought to [be] received with thankfulness, as a boon to the parched Earth—

29th Richard Stears Hubbard, with his daughter, and Wilkies two Daughters, Mary and Emeline, left us this day, for NewYork—their home—

•

August comes in very warm—

Cleora, with her Husband & family, with us, from N.York—

I forgot to observe that a Mr. William B. McFarlin came to stop with us on the 15th July [415] and continues with us—He is studying the profession of the Law—We think him to be a young man of abilities, and much promise—

Aug. 7th A.M. Foggy—P.M. Melting warm—

A grandchild of ours, an Infant child of James McNeills died last eve—18 months old

Sweet Babe—Soon—Soon to you 'twas given

To be an Angel bright in Heaven—

17th Our York boarders left us on the 11th—Maria Woodford left with R.S. Hubbard—

The Steamboat Clifton came to our (Dyers) wharf this day, It being the first time a Steamboat ever visited us, at our landing—

From 18th to the 24th one continued course of dry winds from S-W- to N-W—Some think that the present summer is the driest since 1799—When the drouth was severe—

This 24th We had a thunder Shower of an hour or so—

[416] August 24th 1838

29th McNeill, Cleora & family left us this day for their residence—N.Y—Sidney's FatherinLaw, Rogers Williams, left us with McNeill—

Sept 1st & 2nd A Capt. Fowler, from Guildford, with a Mr. Meigs, stoped with us—

3rd Training at my House—Comfortably cool—Thomas Tuthill of Ramisland, with us—

8th Septem. 1838 Wm. McFarlin, who has been with us since the 15th July, left us this day for new Amsterdam, State of N.York—his residence—

Friday 15th Thomas Tuthill was married to Miss Esther Taber—She is his 2nd wife—Mistake, they were married on the 10th Sabbath—

[417] It rained on the 15th—

16th A hard Easterly rain Storm—

18th A Man & Woman passed my house on foot, in social chat, and good Spirits, this day—The Man was over 91 years & the woman over 89 years—Rufus Tufhill & Esther Taber Senr.—

26th Some rain—

27th Drizly weather—

28th Weather as yesterday—

29th Variable weather—Mr. White raised Sidneys house, on the corner

of my street lot on the 25th—It is designed for a tenement, for Wilcox &
Honora—

Oct. 9th Some white Frost last night—It has been pretty wet since the
15th Sept.—
12th Squally weather—Wind S-W—
From 15th to the 30th It has rained about every 3 or 4 days—And some
times hard—

[418] November 1st 1838 Rainy weather—
5th A rain Storm—It has been an uncommon wet Autumn—
20th Cold, and quite uncomfortably so—
25th continues cool—
26th Cold increases—
27th Weather as yesterday—
On the 16th this Inst—My Brother James Griffings wife, Mehitable,
died—She was truly one of the Excellent of the Earth—An affectionate, tender, and an endearing Wife, Mother, neighbour, and Christian—
I might have noted that we had some Snow on the 20th—and some more
on the 23rd—

Decem. 1st Very windy—
Up to the 20th Some rain—some Snow—& much blowing, high
winds—Some of them was near allied to Hurry Canes—
[419] Sold my Carriage shed in Decem. to Zilla Young, for 9 dollars & 1
bushel corn—
Noah Tuthill was married, to Arletta Youngs, daughter of Lemuel & Fanny
Youngs—Noah is Son to Nathaniel Tuthill—this took place on the 25th

1839

January 1st 1839—Samuel Wiggins was married to Hannah Youngs—
From the 7th to the 12th It was pleasent and mild—
13th As warm as It often is in May—
14th A light Snow, which disappears rapidly before the warm S- Wind—
On the 20th My beloved (I ought to have said our) dear, and greatly
endeared daughter Deziah Preston, departed this life—She has been a suffering mourner, ever since her invaluable Husbands death in Apl. 1833—
Much of the time since that afflicting stroke of Providence, she has been

On the 13th
October 1838 Capt
David Pool, of this
place (Orient) was
drowned, in the
Hudson River,
near Albany—We
believe he always
sustained a char-
acter for [honesty
and?] (page
trimmed)

confined to her house—Her Faith in her God, and Saviour, was brighter, and brighter untill she was admitted to join the Church Triumphant, whose [names?] are written in Heaven

[420] 26th January 1839—A very severe Storm—This Storm is noticed in Thompsons Long Island history—

27th Cold—our harbour is freezing up—

Feb. 1st comes very cold—This evening, Lemuel Youngs Jr. was married to the aimable Miss Fanny Vail, daughter to Jasper Vail, of Riverhead—

Monday 18th A moderate day—light wind N-N-W—The ice appears to be moving out of the Harbour—

Feb. Is going out, as the saying often is, like a Lamb—

March 1 rather cool—

2nd Continues cold—

3rd Weather as It has been this some days—

4th Piercing Cold—

5th Ditto Ditto—

6th Winter weather—

7th Dreary Cold—

8th 9 & 10th and cold as this 8 days past—

[421] Up to the 18th it was cold tedious days—Silas Preston, our late Soninlaws (James H Prestons) Brother, came over, and took upon himself the guardianship of our Orphan Grandchildren, viz. Deziah—John Augustus—Harriet Matilda, & James Hervey—

Two of said Grand Children, leave us with their uncle Silas, for Ashford— Our blessing attend them—

Monday 25th A.M. A brisk Storm of snow—P.M. It clears off—

Apl. 1st A pleasant day—

2nd Mild as yesterday—

3rd Sidney & wife came, and stoped with us until the 7th, when they left us, and took the Stage for Riverhead—

Mr. Jonathan Youngs died, on the night of the 6th aged 75 years—He was never married—was the Son of Jonathan Youngs (who died about 1809) who was the son of Jonathan Youngs (who died 1773) who was the son of Jonathan Youngs (who died 1776 aged 92)—The last said Jonathan Youngs was son to Gideon Youngs, one of the first settlers of our Town—probably son to the first Youngs of this place

Apl. 9th a Snow Storm

[422] 13th April 1839—It was rain—

14th Continues moderately to rain—

15th It still is wet weather—

17th A hard rain Storm—Wind E-N-E-This eve It snows brisk—Wind N-E—

19th Heard this day of the sudden Death of Capt. Gabriel Havens—Died in N.York on the 7th Inst—He was an affectionate cousin of Mrs. Griffings—

23rd Capt. Joseph Griffing paid us a visit of one night—He was now just from Guilford, Connecticut—where he has resided for near 50 years—His birth place was at Riverhead, where he is now bound, and where he intends to locate, and spend the few remaining days of his eventual life—He was born in 1755—He has been a man of uncommon strength, activity, & spry or supal [supple] to admiration—has leaped over a string, or rope, 6 foot & 2 inches high—His figure is now at 80 noble, and commanding—

[423] May 2nd A rain this morn—

3rd Another Shower—

6th Wind high this morn—

7th Very blustering, wind W-N-W—

Up to the 20th we have had it sufficiently wet—with some warm & pleasent days—Finally, the month thus far has been generally pleasent—

21st to 25th Wind E—Some Showers—Some thunder Showers—

26th Easterly weather—

27th Foggy,with some rain—Some thunder Showers—

June 1st Wind N-W—Some rain—

A number of rains from the 2nd to the 20th June and some cool weather—

A Capt. Seth Baker from the State of Massachusetts, Gowanus, stoped with us a few days—I am much pleased with him, as I find much of a Gentleman, pleasing in his address, and entertaining in his conversation—

[424] June 1839 has in general been [a] pretty wet month—

July 1st 1839 to the 16th we had a number of good refreshing Showers— One or two good ground rains, as old Sambo use to say—

It continued very warm, and close up to the 25th—

A Mr. Latham, from N.York, staid with us last night—

July has been, take It altogether, a very warm & wet month—

•

August 1st Was visited by my Friend Thomas H. Genin Esq—It is now about 23 years since he was at our house, which was the last interview I have had with him unto this day—He has been successfully a practitioner, as councillor at Law, in the State of Ohio, at St ClairsVille, now more than 20 years—

[425] In this month August 2nd Zilla Youngs wife was put to bed, or confined with a fine boy—They call him Julius—

10th & 11th was two cool days—

12th A hard thunder shower—Our youngest Brother, Samuel Caddle Griffing visited us yesterday—

What a little speck am I in the creation of the great Jehovahs mighty works! What a little moment is my chequered life!—But immortality gives them unspea[ka]ble weight—

16th Wind, E-N-E—It has been from that point this 3 past days—Wind is very high to day, with a flood of rain, which continued to pour down for 8 or 9 hours—

17th This morn the corn, in our fields, is pretty much all prostrate, in consequence of the very high wind, & rain of yesterday—Wind light this P.M. N-E—

20th Wind A.M. E—It has been so, much of the time this 8 days—

[426] 21st August 1839 Warm & calm—Mrs. Griffins Sister, Mary Hubbard, visited us on the 18th—

Thursday 22nd Sultry hot—Wilcox arrived home from N.Y—

A camp meeting at JamesPort—

23rd Very warm, wind S—

24th A cloudy Morn, with scarce any wind—If any It is S—

Gardens look slim, this season, in consequence of the early drouth—Our latter rains could not bring them fully into a revival so as to make them productive—

25th A warm S- wind—

Monday 26th Wind light E-S-E—Mrs. Griffing gone to Brother Rufus Tuthill on a visit with her Sister Mary Hubbard—

27th Wind S—and very Warm—

28th Rained considerable last night, and so It does—Wind E-N-E—Grows cool—

[427] Richard Peters, & George Jennings, took dinner with us—

This Mr. Peters is the grandson of the late Richard Peters, who was sometime a Merchant of some consequence in Southold—He was very eccentric, and singular (perhaps sometimes vain) in his many observations—Yet we hope, at heart, he was aiming at the thing, that was right—He died somewhere about 1802 or 3—

His only child & Son, Henry, Married the grand daughter of the widow Abigail Moore, who was a woman of superior abilities, virtue, and sterling piety—She was once the Widow* Ledyard, and Mother to the celebrated Traveler, John Ledyard. She died about 1805 or 1806. The said Henry Peters died young—somewhere about 1815—

*Brother to Col Ledyard who was killed at Groton Fort

29th August Wind E-N-E—Cool—Sister Hubbard left us this day for Mattituck by the way of Southold, where she stops a day or two—

[428] Honora left for our Son Sidneys, at Riverhead, with her little Goodridge—

Caleb Dyer is adding one or two blocks to his wharf that is he is extending It further out into the harbour—He commenced building the said wharf in August 1829—

30th Wind very strong E-N-E- with a copious rain—

I ought to have mentioned that on the 25th Brother Samuel C. Griffin, and his wife, left us, and proceeded on towards their home, at Newburgh—

At 5 P.M. this 30th of August It blows almost a hurricane, with rain pouring down in torrents—this Storm is attended with a very full Tide—

David Petty's barn (which is perhaps 90 or 100 years old) blew prostrate, on the ground with this great gale—Noah G. Beebes Sloop drove on to Shelterisland beach—

[429] 31st August 1839—Wind N-W—this morn, and blows pretty quick—

I have one pair[pear] tree, off of which the wind blew yesterday a bushel or more of pairs—

Sept. 1st Sabbath—Wind N-W—A pleasent, comfortable day—

We got Dinner for seven Men, (travillers)

2nd A Foggy Morn—A calm day—Brother James was with us yesterday—

Company training at my house—We got Dinner for thirteen of the trainers—

Some time before this we quit (from principle) selling any kind of intoxicating liquors—We now lament with sorrow, and contrition of heart, that we did not view 20 years ago the trafick in alcoholic Spirits as we do now— What a sea of wretchedness, we should have escaped of being in some respects the means of—May our Father in Heaven forgive us, although in following the custom of those times, we did not conceive the heinousness of dealing out <u>poison</u>, <u>misery</u>, distruction and death—

[430] September 3rd 1839—very little wind through the day—Northern lights this eve

A Mr. Igmire preached at the upper Church this Evening—

Uncle Jared Griffings daughter, Mary, with Brother James, took dinner with us

4th Light wind E—This eve Narcissa set out for NewYork, took passage in the sloop Sarah Brewster—Capt. Sidney R. Racket—

5th Thick, hazy weather—Wind E-S-E—It rained pretty hard for about 40 minutes—

How few good Samaritans have we in this region!—

6th Wind W—Theodore N. Brown, Son to our new Deacon Peter Brown, and grand Son to the late Capt. Christopher Brown, is now keeping a store, on the main road near his Fathers residence—Is doing a small but we believe a safe buisness—He opened his store about 2 years since—

[431] Saturday 7th Septem. 1839—Some rain last night, attended with lightning & Thunder—I am settling the estate of the late Mr. Jonathan Youngs, as one of his Executors—Thomas V. Youngs, the other—

The energies and warmth of my past youth, middle age, sensibly decrease, and the goal of threescore years & ten, point with a brilliant Index to the Solitary house, appointed for all the living—

8th A ground rain this morn, with heavy Thunder—Wind E by S—

Monday 9th Sept. Cloudy, with some little wet—P.M. clears off warm, with wind S—It has been a wet Season—Weeds, have sprung up in great abundance—

10th A pleasant Morn, with wind light W-S-W—Charles Kingly Hobart (son to the late Capt. Henry Hobart) left for N.Y. to day—Intends to go to Sea, as a Sailor, and do his future buisness of life on the mighty waters—Success, and good conduct attend him, in all his voyges, untill he arrives to the Haven of rest

[432] Wednesday 11th Septem. 1839—Cool Morn—Wind W-N-W—

12th Wind N-W—continues cool—

Temperence, has become considerable the order of the day, in this place—A goodly number amongst us, has pledged themselves, to wholly and <u>actually</u>, abstain from the use of any, and every kind of liquor, or liquors, which can, when indulged in, intoxicate—A glorious, and, I believe, a heavenly resolution—Worthy of the best of causes—If we look back a few years, what wretchedness, misery, distress, and poverty Rum, Gin, & Brandy has brought on many families, in this place—Mothers' tears and children's woes, have been sufficient, if it were possible to make Angels weep!—The traffick in these above noticed ingredients, we now begin to see is accursed—Would to God we could have seen It sooner.

[433] 13 Septem. 1839—Wind, E-N-E—Quite a cool day—Lewis Tuthill (Son to the late Mr. David Tuthill) has built himself, a comfortable dwelling house, & barn, this past Summer. His house stands on the southside of the road, a little west of Deacon Wm. S. Hobart—

Capt James Smith, late from N.York, is now building a convenient home on the road leading from Orient or Oysterponds Landing, at the harbour, to the main road—

Last season, Doct. Seth H. Tuthill built his son Lewis a house, just to the westward of the bridge, long known as the dam bridge.

James Winters Sen. is now building a house, opposite the site of Lewis Tuthills, Rocky Point, on the southside of the road, near said Dam Bridge—

4th A cool morn, with a N- wind—12 at noon near calm—Ill with a severe head ache—The seeds of mortality are sown in our wonderful system—they will grow, an[d] in the appointed time burst the shell—

[434] Sabbath 15th Septem. 1839—Wind E-S-E—Clear weather—

Received a letter, from our Sister Mary Hubbard, last eve—Answered this day by the Stage—She is now at Smithtown

16th Light wind W-S-W—Our affectionate Grand daughter, Deziah L. Wells, with a Miss Prince, visited us this very pleasant day, made more delightsome by the presence of this solaceing, pleasant grandchild—

About 4 P.M. It set in raining—It cleared off about 6 P.M.—

17th A Foggy morn—Warm all P.M.

18th Rain, with lightning & Thunder, this morn—In the evening just so—

19th Wind quite brisk from N-W- this morn—The two Glovers—David L & Ezekial N. with their Vessels, started for N.York, this eve

20th A pleasant day—

[435] 21st A calm, mild, pleasant day—Visited this day, by our Son Sidney, & wife—

Sabbath 22nd Wind similar to that of yesterday—Sidney & wife left this morn, for Riverhead—P.M. Blustering—Wind S-W—

If you are angry, count 1000 before you speak—If you can possibly govern yourself, wait a week, with much serious reflection on the shortness of time, before you say any thing relating to the affair or its cause—

23rd What is called fine weather—Wind W-S-W—

24th Wind W- & Cool—Narcissa arrived home from N.York, yesterday—

25th A Shower, last night—This morn Wind N-W—cool—P.M. It dies away to calm—

26th Rained some last night—Today it blows a gale, N-W- by W—

27th High wind S.W—Heard this day of the tradgical death of Mrs. Jemima Morgan, She was murdered by her Husband, last Wednesday [436] night, in NewYork—He was subject to having, pretty often, a drunken frolick—In one of these hellish sprees, he destroyed a tender, and affectionate Mother, an obedient kind, industrious wife—and filial Daughter—

O rum, rum, thou curse of our Country! Thou bane, and <u>besom</u> of distruction! When will thou cease thy devastating poisins, which are more fatal then the <u>Behenupas</u> of Java—

Mrs. Morgan, was the daughter of Mr. Joshua Hobart, and grand daughter of the late Mr. Samuel Hobart, and great grand daughter to the late Mr. Benjamin King, known, through the Town, by the appellation of Uncle Ben—This was from 1774 to 1794—

28th A rain Storm last night—This morn cool N-W- wind—

Sabbath 29th pleasent weather—Wind light, went near round the compass in the course of the day

[437] 30th Wind E-N-E—with a hard rain storm—which continued until near midnight—

Tuesday 1st October 1839 commences with moderate weather—Wind light A.M. N—P.M. S-W-

Disagreed, this day, with Mr. Abner White, respecting a just debt, which he acknowledges he owes me—As he and our Son, Sidney, differs respecting the house, built, by White, for Sidney, White refuses to use me, as he would wish to be used—He has wronged me, and he must see to It—

3rd Wind S-S-W—warm & cloudy

4th More cool—Wind N-W—Our Wind Mill, in going quick, struck George Champlins Horse, with such force, as to break one of the points off some 8 or 10 feet—It will cost severel dollars to repair damages—How the bruised Jade will get along, we are yet to learn—

5th High wind N-E- & cool—

6th So cool that a fire feels comfortable

There may be such a thing, or Spirit, as is disinterested but alas, who posesses It—

[438] 8th Octo. 1839—Calm & warm—

Inconsiderate, and hasty expressions, are pregnant with much foolishness, as well as weakness—Their produce is bitter reflections—

9th A Cloudy, yet moderate day—Our dear daughter, Harriet, visited us—She left us this eve—

Wrote a Letter, to Jeremiah Horton Esq of Orange County—N.Y—Mr. Horton was a resident in this place, in the years 1772- 3 & 1774—It is now forty years, since our last interview—He is a good Man, and a Gentleman, of sterling veracity—

Monday 21st A cool morn—Wind N-W- by W—Frost last night

22nd A large white frost last night—Wind S-E—but very light—

23rd Wind light S-W- by W—

[439] How many useless words do we speak, to one that is useful? A fair question—Echo answers, "How many!"—

24th Smoky, thick weather—Wind W—Wilcox, bought his first coal stove—It cost him 19 Dolls—

James Shenick, a shoe maker, began to work with Wilcox—Yesterday—

25th Fine weather—Wind light N—Capt. Jonathan F. Latham, and his sons Joseph & Elias have sold this day 1000 bushels of potatoes to a Capt. Coe of Connecticut—The sloop is now takeing them in at Dyers wharf—

In Oct. 25th 1739 just 100 years ago, my Father, James Griffing, was born—

Saturday 26th October 1839 A pleasent day, comfortably warm—Very light wind, S-E—

He that says good, and does good in all his actions, and buisness, is assuredly a valuable member of Society—

Sabbath 27th As fine weather as yesterday—

[440] Wrote this 27th Octo. 1839 to our late boarder, Cap'n Seth Baker, of and belonging to Hyanus[Hyannis], State Massachusetts—I some time since received one from him—

28th Foggy, thick weather—Many of our Banks, in these States, are now failing—People, especially our hardworking Farmers, are losing their confidence [in] the soft, light rag money—We have heard our Fathers mention the famous Continental money, 1776 and on—

29th Mild & pleasent weather—Mrs. Griffing, much distressed with a pain in her left Eye—

Wednesday 30th Wind, N-N-W—which brings It cool, and It is the say, that winds are healthy & braseing—

An Eastern Vessel, is at Dyer's dock, supplying the people in this region, with homemade Salt of the first quality—at about 40 Cents

[441] I think It shews lack of prudence, to speak very <u>loud</u>—very <u>earnest</u>—very <u>absolute</u>, to anyone, not hard of hearing—Just so In being too <u>confident</u> of <u>that</u> which is not absolutely certain—

31st Some rain last night—

Friday 1st Novem. 1839 A cool high wind from N-N-W—Rain again last night—John Vail, son to <u>Nath'l Vail</u>, of Riverhead, who was a playmate of mine, in the days of our boyhood, staid with us last night—He, John, is now a travilling merchant—A nephew to my late very dear friend Silas Vail—

2nd cool—Some frost last night—

3rd Wind light N-N-W—of course cold—Mr. Ezra Youngs, preached at our upper Church this day—He is a decendent in a regular line from the Reverend Joshua Youngs, who was the first Preacher, in Southold, about the year 1650—Mr. Youngs, is a Man of Coledge education, yet very moderate, in his movements, doings, and conversation—[442] As a preacher, or pub-lick speaker, <u>he</u>, whom I esteem as a worthy exemplary man, he stands about second to the midling class of your <u>note[d]</u> Ministers—

Monday 4th Novem. 1839. Wind from the N—Ellection at our house for the 31st or 32nd time, since 1809 or 10—Nine, I believe, as I am pretty certain I took out my first Tavern license that year—If so this is the 32nd Ellection, as there was two, or 3 one year, or 2 for two years. About Ninety Votes taken in at our house this day—nearly all of them Democratic—This Orient is all, with the exception of one or two, of that stamp—

5th A cloudy cold morn—Who is there, that has agility, and bottom suf-ficient to keep up with time?—Who, and what can stand against its rav-ages—<u>Pyramids</u>, and <u>Babylonion Walls</u>, fall into crumbling ruins before Its all powerful sway—[443] Then alas! What is Man composed of Flesh, and, but a vapour! A thing that was—Was here—Is gone—gone—gone, forever!

Wednesday 6th November 1839—Last night was a rainy one, with wind S-E—This morn wind W—And cloudy—

7th High winds from W-S-W—Very full tides this some days past—

We are apt to think strange to see a Man, that is worth ten thousand dol-lars, make use of right whale oil, which gives but an indifferent light in his common tin lamp—Oil, with its stench and sediments, costs 37½ Cents— I say we think It strange, that a man of that caliber, should deprive himself of such a necessary comfort, as sweet refined light, which would cost him 75 or 100 Cts per gal'n—But so It is—For the want of a heart, we hug that to us which our avarice will never let us enjoy—Doctor Watts Says (and Its Truth) "He is but a wretch with all his lands that wears a narrow Soul"

[444] 8th Novem. 1839—Narcissa, and Chatham Augustus, (our Son Sidney's first son) left us for Riverhead, this morn—

Mrs. Griffing, is very feeble—Is much distressed with sharp, and accute pains In the ball of her left Eye—Such is her distress, that It strikes her stomach and brings on a pukeing, almost every day, and sometimes 2 or three times a day—

Saturday 9th Wind E-N-E—Some little Flakes of snow this morn—

Sabbath 10th A cold North wind—It blows fresh, or high, or quick, as you please—

Mrs. Griffing, continues quite unwell—Our Sister, Lucretia, is attending with us—

11th Hard frost last night—

12th A large white frost, has with its unsullied, brilliant, but cold mantle, overspread the Earth in our favoured, and highly exalted region—

[445] Married last evening, Deziah Tuthill, youngest daughter of my Sister, Lucinda, the affectionate wife, of Capt. Rufus Tuthill Junr—Deziah, married a Mr. Perkins, who appears to be a worthy, industrious, considerate Man—He is from some part of Connecticut, but perposes to locate in Southold—

13th Pleasant—Wind light from E-S-E—Narcissa arrived home, from Riverhead—Mrs. G- remains unwell—

14th Rain last night—Clears off this morn, with Wind S-W—

15th High wind S-W—P.M. a rain untill 12 midnight—

16th Clear weather—Wind N-W—Rusia Turnips dull at 16 Cts—potatoes 22 Cts

17th Wind high, and cold from S-S-W—

Mrs. Griffing continues very unwell—of course She is unable to go out, much less to attend Church—so I conceive It my duty to tarry at home with her—To know our duty, and do it, is wisdom

[446] Monday 18th Novem. 1839—A high wind from N-W—

Mrs. G- very much distressed this eve—Of late, she has much of the time been familiar with accute pains In her Eyes, which greatly affects the whole System—The Doctors, in attendance, fear, as circumstances are, and continue, She will eventually lose her sight, intirely—

19th Blustering & very high wind, N-W—Butchered our swine, this day—he weighed 310 Lb with the gut fat—

20th The coldest day this season thus far—It has froze in the Sun through the day

21st Continues as cold as yesterday—

22nd Blows from N-W—as It has done this some days—

23rd Wind as Yesterday—and as cold—A day or two since, our Grand daughter, Maria L Prince, was confined with a Son—they name Henry Wells—

[447] Mistake—page 282 ought to have been on this page, & this on that

27th Novem. 1839—This morn wind S-S-W—of course more mild and warmer—

Received a letter, this morn from Jeremiah Horton Esq, an old Friend, once a resident in this place (as I believe I have before observed,) now of Orange County, N-Y—This letter, was in answer to one I wrote him in Oct. last—In mine to him, I requested to be informed respecting those families, and the heads of them, which compose the district, in which I taught school, in the years 1791, 92–93 & 1794—In my Diary, of those dates, I often mention the names of my then Employers—Their marked attention, and affectionate civilities, shown me, while so pleasently situated amongst them—Friend Horton, observes in his answer, that those agreable Fathers, (except himself) were all gone to that bourn whence no traviler returns—The hospitable Mothers were likewise all gone, except one—A Mrs. Ruth Coleman—He says they all died betwixt the years 1815 & 1835—

[448] 24th November 1839—Wind, E-S-E—with a moderate rain—

25th Wind S-E—With a copious rain, with a tempestuous wind—

This day is considered, as a day to be remembered, in the annals of the History of N-Y- City—It was on the 25th of Novem. 1783, the British Army left the City, of NewYork, and repaired to the land of Lord North, and other impolitic advisers of George the Third—We have gained our Independence, and the British Nation, lost their credit, their Colonies, and Milions of Dollars—

26th It blows a gale from N-W—with extreme cold—Wood, at this time with us, at the Dock (oak) is from five to six Dollars—

There is, or has been raised this season, in Orient, and now for sale, from 6 to 8000 bushels potatoes, and near 14000 bushels Turnips—Corn—Rye— Wheat—Oats—Barley etc etc

[449] 28th Novem. 1839 Wind light W—P.M. calm—A large white frost covers the ground this morn—Wilcox left for NewYork, in Smiths Stage—

29th Wind very light all day—Haste, It is said makes waste, howsomever, It wont apply in getting out of the brush, which surrounds you, at the time It is on fire—Its probable we cannot be to much in a hurry in getting out of a bad scrape—No—nor out of hot water—

30th Light E- Wind—Ellection, at our house, to chuse Militia officers, this P.M—

•

Sabbath 1st Decem. 1839—A hard N-E- Wind—Some little rain—It appears to be a Storm of Wind

2nd Wind, continues high from N-E—Man, says Doct. Young, to Man, is the surest Ill— ·

[450] Tuesday 3rd Decem. 1839—It blows a gale from E-N-E—and has continued so since Saturday—

4th A gale—about as yesterday—or more severe—Sea Vessels, many of them will feel Its powerful effects—Alas! And Sailers to—

Ellectionering runs high, at this time—The Federal delegates meet this day at Harisburgh, to nominate a person for their candidate for the Presidency—It will, no doubt be Mr. Clay, or General Harrison—But who will be the President, we are unable to tell, until after Ellection—When a beef is weighed, we know Its weight—

To be over anxious about matters, and things, that are assuredly, at any rate are not to yield us the least benefit in purse, or comfort, shows lack of judgment

[451] Thursday 5th Decem. 1839 comes in with the Wind, Easterly, as It has been this number of days past, but not quite so boistrious—

Some of our old shrewd, hardy Captains who have seen London, and tremendous Gales, on the Mightly deep, observe, with emphasis, that they never knew such a Eurochlydon for five or six days in course, while on shore, dwelling amongst land sharks—

Capt. John Brown (some time Master of the good Ship Douglas,) said the other day that this gale in continence, and power, was certainly worthy of notice—

Rye, & corn, which have been selling, for 6 & 10 Shillings, are now slow Sale at 6 Shillings—

A handsome bow, cost nothing except a little pain if we chance to have a lame back—Politeness, and suavity of manners, are well received, if they are properly timed to those wise, and well bred—

To be silent towards whose whom we don't esteem is wise

[452] Friday 6th Decem. 1839—Wind N.E. but much more moderate, than days past—

Patience is a virtue of the brightest hue to the possessor—It is a treasure that is of more value than gold, and he, or she, is poor who have It not—

Saturday 7th Wind E—Weather thick—Although the wind is very light—It looks, If we may Judge of the weather, by what we call signs, we should say a rain is hatching—

Some people appear always calm, and collected—At the same time, they may be inwardly ruffled, and painfully perturbed, yet they have a particular gift, and faculty, of displaying a serene, composed, and complacent out side-In some, this temper, and disposition appears to be consitutional—Are not such persons fortunate?

[453] Sabbath 8th 1839 A rain storm, with wind E—It has been from that corner for about ten of the last days—Four days of said time It blew a hard, very boistrious gale—As the Sailors of long yarns say, "It blows like ten thousands topsailsheet blocks, all tied up in a piece of spun yarn"—A sentimental Sailors Vocabulary, and his gifted use of It, is a caution, they say to land Sharks—

Monday 9th Decem. 1839—Wind S—Very foggy, of course Its dark thick weather—We had a copious rain from yesterday morn—up to 10 Oclock last eve—this P.M. It Thunders, & rains again—

Politics are the order of the day—Democrats, and Feds, are all exitement—Both appear determined to carry their points—After Ellection it will be known who is King

[454] Tuesday 10th Decem. 1839—Wind high this morn W-N-W—

When the wind shifted, last evening into the W-N-W- about 8 Oclock, It blew a tremendous gale, whose furious puffs, continued to almost prostrate every Tree, & bush in Its course, for near two hours—

This evening, Wilcox arrived home from N.York, with a handsome assortment of Leather—He has now a good Journyman, and appears to be doing some buisness in the Manufactory of Boots, Shoes, Slippers and Brogans—That he may succeed, prosper, and be wise unto Salvation, is our daily prayer—

Our Children, we know, can never find consolation, and permanent tranquility in any situation but those of virtue, and unsullied filial propriety—

[455] Wednesday 11th Decem. 1839—A mild, tranquil, and very pleasent day—

An emblem of a calm, composed, virtuous, resigned, and Sanctified Soul, whose hopes are founded, and built on the Rock of ages—

Thursday 12th A rainy night, and It continued to pour down, untill 10 A.M.—

Capt. Dyer leaves, this day, for Nantucket, with near three Tons of pork—with pigs, poltry etc. etc. etc. etc—This is the Caleb Dyer, mentioned in my Journal of the Summer of 1798 & Decem. 1799—He now owns Five dwelling houses, in this place, (Orient) worth, altogether, about 5000 Dolls—Outhouses, Barns and Shops, worth 1000 dollars—Vessels 2000 Dolls—

Lands, and buildings in Nantucket worth 4000 Dolls—This property, he now possesses—what he is actually worth we know not—

[456] Capt. Dyers present situation, discovers a great contrast, from that he was in, now forty one years since—He was then a boy of 17 years—A shoemaker, on his own hook—sit[t]ing on his bench, singing & whistleing, over his awl, Last, End, and Sole—Then, as he was, Its probable his cares, and anxiety, were a feather, in weight, compared to a Millstone, at this his present time— He knows how It is, and a Stranger ought not to attempt to medle therewith—

Friday 13th A very heavy gale of wind, W-N-W- yet not cold—

Saturday 14th A beautiful pleasent day—Our pleasent daughter Harriet, leaves, this day, for Southold, her home—

[457] Wednesday 18th Decem. 1839—

Wind W-N-W—Extreme cold pinching weather—Midling good Sleighing, with every thing like a Bell, is set a gingleing, to give life & vigor to the ride—

Old Dobbin & lame Roan, feel the affects of the snow, and Katty & Dollys disposition to have a ride—

Thursday 19th Cold—Very severely cold

Auction this day at Mr. Abner Whites, who is now clearing out from Caleb Dyers Farm, down near the Narrow River—C. Dyer, and A. White, have had a quarrel—have Lawed It, and both felt the pains, and penalties of a sad disagreement—White, being poor, suffers, I should suppose, the most—No doubt they are both in fault, and have deviated from the paths of rectitude—That either of them are over punctilious—I doubt—

[458] Sabbath 15th 1839 Rains this morn for an hour or two—It then set in to Snow, with E-N-E—

This eve, we have a tremendous gale of wind—A Capt. Coe, and another gentleman, stoped with us last night—

Monday 16th Wind continues to blow a gale W-N-W—Snow drives into banks—those two men took breakfast with us—

Tuesday 17th Decem. 1839—Wind not so high—yet W-N-W—

Mistake turn back to 291st for the 18th Decem.[?]

Friday 20th Decem. 1839—Extreme cold—Wind N-N-W—

Departed this life, this evening, at 6 OClock Ebenezer Conkling Hedges, aged about 36 years—His native place was Easthampton—He came to this place, (Orient) about Seventeen years ago—[459] With us, all that time, he has sustained an irreproachable character—Industry, prudence, economy, with the most aimable civilities, were conspicuous traits, to adorn all his movements, and buisness, through his brief stay on Earth—

His last Illness, which was long, distressing, and severe, showed him to posess a patience, resignation, and a composure of mind, not inferior to the Holy Man of Uz [Job]—Suffice It to notice this fact, that, Ebenezer Conkling Hedges, was an ornament to society, and an honor to his associates—

Saturday 21st Very severely cold, with good sleighing—wind light N- Sabbath 22nd High wind E—Mr. E.C. Hedges remains were interred this day—

Monday 23rd A Snow storm, which commenced last eve, and continues— 24th Continues Snowing—

25th Mild, and serene everywhere—Good sleighing—Bells tingle

[460] Tuesday 26th Decem. 1839—Light wind E- by N—A cold, moderate day—Sleighs, sleds, & pungs [one-horse sleighs], called in days of yore, Tom Pungs, are flying through our streets, with the haste of an extra express, as though they were carrying the sad news of the declaration of War by Mother Britain, with her American Children—We are happy to say there is no such news—

John B. Youngs (Son of my late, very dear Friend John Youngs*) was married, on the evening of the 24th Just—to Mary, daughter of Deacon Peter, and Phebe Brown, of Orient—

Friday 27th A.M. Cloudy, with wind very light E-S-E—P.M. Wind increased to a gale, with torrents of rain—Tide much higher than common—perhaps, the waters are higher than they have been this 24 years— that is since 1815—A fine little black fish, found Its way up, with the tide, nearly opposite Mr. Vincent Youngs, where It died, and we found It—

Saturday 28th Showers, untill 2 P.M. when It cleared

[461] Sabbath 29th 1839 A gale of wind from S-W- and W—

Died this Evening, Mr. Zilemus Beebe, Son of the late Mr. Silas Beebe, of Plumisland—Mr. Z.B. was about 63 years of age—He sustained the Charracter, (and Justly,) of a peaceable, quiet, Industrious innofensive Man— From some, with whom he had done buisness, he was har[d]ly dealt with, and suffered much—But he is gone to his reward, and they will soon follow where he, and they will see, and know, as they are known—His last moments brightened with strong Faith, and a glorious hope, of a happy immortality—

Monday 30th—Blustering, cold weather—wind N-W- by W—

Tuesday 31st Mr. John Armstrong, a native of Europe, and for some two, or three years past, a Methodist Preacher, on this Circuit, of good standing, and of good report, departed this life, after a few hours illness this morning—He was a mild, sincerely pious, good Man—Instant in season—out of season, [462] reproving with all long suffering, those who

*He was the son of the late Judge Thomas Youngs, of Southold—A man of abilities, integrity, sound Judgement, and an invaluable friend to the poor— Sometime a Representative [page trimmed] State

stand in perishing need of that Grace, without which Man is of all creatures the most miserable—

His age was about 24 years—ripe, we trust, for the shores, and regions of
everlasting Spring, and endless rest—

> Dear Man, a short Farewell, to you 'twas given
> To early reap a rich reward, in Heaven—

The weather is tediously cold—

Thus ends the year one thousand eight hundred thirty nine—Its gone
with those years, which composed the years of Adam, and Noah—
Mathusalalom[sic], and Lot of Zoar—

This Journal, commenced 12th October, or more properly 17th
September, 1800, and has made some notices of my movements, doings,
and remarks, on neighbors, acquaintances, and friends, up to this 31st
Decem. 1839—Being Forty years—A large space in our short existence, and
of the utmost importance to poor, frail, dying, wretched Man—[Griffin had
moved back permanently to Oysterponds in 1800]

1840

(463) 1840 January 1st—Wednesday—a very cold N- wind, with a clear,
or, as they all It a "cloudless sky"

Thursday 2nd Wind N- and intensly cold—

Our Orient Harbour, is fast shut[t]ing in with Its own waters congealed
by the air first cousin to the Frigid Zone—Vegetables at this time with us,
at Orient, are very plenty, and cheap—Wheat 87½ to 100 Cts per bushel—
Potatoes 19 to 25 Cts—Turnips 12½ to 16 Cts etc etc—

Friday 3rd Cold continues—Our harbour closed with Ice—Departed this
life, this evening, Mrs. Maria Tuthill, the wife of Doct. Seth H. Tuthill, after
a long, and distressing Illness, which she submitted to with much patience,
and humble, pious resignation—Aged 48 years—

> Heavens will be done—The Christians path is best
> Tis that which leads us to our long sought rest—

Saturday 4th A light N-W- wind, and as cold as ever

Sabbath 5th Wind W—Our harbour is handsomely closed up with Ice,
and cold continues—

[464] Monday 6th Jan. 1840—Wind W. A cloudy cold day—Narcissa, our daughter, quite sick—Doct. Skinner attends her this day—

Tuesday 7th A W- wind—People, now cross the harbour, to Rockypoint, and longbeach, on the Ice

Wednesday 8th Wind N-N-W—and to a severely freezing point, as our fingers shew, amid the blast without mittens—

This day 25 years ago, Andrew Jackson, was gathering laurels, that will remain fresh, while heroism, and virtuous Liberty are the glory of our republic—

Thursday 9th A cloudless calm day—

Friday 10th Wind W- by N- and a cloudy day—

Saturday 11th Commences with rain, or rather hail, as the rain freezes, as it reaches the Earth—P.M. A snow storm—

[465] Sabbath 12th January 1840 the storm clears off with High wind N-N-W- and as cold as any time within 20 days past—Slaying [sleighing] or sleding is the first role—It is so, says old dobbin, after having been driven 20 miles, in quick time, without stoping, or feeding

Narcissa, continues sick, and attended by Doct. Skinner

This eve, Thom. V. Youngs wife was confined with a Son—

Monday 13th A moderate Snow, with wind W—Wilcox & wife, gone to Southold, in G. Champlins Sleigh

Tuesday 14th Wind light W—With the exception of a day or two, It has been extremely cold since the 15th of Decem. Last—

Wednesday 15th A light N-N-W- wind—P.M. some Snow Squalls—Cold—Cold—

Thursday 16th An intensely cold morn—wind N—

Calvin King, (who has by illness, some no doubt of body, and much of mind) has this day, by his wife, a son born to him, which we hope will prove a blessing—He has not walked the floor, very little, if any, this two years—generally kept his bed—the mind is the Man—

Friday 17th A calm, cold day—

Saturday 18th A tedious N-W- wind—Harbour shut up with Ice, as before said—

S.V. Youngs child died this day—

[466] Sabbath 19th January 1840—Wind N-W—

Monday 20th Wind W-S-W- and warmer than many days past—and yet it freezes through the day

David Terry's (our cousin) wife was confined with a Son, this morn—This Eve, Marcus Brutus Brown was married to Cynthia Taber, daughter of Frederick & Polly Taber—

The act is solemn, Joyful, and divine—
At such a scene, the Waters blushed to wine!
Mildness—Sublimity! Every care was hushed!
And Pots of water, saw their God, and blush'd!

Tuesday 21st Wind S—Of course not so cold—

Wednesday 22nd Wind N-E- with a Snow Storm—About 8 P.M. It commenced a rain Storm—

Thursday 23rd Last night was attended with much rain, and a gale of wind S-S-W—It clears up about one P.M. with a blustering West Wind—This eve, wind hauls to the N. and a gale, with severe cold—

Last Monday 13th Inst. The Steamboat Lexington, bound to Stonington, while off East of Eatons neck, took fire, and out of 111 souls on board, only 3 or 4 were saved—

[467] Friday 24th Wind continues boistrous from N-W—

Saturday 25th A westerly wind, and not quite so freezing—Rec'd a letter, from our affectionate Grand daughter, Deziah Preston—

Sabbath 26th Wind very light W-N-W—Our harbour continues closed with Ice—

Monday 27th Calm & cold—

Tuesday 28th It snows with wind very light E—

Wednesday 29th Foggy, and It thaws some—Our Brother James Griffing, with our kind brotherinlaw, Rufus Tuthill, was with us some time, this day—

Thursday 30th Fog continues, with considerable thaw—Wind S. this eve, with rain—We have now had about 45 days of severe cold weather in succession—It now appears as if a thaw was near

Friday 31st A gale of wind W—not so cold as days past—

Saturday 1st Feb. 1840—A Snow Storm, with a light N-E-wind—A letter from Sidney this eve

Sabbath 2nd A mild day—Snow covers the Earth about 6 inches—good sleding—

Monday 3rd A squally cold day—Sidney & wife, and Augustus with us this eve—

[468] Tuesday 4th Feb. 1840—Amidst the many cold days, and nights we have experienced this winter, and we have had many of them, this may be safely set down, as the coldest—At least, we fully believe so—Wind N-N-W—

Wednesday 5th Very light wind S—Sidney, our Son, with his wife, & son, Augustus, left us for his home, at Riverhead—Weather cold

Thursday 6th South Wind—moderate—

Died, very suddenly, this day, David Brown, Son of John & Phebe Brown, aged 29 years—He was a young man of excellent acquirements in all that is taught in our English, common Schools—He stood in a respectable station as a Schoolteacher—Taken him all in all he merited, and received the most respectful consideration of all who know how to appreciate worth, and merit—He was lecturing in his School 48 hours previous to his death—

Friday 7th A rain storm last night—A clear sky this day, which is the warmest we have had this 50 days past—the Snow goes off rappid—

[469] Saturday 8th A.M. Rain—P.M. Foggy—The travilling, amid the mud & splash, is a caution to the dandy in his silk stockings, and corset vest

Wind S- and light—

Sabbath 9th Very mild & pleasant overhead, but the Earth, in our roads, is carpeted with mud, and more

Monday 10th There is thick fog through the day—

Tuesday 11th clear, & high wind W—more moderate as to frost—

Wednesday 12th A calm day, wind S—Ice in a large body begins to move in our harbour

Thursday 13th Pleasant, and comfortable as to warmth—

Friday 14th Wind E—The Ice, which has blocked up our harbour this 2 or 3 weeks past, has moved pretty much off this day—

Saturday 15th Continues pleasant—about 1 A.M. this morn, we had a short high wind, with Thunder & rain—Rec'd a letter from our Grand Son John A. Preston—

Sabbath 16th wind N-W- & Pleasant—

Monday 17th Pleasant—Wind S-W—

Tuesday 18th Wind E—Cloudy—

[470] Wednesday 19th Feb'y 1840 A foggy morn.

Thursday 20th Wind brisk S—Rec'd a newspaper this day from Doct. George O. Summer, now of Hartford C-t—This gentleman boarded with us in the summer of 1825—In the paper he sends, is a well written piece on our late Soninlaw, James H. Preston, and departed daughter, Deziah—

Friday 21st Wind W- & pleasant—

Saturday 22nd Calm & mild—

Sabbath 23rd A South wind—Pretty brisk P.M.—

Monday 24th A N-W- wind brings cold weather with It—

Tuesday 25th Some Snow this morn and pretty cold—Southgate, a writing Master, with us

Thursday 27th Rains, with wind N-W- moderately through the day—

Friday 28th Pleasent—wind light W—

Saturday 29th Pleasent—This date comes [page trimmed]

[471] Sabbath 1st March 1840—A chilly, unpleasent day

Monday 2nd What is called raw, chily weather Wind S—

Tuesday 3rd A calm, yet a cloudy day—A number of Flatfish, and some other good eatable fish are taken by our neighbour with spears near the wharf this day—Its pretty early, I should say, for such game

Wednesday 4th Very mild, and pleasant—Very little wind, any part of the day—

Thursday 5th A brisk wind N-W—and [?]

McNeil, our Soninlaw, from N.York, with us, this day—Says produce is quite low—Oats 30 Cts—Corn 60—Rye 60—Turnips 20 etc etc—

Friday 6th Wind S-W—more warm than Yesterday—Some thunder last night

Saturday 7th A high, cool N-W—wind

Sabbath 8th As the wind is yet N-W—so it remains cool—

Monday 9th Wind W—and mild—McNeil leaves for New York this day P.M—

[472] Tuesday 10th March 1840 A pleasent day wind S—

Wednesday 11th A blustering cold N- wind—

Thursday 12th A moderate S-W- wind—of course not so cold as yesterday—Narcissa goes to Southold, in the Stage, which stops with us, as It has done this 16 years past—

Friday 13th Snow squalls, with wind N-W—

Saturday 14th A chilly W- wind—Vendue selling articles, formerly belonging to the late Ebenezer C. Hedges—

Sabbath 15th A cool N- wind—John A. Racket, now is owner, and commander of the handsome Sloop William Mitchell, which arrived here from N.York this morn—This is the John A. Racket, who was a boy at my School, in 1818 & 19th mentioned in this Journal 224th page—

Monday 16th It is what people who are buisy in lawful affairs, call fine weather

Saturday 17th a cold Easterly rain storm

[473] Wednesday 18th Wind E—and Pleasent—

Thursday 19th Wind E & cloudy—A Mr. Wheeler, from Stonington, Cow Merchant stoped with us last night—

Friday 20th A hard rainstorm all last night, accompanied with a gale of wind, E—

Saturday 21st Wind, N-N-W- but light—The Mr.Wheeler, above said, leaves this morn for his home—Con't [Conn.]—

This evening, James McNeil, and his wife, our aimable and truly affectionate daughter Cleora, with their 3 surviving Children, arrived to my house from N.York—all well—He has purchased the House, which was formerly owned, and built by Abner Wells, just East of our Congregational meeting house, in Orient—

Sabbath 22nd Wind cold, and high N-N-W—

Monday 23rd Wind E- and cold—McNeil moves into his house this day—

Tuesday 24th It snowed some last night—

Wind E- Cool—P.M. Squally—

[474)] Wednesday 25th March 1840 considerable snow fell last night—Wind N—

Thursday 26th Wind N-W—Cold evenings & mornings—Mrs. Esther Taber, over 90 years of age, is this cold morn hanging out clothes, in order to dry them—It is certainly worth observing—

Friday 27th A fresh S-S-W- wind—and warmer—We are informed that Mr. Hezekiah Jennings, of Sagharbour, died yesterday—

Our neighbour Ezekial N. Glover Junr. had a daughter born to him, this day—They name her Virginia Cook—

Saturday 28th A calm, pleasant day—

Sabbath 29th High wind S- with some rain—

Monday 30th Squally, with rain—P.M. Wind, blows a gale—

Tuesday 31st The gale continues W-N-W—

Wednesday 1st April 1840th Showers all day—Wind E—

[475] Thursday 2nd A cold Northwester—

Friday 3rd Wind high from S-W—

Saturday 4th A.M. It blows a gale S-W—P.M. Its Squally, with wind N-W—Rode to Greenport with George Champlin

Sabbath 5th Blustering weather from N-N-W—

Monday 6th Wind light, N- and Cool—

Tuesday 7th It froze hard last night—A cold N-W- wind this morn—Visited at Southold, and found our dear daughter Harriet, her husband, and Children all well, & glad to see me—

Town Meeting—It was a day of great joy to me, 56 years ago—Then a boy, with my mates—and now where are they? Nearly all gone, never to return—The adults who <u>then</u> composed the multitude, <u>all</u>—all are gone!

Wednesday 8th A cold N-W—blow—McNeil arrived home from N.Y.—

Thursday 9th Weather much as yesterday—

Friday 10th Pleasant A.M. and calm—P.M. A good breeze S-W—

Saturday 11th Warmer than any day this month

Sabbath 12th A rain storm, a pretty hard one—Sidney & his son Augustus, came to us last night—They leave this morn in the Stage—With the Storm, we [page trimmed]

[476] Monday 13th April 1840 Wind N-W-

Tuesday 14th A large white frost this morn—Wind E—Our cousin, and niece, Harriet Wiggins, stops with us this Summer—

Joseph C. Beckwith keeps Dyers House, at the Dock—

Wednesday 15th A calm, pleasant day—Wind, if any, S-E—

Thursday 16th Pleasant—Ploughed a part of my garden—

Friday 17th Wind S-S-W- & hazy—

Saturday 18th Brisk, wind S-W—It is, thus far a backward Spring

Sabbath 19th A wet East wind—

Monday 20th White frost—Wind W—Our set nets have took some fish, within a few days, for the first [time] this Spring—

Tuesday 21st A M. Wind E-N-E- & cool—Visited Brother Rufus Tuthill, & Sister Lucinda—

Wednesday 22nd Cool S-W- wind—

Thursday 23rd Squally, and rain, with S-W- wind—nearly calm this eve—

Friday 24th Calm & warm—

[477] Saturday 25th Apr—1840 Foggy—Christopher M. Tuthill (our cousin) we believe is in a decline—

Sabbath 26th A pleasant day—Narcissa, leaves us this morn for Riverhead—Thunder & lightning this eve, and rain—Wind S-W—

Monday 27th A gale of wind N-W- & cool

Tuesday 28th Wind E—The Jackson Seine took about 4600 Shad yesterday—

Wednesday 29th A Rainstorm with wind E—

Thursday 30th A clear S-W- wind—The Union Seine took about 20000 shad this eve—

Friday May 1st 1840—A fresh wind S-W—Our dear daughter Harriet visited us this day with her little son Walter

Saturday 2nd Wind S-W- Our daughter & grandson left us this P-M-

Sabbath 3rd A pleasent day—Narcissa arrived home from Riverhead—

Monday 4th A cloudy, dark day—

Tuesday 5th Wind N-W—cool—

Wednesday 6th Wind high N-W—

[478] Thursday 7th May 1840. Wind continues hard N-W- as It has done this now 3 days—Wilcox & McNeil leave for New York, in the Sloop Liberator, D.T. Glover Master—

Friday 8th Wind E- by S—more moderate, and pleasant, yet rather cool—

Saturday 9th A hard Easterly rain storm—with now and then snow, & hail—Wind is very high, & powerful—

Sabbath 10th—Quite moderate, this morn, yet some wet, with wind E- by N, and cool—The storm was yesterday certainly powerful, with wind, rain, hail, & Snow—

Monday 11th Clear, with a light wind N-N-W—of course cool—Fruit trees now in their bloom, & perfume—P.M. wind S-E—

Attended as a Jury man, on the body of a Man, found drove on shore, on the north side—We could not tell who he was—

Tuesday 12th A pleasent, mild day—

Wednesday 13th Wind light N—clean weather—Samuel Landons Whaling brig arrived yesterday to Greenport, from whence he sails—

[479] Thursday 14th May 1840—Pleasent—

This day, departed this life, Christopher M. Tuthill, aged about 33 years— He was naturely of a pleasent, good disposition, a likely young man—but he was unfortunate in a strong attachment to company, and ardent Spirit— From such an indulgence, we fear he has now fell Its early victim—

Friday 15th Wind fresh S—Our friend C.M. Tuthills remains were interred this P.M.—"There is no discharge in that war"

Saturday 16th A very Pleasant morn—Last eve, we had a fine Shower— Jackson Seine took this day about 130000 & Union Seine about 200000 fish—

Sabbath 17th A Pleasent fine day—Wind S-W—Wilcox & McNeil arrived home from N.Y.—

Monday 18th Wind fresh S-S-W—

Tuesday 19th Wind brisk E-N-E—

Wednesday 20th Wind E—Our grand daughter Deziah Wells is with us— She is an agreable child, and of much comfort to us—

[480] Thursday 21st May 1840 A hard rain storm, with wind E—

Friday 22nd A heavy rain through all last night—Continues this A.M. with wind E—P.M. Winds lulls to almost a calm—

Saturday 23rd Wind S-W- and pleasant

Sabbath 24th A cool E- wind—

Monday 25th Very little wind S-W—

Tuesday 26th A pleasant morn—Rode today to Riverhead, with Doct. S.H. Tuthill—Found our son Sidney and family well—

Wednesday 27th Returned home this eve—

Thursday 28th very warm, at least much more so than almost any day this Spring—

Friday 29th Wind light W-S-W—

Saturday 30th Clear & warm, Wind E—

Sabbath 31st Springlike weather—

Monday June 1st 1840 Some rain, wind E—

[481] Tuesday 2nd June 1840 Wind E—It has been from that course much of late

Wednesday 3rd—A very chill wind E—about 8 P.M. It commenced a rain storm—

Thursday 4th A severe rain through the past night—It still continues showery, wind E—

Friday 5th Wind S-W—what we call good growing weather—

Our uncle Jared Griffing visited us this day, His age 78 years—He is a man acquainted with many scenes of disappointment, and rever[s]es of fortune, but he murmurs not, appears resigned religiously to his lot, and in an unshaken Faith, awaits the will of his Heavenly Father—I think him a valuable member of Society, and ornament to the Church—

Saturday 6th Calm, & pleasant—P.M. A fresh S-W- wind—

Sabbath 7th A fine rain this morn early, and continued untill 8 P-M—

Monday 8th Wind this morn N-W—Our good Uncle Jared stoped with us last night—left us this morn for his home—Southold—

[482] Departed this life, this morn June 8th Captain James Smith, aged 38 years—He has been a resident of our Orient, about 4 years, leaves a wife, and two children—he had, within 2 years past, built himself a handsome House, cost about 1000, or more, dollars—Was a man, well proportioned, of 6 feet—In short he was a handsome, pleasant, well informed, useful, buisness, and we think an honest Man—To appearance, he was cut off in his full strength, as his <u>illness</u>, with which he died, was of but 2 or 3 days duration—

Tuesday 9th A fine time for grass, if showers & Shines will produce It—

Wednesday 10th Warm, and growing weather

Thursday 11th Wind light S-S-W—I have now kept store about 40 years—I am now winding up—Those few who now trade with me are, many of those few, grandchildren to my first customers—

Friday 12th Pleasant morn—Wind light W—

[483] Saturday 13th June 1840 Pleasant—Rec'd a letter from our Grand daughter Deziah Preston—She is an endearing grand daughter—

Sabbath 14th Wind W-N-W—very comfortable as to warmth—P.M. Wind N-W—

Monday 15th Some rain—not much—

Tuesday 16th Wind W—I went to Longbeach and got 32 Gulls Eggs—

Mr. McFarlin took dinner with us—This Gentleman boarded with us some weeks two years ago—

Wednesday 17th Wind W—Pleasant—Our two Seines Jackson & Union, have taken together about 900000 little shad up to this date—

Sidney, his wife & 3 children- daughters- with us this eve—

Thursday 18th Brisk wind W—McFarlin with us—Went with Sidney & Wilcox a blackfishing this P.M.—

Friday 19th fine rain this morn untill 8 A.M., when it clears with wind N-W—Rode to Greenport, and dined at Capt. Clarks

[484] Saturday 20th June 1840 Showers untill one P.M.—A Show of wild beasts at Greenport—

Sabbath 21st Cool wind N.W—Our Sidney & his family left this morn for Riverhead—

Monday 22nd Warm, with but little wind W-S-W—Wilcox & McFarlin went to longbeach, got 7 Gulls Eggs—

Tuesday 23rd light wind S—Gurdon Vail, of Southold, cut his throat a day or two since—not yet dead—but It is thought It will be a fatal wound—He has been an industrious, harmless young man, but much given of late to gloomy turns—

Wednesday 24th Fresh breeze wind W-S-W—

Thursday 25th Vincent Youngs daughter Polly, now Mrs. King, was confined with a Son—her 2nd child—yesterday, the child was born—P.M. Wind E-N-E—

G. Vail died this day 25th

Friday 26th Wind N-E—

Saturday 27th High wind E—

[485] Sabbath 28th June 1840 A warm day, wind S-W- by W—

Monday 29th Fresh wind W-S-W—Our grand daughter Maria Prince, with her good Husband, with their little Harry, with them

Tuesday 30th Very warm—

Wednesday 1st July 1848 [*sic*] Capt. Rufus Tuthill came to my house this day in a one horse waggen, which he drove himself—he is now about 94 years of age—

Thursday 2nd Not uncomfortably warm—Wind S.W.—Rec'd a letter from our Grandson John A Preston, now at Ashford- Con't[Conn.]—

Friday 3rd July—A moderate rain—

Saturday 4th July, roars of Cannon ushers in this day, conspicuous in the history of our country—Wind S-E—

Sabbath 5th A Pleasant day

Monday 6th Wind E-S-E—

Tuesday 7th A moderate rain—

Wednesday 8th Rain this Evening—Narcissa, and our grand daughter Deziah Wells went to Sagharbour today, and returned this eve

[486] Thursday July 9th 1840—Some rain, with a S- wind—Clears off about 10 A.M.—18 Connecticut young folks took breakfast with us this morn—They left us about 12 noon—

Friday 10th A N-W wind—As yet, thus far we have had but little very warm weather—

Saturday 11th A bright, pleasant day

Sabbath 12th A light wind S-W- and pleasant—Rec'd a letter from our Grand daughter Deziah Preston—A solace indeed to us

Monday 13th Some little rain, hardly sufficient to assist vegetation—

Tuesday 14th A pleasant S-S-W- wind—

Wednesday 15th—This may be set down for a warm day—An Exhibition of shows, In the lot before Aviah Young's door, under a large Canopy, this P.M. and Evening—

Thursday 16th A pleasant S. Wind—Richard W. Smith Esquire stops with us—Is now takeing a census of the inhabitants of our County—Suffolk—very warm

Friday 17th More comfortable as to heat—Wind S-W—Mr. Smith leaves this eve—

[487] Saturday 18th July wind S-W—with some light showers

Sabbath 19th What is called a <u>close</u>, warm day—A W-S-W wind—Towards evening a refreshing Shower—It was much needed—

Monday 20th An invigorating light N-W wind—Wilcox, McFarlin,

and Narcissa, gone to Shelterisland, in pursuit of Cherries—Returned
minus

Tuesday 21st Actually pleasant, with a light wind W—

Wednesday 22nd It grows warmer than some days last—Wind S—Our
Friend Capt. Rufus Tuthill with us, an hour or so—is smart—Sang us a
hymn—is 94 years of age—

Thursday 23rd Continues quite warm—Mr. McFarlin, caught 160 blue
fish, in company with a Mr. Rumrell—

Friday 24th A high S- wind, accompanied with much rain—It subsides
at 10 A.M.—Brother Samuel C. Griffing, with us, from Newburgh—Hewlett
Smith and his wife stoped a few minutes with us—

[488] Saturday 25th July 1840 A pleasent N- wind A.M. This P.M. It is S-
and warm—Brother James, dined with us—

Sabbath 26th A clear sky—wind S-W- by S—

Monday 27th Very little wind the day, which is a warm one—

Tuesday 28th A lively breeze, from W-S-W—

Wednesday 29th Wind W- by S—warm—

Friday 31st A smoky, warm day—Wind S-E- by S—Wm. H. Ellis, Collector
of the port of N.Haven, and Genl. Henman, took breakfast with us this morn

Saturday, August 1st, 1840 Commences with a Flood of rain—It appeared
to come down in torrents—P.M. It clears, with a light N. wind—A Son of
my Friend, Thom. H. Genin, visits us this day—He is from his Fathers, who
lives at St. Clares Ville, State of Ohio—

Sabbath 2nd Some small showers untill 3 P.M.—Our dear Harriet, with
her husband, Abner Wells, with their son Walter, visit us this day—

[489] Monday 3rd August 1840 A warm S- wind—It is not common to
have the wind from that course, any length of time without producing hot
weather—P-M- A Shower—

Wilcox, and the young Mr. Genin went a blackfishing, and took a small
mess—

Tuesday 4th Brisk wind S-W- by W—Clear, this morn—Last night we
had Rain, with Thunder & lightning—

Young Genin is takeing a miniature likeness of Sidney P. Racket, who is
now Master of the good Sloop Motto—

Wednesday 5th A warm S- Wind—Mr. Wm. McFarlin leaves us, for
Montauk, on a fishing Excursion—

Wilcox, Narcissa,and Harriet Wiggins, visited ShelterIsland, after blackberries—Returned with but few—

Thursday 6th Clear, fresh breeze, wind W—for some weeks past It has been, almost continually, rather uncomfortable warm—

Friday 7th A clever rain last night—This morn, a refreshing breeze, W. by N—

This eve, at about 8 P.M. Honora was confined with a daughter—

[490] Saturday 8th August 1840—A calm, & clear day—

Sabbath 9th Wind, fresh, W-N-W- and braceing, as Its cooler—

Monday 10th As pleasent, as yesterday, with wind from the same point—

Tuesday 11th A S-West wind—Politics run high in these days—As the Presidential Ellection is approaching—Harrison and Vanburen (t[w]o opposites) are now the order of the day—

Wednesday 12th A rain last night—

Thursday 13th Very hard Thunder last night, with Thunder & lightning— A rainy day, this may be set down for

Friday 14th It rained nearly all last night—A wet time—Sidney (our Son) with his son Augustus, with us last night—left us this morn—

Saturday 15th A fine clear, refreshing wind N—John A. Racket is now owner and Master of the handsome Sloop Wm Mitchel—This was the boy mentioned in my Diary of 1818 & 19—

[491] Sabbath 16th August 1840 Fine weather—Wind light W-N-W— Our youngest Brother Saml. C. Griffing left us for Newburgh, his residence Hazard Brown, Son to the late Richard Brown, called on us, with his Wife— He is now a resident of Newburgh—

Monday 17th A calm day—

Tuesday 18th Yesterday, and today, is, and has been t[w]o very close warm days

Wednesday 19th As warm as yesterday—John A. Racket, and his wife, are now sitting to our young Friend, Genin, for their Portraits—or as we say, for their likenesses—

Thursday 20th Extremely warm, and calm—Elias Beebe, Son to the late Joseph Beebe, Fell from the Masthead of the Sloop Wm. Henry while on passage from N.York, and was almost instantly killed—As he survived the fall but an hour or two—This calamity took place on Monday, 17th just off Lloydsneck— He was 17 years of age. and the youngest Son of his widowed Mother—

[492] Friday August 21st 1840 As warm a day as any this month— Thermometer stands at 1 P.M. at 90—

Saturday 22nd A moderate wind S-S-W—Mr. Genin gone to EastHampton, today—Sidney & Chatham visited us this eve—

Sabbath 23rd Wind S-W—

Monday 24th A sweet breeze to fan us this morn N—A shower last night with Thunder & lightning

Tuesday 25th A gentle wind W-N-W—Sidney & Chatham left us this morn for their home, at Riverhead—

Wednesday 26th Pleasant, wind N—P.M. wind S—

Thursday 27th A still, or as we say, a calm day—Just passed my door, in a waggon alone, Capt. Rufus Tuthill, the Elder—

Friday 28th wind E-S-E—

Saturday 29th Wind S-E- by S—Our Jackson Seine took last evening about 60 or 70000 fish—

[493] Sabbath 30th August 1840 A moderate E-by S wind—

Monday 31st Some little showers—With Mrs. Griffing, went to Southold—Stop the night at Wells's, with our dear Harriet & family—

Tuesday 1st September 1840—Wind light N-W- by W—Christopher Williams & Mr. Willetts stoped with us the night—We arrived home from S-hold just at Sundown—

Wednesday 2nd Sept—A Squally day, wind S-S-W—Williams & Willets left us this day for N.York—

Thursday 3rd Some rain last night—Wind, this morn, light from the North—

Friday 4th A.M. wind N-E—P.M. S—

Saturday 5th An E-S-E- rainstorm

Sabbath 6th Clears off about 10 A.M. with wind W—

Monday 7th A.M. wind N-W—Training day, that is company training

Tuesday with Wind S-W—Our cousin Wm. H. Griffing with us—

Wednesday 9th Some little rain—Wind S-W—Capt David P. Glover lost a child 13 months old on 4th Inst—

[494] Thursday 10th Sept. 1840 Some little rain today—Cousin Wm. H. Griffing stoped with us last night—left this morn for Guilford his home

Friday 11th Wind, N-W- by W—Some rain last night—

Saturday 12th Last night we had a smart rain, attended with Thunder, and Lightning—Wind this morn N-W—

Sabbath 13th—Wind continues N-W—moderate

Tuesday 15th Wind light W—Dyer, is building another block to his wharf—This wharf was commenced in August 1829, is (in my opinion) something like the house, which the Man built on the sand—not well founded—

Wednesday 16th A small wind S-W—Lewis Edwards Vendues his things

this day—He has made a failure in takeing Dyers House at the landing—
Edwards by the undertaking has realized a loss of near 500, or more
Dollars—And yet, we believe him an honest, fine man—Not the first that
has been woefully deceived—

Our daughter, Margaret [Sidney's wife], and her two daughters visited us
this Eve—

[495] Thursday 24th Sept. 1840 Very still day & pleasant

Friday 25th Wind, light E—

Saturday 26th Warm, and yet pleasant—

Sabbath 27th A moderate S. Wind—Brother James dined with us—He is
a son of consolation—

Monday 28th Rain last night—clear this morn—wind N-W—

Tuesday 29th A pleasant day, for a great Democratic meeting at
Greenport, which is to be attended, by some conspicuous Men—Hon. Eli
Moore, and etc. etc. are to be there—

Wednesday 30th Wind S-W—Pretty warm—

Thursday 1st Oct. 1840 A lowry dark day—Gen'l Training at Riverhead—
Our G—son Chatham visited us this eve—

Friday 2nd Wind E-N-E- And a cloudy day

Saturday 3rd A fresh breeze from S-S-W—Some rain last night—

Sabbath 4th Wind pretty high S-W—

Monday 5th Wind S-S-W- and Pleasant—

Tuesday 6th Wind very light S—Wm. Webb arrived home from Mobile,
this morn—He has been away [page trimmed]

[496] Wednesday 7th Oct. 1840 Wind light N-N-W—P.M. wind hauls to
S-S-E—and pretty brisk

Thursday 8th Dry, and warm—Wind light S-S-W—Corn, with our
Farmers, comes in well this Autumn, and is earlier than common—

John A. Racket sails this day, in his good Sloop Mitchel, for
Appa[la]chicolla, where he expects to spend the Winter—I think him a
decided, generous, noble minded young Man—Thus far, such respectful
consideration I deem my duty to cultivate—

Friday 9th Wind S-W—

Saturday 10th Fine, pleasant day—Wind S-E—Yesterday, our very affectionate Daughter Harriet L Wells and her daughter Deziah, came to visit
us—They returned to Southold this eve—

This eve, Augustus (Sidneys Son) came to us, in the Stage—

Sabbath 11th High wind W—P.M. squally, with wind N-N-W—

Monday 12th—Wind W—

Tuesday 13th Wind N-N-W—and cool—This morn John B. Youngs, and Peter W. Tuthill, had each of them [page trimmed]

[497] Wednesday 14th Brisk wind S-W—

Thursday 15th A fine bright day—wind S-S-W—

Friday 18th Cool wind N-N-W—This eve quite cold, more so than any previous one this autumn—

Saturday 17th Black & white frosts show their force this morn—<u>Our mercies are numerous</u>

Sabbath 18th A cold E- wind—

Monday 19th—Moderate day—

Tuesday 20th A Rainy day, with wind S—

Wednesday 21st—It rained through the night and all this day—A wet Autumn, the old Indians say betoken a hard Winter to follow—

Thursday 22nd After the two last days of almost incessant rain, It clears off this A.M. at 10, with wind N-W—

This eve, our dear Grand daughter, Deziah Preston, arrived at our house, a timely welcome guest—The time she has been from us is near two years, in Connecticut—

Friday 23rd High wind, W- & cool—

Saturday 24th A cloudy, blustering day, Wind N-W—McNeil and his D. Betsey leave for N.Y.—

[498] Sabbath 25th Oct. 1840 A cool N- wind—Wilcox, leaves for N.Y. this morn—Our Grand sons, who have been with us on a visit, Chatham & Augustus, go with W. in the Stage, as far as Riverhead—

Monday 26th A hard thunder shower last night—clear this morn with a gale of wind S-W—

Tuesday 27th moderate wind S-W—

Wednesday 28th A Squally day untill 2 P.M.—after which It moderates—

Thursday 29th Rain with wind E—P.M. very squally—

Friday 30th A hard rain all last night—

Saturday 31st A cloudy damp day—wind N—Wilcox arrived home from N. York—

Sabbath 1st Novem. 1840 A cloudy day, with wind E—

Monday 2nd Wind E-N-E—

Tuesday 3rd Wind continues E—

Wednesday 4th Wind as yesterday—This day closes our Ellection in this State [page trimmed]

[499] Thursday 5th Novem. 1840 A cool wind N. with heavy looking clouds—

Friday 6th Wind N—Very full tides—

Saturday 7th A boistrious North wind, from which course It has come this week past—

Sabbath 8th Some rain,with a tedious blow from the point, It has blown this some days—

Monday 9th Squals, with rain, and wind N-N-W—

Tuesday 10th A rain storm in earnest—Through the intire last night, until 5 this A.M.—with wind N—This P.M. It blows a gale N-N-W—with a very full tide—

Wednesday 11th The gale continues, with much power—The Tides has been very full this ten days past—but the one today exceeds any of them by a foot—

The excitement is <u>great</u>, just now as to the result of the Ellection, which has just closed—It will soon be known, and the unreasonable anxiety over—

Thursday 12th Rain last night, with wind E—The waters & tide came up to Champlins door yard gate—

[500] Friday 13th Novem. 1840—The boistrious gales, which have been tremendous this 10 days a gone, have, in some measure, spent their strength, and now come mild from the W-S-W—

Saturday 14th Wind light S-W—Northern lights bright this eve—

Sabbath 15th A rain storm, all last night—It clears up this morn, with wind N-W- by W—

Monday 16th Light wind W—Put a new pump into my well, this day—

Tuesday 17th Very mild day, more to be appreciated, as we lately had so much rough weather—

Wednesday 18th Very light wind N—with Snow through the day—The first Sled with a Man in It, passed our house this day—This Season—Butchered my pork this 18th—

Thursday 19th A real snow storm, or as we might say a driving one, as the N-W- gale blows the snow up on huge banks—A large snow storm for so early—a little uncommon—

[501] Friday 20th Wind N-W- by W—with cool weather, and plenty of snow—My hog weighed 300 Lbs—Mine of last year weighed about the same—

Saturday 21st Wind light W—It freezes hard

Sabbath 22nd Wind E-S-E—A damp unpleasent day—Last Wednesday 18th departed this life Capt. Daniel Harris, aged 82 years—Of Greenport—In his dealings and intercourse with his fellow Man, he has sustained the carracter of an upright, honest Man—He was all the Father, husband, and Friend, and last, not least, a Christian—

Monday 23rd Last night was one of a steady rain—And this day is a misty wet day—Little wind from N-E—

A Mr. Pedlar Ward, with 2 horses, stoped with us the night—

Tuesday 24th Wind W—G. Champlin goes to N.York this day after goods—

Wednesday 25th A calm day—Rev'd Jonathan Robertson, formerly our preacher, in this place dined with us—he is now about 87 years—

Thursday 26th Still continues calm—It rained much last night—

[502] Friday 27th Novem. 1840 Rain, & hail, a part of last night—Clears this morn with a gale of wind N-W-W—with a freezing cold time—

Saturday 28th—A very cold night, the last one—Wind S- this morn—

Sabbath 29th More Pleasent, and mild—

Monday 30th A.M. High wind S-S-W—P.M. It blows a gale—

Tuesday 1st December 1840—The winds force of last eve, has much abated—P.M. calm, and cloudy—

Our Farmers, in Orient, are now Shiping of their produce for market—

Wednesday 2nd A light wind W—White frost this morn, a large one—Sidney and wife, our daughter Harriet, & Walter her son all with us this P.M. and we were glad to see them—The first is our oldest, and first born child and the last the youngest—

[503] Thursday 3rd Decem. 1840—Wind light, S—P.M. cold and blustering—

Friday 4th Wind N—Cloudy—Harriet and Walter returned home—

Saturday 5th It is a driving snow this morn, untill 10 A.M. after which It continued blustering through the day—Sidney & Wife left this P.M. for A. Wells in Southold—

Sabbath 6th A tremendous Snow Storm, equal to any we have experienced this 2 or perhaps 3 winters past—

Monday 7th Wind N- & cool—The Snow of Yester drives into banks, which obstruct the travilling very much—

Tuesday 8th A calm, cloudy, cold day—A Mr. Spencer, writing Master, stoped with us this night—

Wednesday 9th Wind light W—A smoky day—

Thursday 10th A.M. Wind S-W—The large banks of Snow appear to dissolve before the S- Wind which commences this P.M.

Friday 11th Wind more brisk W-N-W—Not very cold

Saturday 12th A mild S- wind—[?] my two pigs within a day or to since amount of both about [page trimmed]

[504] Sabbath 13th Decem. 1840 A South wind, and rain storm—

Monday 14th The warmest, and mildest day we have known this 50 days past—

Tuesday 15th As pleasent as yesterday with a very light S. Wind—Bought the first coal I ever purchased, this day ½ ton 3 Dolls & 50 Cts

Wednesday 16th A cloudy, calm day—

Thursday 17th A.M. very mild & pleasant—P.M. Snow squalls—

Friday 18th Very blustering, with squalls of Snow, and cold—

Saturday 19th Cold—very cold, with high wind N-W—Spencer has been with us this some days, instructing in writing—a number of our Young Men & Women—He rode out to Southold this eve—

Sabbath 20th Wind N-W- with clouds & cold—

Monday 21st Very cold & blustering—Mr. Spencer returned this eve—

Joseph Latham, a small Farmer, here, has raised this season 1400 or 1500 bushels of potatoes & turnips, with Beans, and other vegetables—

[505] Tuesday 22nd Decem. 1840 A.M. some Snow—P.M. Wind S—damp & chilly—

Wednesday 23rd Very squally with wind W- and cold—

Thursday 24th Wind S-W- and as high as yesterday

Friday 25th 1840 years since the Christian era commenced—

Saturday 26th A Snow storm with wind S-E—Mr. Waldo, a teacher in the Academy, at Southold, stoped with us last night—

Sabbath 27th Very Freezing time—Mr. Waldo left us this P.M.—

Monday 28th Wind W—continues cold—

Tuesday 29th Calm & cloudy—

Wednesday 30th Moderate—but cloudy—Wind light S—

Thursday 31st A cold N- wind—McNeil left for N.York in the Stage this morn—He thinks some of staying the winter—Howsomever Its doubtful, as he for the last 10 years his movements has been many, and not advantageous—Unpleasent for a pleasent [page trimmed]

1841

[506] Friday January 1st 1841 commences with a N-E- Snowstorm—Our friend, Benjamin Clark of Rockypoint, has his Sloop on the Rocks, at or near Blackrock—She is loaded with oats, Beans, turnips & potatoes—chiefly owned by Capt. J. Latham, and Earthenware, of Austin Hempstead, all of which said cargo will probably be lost—

This evening It sets in a hard rainstorm with a heavy gale of wind—

Saturday 2nd Wind W- and very quick—The writing Master, Mr. Spencer, left us this morn—

Sabbath 3rd Moderate, but very cold—

Monday 4th High wind N—Extreme cold this eve—

Tuesday 5th This morn, our harbour is froze 50 rods out from the shore, Wind A.M.—P.M. East by N—Doct. Skinner attended on Narcissa as she is quite ill—He has been to her 3 times within 10 days—

Wednesday 6th A.M. Some rain—P.M. foggy—[?] Jason King[?] [page trimmed]

[507] Thursday 7th January 1841 Some rain, with a heavy fog, and a S-wind—Of course a thaw—Nrs. G- and Narcissa, both quite unwell—

Friday 8th The S- wind continues to increase the thaw—

Saturday 9th A calm day—If any little wind, Its from the E—Ezekial N. Glover, in the Dan.Webster Sloop, sails for N.York, with a load of Sauce this day—

Sabbath 10th A hazy, warm day—David T. Glover in the Sloop Liberator, sails for N.York, with a load of vegetables—

Monday 11th Moderate weather—

Tuesday 12th A clear day, with a fresh Westerly W—A great freshet in the Sound—A part of a house has dove on shore, at Lathams at the point, with some furniture in It—Some loses, while others find—

Wednesday 13th A snowstorm with wind E—

Thursday 14th A cloudy, cold day, with light wind—

Friday 15th wind N—but very light, with some Sprinkle of rain—7 couple of Young Women and Men, have gone a riding to Riverhead, on Sleighs—

[508] Saturday 16th A very still, or calm day, yet a cloudy, dark one—People are now in earnest in the sleding line—Old Dobbin appears not to relish such glee, as arrises from such haste in moving night & day to the tune of many bells—

We have just got the news, that Thaddeus Hobart is lately drowned, on his passage from Gibralter to N.York—He was the Son of Capt. Henry Hobart of this place, who died at Sea about the year 1831—

Sabbath 17th A rain Storm, with wind S—It rained copiously until 10 P.M. when It cleared up with wind N-W—

Monday 18th A clear, and midling cold day—The freshets, in This—Connecticut, and Pennsylvania, have, we hear, done immense damage—A great loss of Property—and some lives—

Tuesday 19th A flattening, still day—

Wednesday 20th Some Snow fell last night—Wind this morn N—

Thursday 21st Snow last night untill one this morn, when It commenced a hard rain untill 9 A.M. when It clears, with wind N—

[509] Friday 22nd Snow again this morn, in a small quantity—It clears again with wind N-N-W—

Saturday 23rd Cloudy—cold, with light N- wind—A little flurey of snow, this day—Abner Wells with us an hour or two—

Sabbath 24th A moderately cold day, just enough to freeze out of the Sun, all day—Wind N—Seth B. Tabers little daughter, Ellen Gertrude, aged nearly 4 years, died this day—

> A pleasant rose—cropped in the bloom—
> To sweeter blush beyond the Tomb—

Monday 25th A very mild pleasant day—Wind S—

Tuesday 26th Very mild weather—A light snow fell last night—

Wednesday 27th A.M. Rain, with wind W—

Thursday 28th A copious white frost covers the Earth this morn—A pleasant day—Our daughter Cleora sets off for N.York this day—She goes in the Stage—

Friday 29th A damp E- wind—rather uncomfortable—At one P.M. It snows—At 3 P.M. It sets into rain & hail—About 10 P.M. It stoped—

[510] Saturday 30th January 1841 What is termed sour, raw weather, Wind W—

Sabbath 31st A clear sky, with high wind, W-S-W—not very cold—

Monday 1st Feb. 1841 A very light wind from E—Mr. Lewis Edwards lost his only child, an infant, last evening, with inflammation on the lungs—She was about 4 months old—

> O what a change, from Earths dark scenes to rise,
> And live a Cherub in celestial Skies—

It snowed, hailed, and rained considerable this night—

Tuesday 2nd A clear cold Northeaster—

Wednesday 3rd A high S-S-W- wind—Rec'd two letters, from my two grand Sons, Chatham A. & Augustus R. Griffin—Riverhead—

May Gods blessing rest upon—If It does, they will be invaluable to themselves, their friends and the world—

Thursday 4th Cool wind W—

Friday 5th Pleasent for winter—light wind E—Sidney P. Racket sails for N.Y.—

[511] Saturday 6th Feb. 1841 Some little snow, but not sufficient to track a gander—The goose, they say—Wind light W—

Sabbath 7th A cloudy, damp, dark day, and emblem of a beclouded, disturbed mind—Wind W—

Monday 8th Rather uncomfortable cold, with Wind N—Auction at the house of the late Capt. James Smiths this day—

Tuesday 9th Dark, damp, chilly day—Northern lights bright last eve—A Mr. Samuel Fenner, from Hartford, stoped with us last night—Mr. Paul Case from Cutchogue, here an hour or so, this day—He professes strong Faith, and great Charity—

Wednesday 10th Considerable Snow fell last, as with Its unsullied garb the Earth richly clothed this morn—Wind N-W- & cold as my unmittened fingers would say—

Thursday 11th Cold increases with a sharp N-W—Sleding pretty good—But tedious to old roan—

Friday 12th Continuously freezing at all points, wind W—

Saturday 13th Very cold for a S-W- wind—As It is excellent sleding, Its up and ride—

Sabbath 14th A light N-E- wind—and cold—

[512] Monday 15th As cold, and as tedious a morn as any one this past winter—Wind high N—

Tuesday 16th Wind W—rather moderated as to the intense cold of yesterday—

Mrs. Griffing is very much distressed, with accute pains in her Eyes—She has been a distressed person much of the passed winter, thus far—What will be the result, our Heavenly [Father] only knows—

Wednesday 17th What is called, by those who observe the weather, a flattening day—Wind, in the course of the day, has been from almost every point—

Thursday 18th A cold N- wind—Cleora returned from N.Y. last eve, in the Stage—

A letter this day, from my G- son A. R. Griffing—he is aged about 7 or 8 years—P.M. Wind S-E-

Friday 19th Cloudy—wind S-W-W—

Saturday 20th A cold brisk wind N-W- By W—

Sabbath 21st Morn light wind S-W—P.M. calm—

Monday 22nd A.M. wind, E-N-E—P.M. clear [page trimmed]

[513] Tuesday 23rd Feb. 1841 Very squally with wind N W- and cold evening—

Wednesday 24th Wind light from N—at a freezing point—

Thursday 25th Mrs. Griffing continues very distressed—My heart bleeds for her deep affliction—If but her finger akes It pains my heart—but our duty is to be resigned—but without great Grace, that is impossible—

Mr. Joshua Hobart died last Wednesday—The remains are intered this day beside his wifes—She died some years since—She Mehitable was a pious good Woman, as we believe Joshua, the Husband to have been a well meaning Man

Friday 26th A mild, fine day—

Saturday 27th A South wind, with rain, & fog—

John Gregory, a man of about 51 years of age, who came to this place, some 4 or 5 years since, we learn just now was drowned, from on board of Sloop Wm. Mitchel (John A. Racket Master) in the harbour of Appalachacola, 3 or 4 weeks ago—Mr. Gregory, we understand has a wife & children near New Haven—He was an uncommon ingenious Man in almost any common buisness, but unfortunately imprudent in indulgeing an inclination to use ardent spirit—

[514] Sabbath 28th Feb. 1841 A brisk S-W- wind and clear—My wife appears some better—May God make me thankful for such a favour—

Monday March 1st 1841. Wind S-W—

Tuesday 2nd Cleora, our daughter, leaves us this day, with her family, and effects, to join her Husband in N.York, as again for the 3rd or 4th time he purposes to locate there again—To some, this appears to be a changeing world, or they often change in It—

Wednesday 3rd Wind E—P.M. calm—

Thursday 4th A cold N-W- wind—It froze very hard last night—

Friday 5th Continues severe, with N-W- wind—

Saturday A blustering E- wind—P.M. It snows untill night when It commenced a smart rain, with a gale from S—

Sabbath 7th clear, and severe gale, so much as to carry the Mill sufficient to ground well without any sails—This is not common—[page trimmed]

[515] Tuesday 9th March 1841 Wind N-W- by W—This eve, our Son Sidney visited us, with his wife—

Wednesday 10th A cloudy and a calm day—Sidney & wife left this morn—It snows this P.M.

Thursday 11th A real blow fromW-N-W- but not so cold as to keep the snow sufficient for sleding untill night—

Capt. Abraham King, lost an aimable, and promising son, last Tuesday, with the Scarlet Fever, his age about 6 years—This is the 2nd Son he has lost in the course of the 3 last years—both about the same age—

Friday 12th A cloudy, unpleasant day—wind E—

Saturday 13th At 12 midnight It commenced a Snowstorm—At 2 A.M. It changed to a tremendous rain with wind as violent untill 2 P.M. when It partially subsided—Evening It snows on

Sabbath 14th A cool, brisk wind W—

Monday 15th It makes Ice, in the sun, all day—of course It is very cold—

Tuesday 16th Wind high N-E- and a real Snow Storm

Wednesday 17th A piercing Clear N-N-W- wind, cold

[516] Thursday 18th Very blustering, and cold—A.M. Rain, & hail—

Friday 19th Wind N-E- A.M. P.M. It comes into the S-S-W- and moderates—

Saturday 20th A mild, pleasant day, more so than many past ones— P.M. calm

Sabbath 21st Wind S-W—moderate—

Monday 22nd A.M. wind S—P.M. S-E—Some part of this day It blew near a hurricane—Absalom King lost, this day his only remaining Son, with the Scarlet fever—aged about 2 years—This was the only remaining child—

Wednesday 24th A light wind S-S-W—and mild—

Thursday 25th Wind S- and warm—

Friday 26th Wind S-S-W- and a gale—

Saturday 27th March like weather—John A. Preston, & his uncle Silas arrived at our house—

Sabbath 28th A cloudy day—[page trimmed]

[517] Tuesday 30th March 1841 A cold E- wind—Vendue at our late son-in-laws house—J.H. Preston—

Wednesday 31st clear, calm, & pretty cold—

Thursday 1st April 1841 A storm of rain—Silas Preston left for his home Ashford C-t—

Friday 2nd A still, or calm day—just at Night wind S—and rain & thunder this eve

Saturday 3rd A blow from N-W—Eve It dies away to a calm—

Sabbath 4th A light wind S—Hubbard Paine & Mr. Waldo, with E.F. Carpenter, with us some time this day—

Monday 5th A storm of rain, with wind S-W—

Tuesday 6th Rain last night again—A clear & Pleasent day this—

Wednesday 7th A rain pretty much through the day—wind S—

News just arrived that President Harrison is dead—He took the oath of office about 4 weeks ago—Alas! What is Man, but a creature of an hour, or of yesterday—

[?]pleasing S wind—[page trimmed]

[518] Friday 9th April 1841 A cold E- wind—some little rain—

Saturday 10th A snow storm, with Wind N-E—

Sabbath 11th A cold N- wind—It is not common to know of a warm North wind—

Monday 12th This morn would answer well for 20th January—Wind N—Snow Storm this P.M.

Tuesday 13th It continued to snow, from last evening, and through near all this day—Its probable its the greatest snow storm we have had, or more properly has been known in any April for 100 years past—It is said that it is on a level 2 or more feet, and the banks from 5 to 12 feet high—

Monday 14th A.M. cloudy, with wind N.W—P.M. clear, & wind W— Edwin Brown arrived from a whaling Voyge of 21 months—Got about 3000 barrels oil—

At ½ past 4 P.M. It commenced Snowing for 2 hours, when It cleared off with [page trimmed]

[519] Thursday 15th Apl. 1841 A clear cool Morn with brisk wind N-W— The snow is deep that the Stage cannot come, nor go—Indeed to travil any way, is very difficult

Friday 16th A calm morn—The sleds pass, which is uncommon so late in Apl.

Saturday 17th A rain storm, which with the abundance of snow on the ground, almost produces a flood—John A. Preston (our G-son) with us this eve—

Sabbath 18th A heavy blow from N-W—

Monday 19th A South W- wind—

Tuesday 20th Pleasent—

Wednesday 21st A S-E- wind, with a hard rain storm—4 P.M. wind N- and It stoped raining—

Thursday 22nd It rains moderately all day—wind E—

Friday 23rd A wet night, and It is so this morn wind E—Almost a flood of rain since last Wednesday morn—That is It has rained with but little intermission 3 days and as many nights—

[520] Saturday 24th April 1841 wind S-E- and light—Occasional Showers through the day—

Sabbath 25th wind E & cloudy—

Monday 26th Very little wind East—A little rain—

Tuesday 27th Some rain, with wind E—P.M. It clears off with wind N-W- and cool—

Wednesday 28th A cool N-W- wind this morn—P.M. wind W—and very light—

Thursday 29th Wind S- & cloudy

Friday 30th Some Showers with wind N—

Saturday 1st May 1841—N-W- wind—McNeil arrived from N.York, this day, and moved into his house, which he left on the first day of March last— This is moving pretty often

Sabbath 2nd cool wind W—a shower P.M.

Monday 3rd Wind N-W- and blows hard—

Tuesday 4th Ice this morn—

Wednesday 5th Moderate Wind S—

[521] Thursday 6th May 1841 Light wind S—P.M. West—

Saturday 8th A cloudy day—It rained about 2 hours this day—

Sabbath 9th A pleasant clear day—wind light S—Capt. John A. Racket in his Sloop Wm Mitchel arrived in our harbour after an absence of 7 months to the South—

Monday 10th A rain storm, which makes it a stormy day—Wind S—

Tuesday 11th A westerly wind, and rather cool—

Wednesday 12th Wind very light W—The Seines took a few fish, this day the first this year—

Thursday 13th A cool morn, with wind N-W—Our grand daughter, Deziah Wells, is with us, came in the Stage last eve—P.M. Wind S—

Friday 14th A calm morn—a heavy dew—A national Fast, recommended by President Tyler—

Was visited this day by our Sister Hannah Howel, from Newburgh, Orange County, N.Y. and her daughter, Hannah, wife of Benjamin Brown Esq.

[522] Saturday 15th May 1841 Some rain, an hour or so—Last night considerable rain fell—Wind scarce any—

Sabbath 16th A Southwest, stiff wind—

Monday 17th Squalls, with rain, and wind which shifted to almost to every point, in the course of the day—Cool this eve—

Tuesday 18th A stiff N-W- wind, of course cool—It has been since the first of March, a cold, wet, windy, very uncomfortable Spring—Sister Howel & daughter gone to Sagharbour this day—

Wednesday 19th A.M. wind light N-E—P.M. calm. Narcissa, returned from Sagharbour, where she has been to accompany her aunt and cousin, who remain there—

Thursday 20th Wind S-W—

Friday 21st Pleasant, with a gentle breeze S—

Saturday 22nd A warm S- wind

Sabbath brisk wind S-S-W- with a light shower accompanied with Thunder

Monday 24th Warm, And wind S—

[523] Tuesday 25th May 1841 A fresh South W- wind—Our daughter Harriet L. Wells, and her daughter Maria, visited us this day—Returned to their home this eve—

Wednesday 26th A South wester—

Thursday 27th Heavy, dense Fogg—Our Sister, Mrs. Howel, and Mrs. Brown, left this day for Newburgh—

Friday 28th A warm S-W- wind—Died this day Capt. Henry T. King, after a painfull illness of 11 or 12 days—Capt. King has followed the coasting buisness this 5 or 6 years past, in the Sloop Gen'l Braidnard—We, and all those with whom he has done buisness, consider him to have been a punctual upright Man, in all their intercourse, with him—His trade, for the last 2 or 3 years has been in cattle, to Nantucket, where we understand he has left a good name, and his early demise is truly and sincerely mourned—He was 37 years of age—Leaves a wife and two Sons—

Saturday 29 A foggy A.M. Wind P.M. S-W—

[524] Sabbath 30th May 1841—Ship Delta, arrived at Greenport last Friday, from a whaling Voyge of 21 months—with 1600 hundred barrels oil, and 400 ditto sperm—Seth Griffing Master (our Nephew)—

Monday 31st Wind E & cool—The 2 Seines has caught up to this time about 80000 fish—This is called [ill?], or poor luck—

Tuesday 1st June 1841—Our aimable, and very affectionate grand daughter Deziah L. Wells went home this day, She has been with us since 12th May last—A cool E- wind—

Wednesday 2nd Southerly weather, yet moderate

Thursday 3rd Wind E-W-E- Thomas Youngs arrived home from a coasting trip of six months—

Friday 4th S-S-W—It is a mistake Thomas Youngs has not yet returned home—

Saturday 5th Warm—Wind S—

Sabbath 6th Dry weather, It begins to be—wind E-S-E-

Monday 7th Our Friend, John A. Racket, goes to Sagharbour in Sloop Wm Mitchel—Wilcox goes with [page trimmed]

[525] Tuesday 8th June 1841—S-S-W- wind—

Wednesday 9th Wind E-S-E—This eve, Sidney (our son) his wife, Augustus & Josephine, all visit us—

Thursday 10th A foggy, warm morn—We went to longbeach after Gulls Eggs—not much success—

Friday 11th A S-W- Squally day, with some rain

Saturday 12th Warm, dry wind S-E—Sidney, with his Family left us this morn, on the Stage—

Sabbath 13th Some rain, this morn, but not sufficient to wet the ground, which is now dry—Twas this morn our Son & family left—

Monday 14th S- wind & cloudy, was visited this day by my esteemed friend Joshua Y Racket—It was him that was associated with me in the Cutchogue Vessel, in March 1800—

Tuesday 15th light wind S—P.M. North and cool—

Wednesday 16th Wind N-W- Friend Racket with me went to longbeach—

Thursday 17th Wind S-E—

Friday 18th An E- rainstorm—

[526] Sabbath 20th June 1841 Pleasant—Wind S-W—

Monday 21st Wind S-E—Fine growing weather, since the 2 rains we have just had—

Tuesday 22—wind brisk S-S-W—a cloudy day—

Wednesday 23—Rain from 10 A.M. to 12 M—Wind S—

Thursday 24th An uncommon heavy dew—This day Capt. Rufus Tuthill, now aged 95 years, passed my house, alone, in a one horse wagon, which he managed well, and drove at a good speed—

Friday 25th A Foggy morn, with wind S-E—

Saturday 26th A Shower of rain this morn—P.M. Foggy with wind S-W—

Sabbath 27th A Southwest wind & cloudy—George Millar, Esquire, stoped with us last night—

Monday 28th High wind S-W—

Tuesday 29th It blows hard from W—Sidney P. Racket was married to Jane Tuthill this eve—Doct. Seth H. Tuthills youngest daughter—

Wednesday 30th A very warm S-S-W- wind

[527] Thursday July 1st 1841 A squally day, with wind S-W—Rec'd letter from our G—son Chatham A G—

Friday 2nd Wind westerly, which we call a dry wind—

Saturday 3rd A.M. a cool N- wind—

Sabbath 4th continues cool—Wind very high N—P.M. S-W—

Monday 5th A swift wind S-S-W—

Tuesday 6th A small shower last night—This morn S-W—Deziah Preston with us—A Thunder Storm this eve—Our daughter Harriet with us this eve—

Wednesday 7th It is this eve when Harriet is with us—

Thursday 8th Very little wind S—

Friday 9th Wind S—Northern lights this eve

Saturday 10th A South wind A.M. with some rain—P.M. clear—Wind N-W- light—

Capt. Rufus Tuthill, aged 95, with his excellent Brother Daniel Tuthill, who is 84 years with his son Baldin, and daughter, was all with us a short time today—Our Chatham [page trimmed]

[528] Sabbath 11th July 1841 Wind W—

Monday 12th It is getting to be dry—Wind S-W—

Tuesday 13th Wind as yesterday—

Wednesday 14th A S-S-W- wind & cloudy—Cherries pretty plenty

Thursday 15th It is very warm—Wind S-S-W—Jeremiah Youngs was married to Mary Case this eve—

Friday 16th A light wind N-W—

Saturday 17th Continues quite uncomfortably warm—

Sabbath 18th A light wind E-S-E—John A. Preston with us—

Monday 19th P.M. Wind quick S-S-W—

Tuesday 20th Wind S-W—

Wednesday 21st A S-W- wind—Ira T. Horton, a likely, very fine young man from Cutchogue, was with us this eve—goes mate of ship Noble, which sails to night—Edwin Brown Master—Ira is Grand son to the late pious, Bononi Horton, an [exhorter?] of righteousness of many years since in this Town—Some 40 years ago

Thursday 22nd Wind S-S-W- cloudy—

[529] Friday 23 July 1841 Very warm Wind W—12 Midnight a Shower

Saturday 24th Wind S-S-W—Departed this life, this day Mrs. Hannah Wiggins, wife of Saml. Wiggins and daughter to Lemuel & Fanny Youngs— She was a pious, good woman and a faithful companion—

Sabbath 25th A fine shower, with thunder this morn—This eve, another small rain—

Monday 26th Breeze of wind N-W—

Tuesday 27th—Some Showers this morn untill 9 A.M. when the wind came to N—cleared off—

Thursday 29th Pleasent—

Friday 30th Wind S-W—Warm—McNeil's Soninlaw with us an hour or so

Saturday 31st Some rain with wind E—Rain again this evening—

Monday 2 August 1841 A very pleasent day—

Sabbath 8th Wind S-W- Warm—

Monday 9th High wind S-S-W—

Tuesday 10th A sultry wind S-E—

[530] Wednesday 11th August 1841—Showers, occasionally through the day—The Hayscales finished today—Peter A. Cowdry Esq. from N.York stoped with us a minute or two this day—

Thursday 12th A fine rain last night—wind this morn N-W—

Friday 13th Very tight wind—

Saturday 14th Wind moderate E—3 young men from N. York with us this eve—

Sabbath 15th An easterly wind—

Monday 16th A cool E. wind—

Tuesday 17th A pleasent warm day—

Wednesday 18th The Hay Scales was put up in July 1836—

Thursday 19th An extreme warm day—

Friday 20th My dear Wife who has endured indiscribile pain in her Eyes, for 12 months past, has now become almost blind—

Saturday 21st—Almost insupportably warm—calm

Sabbath 22nd—White & Willet, boarders left us this morn—

[531] Monday 23rd August 1841 Wind N-E—Our grand daughter, Deziah Preston, left us this day for Shelterisland, where she is teaching school—

Tuesday 24th N-E- wind—comfortably cool

Wednesday 25th N-E- by E- wind

Thursday 26th E—wind N-E—

Friday 27th A Storm of rain with E- wind

Saturday 28th A copious rain all last night—wind E—

Sabbath 29th Wind E—very damp without—A Col. Peck stoped with us last night—The same gentleman was with us in 1837 or 8

Monday 30th Storm of rain, with thunder and lightning Wind E- by S—

Married last eve A Mr. Sing to Chatrine Youngs of Orient—My very respectable and long esteemed friend Jeremiah Horton of Orange County

(NY) died this morn aged 82 years—He was a resident in our place more than 50 years ago—

Thursday 31st South wind A shower P.M.

Wednesday 1st September 1841 Wind W—

Thursday 2nd wind S-S-W—[page trimmed]

[532] Saturday 4th, Sept. 1841—S- Wind And very warm and close—

Sabbath 5th Wind E-N-E—Some cooler

Monday 6th—A light wind N—Training of Orient Militia company

Tuesday 7th Pleasent for N-E- wind—Our Brother Saml C. Griffing was with us to tea this P.M.—

Wednesday 8th Wind N-E—Our brother S. C. G & his wife, and adopted child with us—

Thursday 9th Wind E-S-E- this morn—P.M. Calm—

Friday 10th A damp E- wind—Apples is more scarce this season than they have been this 5 Autumns past—

Our Methodist Church was erected in Orient in 1836—I gave 7 dollars to aid its building—it was but a mite, yet it was a free gift—

Saturday 11th Wind W- by N—Our grand daughters, Sidneys two oldest daughters, have been with us a day or two—they [page trimmed]

[533] Benjamin F. Thompson Esq. stoped with us a short time, this day—Made me a present of Long Island History, one Volume—

Monday 13th A wet drizzly day—Wind E—

Tuesday 14th Last light wind from N—

Wednesday 15th A still, or calm day

Thursday 16th E-N-E- wind—Henry Wells Esq. from Tiogo County, and our daughter Harriet, visited us this day

Cousin Wm H. Griffing's wife Anna & daughter stoped a short time with us

Friday 17th An Easterly rainstorm—

Saturday 18th Wind S-E—

Sabbath 19th Wind E—

Monday 20th wind very light E—It has been from about that point, or near It, with only short intervals for the last 20 days

Tuesday 21st Wind pretty near E—

Wednesday 22nd Wind from the E- board—

Thursday 23rd Wind near the old corner of more than 2 days—

[534] Friday 24th September 1841 A South E- by S—Some rain, with Thunder—

Saturday 25th Rained hard all last night, with wind S—It continues to rain, pretty much this day through, with Thunders—

Sabbath 26th Wind, brisk W—Rode to Southold, found our dear Harriet & family all well—

Monday 27th A.M. wind high W-N-W—Died away P.M.

Tuesday 28th Wind S-W—

Wednesday 29th Showers, with wind S-S-E—

Thursday 30th Squally, with wind N-N-E—A little rain—

October 1st Friday 1841—A cool morn, with wind N-W—

Saturday 2nd A North East rainstorm, with a smart gale

Sabbath 3rd—

Monday 4th The gale has been violent and It yet blows powerful—

[535] Tuesday 5th October 1841 cool—wind N—Two vessels drove on shore on Ram Island—It has been a tempestuous wind—

We are just informed that Charles Terry was lost overboard, from the sloop Liberator, Capt. David T. Glover, in the gale of the 30th—He was a worthy young man—

Wednesday 6th cool wind N-W—

Thursday 7th Wind W—

Friday 8th A showery day—with S- wind—

Saturday 9th Wind W—

Sabbath 10th Pleasant—wind W—

Monday 11th Wind S-W—

Tuesday 12th Some rain, occasionally through the day—

Wednesday 13th Brisk wind N-W—

Friday 14th Wind N-W—rains some—

Friday 15th Rain squalls

Saturday 16th Wind N—

Sabbath 17th Wind N-W—

Monday 18th N-N-W- wind—

Tuesday 19th Squalls N-N-W—

[536] Wednesday 30th October 1841 It rained with wind E-S-E—

Thursday 21st Wind boisterous from N-W—

Friday 22nd Wind W—

Saturday 23rd N-N-W—wind, and pretty stiff—Our g-daughter, Deziah Preston's school, on Shelterisland is out—She has taught about 5 months—and is now with us—

Sabbath 24th Pleasant—Wind S-W—

Monday 25th A cool morn, with wind N-W—

Tuesday 26th Brisk wind S-W—Ice this morn

Wednesday 27th A.M. wind light S—P.M. North & cool

Thursday 28th Very light wind E- by S—

Friday 29th Wind S-W—Our cousin, John Stewards two Sons called on us this day—

Saturday 30th A foggy day with wind S-S-W—

Sabbath 31st a warm clear day—

November 1st Monday held Ellections at my house—Sidney his wife & Josephine visited this eve

[537] Tuesday 2nd November 1841 Wind quick S—with some rain—

Wednesday 3rd A calm, warm day—Sidney & family left this A.M.—

Thursday 4th A brisk breeze S-S-W—Phebe, the frugal, attentive, virtuous wife of John Brown (better known as Capt. John Brown) died very suddenly—aged__ She was the 3rd daughter of Mr. Amon & Sibil Taber, of this place (Orient)—

Saturday 13th Novem. Have been unwell this some days past—

Sabbath 21st Deziah Preston goes to day to assist Mrs. Doct. [Skinner ?]—

Wednesday 27th Mrs. Mariann Havens came and staid with us until 30th & again and staid altogether made 7 days—

Sabbath 28th Nov. Wind E-N-E—P.M. It snows—

Monday 29th A snowstorm with wind N-E—

December 3rd 1841 A hard rain Storm—wind S-E—

Saturday 4th Squally, with rain & high wind S-W—

[538] Friday 10th Decem. 1841 A rain Storm through the day, with S- wind—

On the 6th of this month, an interesting daughter of George & Maria Case, was burnt, by her clothes taking fire so bad as to cause her death, on the 7th—She was 4 years old—

Sabbath 11th Deziah returned home from Doct. Skinners—

Tuesday 13th A storm of rain, with wind E—

Friday 17th Wind S-S-W—A real storm of snow, which drives into large banks—

Tuesday 21st A Snow moderate last night, makes sledding tollerable—

Thursday 23rd A rain storm this day which makes splashing work with the Snow, especially with the traviller, with not any boots—

Tuesday 28th A little Snowstorm of 2 inches

Thursday 30th Some rain—not much—

1842

[539] Tuesday 4th January 1842 A small snow of about 2 inches deep as the wind changed to the Southern brand, by night the Snow was gone—

Friday 7th A S-E- Rain Storm, all last night

I ought to have mentioned that on Saturday the 1st of this month, departed this life, Rosetta, the very affectionate, and well informed wife of John Champlin, and the dutiful daughter of Caleb & Mehitable Dyer of this place (Orient) she was aged__ years—

Monday 10th Some Snow, with wind E—In the eve, some rain—At 9 P.M. Starlight—

Tuesday 11th Some Snow today—

Thursday 13th A cold N-W- wind—

The 17th 18th 19 & 20th were all warm and pleasent days for January—

Wednesday 26th a very mild day—Ezekiel Glover, aged about 84 years, died this day, having been some weeks sinking under infirmities of body, age, and acute rheumatic pains, all which he appeared to bear without a murmur—He has always lived in this place, and bore the name of an honest Man—

[540] James Winters, aged about 35 years, died on the 17th this month—He was an active, industrious peaceable man, of good moral principles, and a believer in the Gospel of our Lord Jesus Christ—He leaves a wife and an Infant Son—

Monday 24th Fanny, the aimable and accomplished Wife of Lemuel Youngs Jr, died this day, after a distressing illness of some months—She was certainly a valuable woman—She leaves an infant daughter—

Thursday 27th A light Snow fell last night—Amanda, the wife of George H. Payne and the interesting and filial daughter of Deacon Peter & Phebe Brown, of this place, died on 26th just—She leaves an infant of a week old—She was aged 20 years—

Monday 31st Wind S. A rain storm—January has been a mild month, for winter

Wednesday 3rd Feb 1842 Squally, with rain—Our daughter Harriet with us

Friday 5th Showers with S.W. wind

[541] Feb.13th 1842 A moderate rain, with wind E—

Wednesday 16th rain, with wind E-S-E—

Thursday 17th A[s] low a tide, perhaps anyone these 20 years past—The wind near a hurricane—

Saturday 19th A copious rain,with wind S- & high—

Tuesday 22nd The Washington Temperence Society, of Orient, ride and walk in a large procession to Greenport, to attend an address of Rev. Mr. Welton—Returned to my house P.M. and sat down, near 100 to an Entertainment, provided for the Occasion—It was a very pleasent day and it was Washington's birth day—

Saturday 26th A rain Storm, wind E—There were 4 of our Sloops, in our harbour, drove on Shore, with the gale of the 19th and they have all been got off within these few days, with the help of 25 men, and not one drop of ardent spirit has been made use of in the buisness—Ten years ago, It could have taken 20 Gall. to do the work of such a sort—Chaplin supplied our Men, with good [page trimmed]

[542] Sabbath 27th Feb. 1842 Snow with wind W-N-W—P.M. clears off

Monday 28th Pleasent—Sidney & Wife visited us—

March 2nd Wednesday, A moderate rain—Sidney (our Son) and wife left us—

Sabbath 6th A East Storm of rain

Monday 7th Continues to rain moderate with wind N-N-E—

Friday 11th Squally, with a North wind—Pretty cold—

Tuesday 15th A mild, Pleasent day—

Sabbath 10th Pleasent—

Tuesday 22nd Snow, then Rain with wind S—

Friday 25th A snow storm last night—This eve It thunder, & lightens, with hail

Tuesday 29th A heavy Squall of wind & rain last night—On the 12th of this month died Joshua Tuthill, aged 50 years—He has been as hard labouring man as I ever knew, to[o] much so for his constitution—I think It has actually shortened his days—he was a peaceable Man—[543] He was the son of the late Christopher & Betty Tuthill of Orient—

Monday 3rd & Tuesday 4th April 1842 were Stormy days with wind E—

Thursday 7th A S-E- rain Storm—

Saturday 9th A hard East- rain Storm—

Monday 11th Wind W-S-W—Deziah Preston (our grand daughter) begins [teaching] school at Rockypoint—Some rain last night—

Tuesday 12th & Wednesday 13th Rain with wind E & cold—

Monday 18th & Tuesday 19th Wind tonight E- with much rain—

Monday 25th Rain last eve—E- wind—Sidney & wife with us—

Tuesday 26th Easterly wind yet—some rain. Sidney & wife left this P.M.
Wednesday 27th Thunder & rain last night—A cool, high N.W. wind

May 1st 1842 Thunder Shower this eve
Monday 2nd Showers, Wind W-S-W—
Tuesday 3rd Showers through the day
Wednesday 4th Light rain, wind W—
[544] Saturday 7th May 1842 Some rain, hail, with Thunder—
Sabbath 8th & Monday 9th two cold blustering days, with high wind
N-N-W—
Wednesday 11th Sharp lightning. with rain & high wind for several hours
this evening—
Thursday 19th Some rain this eve, South wind
Friday 20th A rain Storm, Wind E-S-E—
Saturday 21st April White frost this morn
Monday 23rd A light rain—
Friday 27th Showers through the day—Sidney visited us on the 26th—
The mail stage, which has put up with us once or twice a week for the last
12 or 15 years, has now quit altogether. It now stops with John Clark at
Greenport—
Monday 30th Showers, occasionally through the day—

Wednesday 1st June 1842 Rode out to Southold, with cousin Wm. H.
Griffing—P.M. Took tea with our daughter Harriet and Husband. I ought
to have mentioned that on the 30th of May last my dear daughter Harriet
L. [545] Wells, and her aimable daughter Deziah L. spent the day with us,
and returned home to Southold that evening—[pencil:]this was her last
visit to Orient—
Thursday June 9th 1842 Still considerable rain—
Friday 10th Another rain storm
Saturday 11th A very high N-W- wind & cold
Tuesday 14th A rain through last night—
Wednesday 15th & Thursday 16th Rain, almost to a flood both days—An
uncommon wet time—
Died on the 11th Inst. Mrs. Experience Cochran, the widow of the late
John Cochran—she was aged 75 years—She was truly an excellent
woman—Invaluable as Mother, wife, daughter, and neighbour—and we
hope a Christian—
Friday 17th Some rain—

Saturday 18th Rain again, last night & this morn—
Sabbath 19th Last night more rain—
Thursday 23rd An easterly, moderate rain storm—
Saturday 25th Wind W—clear
[546] Monday 27th June 1842 Rain, with Thunder this A.M. Showers again P.M.—

Monday July 4 1842 After 10 A.M. It was very pleasent—Nearly 100 Men and Women took Dinner, at Tables set under my trees before our front door—Previous to Dining, they attended to a well pronounced Oration, by Mr. Ingles, of Southold—Mr. Franklin Vail, after Mr. Ingles, made a handsome address—This last Gentleman is the Son of my late greatly respected friend, Silas Vail—
Tuesday 5th Some rain—
Wednesday 6th—Rain this A.M.—Honorable Mahlon Dickerson, late Secretary of the Navy, and formerly Governor of New Jersey, took dinner with us this day*
Friday 15th A shower this eve—
Tuesday 19th two brothers E & Joseph Johnson, with [Turney?] L. Whelan, with us
[547] Tuesday 26th A Thunder Shower this P.M.—
Friday 19th A shower this A.M.—
Sabbath 31st Some rain this P.M.—James Wilkie Jr., his sisters Mary & Elizabeth, and Eliza Williams, with Col. James Willetts, all left us in the Stage this day—They have been with us some days—Chatham our G-Son for Riverhead—

Monday & Tuesday 1st & 2nd August—cool E-N-E- wind—
Wednesday Wind E & cool
Friday 5th A gale wind E- with much rain
Sabbath 7th Wind E- with occasionly showers
Monday 8th Rains this A.M.—I rode to Southold—our daughter pretty well & family—
9th 10th & 11th Wind E- with wind Easterly—
Friday 12th Wind cold [warmer?] E—Sidney & wife with us—Mr. Dobbs likewise from N.Y.—
Saturday 13th Some Rain & wind as It has been nearly all this month—
[548] Sabbath 14th August 1842 Some rain Wind N-N-E—
Monday 15th Pleasent West wind—

*He was on his way to Southold village graveyard where some of his ancestors were buried—I directed him to Goldsmith Horton Esq who would give his desired request—He hasn't [illegible]

Thursday 18th A small rain with wind S-W—Rode out to Greenport with Mr. Frederick Dobbs—

Saturday 20th A fine day—

Monday 22nd Light wind N-E—This eve, Sidney, his wife, and his Mother inlaw, Mrs.Williams, visited us—

Tuesday 23rd They left us for Riverhead—Wind S-S-E—

Wednesday 24th A light wind E-S-E—Uncle Jared Griffing & his daughter stoped with us about 2 hours this A.M.—He is in his 81st year of his age—

Thursday 25th Brisk wind E-S-E—

Friday 26th Wind S—Jeremiah Young lost his only child, a son of 8 months old

Saturday 27th Wind S-E—some rain

Sabbath 28th As warm as [any] day this summer—

Monday 29th Some cooler—[549] Mr. Henry Youngs & Wife, from NewYork, visited us this day—He was formerly from Goshen, Orange County—He is now a prominent Merchant in NewYork—His great Grand Father, Henry Youngs, was from this place (Orient) in 1734 or 5

Tuesday 30th Pleasant—Rode out to Southold, with Mr. Youngs & Wife

Wednesday 31st Mr. Youngs & Wife left this morn—

Thursday 1st September 1842 Pleasant

Friday 2nd Fair day Wind S-S-E—

Saturday 3rd A South wind—

Sabbath 4th Pleasant—Mr. Gillett of Lyme was married to Maria Vail, daughter of Gelston & Roxanna Vail of this place—

Monday 5th [blank]

Tuesday 6th Wind N—

Wednesday 7th Wind S—

Thursday 8th Wind N—

Friday 9th Rain with wind S-E—

Saturday 10th cool—[page trimmed]

[550] Wednesday 14th Septem. 1842 Wind E—Wilcox, Honora, and their little girl, Ellen, leave for New York in the Liberator, D.T. Glover

Thursday 15th An Easterly Rain Storm—

Friday 16th Continues to rain, with wind E—

Saturday 17th A little wind N-N-E—

Sabbath 18th Wind W-N-W—

Monday 19th Squally, with showers—

Wednesday 21st Some showers, with brisk wind W—

Thursday 22nd N-West wind, and high

Friday 23rd Cool, with not any frost—

Saturday 24th Walter O. Hubbard, who has been with us some time, leaves for N.York—

The newspapers inform me this day that my Friend John Hallock, of Orange County NY died, a few days since, age 91 or 2 years—This Man, and his aimable wife, showed me the most marked civilities and kindness when a lone stranger, in their vicinity in the year 1790—I at that time was teaching school in their neighborhood—His house was my [page trimmed]

[551] Monday 25th Pleasant

Tuesday 16th A pleasent weather—Sidney and his Son Augustus visited us this eve

Wednesday 27th Sidney, Chatham, & Augustus leave this day—pleasent—

Thursday 29th Wind E—Our best of daughters, Harriet L. Wells, is now very sick—

Saturday 1st October 1842 Foggy day—

Friday 7th Very little wind S-S-W—

Saturday 8th Wind S- & warm—Potatoes sell by the quantity at 20 lbs

Sabbath 9th A calm day—

Monday 10th Wind N-W—comfortably cool

Friday 14th October 1842 This morning at 25 minutes past 7 o'clock, our Eldest daughter Harriet Lucretia departed this life, after a distressing illness of three weeks—As a daughter she was all obedience, and dutiful—as a wife, kind, affectionate, and loving; as a Mother tender, with all those endearing qualities that render the name of Mother Sacred, and Heavenly—as a neighbour greatly beloved

Saturday 15th This day all that was mortal of our [page trimmed]

[552] Wednesday 19th October 1842 Schooner Planet, Lester B. Terry, sails this day for Charleston S.C.—

Sabbath 23rd Abner Wells (our soninlaw) visited this day—

Tuesday 25th A Southeasterly wind, and rain—Deziah Preston goes back to N.Y. this day in the Sloop Liberator D. T. G[lover] Master—

30th Oct. A cool E- wind—Died this month (as we now hear) Daniel Tuthill, youngest brother to Capt. Rufus Tuthill Senior aged 85 years—He was the mildest pleasentest man I ever knew—Likewise a just, benevolent, sensible, strong minded person, greatly & deservedly beloved—

Friday 4th Novem.1842 This morn at 4 oclock our greatly beloved grand daughter Deziah L. Wells departed this life, after suffering some months with an incurable consumption [tuberculosis]—She was a pleasent, interesting [girl], and of the sweetest disposition—Thus she has followed her dear Mother in less than 3 weeks—[page trimmed]

[553] Sabbath 6th November 1842 This day the remains of our beloved Deziah, is committed to the Earth—" And dust to dust, the mourner cries"

On the 30th of May last she and her Mother was at my house—they left us that evening—Deziah had been stoping with us a week or more—

Monday 14th Wind S- with rain—There was a rain storm on Saturday 12th just—

Wednesday 16th A cool E- wind, with cloudy weather

Thursday 24th A rain storm from E—

Friday 25th A Frost last night—calm, wind mild this day

Sabbath 27th Snow squalls, with high wind N-W—Eli Tuthill was married this eve to Nancy Taber, daughter to Frederick & Polly Taber, of our place—

Wednesday 30th A tremendous wind, if not a hurricane, N-W—Some rain this eve with with wind shifted E-S-E—

Thursday Decem. 1st 1842 Blustering, and cold

Saturday 3rd Ezra Young's wife Maria was confined with twins, boys—which they, She names George [page trimmed]

[554] Monday 5th December 1842 Some rain, with very little wind—

Wednesday 7th A light snow, wind N-E—

Thursday 8th Wind E—Some rain—

Friday 9th Rain all last night—

Sabbath 11th Some Snow fell this day—

Monday 12th Our son Sidney & Wife visited us—they leave for Riverhead this day—

Tuesday 13th A snow, rain & hail storm with wind E—

Wednesday 14th A high wind N-W—

Monday 19th Wind, as yesterday and cold

Tuesday 20th A calm, pleasant day

Wednesday 21st Rain Storm, with wind E—

Thursday 22nd A wet, or rainy night the past one—This morn Wind W-N-W-

Thursday 29th Moses Latham was married to Harriet, the daughter of Orange & Harriet Petty, of our Orient—

Capt. Marther, of the Revenue Cutter, called on us this day—

Saturday 31st [page trimmed]

1843

[555] January 3rd 1843 Tuesday A light Snow

Wednesday 4th A very cold night—wind this morning is N-W—

6th & 7th Friday & Saturday was wet & very unpleasent—Maria Prince, our grand daughter is with us—

Sabbath 8th Our Maria, mentioned yesterday, goes home today—John A. Preston, our G-son, is with us—Rain this eve—

Monday 9th Pleasant—Jeremiah Youngs wife Mary was confined with a daughter on the 1st week in this month—

Tuesday 10th Some rain last night

Wednesday 11th Rain again last night—quite warm this day—

Thursday 12th Warm, yet unpleasent, drizzly weather—

Friday 13th A copious shower very early A.M.—P.M. dark, damp, calm day—Samuel W. Hill with us this Eve—

Monday 16th Very pleasent—

Wednesday [Tuesday] 17th & Thursday [Wednesday] 18th Warm & calm—

Thursday 19th Wind light S—

Friday 20th very warm, to much so for Winter—

[556] Tuesday 24th January 1843 Squally, with Showers & Snow—high wind—

Thursday 26th cool—

Saturday 28th Rain—

Tuesday 31st An Easterly rain storm

Wednesday 1st Feb. 1843 A moderate Snow, about 4 inches thick—

Thursday 2nd A cold North wester—This day 76 years ago, I am informed I was born—what a number of years this appears to be to the young man! But alas to those who see them, they appear but a moment—A tale that is quickly told—

Sabbath 5th An old fashioned Easterly Snow Storm—A drifting one—

Monday 6th Wind high W-N-W—

Friday 10th Sidney, wife, and two of his children visited us in the Stage

Saturday 11th A rain storm, which spoils the Sleding—

Sabbath 12th A cold N-W- wind—Sidney & family left this P.M.—

[557] Monday 13th Feb. 1843 Wind light W-N-W—

Tuesday 14th An Easterly blow, with some Snow—Our G-daughters Deziah & Harriet Preston with us—

Wednesday 15th Snow, hail & rain this day, with very cold weather—the trees are dressed off with a dazzling Robe—

Thursday 16th Continues cold—Ground covered with Ice—To see some people attempt to walk, with a little too much in the head is a caution to the te[e]totalor—

Harriet M. Preston has been absent in Connecticut near 5 years—

Monday 20th Weather more mild—The walking grows more safe—This day they our neighbours raised a pole near my front door yard gate—It is near 100 feet high—

Wednesday 22nd A Snow Storm—111 years this day since Washington was born—In many respects he was a wise good man—

[558] Feb. 22nd 1843—Wednesday, Washingtons Birthday was celebrated in this place—Addresses were delivered in the Methodist church by Messrs. Ingles, Huntly, Welton & Henry Racket to a large audience—after which nearly one hundred gentlemen and ladies retired to my house where Wm. H. Wilcox served them up a suitable Dinner, with which entertainment all appeared to be well pleased—The day, take it with its innocent, well timed amusements, and interest, passed off with much satisfaction to every actor—

March 2nd Thursday blustering & cold—Wind N-W—Died about two weeks ago, Capt. Joseph Griffing, at Riverhead, where he has resided __ years—he was 88 years of age—See my notice of his visit to my house in Apr. 23rd 1839 page 422

Friday 10th Some rain, wind East—

[559] Monday 13th March 1843 Rain Storm wind S

Tuesday 14th High wind W—Jesse Conkling, a travilling Merchant, with us—He has often stoped with us this two or 3 years past—

Thursday 16th A real Storm of Snow, with an Easterly wind—

Friday 17th A very high, or gale of wind from S-S-W—attended with a tide uncommon high—

Thursday 23rd—A Snow Storm, with wind E-S-E—At 11 A.M. it stoped snowing, and the wind shifted N-W—a gale, and cold—

Friday 24th Very cold, such a day would answer well for January—

Wednesday 28th Rain Storm, with wind from the South—

Saturday April 1st 1843 Last night considerable rain fell—Continues to fall in profusion all this day with wind N-N-E—

Sabbath 2nd A cold North Wester—

[560] Tuesday 4th April 1843—Pleasant—A great excitement in the Town about granting <u>License</u> to sell rum, and other intoxicating Liquors—The <u>world</u> it appears is just awaking up to the awful consequences of indulging in its traffic, and using It as a beverage—Its use in a family, immoderately, is more wretched and fatal to the peace of the Wife and Children than the poison of Asps—

Wednesday 5th considerable Snow this morn—P.M. It sets in a steady rain—

Thursday 6th A cool, damp day—A man from Lyme, Connecticut by name Lord Wellington Gillett, opens a Store, at the Landng this Spring—He appears a man of veracity—

Wednesday 12th—Some white frost this morn—A mild day—

[561] Thursday 13th Apr.1843—Pleasant

Friday 14th Plenty of rain with wind E—

Saturday 15th—Some rain—Wind from almost every point in the course of the day—

Sabbath 16th Pleasant—Our G-son Chatham A.G- visited us this day—

Monday 17th A drizzly wet day wind East—

Tuesday 18th Rain this morn as It has through the two last nights—Wind E-N-E—

Wednesday 19th continues to rain—wind E-N-E—

Thursday 20th Friday 21 & Saturday were all pleasant, mild days—

Repaired my dooryard fence with new posts and new railings, but retained the old pickets which are about 45 years now in wear—

[562] Sabbath 23rd April 1843—A rain storm—Wind S—Our Chatham left us this day for Riverhead—Deziah Preston (our grand daughter) is now keeping school at Greenport—left us last Thursday to commence the School—

Monday 24th Pleasant—Wind S-W—

Tuesday 25th A Mr. Hayns has hired my Shoe Shop—

Friday 28th Wind N-W- Cool—A Thunder Shower last eve—

Saturday 29th A cool wind East—

Sabbath 30th Wind brisk N-N-E—and cool—Edwin Brown has just arrived from a whaling voyge, Master of the Ship_____with 2200 Gall. oil—

Monday 1st May—A copious rain fell last night—moderate

[563] Sabbath 3rd May 1843—Thunder Shower this morn—

Wednesday 10th Wind E—Cool, unpleasent weather—

Thursday 11th Wind fresh E—

Friday 12th Departed this life Henry Vaill, aged 50 years—He leaves a wife and three children to mourn a kind Husband, and a tender Father—He was a very industrious man, and a professed believer in the Gospel of Jesus Christ—

Sabbath 14th A very pleasent morn, with the harmonious song of the red breast, and soaring lark—

Monday 15th A Pleasent morn

Wednesday 17th A very light rain—not enough to wet the ground—

Tuesday 23rd A good Shower, which began to be needed—

[564] Wednesday 24th May 1843—Another fine shower last night, or rather very early this morn

Friday 26th An East wind with some little rain—

Monday 29th A.M. A moderate rain—wind W-S-W—

30th & Wednesday 31st were some pleasent, on 30 & 31st a small rain—morning—

Saturday June 3rd P.M. a Shower, with Lightning & Thunder—E—Shery Racket, in the Schooner Prentice, arrived in our harbour, from the South, but last from the Westindias—He has been absent about 8 months—

Tuesday 6th June—Some very light showers—Wind E—On the whole It is a rather dry Spring thus far—

Thursday 8th A Pleasent day—

Friday 9th A small sprinkle of rain, with distant Thunder—

Sabbath 11th A rain sufficient to wet the ground which needs It—

[565] Friday 16th Another fine, or good rain with wind S-E—

Monday 19th Pleasent—Rode out to Greenport—While there, visited our Grand daughter, Maria Prince, who, now, with her Husband, Orin Prince, live at G-port—

Alan B. Webb accompanied me, in the ride—He is a young man whose welfare I feel much interested in—And carries with him my best desires for his present & future welfare—Whaleing voyges has been his employ this some years—That he may find it profitable, and rise to offices of consequence, and honorably aquit himself in every station he may [be] destined to fill, is our sincere prayer—He is the Grandson of the late Capt. Thomas Webb, of Cutchogue—

Thursday 22nd Died this day Mrs. Jane Racket, wife of Capt. Sidney P. Racket—She was aged about 22 years—They have been [page trimmed]

[566] Wednesday 28th June 1843 Some small showers with wind W—

Sabbath 2nd July 1843—The 3 last days with this have [been] uncomfortably warm—Sidney (our Son) with his wife & Josephine with us last night & today—John A. Preston with us—came, with Sidney, his uncle—

Tuesday 4th—Mr. Welton, Southold Minister, delivered an address to the people in this place, at the Methodist church—And Sidney (our Son) addressed the assembly—After the Excercises, they, a large company of them, took dinner with us, served up in good stile by Mr. Wilcox—

Wednesday 5th Some little rain—Sidney and family left this eve—Harriet Matilda Preston with us—

July 6th—Pleasent—

12th & 13th Hot & dry—The tears of filial sorrow give the brightest luster and are the most noble of any that are shed by frail humanity—

[567] Saturday 15th A little sprinkle of rain, about as much as a good dew—Cherries with us and beginning to get ripe—

July 17th—Just a small Sprinkle of rain

Friday 21st—Cousin Ludica Dayton & her niece visited us—Capt. Marthen, of the revenue Cutter, with us, an hour or so—

Monday 24th P.M. a Squall of wind, with but very little rain Wind N-W—

Friday 28th Wind S—very warm—A Mr. Turney, from N.York, has stoped with us some days past—leaves this day, with my best wishes—

Saturday 29th S-S-W- wind—very warm—P.M. we have a refreshing rain of about 30 minutes—More rain has now fell in this short space than has fell altogether since the 16th June—Lightning & Thunder with the above shower—

Sabbath 30th Wind E- with some rain—

Monday 31st Rain last night, as It does this morn—

[568] Tuesday 1st August 1843—Our Congregational Church, which was built 26 years ago, is this day being taken down, in order to erect one more suitable to the present generation—

Friday 4th Ludica Dayton & niece left us for N.Y.—

Sabbath 6th A good ground rain last night—Wind E-S-E—

Monday 8th Some little showers, with thunder

Thursday 10th Wind E—Some showers—Col. Willetts, who was with us last July 1842 is with us now

Friday 11th Wind N- Abundance of rain

Saturday 12th Cool wind N-W—

Sabbath 13th Pleasent

Monday 14th Was visited this day by our Friend N.T. Hubbard, the affectionate, a[nd] welltimed civilities, we have from time to time received from this gentleman are abundently numerous and yield [page trimmed]

[569] Tuesday 15th A pleasent day—Rode out with Friend Hubbard— Some small showers this day—

Wednesday 16th Mr. Hubbard and his good wife with us—

Friday 18th Our friend Hubbard & wife leave this day for N.Y.—

Saturday 19th Some, very little rain—McNeill, Cleora (our daughter) and their child Harriet leave us for N.York in the Sloop Motto, Sidney P. Racket Master—

Monday 21st Some showers, with wind South—A Mr. Stephen V. Terry, Grandson of my late dear, and deserving Friends Constant & Sibil Terry, stoped with us this night—He is a preposessing, very well informed, fine young Man—

Tuesday 22nd Showers last night—A Mr. Joy Terry with us last night—

Wednesday 23rd A rain last night—John A. Preston (our G-son) with us

Thursday 24th Some little rain

Friday 25th Sultry hot—

[570] Saturday 26th August 1843—Pleasent—They raise the New Church on the site of the one just taken down—

Monday 28th Some rain this P.M.—

Tuesday 29th Wind light E-S-E—Received this day by the hands of Capt. John Terry a piece of the Rock of Plymouth, on which our Pilgrim Fathers landed in 1620—

Thursday 31st—A warm, light wind W—

Friday 1st Septem. Winds fresh E—Distant Thunder—P.M. It rains

Saturday 2nd Wind W- wind—

Monday 4th Very warm—our friend John King, son to the late Rufus King of this place, visited us this day—He, John King, has lately travilled in Europe, of which account he gave us very interesting particulars—

Wednesday 6th Wind as yesterday E—

Friday 8th East Wind, with some little rain—

[571] Saturday 9th September 1843 Wind N-N-W- and pleasently cool—Capt. Rufus Tuthill, now in his 97th year of his age was with us a short time today—

Sabbath 10th Wind N-N-W—Sidney (our son) & wife wisited us this day—

Monday 11th It rained last night—& some this morn—

Tuesday 12th A damp day—

Wednesday 13th Wind E—Sidney, his wife, and daughter Maria, leave this morn in the Stage—

Thursday 14th A gale E—

Friday 15th A.M. Wind E—P.M. very high S-W- with Showers—Rode out to Greenport with Mr. Abraham Morse, who lectures on Temperence—

Saturday 16th A calm day—if any wind it is S—

Sabbath 17th A warm S- wind—

Tuesday 19th wind S-W—Benjamin Browns Son Henry Field Brown and his sister [page trimmed] our cousin Ruth Beebe

[572] Saturday 23rd Wind S-W- Mr. B. Brown's children leave this day for Goshen, their home—

Sabbath 24th Wind E-, & Cloudy—A Mr. Abbot lectures in my dooryard this P.M.—

Tuesday 26th Wind N-E- with rain & Thunder with sharp lightning

Wednesday 27th Wind N-W—

Thursday 28th White frost this morn—

Friday 29th Sidney & wife with us—Just from a visit to Boston—

Saturday 30th Took Sidney & wife in Zilla Youngs waggon to Riverhead— Dined on our way up at Squire Henry Landons—

Sabbath 1st October, a very hard Easterly rain Storm—

Monday 2nd—Pleasant—returned home—

Tuesday 3rd Wednesday & Thursday 5th Wind N-W- and a gale—

[573] Friday 6th October A pleasant day—wind W-S-W—

On the last of September past departed this life Lieutenant Benjamin Hallock of Southold, Hogneck—He was a kind husband, an affectionate father, and a worthy neighbour—And we believe an honest man—About 78 years of age—

Saturday 7th Oct. 1843 An East Storm of rain

Sabbath 8th This morn is very boistrious with wind E—It rained through all last night—

Monday 9th & Tuesday 10th Cool wind N-W—Chatham with us—

13th Friday & Saturday 14th Some rain, when it clears off with wind N-N-W—Cool—

Monday 16th A moder. Rainy day—Chatham A. left this day for Riverhead

Thursday 19th High wind W—

Saturday 21st Wind brisk S-W—

Monday 23rd Squally with rain and cool

Tuesday 24th A pleasant day—some cool

[574] Wednesday 25th October 1843—some rain, with wind S—

Thursday 26th A cloudy cool day wind N—A Mr. Coe, a dentist has been with us a day or two, leaves this day—

Friday 27th A rain Storm—Wind E—

Saturday 28th Wind cool N—

Wednesday 1st November 1843 Cool weather—

Thursday 2nd A.M. a smart rain from midnight untill this morn, when It clears off, with Westerly wind

Saturday 4th A pretty fair day—I have had a cold with which I have been almost confined this week past—headache & a cough is tedious, but much lighter than I deserve—

Sabbath 5th Clears & cool this eve—Mr. Smith Dewy was married to Susan, the daughter of John & Parnol Wiggins—Harriet M. Preston with us—

Tuesday 7th Henry Haynes, who has worked in my shop 6 months, quit this day

Wednesday 8th The snow which fell yesterday

[575] Friday 10th November 1843 Wind E—Died last night Nancy, daughter of Frederick & Polly Taber, & wife of Eli Tuthill—she was a dutiful child and an aimable wife

Saturday 11th A cold rain Storm—wind East—

Sabbath 12th A powerful wind W-N-W—

Tuesday 14th Some snow last night, wind W—

Thursday 16th A rain Storm, with with S-E—On 13th Wilcox killed his hog, which weighed 324 lbs.

Friday 17th a damp day

Saturday 18th Showers this morn—

On Thursday Evening 16th this Inst. our beloved Grand daughter Deziah Preston was married to Samuel Griffing, of Riverhead—

Sabbath 19th Novem. 1843—A Pleasent

James Preston, our late soninlaws place was sold yesterday for 3680 Dolls—

[576] This eve 19th November 1843 Henry Hayns was married to Mehitable Vail, daughter of the late Henry Vail, and Dolly Vail—

Tuesday 21st A Southerly wind with Rain—

Friday 24th Rains this morn with wind S—

Sabbath 26th A pleasant day—

Monday 27th Wind S-W- Our daughter Honora was confined with a daughter—They call her Honora Seward

Wednesday 29th This day Joshua Payne put on the spindle on the Steeple of our new meeting house—perhaps its 70 feet high—This Mr. Payne is the Son of my Friend Phineas Payne of Southold—

Friday 1st December 1843—A snow this morn with wind N-N-W—It snowed some on 28th last just—

Saturday 2nd Some Snow fell this eve

Monday 4th A damp S- wind

Tuesday 5th A Squally day wind N-W—[577] Died this day, December 5th 1843 Elijah Terry, Merchant at Riverhead—Mr. Terry was a man of talent and of much consideration amid a large circle of connections, and friends, amongst whom his aimable manners and gifts of communication were considered very respectable—His religious profession was strictly Swedenborgian—In the faith of that doctrine he died without a doubt

Thursday 7th A.M. A Snow Storm, wind N—In the afternoon It was a moderate rain—This Eve It Snows again—

Friday 8th Cool, with wind N-W—

Saturday 9th It Snowed, and rained both last night—Harriet M. Preston, our G-daugher, with us—

Sabbath 10th—Wind N-W—Harriet left us this Eve—

Monday 11th A moderate rain Storm—Departed this life this day Capt. Rufus Tuthill aged 96 years 10 months & 24 days—

Tuesday 12th Wind N-N-W—

Thursday 14th Thanksgiving, by proclamation of the Governor

Saturday 16th An Easterly rain storm—

[578] Tuesday 26th December 1843 A light Easterly wind

Wednesday 27th An East, N-E- rain storm, all last night—Some rain this morn—P.M. It [?] off moderate—but cool

Thursday 28th Midling Pleasent—Our new church is dedicated this day—A Mr. Noles of Riverhead preached the dedication sermon from 2nd Chronicles 6 Chap & 40th verse—

Friday 29th Wind N-N-W—

Saturday 30th A blustering cold day—Our two endearing Grand daughters, Deziah and Harriet M. Preston, with us—

Sabbath 31st—Our two children, mentioned yesterday, left us this day with Samuel Griffing, for Riverhead—

There is much excitement in the cause of Temperence about this time— it has brought much comfort, and consolation to thousands who have been made wretched and miserable by the accursed use of intoxicating drinks— the cause of Temperence is the cause of God—

•

[579] <u>Appendix</u>

Richard Goldsmith, mentioned in page 11th of this journal, died 2nd April 1825—He was considered one of the wealthiest farmers in Blooming Grove—He was a useful, benevolent man, and a friend to the poor—A prudent, wise economist—Fifty-five years ago he was all this, and about fifty years of age at the time 1793—Now in 1848 his beautiful place has gone out of the name and his family, (which was one son & 3 daughters) I rather believe are all dead—he was about 80 years old or near that at his death—

Anselm Helm Esquire, noticed in page 5th was a very respectable farmer and Majestrate in Bloooming Grove—He died 9th December 1824

William Hudson noticed in Page 16 died Feb. 4th 1817 aged about 52 years—Capt. Joshua Brown- noticed in page 30th died June 2 1818 aged about 71 years—Samuel Moffat, noticed in page 11th died 14th Oct. 1807 aged about 73 or 4 years—He was a Man of strict integrity, and a valuable member of society—George Brown Esq. noticed in page 59 died Jan. 3rd 1841 aged 84 years—Abner Coleman noticed in page 27th died Jan. 24th 1834 aged about 73 or 4—I always found him friendly and accommodating. He was a kind neighbor, and useful in his situation.

[580] John Hudson, noticed in page 102 died not far from the year 1830—aged about 69 years

John C. Rudd, a young, tallented, accomplished, and justly approved School Teacher, on Shelter island, in 1799 & 1800, mentioned in this Journal of 11 Febr & March 1800 I think—John C. Rudd died on Wednesday 22nd Novem. 1840 at Utica—He has edited a paper in that city this some doz. or more years—I believe it was called the Christian Messenger—After leaving Shelterisland he taught school in New York, and studied divinity at the same time—In possess of time, by the friendship and assistance of Bishop Moore, he became an Episcopalian priest of consideration and in due time was created Doct. Of Divinity—He was also really a Student of great Industry, and I believe a <u>good</u>, as well as a selftaught Man—He named our daughter Cleora, who was born Dec 1799—At the time of his death he was about 70 years of age—

[581] Beriah Moore Cleeve, noticed in 120th page, who was master carpenter of the building of my House in 1798 died in March 12th 1840 within a year or two of 70 years of age—He was through life a peaceable, quiet, industrious, hardlabouring Man, generally at his trade—We believe strickly honest—

Jared Gardner, mentioned in page 118 died, we are informed, at Riverhead about the year 1818 or near that date, at which time he must have been about

50 or 51 years of age—My fears of his future progress in life, as noticed in page 118 were well grounded—He lived about 25 years after the period when I made my observations on him—In these after years his imprudence continued, with not any abatement, except at short intervals, yet with an excellent constitution, united with great animation of spirits his outer Man held on to a full half century. His death was very sudden, about midnight after eating a hearty supper—

[582] Wines Osborne, noticed in page 154, died in New York in 1830 aged about 64 years—

My friend and once Juvenile Schoolmate, Phineas Paine, mentioned in 24th page, Died suddenly at his house, in Southold, 18th May 1849, aged 80 years—He was through life an industrious, well-informed, agreeable Man, and much of the Gentleman—

September 18th 1849 died this evening Capt. William Austin Booth, particularly noticed in 144 page of this journal aged about 75 years

Died on the 16th March 1850 Capt. David Landon, aged 60 years, noticed in page 360. Capt. Landon was a man of much literary information, considering his opportunities—He had some years since commanded a fine Brig, to foreign ports with tolerable success—of late years his path has appeared to be rough—his habits has been industrious, but almost entirely excluded from society—He died a disappointed Man—Possessing a knowledge of the world and its heartless ingratitude—to err is human

[583] Capt. David Sweezy, mentioned in 79th page of this journal, as a kind, accommodating, agreable neighbor, died in 1828 aged about 86 years—It appears he lived after these friendly visits 32 years—As we moved from his neighborhood to Southold, Long Island, in the Spring of 1797, I do not recollect of even seeing Capt. Sweezy after the Spring above said—I think the Doct., The Captains very aimable and greatly beloved Brother, Jonathan, died some years before—

Capt. David Hawkins, mentioned page 11th died around 1825, in Orange County N.Y. where he has resided with his family I suppose the last 40 years of his life—In the war of the Revolution he was a Sergeant on duty at Oysterponds about the time Genl. Wooster was there with his regiment—I think in 1775—At that time being about 7 years old, I remember of his being [?] where I was staying—

[584] Capt. Silas Webb, mentioned page 347, died in New York on the 16th March 1849 in his 91st year—He was born August 1768—

In page 358 is noticed a visit I made to Southold, on purpose to see and become acquainted with a Mrs. Penny, a Widow Lady, of 102 years of age—

I have just received a letter from Joseph H. Goldsmith Esquire, dated 2nd March 1849, which informs me that Mrs. Penny's Christian name was Esther—She was three times married—Her first Husband was Jonah Halsey—Her 2nd Dickerson—3rd William Penny, whose Widow she was at the time of her death, which took place in 1838 at Wading River, where her remains lie interred in the burying ground—She was 102 years & about six months when she died—Its probable she was the oldest person that ever lived in the Town—

[585] George Champlin, noticed in page 317, died on the 17th May 1849— He had become greatly and justly beloved by a large circle of connections, friends, and neighbours—He had been at the time of his death one of our Orient Merchants, for the last 20 years, and a more accommodating, oblidgeing, kindhearted Man we have rarely known in Orient—His age about 47 years—

Joshua Curtis, noticed in 32nd page, died about the year 1824, an honest man

Benjamin Brewster, noticed in page 61 died near the year 1824—A man of strict veracity—

Asael Coleman, noticed in page 14, died at or about 1824—An irreproachable [?] character, and a great blessing to Society—one of Popes noblest works of God—As honest a Man as is known in our World

[586] Died in Bloomingburg, N.York, Thomas Payne, aged about 78— I have noticed his kind attentions to me in page 24th—His Death took place some where near 1840—In the years 1786-7 & 8 Thomas Payne— Grover Moore and Wines Orsborne were what was then called rude, or high boys—Too jovial, and frolicsome, almost to escape censure—After this period, Mr. Payne went to Goshen, Orange County, married a beautiful woman, with whom he lived many years, as we believe in tranquility, as a steady, industrious, prosperous Man—Grover Moore married a fine Woman, settled in Cutchogue, a steady, industrious citizen—He died March 13th 1825 aged about 60 years—Wines Orsborne see page 582—He was married I believe three times—His buisness was School-keeping—He was talented but rather imprudent

[587] Isaac Youngs, noticed in page 108, died about the year 1798 or 9— He was a man of very agreeable address—prepossessing and pleasent in conversation—learned—talented—a fine figure, with marked beauty of the whole Man—But alas! Company, and bad habits destroyed this interesting Charracter at the age of 34 or 5 years—

O Rum, Rum, what a curse, hast thou been to the Human family! Thy path has been marked with sighs, groans, wretchedness, murder, blood and death—

Mr. Henry Youngs, noticed in page 108, died in 1802—

[588] Died on the evening of the 27th November 1852 Caleb Dyer, aged 72 years—This gentleman is particularly noticed in this Journal, pages 112-143 & 455 &6

> "How many sleep,
> "that kept the World awake"

Daniel Hull Wickam, brother to Mrs. Patty Tuthill, noticed in page 29th this Journal, was a Man of deserved respectability—Through a life of fourscore years, he has sustained a character for Integrity, consistency and moral dignity, unimpeachable—This gentleman died on Staten Island, Feb. 3rd 1853 in his 83rd year—He had received a Collegial Education—

[589] Mr. Samuel Tuthill, particularly noticed in pages 9th and 50th of this Journal, died at Elmira N.Y. in 1851, I believe in the month of August—He was in the 86th year of his age—As a Father, Husband, and neighbor he merited much and was greatly beloved—He had become wealthy by Industry, prudence and strict attention to his own affairs—Benevolence, Morality, and sound Christian Faith, greatly supported him when taking his final farewell of Earth and all the fading productions—He was the 2nd son of the late Majors Tuthill of Orient N.Y.—who was the Son of Henry Tuthill Jr. who was the Son of Henry Tuthill Sr. who was the Son of John Tuthill Jr. who was the son of John Tuthill Sr. who came from England to Southold in 1640—he was living in 1681 & 2 at the time more than 80 years of age—

Bar-room Scene
Painting by William Sidney Mount, 1835. This scene by Long Island native Mount, with a flyer on the wall advertising Temperance meetings, perfectly reflects Griffin's ambivalence about serving liquor in his tavern (I: 77 [197]). Courtesy of The Art Institute of Chicago.

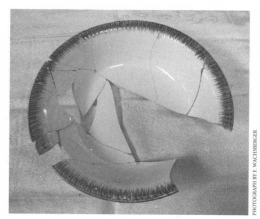

**Leeds bowl,
early 19th century**
This fragmentary bowl, excavated from beneath Village House in 2007, is an example of the sort of everyday ceramic ware, imported from Leeds, England, which would have been used as tavern ware (I: 86-87 [222]). OHS Collections.

**Certificate,
Temperance Fund League, 1847**
Orient was to remain a dry village until after the Second World War. OHS Collections (facing).

VOLUME II

Windmill, Orient Harbor

Before 1898; photographer unknown. This grain mill, which stood at the foot of the present Skipper's Lane, was built in 1810 by Nathaniel Dominy of East Hampton to replace an earlier one that, according to Griffin, had stood there for fifty years (I: 117 [302], II: 240 [16]). It was sold to the Glen Island (New York) Amusement Park in 1898 and burned to the ground in 1909. OHS Collections.

1844

[7] Monday 1st January 1844 comes in with a bright sunshine, cool, yet for the time of year, pleasant—This day 79 years ago, my brother James was born—through all this period of flying time, (since he arrived to years of discretion,) his eventual life has been strictly moral. He has been, at all times, an obedient man, an agreable companion, and an instructive stedfast friend—Well informed—a tender husband and a kind Father—Few men have passed through so many years as well beloved, and with so very few enemies—I am almost led to believe he never had a sentimental enemy— If he had, It must have been one of the old squaws poor creatures—Well— this is my brother—how is it with me? Ah—indeed how Is It—Why, when I would do good, evil has been present with me

[8] Tuesday 2nd Very little wind through the day—Evening, a light breeze from the South—Died yesterday (as I have just heard) at Southold the Widow of my late uncle Thomas Terry, Esther, aged about Eighty Six—She has been through life one of the most excellent of women—Endeared to her husband, children and her numerous connections, by every virtue that constitutes a woman an ornament to society, and a fit subject for a glorious immortality—My above mentioned Uncle Thomas, I have particularly noticed in my journal page 384 and 85—Isabella Moore (daughter of the coloured woman whom people generally call Aunt Genny) died last evening—[9] Isabella was about 66 years of age—She has been one of the most industrious, economical, and laborious of anyone in her situation— prudent, and nice in all her works to a proverb—By her industry and uncommon attention to her earnings, she has accumulated property to the amount of from Ten to twelve hundred Dollars—Its very probable there never was a more faithful, neat and honester person employed as an assis- tant in any buisness of a domestic relation—Her Father, called Cade Moore, was a Slave—His time, she purchased with her first earnings—He died some years since—he was honest, frugal and peaceable—Genny, the widow, is now about 87 years of age—was brought up in my Grandfather Jonathan Terrys family

A Miss Solomon
began to assist
Wilcox in the fam-
ily this day
viz.2nd Jan. 1844

[10] Wednesday 3rd Jan. comes in with a S-E- rain storm. Speaking yesterday of Isabella Moore (the coloured woman,) reminds me of another, in every
particular, as to Industry, prudence, attention, and usefulness to her employers, her (Isabellas) counterpart Dianna Williams, died on Shelter Island March
1837—She was born a slave, in this place (Orient.) Obtained her freedom,
when about 25 years of age, after which, like Isabella, by indefagitable [sic]
continual labour, united with strictest economy, and a wise use of her earnings, she got together property to the amount of perhaps a thousand or twelve
hundred Dollars—Her husband, Williams, was a more than [11] common,
well behaved coloured man. Knew his place with marked precision, and at all
times moved in his sphere, so as to unite the goodwill of all those with whom
his buisness called him to act—He died some years before his wife, Dianna—
Her manners, conversation, and knowledge, in attendence as a waiter, on genteel, good and well-informed company, exceeded any coloured woman I ever
knew—In this view, I am sure I am far from being alone—Thus far, I have
conceived It my duty to pay this small tribute, to these two extraordinary
Ethiopeans, who but for their colour would have had a conspicuous place in
the register of Columbias favourite Daughters. Dianna's Father was Crank,
known in this town, as a manufacturer of Salt from Salt water, by boiling, at
Shelter Island in the revolutionary war. His wife Flora, as a nurse, had hardly
her equal, and in her humble situation many friends.

[12] I understand that in the revival, now at the Baptist Church, at
Greenport, there has had the ordinance of Baptism administered on them,
by immersion over Sixty persons, adults, and children—It is assuredly a
solemn manifestation of the belief of the subjects in the mode of showing
the faith, and iniciation into the church militant—And not any, be their
lives ever so holy, can be admitted to their Sacrimental table, but those
comeing into the door, as themselves—Thus says their teachers, is God's
imperitive commands; and their members must solemnly, and assuredly at
all times this side [of] the grave, adhere to It—Charity, persuades us to
believe those pastors sincere, at the same time in error—for certainly, a true
believer in the gospel of Christ, and a humble partaker of Its rich sources of
love, and holy resignation, and humil [13] ity at the feet of Jesus, is a fit subject to set at the Table of our Lord, wherever It is spread for the absolute
followers of the LAMB—A Mr. Abely is a stated pastor of said Church—but
a Mr. Swan from New London, has been a prominent preacher in said place
this two or three weeks past—Rumor (tho sometimes it lies) says, although
a renowned revivilest [sic], he displays much lack of that, which inspiration
says exceeds faith and hope—"Man to man is the sorest, surest Ill."

Thursday 4th Commences with snow, Wind N-W—P.M. Wind W-S-W—clear—snow goes off rapidly—Walked down to Doctr S.H. Tuthill

Friday 5th High wind from N-W- attended with what some say very cold weather—Selfishness is so interwoven into our natures, that to find a Man whom It does not govern is like Solomon's one amongst a thousand—yes, 10,000—

[14] Saturday 6th January 1844—A light wind W-N-W—much more mild yet pretty cool—Our G-son John A. Preston took dinner with us—We were glad to see him look so well and contented as he appears to be—May the blessing of Jacobs GOD rest upon him and Devils and fanaticks have no power at all, at all, over his body or mind—

Sabbath 7th A cloudy day—a light breeze of wind from the S—Snowed a little this morn—P.M. a light rain—Error, and fanaticism are assuredly abroad at this day in our highly favoured land—The spirit of censure is indulged by those preachers who make loud professions of meekness, godliness and that great Grace Charity—There is says the Bible, a zeal that is not according to knowledge—viz. according to the Spirit with which good old Simeon was filled, when he embraced the infant Saviour, in his aged arms—[15] A Teacher of the people, a preacher of righteousness ought to be clothed with that precious garb of Heaven, Humility—They should be at all times as wise as Serpents, and as harmless as Doves—Revolt at the idea of uttering a sentence, or censure which is derogatory to sound sense, and devoid of every particle of wisdom—If not wise, is It not vain, and if vain, Is It not foolish? And if foolish, is It not sinful? If sinful we are told to shun It, as a deadly poison

Monday 8th High wind N-W- and freezing cold—

Tuesday 9th Very little wind this very cold morn—hazy, or thick weather and we should not be surprised if snow appeared to come soon. Towards evening, It commenced snowing with wind E—

Wednesday 10th Light wind N-W—The ground is covered with about 2 or 3 inches of snow

[16] Thursday 11th What is generally called "a pretty cold morning" Wind N-W—clear sky—

Friday 12th A.M. Clear & cold wind N-W—P.M. cloudy Wind S—Have been transcribing a dream, which I had near fifty years since—which I at the time attempted to describe in rhyme—It will not bear criticism—The poetry I refer to—yet, as a relic It may please some friend, whose goodness of heart will love to put the best constructions on well intended effusions of the moment—Especially those productions coming from one who claims no pretensions to that of a poet—

Saturday 13th Rained pretty much through all last night—clears off this morn with brisk wind S-W—They (the owners of the wind <u>mill</u> in this place Orient) are puting a new shaft in her—It weighs about a <u>Ton</u>—They have to hoist It 30 odd feet to get it in its place—

[17] Sabbath 14th January 1844 A clear cool day—Wind moderate N-W—Rec'd a letter this day, from our son, Sidney, from Hempstead—

Monday 15th Cool & hazy—wind light from N—Our need of watchfulness is great—very great indeed—e'er we are aware, our propensity to err leads us into situations calculated for the most unpleasent reflections—and often, too often, into bitter and briery pathes—If we perceive a spark of anger arise in our bosom, we ought, as we value our peace and our standing in our families and society, count Ten, yes <u>one hundred</u>, before we notice the Demon, which is tempting our tranquility—Always, and at all times, and in all places, "leave off contention before It is meddled with" Attend to these rules, and Heaven will assist you to all the comforts derived from true wisdom—A.G.

[18] Tuesday 16th Last night was a rainy one—It still continues to rain. It has been a constant rain through the day—

Wednesday 17th It still rains, as It has done this 24 hours past—This day Ninety seven years ago, Captain Rufus Tuthill (who died on the 11th of Decem. last) was born—Of course, he was Ninety six years Ten months and twenty four days old at his death—His great uncle John Tuthill, who died November 26, 1754 was Ninety six years and Nine months and 12 days old at his death—Their united ages would be 193 years and 5 days—Died this day an infant daughter of G.M.Tuthill's, whose wife died on the tenth of November last

Thursday 18th Clear, Wind high N-W- and growing cold—To be very careful in giving our opinion in matters of weight is, (in my Idea) a step in the path of providence—A mother that is honored by her children, yea, and respected too, has a special [19] call to bless them—yes, they shall be blessed—

Deeds are fruits, words are <u>but</u> leaves

I might have observed that yesterday afternoon, It blew a tremendous S-W- gale, which drove two of our Sloops on the shore—The <u>Liberator</u>, and Dan'l Webster—the 1st commanded by D.F. Glover—the other—E.N. Glover—

Friday 19th Weather and wind as yesterday—It appears to be much easier to see goodness in those we <u>admire</u> than to find only the least uprightness in those we do not—

It is wise to see how we are to [be] benefited, by what we are about to undertake—

Saturday 20th Last night was about as cold a one as we have had this winter—Wind N-N-W—How much of our conversation in the daily intercourse we have with our neighbours and others will bear a virtuous approbation? Ah, will bear a pleasant reflection? —I fear not any—If so, what account can be given for the time spent—Alas! we are not [considerate?]—not watchful.

[20] Sabbath 21st 1844 A very light wind N-N-E- and very cold—the harbour for some thirty rods out, begins to shut up with ice—This evening it commences snowing very moderately—This day is set apart to worship [of] our Father in Heaven—Alas, how many are they who attend church, amid one thousand, can say (and speak Gods Truth) that they this day have worshipped God in Spirit & in Truth—

Monday 22nd The ground, this morn, is covered with snow about two inches in depth—

He that speaks as he ought discovers more wisdom than loquacious people generally possess—Arguments are often carried on with to[o] much unreasonable warmth—Disputes, altogether more so—If possible, then, shun them, as you would a path full of briers, and thorns—A good word is as easy said, as a bad one—If so, we indulge the bad ones far the most, and of course become guilty—guilty, and condemned already—

Positive persons are often in error.

[21] Tuesday 23rd Comes in with wind E-S-E- and a little flurry of snow—then a light rain—Frank R. Youngs puts the roof upon his Ice house this day—Give those power, whose hearts and dispositions you wish to know—Confine a wolf and he is as harmless as a lamb, but give him his liberty and he is all wolf—

Wednesday 24th A moderate, what is called a pleasant morning in January—Some white frost—We all have a motive in our every undertaking—If its to do a real good, and our aims are to increase our grattitude to our Father in Heaven, we are certainly moveing in a Glorious cause—But alas, how is the past time of our life been? Are our reflections upon It Joyous? Every heart knows its own bitterness, and its own sweets—To be composed, and calm, in the midst of a hurricane, argues wisdom, and true resignation in the Man of sound sense—They who know nothing have no fear.

[22] Thursday 25th Jan. 1844—A cool N-W- wind—Yesterday the roads were mud and mire, this morn they are like the scragged rock—So much from the fever heat to the freezing point.

The railroad which has been constructing through Long Island, very slowly, since about 1840, is now (we are informed) in rapid progress towards

Greenport its destined termination—Its length when completed will be Ninety four miles—

The Sloop Motto, owned in part, and commanded by Sidney P. Racket, was sold a few days since to Greenport—Of course, she has left our Orient Harbour, making one vessel less owned and sailing from the place—

Friday 26th As cold a night the past one as any this winter—It is extremely so this morn—Wind very light N—

Sidney Philander Racket (mentioned yesterday) Is the third Son of my late, much esteemed friend Elisha Racket, who died in November 1822— [23] He, Sidney, was at the time of his Father's death about Nine years old, left to the care of his Widowed Mother, with two elder brothers—John & Sherry—After passing through the scenes and causalities incident to boys who have no Father to watch over their chequered road to Manhood, he reached the age of about twenty—At that early time of life he was selected to take charge of a coasting sloop—In this trust he exceeded the most sanguine expectations—His owners realized substantial advantages by their confidence in a youth scarcely twenty one—How much gratitude, he has found his [?] or first employers to possess, towards him for his untiring zeal and industry for their interest, he (now at thirty years) best can tell— His plans, and intended movements appear to have always been shut up in his own bosom—and only known when submited to publick action— To me, he has in his line shown that he knew no confidents, and if he was never a Washington, he has one of his conspicuous traits, that is, in strictly keeping his own secrets—[24] The short biographical notice of my young friend Sidney P. Racket was suggested from motives as pure as my wishes are for his prosperity and virtue through all his future life—See 22nd June 1843

Saturday 27th Jan. 1844. It continues extreme cold—our harbour pretty much shut with Ice—Wind N—Sabbath 28th Still as blustering and cold as some days past—Monday 29th Colder, if possible—Wind high N—Our John A. Preston with us—To us, It is our Joy, In this our eve of Life— "Children those precious limbs, those tender portions of our flesh, those our dear otherselves, how they dilate the heart to wide dimentions and soften the Mothers sad capacities of pain—of pleasure"

Tuesday 30th Calm—Cold & cloudy, with a few flakes of snow—not so as to cover the ground—People this day have crossed over to ShelterIsland on the Ice, from or near Greenport—This evening more snow

Wednesday 31st Cold as ever—It prognosticates a coming very cold night—

•

[25] Thursday 1st Feb. 1844 As was supposed the past night was as cold
as any one this winter—This morn & clear—People are crossing over the
Ice to long beach after eels—Capt. Wisdom & a Mr Woodruff, from
N.York, are with us—They are to lecture on Temperence this evening at
the upper church—

On the 20th
several men
crossed from
Fannings point
to ShelterIsland

Our grandson John Augustus Preston, left us last evening from
GreenPort—He purposes to set off in a few days for the State of Maine to
attend the medical lectures, which commence about the 19th this Inst—I
do not at this time recollect the town of the School, or college—

Friday 2nd The ground is covered, about 3 inches with snow—Wind S-
E—This is the anniversary of my birth, Seventy Seven years have told their
astonishing revolutions since I commenced my part on this varied scene of
time, and sense—It has passed off like a vapor or a tale that is quickly, and
mournfully told—[26] And now where do I stand? On the verge or shores
of Ocean, on which every son and daughter of Adam have, & must assuredly
launch, and blessed indeed are they who are found righteously provided in
full for the voyge—May my Father in Heaven vouchsafe me (the most
unworthy) a prosperous soil, and a safe arrival into that celestial port "where
the wicked cease from troubling and the weary find immortal rest"

> Quite eleven times seven revolving years
> With all their pains and cares and fears
> I speedily have past—
> How like a vision, or a dream—
> Do all these revolutions seem—
> How vain, from first, to last—

Saturday 3rd Wind light North W—Thaws considerable—Some not very
good sleighing. There has been but very little sleighing thus far this winter—Nathaniel Corwin of Green Port with his wife, and Mrs. Miller (wife
to Priest Miller of Southold) was with us an hour or two this day—

[27] Sabbath 4th Feb. 1844—Very little wind N-E—And moderately
cold—A Mr. or Dr. Hall, Dentist etc.—with us—professes the Knowledge
of phrenology—

Monday 5th A damp, chilly, rather of a thawy day, some hail—Some rain
this eve—Wind E—

Tuesday 6th Considerable rain through the past night—The following
question suggests itself with peculiar insight to me this morn, viz. what part,

or how much of our time do we improve for the actual benefit of ourselves, our Friends, and Society? How much from the age of twelve to thirty five? Does it tranquilize our evening reflections, to scrutinize each action, and conversation of the past day? A look into our barrooms, hotels and boardinghouses gives peculiar weight and interest to these, and many more important and alarming questions—Well, there is no evading the surrender of the Length[en]ing account—and those possessing the spirit of the Publican, may find a merciful Lord—

[28] Martin L. Hallock has been stoping with us occasionally this twelve months past—He was a pupil, or a favourite apprentice to the late Henry Ekford. His opportunities with Mr. Ekford were good, and the improvements he made of them were we hope such as will yield a prolofick harvest—Mr. Hallock is about thirty five years of age—Since twenty one he has passed through severe and thorny pathes, and seen stormy seasons—And yet the clouds have not all passed off—He best knows his own sad past history—that the future may be more pleasent, more mild, and calculated to produce a rectitude in all his movements, productive of that resignation, which constitutes all the happiness which mortals can attain to on this side the grave—the above notice is suggested from pure motives.

[29] Wednesday 7th Quite a thaw, and more mild and warm than any day this month past—Mr. or Doctor Hall left us this morn. He appears to be a man of some considerable acquirements in his possession, as dentist etc. etc.—but whether he cultivates that taciturnity necessary to beget the dignity which we always find accompanying wisdom, A day or two in his presence will correctly inform us—

Thursday 8th Came in with snow falling pretty fast for 30 or 40 minutes—Wind N-N-E—Howsomever, It did not snow hardly enough to make sleighing tollerable—It has been a cloudy, what people say a sour day. We had the sweet repast of an affectionate communication from our very filial G-daughter Harriet M. Preston—

Friday 9th Some snow squalls this P.M. Cool, sour weather—Chancy W. Moore staid with us last night. [30] He is the son of my late much respected friend Usher H. Moore of Aquebogue—Chancy has been a visitor, occasionally since the year 1822—He at that time commenced selling dry goods by travilling with a one Horse waggon—Sometime after that with an elegant two horse one in style—for about 10 or 12 years past, he has kept a large wholesale store in N. York where he is in now doing buisness—We believe him to be well calculated for his profession—Noble hearted, generous, tenderly inclined to actions of Kindness, especially to his connections and friends—for the first of these he has [31] done much—very much—

Saturday 10th Very cold—Wind N-N-W—A profile taker [silhoutte cutter] with us—

It is an easy thing for some people to censure others, but whether the censurer is discovering good breeding, or a virtuous reverence by his, or her language, we can form our own Ideas of—Not favourable, we presume

Sabbath 11th Feb. Clear, and very little wind—not warm—

Monday 12th Wind light, N—Still continues cold—The Sound is full of floating Ice—our harbour is yet frozen up, as It has been since the 24th of January, last past—Tuesday 13th As pleasant a morn as we have seen this 30 days past- A light wind S—

[32] Wednesday 14th February 1844—Morning very pleasant—Day more cloudy—cool—Wind W—

Was deceived this day, and by the deception, put my name to a paper respecting a deputy Collector, at Greenport—Well, I have been imposed upon—let it pass—The duplicity will out and those concerned in the nocturnal move assuredly fall—Those who have knowledge without virtue are like the old Apple tree, which bears blossoms without ever producing any fruit—

Thursday 15th Very little wind, and that varying different points through the day—A Mr. Judd, and another gentleman with us this eve—they have three horses and are traviling merchants—Vending Yankee notions.

Friday 16th The ground this morning covered with snow having fallen last night. It goes off fast with a [33] Clear bright sun and S-W- light wind— Our traveling merchants left us this morn—Mssrs. Judd and Wicks—This Mr. Judd appears to be very active, pretty well informed, buisnesslike young Man—And I should suppose possessing a quantum of the necessary knowledge of the fickleness of Mankind—

Saturday 17th Wind S-S-W—Although considerable frost last night, It thaws fast today—

Thomas V. Youngs, Barzella & Benj. Youngs, Joseph Latham, Elisha Mulford, J. F. Latham, Seth B. Taber, Joseph Terry Esq., Seth H. Tuthill & Lewis Tuthill, Jeremiah Terry & Noah Tuthill, 12 of our neighbours here in Orient have raised for market 3200 bushels of potatoes and 4300 bushels of turnips this year. Total of only 12 of our neighours 7500 bushels—

[34] Sabbath 18 Feb. 1844 Very cold Wind N-W—

Monday 19th Rather more moderate—P.M. wind dies away, & bids fair for a still and pleasant night—

How good it is to be sensible, and thankful for our many mercies.

Tuesday 20th More mild and warm than any day this four weeks past. Raymond shortened my woodhouse, or shed some ten feet—the part taken off was getting much rotten—of course It was taken off—

Wednesday 21st As mild, as pleasant as It was yesterday—Worked with Raymond in makeing a hen roost in my Barn—

[35] Thursday 22nd Still continues mild weather—Quite a gathering of the temperance society, at Orient—An able address at the Congregational Church delivered by a gentleman from Southold—One hundred & 12 years since George Washington was born this day—

Friday 23rd Wind S-E—cooler than some days past—Raymond & myself, at the Hen pen today—

Saturday 24th Fresh breeze E—Cool and cloudy—The Ice left the harbour this morn. It has continued shut up 33 or 34 days.

[36] Sabbath 25th Feb. 1844—A lowry, cloudy day with a very light E-S-E- wind

Monday 26th What we call pleasent—White frost this several nights past—calm this eve—

Tuesday 27th Some sprinkles of rain occasionally through the day—Raymond, with myself finished my hen pen, and covered it in part with old fish seine—Yesterday—

Wednesday 28th This morn there is about two inches of snow on the ground—Cool N-E- Wind—At noon it moderates—Snow goes off, but it bids fair for a cold night—

[37] Thursday 29th Feb. 1844—Leap year—Cool morn, Wind light N—A cloudy and damp day—

Friday 1st March 1844—Much such a day as yesterday, but nearly calm—Where is the rational man that is free from anxiety, or anxious care? If wisely anxious about acquiring a holy resignation to our Heavenly Fathers will, we are assuredly in a blessed employment—

Saturday 2nd Cloudy—damp and chilly weather, with very little wind S-W—Mr. Erastus Wells, from Acquebogue, took dinner with us—He has lately commenced preaching. Bids fair to be a useful Man in the field of the gospel of Jesus Christ.

[38] Sabbath 3rd March 1844—Very little, and a part of the day not any, wind—A cloudy day—

Monday 4th comes snowing briskly, with wind N-W- yet moderate—Deep in the <u>vale</u> of life, accompanied with sensation which attend no one but those who arrive to that thinly sequestered and very lonely situation—

Tuesday 5th A colder day than any this Ten days past—Wind N-W-and brisk—

To bear, and forbear, betokens a good mind—

[39] Wednesday 6th March 1844—Much more moderate, wind light W—Deception and ingratitude destroy much of the comfort of those who would shun those banes of all honest men—The most wary, and best of men, at times, (if they deal much) get grocely [grossly] deceived—

Thursday 7th Continues more mild—Very little wind through the day—Assisted Raymond in moveing the pettion [partition?] in my grain house, about four feet to the east part—Received a letter from our Son Sidney—It was like cool water to the thirsty soul—As they were in health—It was refreshing in deed and in truth—

Friday 8th A rainy, or wet day—Wind S—Worked at the grain house. The steam ship Princeton burst her large gun 29 last month, killing the Secretaries of the State & Navy, and several others.

[40] Saturday 9th March 1844 A cloudy day, uncomfortable day—Bad walking, as it is very muddy—Wrote to our Son Sidney—Doct. Young Justly says "lean not on Earth, 'twill pierce thee to the heart, a broken read [reed] at best and oft a spear, on the sharp point, peace bleeds, and hope expires"—

In advanced life, when the grasshopper becomes a burden, we look to something to lean upon—We cast an affectionate eye upon our children—It is right we should—Yet how little do they know of the weighty, gloomy painful sensations attending the thorny vale of threescore and seventeen years—God be praised, some such parents have filial children, to feel and sooth their parents anxious cares—

Sabbath 10th Wind N-W—Some cooler this morn, Captn Wisdom and Mr. Morse are with us from N.Y—They lecture on temperance this eve—

[41] Monday 11th Very mild, and Spring like weather—The ground appears to settle fast—howsomever, we must expect some cold & blustering weather yet—Spring will return, and with it all its musick, and fragrance, and bloom, but the springtime of Youth can never return to those in the winter of age & infirmities—Their Spring—Their Summer, and Autumn is gone—gone forever—Yes, and each have bourn away Its own load—

Tuesday 12th Wind E—cooler—and cloudy day—Wednesday 13th A rain storm—Vendue at John G. Champlins selling off his effects, Intending to move to Greenport, in a week or two—

Thursday 14th Wind yesterday E—today N- and cool—Wrote to our dear Grand daughter H.M. Preston, in answer to hers of a day or two since—

Friday 15th Cool Wind N- & cloudy—more squalls P.M.

[42] Saturday 16th March 1844—Comes in with an Easterly rain storm—
Capt. Tuthill & Ezekiel Glover got their Vessels off the beach on which
they have been lying all winter—Our coasting vessels, from this place, are
all about starting, in pursuit of buisness, for their season. Raymond (our
soninlaw) entered on board of George Tuthills schooner last Thursday,
when she immediately set sail for NewYork.

Sabbath 17th This morn It continues to rain, as It has profusely, and,
occasionally moderately since last Friday night—About 10 OClock this
morn, It set in snowing about an hour very fast—Partially clears off ½ past
11 A.M. with wind West—

Monday 18th A blustering, or what we call a windy day—Wind W—A
Mr. McDermott is putting up a house [43] in this neighborhood, at this
time. His wife is daughter of Nathaniel Tuthill, who lives near the Dam.

Tuesday 19th Comes in very cold and blustering—It freezes quick this
morn—Wind or gale from N-W—

On the 1st of this month, March, departed this life Ebenezer W. Case
Esq.—He has been for the last twenty years, quite a publick, and in many
respects a useful Man in our Town and county—A Judge of the Court of
common pleas—A Surogate of the County—A member of the Assembly of
our State, A supervisor etc. etc.—All which offices he held with honor to
himself and approbation of his constituents—[44] Although Mr. E.W. Case
was not a man infalible, yet to me, I have always and at all times (and he has
formerly had much to do with my intricate afairs twenty five [years] ago)
found him faithful to me, and mine—

Wednesday 20th Wind S-S-E- and squally—

In the year 1750 It is said there was in the (then Oysterponds) now Orient
about forty dwelling houses, and from 40 to 50 families—In 1780 somewhere about fifty dwellings—Now in 1844 there is about one hundred or a
trifle over—and four stores, two or three shoe factories, and that number of
Joiners shops. The farms are of course small, but the owners of them very
industrious, and their yield is truly astonishing see a specimen of It mentioned in 17th Feb. last in this Diary—

Thursday 21st Wind fresh E—and squally, with some snow

[45] Friday 22nd March Wind E-N-E—It snowed hard or fast through
the past night and continued to snow until 10 OClock A.M. when it partially
clears off with wind W—P.M. A clear suny sky

(The below is a mistake Miss Paine died June 21 1846 Aged __ See page
297)

[The rest of the page is lightly crossed out.] Departed this life about two weeks ago, as we hear, Mrs. Lydia Paine* widow of the late John Paine of Southold—A more experient[i]al and living Christian, is seldom known in our Sinful, and Selfish world—Her conversation amid her friends and associates, was always in strict accordance with her great love and faith in the blessed Jesus—Her exortations in class and prayer meetings were sufficient to melt the most obdurat heart, and console the most afflicted lover of her (as she expressed it) precious Jesus—We looked upon her as a Mother in the church of God—And now she has gone to reap a rich reward of Glory with our Fathers & Mothers who have gone just before her—Her age was about 72 and She was the daughter of Major Barnabas Tuthill, of this place. He died in 1782

[46] Saturday 23rd March 1844—Very cool, rather more than common for the time of year—the ground is covered with a thick coat of snow and sleighs are passing our house merily with their tinckling bells—It is a cloudy, cold and windy day, Wind N—

All our comforts, or enjoyments, which accrue from Earthly productions are assuredly and actually fallacious—There is nothing solid or permanent in them—But the Man whose heart is wraped up in the month of Divine love, and Christian resignation to the methods of Gods holy Providence, partakes of those comforts, and enjoyments which will grow brighter, and brighter, round and round Eternity—

Sabbath 24th March—A clear suny day, after a cold night—Although a bright sun, the North wind, with plenty of snow on the ground, make It uncomfortably cool—"Blessed are the peace makers", And surely they are blessed who merit that Heavenly benediction

[47] It is assuredly distressing to be persecuted without a cause, and more especially at that time of life when the grasshopper becomes a burden—Yet if those who receive hard things, are possessed of a forgiving disposition, they can bless God at all times, and in all circumstances, and pray for them who speak evil (without reason) of them—

Monday 25th Comes with S-S-W- [wind] which carries off the snow which was thickly layered upon the unfrozen Earth—The melting of the snow, the clouded sky, and chilly wind make an out door excursion quite unpleasent—Yet the mind composed with a religious view of the unnumbered mercies of our Heavenly Father, gives a beauty, and comliness to calms, or storms—To such every shrub, tree and plant bears the brilliant impress our Saviours name—

Tuesday 26th A Cloudy calm day—If any wind it is from the S—Received a Letter from our very affectionate Grand daughter Deziah P. Griffin—Her

*Miss Paine we are informed is yet living —The knowledge of her death appears untrue

communications always awaken our tenderest recollections—of course, we read & weep.

[48] Wednesday 27th A cloudy day, Wind pretty brisk E-S-E—Some sprinkle of rain—Capt. John G. Champlin, moved himself and family to Greenport yesterday—He sold his house & lot to L.W. Gillett, some time since—Capt. Champlin lost his wife, She that was Rossetta Dyer, Jan 1 1842 and Married his present wife the widow Sally Roberts Decem. 1843—

We this day received a letter from our affectionate daughter Margaret (Sidneys wife) and their son Augustus—they were read and reread, with those emotions which can never be known, to any but affectionate parents—

Thursday 28th A very moderate rain—Wind light E—Settled up accounts with Marvin Holms, and ballanced all former dealings on book— This evening delivered him (Holms) sixteen dozen & 2 eggs, for which he owes me, now, two dollars & 2 cents.

Friday 29th Forenoon clears pleasant & warm—P.M. cool wind E—

[49] To love home, and the domestic circle, a seclusion from company, and the bustle of the world, Is truly valuable to the Man or Woman who with such retiring gifts possess good Judgement and philosophic reason.

Saturday 30th Comes in with a gale of E-N-E- wind and rain, which continued with considerable violence through the day—Evening, It set in a snowing, with hail, thunder, and lightning—severely cold wind hauling round to the North—

Sabbath 31st As cold a morn as is perhaps seldom known in the last of March—Wind N—Hail and snow covers the Earth about 4 or 5 inches.

A wise old man does three things viz 1st he abandons the world before the world abandons him—2nd He builds his sepulcher before It is time to enter It, and 3rd does every thing pleasant in the sight of God before he is called to his presence.

Mr. Marcus B. Browns wife Cynthia, was delivered of a Son last evening, and appears as yet with the little boy doing well—

Monday 1st April 1844 A very cold N-W- wind—It is uncomfortably cold—Called at Deacon R. Browns and at several neighbours—

[50] Tuesday 2nd April 1844 Wind N—It holds cool—Our neighbours appear much in earnest to attend the Town meeting—It is, and has been much attended to in this Town for one hundred years—Our father and their Fathers, who use to be all attendance on this day alas, where are they? All passed away—and the present buisy generation are fast following in the tract—

Wednesday 3rd Cool, clear, calm and very pleasant—Purchased 330 odd [?] of Hay of Joseph Terry Esq., and got It in my barn this evening—

Thursday 4th A mild day wind S—Captain Wm. Wisdom and family arrived from N-York this morning and hired a part of Sidney P. Rackets house for his present residence—that he may be a useful Citizen, is my sincere [desire?]

[51] Friday 5th April 1844 Cloudy with a light wind W—Walked over the farm of my late soninlaw James H. Preston—It is now owned by Mr. Beers, the Minister in this place, as preacher of the Congregational Church—Mr. Beers has a Man, employed in blowing, or splitting rocks suitable for a stone fence—I was accompanied in my walk by Capt. Wisdom—

Saturday 6th A damp cool E- wind—Some few sprinkles of rain—

Sabbath 7th Much such a day as yesterday Cool E- Wind—rode down to our Brother Rufus Tuthills in company with Brother James—Brother Rufus is very unwell—

Monday 8th Morning Foggy, with wind light E-S-E—Afternoon very mild Wind S—Planted a sage, and rareripe onions—It is more common to rejoice in haveing spoke but very little when in company than haveing spoke much and not to the purpose—"A wise head keeps a close mouth."

[52] Tuesday 9th April 1844—Foggy with thick wet mist—Wind light S-E—Fixt my Asparagus bed, covering It with beach sand, which is said to be good to make It productive—

Wednesday 10th As pleasant, mild and clear a day as we have had this Spring—Wheeled out in my wheel barrow 17 loads of cowyard manure on my Garden—

Thursday 11th Pleasant—Towards evening Wind became E- and It appears as if there is a storm of rain and wind near at hand—sowed, or planted, two onion beds, and some lettece and safron seeds—

Friday 12th Mild, and warm—Our dear Grand Son Chatham A. came— We were truly rejoiced to see him in health—

Saturday 13th Very warm—wind S- but very light—rather getting dry—

Sabbath 14th As mild & as warm as yesterday—Wind W—rather more of it than two days past.

[53] Monday April 15th 1844 Warm for the season—worked rather hard in the garden this morn—perhaps it will be for the best—To use, or cultivate moderation in all our doings.

Tuesday 16th Wind E—Some cooler—Rather smoky weather, and begins to be dry—Planted some potatoes in the S-W- part of my Garden—

Wednesday 17th A.M. Foggy and quite damp—P.M. clear, and very warm—

Thursday 18th Wind E- & Cooler—Worked some in my garden—

Friday 19th Sidney P. Rackett moved his Shop from his back lot to the road, in order to make an addition to It for a Blacksmith to work in—Capt. Wisdom is to occupy it—Our Grand daughter Deziah P. Griffin, and her Husband Samuel Griffin, Visited us this day—They were welcome guests—

Saturday 20th Wind as yesterday E—rather warmer. Our Grand daughter Harriet M. Preston came to us this day—Truly rejoices our hearts.

[54] Sabbath 21st Apl 1844 A foggy, cool morning—Wind E—some rain P.M.—comfortably warm—

This evening our Grand children Chatham A. G. & Harriet M. Preston left us for their homes—the first at Hempstead, the other at Greenport to attend her school—

Monday 22nd Calm & warm, planted onions, carrots, parsnips, beets & peas—Let Gelston Vail have 5 or 6 trees, for which he is to pay me in fish—

Tuesday 23rd Cool E- Wind—Set out several Cherry Trees—and did sundries—This day at about 8 A.M. my brother in law Rufus Tuthill departed this life—A more peaceable, kind benevolent, and pleasant Man, is rarely found amongst the large family of Man—As a dutiful, and obedient Son, I doubt whether there was ever his superior. To be acquainted with him, was to love him. His age was 67 years. [55] As a Father, he was wisely tender, and indulgent—An affectionate, kind loveing Husband—Invaluable as a neighbor, and take him all in all as a Man, he was a blessing to his neighbours and to his Town—

Wednesday 24th Was mild & pleasant—Wind light E-S-E—

Thursday 25th Wind as yesterday—This day our Brothers remains were committed to their final resting place—"Dust to dust the mourner cries"

Friday 26th Wind S—P.M. It set in a rainstorm—This day about 2 P.M. departed this life Mr. Samuel Youngs aged 74 years—Mr. Youngs has been through his life a laborious Man, and for the last thirty years an afflicted infirm Man, enduring almost constant pain from the disorder with which he died—

Friday 26 our Grand daughter Deziah with her Samuel

[56] Saturday 27 Apl 1844—A cool S-E- wind, with cloudy, unpleasent weather

Sabbath 28th Cool, as yesterday—Our time, how fleeting, and It appears much more rappid, with deep shades & pains, at Seventy, than at 25 years—

Monday 29th More warm, with light wind W-S-W—Ploughed my potato ground—and my Garden—Got home 350 [?] of Hay from Lieutenant Jasper Y. Tuthill—

Tuesday 30th Morning mild, Wind E—Afternoon more cool, Wind E—sowed my parsly seed—McNeil planted potatoes & corn on my North lot—

Wed[nesd]ay 1st May 1844—Wind brisk W-S-W—Doct. Watts says "months that are gone are gone forever, and each have bourn away Its own load"—Yes, our pains as well as [57] our pleasures—Well, the end must come—Solem thought

Thursday 2nd Wind continues to blow fresh from the S-W—Wilcox has begun to move his goods and chattles to Dyers Hotel oppisite the Wharf, or dock—

Friday 3rd Wind S-W- but light—Wilcox still removing his effects—Joseph C. Beckwith removed from Orient to Greenport, this day—Planted 40 hills corn, in my garden—Raymond got home today.

Saturday 4th Morning Foggy—Wind very light through the day—Warmer than any day this spring—A thunder Shower last evening—Wilcox got all his articles and his family to his new situation this evening viz. Dyers House at the landing, where he Wilcox opens a Temperence Hotel, on the Te[e]total system—

Sabbath 5th Warm—Wind S-W—How very necessary it is to be watchful.

[58] Monday 6th May 1844—Foggy morn—Wind S- & very warm P.M.—Tuesday 7th High wind S-W—Planted some pumpkin seed in S.E. corner of my orchard—Raymond left today

Wednesday 8th A calm morn—planted Beens, Corn, Squash, & potatoes, In my garden—Together 142 hills—High wind this evening—Had a fine Shower last eve—

Thursday 9th A Cloudy day. Brisk Wind S-W—repaired my board fence oppisite the back door, or East of the house—

It is good to be careful how we speak—especially when we are talking to some Charracters—

[59] Friday 10th Clear, and pleasant—Wind W—Our two seins have caught within the last ten days somewhere in neighbourhood 500.000 boney fish—Our Son Sidney and his dear wife came to us this evening—

Saturday 11th Wind S-W—not a clear cloudless sky—Evening squally with showers—attended with thunder & lightning and rain—

Sabbath 12th A clear N-W- fresh wind—Our Son Sidney & wife left for Hempstead, their present residence. Our dear Harriet M. Preston came to us this morn—dear [?]

Monday 13th Cool W-N-W wind—Matilday left us this morn—Sold 13 Hens to A. T. Glover, for 20 cents a head—Our Grand daughter Mariah Wells Prince came to us, with her Father, Abner Wells

Tuesday 14th Wind S-S-E- and we may set it down for a rainy day— Prudence is always requisite—

[60] Wednesday 15th May 1844—A very pleasent day—Made me a little gate to the East of my Cow yard—Planted some onions—Wind S-S-W—

Thursday 16th Some sprinkles of rain occasionally through the day— Changed away my cow with N.G. Beebe, for one of his—he gave me two Dollars, in cash & 1 bushel of corn for the bargain—

Friday 17th Considerable of a thunder shower about one OClock this morn—This forenoon It appears to continue into a settled rain with wind E—He that rises to fall Might as well not rise at all—It ceased raining about 4 P.M.—Raymond got home today.

[61] Saturday 18th A.M. Continued Showers—Some sunshine toward Evening—Wind W-S-W—

Sabbath 19th Wind S-E—Cool—Mr. Erastus Wells from Aquebogue preached in our Methodist Church twice, and once in the Congregational D[it]to this day—

Monday 20th Considerable rain, Wind S—Evening damp, cloudy, without rain—Raymond to Sagharbor—

Tuesday 21st Wind this day W-N-W—A hard thunder shower about 1 OClock this Morn—A very wet time—

Wednesday 22nd Very cool. Sawed out boards for fence

Thursday 23rd Wind N-W- and some cool—Raymond home today—

Friday 24th Wind W-S-W—Made my fence betwixt my shoeshop & the street—

Warm this P.M.—Raymond left for Philadelphia—

[62] Saturday 25th Warm muggy weather worked on fence as yesterday— pretty much finished It—

Sabbath 26th Thick damp A.M—some drizly, or fine rain. Our grand daughter Mariah Prince with her two children left us for Southold—She has been with us since the 13th—Wind S-S-E—

Monday 27th Pleasent but very warm—

Tuesday 28th Wind fresh S-W—Brother James called on us few minutes this A.M.—Sowed my late cabbage—

Wednesday 29th A pleasent warm day—Our two Grand Sons, John A. and James H. Preston came to us last Eve.

Thursday 30th Wind E-S-E—Wilcox left for N. York this P.M. In the Sloop Liberator Capt. David T. Glover.

[63] Friday 31st Rained considerable through the later part of last night— It continued with ocasional showers through the day. How invaluable is Truth. It will stand with a brilliance immortal when the rocks and mountains shall be dissolved, and melt away—

Saturday 1st June 1844 Wind S-S-W- and a mild day—The vegetable world appears much refreshed by yesterdays showers—

Heard this day of the death of my good Uncle Jared Griffin. He died at Acquebogue, while with his daughter Polly, Some time, as we hear, the first of this week—He was the last surviving child of my Grand Father Griffin, and the last of 17 Children—He died 105 years after his Eldest Brother, Daniel, was born—He was of the best of Men and a Christian—

Sabbath 2nd Brisk wind N—

Monday 3rd A cloudy, and as damp a day as is generally known, without rain. Wrote to Benjn. F. Thompson Esq. last Sunday—Wind S-S-W—

[64] Tuesday 4th June 1844—A pleasent growing day, Wind light W-S-W—Raymond home this eve—

Wednesday 5th Wind very light W—Raymond left this morn—Our G—son James H. Preston left for Riverhead—Been with us since Saturday—

Thursday 6th Wind fresh S-S-W—Our amiable little grandson Augustus G. Wilcox, Is now dangerously sick—We grieve at his distress, and tremble with fear of the consequences—May God endow us with a holy acquiescence to his divine will in all circumstances we are and shall be placed In—

Friday 7th Scarce any wind, not sufficient to stir the popler leaf—of course, we call It a still morn—Caleb Dyer is building a piazza in front of his house at the landing, or Orient Harbour

Saturday 8th Cool N-W- Wind—There was a fine shower last evening—

[65] Sabbath 9th Fresh breeze wind from S-S-W—There is assuredly not any solid satisfaction short of a gospel Temper of mind—An inward holy peace constitutes the only tranquility capable of giving substantial sweetness to our every days existence—To love & be beloved, to live in peace, and good will with all with whom we have to do, is a strong evidence that our lot is cast in places, and we have a goodly heritage—

Monday 10th It appears to be fine growing weather—The ground is sufficiently wet—This evening we had a thunder shower

Sabbath eve, I wrote to my Friend Joshua Y. Racket—

Tuesday 11th We had a cool N-W- wind through the day—Our frailty,

and the decline of life begin plainly to be perceived of. For we measure three
score & ten years—Indeed, I daily know its truth—Some know it earlier—
All who measure four score years feel the ship sinking in which their all is
embarked for Eternity—

Wednesday Very little wind, And that little from the West—We resolve,
& reresolve & where views [?]

[66] Thursday 13th Cool for the season Wind N-W—P.M. W—Rec'd a
Barrel of Molases from N.Y.

Friday 14th Weather as Yesterday—Experience the seeds of Mortality this
day—considerable of pain about the bowels—Weakness and relaxation
points us to the Tomb—

Saturday 15th Weather continues Cool—Feel better some this morn—
Could we but duly appreciate our many mercies we should certainly act
with more humility and gratitude to our Almighty Father in Heaven—

Sabbath 16th A pleasant, rather cool day for the time of year—My years,
and the sensations incident to those far advanced in life, point me to the
house appointed for all the living. This important truth ought to keep me
truely humble—God grant It may at all times have its due effect on me &
all who are born to die—

[67] Monday 17th A.M. Cool W- wind—Have this some days been considerable out of health, yet about—A relax, and pain in the bowels—We are
assuredly surrounded with mercies, but alas, how do we appreciate them—
A sanctified improvement of them, ought to be our constant & daily
prayer—P.M. Some sprinkle of rain—Our gardens begin to need a
shower—

Tuesday 18th A mild and pleasant forenoon—P.M. high wind S—thick
clouds in N-W—Our kinsman (or nephew) Thomas Vincent Tuthill moves
with his family to this place (Orient) again, from Southold—He moved
from Orient, some few years ago—and now returns again to his old natal
spot. He has been away five years last March.

Wednesday 19th A warm S- wind—Our Grand Sons John A. & James H.
Preston visit us this day—My neighbours, and acquaintance—who are they?
Why, they are the children and grandchildren of my mates, and associates
of those with whom I began the rugged Journey of Life—

[68] I have passed the seventh arch of Addison's bridge of life! A miracle!
How many of those who started with me are now my fellow travilers? We
were then many—now alas, few, very few—A thought the most solem, profound, and full of interest—Thursday 20th Warm & begins to be dry—
Raymond came home this eve—

Friday 21st Some sprinkle of rain—about as much as a large dew—It is said (and I believe It is true) that the period between early Youth, & Manhood, is the most dangerous part of human life. Habits with their bands of iron, are then created, and many,—yes many cary the presure of these bands, and evil habits, down to the loneliness of the tomb.

Saturday 22nd A fine and refreshing rain which continued to fall copious untill 12 M.—when the [wind] shifted from E- to W—Set out about 40 cabbage plants—

Sabbath 23rd Comfortably cool wind W—

[69] Monday 24th Visited longbeach, after Gulls Eggs accompanied by our Grand Son James H. Preston—we got about 40—out of which there was 15 or 16 addle ones—In walking to the beach, and on the beach after Eggs—then home—the travil altogether must have been 8 or 9 miles. A fatiguing job for a Man over 70 years.

Tuesday 25th A warm S- Wind—McNeil & Augustus (his Son) went for N.Y. today—Yesterday our affectionate grand Son James H. Preston, left us, for his Uncle Corbins, in Connecticut—Our prayers will attend him, wherever he is, or goes—O may he through all his life possess a double portion of his late blessed Fathers Virtues—

Wednesday 26th As yesterday, Warm S- Wind—A Greenport Ship arrived yesterday 800 barrels Oil—Name is Sarah & Esther—

Thursday 27th S- wind—of course Its a warm one—The LongIsland rail road is nearly finished—at least It is intended to travil on It from Greenport with a week or so.

[70] Friday 28th June 1844 High wind S—To observe winds—rain, and calms every day, is teaching the one that does it the alarming rapidity of his little time, amidst these changeing, and varied scenes—

Saturday 29th Cool N-W- wind this morn—Our brother James tarried with us last night—left us very early this morn—our niece, Lucinda M. Wiggins was married this evening to Rev. George Hollis, one of the Methodist Preachers—

> An institution, God has given—
> O May these have the smiles of Heaven—
> Free from all strife—O may they live
> In every good that Earth can give—

Sabbath 30th Comfortably cool—Wind S-S-E—Rec'd a letter from our Son & Grand Son—Sidney & Chatham A—Wrote to our G-d daughter Deziah Griffing

•

[71] Monday 1st July 1844 Fresh breeze of wind S-S-W—Raymond left for N.Y.—The mind composed in peace and grattitude to our Father in Heaven, for his mercies bestowed—such a mind is an invaluable treasure. The mortal that is endowed with it is blessed indeed, and in truth.

Tuesday 2nd A clear S-W- wind—Had a letter from our Grand daughter Deziah P. Griffin (Riverhead)—An affectionate one—full of filial tenderness—Children & friends are blessings too When God our sovereign makes them so—

Wednesday 3rd A fine shower this morn—hardly enough to wet the earth, which is getting dry.

Thursday 4th July 1844—called the birthday of the nation—Pleasent—

Friday 5th Fresh breeze wind S-W—It is getting dry—Pastureland needs rain. Wrote to Chatham (our grandson)

Saturday 6th A cloudy morn, with a gale of wind S-S-W—About 12 M. it moderated to but very little wind—wrote to our son, Sidney—Our cherries are getting ripe—

Wrote this 6 July to Cousin S.H. Griffin—

[72] Sabbath 7th July 1844 We had a refreshing shower last night—Wind west this morn—and comfortably cool—How blessed is the mortal who is virtuously sensible of the goodness of his Heavenly Father toward him & all Mankind—That I may possess that wisdom, is my daily & fervent prayer—

Monday 8th Wind S-S-W—Not uncomfortably warm—A Mr. Howe, a Methodist Preacher (at this time located in this place) took tea with us this P.M.—

Tuesday 9th Brisk wind as yesterday and from the same quarter—Should we never speak, only when its necessary, and what we ought to say, we should certainly find our feelings congenial with calm tranquility—

Wednesday 10th The brisk W-S-W- wind still continues—Warm—

Thursday 11th Some rain Night—hardly enough to help vegetation—

[73] Friday 12th Warm, with scarce any wind—within a few days, and today altogether, I should suppose there has been gathered from two to five bushels of Cherries off of our trees and there is some left yet—

"Wisdom is the principle thing " And he or she is wise, who only speaks what is necessary, and when it is so—

Saturday 13th Still continues warm, with wind from the sickly S—Great riots, and mobs, in Philadelphia. Several lives sacrificed—This is the second Mob in that City this summer—

Sabbath 14th Weather much as yesterday—How vain, and empty are the amusements of Man!—

Monday 15th Cloudy & calm —& hot—

Tuesday 16th A Rainy day—Wind E—Refreshing to vegetation—

Wednesday 17th Our Cherries pretty much gone off of our trees, which have produced us a good supply this season—A pleasent day this, after our good rain yesterday

[74] Thursday 18th July 1844—Clear, warm & pleasent—The air appears to be much purified by the late copious rain—Edwin Brown, Master of the Ship Washington arrived this morn, from a whaleing voyge, with 1200 barrels of oil—He has been gone about 12 months—

Friday 19th Clear weather Wind fresh S-S-W—What our farmers call fine growing weather—Seasons follow seasons In quick succession—and so does generation follow generation as rapidly, and to the considerate Man, as solemn and as alarming—

Saturday 20th A cloudy morn—A good shower last night—Raymond came home last Thursday left today

Sabbath 21st pleasent

Monday 22nd Clear, and very mild. Messrs Johnson & Twomey stoped with us a few minutes this [morn?]—Our cousin William H. Griffing called on us a few minutes today from Gard[ners?] Island

[75] Tuesday 23rd July 1844 Hazy, or cloudy through the day—

Wednesday 24th An Easterly brisk wind. A man who never goes, but where he ought to go, and never speaks but what he ought to speak, certainly acts, and does, very different from a large number of his fellow Men—A vain, and very unwise curiosity is the predominant passion of our species, and especially of all those who strive hard to live without attending to a useful, & truly lawful livlihood—

Doct. Skinner called on us today—our Grandchildren John A. & Harriet Preston called on us this P.M. They returned to Greenport in the Evening—Our friend N.T. Hubbards Son, Samuel, paid us a visit this day. He has just finished his collegeical studies—

Thursday 25th Some rain this morn—Wind E—12 M. commenced raining pretty strong for an hour or two—

[76] If we were as anxious to make the wisest improvement of every situation we shall at all times be placed In, we should find our road of life much smoother, pleasenter and assuredly happier—We have only to count up our mercies to know how numerous and multiplied they are—Do we merit them? Ah! There is the all important astonishing heart-rending question—

Friday 26th A cloudy day. Wind light E- by S—Wm. A Griffing, called on us an hour—Wm. A. Wilcox's Uncle Samuel Wilcox called on us this morn—He lives at Madison Connecticut

[77] Saturday 27th July 1844 Light wind E—A large company of invited guests steped into the cars, at Brooklyn and rode through the Island to Greenport, makeing the pasage (94 miles) in about four hours—This is the first time that the rail cars have ever gone intirely through. Our friend Nathaniel T. Hubbard, was one of the guests—This evening, it was our peculiar happiness to receive and welcome him to our honorable mansion—It is now thirty six years since he made a part of our family for six weeks—The changes we have passed through, and the part we have acted on the theatre of this chequered eventual life since that time would fill a volume—It would no doubt some of It partake of the <u>romance</u>—In all this time, amid [78] his astonishingly multiplied avocations, and cares (haveing done buisness amounting to Millions in execution.) I have never known him to abate a single marked civility towards me or mine—That his last days may be as tranquil, composed, and peaceful, as <u>virtue</u>, and resignation to providence, can render them is our ardent wish, and daily prayer—

Sabbath 28th A fine morning, wind W—P.M. Rode to Latham's with N.T. Hubbard—Returned in about two hours—Our friend Hubbard left us this evening for <u>Greenport</u>, from there tomorrow morn at 5 OClock he starts in the rail cars for N. York—Henry T. Taber and wife called on us a few minutes.

Monday 29th What we call pleasant weather—not uncomfortably warm. Was called on this day, by Joseph Truman, [79] who has resided some where near Shenang. He left this Town, I might say, this place, with his Father & Mother, William & Mary Truman, when he was about fourteen years old, and is now Sixty seven—His Mother, Mary, was a very pious woman, endowed with prepossessing conversational powers—A <u>Sabbatarian</u> strictly, and a loving Christian—Died some years since betwixt Ninety & one hundred years of age—

Tuesday 30th A small shower of rain this morn, Wind S-S-W—

Wednesday 31st A wet, or what is called a rainy day—Wind S—A pain in my head this day, teaches <u>me</u> that the seeds of Mortality are sown within <u>me</u>, and will e'er long destroy this active frame of humanity—

[80] August 1 1844 Commences with wind nearly as yesterday E-S-E—It has been a stormy night—Mrs. Anna Griffing, wife of our Cousin William H. Griffing, stoped with us last night—She is an Excellent woman, discreet—prudent—industrious—and a Christian—It is common, when

speaking of conspicuously great, and good Man, to enquire who, and what sort of a Mother he had—Believing that the early, and constant advice of the virtuous Mother was the first, and almost only means of the son's future usefulness, and finally becoming a bless[ing] to his country, and an ornament to Mankind. The above Mrs. Griffing, was Mother [81] to Capt Seth Griffin, who died in London on October 12, 1841 while Master of the London Packet Montreal—was aged about 32 years. He was one of the most agreable, loveing, and filial of Sons—prepossessing—intelligent—bland, and punctiliously honest to a proverb. An invaluable consolation to his Parents—but alas—he is gone and left them to mourn the loss of one of the loveliest, and best of Sons—

> Short was his race, brilliant he shone
> To bless his friends, & then was gone—

Mr. and Mrs. Griffing have now one child left, a daughter (Maria) As virtuous, as she is aimable—as dutiful as she is accomplished—She appears to be destined to solace and bless her parents Evening of Life.

[82] Friday 2nd August 1844—Wind very light from the sultry S—A warm day—

Saturday 3rd Not so warm as yesterday—Fresh breeze from S—Col Elijah Johnson and wife, and others, from N. York boarding at Wilcoxes, at the Landing—

O, what great- great need we have of watchfulness, and much more abundantly if we have to give an account to our Father in Heaven, for every idle word that proceedest out our lips—What a thought—! "and has eternal Truth declared it & -Watch-watch Jesus says W A T C H!—

Sabbath 4th August 1844 Commences with showers, and some Thunder—yesterday—Wm. H. Griffing his wife—Daughter Maria and her husband (whose name is Hart) all left here for their home [83] at Gu[i]lford, Connecticut—as they had a fair wind, I hope they got, or arrived save home—Brother James was with us an hour or two this day—We have grown old together—and I trust we have always lived, and loved as breatheren—Attended the Methodist meeting A.M. Mr. Howe preached—

Monday 5th Wind A.M. North—a pleasant morn—Went to the North side and gathered about two quarts of blackberries—

I understand, by the newspapers, that my Cousin Phineas Terry Esq. died very suddenly, about two weeks since. He was the eldest son of my Uncle Noah Terry, mentioned in my 3rd diary 78th page—

Sold my cow Saturday 3rd August

[84] Tuesday 6th August 1844 Brisk wind S—A cloudy day—Settled with Samuel Youngs for a half Ton of Hay Bot[Bought] of him in July—1/2 past 5 P.M. It rains—

Wednesday 7th Light wind N-& W—Fixed a door in the back part of my formerly store room—

Thursday 8th Wind light from S-W—To be composed and reconciled to our common allotments of life, discovers wisdom, and virtue—For certainly, not any one can truely enjoy those great gifts of his maker without being a participater in the Gospel Temper—Those only can drink of that fountain, who are clothed with the same humility which adorned the accepted Publican—I daily regret my want of watchfulness

[85] Friday 9th August 1844 Wind very high S-S-W—Yesterday two Friends or those called quakers, held a meeting in the Methodist church in this place—one of them spoke much to the purpose—

Mr. Hewlett Smith, from N.Y—stoped with us an hour or so this A.M.— He is and has been this two years past as much alive in the cause of total abstinence from all alcohol liquors, as any man I ever knew—No doubt his exertions in the glorious work have done much, very much good—

Saturday 10th Cloudy weather—wind S-W—Better be silent, than to have said to much—

Sabbath 11th A West wind, something cooler than days back—Received a letter from E.M. Griffin, our cousin of Little Falls—

[86] Monday 12th August 1844—Comfortably cool wind W-N-W— Began to dry Apples—paired about one bushel this day myself—As they were rather small in size, and not yet ripe, I found It an unpleasant Job—

Tuesday 13th Wind W—Not uncomfortably warm—Travilers now leave N. York, at 8 A.M. by the railroad through Long Island, and reach Boston at 6 P.M. makeing the time in reaching Boston Ten hours—

Wednesday 14th A.M. Showers—light wind E-S-E—Was visited this day by James Griffin, a grandson of my late esteemed Uncle Jared Griffin—the young gentleman, (said James) is a resident [87] of Little Falls, Herkimer County—His Father, gave him the names of James, to bear up the name of my honored Father

Thursday 15th Wind E—I forgot that last Monday the 12th was Just forty five years since I commenced keeping a School, at what was then called Sterling—The School house stood on the north side of the main road, on the west side of the farm owned by the heirs of the late Judge Thomas Youngs—at this time, and for twenty years afterwards, there was no such a place, known, or thought of as. It has grown up nearly as sudden as a mushroom—It begins to be conspicuous, in trade—has 8 or 9 whale ships—94 miles from N. York & is rode in railroad over in 3 & ½ hours.

[88] Friday 16th August 1844—A pleasant, calm, midling warm day— Not any are found in the road which leads to permanent comfort, but the truely virtuous—

Saturday 17th Pleasent, but rather warm—Wind very light through the day—

Sabbath 18th Not so warm as yesterday—This morn we had a peculiar satisfaction of welcoming our friend N.T. Hubbard to our humble abode— with <u>him</u>, and his two friends, Mssrs. Sedam, & Johnson, who accompanied him from N-Y—I rode to Lathams, and took dinner—At the Table, there was about Sixty set down with us—Amongst the guests was Alderman Under- [89] hill, a venerable gentleman of Eighty years of age—The Lady, and her two Sons, of the conspicuous Col. James Watson Webb. Mr. Leroy, a Gentleman boarding at Lathams, and many others, gave us a very agreable afternoon by their preposessing address, and moral communications inter-spersed with well timed Anecdotes—Mr. Hubbard, left our sequestered abode about five P.M.—

Monday 19th Cloudy—Wind S—If we swerve from the road of rectitude, we find our way amid mire, bogs & thorns—

Tuesday 20th Wind very light from various points in the course of the day—P.M. Cloudy—

[90] Departed this life this forenoon Mrs. Mehitable Dyer, wife of Capt. Caleb Dyer—She has passed through <u>many</u> and severe trials of a domestick nature—From whom they accrued, I am not competent to say—she has certainly drank deep at the bitter fount of domestick disquiet—

> She has done with sighs & tears,
> this Earthly grave—
> Is now exchanged for Heavens
> eternal love—
> This a glorious hope—her sins forgiven,
> And God will have the Glory of her
> Heaven—

[91] Wednesday 21st Wind E- by N—purchased three cords of wood of Capt David T. Glover at four dollars & 25 cts. delivered to the landing—

The saying of Doct. Edward Young viz. "Lean not on Earth, It will pierce thee to thy heart" This is truth In all its vivid colours—

Thursday 22nd Wind S- E—A cloudy day—Has the appearance of gathering for a storm—How blessed are they who are ready, and fully prepared for any event that awaits them in this eventual life

> "All, all on Earth is shadow, empty vain
> Her bed of roses is a bed of pain—"

We this day two cords of wood stowed away in the wood house.

[92] Friday 23rd August 1844—Wind S-E- with rain, which poured down profusely untill 9 A-M—

Saturday 24th A cloudy day—the young people, at least a number of them, have gone on a sailing party to day, in Captn. James Glovers Sloop—Yesterday I received letters, Sidney, (our son) Chatham (our Grandson) and few lines from Benjamin F. Thompson Esquire—This eve about 11 OCk Sidney, (our son) his wife, & daughter Margaret, came to us—The interview was a joyous one to us, in very deed & truth—

Sabbath 25th High wind S- & Cloudy—The mind may conceive, and the heart feel what the pen (in my hand) can never paint—

Monday 26th A pleasant morn—was visited this morning by Mr. Cuningham, and his wife Louise (formerly Wilkie)—[93] This aimable couple was with us a few days in July 1836—Since then they have resided the whole time in New Orleans—These shifting, fluctuating scenes, and Acts on the Theatre of our little point, with me must assured Close. My increasing years tell us in language not to be misunderstood that the curtain of my period must soon soon fall—Our endeared Grand daughter Harriet H. Preston came to stop with us a few days—

Tuesday 27th What we call a fine morn—made charming by the sweet musick of the red breasts congregated in my sequestered Orchard—Their praise is as perfect, as It is accepted by HIM who cares for the sparrow, which falls not to the ground without his knowledge—To be over anxious Is to be without serenity—He who lives upon the future, is blind to the present.

[misnumbered 96]

> "When Tides of youthful blood runs high
> And scenes of promised Joys are nigh
> Health presuming, beauty blooming
> O, how dreadful 'tis to die—"

Wednesday 28th Cloudy—sunshine and a shower—Evening Wind S-E—

Contention breeds strife,
A noisy jar[r]ing sound,
Will ever meet in every street
In an unhallowed ground—

But Peace—peace is the only atmosphere which can produce rest—Foolish talking causes uncomfortable reflections—

Thursday 29th Comfortable weather, Wind light W—Wilcoxes boarders, viz. Walter & Samuel Hubbard—Messrs Wheton—Cunningham—Thompson—And with them Sidney, and several Women They caught a mess of fish in the Sound, took them ashore, upon the beach, & rocks, where they cooked them into an excellent chowder, upon which with keen appetites they partook with much good will, and great good humor—

Friday 30th A fine comfortable breeze from the W—Sidney, his Wife, and daughter Margaret left us this day for their dwelling, at Hempsted—Mr. Dobbs left yesterday—Mr. Wheaton, to day—Saturday 31st Wind light S—P.M. Cloudy—The summer is going—and as the Auctioneer crys "It is gone!" Alas, our little life—what a bustle—and It dies away—Truth says "we have here no abiding City—"

[94] [Monday struck out] Sunday 1st September 1844—And is summer gone? What gone!—yes gone forever! What an important thought—What an alarming Truth—! Well—Immortality, is Just before me—No change there—All is substance, and Eternal.

Some sprinkle of rain this morn—

Monday 2d Sept—By some mistake or inattention yesterday I wrote Monday, instead of Sunday, as it ought to have been—. The error was just discovered (by our young friend Walter O. Hubbard, who with the prepossessing urbanity of the nobleness of true civility, corrected the misconstruction of my head & pen. Walter O. Hubbard is the eldest son of N.T Hubbard, of N. York) [97] This N.T. Hubbards name stands in conspicuous carracters on the first page [of Vol. 2] containing the list of my FRIENDS that are, and those of them who are gone to the beautific regions of immortal FRIENDSHIP—

Tuesday Sept 3 1844 What we call fine weather Wind W-N-W—There was a shower last night—This morn departed this life Mrs. Hannah Havens, the very aimable, and prudent wife of Mr. Caleb Havens aged [blank] Mrs. Havens was a mild, aimable & peaceable woman—possessing, and practicing those virtues which render a wife to be of greater price than Rubies—

Wednesday 4th Fine weather—light wind N-W—Mr. Cunningham took me to Greenport in his carriage this P.M. We had a pleasant time, and his good company, and his marked civilities are duly appreciated by his humble servant AG

[98] Thursday 5th Wind E—Clear, & dry weather—To do right, is to do good—Friday 6th Cool E-S-E wind—Camp meeting at Jamesport—Our Grand daughter Deziah Preston Griffing, became the Mother of a fine daughter, on Thursday 29th August, last

> The little cherub—May the acts all prove
> It is <u>gem</u> from <u>mines</u> of endless love.
> Sweet innocence to us thou art given,
> A bud—a flower, Just dropt from Heaven—

Saturday 7th Cool morn for the time of year, yet I think not any frost in Orient—Humanity [99] produces the <u>seeds</u> of mortality, and every son and daughter of Adam will sooner, or later, find that they, (those seeds) will burst the shell of their tabernacle, and open a passage for the Spirit, to regions where change shall be no more. This P.M. we had cordial consolation of welcoming to our humble mansion the invaluable, and long tried friend of <u>ours</u>, and of <u>all</u> the virtuous of Mankind, Nathaniel T. Hubbard—with him was his good, aimable and very worthy wife, and youngest daughter Josephine—

Sabbath 8th A comfortable day—Attended meeting with our friends Mr. & Mrs. Hubbard. Mr. Beers preached.

[100] Monday 9th Septem 1844—Pleasant but dry weather—light wind S—took dinner, at Wilcoxes with our friends N.T. Hubbard, his wife & daughter—previous to dinner—Mr. Hubbard & myself visited Hog pond—the residence of Doct Seth H. Tuthill—It is the old site on which stood the house of my ForeFathers, of the Tuthill Family, of more than one hundred years ago—My great Grandfather Daniel Tuthill, died there in 1762 aged 83 years—This eve our friends above said left us for Mattituck, where they will spend a day or two, and then proceed to their home at N. York—

Tuesday 10th Very warm—and very dry—purchased me two cords [101] of oak wood, and one of pine—The bill of wood was $9 = 25 cts.

Wednesday 11th Wind E-S-E—and as warm as yesterday—the two days have been as warm, and as uncomfortably close as any two days in succession this season—What a fortune awaits the young Man, or Woman, whose every action, and movement, is guided by <u>prudence</u>—and discretion—

Thursday 12th Cloudy—Wind E—Stowed away our potatoes this day in my Cellar, 12 bushels, being one half raised on a part of my back lot—the ground planted was about 30 rods a part of which was corn—of course there might be 25 rods of potatoes ground. Our friend W.O. Hubbard, presented us with some handsome peaches this eve—this attention to us was duly, and sensibly appreciated—

Friday 13th Wind E- and severe rain storm last night

[102] Saturday 14th Sept 1844—Light wind N-N-W—

Sabbath 15th Wind & weather much as yesterday—Mr. Joseph Lamb called on us yesterday—Wrote this day to our Son Sidney—

Monday 16th Very light wind W-N-W- and uncomfortably warm—

Tuesday 17th Considerable of Wind N-E- & cooler—My Friend of 1800 often noted in that year in my Diary who was often interestedly associated with me at that time, called on us this morn, Just from Hempstead, where he and his family reside—This gentleman Joshua Y. Racket—He has an elegiable [sic] situation amid the circle of the few friends I yet have left on this mundane sphere—

[103] Wednesday 18th Wind very light W—It is what we call pleasent weather—Brother James with us this eve—Matilda Tuthill, widow of the late Hull Tuthill, called on us this day—She now lives in New Jersey, with her children—She was Matilda Racket when a girl, Daughter of Daniel Racket of Rocky Point, who died in 1800, and his wife Bethia (an excellent women) who died in 1816—The above named Hull, died in 1835—He was the son of Jonathan Tuthill who was Grand Son to our Great grand sire Deacon Daniel Tuthill—

Thursday 19th Very mild, and a calm morn—Capt Noah G. Beebe [took?] off 16 head of cattle this day.

[104] Friday 20th Sept 1844 Continues very warm—Wind light—Died last night abut 12 o'clock midnight Mr. John Tillinghast, aged 75 years—Through his whole life he had been industrious, peaceable and strictly honest—We now believe that the blessings that Heaven attached to those estimable virtues now rest upon him. No pain—no sorrow—No sin to cloy—Those streams of life & endless Joy—

Saturday 21st Wind S—and of course a warm one—Last eve, our cousin William H. Griffing, and Charles Stone, from Connecticut, called on us for a short time—This latter gentleman is Grand Son to our late Aunt Betsey Stone, who was Betsey Griffing when a girl—

What an emptiness and vanity, the world shews
Itself to be to a Man in pain & distress

[105] Sabbath 22nd September 1844—Brisk wind E-N-E—Some little sprinkle of rain—The Earth is quite dry, and <u>good</u> ground rain is much needed—

What an alarming Fact It is that Man is so prone to persue those <u>amusements</u> which are sure to yield remorse in retrospection, and often, to[o] often final wretchedness—<u>Habits</u> to deviate from rectitude are awful at the commencement. If continued to be indulged, <u>will</u>, assuredly as God exists, Sting like a Serpent, & bite like an Adder. Life and Death is set before every reasonable Man & Woman. We have our choice—Joy, or Sorrow—

Monday 23rd Scarce any wind—not sufficient to flutter the poplar leaf — Dry—Dry weather—How important it is to possess patience, without It we cannot be in time—

[106] Tuesday 24th Continues windy & <u>dry</u>—and from information abroad, It begins to be distressingly so in all our northern section of the country.

Wednesday 25th Wind S—A cloudy day—a picture of a gloomy mind— To speak to the purpose, is to speak wisely—To give <u>good</u> <u>council</u> to those who <u>will not</u> accept It, is like planting garden seed on a rock—Yes, like giving Jewels to a hungry Swine—To indulge in <u>that</u> which is sure, in the sequal to produce wretchedness, is runing with open eyes into the yawning vortex of degradation & unutterable misery—

[107] Thursday 26th Sept. 1844—Wind brisk N-E—A copious rain, which commenced last Eve about 7 O'clock & continued without intermission untill 8 this morn—A pleasant consideration as well as a peculiar benefit to farmers—Flocks, Hills, Dales, and creation rejoices at the Heavenly Boon—

Friday 27th A cool morn, wind N—Narcissa left to day for N.Y. on board Sloop Lib[e]rator D.L. Glover Master. Raymond (her husband) goes with her. Mrs. Griffin more feeble this some days—her cough, (which has closely attended her, this three years) is very bad, Just now—God can Temper the wind to the shorne lamb—

[108] Saturday 28th Sept 1844 A cloudy day—light W[ind] E-N-E— Evening commenced raining—Our grand daughter Marie Prince with her Husband Orin Prince, Visited us this P.M.—<u>She</u>, Maria, awakens in our bosoms inexpressible emotions!—painful & Joyful—O. how like our dear— dear departed Harriet—the most virtuous, dutiful, loving, and beloved of Daughters—An Angel now! All glorious—

[109] Sabbath 29th This morn the wind is N-N-E—and it blows a tempestuous gale—The water or tide is higher than It has been this year past—

It continues to rain until about 12 Meredian[meridian], the Wind changed to S-S-W- and blew with great violence—

Our Grand Child Maria & Husband left this P.M. for Southold, their residence—Orin, her Husband, is an excellent, open kind, generous, prepossessing, Invaluable partner & friend—

Monday 30th A Gale of wind N-W—Several Vessels drove on shore last night—

Tuesday 1st October 1844 Cool W- wind—Evening Calm—How often—alas, to[o] often, we resolve, and reresolve, and never perform—

[110] Wednesday 2nd October 1844—White frost this morn—the first I have seen this Autumn—light wind this morn E—We hear of much damage by the gale on the 28th & 29th last Inst[ant]—Vessels, goods and some lives lost—How weak, how frail is the Bark In which we sail on the tempestuous ocean of mortality—

Thursday 3rd Wind brisk E—Capt. Lester B. Terry, In the Schooner Planet, Sailed for the South on Monday Eve 30th last Inst[ant]—

Hasty speaches are generally out of place, and do not produce good effects—Gentle reproofs that are well meant should be kindly received. Advice given to benefit us, is an [111] expression of love—It goes greatly to show that the giver would save his friend, if possible from the yawning pit of ruin, into which the course he is persuing will inevitably receive him—The pathes of strict TEMPERENCE, and rectitude, lead to honor, wealth, and real enjoyment, but a course of vain indulgence will assuredly land Its deluded victim, into the black gulf of remorse, wretchedness, and irretrievable ruin—RUIN!—This is Gods eternal Truth! Then Stop!—Shun—O shun the fatal bait—The accursed cup—

>   The sparkling bowl
>   Where adders hiss and poisonous serpents rool [roll]!

[112] Friday 4th Oct 1844 A wet or Rainy morn—Wind light N-N-W Dyer's Wharf received considerable damage, by the storm on last Sabbath morn* 12 M It died away to a calm—and warm and clear—

Saturday 5th High wind W-N-W—Times and seasons continue their onward course, but Man with all his schemes, and inventions passes off! and where is he? For a brief space he kept the neighborhood—The Town, yes, the World awake! And now he sleeps, to wake no more—A truth how solemn! How momentuous—

* It, the wharf is become unsafe to go on to it with teams—It has been a tollerable wharf for about 12 years—

We had two of my nieces with us, this day, makeing me a pair of satinet pantaloons—Caroline & Mahitable Wiggins—Daughters to my youngest Sister, Lucretia, Widdow of the late [113] David Wiggins Jun—After suffering unspeakable distress from a wound received in 1814, he died, exhibiting a patience, humility, and resignation, rarely equalled in our uncertain change-able State—He died in 1828—His widdow (my Sister) has drank deep of the affliction which too often attends the melancholy State of widowhood—Yet in all her sorrows & visible privations, which assuredly have been great, she has displayed a magniminity, and strength of mind uncommon to her Sex—Superior virtue and Gods unbounded goodness must have sustained her or she would have sunk under her mountainous trials—

[114] Sabbath 6th Octr. 1844 Cool, & Cloudy. Wind N—We know that this world is not our abiding place, and yet how do we appreciate that knowledge! Alas! How do we improve by its Truth—"do not actions speak plainer & louder than words?"—

Monday 7th Dark and cloudy with a very light sprinkle of rain—Wind N—

Tuesday 8th Wind light N-W—Potatoes appear to be diseased in many parts of our Northern states—Some of the farmers have lost their intire[entire], large crops—They rot, and soon become nauseous—Hogs that eat them grow [115] sick, and die. It is a calamity that at present we can-not account for—Whether there is a natural cause for this serious provi-dence, perhaps we may yet learn—We are certainly a highly privileged nation, but Its to be lamented that so few of us are found in the ways of righteousness, and the Heavenly Gratitude—God grant that a speedy refor-mation for the better, may enter every heart—of those who compose our entire republic, and our America become as proverbial for holiness as It is for Liberty—

Wednesday 9th High wind W-N-W—Autumn with her sere yellow leaf approaches with all her dreary Aspect—

[116] Thursday 10th Oct 1844—A mild pleasent day—Wind S—Of course warm—General Training at Greenport—A large assembly congregate there this day—Many such meetings I have witnessed more than fifty years ago—With all the ardor of youthful vigour, I use[d] to hasten to attend them—there with buoyant spirits I met my Juvenile companions. Alas! Now where are they? Where, those companions? Officers that on the stately steed pranced the musick field? Alas-alas! Echo says where are they!! To day will e'er long be as that day is now!—[117] A thought sufficiently weighty to damp all & every improper recreation—The two Colonels that superintend the Regiment today were not born at that time—

Friday 11th Wind E- with some rain this morn—Cool—It has finally been a rainy day—

Saturday 12th Cool, and pleasant—Wind light N-W—

Sabbath 13th A mild day Wind very light W—A.M. nearly calm. My dear Sisters Lucinda & Lucretia and brother James called on us this day—We met as brother & sisters, and I trust loved as such—

Monday 14th A cloudy day with ocasionally a little sprinkle of rain—to a mind rather shaded, such dark weather naturally feeds the beclouded vision of the inner and outer Man—

Tuesday 15th Last night was a wet or rainy one—Wind S—It is drizzly this morn—pretty copious showers from 1 P.M. to 4 when it cleared off with wind N-W—

Raymond came home last eve—

[118] Wednesday 16th October 1844—Clear weather—High wind W-N-W—

It appears that the Men fit to be entrusted with power over there fellow Men are in number very small. Especially ab[s]olute power—Well has Doct^r Young observed this fact viz—" Man to Man is the sorest, surest Ill"

Thursday 17th Wind very light S—P.M. more fresh with a cloudy sky & signs of a storm—Chatham & Augustus (our grandsons) with Narcissa arrived at our house last evening, by the rail road, and cars, from Hempstead—Sidney wrote us by them—

[119] Friday 18th This morn comes in with copious showers of rain—to appearences of puddles & pools, It rained considerable last night—

How important, how necessary to our tranquility—Our immediate, and future peace, is wisdom in our conversation, and daily speach—Over the statue of prudence stand, in bold relief, these words in all languages, viz. "A wise head keeps a close mouth" Happy is the man, happy the youth who profits by them—

It is now eventide, and it continues to rain—in short, It has been a very wet day. [120] Saturday 19th Oct 1844—We have a very stormy night—The wind a gale from S—rain in abundance—It continues to shower this morn—wind rather abates this 8 O'Clk Morn—at 11 it changed to W-N-W- and partially cleared off—

This evening Wilcox arrived home from N.Y. and with him our pre-posessing tallented young friend W O Hubbard—As he (W-O-H) advances on the astonishing, stupendous Bridge of Life, may Wisdom mark him for one of her brightest votaries

[121] Sabbath 20th A cool N-W- wind—To walk not to any use, is

worse than to sit still—To speak not the purpose, is not comparable to silence—

Monday 21st Cool wind E—The <u>Millerites</u> are now in an unspeakable excitement—To day & last night and to night they neither eat nor sleep, spending every movement in preparation for <u>tomorrow 22nd</u> which they appear <u>fully</u> and <u>positively</u> to believe will be the final end of all the wicked on this Terraqueous Globe—

Tuesday 22nd A cool E- wind—rode out to Greenport with my Grandson Augustus A. Griffin—For the first time, I visited the rail Road Depot and the arrival of the Cars from N. York—The mode of travilling—Its dispatch, and comfort are assuredly one of the many curiosities, improvements and wonders of the Nineteenth Century—A mile a minute is certainly quick time, a corporal trim says—

[122] Wednesday 23rd Oct. 1844

What is termed by Gents, and [clown?], fine, or good weather. Wind very light E—Great Mass meeting at Patchogue by the Democrats.

This eve was married Mr. Legget, of N. York, to Miss Cecilia Racket, daughter of the late Capt. Grant B. Racket—

> When Adam took the beautrious [*sic*] Eve
> From GOD, he did the <u>boon</u> receive—
> A Marriage that!—Effulgent Feast—
> Angels the Witnesses!! And God the Priest—

Thursday 24th Weather much as yesterday. Our <u>words</u>, and <u>actions</u>, of each day—do they bear an agreable retrospective view? Consideration will answer us—God of his infinite mercy grant <u>us</u> Grace and Wisdom—

[123] Friday 25th Continues moderate, that is, very light wind—Some rain last night—Infirmities, or bodily weakness, will command the sympathy, or tear of commiseration, from <u>all</u> those who are endowed with a spark of humanity, or sentimental affection—

Saturday 26th A calm day—P.M. Cloudy—This morn, at 7'Oclock our dear grandsons, Chatham A. and Augustus R. left us for their home, at Hempstead—they are to take the Cars at Greenport—Stop two or three days at Riverhead—then proceed home—McNeil, and Cleora arrived home last eve—They have been about 5 weeks in N.Y.—

Sabbath 27th Wind cool N-N-E—Our two grandsons John A. and James H. Preston came to our humble abode this morn. Our <u>sensations</u> in the retrospect cannot be [page trimmed]

[124] Monday 28th Oct. 1844—Wind as yesterday N-N-E- and it blows a gale, with rain in copious profusion—Tides very high—Our grandsons John & James, with Harriet Matilda, left us last eve, for Greenport, intending to go to N. York, in the course of a day or two—

Tuesday 29th rain & high winds N-E—untill 2 OClock P.M. when the wind changed S-S-W- with quite a gale—A Mr. West gave a very spirited Lecture on temperence Sabbath Eve—It is said It was one of the most touching, and affectionate of addresses—This eve Chatham G & James H. Preston returned to our house—Our Grand Sons

[125] Wednesday 30th A blustering cold N-W- wind—to age, and Infirmities, these chilling seasons are tedious—yet to support them as creations of our Heavenly parent shows us dutiful Children.

Thursday 31st Cool weather, with high wind N-N-W—

Thursday 31st Weather much as yesterday. Our country is in much, very much agitation on the pending Ellection of a President, the two parties resort to almost every means (some disonerable ones I fear) to gain their point—

Friday 1st Novem. 1844—A mild, yet rather cool day—some frost last night—

Saturday 2nd Weather much as yesterday—Last Thursday morn Chatham AG & James H. P. (our grandsons) left us for Riverhead, from which place they proceed on Saturday next (or I might have said to day) for Hempstead—

Sabbath 3d A calm day—not so with the people of this country, who are in a violent storm, about the approaching Ellection—[illegible]

[126]Monday 4th Nov 1844—Commenced raining early this morn with E [wind]—and continues to storm & rain until 11 OClock at night—

Tuesday 5th High wind N-N-W—A very contested Ellection, throughout our State (N.Y.) this day—Clay, the Whig candidate—Polk, the Democratic, Do [ditto]

Tuesday 6th A blustering cold N-W- wind—Thursday 7th Weather more mild Wind S-S-W—Last evening, sailed on a whaleing Voyge Capt. Edwin Brown, In the Ship [blank]—Our young friend Alanson B. Webb is in her, as third mate—His sensations were shaded with painful reflections on [127] some missteps which he inadvertently took a few days before he left—He observed with tears to me, the morning he took his leave, that he indulged in a recreation of a few minutes, which he felt would cost him a long voyge of stormy commotions in his now trembling, and tortured breast. By one imprudent move, we often lose the game.

Friday 8th Mild W-S-W— weather—He, or She who speaks ill of no one are amongst the small, or few, who are always in the straight and narrow road which leadest to life, & Joy—

[128] Saturday 9th November 1844

A.M. A small breeze of wind W- by N—P.M. Calm—We hear the roar of cannon, from Sagharbor—Its probable its in consequence of Ellection news—although I am of the opinion that the result is not certainly known, how our State (New York) has gone as yet—

Sabbath 10th A hazy or what we call a Cloudy chilly day—Wind E—Our Grand Daughter Deziah, & her husband Samuel Griffing, called on us about four hours, this day, with their little Babe Mary—

Monday 11th Wind light E-S-E—Warm day—Evening a copious rain, with hard thunder, and as hard Lightning—

[129] Tuesday 12th Wind fresh from E—and It has been a cloudy day—If our minds are clear, attended with a conscience void of offence toward God, and Man, it is fine weather with us—Ah, is It so—

Wednesday 13th A moderate rain storm Wind N—

Thursday 14th Blustering, and cool Wind N-N-W—Winter, with all its attendant chills, hails, and snows approaches! Yes, and so does the final, end of all the present Human family—

15th Wind light W-N-W—Sloop Liberator, D. T. Glover, sails for N. York

16th Mild, calm, and clear weather. Got me home a cord of wood of George Champlin, —Price $3=75/100

[130]Sabbath 17th November 1844—Wind S-S-E—This is the Christian Sabbath—All Christendom, profess, this day to worship God—But how shall we worship him?—His word answers the all important question, viz. In "spirit and in truth"—Except we are the children of peace, we can never become heirs of Heaven—

18th A rain storm through the past night—clears off 11 A.M.

19th Cold N-W- wind—Wilcox killed his hog—its weight 270 Lb.

20th Wind W by N—some little rain—calm this Eve—

[131] What a happy circumstance, that in all neighbourhoods there [are] some charracters, that never allow a slanderous expression to contaminate their lips—

21st A pleasent day—

22nd Wind E—A moderate rain—Made a Table to set my desk on—not being a Joiner, the work of course, is rough—

23rd Wind E—It has been a rainstorm all last night—Clears off this noon. Is it not better to keep silence, than to talk to not any profit?—

24th Sabbath—high wind N-W—

25th Squally, and, cold—Tedious uncomfortable weather—It betokens [132] the approach of winter, a semblance of old age, with the chilling frosts of threescore years and Ten—Job says (and Justly) that our "days are swifter than a weavers shuttle"—It was amid the severest losses, accute distress, and pain of body, that he uttered this solemn, and important truth—

Tuesday 26th Novem. 1844—Hazy wind S—Rd [received] a newspaper from my very dear Brother Samuel C. Griffin—living at Newburgh-N.Y— Another paper, from my cousin E.M. Griffin, Little Falls—N.Y—

27th Wind N-W—purchased a small Hog of Wm Youngs—Wt 147 lb [& 5 oz.?]

28th A snow and hail storm—Saml. W. Hill (son to my later friend Ithual Hill) stoped with [us], an hour or so

[133] 29th Wind E- by N—Snow sufficient—for not very good sleighing— Saturday 30th Sleighs, and Ponys pass with a tinkling sound of many bells—

Decem 1st 1844—The snow which fell on the 28th last Inst—has nearly disappeared Wind W—From the anxiety mankind discover, to obtain property, & money, one would reasonably conclude that they were being destined to possess the fruits of mortality Forever—

Heard this day of the Death of Walter Corwin, by drowning, in the Delaware River. By some mistep, he fell overboard, and before assistance could get to him, he sunk to rise no more—He was on board the Schooner Prince, E.S. Racket Master—on the 27th last Inst—He has been [134] a boarder with us, a number of months, for the two years past—In said time, we have always found him a steady, correct, and friendly young Man—our family feel deeply to mourn, with his widowed Mother, his sudden removal from time to the Eternal world.

> Farewell, dear Youth, Just in thy manhoods bloom
> Thou art summon'd from us, to a watery tomb
> Jesus alone, thy precious soul can save—
> Whether on land, or In the ocean wave—
> If justified—you have an entrance given
> To all the glories, and the Joys of Heaven.

Monday 2nd Decem 1844 Wind light N—Our brother James stoped with us the last night

[137- misnumbered] He shows the effects near fourscore years, in a part of said time his trials have been great & severe, in losses* & crosses of his dear family—yet he appears to possess much of the Spirit of Job, is strong in Faith giving Glory to God—

*In June 1825 he lost 4 beautiful sons in one day by drowning—And an excellent wife in 1838. She was the ornament to her sex—

3rd Wind N-E—Benjamin Goldsmith Esq. (son [of] the late Reverend Benjamin Goldsmith, who presided over the Church, at Acquebogue, from 1775 to 1810 or 12) died on the 13th last Inst. aged about 77 years—Mr. Goldsmith was a man of good information, much respected, hospitable and obligingly accommodating to all with whom he had intercourse—untill 60 years of age, he was in respectable circumstances—In the close of his life, adversity embittered his setting sun—Howsomever, we hope his heart was bright—

[138] Monday 16 December 1844 Wind brisk W-N-W—The agitation, bustle, and raging commotion, of the two great parties, the Torywhig & the Democrat is over—the interesting, all important Ellection is gone by—Polk, is ellected President for the next four years—

17th Cold wind N-W—Our Grand daughter Harriet P & Walter C. Hubbard, leave, for Southold

18th A very cold wind N-N-W—

19th Wind more light W-N-W—

20th Wind N-E—The rail cars came through from N.Y. to day in 3 hours & 30 minutes

21st A very calm day—

[139] Sabbath 22nd Decem 1844 light wind S—A light rain—

To bear, and forbear, is almost always best—As much so as peace is preferable to war, or a mild calm clear sky, to a tremendous wind & snowstorm—

23rd Foggy, and unpleasent—Street muddy, wet and heavy walking—Some Hail & Thunder this P.M—

24th Almost a hurricane from N-W—Drove two of our coasting sloops on shore—the Sephrona N.G. Beebe & the Champlin H. Henry Racket—

This eve, we had the Joy of seeing at our sequestered abode, our friend N.T. Hubbard

[140] Wednesday 25th Decem 1844—Calm, clear and very mild for winter—

26th Fresh breeze wind S—of course its not very cold. Our son in law Abner Wells's 2d wife Susan, died this day, she was a good woman—

27th Morning cloudy, damp morning—At one P.M. it commenced a copious rain, with Wind E-N-E

28th Wind N-N-W—this morn about 1 OClock It commenced snowing
and continued briskly so to do untill 4 when it when It ceased—the high
wind has blowed the snow into banks, and spoiled the would have been
sleighing—

Died yesterday at Greenport, Mr. Henry K. Booth, over 50 years of age—
He was a man of very mild, and agreable disposition. And we believe his
motive, in all his intercourses with his fellow men, was to injure no one—

[141] Sabbath 29th Cool N-W- Wind—P.M. more mild

30th Some sprinkling of rain occasionally through the day—Snow wastes

31st High wind W-N-W—not uncomfortably cool

1845

Wednesday 1st January 1845—A new year—Brisk wind S—

2nd Wind very powerful from N-W—

3rd Wind light from N-N-E—

4th A clear sky—wind W—

5th Wind S—Cloudy—

6th A cloudy day—wind N- & cool

7th Wind very light—It appears to have snowed, rained & hailed some
time in the last night, as the ground looks this morn

8th Wind N-N-W—Wilcox leaves for N. York this eve—He, and Capt.
Wm Wisdom go by the way of New London—this eve Sidney, his wife &
daughter, Josephine, came to us—

[142] Thursday 9th Jan. 1845—A moderately rainy day, with some
snow—I mistook It was this eve Sidney & his wife came.

10th Very blustering, wind N-W- by W—

11th As pleasant, clear, and as mild a day, as we generally find in April—
perhaps I might say in May—

Sabbath 13th Wind light from S-S-W—Some little Snow—rather larger
than a white frost—Sidney, and his family left this morn—

14th A clear, bright, mild day—

15th Wind S—A damp day—Abner Wells, and Walter, (our grandson)
visited us.

16th A very little rain, and warm weather. A curious observation, for the
month of Jan.—The frost appears to have left the ground

[143] Friday 17th January 1845—Wind light E-S-E—It appears to have
been a rainy night the past one—Rains hard this evening—

18th Wind very brisk this morn N-W- and a cloudy, cold day—

Sabbath 19th Wind powerful as yesterday—Capt Wisdom arrived home, left Wilcox at Madison, Connecticut—They left Orient together, on the 8th, with the laudable design of Lectureing on Temperence

20th Wind light N-W—Some flights of snow—not sufficient to track a good fat goose—

21st Through the last night, it has rained, hailed and snowed—Wind N-N-E—

22nd Cool & clear this more[n]—Wind W—

[144] January 23rd 1845 A pleasent day with with [wind] light N—

24th A thick cloudy day—Wind S-E—It rained profusely In the past night—

25th A wet, misty atmosphere, nearly sufficient to wet an Irishman to the skin

Sabbath 26th Cool—Wind brisk N- with snow squalls—

27th A mild pleasent day—

28th Much like pleasent May day—

29th Wilcox arrived home—

30th More cool, wind W—

31st Wind N-W—This evening, our Grandchildren, Deziah, with her Husband Samuel Griffin, and their Infant—Harriet Matilda with them, came on a Visit to us—

January has been as mild, as pleasent, and as warm a January, as perhaps we have known this ten years past—

[145] February 1 1845—Cold, and what is called good winterlike weather—

Sabbath 2nd Much such weather as yesterday—This day is the aniversary of my birth, Seventy Eight years have run their important rounds, since I commenced my walk on the wondrous bridge of life—The company, (in this Town,) that set out with me, on that eventful year, (and they were many,) have, alas! nearly all disappeared!—What a dream is mortal life!— A spiritual view of It, is sufficient to stain the pride of all Earthly glory— This evening our <u>children</u> mentioned 31st last just left us—

3rd Light wind—but cold—

Tuesday 4th It commences an E- Snowstorm, with a gale of wind E—It drives & smothers—

[146] Wednesday 5th Feb. 1845—The wind, last night, blew near a hurricane—It continues in snow squalls pretty much the day—

6th Clear, blows, & cold—This Winter, Jeremiah Youngs has commenced building himself a dwelling house—It is to stand about two rods to the south of his Fathers, Thomas V. Youngs—The carpenters have likewise begun to errect a house for Mr. <u>Marvin Holms</u>,* now a store keeper, of this place (Orient). This Man came to my house, In June 1825—At that time out of health—said [147] he was from Connecticut, and in persuit of that inestimable Jewel health—As the place looked agreable, Its harbour, bays, Islands, and prospects were congenial to his mind, he would stop with us some time if It suited our convenience to keep him—We were agreed, and he commenced board the 30th of June, of the year before said—Mr. Holmes is now 1845 one our most prominent Merchants, in our Village—Previous to his keeping store, he kept our district School nearly six years, to the intire satisfaction of the <u>employers</u> and the <u>Scholars</u>—a good recommendation this—

*See my 2d Journal page 315

[148] Friday 7th February 1845—Wind N-W—very cold, as much so as any night we have had this winter—Such intense cold, affects sinceably [sensibly] the <u>aged</u> and the <u>poor</u>—Yet we are told, (and we often see It verified) that God "tempers the wind to the shorne lamb"—

This month we was visited by our friend Chancy W. Moore

The storm of Tuesday night, with the very full tide, has broke through the beach, Just this side of the bridge near Rocky Point, so that the tide ebbs and flows through—A thing that happened once before, which took nearly all the teams in the place, about two days to fill up the chasm—The roads are such that we have no mails these 3 or 4 days past—

[149] 8th A calm, cloudy, cool morn—Wind light N-W-W—

Sabbath 9th Feby 1845—Wind very light, N—It is cold, yet a cloudless sky—The late severe snow, and hail storm, has so filled up the railroad track, that the cars cannot traverse It, and have not passed on said road this 5 days—A heavy loss to the company—

Monday 10th Cold & clear, with winter cheer.

Tuesday 11th Commences with a moderate snow—Wind light S-S-E— P.M. It rains—The rail cars, got through, from N.Y. last night, for the first time since last Tuesday—

[150] Wednesday 12th February 1845—It rains some this morn—Wind S—The snow goes off before the S- Wind—

To be cool, and collected, from a virtuous view of human fluctuations discovers the Man, as he should be—

Thursday 13th Wind N-N-E—and a snowstorm—It has set in very moderate—Yesterday, arrived from a whaleing voyge, the Ship John Jay—On the account of the Ice in Sagharbor, she has put into Greenport—Is owned by the Mssrs. Howels. Has, we are informed, riseing 4000 barrels of oil. She has been absent 28 months.

[151] Friday 14th Wind N-N-E—I mistook, It is this day (not yesterday) It commences a snowstorm [and] covers the ground several inches—And yesterday 13th the Ship J. Jay arrived—

One half of our troubles, and difficulties, come upon us, in consequence of inattention, and unwatchfulness—

Saturday 15th A foggy, wet uncomfortable day—Travilling is intollerable—Streets inundated, with splash, and water—

Sabbath 16th Much such weather, under foot, and overhead, as yesterday—

Is not the prudent person good, if not wise?

It clears off calm, and pleasant, as the sun sets.

[152] Monday 17th February 1845—A clear, cloudless, pleasant day—Wind W—To bear, and forbear shows wisdom—certainly good sense, in a person of such sense—

Tuesday 18th & 19th two very mild days—Wilcox moved from his, Dyers house, at the landing, into our house, from which he removed on the 4th of May last—A world of changes—How solid all, where change shall be no more.

20th Damp cloudy unsettled weather—Ice, with which our harbour has been pretty much shut up, appears to be moving off and breaking in pieces

[153] The fairest morning, is often succeeded by the foulest day—so the brightest Sun, enters into the blackest cloud—A moment since It was all dazzling light, now it is obscure & doleful darkness—But in him, that is Christ, there is no darkness at all—then, that is a truth, those only are blessed, who are in Christ—

21st Cloudy, and as damp, and dark a day as yesterday—It is called (and perhaps, justly) unwholesome weather—

Great—great indeed is the quantum of misery, and sorrow in this our nether world—But grace,—True grace is sufficient for all these things

22nd Mild, and as pleasant, as a fine May day, —Amusement that yields sweet reflections are good

[154] One hundred and thirteen years, this day, since Washington was born!—He lived to merit, (and Justly,) the appelation of "Father of his Country"—The Societies which call themselves after his name, meet this day, to celebrate the Anniversary of his auspicious birth—It appears that these Societies, if It were possible, are adding immortality to his already undying name—

Mr. Richard F. Nicoll, gave us, at our Church, a very excellent, and feeling address, on the glorious subject of Temperence—and so likewise did Mr.

Huntly of Greenport. [155] After Mr. Huntly had given his very excellent address, I returned home—I am since informed, that after I left, Mr. John C. Cook, of Greenport, spoke, and very much to the purpose, and satisfaction, of the respectable and numerous audience.

Sabbath 23rd Feb 1845 A wet, or rainy day, attended with lightening and Thunder—Mr. Nicoll, tarried with us last night

Monday 24th A cloudless, and pleasent day—Wind W—Mr. Nicoll left us this morn, for his home in Shelterisland

[156] I have just heard, that our cousin David Griffing, of Clinton, Connecticut, died last November 16th aged 81 years—At the early age of fifteen, he entered into the service, as a musician, in the army of the United States, to assist in emancipating our beloved country from British Tyrany— He belonged to the Company of his heroic Father, Captain Daniel Griffin. After the peace, he, (David) betook himself to the Sea, which he followed, with credit to himself, and profit to his owners, for more than twenty years—Many years before he left the sea, he commanded, a number of fine Vessels, with an unsullied reputation—In 1830, he joined [157] the Methodist Church at Clinton—Of said Church he has been an ornament, as a Member, and as a Christian—His sun has set on a clear place, and we rejoice to believe that the missteps of his early life, are cancelled, and washed out in that precious blood, which speakest better things than that of Abel—

25th February 1845 As pleasent, and perhaps warmer, than is generally known in almost any May day—Wilcox set off this day to lecture on Temperence, at Southold, Cutchogue, and Riverhead—May his way be prosperous, and the votaries of strong drinks speedily come to their senses— reclaimed, and finally saved with an everlasting Salvation—

[158] 25th February 1845—Jeremiah Youngs (Son to Thomas V. Youngs) raised his house this P.M.—Raymond shiped on board the Schooner Princes[s], E.S. Racket, Master—

26th Wind S—White frost this morn. Arrived yesterday the Ship Triade from a whaleing voyge of _____ months, with _____ barrels of right whale oil & _____ barrels of sperm—Isaac Case Master—

27th Thursday—A Cloudy, damp day, Wind light—Mr. Thompson, a Taylor, is stoping with us a few days, at his trade—A meeting was held at the meeting house, this P.M. In order to devise on the best plan [159] for a better road across the South dam pond beach, than they now have. Some part of said beach has, in consequence of full tides, often overflowed, and occasioned very heavy travilling—Some thousands of loads of sand, earth or loam, stone, pine logs, boards & locas [locust] posts, have been put on said beach, within the last thirty five years. And the tides and water, has washed It, and them all away—

28th continues moderate weather, light wind —

Saturday 1st day of March 1845 Weather as yesterday—Wilcox returned home

[160] March 2nd 1845 A cool, cloudy morn—light wind E-S-E—To have any consistant, alarming view of the rappidity of the days, weeks, and years allotted us, we must take a minute note <u>of them</u> as they pass, swifter than the weavers shuttle!—P.M. Clear, & pleasant—

To be calm, composed, tranquill, and humble, under every dispensation of the providence of God, is an attainment devoutly to be prayed for—Stephen, possessed that spirit, in an eminent degree, amidst a shower of stones—yes, an so did the Shunamite woman, when she said "It is well"—

3rd High wind S- A.M.—P.M. W-S-W—

No amusement can be good, which will not bear an agreable reflection—

[161] March 4th 1845 Open March weather, and midling pleasent—much unlike the 4th of March 1841 when the cold N-W- wind blew near a hurracane, and the gathering at Washington was tumultuous and immense to see, and hear the Inauagartion [inauguration] address of General Harrison, on his takeing the oath of his office, as President of these United States—Alas! Alas, the mutability of all sublinary things! Today in the chair of State, placed there by the free gift of the only free, independent and sovereign people on Earth, the highest office, surrounded with courtiers, flatters, and friends—In the midst of the blaze of this worlds Glory, within 40 days all, <u>all</u>, is exchanged for the coffin, and the winding sheet—

[162] Thus terminated the solem career of President Harrisons campaign in the sublime field of State—Mr. Polk's Occupation of the station, the Chair, and the conspicuous field he is called into, we are yet to learn, Its happy or unhappy, good, or bad results—

5th March 1845 A severe hail & rain Storm last night—and continues this morn—High wind E—Some Thunder attended with sharp lightning—Wind very high this eve—

6th A clear, pleasant morn after the storm—wind W-N-W—

7th Uncommon mild, Clear & pleasant, for so early in the season—White frost last night—Wind S

[163] 8th March 1845 A Cloudy day—Wind Easterly—Capt James Glover, is at this time errecting, or putting up, a very fine, or showy fence before his

house, on the road. Mssrs Eli Tuthill, and Wm T. Conkling, are the builders—The cedar posts, about 7 of them, cost 50 Cents a piece.

Sabbath 9th A cloudy and damp, drizzly day

Monday 10th A.M. thick, hazy, & damp weather—P.M. Snow & Rain—Cool—wind E-S-E—

Tuesday 11th Comes in with a copious snow storm Wind E. P.M. It clears off pleasant—snow from 4 to 6 inches deep—good sleighing.

[164] Wednesday 12th March 1845 Mild and pleasant with clear sky, yet the snow & splash under feet makes the traviling almost intollerable—

Thursday 13th Weather much as yesterday—White frost, this morn—Wind S—the snow goes off—the body of It was so great, that It will take sever[al] such days to take it intirely away.

14th Comes in with a plentiful rain—E- wind & pretty cool—Received a very affectionate, and expressive letter, from our good grand daughter Deziah P. Griffin

[165] This day departed this life, Charles, son of Mr. John, and Mrs. Maria Clark, of Greenport—Charles, appeared to be a young man, of much promise to his doating parents, and to the large circle, of very respectable connections, & friends—He has been this sometime past residing in New York, as Clerk, in an excellent dry goods store, where his prudence, carriage, and industry, was such as to secure him, the utmost confidence, and lasting esteem of his employers—About 8 or 10 weeks ago, he left NewYork, quite unwell—Since then, he has continued to fail—Thus has a bright and an interesting Youth, of about 20 years, been called away from an adoring & weeping mother, whose grief none but a mother can know

[166] Saturday 15th March 1845—Blustering & cool—Dyer, is making a stone wall, at the shore, on the east side of his wharf—This wharf, was commenced in August 1829—A large part of it is built far from solidity—that is, rather light, or slender—the two, or three outer blocks, are more substantial—

Sabbath 16th A very Squally, blustering day, with some snow squalls—Brothers James, Warren and Warrens wife, and Sister Lucretia, called on us this noon—Our niece, Lucinda Hollis, Likewise Asenath—cousin Vincents two eldest girls

[167] 17th March 1845—Cloudy—very little wind S—warmer than days past—yet cool evening

18th Cool, wind N-W—considerable frost last night—A Cloudy chilly P.M.

Wilcox started last night for Cutchogue, to lecture there on Temperence—

19th A cold N-W- wind—What is Justly called raw, chilly weather—Cloudy—

20th Blustering, and as cold as yesterday, & several of the past 5 or 6 days.

21st A severe tedious cold N-W- wind and has been so since last Saturday

22nd The pierceing Northwester, appears to be dying away—The weather has been very unpleasant for six days past

[168] Sabbath 23rd March 1845—A pleasant morn—made more so by a bright Sun, and the songs, and harmony of the feathered chanterers in our orchards & groves—

> How sweet to rise, and hear their lays,
> Melodious, in our Makers praise—

Monday 24th A raw March wind—A cloudy day, with brisk S- wind—Repaired our East line, board fence.

Tuesday 25th A chilly, pierceing, Northwest wind—As clouds obscure the Suns irriadient beams—Our two affectionate Grand daughters Mariah L. Prince & Harriet M. Preston, visited us, which gave us moments of Parental Joy, & gladness—They left this eve—

[169] 26th A pleasant Morn—Raymond returned home on the 23rd & left yesterday—

27th The day has been mild & pleasant, with wind light from S-S-W—Evening calm—a little smoky—How inexpressibly solemn are our views of approaching important events that we know must, and will take place—In them we shall be actors, not spectators—

28th The warmest day this three months past—I expect that more people went to Southold to attend the meeting, to nominate Town officers, than ever attended, on such occasion, at one time before—Several two horse waggons went, full of passengers—In favour of Temperence was the movement

[170] March 29, 1845—A cloudy morn Wind E—rather uncomfortable—

30th Sabbath, Mild, and pleasant, Wind light S—

Who are they that can view Earth, and Its best, and brightest productions, in their Just, and proper light? Knowing this World is not our permanent, abideing place, how ought we to not? How do we act? Why, as to our actions, movements, anxieties, and earnestness in persueing the pelf [wealth], and productions of this World, they carry the Idea, that this life, and World, is all that Mankind has to concern themselves about, or merit their attention—

[171] 31st Smoky, warm S- wind—wrought at my board fence, to the N-

of T.W. Young's barn—Sam'l Taber assisted me—An addition this day to our satisfaction, united to our multiplied obligations to the Father of all mercies, in being once more permitted to embrace our very dear connections—Walter O. Hubbard, and our invaluable grand daughter, Harriet M. Preston—

> "When all they mercies, O my God
> "My wondering soul surveys,—
> "Transported in the view, I'm lost!
> "In wonder, love and praise"—Addison

April 1, 1845 Rather a damp, drizzly morn. Wind S—people, muster out strong to Town [172] Meeting—There appears two parties—Something like Grace & Nature—Virtue, and Passion—Rum, or no Rum—A Supervisor, opposed to the sale of every and any article, that will or can intoxicate, or, one that advocates the vending that, or those liquids, which has brought more misery, wretchedness, and anguish, on the civilized World, than War, Pestilence Ear[th]quake, and Famine, all combined—

2nd April 1845—We hear this morn that the Whigs got the majority of votes for Supervisor—Joseph Moore of Cut [173] chogue, (an anti[tem]perence Man) was their candidate. Hutchinson H. Case (a temperence Man) is the democratic choice—How shall we account for such a course, persued by the temperence Men, in useing their influence in procureing the Ellection of Man, who builds up the Fabric, they are endevouring to pull down!—The inconsistency of many (not all,) is sufficient to astonish the consistant Man, what a fluctuating speck of imperfection man is.

W.O. Hubbard & H.M. Preston left us this A.M.—

[174] April 3d 1845 A very brisk wind from the W—The clouds look black & squally, in the N-W—

4th Rather of a cool W-N-W- wind—Our friend Calvin M. King, is now working out at his trade (house Carpenter) and smart—For the last seven years, he has been confined to his house, and much of said time to his room, & bed—The change in his health, is assuredly great, if not miricileous [miraculous]—

5th Cool N-W- wind this morn—Repaired our Garden, & Orchard board fence this P.M.—was grattified this eve with a visit, of our son Sidney L. G. & Grandson Augustus R. G.

[175] They came from Hempstead, to Sagharbour—from which to Greenport, and on to us at Orient—

Sabbath 6th Some snow this morn—Cloudy, but moderate, through the remainder of the day.

I must believe, Solomon's <u>Wisdom</u>, exceeded many others, <u>only</u> in his first desire for <u>Wisdom</u>, as superior to all things attainable—

Monday 7th A cold S-W- wind—Took our Son, Sidney, and his son Augustus, to Greenport, this morn, in Absalom Kings Carriage—They left there, in the railroad cars, at 9 A.M. for Hempste[a]d—

Greenport, I perceive, grows—where there was only one small house in 1826, there is now 1845 I should say, 2 or 300, besides about 22 or 3 going up—

[176] Tuesday 8th Apl. 1845 A very squally, cold blustering day—some smart snow squalls—This day 77 years ago, my Wife's Father, Nathaniel Tuthill, departed this life—He was one of the best of Men & a Christian—

Wednesday 9th Cold and piercing N-W- wind—It has now been two, or three very Windy, cold, uncomfortable days—

Several of the plannets, have, as our Almanac says, been in conjunction—Thus our weather, has become boistrous—

Thursday 10th High wind S-S-W and Cloudy weather, some few sprinkles of rain—Capt Wm A. Wisdom, moved, himself, family [177] goods, and chattels, into Dyers Hotel, at the landing, faceing the Wharf, yesterday—

11th Friday 1845—Cold & blustering, with a cutting, N-N-W- Wind and heavy black clouds in Northwest—Was visited this day, by Mr. David Carpenter, now, of Southold, where he has been living with his family, eight or ten years, on a small, beautiful, and <u>well</u> cultivated farm—Mr. Carpenter, was (I believe) originally of Westchester, from which he moved into NewYork, and kept a store—was successful—And then repaired to Southold, as before observed. Is an Industrious, hospitable and we believe, an honest Man—

[178] April 12th, 1845—Continues chilly, and raw weather—Wind, although Southerly, blows cold, and uncomfortable—

Our agreable, and venerable Brother James, called on us a short time—enjoys comfortable health, and Spirits—

Received, a day or two since, a letter, from Capt. Jeremiah Glover—now living at Es[s]ex, in Connecticut—Is 81 years of age—Was born in this place (Orient) where he spent the first twenty years of his life, which has been an active, and an honorable one—

Sabbath 13th this morn, is cloudy & cool with wind S-S-W—

Monday 14th Wilcox commenced School today

[179] Tuesday 15th April 1845 Wind, fresh S-S-W—rather cool—Dyer is fixing a blacksmiths shop, near his dock, for Capt Wisdom—

Wednesday 16th A dark cloudy day—Wind E—Raymond (our son in law) was at home some half an hour, this day—then left for NewYork—

Thursday 17th We had, what may be safely called a wet, or rainy night—It rained moderately all night—This day is a dark and Cloudy one, with a cool E- wind—There is now laying with her mast in the water, she nearly all under water, off about two miles [180] A sloop in the Sound, oppisite Browns hills, driving with the tide, and wind—She upset about two days ago—we understand her crew was taken off of her, all alive, but they who succeeded in saveing the men was unable to get the Vessel into any harbour, at the time—

Friday 18th Apl. 1845—Wind cool from E—A cloudy day—Is it not true, that a wise head keeps a close mouth? —In many instances, it is—How can there be a contention betwixt two, when one of them doesn't speak? [181] How can there be fighting where one of the parties make no resistance?

19th Wind E- as it has been this 10 days, with the chilly effects and what is called uncomfortable weather

Mr George Hollice, A worthy Methodist preacher, and aimable wife, called on us this day—She is my Sister Lucretias second daughter—her name Lucinda—

Sabbath 20th 1845—A dark cloudy day, some rain Just at night—Our mercies, ought never to be overlooked—

Monday 21st Wind continues E—It appears to be dying away—Capt James Glover, succeeded in getting his vessel afloat, after useing great exertions to do so, for near three weeks—She has been laying in the bay, near longbeach, the past winter

[182] Tuesday 22nd Moderate, with wind S—Raymond, came home from N-Y- this P.M. Left N-Y- this morn—came in the rail cars—

Wednesday 23rd Morning—the mildest, brightest & calmest we have had this Apl.

24th A cloudy morn—Wind S—Took down our stove this morn—

The women in Orient, advocates of Temperence, have with the best feelings, and the livliest emotions of respect for Wm H Wilcox's exertions, in that glorious cause, presented him with a valuable suit—viz. a dress coat & pantaloons—Worth altogether 20 Doll[ar]s—A handsome present, and properly, seasonably, and Justly bestowed—[183] Miss Cynthia A. Tuthill, we suppose, was one of the first that suggested the virtuous, noble, and patriotic deed of goodness—Assuredly, the spirit of the inspired Dorcas of holy writ must have greatly rested on her, and all those who have come up to the help of the Lord against the mighty—They, all share in Mr. Wilcoxes best wishes, that goodness, and mercies may follow them all their days, and this expression, of their kindness, to him, may be registered, in the records of immortality—As a champion in the cause of Temperence, Wm H. Wilcox has no superior in this region—I think I am Warranted in saying, that He has done more for the suppression of Alchohol drinks, and the success of the Temperence cause in Orient, than any Man living. Like an instrument in Gods hand he, has been a host of good, and deserves a monument of Brass to perpetuate it—

[184] Sabbath 27th April 1845—Wind, which has been blowing from the Easternboard this 8 or 10 days, is now very light S-S-E—We were visited this day by Joseph King, who was born in this place in the year 1764—He married Betsey Tuthill, my Wife's sister, about the year 1789—Removed into the Country, above Utica, in Ontario County, many years since, and is now on a visit to his native land, and home of his boyhood—He now finds everything changes, and his former friends and acquaintance, all gone to the land of silence—He has been through many strange, and [185] trying scenes— and many of the most unpleasant ones has been brought upon him, by his imprudence and unreasonable actions, and hasty proceedings—With all difference[deference?], and the best wishes, that the evening of his life may be more tranquil, and himself wholly sanctified, I forbear to notice farther, on his chequered, rather singular, and often unpleasent life, which is now drawing towards a close—His history would not edefy his friends, and could not be of any use to his enemies—He dwells much upon a future State, and appears strong in the Faith of a glorious rest, where the wicked cease from troubling.

[186] Monday 28th Apl 1845 A pleasent day—Wind light, W—Raymond & myself took sail to Long beach—It was an amusing & pleasent excursion on the water, as we had a neat and good little sail boat—

Capt. Wisdom, moved his blacksmiths Apparatus to C. Dyers Shop, this day—

Last week, a Mr. Charles Tuthill, from the County of Yates, town of Starky, in our State of N.Y. called on us, with his Fathers, and his Uncle Samuels respects, to me, and mine—He is the son of Joshua Tuthill, a native of this place, where [187] he Joshua was born, about the year 1772—His Joshuas Father, was Major Barnabas Tuthill who was some time in the continental army, under General Washington—He was a noble looking Officer—He died about 1782—The above said Joshua, removed into the country with his Brother Samuel, about fifty five years ago—Samuel is a Man of handsome property, a widower, having lost his very excellent and good Wife about three years since—She was, when a girl, Parnol Contine, and one of those daughters, whose price is above rubies.

[188] Tuesday 29th Apl. 1845 A cold, squally day—Wind E—
Wednesday 30th A cool S-E- Wind—

Thursday, 1st May 1845—Comes in with a light wind S-S-W—A cloudy day—

Mr. Foster King, now a Merchant in New York, called on us this day, with his uncle Joseph King—Our young Friend, Mr. F- King, (whom we esteem as one of the noblest of Gods works, an "honest Man",*) brings us the solemn news of the death of his very invaluable Brother John—Says he died, on the February last, at, and in the Celebrated ancient City of Rome—Called by many "the Eternal city"—John, when a boy of six years, at School to me [189] was, from his openness of manner, activity of movement, energy, and willingness to perform his every task assigned him, a deserving favorite of mine—He grew up, and continued such through all the multiplicity of changes allotted him, until he was called to pass that bourn, whence no traviller returns—For more than thirty years, he has resided principly[principally] in NewYork, doing a justly profitable business, in which he was successful—In the year 1841, his health, which has generally been delicate, began to decline, and a European Voyge was urged by his Physicians—He accordingly with his attentive Brother foster embarked for London, where he arrived, after good, and not a long passage—In this tour, he visited many of our classical cities, of old renown, with Egypt, Paris, and Marseilles—After fifteen [190] months of travil in and about the old world, returned to our favoured clime with much better health, and vigour, than when he left—The hopes of his friends were buoyant, and elated—But alas, the mutability of all sublunary things—1844 came, and with its fleeting course the perceptible decline of our Friends Health—In the summer of this year, he stoped some time in this place (Orient) and often indulged me and mine with a call—He always met us with a complacent smile, and with that suavity of manner, and address which appears well designed to show us our lot is [191] cast in pleasent places, and he and we and all of us have a goodly heritage—Growing unwell, he soon left for NewYork, where he shipped again, for Europe—Arrived there after a tedious, and to him, distressing passage, being quite ill on the voyge—He proceeded, on his arrival, almost immediately for Rome, which he reached in a reduced, and low state of health—The result is now known as before observed and to us communicated by our Young Friend Mr. T. King—John King was, as a Son, to his

*In certain circumstances, singular and curious, as an incident satisfied us, that the above remark is in time, and just in all its bearings—A-G-

Widowed Mother, made up of affection, tenderness, and fillial Sympathy, for her comfort, and tranquility—A Son, able, and all accommodation, and disposition to administer the cup of consolation in her weary trial.

[192] This estimable, aimable, and accomplished Friend of ours, (John King) was born in this place (Orient) about the year 1795—From his boyhood, to his last visit to this place, which was about last August, his manner was lively, animating, sociable, with a flow of spirits, mixed with a good will to make a glow of comfort, and enjoyment pervade the hearts of every one with whom he was conversant—

John King was the son of Mr. Rufus King, a very worthy, kindhearted, good Man, who died Apl. 1834—He Rufus was the son of Mr. John King, who died in the year 1792—[193] And he, John King, (last mentioned) was the son of Ensign John King, one of those men whose piety, humility, and examplanary [sic] life rendered him an ornament to the Christian profession, and to the Church militant—He died somewhere about the year 1758 or near that date—He was the son of William King, who was the son of John King, who came to Orient about 1650—

Friday 2nd May 1845—A mild springlike day—Wind light S-S-W—Our grandson, James H. Preston, came to us last evening—looks improved in health, and growth—perposes to attend the Seminary, at Millars place, the ensuing Summer—

[194] Saturday, 3rd May 1845—This is one of the pleasentest of May days—an unclouded Sun, with a very light S-W- wind, these Spring beauties, with the sacred melody of the Lark, Red breast, and a conscience void of offense, are sentimental, and refined comforts—These paths of rectitude are the only ones in which we can walk to the abodes of comfort, and tranquility—All other roads, or highways, lead only to disquiet, remorse and wretchedness—Then, dear Sir, or Madam, whoever you are, that reads this observation given in love, [195] and great goodwill, seek, and at all times secure your walks in that sanctified, purified path, of light, knowledge, and unmingled enjoyment—

Sabbath 4th Much such weather, as yesterday—Evening a shower—James H. Preston left us this eve for Riverhead—

Monday 5th A cloudy & moderate day, wind light W—Wilcox moved to Sidneys house, which stands on the road, north of my house—Mr. Abner White built the house, for our Son, about six years since, for the consideration of two hundred dollars—I paid him extra 35 dollars—

Tuesday 6th Morn wind—E-N-E—Yesterday, Raymond commenced on the seine, for J.C. Havens, for 16 Dollars per month

[196] It is calculated that the fires kindled by the Locofocos [locomotives] in the woods, near the middle of Longisland, which have been rageing last week, and week before, have destroyed property, to the amount of near, or quite 300000 Dollars—A very large quantity of cord wood, fences, Barns, out Houses, & dwelling Houses—The owners of this property, are becoming indignant, and have demanded satisfaction—To day, we hear, that two or three hundred Men, owners, and friends of the property destroyed, have turned out, with loud threatenings [197] that if satisfaction, is not immediately made, for losses sustained by the fires, originating from their engines, they, the sufferers, will stop the travil, by the railroad Cars, instantly—

Wednesday 7th Wind, light W-S-W—Mr. Marvin Holms has this day commenced pulling down his house, in order to, on its site, erect a new one—The old house, which is now comeing down, was built by the late Mr. Daniel Youngs, about fifty two or three years ago—Mr. Youngs occupied and owned said house and about 13 acres of land adjoining It, for more that 40 years, up to the time of his death

[198] Thursday 8th May 1845 Very cold E-N-E—wind—Evening more mild, with a light breeze W—Our Seines have caught but a very few fish, as yet—

Friday 9th As cool a morn as yesterday, with wind E-N-E—P.M. Cloudy—

Our late Friend John King, mentioned in page 100 & 192 to 193 left a Will, which was Read In the presence of this Mother, sister, and his two remaining Brothers, Sylvester & Foster—Its contents were something like this, viz. To his affectionate, and weeping Mother, he [199] has bequeased[bequeathed] five thousand, five hundred Dollars—To his Sister, Margeret Petty, and her Children, 5500, and to his Brother Foster, the remainder of his property, supposed to be about 3000 dollars—It may be 10000, as It was the opinion of many, that he was possessed property to the amount of some 20000—But dear, disappointed anxious Man, It was thy sad, and fatal lot, to die in a foreign, and strange land—far, far from the cheering presence of the most endearing, and tenderest of Mothers, the soothing and lovingest of sympathetic Sisters—Distance prevented them from the consolation of administering comfort in the his dying hour—To wipe off the damp sweat, and give the last, last look of Love, while closeing his Eyes in Death—

[200] Saturday 10th May 1845—A cold E- Wind—There was some frost last night—we fear it will injure the fruit prospects, as our trees are now beautifully arrayed in all riches of odoriferous blossoms, of almost every tint & colour—

Sabbath 11th Pleasant—Wind light- W—

Wisdom points to the dwelling of substantial enjoyment—The family who occupy that Tenement which is built upon a Rock, are all Scholars, to that Preceptor, who teaches as never Man taught—

Monday 12th A warmer day than any former one this Spring—Narcissa is quite unwell—unable to set up very little this two days—

[201] Tuesday 13th May 1845—mild, and warm weather—Worked on the road this day—found It rather to laborious for advanced age, and its attendent aches, and infirmities, which realize daily—

The Jackson Seine, took about 5000 Boney fish this morn—this is pretty much the first draw of any consequence this Spring by this Seine—There has been no very great draughts made as yet in this region—

Wednesday 14th A cloudy, thick morn—Some very little Sprinkle of rain, in the course of the day—Mr. Saml. W. Hill with us this eve—Mr. Hill, presented me with a handsome pinchback cased Watch, this Evening—It is said to be of good old fashioned work—I esteem It as an expression of intrinsic [202] value—and if possible, more so, by having long been the faithful pocket companion of my late Sentimental friend, his revered Father, Ithuel Hill—This day the Jackson Seine took about 145000 fish—

Thursday 15th

Friday 16th An Easterly rain storm—Rode out this P.M. with Mr. Hill, to Wm. H. Tuthills, and John Younger—See, at Mr. Youngers, and conversed with our venerable and valuable female Friend, Mrs. Phebe King (known by the present generation as Aunt Phebe King)—She is, or will be Ninety years of [203] age in November ensuing this date—In acts of kindness, tenderness, and affectionate expressions of charity, she is certainly a Modern Dorcas, and in humility, a Mary—

Saturday 17th The storm continues—Our Friend Hill left us this morn—

On the 9th Inst departed this life Miss Phebe Wiggins, aged 86 years—Miss Wiggins was through a long life prudent, industrious, virtuous, and affectionate—Propriety marked her steps, and especially in her many expressions of tenderness and benevolence towards the orphan Children, of that good, and late pious Man, and friend of ours, Mr. John Wiggins—To these Children, she has with unceasing attention been all the Mother, and Friend—She was a Maiden Lady, never having been married—

Sabbath 18th Wind E-N-E—with rain occasionally—

[204] Sabbath 18th May 1845 Is as before observed a cloudy, damp, or moderately wet day—Evening, the wind E—dies away—

The Mr. George Wheeler, noticed March 1840, called and took Dinner with us, last Friday—He is now 18th stoping a night or two at Wm.Wisdoms Inn, Dyers House, near the Dock—He, Wheeler, for reasons best known to himself, has seldom called on us since the Spring of 1841, although he has visited our place often since that time—Such things will happen—When we observe a change in a persons movements, our views of them undergo a like change—

(205) Monday 19th 1845—A pleasant morn—Wind light W—A fine and salubrious purified air, this morn, after the late refreshing rain—Set out about 20 Early Cabbage plants—A very little Sprinkle of rain this eve—

Tuesday 20th This morn, about 7 OClock I saw the most beautiful cloud rise out of the N-W- I ever before beheld—It spread, and rolled in Majestic grandeur from the S- to the far N- in the purest symetry, and folds of white, surpassing the richest fleecy robes of the harmless and favourite lamb—It was rendered more sublime, and awfully grand, by a stripe of a coal black cloud, underneath, and adjoing It in its intire length, which was across the western horizon—It moved in rapid, suprizing majesty over to the E—and disappeared—P.M. It rains very moderate, light wind S-W—

[206] Wednesday 21st The rain for three, or 4 days past, has given the Earth, in our region, quite a different colour, from what it was ten days ago—Then vegetation began to droop, and languish, now, all is green, gay, blooming, refreshing, and odoriferous, with the matin Song of the Lark, and Redbreast, renders the hour of early riseing enchantingly delightful—Jeremiah Youngs moved into his new House, this day—He raised his house 25th Feb. last—Lester B. Terry was Married last week to Miss__Brown, daughter to Mr. Christopher Brown, of Fish Kill—_____County

Married, this Evening, Mr. Joseph C. Havens, to Miss Hannah Brown, daughter to Deacon Peter Brown, all of this place—

Thursday 22nd Wind S—P.M. Cloudy

How good, how kind is our Creator in bestowing his innumbered mercies on us in his own way, and manner—Not as we see, but as he sees, for our own final, and best good here, and we trust hereafter—Infinite Wisdom has wisely given us, his dependent creatures, but one moment at a time—had he given us two or more at a time Its probably we should use them worse that we do now—and that is bad enough—

[207] Friday 23rd Comfortably cool—Wind E-N-E—

The Jackson Seine took about 50000 Boney fish today—

Saturday 24th Cooler than yesterday, fresh breeze from the N—

Sabbath 25th Wind as yesterday—with Occasional Showers—Woolen clothes, with watch coats buttoned up suitably meets the feelings of those

who stand without excercise aloof from a comfortable fire—We had some
hail this A.M.—When we are tried by misfortunes, privations, and distresses
incident to mortality, then the world will know, and our friends will know
our true character—Our patience, humility, and resignation to the [?] prov-
idences of our Heavenly Father will be fully displayed—"A tree is known
by Its fruit"—Of course our moves, dealings, and every days actions, and
words portrays pretty plainly what kind of hearts we have—

[208] Man in French is <u>Homme</u>, In Spanish[Italian] <u>Uomo</u>, In Greek
<u>Anthropos</u>, In Hebrew <u>Ish</u>, In Chinese <u>Jin</u>—

Monday 26th Wind W-S-W—It grows more mild—We have seldom
known three cooler days in succession, in May, than were the 23rd—24th &
25th of our present May—Howsomever, I have seen not any frost in them
as yet—

<u>Patience</u>, from a virtuous motive, has the benignant Smiles of Heaven—
As It is such a celestial treasure, let us pray that <u>we</u> may posess It in all circumstances, and at all times—

The Jackson Seine took about 60000 fish this morn—I am just informed
that the Seine has took about 100000 instead of 60000.

Tuesday 27th I mistook, It was <u>this morn</u> that the fish were caught—

It is said that the fires about the middle of the L.Island, which were kindled by the railroad cars, have distroyed Barns—Houses, outhouses, wood,
fences and trees, & etc. etc. to the amount of 400000 Dollars. [209] What
will be result of said distruction, time will explain—The owners of said
property are much grieved, and highly offended—If reparation is not in
part made soon, they, the aggrieved, threaten to take such satisfaction as
they shall deem proper—Perhaps Lynch said road, or tracks—

Yesterday a young Gentleman called on us by name (as he said) Thomas
Dodd—He tells me that his GrandFather was Cousin to the celebrated, but
unfortunate Doctor William Dodd, who was executed in June 1777—Doct.
Dodds thoughts in Prison, is a very excellent production—

Wednesday 28th High Wind W—When our neighbour, or any one, with
whom we have to do, wax <u>warm</u>, our bounden duty is to keep <u>cool</u>, calm,
and completely collected—Look sharp before we leap—Count 100 before
we reply to an angry, hasty Man—

Marvin Holms is errecting a new House, which the carpenters, with other
assistance, have raised this P.M.—It stands partly on the scite [site] of the
one formerly owned and built by the late Mr. Daniel Youngs—He Mr.
Youngs built It in about 1787—

[210] Thursday 29th May 1845 Wind as Yesterday, brisk W-S-W—Some

sprinkle of rain this morn—William Webb, (Son to Sandy Webb) arrived here from seven Months voyge to the South—

Two Hotels, or boarding houses, put up this Spring at Greenport—The largest one is Peconic House, conducted by John Webb, Son to the late Captain Thomas Webb of Cutchogue—The other, Greenport House, by a Mr. Terry, I believe, from near Riverhead—John Clark is making an addition to his house, in order to accommodate more boarders—Thus we see, that the World appears to be alive to every means, and invention, to procure the root of all evil—Money, and the consequence it procures, appears to engulf the whole mind of the present generation—Howsomever, Selfishness, has been, and will be, a predominant passion of Mankind, untill that glorious era, when Adams posterity shall all see eye to eye in the Truths of the everlasting Gospel—

[211] May 30th 1845 Wind N—and uncommon cool & blustering—A good fire this morn is much needed to keep the body and temper in their proper, and agreable, tone—Our very affectionate grand daughter Harriet M. Preston is with us—came last Eve—

Saturday 31 A.M. very cold—Wind N—P.M. wind S- & warm—Jackson Seine took about 250000 Boney fish this Afternoon—Yesterday they took about 100000—

June 1st 1845—Wind light from W-S-W—

Doct. Young says "we take no note of time but by its loss"—True—while we attempt to look at its rappidity, behold! Its gone—Our last years—past weeks, and Yesterdays, where are they? With the years in which Noah constructed that wonderful Vessel, which safely rode out and safely survived the most tempestuous flood & rainstorm that our World ever did, or ever will know—

[212] June 2nd 1845 Wind W—How little, very little, do the larger part of mankind appear to be affected with the shortness, and uncertainty of their mortal existence—

"A bubble on the Sea of matter borne
"We float, we break, and to that Sea return."

When the evening has come, the products and what the day has brought forth is, or will be known—

Tuesday 3rd Pleasent salubrious air—A suitable and agreable warmth, and coolness to render morning, noon, and evening excursions pleasant—

It was, (Yesterday,) an impressive and an affecting consideration, in seeing our grand daughter, Harriet M. Preston, kneeling, with the tenderest
sensibility at the Graves of her Sainted Father & Mother—The emotions of
her heart, and sensations, at the eventual moments, were unspeakable, and
only known to her guardian powers above—

[213] Wednesday 4th June 1845 Warm S- wind—

Last autumn, Joseph C. Havens built himself a handsome Shoe Shop,
and set it on the N-E- corner of George Champlins Garden, adjoining the
road—Today has removed said Shop to his own premises, say, about twenty
rods, up the road—

The Jackson Seine has this two days past about 200000 fish—

Consideration is an excellent acquirement—those who possess It at all
times, and in all cases, are greatly blessed—

Thursday 5th As warm, as yesterday, with wind S-S-W- and light—I
might have mentioned (as such events, however trivial to others, to us, at
this time, important) that our Grand daughter Harriet M. Preston left us
this P.M. for Greenport, intending in a day or two to visit N.York

Was visited this day by Mr. __ Hall, a gentleman, Merchant of NewYork,
where he has resided for about twenty years past—[214] Mr. Hall, and his
(at that time) beautiful and accomplished wife, stoped with us some days in
the July of 1833, 4 & 5—Since that time we have not seen him, in these
parts—His aimable wife died about six years ago, and we are informed he
has since married again—

Friday 6th Wind light S-S-W—It is getting rather dry—I fear hay will
come in light this season—

I believe, from what I read in our newspapers, that the distruction, by
fires, has been greater within six months past, than any other six months,
this Country has known since Its settlement—Pittsburg, Quebec, and many
other of our Cities & Towns have suffered the loss of Millions of property—
The uncertainty, and instability, of all sublinary things, is sufficient to teach
us to look for an inheritance where change shall be no more—

[215] Saturday 7th Pleasant, but continues dry—Last eve, Our Grand
daughter, Deziah P. Griffin, with her Husband, and Babe, came to us—They
were truely welcome to our humble, and secluded mansion—

This Morn, our agreable, and sage Friend, Benjamin Brown Esq., from
Orange County, with his two daughters, Mary & Elizabeth, came, and
stoped with us about six hours. Mr. Brown was born in this place (Orient)
in the year 1780—Is the Son of George Brown Esq, who died about two years
since at his residence in Orange County, aged about 82 or 3 years—Squire

George was the Youngest Son of Benjamin Brown Esq, who died in this place in 1774—His father was Joseph Brown Esq—It appears that our friend, now on a visit to this land of his Fathers, is the fourth Generation in which there has been a Justice of the Peace in the family—He being the fourth in succession—

Jackson Seine took about 100000 fish to date—

[216] Our friend, Benjamin, who was with us this day, moved into Orange County, with his Father in 1782—His Father having sold his farm, some short time before to our Uncle, Jonathan Terry, for somewhere about 3500 Dollars—This Farm ajoins the Sound, and Trumans beach, (commonly call hard beach)—The Hills, known by the name of Browns Hills, make a part of said farm—It had been owned and occupied by this family since about 1710—

Sabbath 8th Pleasent, but very warm and dry—

Monday 9th Wind light W-S-W—Our Kinsman, William H. Griffins (of Guilford C-t) daughter, Maria & Husband, Mr. Hart, Stoped with us an hour or two this P.M.—

[217] Doct. Young says "Man to Man, is the sorest, surest Ill" I would that Mankind would so conduct, and act, in their every intercourse with each other, that another Doct. Young might find urgent reasons to publish to the world, that Man to Man, (in the now 19th Century,) is the safest, surest good—May we not Hope, that such an Effulgent season is fast approaching—Such a Mellenium of peace, & serenity, unspeakable, is now at our doors—

Tuesday 10th Continues very warm, and It begins to be seriously considered dry—dry—

Died yesterday morning Eugene, son to our Brother Peter Warren, & Polly Griffing—His age about 30 years—He was an industrious, active, kind, and obedient Son—Strong, vigorous, and healthy, untill about three years ago, when a sudden attack of illness, brought on him, the complaint, which has terminated his life, thus early—

[218] Wednesday 11th June 1845 A refreshing shower this morn—Vegetation feels its salutary influence, and puts on its delightful robe of Green, perfectly suited to the vision of dependant Man—

Deziah P. Griffin, (our grand daughter,) with her husband, Samuel Griffin, left us this P.M. for their home at Riverhead. She has a very interesting daughter, called Mary Preston, about nine months old.

This P.M. the wind hauls to the E—

Thursday 12th Continues very warm.

Friday 13th Wind brisk S-S-W—Jackson Seine took 60000 Boney fish this A.M.—We had a fine Shower this morn—

Saturday 14th Wind this morn S—Some showers—A growing Season

[219] Calamities, if sanctified, prove blessings—A bitter, nauseous medicine, administered to a distressed patient, often affects the sweetest relief—"Blessed are they that mourn, for they shall be comforted"—

Sabbath 15th A pleasant morn, with a salubrous braceing light N- wind—Capt. John Clark, Inn Keeper, at Greenport with his brotherinlaw, Edward, Stoped with us a short time this A.M.—Informs us that the rail road fare is reduced, from $2=25 Cts to$1=75 Cts to NewYork, from Greenport—or 1¾ Cts per mile—likewise they will run three times, or three trains through a day—The inventions, and movements of Man, are a wonder and an astonishment to Man—Yet to those who have passed away from these varied, and exciting scenes, they are, as tho' they were not—

[220] Monday 16th June 1845 This morn comes in with light wind S- and moderate Showers—clears off 10 A.M. and warm

Died this morning Lester R. Tuthill, son to Nathaniel Tuthill Jun.* aged ___ years—A pleasant, mild, obedient, and much beloved Son—Was greatly resigned to his Heavenly Fathers will and full of that Faith which works by Love, and purifies the heart—What yields this world, but vain delusive toys, while tears are mixed with all its fleeting Joy—

*His Mother is Azubah, Sister to the Rev. Ezra King, who has been a Preacher to the Congregation of Middle Island for some years—

Tuesday 17th A heavy thunder shower this morn—Clears off cool—Jackson Seine has took 38000 fish this day—Wisdom is the principle thing. What a treasure it is to the posessor. One of the richest boons of Heaven—

Wednesday 18th Wind this morn—N- and cool. Visited long beach in persuit of Gulls Eggs—got 13—Augustus McNeil, found 5—poor success to us—

[221] Thursday 19th Comes in with a moderate rain, and very light S- wind—

Just behind a few fleeting days, lies a complex explanation of the result, and products of the doings, factions, and undertaking of us, our neighbours, and all who are buisy in schemes, and inventions for profit and honor—The night will come, and then It will be fully know what the day has brought forth—

Friday 20th Comfortably cool, cloudy, and a pleasent morn—The World awakes to all the buisness cares, perplexities, pains, and anxieties which flesh is heir to—

News has just arrived that General Andrew Jackson is Dead—He died on Sabbath 8th Inst.—We can say of him, as the sweet Psalmist of Israel said of

Abner, the Son of Ner, Know ye not that a great Man has fallen in America—
He was a great General, Statesman, patriot, and last, not least, a Christian—
On the Sacred Roll, containing the names of American Worthies, stands in
bold relief on the page with Washington, that of Andrew Jackson—

Saturday 21st It commences with a moderate rain, which continued untill
one P.M. when it clears off very moderate—This P.M. Brother Samuel C.
Griffin & Wife and adopted Daughter came to stop with us a day or so—
They are in good health—

[222] Sabbath 22nd June 1845 A salubrious, clear & pleasent day—Wind
light N—A.M. S-E- P.M.—

Alow yourself not to speak while you are excited or angry—It is better to
keep your mouth shut than to open It to no use—To visit places where we
have not any buisness, is wasting time, and creating unpleasent reflections—

Monday 23rd A copious rain, from 2 A.M. until 7 A.M. when It clears off
with very light wind W—While It continues to rain, the wind was E—

Tuesday 24th Very light wind W—Is it not more common to speak of
our neighbours faults than their goodness?—I think It is—It is assuredly
an evil, and we all ought to shun It as a poison—

Wednesday 25th Considerable rain fell last night It clears off this morn
with wind light—very light N-W—

[223] Brother Samuel C. Griffin & wife, with their little girl, left us this
morn, for rockypoint—Jackson Seine took 50000 fish this day—

A Mr. Lee, a Clergyman, Stops with us this evening—He is selling Maps
of the State, and of the U-States—Is traviling for the benefit of his Health,
which is delicate—

Thursday 26th A fine salubrious, very light N- wind—

Capt. Caleb Dyer was Married last Evening, to Julia, Daughter to Capt.
Elias Terry, all of our place (Orient.) He, the groom, was born In the year
1779, March, and She, the bride, in 1811—Winter & Summer Seldom come
together—When they do, may It produce no inauspicious season—

Friday 27th A clear sky, and refreshing, light wind W—

[224] Saturday 28th June 1845—Light air S—Comfortably cool, and
shady by haze, with clouds—

Silence, is often more productive of tranquility of mind than many words
uttered in haste, and not well timed—

This evening, we learn, from the NewYork papers, that our Grand daughter Harriet M. Preston was Married on Thursday 26th Just to Walter O.
Hubbard, of N.York—May the Benediction of Heaven greatly rest upon her,
and guide her safely through every trial allotted her, in lifes uneven path—

[225] Sabbath 29th June 1845 A cool E- wind, after a rainy night—

Monday 30th A.M. cloudy & very cool, E-wind—P.M. Cloudy—A rain Storm—Brother Samuel C. G- called on us an hour this afternoon—Is stoping, with his wife and adopted daughter, at Rockypoint for a few days—

Tuesday 1st July 1845—Considerable rain fell in the course of last night—

It has been very cool for the time of year, now for these three days past, with a fresh breeze East—This P.M. the wind is N-W- with a tollerable clear sky—C. Dyer has bargained away his house, which was built by the late James H. Preston, and has belonged to Thomas Youngs, the last five, or six years—The house became Dyers about a year ago, and he has now conveyed It away to Edward Prince, of Southold—

Wednesday 2nd July wind S—A Cloudy day—Some fine sprinkling of rain—

[226] Thursday 3rd July 1845—Considerable rain fell last night, attended with lightning and thunder—Days, hours, and minutes pass in rapid succession, and where are they!—gone—gone—and each hour borne away Its own load of cares, perplexities, sighs, Tears, and the woes which flesh is heir to—To be over anxious, is unwise, and renders such moments very unpleasent.

Friday 4th A very pleasent day, rendered moreso by a clear, comfortably cool W- wind—A number of the people of this place celebrate the day, and dine at Wisdoms, at the landing.

Rev. Mr. Ingles of Southold pronounces at the Methodist church—

[227] Saturday 5th Clear, and pleasant Wind W-S-W—and brisk—We received a letter from our Son Sidney, with one from his son Augustus, yesterday—Wrote to Augustus, this P.M—

Sabbath 6th July 1845 A pleasant day. A cool, and braceing West, brisk wind. A lover of peace, and a healer of breaches betwixt neighbours, is a person of incalculable value, in Society—May not such a personage bear the noble appelation of Mr. Popes honest Man—"The noblest work of God"—

Monday 7th wind very light W-S-W—Our cherries, which are plenty, begin to be considerable ripe—a day or two would help them to ripen—

[228] Carnal weapons can never make a Man a humble follower of Christ—they may make hypocrites, and Mahometans—It is love, celestial love, which prepares, fits, and sanctifies the soul, for the regions of a blissful immortality—

Tuesday 8th Warm, clear and comfortable—

Wednesday 9th What is called (and Justly) fine hay weather—Was visited this day by a Mr. __ Parshal, of NewYork—This Gentleman, with his Wife, stoped with us near a week in August 1837—

Thursday 10th Mr. Parshal, and myself, early this morn, visited the ancient buriel ground, up in Browns Hills. While viewing the graves, we copied the following, from some of the headstones, which time has marked with her destroying hand, and moss has over grown—On the wife of William King, who died May 7th 1764 is the following lines

[229] Beneath this little stone, here lies,
The wife of William King—
And though she's dead to mortal eyes,
She will revive again—
Lived four and fifty years a wife,
Died in her seventy seven—
Has now laid down this mortal life—
In hopes to live in heaven—

On the Wife of Samuel Beebes, who died June 10th 1716

Here lieth Elizabeth, once Samuel Beebe's wife
Who once was made a living soul, but now's deprived of life
Yet firmly did believe, that at her Lords return,
She should be made a living soul,
In his own shape and form—
Lived four and thirty years a wife,
Died aged fifty seven,
Has now laid down this mortal life
In hopes to live in Heaven—

Walter Youngs, Son to Gideon Youngs, died 1714
Gideon Youngs, Died in May 1699 aged 61 years
Dorothy Youngs, wife to Jonathan Youngs Died 1753 aged
[230] Jeremiah Vail died 1749 aged 39 years
Capt. William Booth died 1723 aged
Samuel King died 1721 aged 89 years. Of course he was born in 1632 or 3—which was about 6 or 7 years before our ancestors, or any other white men landed at Southold, or any other part of the East end of Long Island—The first settlement of this part of the Island was in 1640—and we have understood in Septem.—

Jonathan Tuthill died in 1741 aged 50—Henry Tuthill died in 1715 aged 24—John Tuthill died in 1743 aged 60 years—This John was Son to John Tuthill 3rd, who was the Son of John Tuthill, Sr. and was with his Father a boy, of five years old, at the time they landed at Southold in 1640—That is, John 3rd, mentioned above, was grandson to the first, or Elder John, which landed, as above stated in 1640—[pencil] This John, who died in 1743, was greatgrandson to John the first of the name to Southold—

[231] Friday 11th A warm S-W- wind—Mr. Parshel is yet with us—He has much of a Byographical, and historical taste, with which I find myself pleasently entertained, as he is sociable, and improvingly communicative—

Saturday 12th Very warm—light wind W-S-W—Mr. James Parshal left us this morn—Raymond took him to Gardeners Island, in a small sail boat—

Sabbath 13th A very warm day—Some company from Greenport—Mr. John Webb, with them—He was the youngest son of the late Capt. Thomas Webb—

Monday 14th The warmest forenoon we have had this season—Some little rain, with Thunder, this 4 P.M.—Our neighbour gathered about 2 bushels of our Cherries this day—

Tuesday 15th Clear, and fresh air—A fine rain last evening, attended with Thunder and Lightning—This rain, began to be much needed.

How very necessary it is for us, at all times, and in all places to maintain a calm, dignified, moral serenity, and composure of mind—

[232] Wednesday 16th July 1845—This is one of the very warm days of our passing summers—In NewYork, it is excessively uncomfortable, and often proves fatal to those who labour hard while exposed to the burning rays of an unclouded, Meridian Sun—

Thursday 17th—More wind than yesterday—If as calm, as yesterday, It would be as uncomfortably warm.

Friday 18th A refreshing West wind this morn—We are passing away, but the cares, anxieties, commotions, excitements, and unspeakable sensations interwoven into our frail system, hedges up our miserable way of heed[ing][233] as we ought, the rapidity of our hours—weeks, and months which compose our little—little life—

Saturday 19th Wind light E—Rode out with our Son, Sidney L-G- as far as Henry Landon Esquire, at Cutchogue—Met on our going, twelve carriages, with a young Gentleman, and Lady, in each—They were in anxious persuit of pleasure—Six months hence, perhaps some of them can tell how much of it they overtook, and possessed, in the intire day, and evening—

Sabbath 20th Still continues very warm—Monday 21st A Copious rain last night, attended with sharp lightning and very heavy Thunder—

[234] Tuesday 22nd Wind fresh and revivingly invigorating, after so refreshing a rain—Took Sidney (our Son,) his wife, and daughter, Maria, in Absalom Kings Carriage, to Greeport, this P.M., from which, tomorrow morn, they take the rail cars for Hempste[a]d—

While at Greenport, I called at the Peconic House, kept by Mr. John Webb—It is finished off in good style, and as a boarding house, I think in finish, convenience, and for comfort, it far exceeds any establishment of the kind in Suffolk County—

Wednesday 23rd Wind, this morn, comfortably cool, from the N—

Thursday 24th weather much as Yesterday—

[235] Friday 25th More comfortably cool, this two days past—Our cherries all but gone off the trees—Wind light W—

Saturday 26th Wind W—Doct. S. H. Tuthill took 5 boarders, yesterday— They are from Hydepark, on the Hudson River, near the residence of the late Doct. Hosack—

Sabbath 17th Wind fresh from E—Considerable rain fell the latter part of last night

Wisdom teaches those who are good scholars, that we are creatures of but a moment—of but yesterday!—Our life, (mortal life) a vapor!—What a humbling, but Eternal Truth—Yet in this brief space, we are to build for Eternity! God be merciful to us Sinners Amen and amen—

Monday 28th Some refreshing Showers this P.M.

[236] Tuesday 29th July 1845—A light refreshing wind N- this morn— "we take no note of time but its loss"—And why not notice It, since it is leaving us with an astonishing rapidity to the silent, darksome grave—

Wednesday 30th A squally day, with wind S-S-W—Some light showers—

Thursday 31st Showers last night, and very warm—More comfortable this day—

Friday 1st August 1845 Light wind W—A gentleman, his wife, nurse, and two children, from Troy, called on us this A.M. He is going to East Hampton.

The wise patient Man is patient & wise—He posesses a treasure, which enriches himself, and which he cannot bestow on his fellow men—

Saturday 2nd Wind light W—A cloudy day—

Sabbath 3rd A gentle breeze from E- by S—and cloudy as yesterday—

Monday 4th Wind very light S—Warm, sultry weather—Dog star rules, as they say—

Tuesday 5th Wind S—It has been very warm this several days—Some say It has not been so steady uncomfortably warm this some summers past— They go as far as 10 or 20—I do not know as to so long a time—

Wednesday 6th We think we are safe in saying this day, with a number which have preceded It is extreme warm—last night was a very warm, sultry night—A light wind E-S-E—

[237] Thursday 7th August 1845—Wind S-E- and cloudy—

Friday 8th Very light E-S-E—David T. Glover arrived in our Orient Harbour this day with his Schooner, he has just purchased her name is ____ and of 120 Tons burden—Saturday 9th Continues extreme warm

Sabbath 10th This morn, to our great Joy we was visited by our Friend N.T. Hubbard, and his good wife Susan, from NewYork—To us it was a season of peculiar satisfaction—From these friends, we have received the most marked and affecting civilities—from such visitors, accrues the most pleasent reflections—

Monday 11th Warm as ever—Rode out with my friend N.T. Hubbard, to Greenport, A.M. to Lathams P.M.—

Tuesday 12th It still, as to sultry warm weather, impersonates Dog days, in all its unpleasent relaxing Colours—Rode out as far as Mattituck, accompanied by our friend N.T. Hubbard, and Wife—On our way we breakfasted at John Clarks Greenport—Called at M. Conklin Cleavelands—was much pleased with the taste, and convenience, which Mr. Cleaveland has displayed in his buildings, gardens, in, and around his spacious, pleasant, and rural Mansion—[238] Our next call was on Mr. Barnabas Orsborne, whose wife was Lydia Webb, daughter of our late friend Capt. Thomas Webb—Mr. Orsbornes flower garden exceeds in the number of its different kinds of flowers, roots, and plants, any other garden I have seen in the Town—and It shows that It has not been neglected by Its kind, and hospitable owner, and proprietor—We stoped again at Mr. William Wickhams—We then proceeded to Mrs. Myra Reeve's, where we took dinner—Mrs. Reeve is the Widow of that late very excellent benevolent, kind hearted Man, Luther Reeve—Mrs. Reeve inherits the place, and old Mansion of her husbands Father the late Thomas Reeve. A visit to this antiquated house, revives in my memory the most solemn, and affecting reflections—Here thirty years ago, I was wont to receive from Mr. Thomas Reeve, and his affectionate, tenderest of wives, every hospitality and civility calculated to render their guests time happy & pleasant—But alas those seasons have passed away, and of the then inmates of the house, only two remain, viz. the widow, Myra, who is the grand daughter, and a sickly daughter, Parnol, who is, and ever has been a total stranger to deceit—[239] I left our friends at Mrs Reeves, about 2 P.M. and arrived home at 6—They take the cars, on the railroad, tomorrow Morn, for N.Y.—

Wednesday 13th Air rather more cool, occasioned perhaps by a light breeze from E—

Thursday 14th August 1845 Calm, or nearly so, and as warm as It has been this 20 days past—For three weeks in course It has been as sultry, close, and uncomfortably warm, as perhaps any summer this five years agone—

This morn, about 3 OClock, departed this Life, Mr. Lewis Tuthill, aged 51 years—His death was after a distressing inflammation of the bowels of about 24 hours—His life has been a peaceable, quiet, industrious useful one, in his family, and his neighbourhood—Honest, and upright in all his dealings—A dutiful son, a kind and affectionate husband—a tender, and indulgent Father, and we believe we are Justified in saying as an individual unknown but amongst his own neighbourhood, and Town, he was one of Popes noblest works of god—"an honest Man"—Mr. Tuthill was the Son of David Tuthill, who was the son of Christopher Tuthill, who was the son of Henry Tuthill, who was the son of Henry Tuthill, who was the Son of John Tuthill, who was one of the first, who landed at Southold in 1640—

[240] Friday 15th August 1845—Wind East. As to coolness, Its more comfortable than any day in three or four weeks past—Joseph Johnson, a boarder of ours some two years since, called on us, a few minutes, this Morn—

Saturday 16th Wind E- and cloudy—The weather as comfortable as yesterday—I have just heard of the Death of Henry Wells Esq. of Tioga county—he was Uncle to my Soninlaw Abner Wells—He died some months ago as we are now informed—He had held some respectable office in his County and was considered a man of respectable Standing and Tallents—

Sabbath 17th Cloudy, Wind E—

Monday 18th Cloudy, damp E- wind—much such a day as It was August 18th 1799—Just 46 years agone—That day was Sabbath—

Tuesday 19th Wind E—Our Grand daughter Harriet M. Preston (now Hubbard) with her Husband W. O. Hubbard came to our Situation this day—

Wednesday 20th Weather, as yesterday—Easterly—Wrote this Day to B.F. Thompson Esq., in answer to one from him, on 17th July last—

Thursday 21st Extreme warm—Our grand Son Augustus R. Griffin, left us for his Fathers, at Hemste[a]d—

[241] Friday 22nd Some wind S-S-W—very sultry hot as It has generally been the last 40 or 50 days—some rain last night

Saturday 23rd Wind S-S-W- with Showers attended with Thunder—

Sabbath 24 A clear pleasent sweet air, after the copious Showers yesterday—Received a Letter from B.F. Thompson Esq last eve—

Monday 25th Continues extremely sultry & warm

Tuesday 26th Weather very warm, as It has been (with the exception of
an hour or two at a time) this more than forty days past—

Wednesday A.M. very sultry hot—4 P.M. wind came from E-N-E- with
a sprinkle of rain, and have a cooler evening than we have had for many
weeks past—N.T. Hubbards Son Samuel L. Hubbard came to us about 1
OClock P.M. He left N.Y. at 8 A.M.

Thursday 28th A cool E- wind, and a Cloudy day—

Friday 29th Much such weather as yesterday—Wind S-E—

Saturday 30th Rather more warm, wind S-E—but light—Samuel
Hubbard left us this morn for his home N.Y.—

Sabbath 31st Wind very light W-N-W—

Monday 1st September 1845 Wind N—Wrote to B.F. Thompson Saturday
& likewise Sidney, our Son—

[242] Tuesday 2nd Septem. 1845 A Cloudy day with Thunder showers—
Wind S-S-W—A camp meeting commenced near Sagharbour, yesterday—

Wednesday 3rd Showers this morn—A number of our neighbours have
left this morn for the Camp ground—

W.O. Hubbard and his wife Harriet M—our granddaughter, left us this
morn, for N.York—they take the cars in the railroad—

Our Son, S. L. G- has wrote a handsome account of his and Wifes visit
to Canada, two weeks since—It is in the Hempstead Enquirer of August
30, 1845—

Died this morning George Clark, a younger Brother, Capt. John Clark,
Inn keeper, at Greenport—George was a truly industrious, fine young Man,
much beloved, and the endearing Husband of a daughter of Mr. Nathanial
Corwin of Greenport—Thursday 4th Scarce wind enough this day to blow
a candle

Friday 5th Wind pretty brisk N-W—The ills which mortality at all times
is subject to are ever surrounding Man, let his situation be what It may—
Not any place this side [243] the grave is secure from the pains, and distresses intailed to humanity in its best estate—Those are truths sufficient to
humble us truly, and stain the pride of all human Glory—

Saturday 6th A refreshing N-W- wind—Camp meeting breaks up this
day, It has continued since Monday last—near Sagharbour—

Sabbath 7th Brisk S-W- wind this morn—P.M. It blows a gale S-S-W—
Lester B. Terry, Schooner Planet—Warren Beebe's Sloop and James Glovers
Sloop Thos. Collier, have all drove on shore—It is what is Justly called stiff
S-S-Wester—It brings plenty of seaweed on shore which give Joy, and buis-
ness to our industrous yeomen—

Monday 8th Wind light N-N-W—

Tuesday 9th A cool E- Wind & Cloudy—Our good Cousin, William H.
Griffin, wife, & Daughter leave for Guilford, this Morn—they have been on
a visit to this place for the week past—He is one of those Men that does
honor to the name of Man—honest, honorable, and upright in all his intercourse with Mankind.

[244] Wednesday 10th Septem. 1845 A brisk S-W- wind—P.M. It hauled
into the N-W—Of course the evening more cool—A small fire in our keeping room makes It look like domestic comfort—A unity in sentiment is
commonly attended with a peace, without which, what is a family, a neighbourhood, a World, but wretchedness and confusion—

Thursday 11th Wind this Morn N-W-W—Dug and housed our potatoes,
about 22 bushels. The yield is moderate, but they are very good—

Friday 12th Wind and weather about as yesterday

Saturday 13th Wind light E—& cool—

Sabbath 14th Wind S-S-E- with a moderate rain. Wrote this day to
Benjamin Brown Esq of Hamptonborough, in the vicinity of Goshen,
Orange County—Who is that wise man that shuneth many of those evils
into which the inconsiderate daily fall? If sorrow is allotted to any of us It
is our bounded duty to acquiesce with a holy, and a humble resignation;
and say with a prayerful spirit, thy will, O Lord be done; on Earth, as it is in
Heaven—Such a frame of mind becomes the wise Man—Who then but
wishes to be wise?—Monday 15th Pleasant—Wind light W—McNeil (our
soninlaw) is moveing his family and effects to N.York, where he perposes to
do business the coming Winter—

[245] Tuesday 16th Wind light, N-N-W—Our very affectionate, invaluable Daughter, Cleora, with her Husband, James McNeil, and their three
children, Augustus, Harriet, and Emma, have all left us for NewYork, this
Morn, In the Sloop Sophrinia, Noah G. Beebe, Master & owner—

Wednesday 17th Morning comes in with light Wind S—It looks much
like a storm of rain gathering—A Capt. Goldsmith, with his Vessel, from
Cutchogue, Is takeing in a load of potatoes, at 45 Cts. Per bushel—This is
higher than common so early in the season—This evening Sidney with his
Wife came to us—Left us for Hempstead this 3 past M—our sensations at

meeting & parting with our children are not easily expressed, yet are sensibly felt.

[246] Friday 19th Septem. 1845—Wind W- and light—Jason King, Son to the late Jason King of Orient, paid us a short visit this A.M.—The Elder Jason moved to MorrisTown, NewJersey, some time before his Death—He died about 1835—His Wife, an excellent woman, died soon after her husband—They had lived together about 50 years—His Mother, Ama, an industrious, peaceable, quiet Woman, died 1814 in Novem. aged over Seventy years—Old, and Young in this place hardly knew or called her by any other name than Aunt Ama, for more than forty five or 50 years—

Saturday 20th High wind S-S-W—

Sabbath 21st Wind N- with rain—

A peaceable, quiet disposition is of more value to the possessor than thousands of Gold & Silver—Moth and rust can corrupt the latter, while the former will retain its brilliance in all seasons, and at all times—

Monday 22nd A cool N-W- wind—Henry Dyer, of the Sloop Shave, with cargo of potatoes, sails this day for N.Y.

[247] Tuesday 23rd Sept. Wind E—

Wednesday 24th Considerable rain the past night—Wind this morn N-W- with flying clouds. Those Vessels Glovers & Terrys have not yet been got off, although considerable efforts have been made to get them afloat—

Thursday 25th Wind cool from N-W- but light—In some gardens there [was] a little frost last night—

Friday 26th light Showers, occasionally through the day—Purchased a cord of oak wood of Mr. Jesse Terry, of red Creek—the price four dollars—Our niece Lucinda, now Mrs. Hollis, with her Sisterinlaw, Miss Hollis, are stoping with us this afternoon—

I ought to have mentioned at the time, viz. on the 15th this Just September, Samuel Racket Junr. of Rockypoint was married to Caroline Wiggin (our niece)

The institution by God was given

And when united, makes a Heaven—

[248] Saturday 27th Septem. 1845 A mild, calm day—Who can comprehend the swiftness of time! The years and days, when Alexander astonished the world with his victories! When Ceaser met the Enemy and they were his—When Napoleon awoke all Europe and caused the Monarchs of the Old World to tremble on their thrones! Those times, and those conspicuous Men have passed away—Yes, away! And their deeds emblazoned on the rolls of Eternal Fame, are spoken of with about as much emphasis as the eccen-

tricities of Sterns Uncle Toby—Heard this day of the Death of Nathaniel Griffin Esq of Guilford Connecticut.

[249] He was aged 78 years, died on the 17th Inst. He had represented his State in the Assembly & Senate, for many years—Was for some time a Judge of the Court—A graduate of Yale Colledge, in 1786, and was truly a Gentleman of the good old School—

Sabbath 28th A pleasant day—Wind very light S—Raymond arrived home last eve—has been absent about 6 weeks—

Sold my rotary Stove yesterday (It being much worn) for Eight Dollars—

Monday 29th A mild morn. Raymond left this morn for Providence— The fluctuous scenes of Earth have a powerful effect on a vast number of Men & Women—Some few, whether from Philosophy, Strength of mind, or Religion, generally appear calm, and collected, amid Storms and devastating commotions—

[250] Tuesday 30th Sept. 1845—Wind fresh S-S-E—This day, a Capt. Goldsmith from Cutchogue took on board his Sloop, at Dyers wharf, 1000 bushels potatoes—The price he gave for them generally was 45 Cents per bushel—I do not recollect of any Vessel takeing so many bushels on board, in so short a time (as one single day) before this one—This said Goldsmith took, about two weeks since, from said dock of our Farmers, 500 hundred potatoes at the same price—makeing in the two trips 1500 bushels—Henry Dyer in his Sloop Shave, has taken off this Septem. 750 bushels of the like Vegetable—

October 1st 1845 A copious rain, which continued nearly through all the past night with wind S-S-E—It clears up this morn about 8 OClock—Lester B. Terry got off his Schooner Planet this Morn—She had lain on shore 24 days

[251] Thursday 2nd A clear pleasant day—Wind high N-W—John Edwards (Son to Sylvia Edwards) moves this day to NewYork—purposes to attend the fish market, in Company with his Brother Isaac—They are grandsons of the late John Brown and Zipporah Brown, of this place (Orient)—

Friday 3rd A very light air of wind from S—All that is mortal is changeable—can there be light without shade? A Shadow without a substance to make It? He is wise who adheres strictly to the voice, and ways of Faith—

Saturday 4th A cloudy, damp day—Wind light E-S-E—Sabbath 5th A copious rain, Wind S-E—Raymond arrived home this morn—

Monday 6th Wind N—misty damp weather—Got into my yard this day two cords of oakwood for the delivery of which I paid Ten dollars—

A Mr. James Brown from near N.York, a Temperence lecturer, and celebrated Singer performed in Our Congregational Church this Eve—He stays with us this night—

[252] Tuesday 7th Oct. 1845 This has been a dark, misty, cloudy day. Captain James Glover succeeded in getting his Vessel afloat, or off from the shore, where she has lain ever since the 7th of Septem., as mentioned in 243 page.

Wednesday 8th This may well be said or called a warm day—Very little wind from S—

A Mr. Hollis, a Methodist Priest, stoped with us a short time this A.M.— Brother James, and Sister Lucretia, set off last Friday for Newburgh, on a visit to our Brother Samuel.

Thursday 9th Showers A.M. wind S—It partially clears off this P.M.— warm and calm. A Temperence convention at Riverhead—great efforts are making by many to check the monster of intemperence in Its raviges through our devoted land—It has to this country, for years past, been a curse of curses—The orphans cries, and the Mothers tears, are melencholly evidence of the blasting influences of the effects of Brandy and its attendants, Rum, Gin,Wine, etc etc—

[253] Friday 10th Very light wind S—and warm, very warm—Henry Dyer is loading his Vessel, the Shave, with potatoes the 2nd time this fall, for NewYork—Takes this time 900 bushels—

Saturday 11th Brisk S- wind, and warm—The Sloop Oddfellow, Appleby, Master, took off from our Orient farmers about 10 days ago 350 bushels potatoes.

This eve, our grand Sons James H. Preston and Chatham A. Griffin came to us, on a visit—Sabbath 12th Very high S- W- wind, with dark & flying clouds—

Monday 13th Wind S-E- but light

Tuesday 14th A very mild day—scarce any wind—Evening Calm—James P our grandson left us this eve for Greenport, and thence to Riverhead— Wednesday 15th Cool Wind N-W- and cool

Thursday 16th Pleasent weather—Friday 17th Wind very light S—Got me home a cord of hickory wood at $5=75 Cts

Saturday 18th Wind S—

[254] Sabbath 19th Oct. 1845—Fresh breeze wind S-S-W—From my actions, and movements, with those of my neighbours connections, acquaintances, & all with whom I know and have to do It would seem we are dreaming away our important, mortal life—While we essay to look at Its complicated fleeting vapour, Its gone! Gone forever!—

Mrs. Betsey Miller (formerly Betsey Brown) called on us this day, from a town called Venece, in the County of Cayuga—This Lady was the daughter of the late Richard Brown and Susannah Brown, of our village (Orient.) She went into the country where, or near where she now resides about 22 years ago—She was Married to this Mr. Miller soon after she left this her natal spot, and is now on a visit here, to her aged Widowed Mother, whose joy on meeting her daughter is such as none can know but Mothers—

[255] Monday 20th Wind E—Thomas L. Youngs moves his family & effects this day to Greenport—

Goldsmith from Cutchogue has took off, in his Vessel, on Saturday last 113 bushels potatoes—Making in his three trips 1500 bushels

We are informed that a woman died in NewYork, yesterday, 19th named Hannah Gough, a Widow, aged 110 years, wanting 27 days—

Tuesday 21st A high N- wind, and cool this eve—Yesterday, our grand daughter Maria Prince, & our grand Son Walter Wells, called on us an hour or two—

Wednesday 22nd Rather more moderate, with less wind N—Yesterday Edward Prince moved his goods, chattels, and family into the house, late the property of Capt. Thomas L. Youngs—We put up the new Stove, this day—

There is now living in the Town of Frankfort, near Utica, a Man, named Hervey, aged 111 years of age—that is he was born in 1734—can walk pretty well—has been a preacher near 80 years. He occasionally explains Scripture at his now great age.

[256] Thursday 23rd October 1845—A calm day, preceded by a large white frost—About the middle of this month Lester B. Terry, of the Schooner Planet, sailed for CharlesTown, S. Carolina—

Died on Sabbath 19th Inst Mrs. Hannah Gough, of Read Street, aged 109 years 11 months & 3 days—She has seen, and conversed with every President of these United States—Commencing with Washington, down to Tyler—

Friday 24th Wind E—and a cloudy day—Raymond left for Philadelphia, with Glover in the Schooner Export this day—

Saturday 25th Brisk E- wind—On the 23rd Two Men from NewYork came to stop with us a day or two—their object is Gunning, or fowling

26th A pleasent Sabbath day—

Monday 27th Wind very light, as It has been this some two days—Warm. Our gunning Gentlemen are yet with us—This eve, they have brought [257]

home 5 good Ducks—last Saturday they brought home 6 making in all 11 &
3 small birds—

Tuesday 28th continues mild and warm—Our two N.York Gentlemen
left this morn to take the cars at Greenport—They are very light coloured
Men, well behaved, and appear to be good moral charracters—have been
employed as Stewards on board of some of our Superb Packet Ships—

Wednesday 29th Very warm for the season—Wind very light S—Henry
Dyer, of the Sloop Shave, arrived here from NewYork, with drygoods & groceries to Marvin Holms—Lord W. Gillet, and George Champlin, Merchants
of this place (Orient)—They, together, received about 350 lbs of butter, to
retail out in our midst—more I presume than ever brought to this place for
sale, at one time, before—

Thursday 30th Mild, and warm—John Terry Junr. & Chatham (our
grand Son) have gone to Orsborns Landing after a load of wood—John
Kellis is selling oysters for [illegible] per bushel at the dock—

[258] Friday 31st October 1845—An Easterly cool wind—with heavy
clouds—Lemuel Youngs was Married last Week at or near Islip, to a Miss
Smith—

The past Summer, the Baptists Methodists & Congregationalists etc
have built themselves a nice little Church which will cost about 10 or 1200
Dolls. It stands about 150 to 200 rods west of the bridge, on the Southside
of the road, and near, at least within 20 rods of the 100 mile stone, from
Brooklyn—

Saturday 1st Novem. 1845 S-S-W—And cloudy day—The Temperence
cause, in the States, we hope, gains ground. May it increase, and grow, untill
not a Man shall have any more countenance in our Legislative Assemblies,
than the Man had to the wedding, who attempted to attend without a wedding garment—Sabbath, 2nd An E-S-E- rainstorm—Monday, 3rd Wind high
S-S-E—It rained much last night—Some showers this day—Very full tides—

[259] To anticipate trials, and sorrows is unwise, as we may not live to see,
and feel them—Our bounden duty is to make constant preparation for
every calamity flesh is heir to—

> "Earth is a shadow empty light & vain
> Her bed of roses is a bed of pain"

Tuesday 4th General Ellection through the State this day—those who
are much excited, and uncomfortably anxious about the success of their

party will soon lose their anxiety, and be as those are who were stormy in the days of Jefferson—"How many sleep who kept the world awake!" There is hardly, or scarcely a Man, who voted in 1804 at our Ellections, now seen at our poles [polls]! They are gone, gone! Never to return—A serious, but important truth—

Wednesday 5th High wind W—Some rain last night—Potatoes, those called <u>merces</u> are now selling with us by retail at four shillings per bushel— Other kinds for about three and sixpence—Higher than I ever knew potatoes in this place before—Thursday 6th A <u>still</u>, cloudy day—the little wind we have is S-S-E—

[260] Friday 7th Novem. Fresh wind W-N-W—People here (Orient) are sending off their Turnips—Are freighting Henry Dyer of the Sloop Shave— Its rather earlier than they have generally sent them to market—The Cutchogue Sloop Capt. Goldsmith—The Sloop Oddfellow, Capt. Appleby, & Shave, Capt. H. Dyer, altogether have taken this [day] of our Orient Farmers, about 3500 bushels potatoes, at an average price of 45 cents per bushel—It comes to 1475 Dollars—

Saturday 8th A cloudy calm day—Wilcox left this morn for N.York and from thence intends to go on a tour of Lecturing on Temperence—This P.M. It rains—

This day, the Cutchogue Sloop, Goldsmith, the sloop Oddfellow, Appleby, and Shave, Henry Dyer, have taken off about [page trimmed] bushels potatoes, in addition to the others they took off some time since—they make the number of ____ bushels they together have took to market, from this place, this far—8th Raymond got home—

Sabbath 9th A cloudy, damp day—wind W- by N—An affectionate tender hearted merciful Man is invaluable in Society, and an ornament to Man

[261] Monday 10th Novem. 1845—This morn It blows a gale from W-N-W—An <u>old Man</u>, that is poorly clad, penniless, and hardly knows of a place where to lay his weary, trembling limbs at night, to <u>see such a Man</u> (late in Autumn, bending over his staff,) without emotions of Kitty, and commiseration, would prove to a demonstration, that the heartless observer was a finished companion for old [Kranks?], in this life, and the society of Demons, where selfishness lands all the votaries—He, or She, that can trifle with the feelings of the aged, and infirm, must have the heart which Nebucadnezer had when he was driven from Men and his dwelling was with the Beasts of the field—Yes in manners, and civilities, they must be infinitely below the Orangutang—

Tuesday 11th A clear morn, the gale has subsided from moderate N-W— Raymond left this morn—

Wednesday 12th A thick cloudy morn, with light wind N—Our Brother James tarried with [us] the past night—Narcissa came home this eve, from Riverhead, & Southold, where she has been on a visit this 12 Days past—

Thursday 13th Pleasant, clear, cool morn—wind W—

[262] Novem. 14th 1845 Wind high W—The precincts of humility and holiness is the abode of rest, and permanent umingled Peace—The Joys which nature and her works produce are of as short duration as they are falacious. The cup of iniquity will be dashed with bitter bowls.

We are Just now, (this evening) informed that Sagharbor has suffered severely by fire, last night—particulars have not yet reached us—report says the great, and new Presbyterian Church is burnt, with a large number of houses & stores—

Saturday 15th Brisk wind N-W—We hear this day that the fire in Sagharbor commenced on the wharf, and extended its destructive element up on each side of main street, on the West Hildreths buildings, which are of brick—It is the most destructive fire ever known on this part of the Island—

Sabbath 16th A pleasant day—

Monday 17th A calm morn—James H. Preston (our grandson) stoped with [us] last night—he, and Chatham, left this morn—This Eve, Sidney & wife came—

[263] Tuesday 18th A calm morn—this A.M. Sidney, and Wife, left for Hempstead—I took them to Greenport, in Champlins Carriage. Raymond left this P.M.—

Wednesday 19th Rain this morn—Doct. Frederick W Lord is now building a fine, spacious house, on a part of the farm, late the property of Judge Thomas Youngs, who died about 1793—This farm, was one intire tract, of about 500 acres, and continued unbroken, from the time his, Judge Youngs, ancestors, to the Judges Son Thomas who died 1816, leaving It to five of his Sons viz. Thomas, Joshua, Ezra, Franklin & Jacob—At this time It is owned by 11 or 12 families—Thus we see, that what the old Judge conceived would be to him sacrilege, is now, after his decease, done to the full, in the cutting up his farm, in parcels, and some pieces of It to strangers!—It is Truth that the penurious, and anxious getter of property knows not whether he is accumulating for a wise man, or a fool—

Thursday 20th Wind fresh N-W- by W—

[264] Friday 21st Novem. 1845 Wind brisk W-N-W—Midling Cool—

Saturday 22nd Wind as Yesterday. It requires a strong & virtuous mind to show a mild, and calm deportment in the midst of a storm—Rec'd a letter this eve, from Wm. H. Griffing, Guilford

Sabbath 23rd Wind S—A rain storm—Some Thunder, and lightning

Monday 24th A cool day—It freezes in the shade through the day—

Tuesday 25th Wind West—Not as chilly—Wrote to B.F. Thompson, Esq., author of the history of Long Island—

Wednesday 26th Wind very light through the day—Henry Dyer, of the Sloop Shave, has just arrived from NewYork, where he has been selling a cargo of potatoes, and turnips, the first he sold for 66 cents per bushel—turnips for about 22 cents—flour is now selling for 7 dollars per barrel—wheat for one dollar & 50 Cents per bushel—

Thursday 27th A profusion of rain last night, and this morn—wind S-E—

Never be in haste except It is to do the works of actual necessity, and celestial virtue—This World gives nothing permanent—It is luxurious in sorrow, and pain.

[265] P.M. Wind changes to the W—but light—It may be set down for a rainy day—Was called on this evening by Peter Booth, a coloured Man, a licenciate to preach, as a Congregational, or more properly, independent—His gifts are good, and we have reason to believe he possesses that Grace, which is a sure passport to a house not made with hands, Eternal in the Heavens. Peters Father was Ruben, a Servant of the late Captain Joseph Booth, who died about 1795—Ruben died about 1811—He had married a second Wife, Dorcas, daughter to John Patoo, an African of true piety—

Friday 28th A cold, brisk N-W- wind—considerable frost, last night—

Saturday 29th A pleasant day, although chilly, with very little wind N— The coldest night we have had this autumn—The sloop Swallow, Capt. Benjamin Wells, of Southold, is now takeing the Orient Farmers wheat—It is now said to be worth in N.York one Dollar & 50 Cents per bushel—good news to our farmers, but bad to the poor laboring man. It is thought Orient people will send off about 2000 Bushels of wheat this season—

[266] Sabbath 30th Novem. 1845—A cold Easterly Wind—P.M. Some rain. Selfishness appears to be interwoven in our natures—Is it not the predominant passion of civilized Man? Our bounden duty and glory is to restrain and subdue the unreasonable sway, with all the energies of our minds, united with watchfulness & prayer—They who do this, will assuredly find the unspeakable consolation of having Heaven on their side—

Monday 1st December 1845—A hard rain Storm through the day—Wind S—Walked down to cousin Jeremiah Terrys, this A.M. He is very unwell— O! what is our mortal life! A shadow, a vapor, a shooting star! Well might

holy Job, exclaim with a spiritual eye, that his days were swifter than a weaving shuttle—

Tuesday 2nd Comes in with a cold N-W- high wind—It made Ice
through the day in the shade—

Wednesday 3rd Wind light, W-W-E—a cloudy day—It rains hard this
eve—

Thursday 4th Considerable snow last night—It goes off this day as fast
as It came—

[267] Friday 5th Decem. 1845—A heavy gale of W- wind—Yesterday I
ought to have noticed was Thanksgiving through the State—

Departed this life yesterday (4th) Jeremiah Terry, aged 68 years—At the
early age of 12 years he gave a lively, and satisfactory evidence, that he had
found the pearl of great price—had found his Saviour altogether lovely, and
the highest amongst ten thousands—His life since that time has left us not
a doubt that his hopes and consolations were built upon the Rock of ages—
He was the 3rd Son of my Mothers Brother Jonathan, and great grand Son
of Deacon Daniel Tuthill, whose life of faith and piety was unsurpassed in
is day & generation—

Saturday 6th—A high W-S-W- wind, not quite so tremendous as
Yesterday, when It blew our sign down—It was put (as we thought) up very
firm, but It seems the wind has tore it off—

Sabbath 7th More moderate, yet cold—Received a letter from Cousin
Wm. H. Griffing, of Guilford, last eve—

The road ambition travils is too narrow for Friendship, too crooked for
love, too rugged for honesty, too dark for science—

[268] Monday 8th Decem. 1845 Wind light S-S-W—Wrote this day to
our cousin William H. Griffing of Guilford—

Tuesday 9th Wind fresh as Yesterday, and from W—It was to day I wrote
to Wm.H. Griffing—

Wednesday 10th A West swift wind—Wheat is now selling at 1 Doll & 50
Cts per bushel—corn at 75 Cts—Potatoes 50 Cts—flour at $7—per barrel—
Bread is said to be the staff of life—Of course the stuff its made of is high,
here & in Europe—

Thursday 11th The boistrous, cold wind of yesterday, and the day before,
has much subsided this morn—though light, it is more N—

Friday 12th was the coldest night we have had this season—And this day
is truly to a freezing point—Wind N—Wilcox leaves for SmithTown this
morn, is invited there, and to Bedding [Baiting] hollows, to lecture
Temperence—A glorious cause—

Died last Wednesday Our Sister, Mary Hubbard, Widow of the late Richard S Hubbard, who died in NewYork, about 1821 or two—They were a united couple and richly inherited all the excellences, and Heavenly virtues of Zachariah, and Elizabeth—[269] Mrs. Hubbard died as she has lived the last forty years of her life, triumphant in that faith, which works by Love, and purifies the heart—

> Now, with the Justified, the Eternal blest,
> Her raptured Soul has found its long sought rest

Saturday 13th Very light wind from S-E—

Sabbath 14th Comes in with a moderated E- rain—Letter last Eve, from our grand Daughter H.M., late Preston, now Mrs. Walter Hubbard—It brought us the mournful news of our Sister Hubbards Death, as mentioned about—

Mrs. Griffing had quite an Ill turn this morn—

Monday 15th It continues to rain through all yesterday, last night, and this morn until 8 OClock, when the wind shifted to the N-N-W—

Tuesday 16th A heavy gale of wind N-N-W—

Wednesday 17th A pleasant, mild, moderately cool morn—light wind W-N-W—Rec'd five newspapers and a letter, all from Nehemiah Foster King, N-York—

Thursday 18th A mild pleasant morn—light wind S—A sprinkling of rain In the evening—Our sister Lucinda, with us this two or three days

Friday 19th A cloudy morn, with wind S-S-W—

Saturday 20th Wind N- and a cloudy day—wrote to N. Foster King—N-Y—Mrs. Griffing more comfortable—

Sabbath 21st a cold whitening day—wind N-W—

Monday 2nd Cold as yesterday—Wind rather harder N-N-W—

Tuesday 23rd Wind very light from W—Got me home, from Greenport, a ton of coal $6=50 Cts

[270] Wednesday 24th Decem. 1845 A moderate snow Storm, with wind light E—Our Grand son Chatham A. Griffing came to us last evening—

We are informed that a Mrs. Rachel Esdras died in NewYork on the 15th Inst, at the advanced age of 102 years & 7 months. It was said of the oldest Man that ever lived "and he died"—Thus we see in that solemn war there is [no] discharge—

Thursday 25th Blustering weather & cold wind N—

Friday 26th Cloudy, and flights of Snow—The ground is thinly covered with that garb—

Saturday 27th Wind N-W—clear & cold—wrote to Benjamin F. Thompson Esq of Hempstead—Rec'd a letter from Brother Saml C. Griffing—Informs of Hazard Browns Death, died on 15th Inst—He was the Son of the late Richard Brown of this place—He was at the time of his Death betwixt 30 & 40 years of age—Died on the 8th of this Inst in NewYork, Mr. John Henry Preston, Son to the late John Preston of Ashford, Connecticut— The said John Henry has been a prominent Merchant in Hartford for some years past—[271] The last 2 or 3 years he has done buisness in that line in NewYork—He was a truely aimable, industrious, affectionate Man—Greatly and deservedly beloved—Courteous, handsome, preposessing, and the poor mans friend—He leaves a wife & two children to mourn their irreparable loss—He was the Youngest Brother of our late very dear Soninlaw, James H. Preston—His age about 35 years.

Sabbath 28th Wind light W—The sleighing is midling, consider the snow is not more than 4 or 5 inches deep, on a level—Received a letter last eve from N. Foster King, of N-Y—

Monday 29th Quite mild & pleasant, with snow suitable of sleighing, which, by some is much improved—Wrote to our Brother Samuel C. Griffin of Newburgh—Tuesday 30th Wind very light this morn from W—White frost this morn

Wednesday 31st Clear and a midling cool N-W- wind—Our high sheriff, Wm.T. Penny of Riverhead, where he kept a large Temperence Hotel, this some time, died on the ___. He has been unwell this some months past— He was an active, useful, buisness Man—Correct in his dealings with the many he was called to act with—a good officer, as a Mililtia Captain—A humane Sheriff—a Gentleman, And last, though not least, a Christian—

1846

[272] Thursday 1st January 1846 A pleasant, mild day commences the first day of a new Year. The old one is now numbered with the by gone ones of the last, and past Centuries—Our Orient young people are having a Fair, at our Congregational Church this day, at least this evening—the house is filled to overflowing—A new thing with us, the first ever held in this old fashioned, all intermarried, Cousining region—

Friday 2nd S- Wind and a wet day, as It has rained pretty much through the day

Saturday 3rd A clear brisk S-W- wind—And not by any means a cold Day—Wrote yesterday to N. Foster King—

If we take a note of time, we become justly allarmed at its unparraled rappid onward course

Sabbath 4th January 1846—A moderate, mild day for Jan.—light Wind W—

Monday 5th As sunny, and as mild a day as a pleasent one in May—Our two Sisters, Lucinda & Lucretia are with us—It rejoices our hearts to once more see and converse with them—

[273] Tuesday 6th As mild, warm and pleasent as Yesterday—This eve It clouds up, as though It was fortasting a Storm of rain, or Snow

Wednesday 7th A hard E- Rain Storm last night and It continues to pour down this morn until 10 A.M. when It partly cleared off, and the wind shifted arround to the N-W—

Thursday 8th Brisk wind W—and not very cold—Friday 9th Clear, not cold—Wind W—

Saturday 19th Moderate for the time of year—Very little frost in the ground—Wind W—There is a Brig cast on Shore, near what is called Pettys bite, at the North or Sound side—She is laden mostly with cotton & pine plank—her name, the Henry Lee—The Capt. Green—

A Temperence Meeting held in the Methodist church, with us, this day— John C. Cook, from Greenport, addresses the meeting—

Sabbath 11th Continues mild—I forgot to observe that our Brother James was with us yesterday some time—We have found him for a long series of years and in all seasons and situations, a Brother indeed and in truth— Monday 12th A cloudy morn—Wind very light W-N-W—Very trifling front this 12 days past—

[274] Tuesday 13th January 1846 A cloudy morn Wind W-N-W—

We have not as yet had any very cold weather, since this month came in—About as warm, and as moderate weather, as It was the 8th 9th 10th 11th and 12th Days of January 1794—Just 52 years ago—

Wednesday 14th the wind light S-S-W—Weather still continues moderately cold—Friend Hazard Racket and his Wife paid us a short visit this P.M.—

Our people, the Seine owners, have raised a Seine house today near the wind Mill at our Orient Harbour—Edward Prince, Master builder—

Thursday 15th A large white frost, which makes a bright dress for our grounds, and the roofs of our out houses, and tenements this morn—The weather is mild,and warm to the particular admiration of our neighbours, who pay but little attention to a number of Januarys within 20 or 30 years last past—

Friday 16th Thick hazy weather—Wind N-N-E—In the evening It commenced a rain storm—

Saturday 17th It continued to rain through the night, and so It has moderately all this day. Wind S-E—This eve about 10 OClock It commenced snowing—

Sabbath 18th Very cold, high wind N-W—Clear weather, and as cold as any day this month—not much snow fell last night—

Thursday 25th Jan.
Roxanna Petty
commenced with
us [illegible]

[275] Monday 19th Jan. 1846 Severely cold last night and this morn—Wilcox left this morn, for Cutchogue, to lecture on Temperence—The cause of wretched miserable and lost Man—Hewlet Smith from New York lectures on Temperence, this evening, in the Methodist Church—

Tuesday 20th Wind quite light N—but as cold, or more so than yesterday—Ice makes fast in our harbour—Our friend H. Smith called on us, a few minutes this morn—He appears to be wide awake in the cause of Temperence—

Wednesday 21st It commenced snowing 2 P.M. Wind E-N-E—Rev. Mr. Gumage stoped and prayed with us. He was our preacher about 7 years ago—We think him to posess much of the spirit of the Publican, noticed in Sacred writ—A Spiritual Man, in society, ought to be accounted a peculiar blessing—

Thursday 22nd A high wind N-W- and very cold—quite a quantity of snow fell last night, which to day is driven pretty much all into peaks, or banks—Of course, in our blustering quarter, the sleighing will be poor enough—

Friday 23rd Clear, and cold—the last night was as cold as any time this Winter—Wind N-W—Our Grandson, J.A. Preston, with a Mr. Richmond, Merchant in N.York, took dinner with us this day—

[276] Saturday 24th January 1846 A clear day, with a brisk W- Wind and pretty cold—Our neighboring Young men are digging out the road, as Its all filled up with snow banks—The rail Cars are unable to proceed to NewYork, this two days past, in consequence of the depths of snow on the tracks—

A Mr. Cogswell, a young man from Connecticut, is now, and has been teaching our School since the 1st of Decem. past—

Wrote to Frederick Chase Esq—last Friday—

Sabbath 25th Much such weather as yesterday—Wind W—continues cold—Rec'd a letter from N. Foster King of N.Y.

Austin Warren Griffin, and Moses Griffin, called on [us] this noon—Sons of my Brother Warren—

Monday 26th weather more mild—snow melts off rappidly—

Tuesday 27th some little snow fell this morn, clears off P.M.—Wind light this eve—"Was there ever a person too watchful"—I doubt It—

Wednesday 28th Light wind N-N-W—

Thursday 29th A very mild and pleasent day for January—Thus far the Winter has not been tediously cold—Friday 30th A snow melting, muddy waking day, Wind S—

[277] In our Methodist Church the meetings, Just now, are well timed, and warm in the excercises of exortation, and petitions to the throne of Grace—

Saturday 31st Some rain last night—Foggy, and a warm damp Morn—David Beebes Wife was confined with a Son night before last and is doing well—

Brother James called on us this Morn—

Sabbath 1st February 1846—Brisk wind N-N-E—A colder day than we have experienced this some days—

Monday 2nd What is called moderate weather—That is, Its scarce any wind, not cold, with shades and shines—

This day is the Aniversary [of] my birth—Seventy nine years this day since I entered upon the bridge of Life! Alas! Where are the thousands, which started with me! What a solemn, what a momentous, yet all important question! Ah! They have nearly all disappeared in that Ocean, over which the bridge of mortal Life is suspended—"What a dream is mortal life"—A little moment of tears & sorrow—

> Near eight times ten revolving years
> With all their pains, and cares, and fears,
> I speedily have past—
> How like a vision or a dream
> Does all these revolutions seem
> How vain from first to last—

Job says, and Justly, "that our days fly as swift as a weavers shuttle"—Astonishing, but true—

[278] Tuesday 3rd Feb. 1846 A cloudy, damp morn, Brisk wind S-S-W—A Spirit of disinterested good will to all mankind, and the love of benevolence, towards our neighbours, as ourselves, is assuredly a bright token of a heart of flesh—

Wednesday 4th What we call a fine pleasent Morn—Wisdom is to the possessor an invaluable treasure—Attend to its precepts, and your dwelling will be in the pleasant paths of peace—

Thursday 5th Brisk wind W—

Friday 6th Uncommmon pleasant, & mild for Winter—

Saturday 7th Wind fresh S-S-E—Rains some this P.M.—Religious meetings held in the Methodist church, in this place, (Orient,) for several nights past, which do not break up until past midnight—Wrote to Foster King this P.M.—

Sabbath 8th Cold & blustering—

Monday 9th Weather as yesterday—Cold

Tuesday 10th Holds cold—Wrote to Sidney (our son) and His son Augustus, this day, in answer to theirs, I received last Sabbath—

Wednesday 11th Hardly wind sufficient to blow out a candle through the day—

Thursday 12th We have had a very cold blustering night with some Snow—With wind N-E—This morn wind more moderate from N-W—Benjamin Prince, called on us an hour to day—He appears to be a pious, well meaning Man—

[279] Friday 13th Feb. 1846 A cloudy cold day with wind W-N-W—The young people have a Faire this evening—considerable preparations are in course to make It prudently acceptable, and worth attention—But its doubtful whether the Methodist part of the community, and especially those Young men, and Women, who are subjects of the present revival, will attend—We understand their Seniors in their meetings are too zealous to countenance Faires Just now—

Saturday 14th Thick damp weather—It looks like a Storm gathering—Wind light N-N-W—

Sabbath 15th A severer N-E- Snow storm, we have not known than the one which now rages, this, (I believe) seven years—some say 20 years—

Saturday evening Samuel Griffin and his wife, who is Deziah, our Grand Daughter, late Deziah Preston, came to visit us—

Hewlett Smith, from N.Y., is attending the Methodist meetings at this time which are held every night

Monday 16th Some pleasant Sunshine this morn, which looks pleasant after such a tremendous storm—The great quantity of Snow which fell in the last 24 hours has blown up into huge banks, which render travilling almost impractible—

[280] Tuesday 19th Feb. 1845 Wind W-N-W—Deziah & her Husband, Samuel Griffin, left his morn, but as the banks of snow were so high &

numerous, I think its doubtful whether they got farther than Greenport, as they were in a Top[less?] four wheeled carriage—

Wednesday 18th Cool N-W- wind—Some flights of snow to day & last night—

Thursday 19th A cold, flattening day—It looks like a gathering for a storm—Wind very light

Friday 20th comes in with a gale of wind from E—with a smothering Snowstorm—P.M. It turns to hail, & rain—Wind S-E—Evening Wind N-W—

Saturday 21st It has been a cold night—Wind this morn W—A patient Man, and a pious Man, are much unlike [alike?], and their enjoyments as much so—

Sabbath 22nd A clear, pleasant Day—Yet the banks of Snow, which are melting fast through the influences of the Suns warm rays, make It splashing traviling on the road—Wet feet is the consequence—

We are informed that there was several Vessels lost in the storm of Sabbath last, on Squaw Beach, and about 60 men perished—Thus far we have heard

Monday 23rd Pleasent as yesterday, overhead, but the walking is intollerable—A Mass meeting, and Dinner at Captain Wisdoms—Mr. Richard F. Nicol stoped with us an hour, this day—He was with us last year, about this time—He lectures this evening at the upper Church, on temperence—

[281] Tuesday 24th Feb. 1846 A sharp W- wind—A chilly, pierceing, searching, uncomfortable time this two or 3 days past—

Heard yesterday of the sudden Death of Doctor Barret Havens, the eldest Son of the late Doct. Jonathan Havens. This said Doct. Barrett Havens has resided in the Country, about 14 miles West of Goshen, Orange County, New York, where [he] has in about 50 years (the time he has lived there) accumulated an estate of perhaps 20 or 30000 Dollars—He leaves one Child, a Son—He was the last of six Sons—The four eldest viz. Barrett, Tyler, Gabriel, & Philetus all lived to gather handsome Estates—But as it was said of Mathusalem, they died—Doct. Barrett died at the age of about 82 or 3—Tyler, 78 in 1835—Gabriel, 76, in 1849, and Philetus about 60 years in 1835—

A great Mass meeting at Greenport this day—After the services, at the Presbyterian Church, they repair to the Greenport House kept by Mr. Terry, and Dine—Its said this eve that the number who took dinner at Terrys Greenport was about 300—The speakers were Messrs. R.F. Nicol—J.W. Case, and Mr. Warren—Rec'd a letter from N.F. King of N.York, & four Newspapers—

Wednesday 25th A still, cloudy, cold morn and so is the day—

Thursday 26th Blustering, very cold day—Wind N-N-W-

Friday 27th Last night was the coldest one we have experienced this Winter—It is seven this morn—

[282] Saturday 28th February 1846—Wind very light this morn—but it is yet very cold, but not so tedious as some day past, as being nearly calm—I believe my Mother was born February 28th 1746—one hundred years this day—

Sabbath 1st March 1846 Wind N-N-W—and continues very cold—It snowed some last night—

Died this day Jonathan King, age 71 years—Mr. King was originally from EastHampton, but has for the last twenty years been a settled resident of this place—He married Phebe, the Widow of Richard Youngs, whose Father Henry Youngs died with his Wife and all his children, 3 or 4, with the Disentary, at the time General Wo[o]ster was quartered in this place (Orient) in the Summer of 1775—I ought to have said, except this Richard—Mr. King was always a peaceable, innofencive [inoffensive], plain, and we believe an honest, well intended Man—

Monday 2nd A blustering, cold, squally day—Wind E-N-E—

Tuesday 3rd Continues extreme cold, as It has been except a day or two, this 16 or 18 days—Wind N-E—

[283] Wednesday 4th March 1846 A pleasant morn, Wind very light S— White frost—Rec'd a letter last eve from our granddaughter, Deziah Preston Griffin—

Thursday 5th Comes in cloudy—Wind S-S-W—

How all important—How sacredly necessary It is for us to weigh our opinions before we give them—think twice e're we speak once—One little hasty, inconsiderate word, has oft brought destruction on Its author—

Friday 6th A cloudy, still morn—considerable Ice in our harbour—A light snow fell this P.M. covers the ground about two inches—

Saturday 7th A clear pleasant morn—Wind very light N-W—Age, and infirmities—the first according to the number of the human family by few even know or experience—The latter, are in number Millions! I have had a turn of the influenza this some time—find such attacks more sensibly affect my system that they did 40 years ago—

Sabbath 8th Wind West—Although it has thawed much this some days past, yet the snow lies in heavy banks with us now—

Monday 9th Wind light W—Appears like Spring overhead, but under foot it looks like winter—

[284] Tuesday 10th March 1846 As serene and as mild a Sunshine as a first rate May day—But Snow, mud, and mire in abundance prevades our Streets

Wednesday 11th As pleasent a morn, and day as was yesterday

Thursday 12th It looks pleasent—Was called on this morn by our friend Mr. Elam Conkling—A better minded, or an honester Man, does not (in my humble opinion) live in our Town of Southold—He wears like a Christian—Mr. Abimel King was with our friend—They are on a Christian visit, arround this place—On the 11th March 1821 this friend of ours, Elam Conklin, held a meeting with us in our District School House—

Friday 13th A cloudy day, wind fresh S—Is It in Man to command his feelings—I think not—Grace can do wonders—but we must have Grace to realize its precious effects—

Saturday 14th Considerable rain this morn, all ended with a heavy fog—Wind S—Towards evening It blows quite a gale S-S-W—with [page trimmed]

Honora, with her two youngest children have been on a visit to her Aunt Lucindas—Vincent & Peter Tuthills, and Joseph Latham—

Sabbath 15th Wind S—A clear day—Mr. Beers, our Congregational Minister, has quit us as our preacher, although [page trimmed]

[285] Monday 16th March 1846 A thick hazy morn—some sprinkling of rain—wind fresh N—

Tuesday 17th A cold N-W- wind—wrote to N. Foster King, N.Y.—sent a newspaper to Sidney

Wednesday 18th More moderate, yet cold—D.S. Glover, in the Schooner Export, sailed for N.Y.—Wind light N—

Thursday 19th Much milder than some days past, Wind S-W- & light—John A. Preston, and Doct. Skinner took dinner with us—

Friday 20th A pleasent morn—Wind light W—We hear that there is a Mr. James Porter living in Kentucky at this time, a Tavern Keeper, aged 24 years—he measures in Height Eight feet six inches, and walks like a giant—

Saturday 21st A cloudy morn—Sidney P. Racket, in the Eliza Ann, sails this morn for NewYork—

Sabbath 22nd A cool N-W- wind, yet light—

Monday 23rd A calm and clear day—It is said to be more wise to always look on the best side of our situation—Count up our mercies—

Tuesday 24th A moderate rain this morn—wind S—A drizzling rain through the day—

Wednesday 25th Much such a morn as yesterday—Wind S-E—Robert Clark is moving his house from off its present situation just west of Jonathan Trumans, He Clark is moving It to Rockypoint, on to the lands of George Tuthill, near said Tuthill's House—Clarks house has been built about 30 years—This P.M. It storms hard, with rain & high E- wind—

[286] Thursday 26th March 1846—About 2 OClock this morn, we had some hard Thunder—We still have the wind E—with a moderate rain—got me home a cord of oak wood—It cost $3=75 Cents—

Friday 27th A heavy fog this morn—wind very light W-N-W—Rode to Greenport with my Nephew, P.W. Tuthill—for his kindness in giving me the ride, he has my sincere thanks—was visited this day by Holland Arnold, son to my late lamented and invaluable friend, Doct. David P. Arnold, of Goshen, Orange County—

Saturday 28th good March weather—Our friend Arnold took breakfast with us, after which he left for Sagharbour—

Sabbath 29th Pleasent Wind W—Attended the Methodist meeting this A.M.

Monday 30th Pleasent for March

Tuesday 31st Pleasent—A very light wind N—rather cool—

Wednesday 1st April 1846 Weather as yesterday—Vincent Youngs putting up a small barn east of his [illegible]

[287] Thursday 2nd Apl. 1846 Cool, moderate wind N-N-W—Worked on the new road P.M.

Friday 3rd Wind and weather as yesterday

Saturday 4th Pleasent yet rather cool, with very light wind

Sabbath 5th A large white frost last night—Wind light from W—Brother Warren and Wife stoped with us an hour this noon—

Monday 6th fresh breeze of wind W—

Tuesday 7th A very pleasent morn—wind very light S-E—Town Meeting, this day—The most publick day in the year, and generally is more numerously attended, far more than any other within the twelve months—Our Fathers, which congregated this day, alas! Where are they!—Alas where!

Wednesday 8th Come in with a moderate rain—Wind in the morn S—P.M. West—Yesterday, my sisters Lucinda & Lucretia took tea with us—Both widows—the first the late Rufus Tuthills—the last David Wiggins Junr.—

Thursday 9th Pleasent—very light wind N—worked some in my garden, that is made a few beds for more parsnips, carrots etc etc etc—

Friday 10th A very still, or calm day—sowed two of my garden beds of onions—

Saturday 11th High wind S—attended with a very thick, or heavy Fog—And so It continues through day—

Sabbath 12th Thick foggy weather, as yesterday—Wind light N—In the course of the day at various points—

[288] Monday 13th Apl. 1846 Rather of a squally cool day, with wind W—Received a Newspaper yesterday from Doct. Hon. Henry H. Cleveland, now a resident of SpringField, State of Massachusets—This Gentleman was formerly a resident of Orient and is particularly noticed in my 3rd Diary, 6th December 1820—and page 96

Snow squalls this afternoon—The coldest evening we have had this 2 weeks

Tuesday 14th A cool blustering N-W- wind—Died yesterday Samuel Tuthill, aged about 70 years—He was grand Son of Jeremiah Tuthill, who died about the year of 1800 aged 84 years—He the said Jeremiah was grand Son to John Tuthill, called in his day Squire John, and often Chalker John—He John was a member of the assembly of this State to New York in the years 1692—1693 & 1695.

Wednesday 15th Cool & blustering with wind N-W—Lewis A. Beach arrived home last eve from a whaling voyge of 22 months—Sidney (our Son) visited us this eve

Thursday 16th More moderate, light wind—Sidney left this morn—leaves his Son Augustus with us a day or two—

Mrs. Polly King, a widow—was the Daughter of the late Capt. Orange Webb, of Greenport, died in NewJersey, 3 months since—She was once a very aimable Woman say 40 years ago—Justly [respected?]

[289] Friday 17th Apl. 1846 A pleasent day—wind S-S-W—

Saturday 18th Pleasent, but its getting rather dry—Wind light West—People in this place (Orient) are buisy in considerable preparations for taking little shad, or moss bunkers for manure—

Sabbath 19th A very mild pleasent morn—Wind moderate W—Children, at adult age, are seldom known to be too attentive to their parents.

The late Rufus Tuthill Jun. was the most dutiful, tender, obedient, kind and affectionate Son, as this place perhaps ever knew—What a Son! How invaluable to his aged Father, the last 10 years of that venerable patriarchs life—

Monday 20th Warm & pleasent Wind light W—

Tuesday 21st Weather much as yesterday—quite warm this morn—took our grandson Augustus R. G. to Greenport, at which at 9 A.M. he left by takeing the cars for Hempstead—

Greenport grows in buildings, but in wealth and profitable buisness I fear not much—

Thursday 23rd A cloudy day—arrived in our harbour Lester B. Terry with his Schooner Planet, from a 7 month voyage to the South Carrobean—He got home last evening, all well—

Planted 36 hills beans, and sowed a bed of Turnips, this morn—carrots & parsnips this P.M.

Friday 24th A hazy foggy morn Wind very light S-W—potatoes, whose price has for the last 40 years been about 30 to 32 Cts per bushel are now 75 Cts—

[290] Saturday Apl. 25th 1846 A cool E- wind—Sun in the Eclips this noon—The wind blew for about 10 minutes last night, about 12 OClock as hard as I have known It for many years—It was truly a brief Hurrycane—

Sabbath 26th Wind very light through the day—The elder Doct. Skinner, Preached in our Congregation Meeting house this day—I attended in the afternoon—He certainly spoke well, as I view his remarks on that text 2nd Corinthians 4 Ch & 5th verse—

Monday 17th A calm, and warm day—Planted 44 hills sweet corn in my garden—

Tuesday 28th Warm day, after a white frost, which shewed Itself this morn—Planted squashes, potatoes & corn in my garden this forenoon—Ellection through the State this day to chuse delegates to revise the Constitution—

Wednesday 29th A cool Easterly wind—Occasionally, a small sprinkling of rain through the day—

Thursday 30th Considerable rain last night—It clears up this morn—A warm day—

Friday 1st May A.M. Cloudy Wind W—P.M. Thunder & rain—

[291] Saturday 2nd May 1846 A foggy, and a damp morn—3 Schooners, are now in our harbour. Two of them heavy laden with coal from Philadelphia, for the Eastern market—Said Schooners loaded are commanded, one by David Edwards, the other by Daniel Harrison McDermott—This last mentioned is the Soninlaw of Nathaniel Tuthill, who is living at the Dam, a short distance from the bridge.

Sabbath 3rd A cloudy cool day—Wind S-E—Wrote to our Grand daughter, Deziah P. Griffin, now living at Riverhead—

Our Congregational Church, in this place (Orient) have this day got a new Priest, commencing on trial—His name is ___ [pencil] Blake about ___ years of age

Monday 4th Foggy Morn—Wind E—planted about sixty hills potatoes in my garden—

Tuesday 5th Much such foggy and damp weather as yesterday—Wrote yesterday to a Capt. John Griffin, of Lyme, Connecticut—A man I never see to my knowledge—Planted a patch of potatoes & corn in my back lot, East of my Orchard—

Wednesday 6th A cool E- wind

Thursday 7th Continues quite cool—brisk wind E—A cloudy, dark and unpleasant day—

If the mind is composed, and right, It produces a solace that is not much affected by winds and storms—

Friday 8th Weather much as Yesterday with wind E—A Mr. Bakeman, a Congregational Preacher, stoped with us an hour this P.M.

Saturday 9th Cool E- wind, and cloudy as It has been this 10 days past— It commences copious rain this Evening—

[292] Sabbath 10th May 1846 Thunder & rain early this morn—It ceased to rain A.M. 5 OClock—Continues a thick fog—Brother James Griffin stoped with us last night—

The lightning struck at Greenport, a house of Mr. Sidney Wiggins, which It injured considerable—the family escaped any hurt—

Monday 11th Very cool, N-W- high wind—

Tuesday 12th Wind as yesterday- Continues cool—I worked on the highway this A.M.—On the Beach, near the Dam—

Wednesday 13th A pleasent mild morn Wind light S—Rec'd a letter from N.F. King—This evening It blows up cool from W-N-W—

Thursday 14th High wind S-W—

Friday 15th Wind as yesterday and warm—

Saturday 16th A warm S- wind—Yet hazy or smoky—so much so as to obscure the rays of the Sun—

Sabbath 17th Considerable rain last night Wind S-E—I am informed the Jackson Seine took 25 or 30000 boney fish yesterday—Some light showers through day

Monday 18th Brisk wind S-W- and warm—Died Saturday night last, Mrs. Desire Youngs, Wife of Mr. Jefferson Youngs—She was an affectionate, peaceable, good woman—leaves a young Son of about 2 years old, and a daughter of 14—Some rain this evening—

Tuesday 19th May 1846 Pleasant—An ellection Through the State (except N.York City) for Licence, or no Licence, respecting spirituous liquors

[293] While at Southold to day, I called on my grand daughter, Maria, now the wife of Orin Prince. She met me with great affection, and tenderness—Wednesday 20th Morning Cool wind N-W—P.M. Wind S-S-W—Received a letter this day from Capt. John Griffing of Lyme, C-t in answer to the one I wrote to him on the 4th Inst—It was well accepted—

Thursday 21st Some rain last eve—This morn, It is a clear cool N-W-wind—Hired out the seats in the church today—

Friday 22nd A.M. Cool & calm—quite a cool night—P.M. Wind S-W—Up to this time, the Oregon Seine has took about 200000 fish worth 75 Cts per 1000—Amount 150 Dolls—

The no licence ticket has prevailed in every Town in the county of Suffolk except one and that is Huntington—I am sorry for the families of that town—

A Mr. Askew, an Englishman, living on PlumIsland, called on us to day—He is a very industrious, economical and (I believe) truly religious Man—And no hypocrite—

Saturday 23rd A cloudy, damp Morn—Wind brisk S-S-W—P.M. Showers—Sabbath 24th May 1846 A pleasant morn—Wrote to N. Foster King of N.York City yesterday—Was agreeable entertained with the company of Orin Prince and his wife, our granddaughter Maria, with their Son Henry—They left this evening—

Monday 25th Warm but not uncomfortable—Rather of a cloudy day—Wind very light S—

Tuesday 26th Light wind S—A cloudy day—

[294] Wednesday 27th May 1846 Some light showers—with now & then a little sunshine—brisk wind S-S-W—Wilcox commenced [teaching] School at Rockypoint last Monday 25th—

Thursday 28th Wind E—considerable rain fell last night—It wets some this morn—It is something a wet time Just now—Has rained some fine rain, or a very wet mist through the intire day—Unpleasant and cool—

Friday 29th A damp, misty, unpleasant day—War is now raging in Mexico—Rational Man (as he is said to be) is killing one another! What a sight for Angels!!

Saturday 30th Brisk wind E—with drizzly damp weather—What is called pleasant overhead, and under foot—This P.M. is a cold driven Storm—

Sabbath 31st Weather as yesterday

Monday 1st June 1846 Wind very light S-S-E—

Tuesday 2nd Morning calm, clear & warm—Evening a light sprinkle of rain, with lightning

Wednesday 3rd A clear warm day, Wind S-W—

Thursday 4th Much such weather as yesterday with wind a little more brisk S-S-W—The Whale Ship Washington of Greenport arrived this P.M. with 2400 barrels right Whale oil, and 30 or 40 Bs of Sperm—

Friday 5th A warm day—Wind S-W—This day the Jackson Seine took about 20 [page trimmed] little shad—the other two Seines, Oregon and Union, took each a goodly number

Saturday 6th Some rain last night—cloudy this morn, with wind N-W—

[295] Sabbath 7th June 1846 A cool N-W- wind this morn—John A. Preston our grandson was with us an hour or two this day—He is an affectionate, tender, invaluable child

Monday 8th A pleasant, moderately cool morn—My sensations, imbecility, increasing lassitude, and age, all loudly warn me that I am nearing the termination of my mortal career, of this little, eventual Life—

Tuesday 9th Pleasant—Rode in the rail cars as far as Hempstead, Queens County, to my Son Sidneys—Arrived at his house about noon—30 odd miles—found his family all well, and to appearance glad to see me—

Wednesday 10th Visited B.F. Thompson Esq—Took an excellent dinner with my old and much esteemed friend Joshua Y Racket—He has an excellent Wife—The most valued of women—His Daughter, now Mrs. Clark, who with her family lives with him, is beautiful, sensible, and accomplished—her husband is at the South doing buisness—I left Sidney's family and Hempstead this P.M. and by rail road reached home about 10 OClock P.M.—

It is said there was in the cars yesterday, on our way to N.York about 1000 men, women & children—all in a train about 14 cars!

[296] Thursday 11th June 1846 Pleasant—This day, with the assistance of 50 odd yoke of Oxen, Benjamin Terry & Brothers had his House, which he purchased of the heirs or administrators of the late Capt James Smith moved to, or within a few rods of the residence of his, (Benjamins) late fathers house—the distance which the house is moved is near a mile—the house, without the kitchen is about 28 by 30 feet—the kitchen is large—they were moved separate—It proved a hard job of 3 parts of days—Wind E—

Friday 12th A cloudy Morn—Wind E—A moderately pleasant day—& cool

Saturday 13th A fresh E- Wind and cold

My most affectionate of Grand daughters Deziah P. Griffin was in the cars with me on my return trip—She stoped at Riverhead, her home—It proved to be our last [meeting?]

Sabbath 14th Wind continues E—Cool last night—Monday 15th Wind S-S-W—and the warmest day this & the past month—

Tuesday 16th Fresh breeze Wind S-S-W—quite warm—

Wednesday 17th Wind S-S-E—It is getting rather dry—From It we ought to learn, and feel, our dependence on our Father in heaven—

[297] Thursday 18th June 1846 Wind S—Sidney P. Racket made me a present of a round, or (as some call them) short Jacket—For this peculiar expression of good will and marked favour to me, I beg him to accept my most sincere acknowledgement—

Friday 19th As warm a day as any we have had this June—A thunder shower this eve although not so much rain as Is needed, yet It [is] our duty to be thankful for every favour—

Saturday 20th A cloudy morn wind S—A light shower Just at night—

Sabbath 21st A small shower this morn—clears off pleasant A.M. 9 OClock—Just before sunset It rained a very small shower—Wind N-W—

Monday 22nd A cool morn—a fire feels comfortable, and a woolen dress today, appears to be suitable and in Time—

Died on 21st Mrs. Lydia Paine, Widow of the late Mr. John Paine, of Southold—She was and has been for many years eminent for her exemplary life of piety and Christian Virtues—Her addresses in Class, and prayer meetings, were powerful gifts, and very affectionate—She was assuredly a Mother in Israel and a Deborah in the Church—Her age was 88 years—She was the Eldest daughter of the late Major Barnabas Tuthill, who died about the year 1782—

Tuesday 23rd Cool Wind

Wednesday 24th A very cool morn—Wind N—

[298] Thursday 25th June 1846 Very light wind E-N-E—Took out our pump yesterday and put in a bucket—The good old oaken bucket that hangs on the pole—quite a refreshing shower last—

Friday 26th Some very little sprinkles of rain—Wrote this day to Capt. John Griffing of East Lyme, Connecticut—Cool wind E-N-E—

Saturday 27th A cool N-E- Wind—It thus far has been a cool June—We think there will be much lack of fruit this season—It is rather dry for vegetables

Sabbath 28th Some small Sprinkle of rain, several times through the day—not all of them sufficient to wet the ground the 20th part of an Inch—I dug the first mess of potatoes, this day—The largest not the size of a hens egg—

Monday 29th This morn comes in with a fine Shower—It has been a damp, cloudy day—

Tuesday 30th A Cloudy day—Our Grandson Chatham and his sister Josephine paid a short visit to day—They came in the rail cars and return this evening to Hempstead

Wednesday 1st July 1846—Considerable rain fell last night—It wets very moderately the morn—Wind E—

Thursday 2nd a foggy morn with wind S—P.M. Very sultry hot, and calm—Received a Letter from N.T. Hubbard notifying us of his intention of visiting on the 4th if life and health permit—

3rd this day Easterly weather—

[299] Saturday 4th July 1846 Wind E—with some light showers—Unpleasant—Rode to Greenport where I meet our friend N.T. Hubbard with his sisters Mary, Ludice, & Olive, with his children and friends to the number of altogether 28 or 9—Our Grand daughter Harriet M. Hubbard with them—James Wilkie Jun. makes one of the number—Likewise Mr. Myers, Soninlaw to N.T. Hubbard—

Sabbath 5th A pleasent day—

Monday 6th After Dinner, waited on Friend Hubbard, and the larger part of his family & friends to Greenport, where they took the cars for N.York—leaving G-port at 4 OClock P.M.

Tuesday 7th Very warm—Wind W-S-W—

Wednesday 8th Continues more warm, Wind S—

Thursday 9th This morn Wind N-W—comfortably cool—Mr. Myers went to N.Y. yesterday—

Friday 10th A very warm day, Wind S-S-W—Took a sail this A.M. in a small sailboat with our young friend James Wilkie Junr.

Saturday 11th Very warm morn—The last night was the most sultry hot of any we have experienced this season—Sabbath 12th Continues very warm—About 5 OClock P.M. we had a refreshing shower

Mr. Myers returned from N.Y. yesterday—

[300] Monday 13th July 1846 Weather rather more comfortable as to excessive warmth

Tuesday 14th Showers this A.M—Our Niece Mary Hubbard what was (sister of our Friend N.T. Hubbard) now the Widow Chute, left us this morn to take the cars at Greenport for N.York—She is one of the excellent of the Earth, full of charity, kindness, and good works—

Wednesday 15th Cool N-W- wind, Rode out to Greenport this morn, with James Wilkie Jun. & his good and aimable sister Mary—they took the rail cars, for N.Y. and I returned home at 6 A.M.—Edward Myres, his very affectionate Wife Susan, their 3 pretty Children (a Son Horatio) and two daughters & Servant girl Sarah all left us this P.M. for Greenport, where they take the rail cars for N.Y.—at ½ past 3 OClock—The above Mrs. Myers was at my house in 1835 in August—She was then the aimable Miss Susan Hubbard, the daughter of our friend Nathaniel T. Hubbard—

Thursday 16th Comfortably cool this two days with wind N-W—With us the Vegetable Kingdom looks rich and healthy

Raymond left this morn—Came home last night

Our cherries are about gone—The trees have produced us much less than former years—

[301] Friday 17th July 1846 Some light sprinkle of rain this day, Wind E— We have just heard of a great fire in Nantucket, which has destroyed a large part of that Town—What number of buildings burnt, and the amount of property hit by the disaster, as yet we know not—

Saturday 18th Moderate showers through the day—Wind E—Continues comfortably cool—

Sabbath 19th pleasant, but damp weather—

Monday 20th Very foggy, especially Mornings & Evenings—

Tuesday 21st Continues foggy, and Showers occasionally—

Wednesday 22nd Showers early this morn—Unpleasant weather for harvest—

Thursday 23rd Showers this morn—A warm P.M.—

Friday 24th very pleasant until 8 A.M. after which It was cloudy, and some light showers—

Saturday 25th A cloudy Morn—Elisha Mulford is building a house for his son Benjamin, It stands perhaps 40 rods South of where Buel Petty now lives—Benjamin Mulfords Mother, Fanny, is the grand daughter of the late Col. Thomas Terry, who died at Saybrook, Connecticut, about the year 1777—Elisha Mulford now owns the farm & homestead which was Col. Terrys, and so It is, that the grand daughter is now, with her husband possessing her grand fathers estate, which has passed through a number of different owners since the Col.s Death—

Sabbath 26th A Cloudy and dark Morn—Cool

Monday 27th Much such weather as yesterday

[302] Thursday 28th July 1846 Pleasant weather but not uncomfortable warm—Thus far we have had but a very few extreme warm days—

Wednesday 29th Much such weather as yesterday—Wind S-S-W—

Thursday 30th Wind S-S-W—warmer than some days past

Friday 31st A very warm S-S-W—wind

•

Saturday 1st August 1846—As warm as yesterday but not so much wind—
Bought me a half cord of wood yester[day] of Oliver Davis

Sabbath 2nd Wind E-N-E—Pleasant—A.F. Glover arrived home from
Providence—

Monday 3rd A pleasant Morn—Wind E—P.M. Wind S-S-W—very
warm—Raymond left—

Tuesday 4th Warm S- wind—Wood is now selling at 4 Dolls & 50 Cts—
40 years ago It was about 3 Dolls—

Wednesday 5th What is called very warm weather—Charles B. Moore
called on us, this A.M. He is the eldest Son of the late Col. Jeremiah
Moore—In 1819 he was at my School, a boy of 11 or 12 years of age—Now
he is a Lawyer of eminence, and much respectability, residing in NewYork

Thursday 6th Extreme warm—Our Grandson C.A. Griffin came to us
this Eve—Franklin S Vail [303] Son to my late friend Silas Vail, called on
us this eve—he is now a Preacher of the Presbyterian order—A man of
tallents—

Friday 7th Wind this morn N-W—light—

Saturday 8th Continues very warm—It has been generally so this 10 days
past—P.M. wind—

Sabbath 9th Considerable of a shower of rain last night—A cloudy
day this—

Monday 10th Some rain last night—Dark and cloudy this morn—

Tuesday 11th pretty comfortable as to warm—light Wind E—

Wednesday 12th Weather much as yesterday—Very light wind E- by S—

Thursday 13th brisk wind S-S-W—very warm—

Friday 14th Wind S-S-W—a very warm night preceeds this morn—

Saturday 15th Continues warm—The two past days may safely be set
down as two very very close, warm days—Not any two this season I should
say to exceed them—

Sabbath 16th Continues warm—Died on StatenIsland about the 10th Inst
Benjamin Wells Case, of Southold—at the time of his Death, he was Master
of the Schooner Napoleon of NewYork, and now from the South—He lived
but a few hours after landing—He was the Son in law [of] Abner Wells—
He was aimable and very handsome, aged about 26 years—

Monday 17th Considerable rain this P.M.—E. Shery Racket has a
Schooner launched today—

[304] Tuesday 18th August 1846 Chatham (our grandson) and myself
repaired our old horseshed yesterday & today—Wind E-N-E—but very

light—William H. Griffin & James Bartholomew were at our house this eve—the latter is Son to my Cousin Sally, daughter to my Aunt Mary Stone, who was the youngest daughter of my grand Father Samuel Griffin—

Wednesday 19th Wind light from E—Raymond home this Eve—

Thursday 20th Very light wind E—Sherry Rackets Schooner goes to Sagharbour with perhaps 150 passengers, all of whose passage is free—The name of this new and Ellegant Vessel is Expedite—

Friday 21st An Eastern Storm—Was visited this day by Mr. F. Dobbs— This gentleman was with us in August 1842—

Saturday 22nd Scarce any wind—The little is from N-E—with a copious rain until P.M.—

Sabbath 23rd rains profusely—Monday 24th Wind E-N-E—Wm. H. Griffin & & James Bartholomew left this day for Guilford—

Tuesday 25th Easterly weather continues—About such an August Storm, this, as we had 47 years ago—And probably many such since that time—

[305] Yesterday, (Monday) the new Schooner Expedite, Sherry Racket, Master, and part owner, left our harbour—Orient, for Philadelphia—

Wednesday 26th Wind E- with a copious rain through the night & this morn—Chatham left for Hempstead this morn—The rain continued to fall plentifully until 12 at noon, when It ceased—

Thursday 27th A cloudy morn, with wind very light S-E—

Friday 28th Calm, but not uncomfortably warm—

Saturday 29th A cloudy day—very light wind S-W—Evening went to Greenport where I met N.T. Hubbard & wife—Sidney (our Son) & wife and Daughter Maria—They all accompanied me home, where we arrived about ½ past 9 OClock

Sabbath 30th Attended meeting with our friends—Evening Our friend Hubbard & wife left for N.Y.—

Monday 31st Calm as It has been the two past days—Sidney, wife, & Maria, left this eve for their home, intending to stop at Riverhead & Greenport—

September 1st 1846—Wind this morn S-S-W—very warm this three or four days past—

Wednesday 2nd Continues uncomfortably warm—

Thursday 3rd A thick, misty morn—light wind S-S-E—continues warm—yes, hot—

Friday 4th Wind fresh this morn S-S-W—a short shower of rain— Continues extremely warm—

Saturday 5th Clear, with a S- wind—warm—This evening David Vail (son to Gelston Vail) was married to Sally Brown, daughter to the late Jeremiah of Rockypoint—

Monday 7th Septem. 1846—Wind S-S-W—It has been nearly from this warm point for 10 or 11 days past, and as warm, Its my opinion, as any 11 days in course for 10 years—

[306] Tuesday 8th Septem. 1846—Continues as warm as It has been this near two past—perhaps this day and the last night is in extreme heat equal to any of those of the last 10 or 12 days—

Wednesday 9th A change of weather this morn—Wind brisk N-N-E— of course cooler—Brother Samuel Caddle called on us this day

Thursday 10th Wind as high and from the same point as yesterday— Solomons choice to be endowed with in preference to all other things was assuredly the wisest choice ever made—

Friday 11th Wind light from N-N-E—Raymond left last Monday Eve

Saturday 12th A small thunder Shower last night, with sharp lightning—

Sabbath 13th Very light wind—Evening calm—John & James Preston with us—

Monday 14th Our grandsons, above said, left us early this morn— Received a ½ barrel flour this day at about 2 Dollars & 75 Cents—Wilcox left for a Mission on Temperence—Is sent out by the United Brothers of that order—May God add his blessing to this most glorious cause

Tuesday 15th A warm night has past—Wind this morn West, rather more comfortable—This P.M. High wind N-N-W—A good clear brace-ing wind—

[307] Wednesday 16th Wind N-N-W—Pleasent and comfortable weather—

Thursday 17th Wind-S-W—more warm—Mr. Barns, a conspicuous member of the Brothers of Temperence in N.York, left us yesterday with his Wife & family—They appear to be an excellent virtuous couple, united—

Friday 18th Wind this morn S-E—Died yesterday morning Mrs. Hannah Pool, widow of the late Capt. David Pool—Mrs. Pool was aged 72 years—She was a kind, tender, and good Mother—Faithful in all her duties, as wife—neighbour, and friend—Her Husband, the late Capt. David Pool died by drowning in October 13th 1838 as noticed in my diary of that date—

Saturday 19th Morning light wind N—Mr. Adam A. Mount, of NewYork, died on the 6th this Inst, aged 91 years—in 1798 two of his Sons, viz. William & Dobbs, boarded with us some months—Mr. Mount was a Soldier of the revolution, An active, buisness, noble hearted, and I believe an honest Man—to us he was a friend indeed—

Sabbath 20th A mild morn—Wind light S—

Monday 21st Much such weather as yesterday

Tuesday 22nd Pleasant—Took a sail to Greenport with Henry Dyer, purch[as]ed sugar—tea, rice, dried Beef, paper, candy—Hat, etc etc etc-

[308] Wednesday 23rd Rather warm for so late in the season—

Thursday 24th Weather much as yesterday, wind S-W-

Friday 25th quite warm—wind S-S-W—Brother Sam'ls Wife and little adopted girl left us this day—They have been two nights with us—have staid in Orient with their friends and connections, since Friday 11th—

Saturday 26th Morn wind S-S-W—P.M. Shifted around the N-N-W-with some sprinkling of rain—gathered all the peaches we raised this year, which did not amount in number over 3 dozen—

Sabbath 27th Light wind W-S-W—Attended the funeral of our Cousin Jesse Terry, son to my late Uncle Daniel T. Terry—Jesse died last Friday, aged 50 years—He was a peaceable quiet man, very retired in his manner of life and we believe died in peace with all who knew him.

Monday 28th Brisk wind N-W—

Tuesday 29th Wind S-W—Fresh—Sold 20 Hens to Henry Dyer for $2.96

Wednesday 30th Wind in course, and power as yesterday—Take the Month altogether, It has been a very warm one—

Thursday 1st October 1846 Wind S-W—light—Training at Greenport—General muster for this season—Received a Letter from [309] Sidney & Chatham—

Friday 2nd October 1846 Wind E- Cool—Wrote to Sidney, and Chatham

Saturday 3rd It begins to look some like Autumn—Wind N-W—

Sabbath 4th It is certainly dry—Very little rain has fell this 4 weeks past—Our brother Sam'l Caddle G. called on us last Thursday—Expects to set off for Newburgh, his residence, in the course of a few days—He is now stoping at Rockypoint—

Monday 5th Wind N-W—potatoes are now selling at 70 Cents—rather Dull—

News arrived last evening that William Youngs, Son of Thomas V. Youngs of our place (Orient) is Dead—It is said he died last Decem. At Sea—He was on a Voyge Whaleing—A more pleasent, agreable, kind hearted young Man is rarely to be found—He was handsome, virtuous, united with the graces of fillial suavity and Love—

Tuesday 6th Some white frost this morn—the first we have seen this Autumn—Raymond came home this morn—

Wednesday 7th Warm West wind—light—Commenced burning Coal in the Stove for the first this season—Narcissa has been quite sick this some days—is some better we hope—

Thursday 8th A very pleasent Morn—And a very warm day—

Friday 9th Wind light this morn E-S-E—P.M. Very warm—uncomfortably so—

Saturday 10th Cool S-Wind—Wilcox left for N.York in Sloop Daniel Webster, Ezekial Glover Master

Sabbath 11th Continued cool, wind as yesterday

[310] Monday 12th October 1846 A brisk S-Wind

Tuesday 13th Wind increases to about a gale—

Wednesday 14th Considerable rain, in very light showers through the day—Some 50 Men & women took dinner at Capt. Wisdoms this day, after hearing our friend Richard F. Nicol, and Mr. Collins, address the Company convened at the Congregational Church on the Subject of Temperence—

Thursday 15th Our brother Samuel Caddle leaves Greenport with his family for Newburgh this morn—He has been very ill, this some days, at Greenport—

Wind this morn W—I ought to have noticed that we had a tremendous gale of wind, on the evening of the 14th—for two hours or more. Wind S—

Friday 16th light wind S-S-W—

Saturday 17th Raymond engaged a Miss Jane Terry to assist us in housework at three dollars per month—Wilcox got home this eve—

Sabbath 18th a N-E- Rain storm—Monday 19th Cool wind N-W—Wilcox left this morn in the cars, for N.Y.—

Tuesday 20th Cool, light wind Easterly

Wednesday 21st Wind light W—

[311] Thursday 22nd October 1846 A cloudy day—Wind fresh South—It is reported that the Steam ship (the largest in the world) Great Britain, is lost on the coast, Ireland, Passengers & crew saved—Some rain this P.M.

Friday 23rd Considerable black frost to be seen this morn, in Ice & frozen ground with a stiff N-W- wind—

A wise person gathers that which the foolish & vain person throw away—Pain, Sorrow, and misery are congenial to mortality—The days of Mans life fly as swift as a weavers shaft

Saturday 24th Wind fresh West E-W—Vanity, and amusements which can yield us no pleasant reflections crowd out those thoughts and actions which are only calculated to favour us with solid comforts—

Sabbath 25th Pleasant weather—Rec'd a letter from our Grandson Chath[am] A G—yesterday—

Monday 26th Wind light A.M.—E-N-E—P.M. S-S-W—Raymond left for NewYork, having been home 2 weeks, which time he has lost since 18th of March—He had then completed 6 months & 15 days

Tuesday 27th Brisk winds W-S-W—Wrote to our Grand son Chatham—

Wednesday 28th A N-E- Storm of Wind, with not [an] abundance of rain—Sent a Newspaper, the Watchman, to Doctor Allen of Deckertown, Sussex County, N. Jersey—His wife is my Cousin Lydia, daughter to My Uncle, the late Noah Terry—

Thursday 29th A clear N-W- not very high wind—Flour and bread stuff higher than some months past—flour 7 Dolls per Barrel—

Friday 30th Very moderate mild A.M.—P.M. Cloudy Wind from the Easterly board—Some rain this evening—A Mr. Lamphere, of Greenport, was drowned last Wednesday in our harbour—Our Grand Son John A. Preston with us a short time on the 21st

[312] Saturday 31st Oct. 1846 Wind N-N-E—Brisk—A cloudy blustering day—Some rain last night—

Died at Southold on 29th Esther Wells, wife of William H. Wells, Merchant. She was the daughter of Joseph C. & Phebe Albertson, and grand daughter of the late Capt. Thomas Terry—

I received a letter this Eve from N.F. King—

Sabbath 1st November 1846 High Wind N-N-E- with full tides—Ten years ago there was not more than, perhaps five families in the Town using hard coal, for a winters fire, now I should say there is not less than 200—So much for a few years—

Monday 2nd A cloudy moderate day—The brisk N-E- Wind which lasts this some days past, appears to be pretty much spent—

Tuesday 3rd A warmer day than any this some weeks—Ellection held at my house this day—Got me a barrel flour this day cost 6 Dolls 75 Cts—

Wednesday 4th A Cloudy day, wind N-N-W—Last evening at Sundown the poles at the Ellection in this State (N.Y.) closed—The votes were perhaps finished canvasing by 10 or 11 OClock P.M. The result was [313] known in N.York by the Telegraph this morn from almost all the small Towns from Buffalo to Brooklyn, and It reached Greenport by 1 OClock P.M. to day—Who could have believed such a discovery 20 years ago, would have even been made! What next!! The question is does mankind gain on the great whole by inventions more than they lose!—Report says the whigs have carried their Ellection for the Governor—

Thursday 5th Brisk wind N-W—Clear weather—

Friday 6th Wind light N—Doct. Young Justly says, "We take no note of Time but by its loss"—The fleetness of our days weeks & months are considerations of the highest moment—Our Spring, our Summer, our Autumn, where are they!!

Saturday 7th Wind fresh E—Some rain—Sabbath Wind as yesterday

Monday 9th Wind E—with Showers untill Noon—Flour is now about 7 Dolls per Barrel and It is thought It will yet be higher—Wrote to Saml. W Hill to day in answer to one from him some days since—

Tuesday 10th Wind very light N—Cloudy—We understand that we have a whig Governor, viz. John Young—He has got the office over Silas Wright, the present incumbent, by a large majority of Votes.

[314] Wednesday 11th A cloudy, misty, moderate day, with light Wind N-E—

Thursday 12th A light drizly day—hardly rains sufficient to wet one much more than a very copious fog—Wind E-N-E—Received an affectionate letter from our dear Grand daughter Deziah Preston Griffin

Friday 13th High wind E—with about rain as yesterday—

Saturday 14th Much such a day as yesterday but not quite so wet—wind as high, and E—Wrote to our Grand daughter Deziah P. Griffin

Sabbath 15th Wind continues fresh from E—with high tides—Our daughter Narcissa continues quite sick—has been much out of health since the last of Septem.—

Monday 16th It Comes in with an Easterly rain Storm—The wind has now been from the Eastly board since the 30th of October, except perhaps an hour or two—It is now about 18 days, and much of said time It has blown pretty brisk, attended with rain—Cloudy, dark weather has made up the last 3 weeks—this eve informs us that it has been a very Stormy day 16th Nov. 1846—Very pleasent this P.M. with scarce any wind—Tuesday 17th Wind East, but very light—Evening Calm—Had a letter from Sidney, our Son & Chatham, his Son

[315] Wednesday 18th Nov. 1846 Wind light E-S-E—A moderate but cloudy day—

Thursday 19th Wind very high S-E—with a hard rain until 12 midnight—

Friday 20th It then cleared off and set in with a tremendous gale of wind S-W—

Our friend Samuel W. Hill with us—The wind was much more high through the day

Saturday 21st More moderate this morn Wind N-W—Mr. Hill left yesterday—He came 19th left 20th

Sabbath 22—Wind light W—wrote to our Grandson Chatham—

Monday 23rd A gale of wind, N-N-W—It grows colder—A Sloop was cast ashore at Moores Point, what we call Rockypoint, near Greenport, on the North side, and is a total loss, with as we hear every soul on board— One Man found dead, lashed on deck—The vessel has gone to pieces— Another Vessel, a Schooner, is lost on Plumisland. These disasters happened Sunday night, or more properly Monday morning about 4 OClock—

Tuesday 24th Wind not so high as yesterday, yet pretty fresh N-N-W— & cool—A cloudy day

Wednesday 25th Comes in with a S-E- rain storm

Thursday 26th A tremendous gale of wind W-N-W—This is the 3rd great gale since Friday the 20th counting that as one of them, which was fully equal to the two last—At any rate we seldom if ever know 3 such almost Hurricanes near together

A Capt. Sylvanus Covel, from Cape Cod with a small sloop drove on our Shore, at our landing this morn—himself, wife & son are at my house this night—

Friday 17th Wind yet high but not so boistrous as yesterday—towards night It appears to die away—It has been a severe gale, and no doubt as the other 2 mentioned above, It has been disastrous to many—

[316] Saturday 28th Novem. 1846 Wind S-S-W—Brisk

Is It right to be very anxious and deprive ourselves of rest and common comforts, that we may die rich? I know not—The shortness of mortal life is duly appreciated by a wise Man dying at the age of 90 years—It is a tale that is quickly told—

Sabbath 29th It Rained this morn until 10 A.M. when it subsided, with very light wind N-W- and warm—

Monday 30th A very high Wind N-W—This makes the 4th gale of wind we have had since the 20th Counting the 20th for one of them—The three first were Tremendous—This was severe—The Vessels lost, & the destruction of Men, Women, & children in these storms is a solemn consideration of the mutability of every subject that is human—

Tuesday 1st Decem. 1846 more moderate, Wind N-W- by W—

Wednesday 2nd Very light wind E-S-E—with some little Snow, Hail & rain—Capt. Covil, his wife, and boy leave this P.M.

Thursday 3rd Rain this Morn until 12 noon when It partially cleared off—Covil did not leave yesterday—Is yet in the harbour—Rec'd a Letter yesterday from George Bartholomew of Hartford

Friday 4th Pretty high Wind W-N-W—

[317] Saturday 5th Decem. 1846 Fresh breeze—Wind W—Considerable Cool—The Steam Ship Atlantic, one of the largest boats in our Waters, was wrecked on Fishers Island on the evening of the 24th, and about 41 or 2 of the passengers & crew, with the servants and cooks, perished—

Sabbath 6th A cool moderate N-W- wind—

Monday 7th A cloudy day, wind varied from N- & E- to S—people are now Sending to Market (N.Y.) several Vessel loads of Turnips, potatoes etc. etc.—One Man, Joseph Latham, loads a large Sloop, pretty much of his own growing, or raising—Orient is certainly conspicuous for its abundance of vegetables—Its thousands of bushels yearly—

Friday 8th Weather very thick, and damp—wind S—A light sprinkle of rain this eve—

Wednesday 9th Commences with copious showers—Four Vessels in our harbour (Orient) are now takeing in turnips, potatoes, Beans, oats for N.York, as above noticed—They will take in from 2 to 3000 bushels, each Vessel—The Commanders of said Sloops are William Potter of the _____, Thomas Pool of the _____, Warren Beebe of the _____ & Henry Dyer of the Oddfellow—

Thursday 10th Wind this morn light E-N-E—Commenced rain 4 OClock P.M. with wind light S—Friday 11th A moderate Storm of rain all last night Wind S-S-E—A thick, misty, cloudy morn this—

[318] Departed this life this morn (Friday 11th Decem. 1846) Mr. Hazard Racket of GreenPort aged about 72 years—He was and had been through life, an industrious, prudent, upright, truly honest man, and a Christian— He was the 3rd Son of the late Absalom Racket, and the Grandson of Judge Thomas Youngs, late of Southold—

Saturday 12th A high wind from N-W—and so cold as to freeze through the Day—

Sabbath 13th A cold night, the last one—High wind continues N-W— Cold evening—

Monday 14th Wind as yesterday and very cold—

Tuesday 15th Very cold, with wind N-W—not quite as brisk as the last 3 days—

Nathaniel Racket died last night, after a tedious illness of some months,

Captain Covel is from Cape Cod County, Barnstable Town, South Downs, Massachusetts

yet but a week or two of confinement to his house—He has sustained the aimable charracter through life of an honest, peaceable, industrious, active Man—In his youth, and middle age, he was one of the handsomest of his sex, in figure, deportment and features—"Dust Thou art, and into dust Thou must return", Says Eternal Truth—

Wednesday 16th Very little wind N-W-

Thursday 17th Wind N-E- by E—About 12 noon It commenced Snowing—brisk, with wind high, and cold—Bad for Vessels—the coast—[?] it is [?] and will suffice

[319] Friday 18th Decem 1846 A damp misty, thawing day—Snow, which fell considerable plenty yesterday, goes off rapidly to day—Wind light N—

Saturday 19th Very high wind W—

Sabbath 20th Wind as yesterday—Cloudy—We pass away and the memory of us is lost in the laps of ages—

Monday 21st Snow squalls this morn—Wind W—The collector of taxes for our Town, Southold, met the inhabitants of Orient, at my house, this day, to receive their taxes—James Richmond, Collector

Tuesday 22nd Wind very light this morn, W—

Wednesday 23rd Cool West wind—

Thursday 24th Cloudy, chilly S- Wind—

Friday 25th Wind S—Cloudy—

Saturday 26th Wind S-W- by W—Was visited, this eve, by our Grand daughter, Mariah Prince, Eldest daughter to our lament[ed] daughter Harriet Lucretia, late the wife of Abner Wells—Orin Prince, Mariahs Excellent Husband, is accompanying his wife—One of the best, industrious, and finest of Men—

Sabbath 27th Winds-W—Our agreable visitors left us about 12 at noon this day—

Monday 28th Commences with a S-S-W- rain Storm, wind not very high—Evening Calm & foggy—

Thursday 31st As pleasant and as mild a Morn, as a sunny one in May— Rec'd letters from Sidney, our Son, and his Sons Chatham & Augustus, yesterday—

1847

[320] January 1st 1847 A new year! Ah, where is the old one! Gone—numbered with those which made the age of Methusalem—

A very mild pleasant Morn—

Saturday 2nd Weather as moderate as Summer, but very thick, and foggy, in the Morn—P.M. clears off calm & pleasant—

Sabbath 3rd Much such moderate day as yesterday—Raymond arrived home having been absent since 26th of last October—

Monday 4th A calm, cloudy A.M.- P.M. commenced a rain storm Wind E—Wrote to our Son Sidney & his two sons Chatham and Augustus—

Tuesday 5th A clear morn, Wind S-S-W—and warm—A large quantity of rain fell last night—

Wednesday 6th As warm as a pleasant May day—some of our neighbours I learn are ploughing their ground—viz. James W Youngs & Jonathan F. Latham. Rather uncommon for January—

Our friend Sidney P. Racket arrived home from Virginia Yesterday—Has been gone about ten weeks—He leaves for that region, this P.M. with our best wishes—

Thursday 7th Warm, not any frost in the ground—rather foggy this morn, Wind very light S—P.M. high Wind S- with rain, Thunder & lightning—

[321] Friday 8th January 1847 A cold (midling) blustering, clear N-W-wind—Saturday 9th wind not high W—As to cold, about midling—A Letter, from our very affectionate daughter Cleora—she writes her husbands Son Joseph McNeill died on the 5th Decem. Last—He was a bright, active man of handsome abilities—In Decem. 25th 1845 he had a wife, very beautiful, and accomplished, with three aimable, promising children and this Decem. 5th Himself, wife and the 3 children were all consigned to the Silent tomb—Alas the Mutability of sublinary things—

Sabbath 10th Some snow occasionally through the day—Wind light N-W—

Monday 11th Quite a quantity of Snow fell last night, and It continues to fall this morn—Evening clears—

Tuesday 12th Clear N-W- wind—snow drives into banks

Wednesday 13th Moderate—P.M. wind hauls into the S—This eve I received a piece of Excellent Beef of Moses & Daniel Terry (sons of the late Daniel T. Terry)—It contained 86½ Lb—Sleighing pretty—

Thursday 14th A cloudy damp thawing day, wind S—Cut up and salted my small quantity of beef—

Friday 15th Wind S—Cloudy and what we call a thaw, and muddy traveling—Hasty promises are seldom seasoned with rational performances—Vows made in Storms are not often fulfilled in calms—

Saturday 16th Rain, with Wind S—the rain S- wind and the disolving Snow makes splashy walking, where e'er we go—

Thursday 15th Jan.
1847 My two
Sisters Lucinda &
Lucretia [page
trimmed]

[322] Sabbath 17th January 1847 A cool N-W- wind, but light, with a bright Sun—Mr. Hewlet Smith, of N.Y. stoped with us an hour this noon—

Monday 18th A dark, cloudy, drizly day,with wind S—Evening showers—

Tuesday 19th A pleasent sunshine this morn, with light wind W-N-W—Sent a newspaper this morn to Thomas M. Perry, Printer, at Mount Clemens, Michigan State—Quite cool this eve, wind Brisk N-W- by W—

Joseph C. Havens' wife Hannah (she being second Wife) was confined with a Son this morn—Just sprung to life, the Infant views the scene—The Ice bound fields, with not a flower that's green—

Wednesday 20th Cold, wind N-W—

Thursday 21st An unclouded Sun through the day—Wind light W—Not as cold as yesterday—yesterday morning William Terry's wife, Phebe Ann, was confined with a boy—

Friday 22nd Last night and this morn we believe the weather the coldest, by far, of any this season—This we set down as a severe cold day

Saturday 23rd Wind W-S-W—not as cold as yesterday—Some Ice has made in the harbour

Sabbath 24th Pleasent, with Wind S-W- by S—P.M. Cloudy, damp weather—What is so valuable as Time? Ah, and what is so profusely wasted?

Monday 25th Moderate, weather, wind S-W—

Tuesday 26th Calm weather, and cloudy—

[323] Wednesday 27th Jan. 1847 Fresh breeze wind W-N-W—Narcissa (our daughter) remains quite unwell—

Thursday 28th Wind very light W—continues pretty cool—Considerable Ice in our harbour—

Friday 29th Weather much as yesterday, except Just at night It commenced a rain storm, which continued until about 12 midnight—This morn Saturday 30th It blows quite a gale, Wind W—

This morn, Capt. John A. Rackets wife Henrietta was confined with a girl—Last Wednesday 27 Inst. Capt. Elisha Shery Rackets wife was confined with a boy

Sabbath 31st Wind light W-S-W—

Monday 1st February 1847 Some Snow, about sufficient to cover the ground perhaps for not two inches—Wind S-E—Sidney P. Racket has bought in this vicinity and Town, from 5 to 6000 bushels Corn at about 70 and 75 Cents per bushel—It is thought he will realize 95 Cts the bushel for It—If so, It will be a handsome profit—

Tuesday 2nd The Snow melts off intire—light wind S—Wrote to George

M. Bartholomew of Hartford, in answer to his of Novem. last—Walking is very unpleasent, as mud & splash line our streets Just at this time—

Wednesday 3rd Wets some this morn, Wind fresh S—P.M. A hard rain Storm, with high wind—

Thursday 4th High wind W—this morn, with snow squalls—Very cold this Evening—

Friday 5th Brisk wind this morn and tediously cold—A clear, unclouded day—Winter—

Saturday 6th Very light wind N-W—Evening calm—Weather not so cold—

Sabbath 7th Quite moderate, and Pleasent

Monday 8th Some Snow, just to cover the ground—before night It was all melted off—Wind S-W—

[324] Tuesday 9th Feb. 1847 Pleasent—Last eve, Margaret, our Sons Sidneys wife, and her Son, Chatham, came to our humble tenement—Narcissa, remains very low—Is very feeble, and as weak almost as an Infant—Chancy W. Moore, stoped with us an hour or so on Saturday last, 6th Inst—

Wednesday 10th Snows some this morn—Wind E- light—Some rain P.M.—

Thursday 11th Pleasent Weather—Rode to Greenport this morn with Sidneys wife (Margaret) & Chatham, our grandson—Margaret took the cars for Hempstead—Chatham returned with me. Got us a half cord wood, this day—

Friday 12th Wind light S-S-W—Moderate.

Saturday 13th A cool West wind—Maria Prince, our granddaughter, who [has] been with us since last Sabbath, went home today with her Father, Abner Wells—

Monday 15th (Yesterday 14th was pleasant and clear) Today as yesterday, with wind W- and what is termed good moderate, winter weather—Evening calm—A fair at the Congregational Church this eve

Tuesday 16th Wind E-S-E—Some snow this morn—cold & raw this P.M. and looks as if it would snow or rain soon—Our grandson Chatham A. left us this P.M. for Hempstead—

Wrote this day to Judge Nathan H. White, of Orange County a Man whom*

[325] Wednesday 17th Feb. 1847 A cloudy damp, thawy day—the snow & hail which fell last night has pretty much melted off—Wind W—

Thursday 18th A cloudy damp day—very muddy traviling—Wind light

*I have not seen for about 50 years—[in pencil] He died in 18??

and variable, from W- to N—The sloop Oddfellow, Henry Dyer, left for N.York with Rye, Corn, Eggs, & poultry etc—

Friday 19th The snow covers the ground this morn, with a garb of unsullied whiteness, about 6 inches thick—Wind very light N-E ½ E—William H. Wilcox (our soninlaw) arrived from Vermont after an absence of four months—His vocation in said time has been lecturing on Temperence, and forming Temperence societies of the Brothers of Union or United Brothers—

Saturday 20th A very mild day—Snow goes pretty fast yet the sleighs fly merrily—wind E—very light—evening calm—

Sabbath 21st Feb. A regular snowstorm, wind not very high E—Continues through the day, a part of the time It hailed, then rain—

Monday 22nd Snow this morn, yes through the day—It is the first snowstorm on the 22nd we have had since 1843—The anniversary of Washingtons birth—115 year this day since that extraordinary Man was born—

Tuesday 23rd This morn the sun shines in all her chearing enlivening ways—the snow covers the ground with as thick a coat as It has had of snow at any one time, its probable this two Winters past—wind this morn N-, calm this eve—

Wednesday 24th Cold, and first rate sleighing, and It is universally improved—calm day—

Thursday 25th A cloudy morn, Wind light N-E—P.M. Partially clears off—wind continues N- and quite cool—

A great famine in Ireland—Many are starving [to] death—Heart rending

Friday 26th A pleasent winters eve—P.M. calm—Got me home ½ cord wood, this eve—

[326] Saturday 27th Feb. 1847 Commences with a snow, hail & rainstorm, Wind E-S-E—It has been and Is now 5 P.M. a severe windstorm—sharp lightning this eve—It ceased to storm about 11 P.M.

Sabbath 28th High wind S-W—Walking very splashy

Monday 1st March 1847 A very high wind W—

Tuesday 2nd Wind W- not so high as yesterday

The brevity of mortal life cannot properly be comprehended by the healthful man, untill he finds to a demonst[rat]ion his days are numbered—The Man of fourscore looks back on the past as a flitting dream—It appears but a little moment and It is gone! Gone forever.

Corn is now selling in N.York for one Dollar per bushel—wheat at one dollar & 75 Cts—Pork 16 Dollars per barrel

The famine in Europe [illegible] to raise prudence in our Country—

Wednesday 3rd A beautiful, clear & pleasant morn, at the same time there is much snow & Ice on the ground—P.M. light wind—S- and dark & cloudy—It looks like a storm near at hand—Our daughter Narcissa remains very sick. She has been confined to her room about four months.

Thursday 4th What is called pleasant weather overhead, but travilling in mud, snow & water is very unpleasent—A wharf meeting at George Champlins this P.M. The Orient farmers and boatmen are about buying Dyers Wharf—This wharf Caleb Dyer commenced building in August 1829

Friday 5th A pleasant and an enlivening bright Sun this morn, while mud & mire cover all the pathways of our common roads or highways—

Saturday 6th A large white frost this morn, as there was yesterday morn—Pleasent this two days past—

Sabbath 7th White frost again this morn—Rec'd a letter last eve from Hannah L. Brown (our niece) Benjamin Browns wife of Orange County, in answer to one I sent

[327] Our grandson James Hervey Preston, (now a Clerk in Lion L. Corwins store Greenport) stoped with us 5 or 6 hours this day—Our grand daughter Maria L. Prince came to stay with us a few days, at the request of our sick Daughter Narcissa—Hazy, with a sprinkle of rain the P.M.—

Monday 8th A foggy morn, with some sprinkles of rain—moderate through the day—clear P.M.—

Tuesday 9th Cloudy morn—light wind N—great temperence meeting at Riverhead this day—

Wednesday 10th Commences a rain storm this morn—Wind S—

Thursday 11th A cold N-N-W- wind—Our grandson Chatham A. G. came to us this day

Friday 12th Continues cold—Wind as yesterday not quite so high—Rec'd Letters from our Son Sidney, and grandson Augustus R. A[G]—

Saturday 13th A cold N- Wind—some snow this morn—Sabbath 14th Wind W—yet cold

Monday 15th Wind W—Cold & raw, as we say—P.M. squally—

Tuesday 16th A blustering W-N-W- wind, with cold so as to freeze through the day—Some snow squalls, as there was yesterday—Our grand-daughter Maria Prince left us this day for her home at Southold—She has been with us since the 7th

This evening ¼ before 11 OClock our Daughter Narcissa Lee, the wife of Janus Raymond, departed this life, after a distressing Illness of 5 months, which she bore with Christian resignation—Much of the time of her sickness, she was the subject of accute pain & distress, yet in the midst of this afflicting dispensation of divine providence she maintained an unshaken faith in the promises of God, and a love for her Saviour unspeakable and full of Glory—Death appeared to have no terrors for her while she expired as in a gentle sleep—

[328] Wednesday 17th Mar. 1847—A squally, cold day, wind N-W- by W—Evening, wind died away—

Thursday 18th A.M. Clear & Pleasant—P.M. cloudy, with some rain, and Snow—Wind varies from W- to N—

Friday 19th A pleasant clear morn—yet a cool N-W- wind—the snow which fell last night disappears quick this A.M.—

Saturday 20th A pleasant day, Wind very light S—The remains of our daughter Narcissa were committed to the dust this P.M. 2 OClock—A large number of the inhabitants and connections attended the funeral, from our house—A sermon was delivered by Rev. _____ Blakeman, from these words "Be ye also ready, for in such an hour as ye think not the son of Man cometh"—The Tex[t] was selected particularly by our dear deceased daughter, herself, a short time before her Death—

Sabbath 21st It comes in with a Southern rainstorm, attended with some Thunder—Rain continued through the day—

Monday 22nd The storm continues pretty severe, with winds N-N-E—James H. Preston, our grandson, stoped with us last night—left this morn early

Tuesday 23rd The storm partially clears off—Wind continues N—Calm this eve—Our Vessels of Orient, which have been laying up for the winter, are leaving to commence their Summers work—John Terry—William Potter—McDermot—David T. Glover—Sidney P. Racket—E Sherry Racket—John H. Racket, Henry Dyer, Thomas Pool etc etc have all left within 10 Ten days

[329] Wednesday 24th March 1847 Snow covers the ground with a coat of about 1½ inches thick—some rain follows—Wind N-W—

Thursday 25th A pleasant day—

Friday 26th A cloudy dark day—Early, rode out to Greenport to wait on my affectionate daughter Cleora, and my Grandson Chatham—They have been with us, Cleora since Friday 19th Chatham since 11th Inst—They leave this morn for their homes, Hempstead, & Williamsburg—Returned home from Greenport 11 A.M.—Rain P.M.—in light showers—Wind S—

William Terry, Son to Capt. Elias Terry, is building himself a house on our road leading to the landing, Orient Harbour—It stands within about 20 rods of what was Dyers wharf—

Saturday 27th comes in with a tremendous gale of wind west—with Snow, & hail squalls—A very full tide—

Sabbath 28th A cold W-N-W- wind—Tedious—

Monday 29th Continues cold—Wind light E-S-E—P.M. wind very light S—Looks like a storm coming—

Tuesday 30th Very little wind through the day—A dark cloudy eve—

Wednesday 31st comes in with hail & rain—Ground covered an inch or two—Wind E-N-E—Looks like Winter in its chilly colours this day—some sleds, with bells tingling, have passed my house this day—

Thursday 1st April 1847 Snows & rain this morn—A damp calm P.M.—

Friday 2nd much such weather as yesterday—Fast day with us in this place—Janus Raymond left us last Thursday 1st and takes board with Joseph C. Havens—It is very foggy this eve—

Saturday 3rd Quite a mild pleasent day—Wind light W—

Sabbath 4th Wind E and cool—

Monday 5th A mild pleasent day Wrote to Sidney

Tuesday 6th An unpleasent day for Town meeting—In the course of the day it rained and hailed—Wind high E-S-E—

Wednesday 7th More pleasent Wind light W—

[330] Thursday 8th April 1847 A pleasent day—an unclouded sky, wind S-S-W—Friday 9th Much such weather as yesterday, Wind light S-W-

Saturday 10th Wind high W- with a clear sky—got me home from E.Hampton ½ cord wood at 2 dolls & 20 Cts yesterday—P.M. this day squally, & some showers—

Sabbath 11th A very blustering cold day, Wind N-N-W—

Monday 12th Wind fresh S-S-W—tollerable clear weather

Tuesday 13th A cool cloudy morn, Wind N—more mild this P.M.— Henry Dyer, In the Sloop Oddfellow, left for N.York this morn—By his mate viz. Luther King, I wrote to Nathaniel T. Hubbard—

Wednesday 14th Wind pretty fresh S-W—clear weather, rather cool

Thursday 15th Very cool Wind N-N-W—A small shower of rain this eve—

Friday 16th Continues cool—Black frost this morn—

Saturday 17th High wind S-S-W—

Sabbath 18th A very cold N- Wind, ground froze this morn—I do not recollect of ever experienceing a colder day in Apl. than this is—

Monday, 19th Ice in our kitchen this morn & the ground is frozen—It was certainly a very cold night this past one—This morn the wind hauls round to the South

Tuesday 20th much warmer than some days past—Wind light S—

Wednesday 21st A pleasant, mild day—Wind light S—Plankd 81¼ Lbs of potatoes

Thursday 22nd Much such a day as yesterday—I sowed my onions & parsnips—

Friday 23rd Some Thunder, this—light showers through the day—Wind E—More cool than some days past—

[331] Saturday 24th A cool E- Wind—I rode out to Greenport—Sidney (our son) & wife, and their daughter Josephine came to our house last Eve—

Sabbath 25th Wind as yesterday, and Cool—From N.T. Hubbard, I received a letter yesterday—

Monday 26th Pleasant—Wind S—

Tuesday 27th A little squally this P.M.—Wind N-N-W—Sidney, Wife & daughter left this morn for Hempstead—

Wilcox (our Soninlaw) moved his family goods and Chattles in to our tenement this day

Wednesday 28th Cool, but midling pleasant—Our Granddaughter, Harriet M. Hubbard, came to us this evening—

Thursday 29th Warmer, Wind S—planted my peas—Harriet left this P.M.—

Friday 30th Cool Wind A.M. N—P.M. W—

Saturday 1st May 1847—Quite cool—Wind as yesterday—Sabbath 2nd May, Wind E-S-E—A Rain storm—It continued to storm untill night when It cleared off with wind N-W—

Monday 3rd A.M. wind N—P.M. S—and warm—sowed my curly cabbage—

Tuesday 4th Wind S—sowed turnips, beets, sallad, carrot & beet, & pepper seeds in my garden

Wednesday 5th A pleasant day—We have had not one to [blot] exceed It in spring like beauty this, nor the former month—Wrote to Sidney (our son) this morn by mail

Thursday 6th A.M. Warm & calm—P.M. Cool wind E—

[332] Friday 7th May 1847 A cool E- Wind—Repaired my old Wheel barrow, which was built by my late friend Hazard Racket about 10 or 12 years ago—

Saturday 8th Wind A.M. E-N-E—& cool—P.M. calm—two of our Seines took about 150000 of boney fish this day, which are the first they have taken of consequence this season—

Sabbath Cool, yet midling pleasant—Wind N—

Monday 10th Mild & warm—Wind N-E—A great show of wild beasts at Greenport, this day—

Tuesday 11th Foggy, with light wind E—Planted corn & beens in my Garden—

Wednesday 12th Continues foggy, Wind E—Some small, or few sprinkles of rain in the P.M. & It grows cool—

Thursday 13th A cool E-N-E—Wind—Some little rain last night—Friday 14th continues cool E-N-E—wind

Saturday 15th Weather & wind as yesterday—On Saturday the 8th, the same Mr. Askew, mentioned 22nd May 1846, called on us again, and made us a truly religious Visit—

Sabbath 16th The cool E- wind which has been from this course this near 20 days, still continues—wrote to Sidney—

Monday 17th Weather much as yesterday

[333] Tuesday 18th May 1847 Wind light S—It has now been pretty much from the Easterly course about 20 days, and with It cool, unpleasant weather—It is now getting dry—Calm this eve—The Union Seine took about 100000 fish this day—The Oregon Seine has up to this time took about 300000—

Wednesday 19th A pleasant morn, wind very light S-S-W—

Wednesday 19th A warmer day than any previous one this month—Wind light S—

Thursday 20 20th More cool, wind moderate E-S-R—Wrote to my grandson Augustus R. Griffing

Friday 21st A cool day, wind E-S-E—

Saturday 22nd Pleasant but very dry—Have quite an ill turn this day—A warning, particular at my time of life "be ye also ready"

Sabbath 23rd A foggy morn, as It is as last eve—Wind S—Monday 24th—A foggy morn—

Monday 24th A foggy morn, with wind S—

Tuesday 25th Warm, and a clear sweet air, light from W—Yesterday the Oregon Seine took about 200000 fish—

Benjamin Brown Esquire's Son Tompkins, from Orange County, stoped with us last night, leaves this day for Boston, from which he will proceed home—

Thursday 27th Wind light W—some sprinkle of rain—nor sufficient to wet the dry ground—

Friday 28th Very little wind, and much of the day It was calm—quite warm—Planted some bush squash seed this day in the corner of the Orchard—

Saturday 29th Warm and pleasent—And etc etc—

[334]Sabbath 30th May 1847 Cool, some showers—Wind N-E—Monday 31st Wind S-E—Cool—P.M. A moderate, but steady rain, which is needed.

Tuesday 1st June 1847 Rain this morn until 11 A.M. Wind shifted S— Foggy this eve—

Wednesday 2nd Early this morn, a smart thunder shower—clears off with wind W—

Thursday 3rd Warm, most of the day calm, Just at night light wind S—

Friday 4th A plentiful rain, with lightning & Thunder about 3 OClock this morn—The ground which was lately parched with drouth is now drenched with water—This eve wind W—

Saturday 5th A pleasent day, Wind W—Rode out to Greenport with Mr. Samuel King a Methodist clergyman—

Sidney P. Racket, now commands a New Schooner lying at this time at Dyers wharf—It is about 160 Tons, and is the handsomest, and we think the best Vessel of her size that has braced our harbour for a long time—Her name is Buenavista—

Sabbath 6th A cool N-W- wind—This morn uncomfortable without a fire—Singular for June—P.M. Wind S-W—

Monday 7th A mild, pleasent day, wind light W—Sidney P. Racket sailed in his elegant schooner Buenavista this day for N.York—Ellection at my house—took in 83 votes—

Tuesday 8th Wind S—light—not any very warm weather yet—Sewed my late cabbage bed this day—

Wednesday 9th Wind S- and pretty brisk—Jackson Seine took nearly 200000 Boney fish-

[335] Thursday 10th June 1847 Brisk wind S-S-W—Rec'd letters from Son Sidney, and his son Chatham

Friday 11th High wind as yesterday S-S-W—

Saturday 12th Wind continues brisk, about W—Visited Long beach this A.M. In pursuit of gulls eggs—with much fatigue I got 11—I suppose my whole travil after them was near 6 or 7 miles, and the larger part of It on soft sand & beach—a severe jaunt for a Man of 4 score—This evening, the powerful wind which has now blowed near four days, subsides into a tranquil calm

Sabbath 13th A pleasant day—Rec'd a letter from our grand daughter Maria L. Prince—

Monday 14th Some showers, and Thunder—Our several Seines have within a few days past took good draughts of Boney fish—

Tuesday 15th Very brisk wind this morn W- and as cold as is seldom known on any 15th of June—A winter dress on is not uncomfortable this morn—

Wednesday 16th A cool Morn—Wind West—

Thursday 17th Wind W—Clear, and cool—Rec'd a letter yesterday from George M. Bartholomew of Hartford, C-t—Son to our cousin Sally, the daughter of my aunt Mary Stone, who when a Girl was Mary Griffing—

Friday 18th A pleasant but cool morn, wind N—Squire Benjamin Browns daughter Hannah Michael visited us a few hours this day, from Orange County—

Saturday 19th Cloudy—Wind S—A little rain this eve—

[336] Sabbath 20th June 1847 A cloudy, damp morn—I rose early, and took a lonely walk, with deep, and solemn meditations on the mutability, and instability of all sublinary things—Our aims, and anxiety, for peace, rest, and solid comfort in this mundane sphere, are, (if possible) worse than useless—The productions of Earth, and Its richest gifts are all mixed with tears & disappointments—A steady rain this P.M. Wind S—

Monday 21st It rained all the last night, and moderately this morn—at 10 this morn the wind shifted from S- to N-W—

Tuesday 22nd Wind S-E—A damp cloudy day

Wednesday 23rd Wind light W—A pretty clear day, and warm—

Thursday 24th Clear & warm—Wind W—Samuel W. Hill stoped with us last night—left this morn—

Friday 25th With [what] is called a pleasant morn—P.M. wind W—a sweet clear, salubrious breeze—

Saturday 26th Wind W- & pleasant—Rec'd a letter from our daughter Cleora—all well—

Sabbath 27th A pleasant morn, wind W—We had a small Thunder Shower last eve

Monday 28th Calm, pretty much throughout the day—

Tuesday 29th Wind E-N-E—Wilcox left for N.Y. last eve—

Wednesday 30th A rain Storm this morn—

[337] Thursday 1st July 1847 A cool, cloudy day Wind N-E- ½ E-

Friday 2nd Wind N-E—& a cool morn—This eve 14 young people from

John Racket, son to Noah & Penny Racket, died about the last of June of this year—near 50 years of age— At his arrival to Manhood, he was one of the likeliest, and most promising of Men, but [?] intemperence destroyed the fairest and most honorable of sons.

Lyme Ct took lodging at our house—N.T. Hubbard, Wife, & son, Cyrus— They were visitors, truly in time & place—

Sabbath 4th Rode out to Mattituck with Mr. Hubbard—A.M. on our way stoped at, and attended the Congregational meeting at Southold—Took dinner with Widow Myra Reeve, at Mattituck—on the way home called on Barnabas Orsborne—John Hurt, & Abner Wells—

Monday 5th A pleasant day—A number of our Orient folks are celebrating Independence at Greenport—they dine at Terrys Greenport house— This morn our friend Hubbard, his wife & son left for N.Y.—took the cars at Greenport—

Tuesday 6th very warm—Wind light S—

Wednesday 7th A calm, warm morn, & as warm this evening

Thursday 8th Weather much as yesterday—Wrote to Sidney and Chatham—Our Son & grandson—Rec'd a letter from Tompkins Brown of Orange County—

[338] Friday 9th July 1847 Warm, with very light wind W-S-W—

Saturday 10th A damp smoky day, Wind E-N-E—

Sabbath 11th Winds-S-E- and light, & warm

Monday 12th Wind light S-E—

Tuesday 13th A.M. Wind W—P.M. Thunder showers, with wind N-W— Gathered this day about 6 quarts cher[r]ies—the first this year off our trees—they have born a less quantity this year, than I have known this some years past—

Wednesday 14th wind (this morn) N-N-W—P.M. Wind light W-W-E—

Thursday comfortably cool last night—Pleasant this morn—P.M. Wind brisk S-S-W—

Friday 16th Warm, with wind S—Wrote to James Hallock Esq. Mattituck—

Saturday 17th Wind S-S-W—Pleasant—"What a dream is a mortal life!"—Mr. Sylvanus Mulford called on us last Thursday—He is from Montrose—See a notice of him in 3 Diary, page 51—

Sabbath 18th Pleasant but uncomfortably warm

Monday 19th Wind W—very warm—Visited Brothers James & Warren, and several others at Rocky point—

Tuesday 20th Very warm—Gathered off our trees (Chery) about 12 or 14 qts this day—they were not plenty as some seasons—

Wednesday 21st wind W- as yesterday—Continues warm—Our grand daughter Maria L. Prince, her husband Orin, and daughter Harriet visited us this day—

[339] Thursday 22nd July 1847 High wind W-S-W—Evening some rain, which begins to be needed

Friday 23rd It has been a cloudy day, with some little rain in the fore part of the day

Saturday 24th A cloudless sky and very warm, Grain, Wheat, Rye etc. come in plenty—James H. Preston is with us this eve—

Sabbath 25th Wind high W-S-W—and a cloudy day—Samuel Griffin, with his daughter Mary Preston, our Great grand daughter, called on us a short time this P.M.—This little plege is much like her dear Mother, our late affectionate grand daughter, Deziah Preston Griffin—

Monday 26th A very warm forenoon—Afternoon we had a copious shower, which was much needed—We gathered about 4 qts cheries—

Tuesday 27th Wind brisk E-N-E—and cool—A great change from very warm to almost uncomfortably cold—James H. Preston left us last eve—

Wednesday 28th A cool morn, wind N—Caleb Dyers 2nd wife, Julia, was confined with a Son yesterday—this evening J. Hull Goldsmith Esq, son to my late much esteemed friend Zacheus Goldsmith called on me an hour.

Thursday 29th Wind light N-E—Cool

Friday 30th Cool wind E-N-E—some little

[340] Saturday 31st July 1847 A severe rain storm last night & this morn until 10 A.M. with wind E-S-E—P.M. It clears off and wind S—Rec'd Letters from our son & his sons—Sidney & Chatham—

Sabbath 1st August 1847 Wind S-S-W—A small sprinkling of rain, occasionally through the day—Altogether It would not equal a smart shower—

Monday 2nd It has been a pleasant day—a comfortable moderate N-W-wind—This morn William Webb was married to Harriet Deziah Wiggins, our niece—

> Marriage—a solem act—the first law given
> In paradise! A union made by Heaven!
> Triumphant love, graced this wedding feast
> Angels were witnesses and god the Priest

This eve a Mr. Blackwell from N.York came to stop with us a few days— He is a descendant of the Blackwells, who was the first owners of Blackwells Island in 1666—

Tuesday 3rd Pleasent—wrote to Sidney and Chatham—

Wednesday 4th A pleasent day—comfortably warm, wind W—

Thursday 5th Wind N-N-E—Cloudy day—P.M. A rain Storm—Wind E—

[341] Friday 6th August 1847 After a severe Easterly rainstorm through the night It clears off this morn with wind N-W—Our fields of flourishing corn lies prostrate by the force of the boisterous gale of last night

Saturday 7th comes in with a hard Easterly rain Storm, and continued in copious showers through the day—It has certainly been a very rainy day—

Sabbath 8th Wind moderate S-S-E—some light rain

Monday 9th After continuing to rain pretty steady through all yesterday, and last night, until 8 the morn the wind changed from the E- to S-S-W and It partially clears away—The ground is drenched with rain—

Tuesday 19th Warm, and what we call muggy weather—wind S—our neighbours are gathering blackberries by bushels—

Wednesday 11th A refreshing breeze of wind S-S-W—Pleasent, and comfortable—Schooner Sarah Strong of Greenport was lost off south of Montauk on the 5th Inst, John Fournier Master, who was lost with 4 others, the 6th man was saved in the long boat—

Thursday 12th Wind W—A pleasent day—

Friday 13th Very light wind, and warm—

Saturday 14th Wind E- by S—cooler than yesterday—Walked on the Hills with Mr. Blackwell—

Sabbath 15th Cool N-E- Wind—N.T. Hubbard & Wife came to us last Evening—

[342] Monday 16th August 1847 Set off this Morn at 7 OClock for N.York, in company with N.T. Hubbard & wife—We took the railroad cars at Greenport ¼ before 8 and arrived at N.York ½ past 2 P.M.—On our way we stoped at the following stations, as they are called—viz. 1 Southold— 2 Hermitage— 3 Cutchogue— 4 Mattituck— 5 Jamesport— 6 Riverhead— 7 St. George Mannor— 8 Yaphank— 9 Medford— 10 Lakeroad— 11 Suffolk Station— 12 Thompson— 13 Deerpark— 14 Farmingdale— 15 Hicksville— 16 Westbury— 17 Carl place— 18 Hempstead branch— 19 Hyde Park— 20 Brusville— 21 Jamaica— 22 Woodville— 23 Race course— 24 East New York— 25 Watering place— 26 Bedford—Took lodging with N.T. Hubbard—

Tuesday 17th Pleasent rode out with Walter O. Hubbard to the Coffer dam, or as some call It "the High bridge" over Harlem River; on our way visited aunt Genny, as they call her—She is a Colored woman of 91 years, was brought up in the family of my Grandmother and Grand Father Terry. While out on this very pleasent ride I took an interesting view of the two

reservoirs—The stupendous bridge, over which is to pass the pipes for leading the Croton water to supply the City—

[343] Wednesday 18th Visited our daughter Cleora McNeil, at
Williamsburgh—Thursday 19th called on James Wilkie & family—Ludice
Dayton, and Mr. R. Williams—Spent ½ hour with my old friend Henry
Youngs in walking over the [ruins?], and viewing the Trinity Church, and
its carved work, with Its massy doors—

Friday 20th left our friends Hubbard and his very affectionate wife and
family with our dear Grand child Harriet M & her husband Walter O. and
repaired to the Ferry, crossed to the railroad depot, took the cars for
Hempstead, with my G-son Chatham, arrived at our Son about 11 OClock
A.M., found Sidney & family all well

Saturday 12 OClock Noon, left for Orient—Chatham accompanied me
to Hempstead branch—I arrived at my home (Orient) about ½ past 7 P.M.
The intire week has been very pleasant, agreable, and comfortable, considering my absence from my afflicted wife

Sabbath 22nd pleasant

Monday 23rd Continues fine weather—Our Seines are takeing plenty of
fish for Manure, many of which they are sending off west on the rail cars at
about 87 Cents per 1000—

This evening Mr. Frederick Dobbs of N.Y., a former boarder of ours
stoped with us—with him is a Mr. Charles Webb, Grand Son of the late
Capt. Thomas Webb of Cutchogue—

Tuesday 24th Pleasant Wind light N-E—

Wednesday 24th Weather much as yesterday—cool—comfortable

[344] Thursday 26th August 1847 Pleasant, wind light E—

Friday 27th Wind W—comfortable weather

Saturday 28th Wind S—some sprinkling rain—

Sabbath 29th Fresh breeze, wind S-S-W—& warm—Edwin Brown, of
the Ship ____ sailed on a whaleing voyge Yesterday—his wife goes with
him—Our grandson James H. Preston called on us this day—

Monday 30th Morn wind E-N-E—P.M. S—Visited the old burying
ground in a hollow amid Browns Hills, with Mr. Joseph Blackwell, who with
his pencil took off the inscriptions of a large nunber of the headstones,
marking the resting places of those who departed this life (many of them)
more than 100 years ago—

Tuesday 31st Wind W—Warm—It is probable that more blackberries
have been gathered on Ram & Shelter Island, this month than any other
August since those places were known by white people—perhaps from

one to two hundred barrels would not be too high an estimate—I think not

[345] Wednesday 1st September 1847—Morning Wind light N-E—1 P.M. light rain, Wind S—

Thursday 2nd Wind light S-S-W—Rather hazy through the day—Wilcox & Blackwell gone this day to Camp meeting at Jamesport—Wilcox, Blackwell & with them our Grandson Chatham A.G. all arrive at our house this eve, from Camp meeting—

Friday 3rd Warm S- Wind—Our Chatham left us about 10 this morn, for Hempstead—

Saturday 4th Wind S—and as warm a day as any one this 4 weeks past—

Sabbath 5th Wind brisk S-S-W—

Monday 6th A copious rain early this morn—about 10 A.M. It cleared off—with wind N-W—

Tuesday 7th Wind N-E—and cooler than It has been for 3 weeks past—

Wednesday 8th A thick misty day, Wind E-S-E—Mr. Zilla Youngs wife was confined with a daughter last Sunday—

Thursday 9th Wind S—a good breeze, and very warm—Evening It rains—

Friday 10th Wind N-E—and a rainstorm through all last night, and all this day—

Saturday 11th A damp, cloudy day, wind N-E—

Sabbath 12th Wind as yesterday, attended with rain occasionally through the day—

Monday 13th Wind brisk N-W—comfortable weather—

[346] Tuesday 14th Sept. 1847 High wind N-W—

Wednesday 15th Wind N-W- road[rode] to Rockypoint with Cousin William H. Griffing—

Thursday 16th A chilly morn, but a mild day, rode out to Southold with our Friend William H. Griffing, made calls on Abner Wells—Our Grand daughter Maria Prince (her husband not at home)—arrived home Just at Sunset—On the 1st of June 1842 I visited Southold with our above said cousin William H. Griffing—Alas! What a change has taken place since that eventual period—Honora goes today to N.Y.

Friday 17th Very little wind this day—got me home a cord of hickory wood—

Saturday 18th Wind light E—Yesterday Wm. H. Griffing (our cousin) left for Guilford, C-t his residence—Honora and her daughter Ellen set off for N.Y. last Thursday 16th—

Sabbath 19th Wind E—& brisk—

Monday 20th Wind N-E—Cool, & some rain

Tuesday 21st Wind N-W—cool—Our Grandson, John Augustus Preston, was married to Emily Richmond 8th this Inst, Wednesday

[347] A pleasent day with light wind W—There has been much sickness in Greenport this some weeks and It continues as yet its mournful effects—The disentary is the most distressing of the complaints now prevailing in Greenport, and in Orient—Thursday 23rd Pleasant & clear weather—Wind light S-S-W—Honora & Ellen arrived home this eve

Friday 24th Wind E-N-E—Thick weather—

Saturday 25th Commences with an Easterly rainstorm—Purchased a cord of hickory wood this morn—Cost at my door $5=87 ½—Purchased me a cord a day or to since at 6=12 1/2 Amount $12=00

This has been as boistrous an Easterly rain storm, with a very high wind, and tide as we but seldom see—

Sabbath 26th Wind N-N-E—& thick—damp weather, and rather cool—

Monday 27th Much such weather as yesterday, with wind N-W- by N—

Tuesday 28th Very little wind through the day—some little rain

Wednesday 29th Fresh breeze Wind W—Evening squally, with wind N—with Northern lights

Thursday 30th Light wind W—The grape vines heavy—we have some frost—

Friday 1st October Fresh breeze wind S-S-W—

Saturday 2nd A calm day—

[348] Sabbath 3rd October 1847—Wind light E—

Monday 4th Wind N-, very light through the day—Died at Greenport yesterday Widow Abigail King, aged 91 years & Nine months—Mrs. King was the Widow of the late Josel King and daughter of Mr. Isaiah Brown, who died about 1800—who was son to the Daniel Brown, who was Master Builder of the Orient Meeting House, which was built in 1717—

Died yesterday at Rockypoint, Widow Penelope Wiggins, aged about 80 years, relic of the late William Wiggins—

Tuesday 5th What is called a flattening day, and a calm one—

Wednesday 6th much such weather as yesterday—Calm—"Mans life is a vapor"—

Thursday 7th A fresh breeze of wind E—& cool—The two cords and one foot of hickory wood I purchased a week or two since, I have sawed one cord & one foot of It twice, making 3 stacks of one, which is equal to sawing

2 cords & 2 foot—This wood is nearly as hard as lignumvitae—At 4 score this is not so bad as If It was worse—

Friday 8th Squally with rain, Wind S-S-E—

Saturday 9th Cool fresh N-W- wind

Sabbath 10th Oct. Wind brisk W- with a cloudless sun

Monday 11th Wind high N-W—Cool

Tuesday 12th Wind W—and pretty brisk—

Wednesday 13th Squally, with rainstorm—wind Morning very high S—P.M. N-W—Thunder & lightning, with a gale of wind in the night—wrote to Wm. A. Overton this day

[349] Thursday 14th White frost this morn—very light wind through the day S—

Friday 15th Weather much as yesterday—

Saturday 16th Calm weather, Sidney and Margeret (our son & wife) came to us this eve—

Sabbath 17th Light wind E-S-E—

Monday 18th A calm day—flattening weather—

Tuesday 19th Very moderate Southerly wind—Took Sidney, Wife & daughter Margeret to Greenport to the rail Cars—He attends Court at Riverhead—On Monday Wiggins sons Will case—The Validity of the Will is contested—

Wednesday 20th Wind light N-N-E—William Webb in the Sloop Sarah Brewster sails for Kingston North [Hudson] river, after a load of coal for our neighbours

Thursday 21st A mild, and almost calm day—

Friday 22nd Much such weather as yesterday, except rather more wind from the S-W—

Saturday 23rd A light sprinkle of rain in the morn—Two Vessels are now taking in potatoes, at our landing, one at 42 Cts per bushel & the other at 50 Cts—flour 7 ½ Dolls barrel—

Sabbath 24th Wind brisk E—cool with some rain—

Monday 25th Rode to Greenport with Joseph Blackwell who has been with us 12 weeks—he leaves for N.Y.

Tuesday 26th Wind S-W—I forgot to observe that there was some showers yesterday & It wet me on my return from Greenport—

[350] Wednesday 27th, October 1847 Calm weather

Thursday 28th Cold N-E- wind—

Friday 29th Continues quite cold—Ice ½ inch this 2 past mornings—This evening, Richard S. Hubbard paid us a visit—This nephew of Mrs

Griffings has not been with us since 29th July 1839—He is much a Gentleman, and merits (truly) our respectful consideration—I mistook It was last eve, Capt. Hubbard stoped with us—This morn I took him in a carriage to Greenport to the railroad Depot—We took breakfast at Capt. J. Clarks, after which he took the cars, and I returned home

Saturday 30th What is called a pleasant day if a very light S- wind, and a clear sky makes It so—Jemima Vail died on Sabbath 26th just, aged 59 years—

Sabbath 31st Wind S—Brother James called on us a few minutes this noon

Monday 1st Novem. 1847 A pleasant, mild, calm day—purchased a ½ cord pine wood

Tuesday 2nd Much such weather as yesterday—quite warm—ellection at our house, where it has been held, with the exception of a year, for 40 years—

[351] Wednesday 3rd Novem.1847 This is the 3rd day of calm, warm, clear weather—It is Just and true as some observes viz. "Shadows we are, and Shadows we persue"—

Thursday 4th Another warm calm day—Rec'd a letter from Wm. A. Overton in answer to one I wrote him a week or two since

Friday 5th Wind W- A.M.—P.M. N-W- and more cool—Evening Wind, brisk or as we call It a fresh breeze—Was any Man ever to[o] watchful of his words & actions?—

Saturday 6th High wind N-W—and quite Cool—Potatoes are selling wholesale in Orient at 60 & 70 Cents—Higher than known before, occasioned by the rot—It is said that the Irish in Ireland are in great calamity for so out of provisions—

Sabbath 7th Pretty fair weather as to warmth & wind N-W—

Monday 8th Wind light S—Wilcox & Hampton Mulford leave this morn for Pokipsie [Poughkeepsie], on a mission as delegates to Temperence League

Tuesday 9th Cloudy, but moderate weather

Wednesday 10th Wind fresh W- Rec'd a letter from grandson James H. Preston

Thursday 11th Wind N-N-W—Wilcox returned home

Friday 12th Wind N-W- by W—midling cool

Saturday 13th A cloudy day Wind W—wrote to our grandson J.H. Preston—

Sabbath 14th Nov. considerable rain last night and morn—How imperceptibly our life passes off—And with what a stupor we view the awful truth!

[352] Monday 15th Novem. 1847 A squally day—wind W-N-W—Potatoes are now selling to load a Vessel, at Dyers Wharf, for 70 Cts—Turnips at 15 Cts. Per bushel—

Tuesday 16th Fresh breeze N-W- by W- wind—

Wednesday 17th Wind W- & warm—died this evening Mehitable Petty, widow of the late Daniel Petty—She was a Woman of professed, and we believe, real Piety, and true faith in the Lord & Saviour, Jesus Christ—Likewise died this same Evening, Mary, the endearing, and affectionate wife of John Youngs—Mrs. Petty was born in January 1767—Making her 81 years wanting about 6 weeks—Mrs Youngs was about 27 years—

Thursday 18th As warm as a pleasent May day—wind S—Rec'd two letters this day, one from our daughter Cleora, the other from D. Tompkins Brown—

Friday 19th Commences with a moderate rain storm with [wind] S—Just at Sundown It appears to be clearing off as light up in the N—

Saturday 20th A blustery, cool morn—wind N-N-W—

[353] Sabbath 21st Novem. 1847 was a cloudy day, with occasionally a small sprinkle of rain—Wind light S—Received last eve a letter from our grandson Chatham—As he has been with us in our late deep affliction, in the sickness & death of our dear Narcissa, and the sensible, solem interest he appeared to take in our calamity at the time, renders his communications, breathing affectionate expressions of kindness, of great worth—That he continues to feel for us, gives sensations indescribable and strong desires that Heaven may make him a blessing to his parents, himself, and Country—

Monday 22nd A cloudy, warm day—Very light wind—wrote to Chatham this Eve—

Tuesday 23rd Much such weather as yesterday—Wind E-S-E—Wilcox goes to Madison C-t this day—

Wednesday 24th Wind S—Showers, occasionally—In the Evening a severe gale of wind, & rain, from the South, with Lightning & Thunder—

Thursday 24th A damp, dark, cloudy day—Thanksgiving through the State—Wind S-E—

Friday 26th Wind W-N-W—

Saturday 27th wind N-W—Cool—

Sabbath 28th Squally, with small flurrys of snow—Wind N-W—

Monday 29th A blustering N-W—cool wind

Tuesday 30th A very cold morn—The first was severe last night—more so than any this season—Wind N—

[354] Wednesday 1st Decem. 1847 Wind S—cloudy—A Mr. Ell, who with

his wife moved into our place, about 3 years ago (I believe he is a Scotchman) is this day moving with his family & effects to N.York. He is in moderate circumstances—a shoemaker, and we believe industrious and honest—

Thursday 2nd A severe Southerly wind & rainstorm—Commenced about 2 A.M. & continued hard untill 4 P.M.—

Friday 3rd This morn thick, and dark—some sprinkles of rain—Wind very light S—As the day closes, we can say It has been as dark a day as we have known in a year past—Probably more so—all the latter part of the day it has rained moderately—partially clears off about 5 P.M.—

Saturday 4th Wind fresh N-W—Rec'd a letter from our Son Sidney, wrote yesterday, when they were well he says—

Sabbath 5th Very light wind S-S-E—

Monday 6th Clear & pleasant, with light Wind N-W—

Tuesday 7th Very moderate weather—Abner Wells, wife & son Walter visited us this day—

Benjamin Wells of Southold is taking in the Orient Wheat perhaps there will be 10 or 1500 bushels at about $1=25 Cts per bushels—

Wednesday 8th Very mild weather—Wind light S—

Thursday 9th Weather much as yesterday Wind S-S-W—

Friday 10th High wind S—Cloudy, with some little rain

[355] Saturday 11th High wind S—with some little showers—Rode to Greenport with Capt. John A. Racket—Purchased some few articles—returned home about 1 P.M.—

Sabbath 12th A cloudy day—wind E-S-E—Some little sprinkle of rain—

Monday 13th Warm for the time of year—

Tuesday 14th Warm as May—& foggy, wind S—

Wednesday 15th Foggy & very damp—Wind S—

Thursday 16th A cold N-E- wind—P.M. rain

Friday 17th Last night was a stormy one—This morn It continues to blow and storm, but more moderate—wind N-E—

Saturday 18th This morn the ground is covered with snow—Wind as yesterday—

Sabbath 19th Snow melts off yesterday, one or two sleighs passed us—

Monday 20th Snow which came Friday night has this eve pretty much all disappeared—Wind S-E—

Tuesday 21st Very cold wind N-E—

Wednesday 22nd Wind N-E—Pretty severely cold—A Mr. Whitiker from Babylon L.I. stoped [with] us tonight—He says he often sees our Son

Sidney—visitors with such communicatons, generally gain the attention of Parents and certainly Mothers—

Thursday 23rd A squally day with flight of snow A cold day—P.M. Wind High S-S-W—

Friday 24th A chilly S- wind—

Saturday 25th A light snow, wind light N-W—

[356] Sabbath 26th Decem. 1847—A cold blustering day, wind high N-N-W—The snow which [fell] yesterday, now drifts into small banks, as there is not much of It to drive—

Monday 27th Extreme cold yet less wind than yesterday—

Tuesday 28th A light Snow covers the ground this morn—Wind light W—

Wednesday 19th Wind S—and very little of It—Thursday 30th Foggy—and splashy underfoot—

Friday 31st A thick dark morn, with now and then a sprinkle of rain—

1848

Saturday 1st January 1848 Weather thick, foggy, Southerly, with occasionally some rain and very muddy—

Sabbath 2nd thick weather—some little rain—Wind S—

Monday 3rd Pleasent, and clear, and not cold

Tuesday 4th Pleasent—A great Temperence Meeting at Riverhead this day—The cause I think looks a little more up than sometime past—

Wednesday 5th High wind S-E—Evening rain—Potatoes are selling in Orient for 80 Cents per bushel by the hundred bushel—

Thursday 6th Good weather—Orient people hold a meeting in order to build a wharf—Dyers wharf appears to be going down, and the inhabitants cannot suit themselves in a bargain with him, for his, they intend to build one as a company, by shares—

Friday 7th A cold N-N- West wind—

Saturday 8th A rain, and Snowy day—

[357] Sabbath 9th June 1848 Winter like weather [superscript illegible]

Monday 10th A cold N-N-W- wind—A severe frost last night—

Tuesday 11th This morn & last night is the coldest weather we have had this season

Wednesday 12th Weather more mild, a light wind S—Calm In the evening—

Thursday 13th Wind N-E—A thick cloudy day—this day a company of Orient Men, chiefly Farmers, have purchased Dyers Wharf, for which they are to pay him 500 Dollars—The company is to be incorporated under the firm of the Orient Wharf Company—they are to hold it in Shares of 25 dollars per Share—There will probably be 80 shares, making the sum of 2000 Dollars.

Friday 14th & Saturday 15th Thick foggy weather—Ocasionally some few drops of rain—two pretty dark days—

Sabbath 16th Monday 17th Very warm—Ground settled like May Weather—

Tuesday 18th Wednesday 19th were blustering days, especially Wednesday, when It blew a gale N-W- by W- and very cold—Received a letter from Chatham A. our Grandson on Saturday 15th—A token to us of consolation—

Thursday 20th Wind S-W—Not so cold as the last five days past—We hear Just now that Samuel Griffing (our late dear Grand daughter Deziah Prestons husband) was married a few days since to a woman of Southampton—

Friday 21st, Saturday 22nd were pleasent, and mild—

Sabbath 28th Wind N—and a cool, cloudy day—wrote to our Grandson Chatham A. Griffin—

Monday 24th Tuesday 25th were moderate, calm days—Very little frost in the ground at this time—Last Evening, William Corwin, of Mattituck was married to Elizabeth Brown, daughter to Deacon Peter Brown of this place—Orient—

[358] Wednesday 26th January 1848—very moderate mild weather, little or no frost this some days past—

Thursday 17th A rainstorm from 2 A.M. to 2 P.M.—A wet time—

Friday 28th A pleasant day—A handsome donation was this day given to our Congregational Minister, Mr. Blakeman—The articles, with the money sent in, were some 70 Dollars—The cash, itself, was 50 Dollars—The other things, at the lowest, were worth 20 to 25 Dollars—A civility shewn, where I deem it was deserved, and will be duly appreciated—

Saturday 29th A very squally day, wind N-W—

Sabbath 30th & Monday 31st Pleasent days—and scarce any frost—

Tuesday 1st February 1848 A.M. Hazy weather P.M.—Snow wind N-E—

Wednesday 2nd Clear & pleasent—

Thursday 3rd A flattening day, Wind N-E—

Friday 4th A snow storm with wind E—Rain in the Evening—

Saturday 5th Rain & Snow, very splashy underfoot—Wind N—Evening wind blows in gale N-N-W—with cold increasing—

Sabbath 6th Some flurries of Snow, with cold N-W- wind

Monday 7th A very blustery N-W- wind—Considerable Ice on the ground—bad walking—

Tuesday 8th Wind has very much died away—clear—

[359] Wednesday 9th 1848 Wind light N-N-W—A cold night, and this morn is much so—

Thursday 10th A brisk wind W-N-W—Evening wind N- & very cold—

Friday As cold a morn as any this winter—A clear sky—

Saturday 12th A very cold night was the last—more moderate this morn—Wind very light N-E—

Sabbath 13th A cold N-W- wind—

Monday 14th More moderate—Sent a Newspaper this day to N.T. Hubbard & Henry Youngs, of NY—It contained Chathams 6th Chapter—A marriage of bygone days—Chancy W. Moore called on us this day—

Friday 18th Midling cool with a light wind N—It has been much such weather since Monday last—

Sabbath 20th A moderate rain last night—Continues so to do very moderately through this day—Wind light E-N-E—Died this morning Sandeforth Webb, aged 52 years—He has been a Man of sincere piety, and lived a life adorned with the profession of sound Evangelical Faith—He was, and has been a Member of the Baptist church, for many of the last years of his life—

Tuesday 22nd A dark cloudy morn—PM. It rained & snowed considerable—

Thursday 24th Ezra C. Terry Esq. & wife gave us a call—Weather continues moderate, and muddy—

Friday 25th Saturday 26th & Sabbath 27th Weather pretty cool, with wind Westerly & some part of the time N- & E—Received Letters from Sidney (our son) and his son Chatham—

[360] Monday 28th Feb. 1848 Some rain and some snow fell in the course of the day—Take the day through, it was a damp, uncomfortable one—Wind light S- & part if the time W- & S-W—

Tuesday 29th & Wednesday 1st March were squally, blustering, and cold days—wind W-N-W—

Thursday 2nd [March] Moderate dark and misty—Wind light W-N-W—

Friday 3rd This morn the ground is covered with a coat of Snow 3 or 4 inches thick—Wind light, varied through the day from N-E- to S-S-W—

Saturday 4th Wind brisk W-N-W—the sleighing midling good—It is improved in our Orient—

Sabbath 5th A cold wind N-W—Evening very cold & bids fair for a tedious freezing night—

Monday 6th A cold high wind N-W-

Tuesday 7th Wind light S-S-W—John A. Racket, Elisha Sherry Racket, & Sidney P. Racket all leave this day for N.Y. to commence the Season freighting buisness with their Vessels, which they each now command, being handsome schooners of 100 or more Tons—These Captains were some years since boys, at my school, in Orient—they are now Men of the first respectability

[361] Thursday 9th March 1848 A rain storm, moderate, with light wind E-N-E—

Friday 19th It continued to rain very moderately until 12 M. to day when the wind shifted to N-W—and cleared up—Our Brother James visited us Wednesday 8th

Saturday 11th & Sabbath 12th & Monday 13th Wind S—but cloudy & some rain—Tuesday A cold N- Wind—Saml. Hill visited us last eve—left us this morn, which is very cold—

Wednesday 15th The last night was as cold & one as any previous one the past Winter, In my opinion—Wind this morn N-N-W- and very cold

Thursday 16th Continues very cold—Received Letters, last eve—One from our daughter Cleora, and another from D. Tompkins Brown, of Orange County N.Y.—A Physician—

Friday 17th Wind N-N-W—It has now for four of the past days, been as freezing pierceing cold, any four days I ever knew in any previous March—

Saturday 18th More moderate—Wind light, varying from N- to S-E—

Sabbath 19th Pleasent—Monday 20th & Tuesday 21st Moderate, and not cold—

[362] Thursday 23rd March 1848 A cloudy dark day, with rain occasionally—Wind E-N-E—Last evening was Married, John Brown Junr. to Betsey, the daughter of Wm. H. & Sophia Tuthill—

> It was at a weddings sacred hour
> The Saviour shewed Almighty power
> The waves & winds, to peace, he hushed,
> The Waters saw their God, & blushed.

Saturday 25th Weather much warmer than some days past—Hannah M. Brown left us for Southold—Our dear Grand daughter Maria L. Prince,

6th March 1848 Died Widow Phebe King aged 92 years & [?] months

with Walter, her brother, and her daughter Harriet, visited us this day—Walter goes home this evening—

We have Just heard of a revolution in France—It is said that the King and his household have fled—

Tuesday 28th A dark, cloudy day, with occasional light showers—Wind light E- N- E—

A man by name Ryly, Genl. Rily as he is called, Lectured in our Methodist church last Saturday Eve on Temperence—He certainly did the subject ample Justice—

Thursday 20th Friday 31st were pleasent days—One ½ of each of these days wrought on the highway—Joseph K. King, who many years since married Betsey, my wifes Sister, but has not lived with her for near 40 years, he was at my house this 30th is now in his 84th year—

Saturday 1st Apl 1848 A high S-W- wind & rain

Tuesday 4th A cloudy day, some little rain—Maria, our Grand daughter, with her daughter Harriet, left us for Southold

[363] Wednesday 5th Apl. 1848 As pleasent a day as any this Spring—wind light W—

Up to this day 10th Monday Apl. It has been warm, & pleasent—I have been setting out a dozen or more chery trees—My time of life induces me to plant trees, of which It is inconsistent to even think of ever seeing their fruits—well—I have planted I hope some virtuous ones will do me Justice, (if deserved,) reap the benifit—

Tuesday 11th & Wednesday 12th were clear and pleasent days—Thursday 13th & Friday 14th cloudy, and what some term sour, chilly days—Some little rain, which is much needed—wind variable, from N-E- to S-W—

Saturday 15th Pleasent—Sidney (our son) & wife, with their daughter Maria, Visited us this day—

Monday 17th Pleasent, with cool wind N-W—Took Sidney & his Family (as mentiond) to GreenPort, to the cars, this morn—

Wednesday 19th A cold E-N-E- storm, of high wind, with rain, hail and snow—

[364] Thursday 20th Apl. 1848 this morn the ground is covered with a light snow—It melts off pretty fast in the course of the Day-

Friday 21st But little snow to be seen this morn—Yet the west wind is cold—

Monday 24th Fresh breeze wind W—planted my peas—Planted 105 hills of potatoes about the 10th this month—

Thursday 27th Some rain last night, which the Earth very much needs— Now very narrow, limited, and contracted are our views of the goodness, and wisdom of Gods mercies towards us—

Friday 28th Cool E- wind—Our grand daughter Maria L. Prince & her Husband stoped with us about an hour this P.M.—

Wednesday 3rd May A cool N-N-E- wind—We had a copious rain all the past night—Considerable light rain through this day—Our friend N. Foster King visited us yesterday—

Saturday 6th foggy—Our Seines have taken since Monday 1st May—the Oregon and Genl. Jackson, about 25000 fish—

[365] Monday 8th May 1848 A warm S-S-W—The Jackson Seine took this Eve about 250000 fish (Boney)—John A. Racket arrived here from Philadelphia in his Schooner—

Thursday 11th A high N-E- Wind this morn, with a severe rain Storm & high tide—11 A.M. Wind changes to N-W—& It ceased raining—

Monday 15th Wind continues W-N-W—as It has been this 3 days—A part of that time It has been quite cool, & blustering—Unpleasent—

Thursday 18th The blustering W-N- Wind for several days past is dying away, & It appears to be growing warmer—

Friday 19th Quite warm, with wind S-S-W—Sam'l W. Hill was with us last Monday, an hour or so—On Tuesday 16th this Inst, Harriet, the wife of Wm. Webb, was confined with an infant son—

Sabbath 21st Wind E—cool—

Thursday 25th More mild, with very light wind S—It has been an Easterly cool wind this some days past—this Evening our Grandson Augustus R. Griffin came to us—

Friday 26th A rainy, squally morn with Thunder—

Saturday 27th Some rain last night—Wind S—Sabbath pleasent—

[366] Monday 29th May 1848 Wind brisk S-S-W—Tuesday 30th Rain last night, continues this day—Wind S-S-W—

Wednesday 31st Very blustering & cool wind W-N-W—Augustus R. G. our grandson I accompanied to Greenport, where he took the cars for Riverhead—

Friday 2nd June 1848 The severe W-N-W- wind, which was cool for June, appears to be dying away—this morn, Mrs. Mary Terry departed this life, after a painful Illness of three weeks—She died in the enjoyment of the Christians Triumphant Hope of a blessed immortality—At the time of her Death, she was the 2nd Wife of Elias Terry, who was her 2nd Husband—One being at the time of marying Mr. Terry, the widow of the late Phineas Brown—

Wrote this day to our son Sidney, and his son Chatham—

Thursday 8th Ocasional showers through the day—Wrote yesterday to Charles Tuthill, of the county of Yates Town of Starky—Son of Joshua Tuthill, formerly of this place—Charles was at my House in Apl 1845—

Saturday 10th It continues cool, & cloudy, as It has been, with occasional sprinkles of rain this some days past—We have had not any warm weather of note this spring—

[367] Our Son Sidney L. & wife, came to us yesterday 9th & to day, 10th, left for Hempstead—I accompanied them to Greenport—

Monday 12th June 1848 A very high W-N-W- wind & much cooler than common for June—

Tuesday 13th Continues cool, with wind as yesterday, and as brisk—Last Evening, Luther Tuthill was married to Polly Terry, daughter of Capt. John & Priscilla Terry, all of Orient—The Marriage ceremony was at, and in the Congregational Church—

Thursday 15th The violent W-N-W- wind which has continued blowing this 3 or 4 days past, has now died away, and this is a calm one, and warm—

Saturday 17th Very warm—Rode to Greenport, where I met N.T. Hubbard, Wife, & son Cyrus—took them in my carriage with me to my family, which gave us all a joyful meeting—

Monday 19th took our above mentioned friends to Greenport this morn where I parted with them in the rail cars in which they proceeded to New York—

Tuesday 20th Some little rain, which is much needed—Yesterday, on my arrival home from Greenport, I met with our cousin Hannah L. Brown, wife of Benjamin Brown Esq.—She stayed with [us] until 5 P.M. when she left us—

[368] June 30th 1848 some rain last night, with thunder—It has been very dry this two weeks past—A Mr. Jagger, from South Hampton is with us taking likenesses, by Daugertypes [daguerreotypes]—

July 1st (Saturday) Last night, was marked with as copious a rain, as is seldom known—It, for two or 3 hours, appeared to pour down almost in torrents, attended with heavy thunder—

This eve Walter O. Hubbard, with his affectionate Wife (our endearing Granddaughter Harriet Matilda,) their little son, and nurse, came to us—The meeting was a Joyful one, abundantly so, to their Grand parents—

From the 1st to the 3rd (Monday) It has [been], and is cloudy, Foggy, damp weather, with wind N-E—

July 5th Wednesday, Pleasant—Waited on Walter O. Hubbard & family to Greenport, where they will take the Cars on the rail for Hempstead tomorrow—On the next day they leave Hempstead for N.Y.—

Saturday 8th was visited this evening by our affectionate Grandson, John Augustus Preston, from whom we have not had a visit since October 1846—

Tuesday 11th James H. Preston, Johns Brother came to us—In the evening they, John A. and James H, left for Greenport

[369] July 20th 1848 Alanson B. Webb arrived home last week—He having been absent since October 1844 on a whaling Voyge—The weather these some days past very warm—the weather up to July 29th was mildly warm—some high S-S-W- winds—We have had from 2 to 7 boarders this 9 weeks past

30th & 31st July—wind E- with some little rain—On the 24th & 25th we had fine Showers, which were much needed—

August—Tuesday 8th Sidney P. Racket, in the Schooner BonaVista sailed for the State of Maine, to get a Cargo of Lumber

On the 11th Messrs. Dobbs and Joseph Johns stoped a short time with us—They were with us in 1842—& several Augusts since that date—they have stoped with us a short time—

Monday 14th A fine shower, which is much needed—Not any rain since 25th July—On the 12-13th & 14th we had a moderate Easterly wind—On the 12th of this month, It was Just 49 years since I commenced teaching a School near now what is called Greenport—See my diary of that date—

From 7th of this August to the 18th It was very close warm weather—this day 19th It is some cooler with wind N-E—

We were quite disappointed at our Grandson Chathams not visiting us this week, as he had informed us we might expect him—We feel more painful as thus far he has been an affectionate Grand child—We know not the present cause—

On the 18th I rode to Greenport with Alanson B. Webb—

[370] Tuesday 22nd August 1848 Wind continues Easterly, and some Cooler—Our Chatham, with his Uncle George Williams came to us Saturday 19th Eve—

Wednesday 23rd Wind yet Easterly, and very dry—Departed this life, last evening Capt. Gamaliel King, aged 63 years—He was a man rich in the Faith of the gospel of our Lord Jesus Christ—His life was truly the life of the righteous, and his Death was triumphant in the Joyous hope of a Glorious Immortality—

> "There sits the dear departed Saint,
> There rests the Father, Husband, brother, Friend,
> Then let us cease the sad complaint,
> Or mingled with our sighs, let notes of praise ascend"

Monday 28th Chatham & his uncle George Willams left us for their homes—N.Y.—& Hempstead—

Tuesday 29th Light wind S—It has been on the Easterly board almost the whole time since the 12th Just—On this day Wednesday 30th Our Grand daughter Emily McNeil left us for her home in Williamsburgh N.Y.—She has been with us about 3 weeks—

[371] Wednesday 6th Septem. 1848 Pleasant, but very dry—this Eve we were visited by our truly kind, affectionate and beloved daughter, Cleora, who with her Husband, James McNeil Intend us a kind visit of some week, or two—The weather is very dry—Seldom more so—

Saturday 9th A small, but refreshing shower this Eve—

15th Friday to 18th was Easterly, and squally weather—A good round rain on the night of the 17th—on the 15th Cleora (our daughter) with her Husband left for Williamsburgh N.Y.—The weather has been cool for a number of days past—

Septem. Tuesday 19th Wilcox & all his Family Went to Madison (Connecticut) to accompany his Cousin Elizabeth Nash, who paid him a visit of 3 days—She lives in Vermont—Is on a visit to her friends at Madison & Newhaven—Wilcox and family returned home this day 21st—

Sabbath 24th This eve John Beulah was married to Esther Tuthill of Orient—Wednesday 27th Some frost this evening—the first this Autumn—

Monday Oct. 2nd 1848 An easterly storm—received a letter from Chatham last Eve—This storm continued heavy untill 4th

[372] Saturday 7th Oct. 1848 Wilcox, & Son Goodridge, set off for NewYork—Saturday 14th Cool, with Wind N-E—The weather has been cool this week past—Potatoes are selling with us in Orient by the quantity for 75 Cents per bushel—It is said there is more than 10000 bushels in the place for Sale—T.V. Tuthill has raised over (as It is said) 900 bushels

Thursday 9th [an error] Oct. Yesterday & to day, Is a storm of rain—Wind E—

Tuesday 17th Benjamin Browns daughters, Hannah M. and Sarah J. was with us a few hours—the last one has her husband with her—his name is ___ Mowbrey—

Thursday 19th Weather midling cool, and windy this some days past—some rain ocasionally—of course the ground is sufficiently wet—This day, our Son Sidney & wife visited us—

Saturday 21st waited on our Son & wife to Greenport, on their way to their home, as they take the Cars for Hempstead—

Sabbath November 5th A very blustering day, Wind S-E- with rain—

[373] Died Friday 3rd, very suddenly, Mrs. Hetty Moore, widow of the late Mr. Shadrach Moore. She was about 70 years of Age—

Sabbath 12th Novem. 1848 A rain storm Friday last—that is the 10th Inst—Our friend Benjamin King (brother to the late Edward C. King) made us a short visit—

I received a letter from our brother Samuel C. Griffin, yesterday 11th

Wednesday 15th Marvin Holms (our Storekeeper) moved the Select Schoolhouse to a place opposite his House, on the west side of the road—He has purchased the Schoolhouse of the owners, which was in Shares—

Saturday 18th Wind N—and Cloudy—Henry Dyer, In the Sloop Oddfellow, left for N.York, yesterday, with potatoes, and turnips

Monday 20th Commences with pretty smart N-E- Snowstorm—the snow drives in banks—of course It makes but poor Sleighing—

Up to this day, Thursday 30th Nov., the weather has been moderate, wind light, some Evenings calm—Wind today rather fresh S-W—

Finished family Record for John A. Racket, this morn—Received a letter last week from Brother Samuel Caddle, who now lives in Newburgh—

[374] Saturday 2nd Decem. 1849 A fresh breeze wind S—Some rain—Came to our house last evening, our great grand daughter Mary Preston, the very interesting Child of Samuel Griffin, of Riverhead, and his invaluable late wife, who was our grand daughter Deziah, the daughter of James and Deziah Preston of Orient—This little prepossessing pratler is now four years of age, and is an affecting, impressing likeness of her Justly esteemed and greatly beloved mother, whose virtues, and sterling accomplishments, will be held in cherished, sweet remembrance by her numerous friends, until they Join her in those regions of immortal Friendship—She, Mary, is

under the kind and fostering tender charge of her Aunt Mehitable Griffin, whose attentions are marked with the most tenderest solicitude for her innocent charge—

Died about 2 weeks ago Moses Cleveland Esq. aged about 80 years or near that—In 1781 & 2 he was a Schoolmate of mine at Southold where my Father lived at the time

Thursday 14th Decem. A cloudy, what is called uncomfortable damp weather—It has been moderate, with occasional Showers, and wind varying from E- to W- this 10 days past—Henry Hayns, and David Edwards wives have been confined with each an Infant, Boys—

Saturday 16th Cloudy, wind E—Yesterday our Brother James Griffin was with us some time—Wrote to George S. Williams, and Sidneys daughter yesterday

[375] Thursday 21st Decem. 1848—this afternoon, we have quite a E-N-E- Snowstorm—It commenced snowing about 10 OClock P.M.—Continued moderately untill Friday 22nd—We received an agreable letter from our Grand daughter Harriet M. Hubbard—It states that they are all in Health—Agreable news

Sabbath 24th Excellent sledding

Monday 25th A dense fogg—Wind S—occasional showers—A truly shady day—1848 years since the glorious Morn on which the Angels sung "Glory to God on the highest, peace on Earth and good will towards Man"—

I have this two days past had a very Ill turn of the bowel complaint—truly a warning to a Man of fourscore—Alas now they are gone, they do appear as short as one—

Vanity is written in letters, which stand out in bold relief, on all terrestrial things, but Man is so infatuated with the bubbles of the moment that he pays no attention to those charracters, though they are inscribed with a pen of Iron—

Wednesday 27th This P.M. It snows moderately, Wind light S-S-E—Some Rain yesterday

Friday 29th Morn, wind S-E—P.M. N- with moderate Snow—It continued snowing, hailing and raining, until Saturday 30th—

Monday 11th Decem. Emma Wilcox commenced going to School in my [illegible] days she attended—[cross-hatched: 12] 12th today

1849

Monday 1st Jan. 1849—Not a very cold day—This day my brother James is 84 years of age-

Tuesday 2nd & Wednesday 3rd—Extreme cold weather—

[376] Thursday 4th Jan. 1849 Very cold with high wind N-W- Saturday received a letter from our Son Sidney, at that time all well—

Monday 8th The extreme high wind, with its intense cold, has much subsided—sleighing is yet pretty good—It is an Icy time—Two women in Sagharbour have fell while walking the streets, and broke each a leg, as we understand—The ground being covered with Ice—

From the 8th to the 13th It was extreme cold—This day Saturday 13th the weather is rather softer, with wind light S-S-W—and cloudy—Wrote a Letter to A. Tompkins Brown of Hamtonburgh, Orange County—and one to our kind and affectionate Daughter Cleora, now in Williamsburg, near NewYork—Our Harbour pretty much shut up with Ice—

Monday 15th Yesterday, High wind S- with considerable rain about 2 OClock A.M.—this Morn is a Cloudy one with wind N—some little hail— Weather cool, and blustering until Sabbath 21st, when It became more mild. Little or no frost on the 22nd-23rd 24th 25th & 26th—This Friday Eve we have a brisk W- wind—

At this time, (and It has been so for 2 months past) the whole Northern & middle States, perhaps I might say all North America, are aroused and astonished at the news of Gold, found in profusion in California—Thousands have gone, and tens of thousands are going to procure that root of all Evil.

[377] Saturday 27th Jan. 1849—Weather moderate—Wind W—Very little Frost this some days past—Rec'd a letter this day from our Grandson Chatham A.G.—now in N-Y—

Monday 29th Some rain, with wind S—

Tuesday 30th A.M. rain—P.M. partially clears off—It ceased raining— continued dark & cloudy—A fair at our house—Its probable over 100 Men, women, with boys & girls attended—they took in near 70 Dolls—Broke up about 2 OClock in the Morning of the 31st—

Company so late, is not very pleasent to us, now over fourscore, especially Mrs. Griffin, who continues greatly afflicted, with a Cough of 5 or 6 years, with but little abatement—She has other accute distresses, and pains, which greatly affect her strength, and Spirits—Once a flower of conspicuous radiance, and perfume, now faded by time, decay and fell disease—"All, all on Earth Is Shadow"—

Thursday 1st February 1849—Commences with moderate Snowstorm— Wind light S-E—Yesterday, our Friend, Foster King, stoped with us an hour—He has been stoping in Orient this six months

Friday 2nd Cloudy, with some Snow, and rain—I am this day 82 years of age—Astonishing for our young men to look at! Yet fourscore years, when they are gone, Now appear as lost as one—Eternal Truth says, "This is not the place of your rest"—

Monday 5th Commences with a Snowstorm—Wind light N—Rec'd Letters from Our children at Hempstead—[illegible] Of course they think they have yet time enough—

[378] February 6th 1849 Pleasent—Excellent sleighing—A level snow, evens the ground from 4 to 6 inches—The papers Just inform me of the Death of Julia Seward, of Goshen, Orange County—I knew her as a single woman, when I lived in that County in 1794 and 6—She was the youngest daughter of Capt. Phineas Rumsey, who is noted in my 2nd Journal, page 73rd—It was on March 1795—Miss Julia was aimable, and was esteemed as a fine young Woman, well calculated for a respectable situation—She Married Doctor Daniel Seward, a Physician, well approved of in Orange County—He died some years since—Died at Montrose, State of Pennsylvania, Mrs. Francis Lucella Reid, the daughter of Elisha & Fanny Mulford, of this place (Orient)—She was aimable, accomplished, and greatly beloved, as daughter, wife, neighbour, and acquaintance—She died in strong faith of a blissful immortality. Aged 31 years—She leaves a husband & 2 children—

Thursday 8th Cold—light wind S-S-W—Died at Greenport on Tuesday 6th Mr. John Beckwith, formerly of Lyme, Connecticut but of late years of Greenport—Mr. Beckwith was the Son of the late Col. Watros Beckwith of Lyme—The son John has been rather unfortunate in his buisness, and for [379] some of the last years of his life he appeared something like a disappointed Man—In his deportment, and movements in life, he was much of the gentleman—But he has gone, and very sudden, with but a day or two sickness, to a World where sickness, sorrow, nor reverses of fortune are ever known—his age was 57—

Friday 9th High wind W—Chancy W. Moore called on us a few minutes this day—

The Ship Sabin, sailed from Greenport last Wednesday 7th for California, after Gold—The company of adventurers in said Ship are from Sagharbour, Southold and the adjoining Towns—Henry Green, a former Whaling captain has charge of the Ship—Her Voyge is intended for two years—at, or before that time their success in the undertaking will be known—

Monday 12th February 1849—Commences with a N-E- Snowstorm—Tuesday 13th This morn is clear, cold with a large quantity of Snow on the

Earth—Of course the sleighing is good—Horses may view It not so good for their ease—

Thursday 15th Extreme cold—A court of inquiry, at my house to see to the situation of our cousins Shadrach & Cynthia Terry, who for some time have been unfit to take care of themselves—A Jury of 24 Men advise the Town to act for them—[380] Joseph Hull Goldsmith Esq. was employed as Councillor in the proceedings of chuseing two trustees to superintend the property, and care of providing for our Cousins, before mentioned. Mr. Goldsmith is the Son of my late, deservedly esteemed friend Zacheus Goldsmith.

Sabbath 18th Feb. Continues very cold—With the exception of now & then a day of moderately mild weather, It has been a severely cold, freezing time—Our harbour has been partially closed this 6 or 7 weeks with Ice, yet not of sufficient thickness to bear walking on It any distance from the shore—wind this some days from the cold North—We hear that Mr. McNeil sailed for California, on the 8th of this Inst—

Thursday 20th It is yet very cold—Extremely so last night—Almost calm to day, and cloudy—Sleighing is very good, and has been so (except for a day or two) this six weeks past—

N.T. Hubbards daughter Julia Augusta was married to a Mr. Francis H. Salstus, on the 6th of this month—

Wednesday 21st Scarce any wind, and weather more mild—

Friday 25th A thaw, or melting off of the Snow—Our daughter Cleora McNeil came to us this day, to administer to her very sick Mother—She was much needed.

Saturday 24th A hard N-E- rainstorm—

[381] Feb. 28th Wednesday 1849—Yesterday & to days weather much the same—Cloudy—with a raw N- Wind, yet not so cold as to freeze—The streets are clothed with mud, & melting Snow—Uncomfortable traviling—Truely bad—

March 1st 1849 Cold N- wind—

Sabbath 4th—Weather Cloudy—Chilly, and what is called uncomfortable—above & below—Early this morn, Departed this life Mrs. Mary Spicer, the daughter of the Late David & Hannah Pool—She was an aimable, industrious, pious Woman—A valuable wife, dutiful daughter, and a Christian—Aged 28 years—Her Husband, who appears to be a mourner indeed, is by name Austin Spicer, an industrious, inoffensive, peaceable Citizen—

Wednesday 7th Weather much as some days past—chilly winds, and such melting of the snowbanks as to make the walking very bad—mud & mire—

50 years this day since we moved into this our house, which was then new—That term appears, now Its past, to have gone like a dream—With its passed years, what a multitude of our fellow mortals have gone with them!

Monday 12th March 1849 Our dear daughter Cleora McNeil left us for Williamsburg—She has been with us since 25th Feb—She has been with us since but now must leave us from [illegible]

[382] Wednesday 14th March 1849 Wind S—And cloudy—The two past days 12th & 13th have been more Spring like than any previous ones this season—

Alanson B. Webb, (our Esteemed young friend) sailed for California about the 10th or 11th—

15th wet, or drizzly day—Wind East this 3 days past—

Saturday 17th Moderate—Wind light S-W—Spring begins to open her cheering affect—

Sabbath 18th Wind N—Cloudy—My dear wife has this 4 weeks past been quite feeble, remains much so—

21st March 1849 Last night and this morn was and is a severe South rain and wind storm—About midnight It blew a tremendous gale—Our Grand daughter Mariah Prince is with us—Came yesterday with her brother Walter and their Mother in law—

Friday 23rd March a cold N-E- Wind—___ Booth Esq from Goshen, Orange County, stoped with us an hour or two—His visit was to ascertain, who was the first of his family that came to this country from Europe, and when they came—From [?] records, and other sources, he says he now believes John Booth, who landed at Southold about 1656, was the Father of his family, now in & about Orange County, and those with us on Longisland

[383] With this gentleman, I was much pleased—In his manners, address, and conversation he was agreable, and pleasing—More than 50 years ago, when I lived in Orange County, I knew some of the family—They were respectable and good farmers—He, I suppose was at the time an Infant—His aunt Polly, then a young interesting Woman, was Married in 1791 to Samuel Watkins, a Young Man of a good family—

Monday 26th March—Wind E—a rain and Snow storm—

Tuesday 27th The ground covered with Snow—Cold N- wind—It rained all through this profusely—Wednesday Morn, about 1 Oclock It blew almost a hurricane—Jefferson Youngs's barn Is this morn much blown to pieces—that is unroofed, and otherwise injured—Wind this day more moderate, but cool from N—Sidney P. Racket sails for N-Y- In the fine Schooner Robert Bruce this P.M.—

Friday 30th Cool, with wind N-E—as It has been near that point this 10 days past—My wife is more comfortable than 7 or 8 weeks agone—Continues weak, but her distress in body has much subsided—

[384] April 1st 2nd & 3rd were cool, with wind E- & N-E- except Tuesday 3rd towards Evening It changed to S-S-W—The Nights of said time have been quite uncomfortably cold—

Tuesday 10th Wind E—cool—Received a letter from Chatham (our Grandson) last Friday 6th—Wrote him yesterday, (Monday 9th)—Mrs. Griffin continues quite feeble, as she has been this 2 months past—to appreciate my mercies—

Wednesday 11th Apl A rain storm last night—this morn a cool, brisk N-W- Wind—

Saturday 14th Sabbath 15th & Monday 16th Apl 1849 the wind blew a gale from W-N-W—and a part of time N-W- with very cold weather—Ice made past Nights, and in the shade through the day—We seldom experience three days of such high, and cold Winds, in Apl—

Sabbath 22nd A cloudy day—Wind light from the Eastern board—From the 16th to this 22nd It has been chilly, unpleasent weather, with cold nights—

My wife, who from extreme weakness has not been able to walk this 2 months, remains much as weeks past—To appearances, as her weakness does not seem to increase much, she may continue in her debilitated state some time, and need that attention which she Justly merits from her friends, and surely from her children—

[385] Sabbath 29th Apl 1849—Pleasant—Thus far, the Spring has been as cold as any have known this many years—There has been three houses built in this vilage within the 4 months past—viz. one for Henry Hayns—ditto for David Vail—and ditto for Ezra K. Youngs—

Within the last week I have received Letters from Son Sidney & Grandson Chatham—

From Tuesday 1st of May 1849 to the 10th Thursday, It was cold, cloudy, Easterly weather—What is Justly called unpleasent sour air—We had a visit last Tuesday 8th from Thomas M. Perry, and his wife Jerusha—Who was the daughter of the late Joshua & Mehitable Hobart of this place, Orient—Mr. Perry now resides in the State of Michigan—Is a Man of a good mind, much esteemed and Justly—Is a Printer by profession, but now is prosperously in other buisness—

[386] Saturday 12th May 1849 Wind fresh from E-N-E—It has now been from near that quarter, since the 8th—Died Yesterday, a very interesting child, a Son of William and Harriet Webb, died, aged about 12 months—

This Eve Sidney (our Son) and Margeret (his wife) arrived at our house—He found his affectionatest of Mothers very sick & feeble—

Monday 14th This eve, Sidney & Margeret left for Hempstead—Weather this two or 3 days past more mild—On the 11th Friday we had a severe E-rain Storm—

Friday 18th At 30 minutes past 12 OClock P.M. my Wife—The invaluable Wife of my Youth and old age, departed this Life—Alas with her has gone all my Earthly rational enjoyments—My time of life warns me of but a short sojourn in the world she has now left forever—A more tender, affectionate companion, never died—

> "When ever I was in pain she felt the smart,
> If but my finger ached It pained my [her] heart"

Thursday 24th Wind E—& cool—Cleora, our daughter, and Chatham, Grandson are both with us—

[387] On 21st May 1849 The funeral of my dear Lucretia was attended by a large number of friends and aquaintances—The Rev. Daniel Beers, made an affectionate and moveing address from these words, viz. "Why should we mourn"—

Tuesday 25th With my Daughter Cleora and grandson Chatham A. Griffin, I left Orient and took the Cars for Hempstead, where we arrived about 4 OClock P.M.—found our Son Sidney, and family, all well—From 26th the first of June the wind was Easterly—cold, very damp, and dark weather—Thus situated, amid intire strangers, (with exception of my Son & family) with a grief no tongue can express, I passed a week at Hempstead—[388] While at Hempstead, I became acquainted with a very aimable, and Industrious young Man, [superscript- Bartlet?] who is studying law, with my Son—I think him a young man of promise, and one that will escape the innumerable paths in which very many of our tallented young Men proceed to swift destruction

June 1st I rode, in the Cars, (Sidney & Wife with me) to Brooklin [Brooklyn]—crosst to N-Y—and then crosst again to Williamsburgh to my daughter Cleora—With her, I could find some small relief in weeping our irreparable loss—With Watts, I say of my late dear companion

> She was my guide, my friend, my earthly all
> Love grew with every waning moon
> Had Heaven a length of years delayed the call
> Still I had thought it called to[o] soon—

[389] June 2nd 1849 Visited N-Y- City 2 or 3 hours—While there called on Mr. R. Williams & family—

Sabbath 3rd At Williamsburgh—Attended Church, twice—

Tuesday 5th Visited N.T. Hubbard, tarried with him the night—

Wednesday 6th Took passage, by steamboat for Newburgh, where I arrived about 9 p.m. and stoped the night—

Thursday 7th about 5 A.M. rode to David Cooley, 3 ½ miles, where I met our Sister Betsey King, who is a Widow of great trials, but of sound faith in the promises of the Goodness of God—Evening rode to Rensaler Howels— [390] At Howels, met our other sister Hannah Howel—those two sisters met me with much sympathy, and we wept, for our late bereavement, which may god in his great mercy sanctify for my Eternal good—

Friday 8th some rain, wind S-S-E—

Saturday 9th Bejamin Brown Esq. & wife Visited Howels—with them, at 6 P.M. rode to Hamptonburgh—

Sabbath 10th Rode out, 3 miles, with Doct. Tompkins Brown—A.M. It rained—Wind E-S-E—

Monday June 11th Rode,with Squire Brown, to the Village of Goshen, which is much enlarged [391] and improved since my residence in this part of the Country, from 1789 to 1797—The land remains, but its then owners have nearly all gone to that bourn whence no traviler returns—While out on this ride, we called on Judge Booth—Gen'l Abraham Vail, who is about 79 years of age—Called on James Dur[y]ea, aged 73—On Ruth Coleman, Widow, in her 78th—On Saml. Moffat, 70 years—Joseph Moffat 66 years— On Jonathan Owen, 70 years—John Decker, aged 73 years—Joseph Decker 63 years—returned to Squire Brown 7 P.M.—having rode near 25 miles—

Tuesday 12th Walked out with Squire [392] B. Brown to the residence of the late Calvin Steward, whose Widow, is yet living, at the advanced age of 91—She is of good health, and Spirits, with her mental faculties unimpaired—Her name Anna—Her Sister Dolly, the Widow of the late Hezekiah Watkins—She was 93 years old last Jan—She is well and bright, and would be good company was It not for her deafness—It is very difficult to converse with her—She was now with her sister Anna—These two old Ladies are great grand daughters to John Tuthill, late of Orient, who was known as Squire John—Chalker John, etc.—He is mentioned in Thompsons History of LongIsland—

[393] Widow Ruth Coleman, noticed in page 391 is grand daughter to James Tuthill, who settled in Orange County in 1749—He was grandson to John Tuthill, of the oppisite page—

Friday 15th rode out with Doct. Tompkins Brown to PhilipsVille near MiddleTown—Was agreably entertained at the house of Mr. Walter Moore—Mrs. Moore, Dolly, was daughterinlaw to my late friend Constant Terry—She, and her Son paid me every attention for my comfort—Returned to Squire Browns about 6 P.M. having rode over 20 miles—

I should have observed that on Thursday 14th I was at the House of a Mr. Hulse, whose very aimable and accomplished Wife is the Mother of three pretty girls, born at one birth—they were 4 years old on the 13th Inst—their names are Sarah Augusta—Catherine Pamela, and Mary Isabel—

[394] Saturday 16th June 1849—rode about 4 miles to the residence of Mr. Ebenezer Bull, a grandson to the aged Mrs. Bull, mentioned In Edgars history of Goshen, (Orange County)—She died in 1796 aged over 102 years—Mr. Bull shewed me marked civility, and entertained us with interesting observations of his grandmother, and her family—She was the first white woman that came to this part of the Country—He shewed me her grave—The house, in which Mr. Bull lives is of Stone, and was built in 1721—The old Lady lived in It 75 years, when she died—Her name was Sarah, born 1694—died 1796, and as before observed died in her 103rd year

[395] Mr. Bull, has a very agreable family—an accomplished wife, with well behaved sons and daughters—This Eve, took an affectionate leave of Squire Brown, and his very dear family, and rode to Rensaler Howels—

Sabbath 17th Clear weather—I must acknowledge, I received the most interesting attentions from Squire B. Brown, his good Wife, daughters Hannah M., Fanny & Sarah, likewise Henry, and Doct. Tompkins B.—this last most aimable of Young Men appeared to make It his pleasure to contribute to my comfort the whole of my sojourn with them—

Monday 18th Very warm—Visited the residence of the late Charles Howel—This [396] House was once a respectable Inn, Kept, by our Brotherinlaw the late Silas Howel, and his distinguished excellent wife, our Sister Hannah—Here was the stoping place of the Governors Tompkins,

Dewitt Clinton, and other Officers of consideration—Alas! The change! Five orphan children now occupy the dwelling, as a private, secluded situation—3 pretty daughters—eldest 18 years—2nd 16—3rd 6 years—two boys 12 & 9 years—

Wednesday Took an impressive leave of our Sister Hannah Howel—and rode to David Cooleys—weather very warm—

21st at Mr. Cooleys—

Friday 22nd After takeing an affectionate leave of our [397] dear Sister Betsey King, her daughter Mrs. Cooley, and Amanda, their kind and attentive daughter, with two pretty sons, I rode, with Mr. Cooley, to Newburgh, where I met my brother Samuel C. Griffin, and his good wife—I acknowledge with thanks Mr. Cooleys civilities, which to me, situated as my mind is, were in true time—He has my best desires, with his kind family—

At parting with Sister Betsey, we found relief in weeping, but not with out hope—Saturday 23rd extreme warm

Sabbath 24th With my Brother, attended meeting—In the course of the day & night I heard four Sermons, at 4 different Churches, and as many different Denominations—

[398] Monday 25th June 1849 At one P.M. left my kind Brother Samuel & wife, and took passage on board the Steamer New World (which is 300 feet long) for New York, where I arrived about 5 P.M.—Walked across the City, to Grand street fer[r]y, crosst to Williamsburgh, found Cleora (our daughter) quite sick—

26th Weather not so intense warm as some days past—

Thursday 28th visited N.T. Hubbard—met there with our dear and much loved grand daughter Harriet M. Hubbard—She is very weak with a slow decline, yet a confirmed consumption—Our interview was impressive—

Friday 29th visited Ludice Dayton (our niece)—stoped this & the last night with N.T.H

[399] Saturday 30th rode round the City with Mr. Hubbard—Evening, crosst the Ferry to Cleoras—

Sabbath 1st July attended meeting Morning & Eve

Monday 2nd Visited Wilkies family, and other friends in the City—

Tuesday 3rd Its getting quite dry—

Wednesday 4th July—A warm day—with a Mr. Navis, a Gentleman of about my age, I visited the Navy yard, at Brooklin—Took an earnest Observation of the Dry Dock, which is now in rapid progress of completion, having a large number of Men employed on It—I think It the most expensive, and greatest piece of work I ever see except the high bridge, or coffer Dam, at Harlem—

Thursday 5th Warm & Dry—

[400] Friday 6th July 1849 At 8 A.M. I took leave of my affectionate Cleora & family, at Williamsburgh, and set off for Hempstead—stoped at Brooklin, and took dinner with Madison Griffin, after which I took passage in the Hempstead Stage, where I arrived about 6 P.M.—found Sidney, & family, well—

Sabbath 8th Attended Meeting—

Tuesday 10th Visited a Mrs. Clouse, Mrs. Thompson, Mrs. Gildersleves, & Doct. Webb—

Wednesday 11th Left Hempstead and took the rail Cars for Riverhead—

Thursday 12th Stoped last night with Mrs. Wells Griffin—Was much gratified with our little interesting great grand daughter, Mary Griffin, daughter to my [401] late greatly, and Justly beloved grand daughter, Deziah Preston Griffin, the worthy wife of Capt. Samuel Griffin—Our Son Sidney, has two Children boarding at Riverhead—viz. Augustus R. & Maria Louisa—

Friday 13th rode in a private carriage to Southold—took Dinner at Ezra Terry's Esq—He is now very low with the dropsy consumption—Stoped with my dear a[nd] kind Grand daughter, Maria, and her accommodating Husband, Orin Prince—

Saturday 14th Our Cousin Ezra Terry died 2 OClock this morn—He was truly a valuable member of Society—A kind Husband, and beloved Father—aged __

Sabbath 15th Returned home after an absence of about 8 weeks—

[402] Returning home

> Yes to the land, I once did tread,
> I bend my weary steps once more
> Where Hills, and dales, now overspred
> The Bays, and plains, that stretch before.
>
> Passion is dim, forlorn is hope,
> Thought deepens o'er my saddened brow,
> What is there, too, my spirits drop
> When what was love is memory now—

From the 1st of July to the 28th It has continued to grow dry—

Saturday 21st Last night, and this morn, a pretty reviving rain—Wind

S—howsomever, the ground is so dry , that our Farmers say the rain does not wet the ground but about 2 inches deep, and It will dry out in a day or two of sunshine—

Thursday 26th Sidney, (our Son) came down last eve—left this morn for Hempstead—some rain this evening—

Friday 27th Went to Sagharbour for the first time this 15 years—

[403] Monday 30th July 1849—Weather, very warm, and extremely dry—spent most of this day at Greenport—dined with, at Brinzon B. Wiggins's—Returned home about 6 P.M.—

This day, at near 10 A.M. Died Mrs. Lydia Youngs, Widow of the late Capt. Jeremiah Youngs—She was to the letter, the invaluable Wife, Mother, Daughter, Neighbour & Friend—yes, the Christian—Her age 78 years—

Wednesday 1st August 1849—this Morn we had a refreshing rain, with wind N-E—It finally proved to be but a moderate rain, not sufficient to wet the very dry ground more than an Inch or two—

Friday 3rd A publick fast, requested by the President of U.S.—Orient Sunday Scholars went to Shelterisland yesterday, [en mass?]—Took Dinner in the grove—

[404] Friday 10th August 1849 A very refreshing rain this Evening, attended with some Thunder & lightning—It is the first rain, sufficient to wet the ground, we have had in Orient this two months—

Monday 13th August—Pleasant—walked in company with our Grand daughter, Harriet McNeil to Peter W. Tuthills—on our way called on Mrs. Jeremiah Hobart—Nath'l Tuthill—Mrs. Patty Terry—John B. Youngs—Elisha Mulford—and Widows Sally King & Prudence Petty—Stoped the night with P.W.T—

Tuesday Dined with my sister Lucinda Tuthill, after which we called on David Terry, widow Maria Terry, and Daniel Beebe—Stoped the night with Joseph Latham—

[405] Wednesday 15th August 1849—Returned home about 4 P.M. where I agreably met my affectionate daughter Cleora & Emily, her daughter—It rained some Tuesday night—

Friday 17th wrote to Chatham A. In answer to his of the 9th last—Was called on this day by Green M. Tuthill, of Elmira, Tioga County N.Y.—This Mr. Tuthill is Great grandson to James Mentioned in my first Journal, page 151—

Monday 20th Pleasant, but dry weather, having not had a rain sufficient to thoroughly wet the ground since last May—Was visited this day by our cousin

Sally Bartholomew of Hartford with her son James, & daughter Harriet—
This Lady is mentioned in my first Journal, page 22—They left Tuesday 28th
for their home, Hartford—Frederick Dobbs of N.York was at my house a
short time—this gentleman has visited us once a year this some years—

[406] Thursday 30th August 1849 Very warm, as It has been this some
days past—the disentary prevails much in this place Just now—A child,
son Gilbert of Jeremiah Youngs, about 4 or 5 years old died this day—a
daughter of Zilla Youngs, Mary, 2 years old died within a few hours of the
other—Friday 31st this morn a Mr. Stantons Child died—a daughter, nearly
2 years old—

This day we had a copious rain, with brisk wind from E-N-E—I was
introduced to Mr. Ladd, a Minister of the Baptist order, residing
Sagharbour—To appearance and address, I should think him deserving the
respectful consideration of the good & benevolent—

September 2nd died last night Edward, the Son of Samuel Tabor, [407]
aged about eleven years—A very promising, pleasent child—

Monday 3rd Septem. Pleasent Wind light S-E—Wm. H. Wilcox arrived
home from Bangor, State of Maine—He has been absent three Weeks—

Wednesday 5th Rain this morn, wind E—Thursday 6th Wind continues
Easterly—Allen Tuthill's son, aged 3 years old, and James R Glovers Son
Howard, aged about 2 years—Both died this day with the Disentary—

Monday 10th, Wind E—Died last night about 11 OClock Benedic B. Havens
aged ___ years—An industrious, peaceable, quiet neighbour—an invaluable
husband and tender Father of three children, with a Wife to mourn this sudden
departure—Sick about 6 days with disentary—Died this morn Francis, Son
of Lewis A. Beach, aged about 16 years—with the above said illness—

[408] Thursday 13th Septem. 1849—The wind which has been nearly all
the time or 3 weeks past, is very light from the S-S-W—I visited Greenport
this day, where I gladly met my old friend, Frederick Chase Esq—

A daughter of Mr. Francis Hill, a Methodist Minister, died last evening
about 10 OClock—aged four years—

Saturday 15th Calm weather—Received letters from our Cousins Mrs.
Bartholomew, and son James, who were with us in August, some days—

Tuesday 18th Some rain last eve—Wind this day W—Sidney P. Racket, in
the Schooner Robert Bruce, left for Philadelphia

21st Friday, Septem. An infant daughter of ___ Coffin, died, aged about
7 month—Ann Eliza by name

22nd Wind to day as 3 or 4 days past E—

[409] Monday 24th Sept. 1849 High wind N-W—as It was yesterday—Rode out to Greenport, this A.M. with our daughter Cleora. On our return, called on my Brother James. He is yet unwell, but hope as comfortable as sometime past—

Tuesday 25th Wind W—Cleora (our daughter) and her two children, Harriet & Emily, left us this P.M. They go to Greenport, from which they take passage in the Sloop Swallow Ben. Hills Master—

Wednesday 26th Wind N-W—died this, a daughter of David Edwards, Aged 3 years, name Arrabella—Likewise a Child of Smith Dewy, a son about 2 years of age—name ___

Friday 28th wrote to J.H. Goldsmith Esq.—Sidney P. Racket arrived home 28th Friday

Monday 1st Oct. 1849 A severe N-E- rainstorm—died this day Capt. Noah G. Beebe, aged ___ An oblidging, kind, good Man—he was son to Noah Beebe, see first Journal page 143—

[410] Wednesday 3rd Oct. 1849 Cloudy, Wind E-N-E—Died, the 1st of this week, a daughter of Thomas Pool, about a year old

Thursday 4th An Easterly rainstorm—Died last Saturday 29th Sept. Mrs. Cynthia King, widow of the late Capt. Frederick King—She was an affectionate, virtuous, faithful Wife, and Christian—Aged 78 years—

Saturday 6th Rain last night, and continued to storm through the day, Wind E—

Sabbath 7th A cold, wet, moderately stormy day, wind N-N-E—An Englishman by Name Flint—A Baptist priest—stops with us to night—wind continued Easterly until this morn Thursday 11th when It changed to Westerly, with an hour or two of rain—

Rev. Daniel Beers is appointed Post Master at our Orient—Joseph Terry Esq. is removed from the office he had held near 30 years—

11th cold—Rec'd a letter from Cleora—

[411] Monday 15th Oct. 1849 A white frost to be seen this morn—the first this autumn with us. I wrote to Brother Sam'l C. G. last Saturday—

Wednesday 17th Weather moderate, wind light S—Wrote by Sidney P. Racket to Cleora.

Died this Morn, Fanny, the widow of the late Lemuel Youngs, who died Apl. 26 1844—She was an affectionate, kind Mother, faithful wife, and a true professor, as member of the Congregational church in Orient—she was aged ___.

Died last Monday, at Greenport, Silas Webb Junr., aged about 44 years—He leaves a Wife, and several children to mourn his loss in the midst of a life of great usefulness to his family—He was in good health and strength, about 10 or 12 days ago—

Sabbath 21st I rode to Southold with Walter A. Wells—Stoped the night with Orin Prince, and my granddaughter, his wife Maria—

[412] Thursday 25th Oct. 1849—Still at Southold—Visited some of my old Schoolmates of days long gone by—viz. Benjamin Boiseau, now near 80 years of age—Mrs. Julia Case (when at School Julia Moore)—now 82 years old—My schoolmates of that day, 1781 & 2—alas! Where are they! These two are left—

Sabbath 28th rode to Orient, took Ellen Wilcox (our Grand Child,) and returned to Southold—

Tuesday 30th with Walter & Ellen, took the rail Cars for Hempstead, where we arrived about 3 P.M.—Stoped with our Son Sidney—

Thursday 1st Nov. rode to Williamsburgh—Stoped with our dear Cleora Friday 2nd Visited N.T. Hubbard—Saturday Evening at Cleoras—

Sabbath 4th Attended Church, Doct. Potts preached—

[413] Monday 5th Took Dinner at James Wilkies—Evening at Cleoras—

Tuesday 6th Evening & night at Mr. Williams's—Sidneys Fatherinlaw—Mistake 6th Stoped the night with Cleora—Wednesday 7th night at Mr. Williams's

Thursday 8th Visited Greenwood Cemetery—A place where art, expense and ingenuity have united to render a resting abode for the dead superior to anything of the kind, I ever saw—Evening at Mr. Hubbards—

Saturday 10th rode to Jamaica—stoped with Mr. Hewlett Smith, and his affectionate Wife, my niece, Henrietta—

Monday 12th at Sidneys, Hempstead

Wednesday 14th Rode in the cars to Southold—Stoped with Orin Prince—Saturday 17 Rode home to Orient—having been gone since 1st Oct.—much rain in said time

[414] Monday 19th Nov. 1849 An E- rainstorm, with high wind & high tides—It clears off with light wind W- on Wednesday 21st—Thursday 22nd warm—

On Thursday 8th of this Nov. died Mrs. Mehitable Prince, the Excellent Wife of Edward Prince, of Orient—

Monday 26th Nov. a hard Easterly rainstorm—

December 1st 1848 We have not had much cold weather thus far, this Autumn—Very little frost indeed—

Monday 3rd Decem. 1849—A severe Rainstorm, the first hour of which was Snow & hail—Wind high E-N-E—On the Evening of the 2nd of this month, we had a hard frost—Wednesday 5th some rain—

Friday 7th My Sister Lucinda Tuthill died this morn about 6 OClock

[415] Sabbath 9th Decem. 1849—Considerable rain—the remains of our beloved Sister Lucinda was Interred this noon, or about 12 N. beside those of her late Husband—In kindness, benvolence, and Christian Charity, with all the graces of a Mother, Wife, Sister, and neighbour, we cannot find her superior—rarely her equal—

> From Widowhoods state, lonely, distress't
> She's found at last, her long sought rest.

On the 10th &11th We had some snow, sufficient to cover the ground—cold N-W- wind on the 12 & 13th̄

Sidney P. Racket sailed on 14th for N.Y. with a cargo of sauce in the Sloop-Scow Mermaid

Saturday 22nd Dec. wind very high N-W-by W—

Friday 21st a hard S-W- rainstorm—Received a letter from our dear Cleora—one from Lewis A. Beach, one from Grandson Walter A. Wells—

Thursday 27th Snow last night—Rec'd a letter from Brother Samuel, and one from Chatham A.G. this morn—Visited Brother James this day—

Saturday 29th About 4 inches of snow on the ground this morn—

[416] December 31st 1849 Snow covers the ground this morn—

1850

Thursday 3rd Jan. 1850 Some snow last night—

Tuesday 8th A rainstorm through last night—Wind S-E—Schooner Export, James Glover, Master, was lost about two weeks ago, not far from Eggharbor, her crew saved—7th 8th & 9th Some rain—very thick drizly uncomfortable weather—

Friday 11th rain

Friday 18th Some snow—

Monday 28th considerable hail & then rain—

Sabbath 3rd Feb. Some rain last night—Yesterday, 2nd, I was Eighty three years of age! I feel lost in contemplation when viewing my past life, with its swift and astonishing career, and inconceivable incidents—Those years, alas! How soon they are gone—And now they appear as short as one—

8th Friday Chancy W. Moore called on me, an hour or so—He has done so once a year this many seasons past—

[417] From the 8th Feb. to 26th The weather was uncommon mild—Therefore, this Winter, the ground [in] Orient has had but very little frost In It—We believe there has not been a milder winter in the last thirty years—

Rec'd a letter from Joseph H. Goldsmith Esq. on the 23rd—

March 2nd 1850 A small snowstorm

April 3rd I returned from Southold yesterday, having been there, at Abner Wells's, and with my grand daughter Maria Prince, this three weeks past—In said time we have had three snowstorms, with considerable cold blustering weather—It has been this 3 days past more mild—Rec'd an affectionate letter from our Son Sidney, yesterday—

Friday 5th A severe Snowstorm Wind N-E—

Wednesday 10th I received a letter from our daughter, Cleora, She writes that her son Augustus writes her from California that Samuel Hobart is dead—died in Feb. 9, at SanFrancisco—He was the only Son of Capt. Nathaniel Hobart of Orient—Suffolk County—N.Y.

About the 16th I received a letter from James Bartholomew, Hartford, It invites me to visit them—

[418] On Monday 22nd Apl. 1850 I left Orient to visit Hempstead—I stoped two nights at Southold, with my dear, and Justly beloved Grandaughter, Maria Prince, whose Husband, the most deserving of Men, is away, doing buisness on the mighty waters—Wednesday I rode on the cars to Riverhead—found our little Mary well—She is the most interesting of children—Her features are much like her dear departed Mothers—Deziah P. Griffin, the late, invaluable wife of Capt. Samuel Griffin—

Friday 26th Arrived at Hempstead, Found our sons family in health—

May 11th Saturday—Weather this 2 weeks past has been generally quite unpleasant cold, backward, and some rainy and [?] days—

18th Saturday, cold N-W- wind—I am now at Hempstead, where I arrived on the [page trimmed]

Tuesday 21st A white frost last night—

22nd Wednesday A white frost this morn—this a cold day for the [season?]

The last week in May I spent at Williamsburgh, & at N.T. Hubbards, NewYork—

•

Tuesday 18th June, I took tea at, and with Mary Clows, widow of the late Timothy Clows, A Divinity Etc—Miss Mary L. Gardner, the poetess, was of the party—Left Hempstead on Wednesday 19—arrived at [?] Sabbath 22nd

[419] Monday 24th June 1850 [cross-written]

A whale, about 30 feet In length, was taken, and killed in the harbour, at Southold—It appears he had by some accident lost his way, and companions, and found himself bewildered in our contracted bays, where our whaleman at Greenport, persued, and after a few hours Industry, and sport, took him, and landed the monster of the deep at Greenport, where he was exhibited, as a curiosity, for one shilling admitance—Some of our Inhabitants suppose him the first of the kind ever taken in or near Southold—Others say there was one such a thing within the last 150 years

[420] Died on the 16th July 1850 Thomas Tuthill aged 73 years—He was the 2nd son of the late Adjutant Daniel Tuthill of Orient—Doct. Seth H.Tuthill, Brother to the above, Died June last aged 66 years—

July 30th 1850 James H. Preston, Jun. with us an hour this day—we have not seen him since March 1847

August 12th 1850 Was called on this morn by Capt. Robert Brown, Son of the late John Brown of Oysterponds—

30th Frederick Dobbs, from N-Y- with us—It is now about 8 years since he has stoped with [us] a day or so, once in each year—George Bartholomew and his wife from Hartford stoped with us an hour or two this Week—

Tuesday 24th Rode to Greenport and stoped the night with Calvin C. Wells—was hospitably entertained—

Wednesday 25th took the rail cars at ½ past 7 A.M. Arrived at Brooklin about 1 P.M.—At 4 P.M. took the cars for Hempstead, where I arrived [page trimmed]

[421] Septem—Stoped with Sidney, & family, until Monday 7th Oct.— morning took the Stage for Brooklyn, from which I proceeded to Williamsburgh, where I arrived about 2 P.M. Found my dear Daughter Cleora & family all in good Health—Thursday 10th visited N.T. Hubbard— Stoped with him & his dear family until Monday 14th—Stoped with Mr. R. Williams that night—Wednesday night 15th Stoped with friend James Wilkie—Saturday 19th Left Williamsburgh—Visited Mr. Hewlett Smith, Jamaica, & stoped with him, and his good Wife & family until Monday 21st,

[Crosswriting]: The following books I took with me to Sidney, Hempstead, the 26th April 1850, viz. Morses Universal Gazetteer Bible, which was present, It observes My 1st & 2nd Journals, with the 3rd one [this volume] Two small books containing my fugitive pieces 1 book with [histories?] & etc. to Cleora McNeil [in OHS archive] A Documentary History of New York a borrowed book Number of books—

when I proceeded to my Sons at Hempstead—Wednesday 23rd left for Riverhead—stoped there one night—then left for Southold—left Southold 28th arrived that Eve—Pretty Well—

[422] While at Hempstead, on 2nd October Wednesday and Sunday 6th On these days, I attended the Friends (quakers) meeting at Jerico—Mr. John H. Townsend oblidgeingly took me In his Carriage—It is about 5 miles—I certainly approve of their mode of Worship—A silent meeting, to those whose heart is right, must be virtuous & solemn.

Our Brother Samuel C. Griffin was with us on the 30th & 31 October— We believe him a sincere, and truly pious Brother—

Decem. 29th 1850 Died this day at Southold Reverend Nathan Hunting, aged about 72 years—An exampleing [exemplary] Man, and sound in the faith of the Gospel of Christ—has been a preacher some 40 years, much of said time at Southold—

Died at Southold about the 28th Decem. 1850 John Wells, brother to my Soninlaw Abner Wells—He had been a man of considerable buisness, but has gone It appears before It was settled to his [?], he had just launched a fine Sloop—

[423] Died this month, at Southold, Matthew Orsborne aged about 83 years—Albert Goldsmith about 60 years—John Wells was about 68 or 9 years—

Decem. 1850—Reverend Jonathan Hunting died on (I believe) the 29th Decem.

The above Mr. Orsborne died on the 27th—John C. Wells on the 28th—

1851

Sidney Griffin visited us 18th Feb. 1851

Edmund Latham died on the 7th Jan. 1851—Joseph King mentioned in 362 page, died at Sagharbour Jan. 1851—aged 86 years

[pencil] Apl. 8th 1851 I visited my Grand daughter Maria L. Prince at Southold—Returned home to Orient on 26th same Inst—

[424] Wrote to Mr. S. Roberts N. Jersey about the 1st Nov. 1850—To Henry Youngs N-Y- 20th

To John H. Townsend 26th

To Margaret L. Griffin Decem. 15th

To Green M. Tuthill Esq—24th—

Rec'd Answer from Henry Youngs and from J.H. Townsend

Jan. 4th 1851—Jan. 7 1851 Wrote to Rev. Ezra King—9th

To Anna J. Griffin—11th

Rec'd a letter from S.C. Griffin 18th

Rec'd A[ls]o from Walter A. Wells—18th

Rec'd A[lso] from Maria L. Prince 16th

Wrote her in Answer—18th

February 11th wrote to John H. Townsend

Answered Walter A Wells 1st Feb.

20 Rec'd a Letter from Chat[ham] A.G—

[pencil] 26th Answered It—

5th Apl. 1851 Rec'd letter from Sidney's three daughters Margaret Maria & Anna

[425] Rec'd a letter from grandson Henry W. Prince Jan. 18th 1851—Answered It Feb. 1st

[426] [pencil] May 12th 1851 Left Orient for Williamsburgh—Took passage on the Bonavista Schooner, Sidney P. Racket Master—Arrived at Williamsburgh on Wednesday 14th to My Daughter Cleora's—Stoped with her Untill Saturday 17th, on which day I took the Stage for Hempstead, where I arrived that Eve & found my Son Sidney and family well—In this visit, I spent about three days in New York—about six in Williamsburgh—and the rest of the time at Hempstead until the 24th June, when I took the Cars for Orient, where I arrived on the Evening of the 24th—found [Honora?] and family well—

• • •

[The page numbers of the last three diary entries bound into Volume II duplicate previous page numbers, and the pages, as bound, are not consecutive.]

[420] May 12th 1851 Left Orient for Williamsburgh—Took passage with the Bonavista Schooner, Sidney P. Racket Master—Arrived at Williamsburgh Wednesday 14th to My Daughter Cleora's—Staid with Her Untill Saturday 17th, on which day I took the Stage for Hempstead where I arrived that eve—Found my Son Sidney and family well—In this visit I spent about three days in New York—about six in Williamsburgh and the rest of the time at Hempstead untill the 24th June, when I took the cars for Orient, where I arrived on the Evening of the 24th—found Honora and family well—

[421] 1851 Our Son Sidney, wife & daughter Maria, visited us at Orient June 25th. 26th left for Hempstead

July about the 27th 1851 our grandson Chat A.G—visited us at Orient—Staid but a few hours—

August 26th 1851 Visited Southold Staid with my Grand daughter Maria Prince & Husband until 27th Septem when I returned to Orient—

[?] daughter and son at my house on the 7th & 8th September Sabbath 21st Septem 1851 Rode out to Southold—stoped with my granddaughter Maria L. Prince—22nd rode in the cars to Hempstead, to my son Sidney's

[?] October Visited my daughter Cleora at Newburgh—After visiting friends in NY—[?] to Hempstead—On the 26th returned to Orient—was absent 5[?] [?]

1852

[422] May 1852 Set off PM for Hempstead—

On the first June, on Wednesday, Set off for Newburgh, where I arrived about 9 OClock P.M. Staid with my Brother Saml until the Thursday—[illegible]

Saturday, Went to Benjamin Brassons Esq—Staid with them about 7 weeks—then went to Newburgh to my Brothers Son—Then back to Williamsburgh to Cleora [illegible]

View toward East Marion from Orient (detail), c. 1900
Photographer unknown. OHS Collections.

PHOTOGRAPH BY F. WACHSBERGER

House, Main Road, East Marion
The oldest part of this house was built around the same time as Griffin's house in Orient. It is a half-house that looks much as his would have looked before he added a second floor. The house is on the bay side of the road, west of the causeway between Orient and East Marion, and was in the Griffing family in 1873, according to the Beers map of Southold Town.

PHOTOGRAPH BY F. WACHSBERGER

House, Skipper's Lane, Orient
This mid-nineteenth-century house, with its eyebrow windows, reflects what Griffin's house might have looked like after his second-story addition. It was built by James Henry Young and originally stood on Village Lane, north of the Methodist Church.

Cynthia Brown King

Portrait by Abraham G. D. Tuthill, c. 1810. Tuthill, born in Oysterponds in 1776, was sponsored by Sylvester Dering of Shelter Island and then—financed by Aaron Burr and Alexander Hamilton, among others—sent to England to study with American painter Benjamin West. After a short return home, during which he created this portrait, he became an itinerant painter, working the route from northern New York State to Ohio. In 1808, Tuthill painted Augustus and Lucretia Griffin; the whereabouts of these portraits is unknown. OHS Collections.

Captain Frederick King

Portrait attributed to Charles Delin, c. 1800. King was an adventurous captain and privateer who sailed the trade routes to the Caribbean and to Europe. This portrait was probably painted in Holland. King lived opposite Griffin on what is now Village Lane. He drowned in Orient harbor (I: 123 [316]). OHS Collections.

Henrietta King Racket
Captain John A. Racket

Portraits by Sylvester Genin, 1840. "Wednesday 19th . . . John A. Racket, and his wife, are now sitting to our young Friend, Genin, for their Portraits— or as we say, for their likenesses—" (I: 193 [491]). Racket was owner and master of the sloop William Mitchel; *he had been one of Griffin's students. Sylvester Genin was influenced by Orient painter G.D. Tuthill. OHS Collections.*

The *Northern Liberties*
Ink drawing, perhaps by Frederick King; Memento Mori, 1800. This frigate, captained by King, went down with her cargo on a voyage to the Canary Islands in 1800. Although King survived, it is likely that some crewmembers were lost. OHS Collections.

PHOTOGRAPH BY E. WACHSBERGER

Home of Captain Frederick King, as it looks today
This house was built c. 1810. Some time after King's death in 1824, it was occupied by Griffin's daughter Deziah Preston and her family (I: 127 [322]). The house was bought by John Brown Young in 1853 and later became Young and Racket's general store.

Miniature of Cleora Griffin
Painted by J. W. Dodge, 1820. Cleora, Augustus Griffin's third surviving daughter, was born in 1799. OHS Collections.

Cynthia Tuthill
Portrait by William Hillyer, Jr., 1832. Born in 1797, Cynthia was one of the three diminutive daughters of Griffin's sister Lucinda and Rufus Tuthill, Jr. She was a dressmaker, and apparently a strong supporter of the Temperance movement (II: 287 [183]). OHS Collections.

1845 home of Marvin Holmes, as it looks today
"This Man came to my house, In June 1825—At that time out of health . . . As the place looked agreable, Its harbour, bays, Islands and prospects were congenial to his mind, he would stop with us some time if It suited our convenience to keep him . . . Mr. Holmes is now 1845 one our most prosperous Merchants, in our Village" (II: 279 [146-47]).

Bay House and dock

Undated postcard. The dock was built by Caleb Dyer in 1829 and was later purchased in shares by the Wharf Company (II: 366 [356]), which still owns it today. OHS Collections.

Bay House

Postcard, c. 1910. Built in 1837 by Caleb Dyer, opposite his dock, it was rented by Lewis A. Edwards, who "opened a tavern or Inn in said house—Rent 200 dollars a year—An extravagant rent—" (I: 158 [401]). As Griffin predicted, Edwards lost money and gave it up in 1840. In 1844, Griffin's son-in-law William Wilcox opened a Temperance hotel here "on the Te[e]total system" (II: 253 [57]). On the Beers map of 1873 it is called the Merriman Hotel. It remained a hotel until the 1960s. OHS Collections.

Explosion of the Steamship *Lexington*
Lithograph by W.K. Hewitt and N. Currier, NY, 1840, entitled Awful conflagration of the steam boat Lexington in Long Island Sound on Monday evening, Jany. 13th, 1840, by which over 100 persons perished. *These disasters were unfortunately not uncommon in early steamboat history (I: 183 [466]). Courtesy of The Library of Congress.*

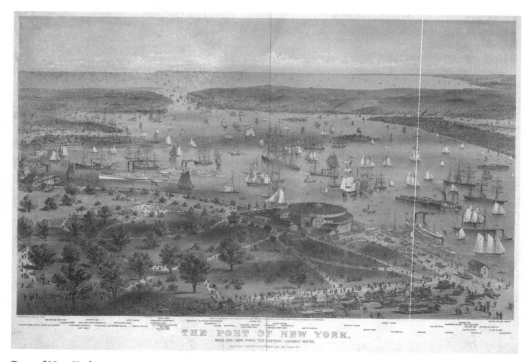

Port of New York
Lithograph by Currier and Ives, 1872. Although this print is later, the harbor would have looked much the same when Griffin made his many visits to New York. Courtesy of The Library of Congress.

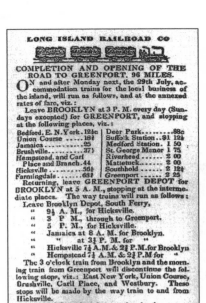

**Advertisement, Long Island Rail Road
Co.**, The Brooklyn Eagle, *1844.*

FIRST CAMPBELL LOCOMOTIVE, 1836.

First Campbell Locomotive, 1836
Emory R. Johnson, American Railway Transportation, *2nd
revised edition (NY and London: D. Appleton and Co., 1915),
p. 43. Note that the engineer rides outside.*

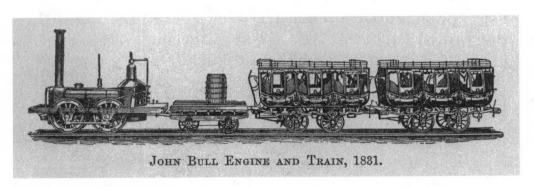

JOHN BULL ENGINE AND TRAIN, 1831.

John Bull Engine and Train, 1831
This sketch from American Railway Transportation, *p. 42, looks like the image in the 1844 advertisement
in* The Brooklyn Eagle. *The early "carriages" were in fact based on horse-drawn carriage design. But they
might not have been in use by the time the railroad reached Greenport; there is evidence that the LIRR
had acquired an eight-wheel Campbell engine in 1842 (John H. White, Jr.,* A History of the American
Locomotive, *Dover, 1968, p. 48, n. 11), and Griffin mentions a train of fourteen cars carrying one thousand
passengers in 1846 (II: 331 [295]).*

The Brown's Hills Cemetery, Orient

The earliest graves here date from the late seventeenth century. Griffin transcribed some of the epitaphs (II: 301 [228]), and, in his Journal *(p. 187) he complained that this ancient cemetery had been shamefully neglected. Today, the cemetery is maintained by the Oysterponds Historical Society with significant assistance from Southold Town.*

Cemetery, Main Road, Orient

The Griffin gravestones (pictured below) are among the most impressive in this early cemetery. The two simpler slabs to the right mark the graves of Griffin's daughter Deziah and her husband, James Preston. The Congregational Church in the background was built to replace an earlier one in 1843. The steeple was replaced after the 1938 hurricane.

The gravestones of Augustus and Lucretia Griffin and of their son Sidney and his wife, Margaret

The wives, who predeceased their husbands, are commemorated on the principal faces of the gravestones.

Margaret Griffin's gravestone

The inscription is singular:
Who am I?
My Husband
What is my name?
Sidney

APPENDICES
NOTES
INDEX

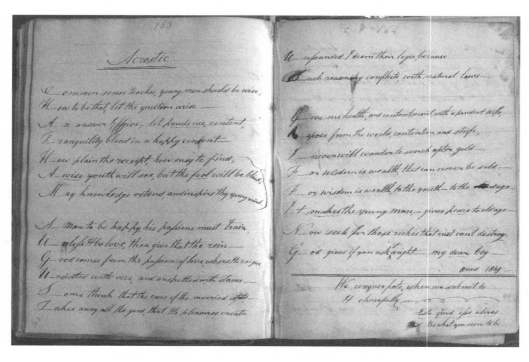

Poem for Cleora
Acrostic for Griffin's grandson
Chatham Augustus
Augustus Griffin wrote many poems and acrostics, some of which are bound with the Diaries but not included in this transcription. These two were among those bound with the "Diary for Cleora" (Appendix A). OHS Collections.

APPENDIX A

Griffin's "Diary for Cleora"

In the archives of the Oysterponds Historical Society is a manuscript bound in marbleized cardboard, with a front page that reads "Augustus Griffing's Diary, Containing some Sketches etc etc 1830." The contents, however, are of various dates and not limited to "sketches." Included are family genealogies, a list of books Griffin owned (see Appendix B), and many of his sentimental poems and some acrostics. These pages were bound together by Griffin in 1850 and given to his daughter Cleora (signed "by your bereaved Father"), with a description of the contents and a note of appreciation for the care she gave, in 1849, to her dying mother.

The selections from the manuscript that are printed below are from 1827. They are carefully written in a lively and entertaining style, and with more standard spelling than Griffin used in the present volume, *The Diaries of Augustus Griffin, 1792-1852*. The first selection is a description of his father's escape from the British and is quite different from and much more colorful than its retelling in the *Journal* published in 1857. The second, stories of his childhood and youthful experiences, are revealing of his character at the time as something of a "mama's boy" but also interesting for the details of indenture. In the third selection, his depiction of the humiliation of bankruptcy is graphic and heartfelt. The final selection is Griffin's description of the rapid growth of Greenport.

Griffin's father's escape from the British

[10] My Father, in the year 1764, (being then 25 years of age) Maried Deziah Terry, of whom I shall speak more fully in the course of these observations—He located a short time at Sagharbour, then at Southold, (where I was born,) from which last place he repaired to Oysterponds. Here his lively hood was following the Sea, or his trade [he had trained as a tailor], untill the British, whose Tyrany became insupportable, undertook to whip us, her then Colonies, into abject submission—The Americans flew to arms, to repel the invading, unreason [11] able foe—My Father was one of the first

*An old Gun, by that name, which he had used to kill scores of wild fowl with—#His whole time of service in the war of the revolution was 15 months

that shouldered his old Kings arm,* took an affection[ate] leave of my weeping, tenderest of Mothers—I well remember the gloomy morn, when (his soul to[o] full for utterance,) he stood transfixed at the door—my Mother weeping, hung upon his arm, breathing her fears for his welfare, in strains more tender, more pathetic, than those sublime ejaculations of the Mother of Moses, when she commited the moaning infant to the waters of the Famed Nile—

For his preservation, Heaven heard her prayers—He was at the battle on Long Island—One man fell near his side, mortally wounded—After being in several skirmishes, going to Ticanteroga Crown point etc. etc., in a nine months service, his time of enlistment being expired, he returned home, where my Mother met him with those emotions of rapturous Joy, known only to such as are sentimentally united#—At the time of his arrival at home, [the] East End of Long Island, was invaded by the british, and Tories, and the [12] habitants of Southold, were moving off to Connecticut, in great agitation—of course my Father, followed suit—He removed his Family to New London, late in the year of 1776—In 1777 he returned to the Island, which was still in possession of the british—but the Tories, the fag end of the unprincipled, were continually distressing, insulting, and robbing the unoffending families which had returned to the island, and those that had remained—My Father, having been in the American Army for about 15 months, now wishing, as his family was circumstanced, to live with them, as a neutral—Yet his mind, as well as his wishes were well known to be for his beloved Country. Thus situated he staid with his family as much as prudence would admit—When they threatened to take him off (and imprison him) as they often did, he like David of old would flee into solitary & unfrequented places, and hide himself for weeks, until they would relax their threats! [13] and permit him to return home unmolested for a few days, but generally dare not tarry at home through the night—Once I remember (although a boy of Nine years) they persued him, and he betook himself to a large hollow tree, into which he let himself down near 20 feet—the file of enraged Soldiers came under the very tree in which he was secreted—talked loud, and angry about the Damned Rebel, as they called him, and threatened vengence should they succeed in taking him—this conversation he heard having only the thickness of the rotten tree betwixt them—He escaped them this time—At another time, they persued him to what we call Peters neck, where, as providence ordered It, he found a small skiff, or canoe, into which he sprang, and paddled her over the stream 18 rods to the long beach shore—they on horses, being close upon him attempted to swim their

Horses over, but he resolutely called to them to come if they dare, as the water was deep & the current very rapid, they would unavoidably perish, before reaching the shore, where their victim felt himself secure—In getting into the boat his hat fell off, which the persuers got, stabbed it full of holes then brought It to my mother, & to distress her, told her they thus had secured him—

[14] After these almost miraculous escapes, he lived, in some measure, as a Partridge hunted upon the mountains—If I mistake not It was in the latter part of the year 1778, my Father having lodged out from his house for a long time, concluded one evening, It being a severe N-E- rain storm, to venture home, and stay with his family through the dreary, stormy night—but alas there was not many hours of rest for him, as yet in the bosom of his beloved family—Unexpected, unthought of, amidst the torrents of falling rain, and the howling fury of tempestuous Wind, at Midnight!! The house was sur-rounded with an enraged, armed and savage foe (at least made so by a to[o] free use of ardent spirits) Soldiery—My Father, lodged up chamber and as It was very dark, and raging as they were to get possession of his body, It was some time before they could procure [15] a candle, in which time my Father, ran to the chamber window under which he observed a Man with his bay-onet fixed on his gun—by this time the men in the House had got to the foot of the stairs, and were mounting towards the chamber—It was now an awful moment! My Father, with nothing on but his shirt, looked out of the window, again, saw the armed centry ride round the corner of the house to avoid the pelting torrents of rain—in a moment he leaped from his then desperate situation to the ground near 20 feet—He landed without broken bones or dislocated limbs, and fled, naked as he was, undiscovered to the neighbouring forests, which of late had been often his solitary home— These fiends in human form, a moment after my Fathers heroic escape, gained the chamber, uttering oaths, and vengence, should they find him— They ordered my Brother James and myself instantly out of our beds— brandished their glittering broadswords over our heads, and said with odious expressions, they wished "these lads a little larger"—The awfulness of that night, with its [16] attendant distresses, and the countenance of my anxious Mother, which resembled the composure of Elisha, when he told the affrighted Youth, (in the presence of an enraged Captain & 50 Soldiers, who were ordered to seize the Man of God) "Fear not for they that be with us, are more than they that be with them"—Yes, her looks, actions, and expressions, on that eventual night, in the chamber, surrounded with armed infuriated ruffians, will remain fresh in my memory, while the tablet of rec-

ollection remains unbroken—Their frothy breathings of vengence, and Death, against the Man whose life was dearer than her own, she appeared to bear, with a calmness, which while It astonished her weeping, affrighted children, softened those wretches, into a silent admiration of her superior virtues—In the presence of such excellence, such angelic graces, such majesty, and harmony of soul, their Tigerlike Spirits could not abide-[17] They left the house, muttering praise of a woman, whose mild, yet determined protection of her lord, unarmed and blasted the unhallowed purposes of their wretched souls—

Stories of childhood and youthful experiences

[27] In page 21 I noticed my birth, Its date etc. I have no recollection of any circumstance previous to my being 3 years old—at about that time I was at my Grandfather Terrys—He was digging a well, at the house, now owned by Joshua Vail—The workmen frightened me, by threatening to throw me into It—The impression was so powerful, my being [28] but a child, that I perfectly remember the circumstances to this day, a period of 60 years—After my Grandfather Terrys death, which as before observed was in 1775—I, being then seven years old, I was often at my Grand Mother Terrys, where I used to stay for a number of days at a visit, and was always feasted with the best the house aforded—I well recolect her nice and pious admonitions— one was never to eat bread & butter near the fire, for fear the crumbs might fall into It & be lost, whereas she observed "let them be thrown out the door, and Hens will get them . . .

[29] In the autumn of this year [1775] I went into Connecticut State (Saybrook) with Adjt. Daniel Tuthill & family—lived with them some months, then went to New London, to my Father, In the next year my Father moved his Family on the Island—In 1782 I lived one season with Timothy Wells, at Cutchogue—In 1784 I went to reside at Stonington, with Mr. Nathan Fellows, a pious Deacon of the [30] Baptist Church—He was a ship Carpenter, and It was My Father's will for me to learn that trade of him— I staid there some months, worked hard, steady, and faithful—My constitution was from a child rather slender, and young as I then was, I believed the trade would be to[o] hard for me, & from such an increasing Idea, I felt determined to quit when my Father should come to bind me out—He came after a number of weeks, prepared for my indentures—I remonstrated with all my might against staying—my oppisition appeared to hurt him, and at

first he sternly refused to comply, but his noble and generous Heart, at last yielded to my tears, and entreaties—with him I left the place, and was once more previledged to live in the blessed society of my tenderest of Mothers— I now went into the windmill, standing at that time a little west of the Oysterpond landing, at the Harbour—Assisted my Father in grinding, untill the winter of 1785—In January or February 1786 I with great, urgent intreaties to my Father, was admitted to go to RamIsland, and be inoculated for the Smallpox—I suffered much with It, being nearly blind for several days, howsomever, through the tender mercies of my Great Preserver, I was spared, and in six long weeks returned to the House of my parents—In April of this year my Father put me to Sterling [now Greenport], to reside with a Mr. Jehiel Wheton, to learn the Tanning, Currying, & Shoemaking—I staid my time out faithfully, which was one year—But that term was to[o] short to become a workman—therefore I could never claim to be an adept in any of those branches————In 1787 I lived at home with my parents—[32] In March, about the 27th 1788, I went to New York, In company with Samuel Brown, (a neighbor mate of mine)—Arrived in Town, we put up with my old preceptor Doct. Thos. Vail—This gentleman was nearly the first Schoolmaster I ever went to School to—His abilities as teacher were considered of the first order in Southold & Oysterponds, in which places he had taught a number of years—His fame soon procured him an invitation to open a School in that growing City—A number of very respectable families, soon committed their children to his care, and the rapid improvement they made speedily procured him 80 or 100 pupils—One of them has since figured conspicuously in our American Navy—A Commodore Chancy— General Washington at that time President of these U. States, lived in the Franklin [33] House, Chery Street—within a few rods of Doct. Vail's School and residence—After staying with the Doct. 2 or 3 days, having been treated by him & his good Wife with the kindness of a favorite Son, I left them, and alone, unexperienced, and with scarce any knowledge of how to conduct myself among strangers, and sharpers, far, far from the hospitable roof of my tender, affectionate Mother—Went on board a North River Sloop, bound up—not a soul on board had I ever heard of before—The first day we reached Tarry Town (famed as the place where the accomplished Andre was taken)—lodged on shore that night in a mill, with the Millar, a Young Man, who kept his loaded Gun at his bed side—I felt some suspicious of the man, but found myself alive next morning, with sensations, such as accrued from finding yourself in the midst of a people of whom you have no knowledge—and surely of their interest in your welfare—The next night we moored our vessel at a Dock a mile or two above the vilage of New Marleborough—The next morning, in company with the two men with whom I had taken passage, they being owners of said vessel, [34] I set off for their residence, which was about two miles from where the vessel lay—We had not proceeded far, when It commenced raining very hard, I was soon drenched to the skin, having my pack of Clothes on my back, I must have resembled a forlorn outcast—My sensations were as gloomy as was my situation, not knowing in what manner I was to be received, wet, and hungry, In the midst of the [?] and who from the appearance of the two Men (brothers) would feel no interest in the comfort of a heedless, and an inexperienced Youth—We arrived at the Parents of the said two Men, about 10 A.M.—They appeared to be dutch people—A large overgrown, rough looking family, of 4 or 5 Sons, and one or two huge Daughters—This family (I learned afterwards) was proverbial for their attachment to the cause of Britain, and the Father, had become superannuated [35] in grieving at the failure of the royal cause—Altho an uncommon stout, hearty man, not much turned of 70, his anxiety had been so poignant, that rest, property, and his domestic comforts had been chearfully sacrificed in endeavoring to aid his beloved England—At the time of dinner, I was invited to the Table, without ceremony, and as little apparent notice from any but the old Gentleman—He eyed me with something like a vacant stare—at last he broke the silence,with a frown which indicated he could not allow himself to be contradicted—Says he, "Young Man, you say you are from Long Island, what do they think there of this wickedness rebelious peoples takeing up arms against the Lords anointed?" I without premeditation, without Judgement, & without a proper reverence for old age, with emphasis observed, we (Long Island folks) believe that Washington was inspired to lead our armies to victory, and those brave Men, who had sacrificed their lives in the cause of Independence, had died [36] Martyrs in a glorious cause—The old Man had scarce heard the sentence through when eyes flashing fire, and indignation, he arose from the Table, with, to appearance, all the fury of a trouble Saul, when he darted the Javelin at the inoffensive Jonathan—He, the old gentleman, bellowed forth with a voice of Thunder, "You young ignorant lad, you beardless boy, know you that all those who have fought against Britains anointed of the Lord, have lifted up their weapons against Heaven, and all those who have fell in the ignoble cause, have gone with Judas to Hell"—I was affrighted at the manner, and adgitated actions of the Man—I left the Table—his youngest Son, beckoned me to the door, and entreated me to be more watchful for the future, said he felt glad that his Father had let me escape thus safe—I promised amendment [37] while I acknowledged my observations at his Fathers Table (situated as I was, a lonely unprotected stranger) were truly reprehensible, I should hope that while he would try to soften his Fathers wrath towards me, I would endeavor through my life ever after to be more watchfull—more reverential, even (I thought) if assailed by the most bigoted of Tories—With the Young Man before mentioned, I engaged to work six months—Farming, assisting in the Tan Yard, etc. etc. was my employ—In this time I never saw a man, woman, or child that I had seen before, neither did I see one that has ever heard of me—thus I was a stranger amidst the mountains, or Rocky Hills, near New Paltz, where I could plainly see the Catskill Mountains—Here It was, as it were hid from all aquaintance, I learned truly the inestimable worth of a Mothers Fostering care—While often sleeping (or attempting to sleep) nights in a kind of workshop, with no bed under me to soften my repose, the thoughts of having left a home, which contained a Mother, whose comforts was interwoven with that of her children, caused many weeping, & wakefull nights—O home—sweet home—methought [38] the time for which I engaged ended some time in October—With hope elated, I repaired to the landing, where I engaged my passage for NewYork—To that City we arrived, with about two days passage—Tarried in N-York about one day—Had only about 12 hours from the wharfs at N.York to Sagharbour wharf where we landed—staid one night, reached my home next day, where I met my Parents with feelings of satisfaction indiscrible—Welcomed with a tear trembling on the cheek of Heavens best & richest boon—A Mother—

Bankruptcy

[57] The difficulties I had conceived to be approaching were realized In 1817—In May I was arrested (for the first time in my life) at the suit of a Mr. Tredwell Seamen, Dry Goods Merchant, N.York, for over 200 Dollars—Here commenced a scene of unpleasant sensations and sorrow, the effects of which produced impressions on my sensibility as lasting as will be my che-quered life—Ruin, now with her haggard aspect stared me full in the face—This Iron call which with a palpitating heart, I had [58] trembling seen approach, I knew would arouse Instantly, with my host of creditors—I repaired, forthwith to my Friend and Counsellor, Thos. S. Lester Esq—His advice was to write immediately to all my creditors, stateing as near as pos-sible my complex affairs—Offer the whole of my property to be divided

amongst them—viz. assign over all my goods on hand—Notes—book debts etc etc to some person they should name—said person should sell the property so assigned at auction—collect in the debts & make a dividend—previous to which they the creditors should sign a release to me accepting the above conditions in full satisfaction of all future demands as those dues—Letters to this effect were sent on by my Daughter Deziah—Mrs. Griffing followed her a day or two afterwards, using all her influence with her cousin, Capt. Gabriel Havens, a conspicuous creditor—[59] her story affected him—He kindly undertook to touch the feelings of the others, and with good success—With the assistance of my friend Lester, who (providentially for me) arrived in N.Y. at the time, they procured nearly all the signitures required to the release—Mrs. Griffin visited her Mother & Sister, at or near Newburgh, and returned in June—In that month an Inventory was taken of all my Goods & Chattles, & Household furniture (wearing apparel etc. excepted)—Mr. Lester was appointed assignee—My acquaintance, which was considerable extensive, received the news of the day, respecting my beclouded situation, a set of diversified comments, agreable to each ones Ideas of the opinion they had been wont to form of the Man, now in troubled waters—My harrowed up feelings can only be conceived by those sentimental souls, whom blind Fortuna has been pleased to place in a similar situation—Let the envious slyly look contemptuous, the self confident strut a show of his ingenious calculations—Time can only [60] teach them that nothing is truly permanent but virtue—and nothing Joyous, but that peace, which flows from knowing that our sins are done away through the blood of Jesus, the immaculate Lamb of God—possessed of that love we have all things—Deprived of that, combined worlds cannot lend the smallest comfort, or mitigate one moments sorrow—On the 3rd of July 1817 at 10 OClock A.M. My goods etc etc were sold at auction, they (as I have before observed) were sold at a great sacrifice—Pleasing to those selfish souls, who could chuckle at the opportunity of purchasing articles (at their neighbours expence) for less than ¼ there first cost, observing with a supercilious smile, of Donquixotical importance "It's a fair vendue"—one of my neighbours very cruelly thus exclaimed—The clouds and darkness, attendant on adverse fortune, are ever near to teach us that the light of nature is liable every moment to be lost in unutterable darkness, wretchedness, and misery—"Let him that standest take heed lest he fall"—On the 4th July (a conspicuous day in the History of America) a party of Ladies and Gentlemen [61] from N.London, near 30 Couple, come to my house—were entertained agreeable to their wishes, and appeared well satisfied with the civilities shown them—on the 5th they left us leaving with me for their fare near 50 Dollars, which at this important period of our experience appeared truly wonderful—Just writhing under all the painful impressions of but yesterdays spectacle, for people 10 miles around to have such a sum, unthought of, unexpectedly handed into our hands for the benefit of my family, was affecting in very deed—Tears of grattitude accompanied the consideration, while I observed to my astonished friends, "this assistance came straight from Heaven"—I have thought, and perhaps Justly, that this extraordinary interposition of providence in my favour, at this crisis was to convince me of the importance and safety of reposing our whole trust in that Almighty being, who says "there is not a Sparrow falls to the ground without his knowledge"—For the sweet influences of his blessed spirit to assist me to rest all my confidence in Him, and to live wholly swallowed up in his Glorious will is my daily prayer—O may I feel to exclaim Alleluia, the Lord God Omnipotent reigneth—Amen & Amen

[63] In July of this year [1819] commenced a school at Sterling—Having taught in that place 2 quarters 20 years since—The parents of those children under the present tuition were at the above period my then Scholars—Alas, what changes I have beheld in that course of time! Vicisitudes & scenes, if not interesting to others, they truly to me have been astonishing—I have launched out into a tumultuous ocean of business—care etc etc—not completely freighted with the produce attached to my own property—I felt to start with a fair wind, and serene [64] Sky—But either the variation of the compass of imprudence, or not, adhering strictly to the pilot of good calculations—In the course of 17 years tossed to & fro, with the waves of adverse Fortune, Trading, as occasion offered, to the value of nearly 100000 Dollars, unforeseen accidents, united with contrary winds of increasing hard times, rendered It absolutely necessary to run the vessel on shore, in nearly the same situation as when she first set sail—Should the clouds dispense—the winds subside—the Sky become again serene, and mild, perhaps prudence would Justify an attempt on another voyage—

The rapid growth of Greenport

[165] On the 23rd day of March 1820 I, Augustus Griffin, attended, as I was a licenced Auctioneer, to the selling of a part of the Farm, of the late Capt. David Webb, which lay on the south East side of the street, which now runs from the Presbyterian Church, to the large, and first wharf built in what is

now called Greenport—A part of the farm lot sold at the time lies on the west side of said street—At the above said time when the land was sold, there was neither road, street, nor house on the premises—I struck It off to the highest bidders—They were three, who bought It Jointly, but soon one of them sold out—The purchasers, were Daniel T. Terry Esq.—Silas Webb, and Joshua Tuthill—It was struck off [166] for less than 2500 Dollars!! I am now writing this, Oct. 1849 Twenty nine after that eventual day—Now, on said pasture field, whereas before noticed there was not a solitary house, road, or street, you can see a doz. Or more stores, a number of Hotels, five or more churches—A printing office—Post office—Collectors office—Several Whale ships—Hundreds of houses—a great number of Streets, Wharves, etc. etc.—What a change! And in so short a Time!—Verily, this is a World of astonishing alteration, Incident, and wonder——

APPENDIX B
Griffin's Library

W HEN AUGUSTUS GRIFFIN decided to become a schoolmaster, he taught himself arithmetic, but he had received a good foundation in literacy before he left Oysterponds. His first teacher, Thomas Vail, was impressive enough to have been invited to open a school in New York City (see Appendix A). Griffin often mentions his reading within the text of *The Diaries;* and at the beginning of Volume II, he lists the books he has read during 1844 and 1845. In his earlier "Diary for Cleora," on the verso of the title page, he gives an inventory of the books that belonged to him in 1839. His personal library reveals that he continued to prepare himself for teaching and that he frequently reread the books that he possessed.

I. Griffin's Library, 1839, from "Diary for Cleora"

Written on the verso of the title page:
Which belonged to him May 1839
A Catalogue of Augustus Griffings Books

1 Biographical Dictionary
Biographical Dictionary. Boston: Edward Oliver and Salem, Cushing and Appleton, 1809.

1 Ellegant Epistles
Elegant Epistles, or a Copious Collection of Familiar and Amusing Letters, selected for the improvement of Young Persons and for general entertainment. London: Charles Dilly, 1790.

4 Paynes Geography 4 volumes
John Payne. *Universal Geography.* London: J. Johnson and C. Stalker, 1791.

1 History Quadrupeds
Thomas Bewick. *General History of Quadrupeds.* New-York: G. & R. Waite, 1807; first published Newcastle upon Tyne: Hodgson, Beilby, and Bewick, 1792.

1 Pilgrims Progress

John Bunyan. *A Pilgrim's Progress from This World to That Which Is to Come.*
   First published London: Nathaniel Ponder, 1678. Many later editions,
   including Philadelphia: Jonathan Ponder, 1814.

1 Pamphlets bound No 1 Andre [?] etc etc

3 Volume laws—State N.York

Laws of the State of New-York. Albany: Webster and Skinner, 1807.

1 Pamphlets No 2

2 Volumes Military/Naval Heroes

Thomas Wilson. *Biography of American Military and Naval Heroes During
   the Revolutionary and Late Wars.* New York: John Low, 1817.

1 Stiles Judges

Ezra Stiles. *A History of the Three Judges of King Charles I.* Hartford, Conn.:
   Elisha Babcock, 1794.

1 Volume Not in English

1 Discourses concerning Resurrection of Jesus Christ

Humphry Ditton. *A Discourse Concerning the Resurrection of Jesus Christ.*
   London: J. Darby, 1712. Many later editions, such as London: T. Cox, 1740.

1 Volume History N.York

Diedrich Knickerbocker, a.k.a. Washington Irving. *A History of New York
   from the Beginning of the World to the End of the Dutch Dynasty.* First
   published 1809; New York: Inskeep and Bradford, 1812.

1 Guide to Domestic Happiness

W. Giles, Esq. *Guide to Domestic Happiness.* London: J. Buckland, 1781;
   Charles Tilt, 1836.

1 John Freeman

John Freeman. *A Method of Teaching Adult Persons to Read.* London: H.
   Teape, 1813.

1 Pamphlets—Paul Jones Etc Etc

1 Ann of Britain

Perhaps Anne, Queen of Great Britain. *The Life and Reign of her Late Majesty
   Queen Anne.* London: B. Buckeridge, 1715; or A.B. Gibson. *Memoirs of
   Queen Anne.* London: 1729.

1 8th Volume of Shakespears plays
William Shakespeare. *The Plays of William Shakespeare, Vol. 8.* London: Rivington, 1765, 1820.

1 Notes on the Parables
Thomas Whittemore. *Notes and Illustrations of the Parables of the New-Testament.* Boston: Whittemore, 1832.

1 Herveys Meditations
James Hervey. *The Meditations and Contemplations of the Rev. James Hervey.* First published London, 1746–1747; Edinburgh: Thomas Nelson and Peter Brown, 1832.

1 Geography for Schools
Jacob Willetts. *An Easy Grammar of Geography for the Use of Schools.* Poughkeepsie: P. Potter, 1814.

1 Cornelii Nepos
Cornelii Nepotis. *Vitae Excellentium Imperatorum.* Amstelodami: Boom, a Someren, & Goethals, 1687; many editions.

1 Ahiman Rezon
Laurence Dermott and J. E. Weeks. *Ahiman Rezon, Or a Help to All that are Or Would Be Free and Accepted Masons.* Printed for the editor, 1756. Probably the first American edition, from the third London edition; New York: Southwick & Hardcastle, 1805.

1 Abelard poetry
Perhaps Peter Abelard and Alexander Pope. *The Unfortunate Lovers; Two Admirable Poems.* London: 1756.

1 Night Thoughts
Edward Young. *Night Thoughts on Life, Death, and Immortality.* First published as *The Complaint, or Night Thoughts*; London: R. Dodsley, 1742. Many later editions.

1 Life of Fletcher
John Wesley. *A Short Account of the Life and Death of the Rev. John Fletcher.* Baltimore: Abner Neale, 1804.

1 Royal Captives
Ann Yearsley. *The Royal Captives: A Fragment of Secret History.* London: G. G. and J. Robinson, 1795.

1 History Longisland

Benjamin Franklin Thompson. *History of Long Island.* New York: E. French, 1839. This was a gift to Griffin by the author, see Vol. I, 211 [533].

1 Reeve Arithmetic

Shepherd A. Reeve. *A Key to Reeve's New Practical Decimal Arithmetic.* Philadelphia: Dennis Heart, 1812.

1 Napoliad

Thomas Hedges Genin. *The Napolead.* St. Clairsville, Ohio: H.J. Howard, 1833. Genin was a friend and may have gifted the book, see Vol. I, 168 [424].

1 G.J. Howet[?] Warr

1 Life of Joseph

John Macgowan. *The Life of Joseph the Son of Israel: In Eight Books: Chiefly Designed for the Use of Youth.* Hartford, Conn: Elisha Babcock, 1796.

1 Du Fresnays

Perhaps Henri Hercule Champagne du Fresnay. *Quaestio Medica.* Paris: Quillau, 1779.

1 Brownlee's papers

W.C. Brownlee [minister of the Collegiate Protestant Reformed Dutch Church, New York City] was a prolific writer of religious treatises, many for young readers.

1 Wessley's Physick

John Wesley. *Primitive Physick, Or An Easy and Natural Method of Curing Most Diseases.* Bristol: G. Woodall, 1747; republished often, including London: J. Paramore, 1781.

2 Volumes Holmes England

John Holmes. *The History of England.* London: A. Parker, 1737.

1 Wesleys Sermons

John Wesley. *Sermons on Several Occasions.* Philadelphia: Henry Tuckniss, 1800. Volume 3 is in the OHS archive.

1 Websters Grammar

Noah Webster. Probably *An Improved Grammar of the English Language.* New-Haven, Conn.: Howe & Spalding, 1831, although *A Grammatical Institute of the English Language,* Hartford, Conn.: Hudson and Goodwin, 1787, was specifically designed for teaching English in American schools.

1 Coopers N. America
W.D. Cooper. *A History of North America.* First published in 1789, London:
E. Newberry; many editions including Hartford, Conn: W.S. Marsh, 1814.

1 Walham Dictionary

1 Apes Experiences
William Apes. *The Experiences of Five Christian Indians of the Pequod Tribe.*
Boston: James B. Dow, 1833.

1 Watts Juvenile Essays
Isaac Watts. *Reliquiae Juveniles: Miscellaneous Thoughts in Prose and Verse.*
London: First published Ford and Hett, 1734; many editions.

1 Hazards poems
Joseph Hazard. *Poems.* London: L. Hassall, 1771; or New York: self-published
by author, 1814.

1 Blairs outlines
Rev. David Blair. *Outlines of Chronology, Ancient and Modern, Being an
Introduction to the Study of History.* Boston: Richardson, Lord & Holbrook,
1832, or Conn.: S.G. Goodrich, 1826.

1 Howards Life
John Howard. *The Life of the Late John Howard, Esq.* London: J. Ridgeway, 1790.

1 Young Gentleman' etc
J. Hamilton Moore. *Young Gentleman and Lady's Monitor and English Teacher's
Assistant.* London: Richardson and Urquhart, 1790. Many editions.

1 Watts L. poems
Louisa Watts. *Nature Displayed, Being a Collection of Poems for Children,
Explanatory of the Operations of Nature in a Style Suited to their
Capacities.* London: James Dinning, 1831.

1 Grace unfolded
John Bunyan. *The Doctrine of the Law and Grace Unfolded.* London: N.
Ponder, 1685; many editions. Possibly Boston: Manning & Loring, 1806.

1 Hallers Letters
Baron Albrecht von Haller. *Letters to his Daughter on the Truth of the
Christian Religion; Letters to the Jews, Inviting them to an Amicable
Discussion of the Evidences of Christianity.* London: J. Murray, 1793; several
later editions.

1 Newtons Letters

Isaac Newton. Probably *Four Letters from Sir Isaac Newton to Doctor Bentley containing Some Arguments in Proof of a Deity*. London: R. and J. Dodsley, 1756.

1 Latin Grammar

Perhaps Alexander Adam. *The Rudiments of Latin Grammar*. Albany: Parker and Bliss, 1809.

1 Ann Royal B.B.

Anne Royall. *The Black Book, or A continuation of travels in the United States*. Washington: for the author, 1828–29.

1 Poet Epitome

Vicesimus Knox. *The Poetical Epitome; Or Extracts, Elegant, Instructive, and Entertaining*. London: Charles Dilly, 1791.

1 Christian Messenger

The Christian Messenger. Baltimore, MD: Joshua T. Russell, 1817; three editions.

II. Books Griffin read in 1844 and 1845,
from *The Diaries of Augustus Griffin, 1792–1852*, Volume II [3]

Have read the following Books since the 1st of January 1844 through 1845: [numbers at right are presumably number of pages read]

Holy Bible two times through pages both times. 1814

Alleine's alarm . . . 202[?]

Joseph Alleine. *An Alarm to Unconverted Sinners*. London: E.T. and R.T., 1672; many editions.

Baxter's Rest . . . 271

Richard Baxter. *The Saints Everlasting Rest*. London: T. Underhill and F. Tyton, 1650; many editions.

Watts Esays . . . 292

Isaac Watts, probably *Philosophical Essays on Various Subjects*. London: J. Brackstone, 1742.

Young's Night thoughts [the rest of the numbers associated with the books are illegible]

Edward Young. *Night Thoughts on Life, Death, and Immortality*. First published as *The Complaint, or Night Thoughts*. London: R. Dodsley, 1742; many editions.

Hervey's Meditations
James Hervey. *The Meditations and Contemplations of the Rev. James Hervey*. London: 1746–1747; many editions.

British Pulpit
Rev. W. Suddards. *The British Pulpit: Consisting of Discourses by the Most Eminent Living Divines*. Philadelphia: Grigg & Eliot, 1836.

Pilgrim's Progress
John Bunyan. *The Pilgrim's Progress from this World to that Which is to Come*. London: 1678; many editions.

Proofs of the Resurrection of Christ
Probably James Dore. *An Essay on the Resurrection of Christ; in which proofs of the Fact are Adduced, Its Import is Explained, and its Beneficial Influence Illustrated*. London: M. Gurney and W. Button, 1797; London: James Robertson and Co., 1823. (There were many works on this subject.)

Tales of a Grandfather
Walter Scott. *Tales of a Grandfather*. Philadelphia: Porter & Coates, 1827.

Two Years Before the Mast
Richard Henry Dana. *Two Years Before the Mast*. New York: Harper Bros., 1840.

2 Vol. The Flagship Columbia, around the world
Fitch W. Taylor. *Flagship: or A Voyage Around the World in the United States Frigate Columbia*. New York: D. Appleton & Co., 1840.

Watson's Apology for the Bible
Richard Watson. *An Apology for the Bible, in a series of letters addressed to Thomas Paine*. New York: T. & J. Swords, 1796; many editions.

Hinton on the Prophets
Isaac Taylor Hinton. *The Prophesies of Daniel and John*. St. Louis, Missouri: Turnbull & Pray, 1843.

Bible again [in ink]

Dodriges Rise and Progress
Philip Doddridge. *Rise and Progress of the Soul*. Leeds: J. Binns, 1795. Many editions.

Tales of the Revolution

Tales of the Revolution, being rare and remarkable passages of the history of the war of 1775. New-York: Harper and Brothers, 1835; or John H. Mancur. *Tales of the Revolution.* New York: W.H. Colyer, 1844.

III. Volumes in the Oysterponds Historical Society archives with Augustus Griffin's name written on the flyleaf.

James Beattie, *An Essay on the Nature and Immutability of Truth in Opposition to Sophistry and Skepticism.* Philadelphia: Solomon Wieatt, 1809.

Rodolphus Dickinson, *Compendium of the Bible; with a separate moral election from the Apocrypha.* Deerfield, Mass.: Newcomb & Wells, 1817.

Melville Home, *Posthumous Pieces of the Late Reverend John William de la Flechere.* Albany, NY: Barber and Southwick for T. Spencer & A. Ellison Booksellers, 1794.

APPENDIX C

Griffin Genealogy

AUGUSTUS GRIFFIN GIVES DETAILED GENEALOGIES of his own family and those of his friends in his *Journal* (1857). The following is meant to be a guide to some of the members of Griffin's immediate family who are mentioned in the *Diaries* and their descendants and is based primarily on incomplete evidence in the *Diaries* and in *Genealogy of the Descendants of Jasper Griffing*, compiled by Clara J. Stone (New York: DeBaun & Morgenthaler, 1881) and *Stephen Griffing, His Ancestry and Descendants*, compiled by Edith Willoughby West (Warrensburgh, New York: Henry Griffing, 1911.) It does not include the numerous cousins, uncles and aunts.

Augustus Griffin (February 2, 1767–March 10, 1866)

Augustus's father, James (1739–1824)
    m. Deziah Terry (1745/6–1814), daughter of Jonathan Terry and Lydia
    née Tuthill

Augustus's brothers and sisters:
James (1765–1852)
    m. Mehitable Moore (?–1838)
        four sons died at sea, 1825
        other children?
Deziah (1768–1794, died of smallpox)
Elisha (1770–1819)
    m. Hannah King
    m. Phoebe (?)
        Harriet
        Augustus
        Peter
        Samuel
        John Orville

Lucinda (1773–1849)
    m. Rufus Tuthill, Jr. (1771–1844)
        Cynthia (1797–1881)
        Thomas Vincent (1800–?)
        Peter Warren (1802–1872)
            m. Fanny Tuthill (1819–?)
            m. Laura Terry, daughter of Daniel (?–1865)
                Rosalie Lavinia (1830–?)
                Emma (1833–1882)*
                Daniel Terry (1836–?)
                Florence Lyle (1838–1861)
                    m. Jas. Henry Young
                Addison (1841–?)*
                Lucinda Terry (1843–?)
        Polly Maria (1805–?)
            m. Joseph Latham
        Lucretia (1808–1888)
        Asenath (1809–1875)
        Deziah Griffin (1811–1891)
            m. Elias D. Perkins (?–1868)
Moses (1774–1796, lost at sea)
Parnol (1777–1791)
Peter Warren, referred to in diary as Warren (1780–?)
Samuel (1782–1784)
Lucretia (1784–1866)
    m. David Wiggins Jr. (?–1826)
        James Edwin (1809–1849)
        Caroline (1811–?)
            m. Samuel Racket, Jr., in 1845
        Mehitable
        Lucinda (1813–?)
            m. George Hollice (or Hollis), Methodist preacher, in 1844
        Harriet (1824–?)
Samuel Caddle (1787–1854)
    m. ?
        adopted female child
Austin (1789–1791)

---

*Emma and Addison, not mentioned by Griffin in his *Diaries,* were under three feet tall, later erroneously referred to as "the Tuthill dwarfs."

Augustus Griffin married Lucretia Tuthill, daughter of Nathaniel Tuthill and Mary Havens, in 1790 or 1791

Lucretia's sisters included:
 Polly, Mrs. Richard S. Hubbard (mother of Nathaniel T. Hubbard)
 Betsey, Mrs. Joseph King (m. 1789)
 Hannah Field, later Mrs. Silas Howel

Augustus and Lucretia's children:
 Harriet Lucretia (1791/92–1842)
  m. Abner Wells, in 1815
   Deziah L. (1820–1842)
   Maria Lucretia (1816–?)
    m. Orin Prince, in 1839
     Henry (Harry) Wells (1839–?)
     Harriet Deziah (1843–?)
      m. Andrew J. Beebe
     Maria Louise (?–?)
     Charles Orrin (1847–1848)
     Orrin Abner (1849–?)
      m. Hattie A. Hobart
     E. Stanley (1858–?)
   Walter Abner (1834–?)
    m. Elma A. Young
   Augustus Griffin (1818–1819)
 ? Son (b. 1794, died in infancy)
 Deziah Narcissa (b. 1796, died at 8 months)
 Deziah (1797–1839)
  m. James H. Preston (1800–1833)
   ? died in infancy, 1821
   John Augustus (?–1853)
    m. Emily Richmond, in 1847
   Harriet Matilda (?–1849)
    m. Walter O. Hubbard
     Nathaniel T. Hubbard
   James Hearvey (1830–1852)
   Deziah
    m. Samuel Griffing, in 1843

Mary (1844–?)

Harriet Matilda (1844–?)

Cleora (1799–?)

  m. James Hemel McNeill, in 1830

  Betsey

  Harriet

  ? died at 18 months, 1838

  Emily

Narcissa Lee (1801–1847)

  m. Janus Raymond

Honora Seward (1804–?)

  m. William H. Wilcox, in 183?

    William Augustus Goodridge (1838–?)

    Ellen (1840–?)

    Honora Seward (1843–?)

Sidney Lorenzo (1805–?)

  m. Margaret Williams, daughter of Rogers Williams, in 1828

    Chatham Augustus (1829–?)

      m. Delia S. Griswold (1833–1871)

    Augustus Rogers (1831–?)

      m. Anna Eliza Hewlett (?–1856)

      m. Elizabeth A. Smith (1843–?)

        Margaret E. (1869–?)

    Sidney (b. 1834, died at 9 months)

    Maria Louisa (1835–?)

      M. Henry Irish

        Augustus (1863–?)

        Anna Josephine (1865–?)

        Laura Frances (1866–?)

        Robert Hendrickson (1868–?)

        Leslie Morgan (1870–?)

        Rosamond Shotwell (1871–?)

        Edward Francis (1874–?)

    Margaret and Josephine, twins (1837–?):

    Margaret Lucretia

      m. Hiram Bedell

        Sidney Griffin (1856–?)

          m. Annie Jewett

Augustus Seymour (1858–?)
   m. Ada Allen
Chatham Franklin (1861–?)
Cyrus D. Foss (1864–?)
Hiram Green (1867–?)
Edwin L. Janes (1868–?)
Albert Marten (1872–?)
Anna Josephine (1874–?)
Anna Josephine
   m. Robert Foster
   Daughter

NOTES

The notes are keyed to the page number of the present volume and to the page number (shown in brackets) of Griffin's original manuscript.

Volume I

1792

3 [1]. *by inoculation* Before smallpox vaccine was invented in 1796, a process called "variolation" was used. It involved an inoculation of pus from an infected person and caused a mild form of the disease, from which most people recovered. Griffin mentions his own inoculation as a teenager in his *Journal*, p. 69, and in his "Diary for Cleora." See Appendix A, where he reports experiencing temporary blindness.

Blooming-Grove Blooming-Grove is about eight miles east of Goshen.

1793

8 [14]. *"noblest works of God"* "A wit's a feather, and a chief's a rod / An honest man's the noblest work of God." Alexander Pope, *An Essay on Man*, "Epistle IV," line 248 (London: George Faulkner, 1745).

10 [18]. *Edwards history of redemption* Jonathan Edwards (1703–1758), the Yale-educated revivalist theologian and prolific author. *The History of the Work of Redemption* was published posthumously in 1774, then republished many times, e.g. in Worcester, Mass. (Isaiah Thomas, 1792).

11 [20]. *Andre* Major John André (1750–1780), Adjutant General of Sir Henry Clinton, collaborated with American General Benedict Arnold (1741–1801) in his scheme to deliver the garrison at West Point to the British; he was captured with plans of the garrison in his sock. Although a liked and admired adversary, he was hanged as a spy.

13 [26]. *Peace is the blessing that I seek* From Psalms 120.

15 [31]. *Brother Richard S. Hubbard* husband of Lucretia Griffin's sister Polly.

17 [37]. *Youngs Night Thoughts* Edward Young, L.D.D., *Night Thoughts on Life, Death and Immortality*. First published as *The Complaint, or Night Thoughts* (London: R. Dodsley, 1742). Owned by Griffin and frequently quoted by him; see Appendix B.

21 [47]. *John Westley' life* John Wesley (1703–1791), English founder of Methodism. Griffin probably read Thomas Coke and Henry Moore, *The Life of the Rev. John Wesley, A.M.: Including an Account of the Great Revival of Religion in Europe and America, of which he was the First and Chief Instrument* (Philadelphia: John Dickins, 1793). There were two books by Wesley in Griffin's library in 1839; see Appendix B.

1794

24 [57]. *stormy time in France* The Reign of Terror had begun in 1793, following the French Revolution.

25 [58]. *Esau*   In Genesis, the son of Isaac who sold his birthright to his brother Jacob.

28 [67]. *ague*   Usually refers to a fever with sweating and shivering, like malaria.

28 [68]. *"to err is human, to forgive is divine"*   Alexander Pope, *Essay on Criticism*, line 525; first published in 1711 and frequently quoted.

1795

30 [73]. *Palsy*   Various forms of paralysis.

1796

35 [85]. *Dorcas*   A common name for women's church societies, derived from the biblical dressmaker who clothed the poor (in Acts of the Apostles).

37 [89]. *Rollins Ancient History*   Charles Rollin. *The Ancient History of the Egyptians, Carthaginians, Assyrians, Babylonians, Medes and Persians, Grecians and Macedonians*, first published in 1730, in French; English translation published in London (A. Dodd, 1730); many republications.

38 [93]. *Rollins*   See note above, 37 [89].

40 [101]. *There Jonathan has his David met*   Griffin quotes this poem he wrote for Absalom Racket again, on the death of Silas Vail; see p. 108 [280].

And Watts   Dr. Isaac Watts (1674–1748), English writer of books of hymns and psalms, published an elegiac poem on the death of his friend Thomas Gunston in *Horae Lyricae II*, first published in London (John Laurence, 1706); (Boston: H. Ranlet, 1795).

41 [104]. *Doct. Isaac Watts*   See note above, 40 [101].

1797

44 [110]. *John Young*   Young, an English musician who shot Robert Berwick as he was being escorted to prison for debts on August 17, 1797: see Daniel Allen Hearn, *Legal Executions in New York State 1639-1963* (Jefferson, N.C.: McFarland & Co. Inc., 1997).

1798

44 [112]. *Caleb Dyer*   Dyer became a major landowner in Orient; see p. 178 [455].

48 [121]. *Blackrock*   Now part of Bridgeport, Connecticut.

1799

48 [122]. *Doc. Watts*   See above, note 40 [101].

50 [127]. *Yellow Fever*   The epidemic in New York City from 1791 to 1799.

1800

61 [155]. *Genl. Dering's*   General Sylvester Dering (1759–1820), of the powerful Sylvester family of Shelter Island. In 1799, he was instrumental in introducing Oysterponds' Abraham G.D. Tuthill, a young aspiring painter, to a group of influential men in New York City—including Alexander Hamilton and Aaron Burr—who sent Tuthill abroad to study with famous American painter Benjamin West. See Helen Zunser Wortis, "Abraham G. D.Tuthill of Oyster Ponds," in *A Woman Named Matilda and Other True Accounts of Old Shelter Island* (Shelter Island, NY: Shelter Island Historical Society, 1978). In 1803, Dering became a member of the New York State Assembly.

62 [159]. *Caleb Brewster*   Caleb Brewster of Setauket (1727-1827) was wounded in a naval battle off Huntington; he later led a successful attack on the British vessel *Fox* off Fairfield, Connecticut.

Revenue Cutter   A branch of the military, established by Treasury Secretary Alexander Hamilton to enforce maritime law. It later became part of the United States Coast Guard.

63 [160]. *John Sloss Hobart*   Hobart (1738–1805) served in the New York State Supreme Court from 1777 to 1797 and was appointed to the Federal bench by John Adams in 1798.

65 [167]. *Company training*   Local militias were meant to supplement the standing

army (as per the Second Amendment). The practice survived for a long time on the East End; see Vol. II, p. 270 [116].

68 [175]. *Bloomingdale* Generally the present Upper West Side of Manhattan.

69 [178]. *had been to Albany to vote* Votes for U. S. President were cast by state electors. Thomas Jefferson was elected President.

1804

74 [191]. *I had once before passed through the Island . . . on foot* Griffin's 1789 walk to New York is recorded in his published *Griffin's Journal*, (Orient, NY: 1857; facsimile edition Orient, NY: Oysterponds Historical Society, 1983), p. 74.

1809

77 [197]. *long embargo* An embargo of foreign goods, imposed by President Jefferson and Congress in 1807–09.

1811

78 [199]. *rainwater doctor* An educated physician and German immigrant who signed himself "Sylvan, enemy of human diseases." His practice was mainly herbal. He maintained a Brooklyn practice during the year of 1811 only, located in an office near Fulton and DeKalb. He then moved to Providence, Rhode Island. He died in 1814 or 1815. Henry R. Stiles, *History of the City of Brooklyn* (Brooklyn, N.Y.: Published by Subscription, 1869), Vol. I, p. 393 and Vol. II, pp. 165–6. It should be noted that doctors had few medical resources at their disposal.

1812

80 [205]. *War was declared* The War of 1812, which lasted until 1815.

Mr. Odell's Jonathan Odell's inn was located in present-day Irvington, named after Washington Irving; drawings and photos of the structure are available on the Library of Congress website, HABS (Historic American Buildings Survey).

81 [208]. *Townends iron works* Peter Townsend was proprietor of the Stirling Iron Works, the first steel producer in the New York colony and creator of the Hudson River Chain that was intended to protect West Point and the river from the British Navy during the Revolution.

Nail Factories called Piersons's The Piersons, who had a factory in New York and manufactured nails by hand, invented a technique for machine-manufacturing cut nails and built a factory on the Hudson at Ramapo, New Jersey. Edward Harold Mott, *Between the Ocean and the Lakes: the Story of Erie*, (New York: John S. Collins, 1899), p. 46.

81 [209]. *Major Andre* See note 11 [20].

81 [210]. *74's* Gunboats carrying seventy-four guns.

Commodores Hardy and Capel Sir Thomas Hardy, with Captain Thomas Capel, was in charge of the blockade of Long Island Sound. Hardy had been a close associate of Lord Nelson, who famously died in his arms at the battle of Trafalgar. He was a respected adversary who treated Long Island citizens well and was therefore able to purchase supplies from them. Rocellus Sheridan Guernsey, *New York City and Vicinity During the War of 1812-1815*, Vol. I (New York: Charles L. Woodward, 1889), p. 273, p. 291; Henry M. Brackenridge, *A History of the Late War between the United States and Great Britain* (Philadelphia: J. Kay, 1844).

Joshua Penny Penny was taken on suspicion that he was planning to torpedo British vessels. He was imprisoned on Hardy's flagship *Ramillies*. Guernsey, op. cit., pp. 283, 293.

novascotia privateers Private, armed vessels with governmental commissions to interfere with merchant shipping. See gov.ns.ca/nsarm/virtual/privateers; and Guernsey, op. cit., p. 78 ff.

1815

83 [215–16]. *a severe Easterly rainstorm . . . blew a hurricane* The Great September Gale of 1815 was one of five "major hurricanes" (Category 3 on the Saffir-Simpson Hurricane Scale) to strike New England since 1635, and it was the first hurricane to strike New England in 180 years. David Ludlum, *Early American Hurricanes 1492–1870*, (Boston: American Meteorological Society, 1963), p. 77.

1816

85 [218]. *European goods fell* A result of the reopening of trade following the end of the War of 1812.

1817

86 [220]. *Christians* The Christian movement of the first half of the nineteenth century was anti-denominational, professing "no creed but the Bible." Daniel Walker Howe, *What Hath God Wrought* (New York: Oxford University Press, 2007), p. 182.

1818

87 [223]. *"Blessed are the dead who die in the Lord"* Revelation 14:13.

1819

88 [227]. *The children of Jonadab* The biblical Jonadab, a nephew of David, admonished his children not to drink wine.

1820

89 [228]. *bunkers* Atlantic menhaden, a small oily-fleshed fish, were caught in seines and used as fertilizer; the seines were owned collectively by fishermen in shares. There is a vivid description of a haul in *The Autobiography of Nathaniel T. Hubbard* (New York: J. F. Trow, 1875), p. 23.

90 [230]. *DeWitt Clinton* DeWitt Clinton (1769–1828) became governor of New York on July 1, 1817, and was reelected in 1818, defeating the sitting U. S. Vice President Tompkins. Clinton served until 1823 and again from 1825 to 1828. The Erie Canal was built during his administration. Previously, from 1803 to 1815, Clinton had been mayor of New York City. In 1812, he had narrowly lost the race for U. S. president to James Madison.

96 [246]. *Battleship Franklin* Named for Benjamin Franklin.

96 [247]. *Andre* See note 11 [20].

98 [252]. *Washington Hall* Washington Hall was built in 1812 at 598 Broadway; a lively description of the hall and a dinner given there in 1813, by the New York State Society of Cincinnati, in honor of Captain James Lawrence of the *Hornet* and his crew, is in R.S. Guernsey, op. cit., p. 208, also p. 103 ff. for a Federalist/Democratic riot at the hall.

98 [253]. *Mr. Clausons spacious Mansion* Isaac Clason was a wealthy merchant. The site of his mansion is now in the Bronx, still known as Clason's Point. According to some reports, the house later became Clason's Point Inn and was razed in the 1930s.

102 [263]. *Lathams* Latham's inn was located at what is now Orient Point. Like Griffin's inn, it had access to a wharf. In 1834, it was enlarged and renamed Orient Point House; see Griffin's *Journal,* p. 34. It was later known as the Orient Point Inn and is reported to have had as guests Sarah Bernhardt, Walt Whitman, Grover Cleveland, and James Fenimore Cooper, who wrote *The Sea Lions* there.

1821

105 [270]. *Post Master* A coveted federal position. Appointments were made by the Postmaster General on the basis of a recommendation by the community or local congressman. Postal employees accounted for the largest percentage of the civilian federal workforce. Terry remained postmaster for 30 years; see Vol. II, p. 389 [410]. The mail stage originally stopped at Griffin's house.

105 [271]. *meeting house*   The Congregational church.

107 [276]. *old sugar house*   The Livingston Sugar House on Crown Street (now Liberty Street) was notorious for horrendous conditions and many deaths of the prisoners. It was razed in 1840. Edwin Burrows, *Forgotten Patriots: The Untold Story of American Prisoners During the Revolutionary War* (New York: Basic Books, 2008) p. 25.

108 [280]. *There Jonathan has his David found* and *Watts*   See note 40 [101].

109 [282]. *Postmaster*   See note 105 [270].

110 [286]. *Comodore Decatur*   Stephen Decatur. This incident probably took place in 1813, on the way to New London, where Decatur was trapped in the harbor by the British fleet.

111 [287]. *Hamans*   In the Book of Esther, Haman plotted to murder all the Jews in Persia; he was ultimately hung by King Ahasuerus.

112 [290]. *Ellection*   New York State elections were held in April until 1822.

113 [290 *bis*]. *GidionsIsland*   Now called Gid's Island, in Hallock's Bay in Orient.

115 [295]. *Revenue cutter*   See note 62 [159].

116 [299]. *"Lean not on Earth, 'twill pierce thee to the heart"*   Edward Young, op. cit., from "Narcissa" in "Night III."

118 [303]. *A Mrs. Green. . . . A connection of the patriot American General of that name*   Nathaniel Green (1742–1786), a Rhode Island native, was a major-general in the Continental army.

118 [304]. *Tayloress*   A seamstress. It was not uncommon for a seamstress to spend time with a family to make their clothes.

120 [307]. *George the 2nd*   King George II (1727–1760).

old French war   French and Indian War, 1754–1763.

120 [308]. *In 1814 we, jointly, . . . by the british off New London*   Thomas Capel, with Sir Thomas Hardy, was in charge of the British blockade of Long Island Sound. See note 81 [210].

1822

122 [312], marginalia. *great embarassments*   Refers to the necessity of Griffin's selling all his property to reimburse debtors, a situation described in Griffin's "Diary for Cleora." See Appendix A. This manuscript is in the archive of the Oysterponds Historical Society.

1825

125 [319]. *Temperance habits and principle*   Abstinence from alcohol. The movement was to become extremely strong in New York State and particularly in Orient.

1829

127 [322]. *a wharf at the landing at the foot of the lane*   The wharf was later bought by a consortium of farmers and is presently the site of the Orient Yacht Club; see Vol. II, p. 366 [356].

1832

129 [327]. *"An honest Man is the noblest work of God"*   Alexander Pope. See note 8 [14].

buriel ground of this place   Refers to the cemetery on the Main Road, east of the Civil War monument, where Griffin is also buried.

1834

133 [337]. *the campaign on Longisland*   The Battle of Long Island (in Brooklyn, August 27, 1776) was the first major battle of the Revolutionary War.

134 [337]. *famous Meeting House at Southold*   This would have been a Congregational church; the Congregational Society was incorporated in 1784. The church later became Presbyterian.

134 [339]. *Albany boards* Albany was a major center of lumber production. There was a huge increase in the commerce of boards as a result of the opening of the Erie Canal, see Joel Munsell, *Annals of Albany*, Vol. 10 (Albany, New York, 1859), p. 385.

135 [340–341]. *Celebrated and unfortunate Robert Emmet, and his Brother, Thomas Adis Emmet* Robert Emmet (1778–1803) was executed for leading an aborted rebellion against the British. His brother Thomas Addis Emmet, who emigrated to the United States, later became New York State Attorney General.

135 [341]. *"There is no discharge in that war" "No exemption from Death"* Ecclesiastes 8:8.

135 [342]. *wild Beasts* Traveling circuses with exotic animals began in the 1830s and were popular up and down the east coast.

Man who is to be hung Public hangings for murder were common until the 1830s; New York State stopped the practice in 1835.

136 [343]. *"bourne whence no traveler returns"* From Hamlet's soliloquy and frequently misquoted. The correct quotation is "the undiscovered country from whose bourne no traveler returns."

136 [344]. *"What I say unto one, I say unto all, Watch"* George Fox, *A Collection of Many Select and Christian Epistles* (New York: Isaac T. Hopper, 1831), Vol. I, p. 140. See also note 146 [366].

138 [347]. *Mr. Orange Webb, Inn Keeper* The inn at Sterling (Greenport) was later moved to the Main Road, and in the 1950s to Orient by George Latham, who bequeathed it to the Oysterponds Historical Society. It is known as Webb House.

1835

141 [354]. *Aul[d] Lang Syne* Loosely, olden days. The poem was written by Scottish poet Robert Burns in 1788.

1836

142 [357]. *a religious revival in our vilage* An evangelical revivalist surge around this time that later was called by historians "The Second Great Awakening." See Howe, op. cit., pp. 186–202.

measles . . . left her eyes very weak Clearly, measles was already recognized as infectious and was known to have very serious consequences, among them what is now known as conjunctivitis, which, if untreated, can lead to blindness.

143 [359]. *A Man . . . condemned to be hung* See above, note 135 [342].

Doctor Rush's essays Griffin is referring to Benjamin Rush (1745–1813), a signer (from Pennsylvania) of the Declaration of Independence, a physician and professor at the University of Pennsylvania, who advocated the abolition of both slavery and capital punishment; see Benjamin Rush, M.D., *Essays, Literary, Moral and Philosophical*, 2nd edition (Philadelphia: Thomas and William Bradford, 1806), p. 164 ff.

India rubber India rubber, still widely in use, is a latex from a species of *ficus* found in southeast Asia; its use for overshoes (rubbers), which Griffin's peddler was probably selling, began in the 1830s. It was also used for gloves and was the initial product of the Goodyear Company.

144 [361]. *first Methodist church* The church still stands at the corner of Village Lane and Orchard Street.

144 [362]. *"What a dream, is mortal life!"* Mrs. Rowe, Countess of Hertford, in *Elegant Epistles*, "Letter LXXX" (London: Charles Dilly, 1790), p. 595. See Appendix B.

145 [364]. *Tract- Dorcas- Benevolent- Washington- Fayett- Jackson* The American Tract Society, which still exists, was founded in 1825, in New York City, to publish and distribute evangelistic Christian literature and was involved in the temperance movement.

The Dorcas Society, founded in 1834 in Great Britain and essentially church-based, distributed clothing to the poor. The Benevolent Society was a social service society. Fayett: probably Lafayette, hero of the American Revolution. It and the Washington and Jackson Society were patriotic societies.

146 [366]. *"What I say unto one, I say unto all, Watch"* See note 136 [344].

"First cast out the Beam, out of thine own Eye . . . or Brothers Eye—" Matthew 7:5; quoted in John Wesley, *Sermons on Several Occasions*, Sermon XXX (Philadelphia: Henry Tuckniss, 1800); *Sermons* was in Griffin's library; see Appendix B.

149 [375]. *"that Gods tender mercies are over all his works"* Psalms 145:9.

150 [378]. *N. T. Hubbard* Nathaniel T. Hubbard (1789–1875) was born in Mattituck and moved with his family to Orange County and later to New York City, where he became a wealthy, influential merchant and a patron of the opera. His mother's sister was Griffin's wife, Lucretia. Hubbard was a lifelong friend of the Griffin family. He discusses Griffin's *Journal* in his own *Autobiography* (New York: J. F. Trow, 1875), p. 29.

1837

156 [393]. *invaluable friends* Southold legislators who had served in Albany.

157 [396]. *the Tunnel, at Harlem* This portion of the railroad tunnel from New York had just been completed. Through this tunnel ran a branch of the New York and Harlem railroad that opened in 1837; it is now part of the Metro-North Railroad, Harlem Line.

157 [397]. *residence of the once Governor Cadwalder Colden* Cadwallader Colden (1688–1776) was born in Ireland. He was acting governor of New York from 1760–61, 1763–65, 1769–70, and 1774–75. His estate was at Spring Hill, near Flushing, Queens.

159 [402]. *"There is no discharge in that war"* See note 135 [341].

159 [403]. *"Children and friends are blessings . . . makes them so—"* Isaac Watts, *The Psalms of David* (London: J. Clark, 1719), "Psalm 127"; often republished, as in *Psalms, Hymns, and Spiritual Songs* (Boston: Crocker and Brewster, 1834), p. 254.

160 [404]. *"To err is human, to forgive is divine"* See note 28 [68].

1838

161 [409]. *A revival of Religion* See note 142 [357].

162 [410]. *Scarlet Fever* A streptococcus infection, most likely to attack children.

163 [412]. *"You . . . know not what manner of spirit you are of—"* Luke 9:55; *"To obey is better than sacrifice—"* 1 Sam. 15:22.

164 [415]. *The Steamboat Clifton* Robert Fulton had built the first successful steamboat, the *Clermont*, in 1807.

1839

166 [420]. *Thompsons Long Island history* Benjamin F. Thompson's *History of Long Island* was published on January 1, 1839. The storm referred to by Thompson is dated 1837. Griffin was given the book by Thompson in September, 1841; see p. 220 [533] and Appendix B. In 1842, Thompson published a second edition in two volumes. In 1918, a third edition in three volumes was published posthumously and then reprinted in 1962.

168 [424]. *Thomas H. Genin Esq* Thomas H. Genin (1796–1868), lawyer and poet, was born near Aquebogue in Suffolk County, Long Island. He taught school in Orient for three months, where he began his lifelong friendship with Griffin. He went to New York (with a letter of introduction from Griffin to Elisha W. King), where he became close to DeWitt Clinton. He studied law and was admitted to the bar in 1816. A year later, he moved to St. Clairsville, Ohio, where he became a prominent abolitionist; see *Selections from the Writings of the late Thomas Hedges Genin* (New-York: Edwin O. Jenkins 1869), pp. 6 ff.

169 [427]. *celebrated Traveler, John Ledyard* Ledyard (1751–1789) was born in Groton, Connecticut, and was a Marine corporal on Captain Cook's third voyage in 1776. He published *A Journal of Captain Cook's Last Voyage to the Pacific Ocean* (Hartford: Nathaniel Patten, 1783).

170 [432]. *Temperence, has become considerable the order of the day* Temperance became a major movement and ultimately led to Prohibition. Griffin was obviously conflicted from the start about selling liquor (see pp. 77 [197] and 169 [429]). Rum was particularly prevalent locally, as it was a product of the Shelter Island Sylvesters' Caribbean plantations.

173 [439]. *first coal stove* The first practical coal stove was invented in 1833 by Jordan Mott; it introduced a significant transition from fireplace cooking to stove cooking.

173 [440]. *Many of our Banks . . . are now failing* A five-year depression began in 1837. Andrew Jackson, who was against paper money, refused to renew the charter of the Second Bank of the United States. See D. W. Howe, op. cit., pp. 390 ff.

Continental money The Continental government had printed millions of dollars worth of paper money, which became almost worthless after the Revolution, causing the soldiers who had been paid with it to sink into debt.

174 [442]. *Ellection* Democrat Martin Van Buren was defeated by the Whig candidate, William H. Harrison.

174 [443]. *Sweet refined light* "Refined light" usually refers to kerosene. Since kerosene was not commercially available until the 1850s, Griffin is probably referring to camphene.

Doctor Watts Isaac Watts (1674–1748), whose *Reliquiae Juvenilis* is listed by Griffin as being in his library in 1839; see Appendix B and above, notes 40 [101] and 159 [403].

177 [450]. *candidate for the Presidency* Harrison was the nominee and eventual winner.

1840

191 [486]. *Exhibition of shows* Probably a circus. See note 135 [342].

192 [488]. *Son of my Friend* Sylvester Genin (1822–1850), son of Thomas H. Genin (see note 168 [424]). A respected painter, Sylvester Genin was particularly influenced by a portrait of his father by Orient native Abraham G. D. Tuthill. See *Selections from the Works of the Late Sylvester Genin, Esq.* (New York: Maigne and Hall, 1855), pp. 17, 28 ff.

193 [491]. *For their portraits* In a letter to his father, dated Orient, August 26, 1840, Sylvester Genin wrote, "I have painted a miniature and two portraits in this place, and received forty-eight dollars." *Selections from the Works of the Late Sylvester Genin, Esq.,* op. cit., p. 31.

194 [493]. *company training* See note 65 [167].

197 [499]. *result of the Ellection* William Henry Harrison won.

1841

199 [506]. *Earthenware, of Austin Hempstead* Hempstead started his pottery in Greenport at Mill Creek around 1825. He shipped his wares to the West Indies, as well as providing utilitarian articles locally. The pottery closed in 1868. See W. P. Jervis, *A Pottery Primer* (New York: The O'Gorman Pub. Co., 1911), p. 170.

200 [507]. *load of Sauce* Probably preserved vegetables or fruit.

210 [530]. *Hayscales* These scales were capable of lifting and weighing a loaded wagon. A description of hayscales can be found in John J. Currier, *History of Newburyport, Mass., 1764-1905* (Newburyport: Currier, 1906), p. 78.

1842

220 [553]. *"And dust to dust, the mourner cries"* John Logan, "On the Death of a Young Lady"; in *Elegant Extracts,* Book VI, p. 241 (Boston: Wells and Lilly, 1826).

1843

225 [568]. *Congregational Church . . . more suitable to the present generation* "It appears that the money part of the members of the Church wished a handsomer and more stately place of worship." This explanation of why the church is being rebuilt is taken from a manuscript by Griffin, entitled *Journal Containing Sketches of the Griffin Family*," p.184. The manuscript is in the OHS archives.

229 [577]. *Thanksgiving, by proclamation of the Governor* From 1817, a Thanksgiving Day was designated annually by the governor of New York State. The national holiday on the fourth Thursday in November was established in 1863 by Abraham Lincoln.

Volume II

1844

237 [7] *Monday 1st January 1844* Although Griffin numbered this as page 7, it is in fact the first page of diary entries. It is preceded by a listing of the books he has read, which are presented here in Appendix B-II, and by a "Contents," an index of names in the diary that has been incorporated into the general index of this present edition.

237 [9]. *Slave* New York adopted gradual manumission of slaves in 1799, and passed a law freeing all slaves in the state in 1837. Slaves were occasionally able to purchase their freedom or were sometimes voluntarily freed by owners.

238 [12]. *revival, now at the Baptist Church* There was a rush to baptism in preparation for Judgment Day, predicted by Captain William Miller to take place between March 1843 and April 1844. The Millerites were part of a large mid-century millenarian movement anticipating the Second Coming. Griffin, raised in the Calvinist Congregational Church, is obviously skeptical. See also below, note 272 [121] *Millerites.*

238 [13]. *"Man to man is the sorest, surest Ill."* From "Narcissa" in "Night III"; Edward Young, L. D. D., *Night Thoughts on Life, Death and Immortality*. First published as *The Complaint, or Night Thoughts* (London: R. Dodsley, 1742). Quoted often by Griffin.

"Solomon's one amongst a thousand" Song of Sol. 5:10: "My beloved is white and ruddy, the chiefest among ten thousand." Widely interpreted as a reference to the messiah.

239 [14]. *Error, and fanaticism are assuredly abroad* Many new Christian denominations appeared during the mid-century evangelical revival. See above, Vol. II note 238 [12].

240 [17]. *"leave off contention before It is meddled with"* Proverbs 17:14, 20:3.9.

241 [22]. *The railroad* The original intention was to create a route from New York City to Boston via Greenport and by water over the Long Island Sound; within a few years, a continuous route by rail was developed along the Connecticut shore and the Long Island Railroad went temporarily bankrupt. Mildred H. Smith, *The Early History of the Long Island Rail Road, 1834–1900* (Uniondale, NY: Salisbury Printers, 1958).

243 [26]. *"Where the wicked cease from troubling . . . immortal rest"* John Wesley, *Sermons on Several Occasions*, Sermon XLI, 6. Vol. 3 (Philadelphia: Henry Tuckniss, 1800) was in Griffin's library. See Appendix B.

243 [27]. *Phrenology* Phrenology was a popular (and widely credited) pseudo-science that inferred personality and character traits from reading the bumps on the skull.

244 [29]. *Chancy W. Moore* Moore, Hutchinson and Moore was incorporated in New York in 1835; previously it was Hallock and Moore. Moore applied for bankruptcy in 1868.

245 [32]. *Yankee notions* A miscellany of small wood and metal domestic goods man-

ufactured in New England, such as toothpicks, pans, pins, buttonhooks, combs, and portable stoves; sold by traveling Yankee peddlers. George E. Walsh, "Millions in Yankee Notions," *The World To-Day,* Vol. XVI (Chicago: The World To-Day Co., 1909). Walsh discusses the eventual importance of such wares in European trade; the term is the origin of our "notions" department, now hard to find.

246 [34]. *Raymond*   Janus Raymond was the husband of Griffin's daughter Narcissa.

247 [39]. *The steam ship Princeton*   On February 28, the USS *Princeton,* carrying President John Tyler, his Cabinet, and about two hundred guests, was damaged by a gun that exploded when fired during a pleasure trip on the Potomac. (The dead included David Gardiner of New York, whose daughter later married the President.)

247 [40]. *"lean not on Earth . . . and hope expires"*   Edward Young, L.D.D., op. cit., "Night III."

248 [43]. *Ebenezer W. Case Esq.*   A New York State Assemblyman from Suffolk County, 1819–20.

249 [46]. *"Blessed are the peacemakers"*   Matthew 5:9.

250 [48]. *Marvin Holms*   See below, note 279 [146].

251 [50]. *Captain Wm. Wisdom*   Captain William A. Wisdom (1803–73) was an Irish-born blacksmith.

251 [51]. *Farm of my late soninlaw James H. Preston*   The Preston estate was auctioned on November 14, 1843; the underbidder was Captain Edwin Peter Brown of Orient. See letter, "Catherine Beers to Mrs. Jane Beers," in the OHS archive. The Beerses had hoped the railroad would go through the property, but it terminated in Greenport.

252 [54]. *Rufus Tuthill*   He was married to Griffin's sister Lucinda.

252 [55]. *"Dust to dust the mourner cries"*   From "On the Death of a Young Lady," by John Logan, in Vicesimus Knox, *Elegant Extracts: A Copious Selection of Instructive, Moral, and Entertaining Passages* (Boston: Wells and Lilly, 1826), p. 214.

> *Alas! The cheek where beauty glow'd;*
> *The heart where goodness overflow'd,*
> *A clod amid the valley lies,*
> *And "dust to dust" the mourner cries.*

253 [56]. *"months that are gone . . . Its own load"*   Isaac Watts, from "To Sarissa," in *Horae Lyricae* (London: N. Cliff, 1709). See Vol. I, note 40 [101].

253 [57]. *Dyer's Hotel*   Later known as Bay House, it still stands opposite the wharf. See illustration, p. 401.

Te[e]total system   Complete abstinence from alcohol.

256 [68]. *Addison's bridge of life*   Joseph Addison (1672–1719), "The First Vision of Mirza," Sept. 1, 1711, in *The Spectator,* No. 159 (London: Sam. Buckley, 1711–1714).

258 [73]. *"Wisdom is the principle thing"*   Proverbs 4:7.

Great riots   In May and July, 1844, Catholic and Protestant working classes confronted each other over jobs, following increased Catholic Irish, German, and French-Canadian immigration.

259 [74]. *Edwin Brown*   Brown's whaling logs are in the archives of OHS.

260 [77]. *Nathaniel T. Hubbard*   See Vol. I note 150 [378].

260 [79]. *Shenang*   The city of Shenyang, in northeast China.

263 [91]. *"Lean not on Earth . . . to thy heart"*   Edward Young, L.L.D., op. cit., from "Narcissa" in "Night III."

"All, all on Earth is shadow . . . bed of pain"   "All, all on Earth is shadow" is from John Milton's *Paradise Lost;* the full quotation is in Young, op. cit., "Night I."

264 [93]. *"When Tides . . . O, how dreadful 'tis to die"*   Joseph Addison, from "Rosamonde," in *The Miscellaneous Works of Joseph Addison,* Vol. II (London: J. and R. Tonson, 1765).

269 [111]. *Where adders hiss and poisonous serpents rool*   William Mason, adapted from "Sappho," in *The Works of William Mason, M.A.,* Vol. II (London: Cadell and W. Davies, 1811). The exact line is "Where adders hiss and scorpions sting."

270 [114]. *Potatoes appear to be diseased*   This fungus (*phytophthora infestans*) was soon carried across the Atlantic in trading ships and caused the disastrous Irish potato famine that began in 1845.

270 [116]. *General Training at Greenport*   Local militias were meant to supplement the standing army.

271 [118]. *"Man to Man is the sorest, surest ill"*   Edward Young, L.D.D., op. cit., from "Narcissa" in "Night III."

272 [121]. *Millerites*   An Adventist sect led by William Miller, who preached that the Second Coming of Christ would be sometime between March 1843, and April 1844, and then recalculated it as October 22, 1844. See also above, Vol. II note 238 [12].

corporal trim   A character in Laurence Sterne's *Life and Opinions of Tristram Shandy, Gentleman,* first published in London (Becket: Dehondt, 1760–67).

273 [125]. *pending Ellection of a President*   Democrat James Knox Polk defeated Henry Clay.

275 [132]. *"Days are swifter than a weavers shuttle"*   Job 6:6.

1845

279 [146]. *a house for Mr. Marvin Holms*   This house still stands, opposite the Orient Country Store. See illustration, p. 400.

281 [159]. *better road across the South dam pond beach*   A reference to the present causeway between Orient and East Marion. Flooding remains a problem today.

282 [160]. *Shunamite woman*   In 2 Kings; her son has died, but she has confidence that Elijah will restore him to life.

282 [161]. *Harrison*   He died of pneumonia forty days after the inauguration. His vice president, John Tyler, filled out the term. James Polk became President in 1845.

285 [171]. *"When all thy mercies . . . love and praise"*   From a poem by Joseph Addison, in *The Spectator,* No. 453, August 9, 1712; reprinted in *The Spectator: A New Edition Corrected from the Originals,* Vol. VIII (New York: E. Sargeant and M. and W. Ward, 1810).

287 [183]. *Miss Cynthia A. Tuthill*   The daughter of Griffin's sister Lucinda and Rufus Tuthill, she was one of three diminutive sisters (about four feet tall) who lived on Village Lane. She was a dressmaker. See illustration, p. 400.

290 [194]. *Sidney's house*   The house was just north of Griffin's property, one plot south of the present corner of Orchard Street and Village Lane.

291 [196]. *fires*   In the Pine Barrens, caused by sparks escaping from the wood and coal burning engines of the Long Island Railroad; a particular loss was the cord wood which made up the principal value of the woods. Nathaniel S. Prime, *A History of Long Island from its First Settlement by Europeans to the Year 1845* (New York: R. Carter, 1845), p. 60.

Locofocos   A play on words: it was a name given to a group of New York Democrats who supported Martin Van Buren in 1840 and was the name of an early striking match.

Mr. Marvin Holms   See Vol. II note 279 [146].

292 [201]. *pinchback*   Pinchbeck, a copper/zinc alloy simulating gold.

293 [207]. *watch coats*   A greatcoat or overcoat; the term comes from the coats issued to soldiers on patrol.

294 [209]. *Doctor William Dodd*   William Dodd (1729–1777) was a high-living English Anglican Doctor of Divinity, hanged for forging a bond in the name of Lord Chesterfield, one of his students.

Dodds thoughts in Prison   William Dodd's *Thoughts in Prison* was first published in London (Edward and Charles Dilly, 1777); reprinted in 1815 (London: T. Miller).

295 [211]. *"we take no note of time but by its loss"*   Edward Young, op. cit., "Night II."

296 [214]. *the distruction, by fires*   On May 28, 1845, Quebec lost almost 1700 buildings; another 1300 were lost in June. On April 10, half of Pittsburgh was destroyed; another fire followed in May. In Pittsburgh, a combination of open fires, overcrowding, coal soot, timber frame buildings, and strong winds contributed to the disaster. Volunteer fire-fighting was hampered by inadequate water and engines. Peter Charles Hoffer, *Seven Fires* (New York: Public Affairs, 2006).

297 [217]. *"Man to Man, is the sorest, surest Ill"*   See Vol. II note 238 [13].

298 [219]. *"Blessed are they that mourn . . . comforted"*   Matthew 5:4.

303 [234]. *Peconic House*   See Vol. II, p. 295 [210].

305 [239]. *Popes noblest works of god*   See Vol. I note 8 [14].

309 [248]. *Sterns Uncle Toby*   A character in Laurence Sterne's *Life and Opinions of Tristram Shandy,* see Vol. II note 272 [121].

309 [249]. *Sold my rotary Stove*   The Stanley rotary stove was invented in 1832. Its round top, which had five griddles, could be rotated to bring a griddle over the hottest part of the fire. Frederic Delos Barber, Merton Leonard Fuller, John Lossen Pricer, and Howard William Adams, *First Course in General Science* (New York: Henry Holt and Company, 1916) p. 147, Fig. 11.

312 [258]. *a nice little Church*   Now the Methodist church, on the Main Road in East Marion.

312 [259]. *General Ellection*   State elections. Democrat Silas Wright was elected Governor.
"How many sleep who kept the world awake!"   From John Milton's *Paradise Lost;* in Edward Young, op. cit., "Night IX."

313 [261]. *Nebucadnezer*   Nebuchadnezzar was the king of Babylon ca. 605–562 B.C.; he appears in the Book of Daniel.

317 [268]. *Zachariah, and Elizabeth*   The parents of St. John the Baptist.

318 [270]. *Benjamin F. Thompson Esq*   The author of *History of Long Island* (New York: E. French, 1839); in Griffin's library, see Appendix B. For Griffin's obituary of Thompson, see Griffin's *Journal,* op. cit., Appendix, p. 247.

1846

320 [275]. *the Publican*   In Luke, cited for humility.

321 [277]. *"What a dream is mortal life"*   Elizabeth Rowe, "Letter LXXX," *Elegant Epistles* (London: Charles Dilly, 1790), p. 595. See Appendix B.

Job says   See Vol. II note 275 [132].

324 [282]. *General Wo[o]ster*   American general quartered at Orient Point during the Revolutionary War; mentioned by Griffin in his *Journal,* op. cit., p. 68 ff.

327 [288]. *Chalker John*   He was a surveyor, hence the nickname.

330 [293]. *No licence ticket*   Temperance platform.

330 [294]. *War is now raging in Mexico*   President Polk had declared war against Mexico in May, principally in conflict over the annexation of Texas. The war was very unpopular in the North.

334 [301]. *a great fire in Nantucket*   Edouard A. Stackpole, "The Great fire of 1846," in *Proceedings of the Nantucket Historical Association* (1946).

339 [311]. *Steam ship . . . Great Britain* The *Great Britain*, designed by I. K. Brunel, was launched in Bristol by the Great Western Steamship Company in 1844. It was built of iron, with a length of 290 feet and weighing 1,930 tons.

340 [312]. *hard coal* The cast-iron coal stove became popular in the early 1840s, and wood stoves were gradually replaced.

340 [313]. *the Telegraph* Samuel Morse had first demonstrated his telegraph in 1838. In 1844, the first national line, between Washington and Baltimore, was completed; "What hath God wrought?" was sent in Morse code. The line was then extended to New York.

Doctor Young Edward Young, op. cit., "Night I."

343 [317]. *The Steam Ship Atlantic* Part of the Norwich and Worcester Railroad fleet, this ship made its first voyage in August 1846, and was meant to link New York with the Norwich and Boston rail service. Three months later, on November 25, it sailed out of New London into a strong northeaster, was disabled by a main steam pipe explosion, and broke up off Fisher's Island. David E. Philips, *Legendary Connecticut* (Willimantic, CT: Curbstone Press, 2001).

344 [318]. *"Dust Thou art, and into dust Thou must return"* Genesis 3:19; quoted by John Wesley, "Sermon LXII," *Sermons for Several Occasions*; see Vol. II note 243 [26].

348 [325]. *famine* The Irish potato famine; see Vol. II note 270 [114].

349 [326]. *A wharf meeting* The Wharf Company, founded June 13, 1848, still exists; the Orient Yacht Club occupies the wharf. See also Vol. II, p. 366 [356].

357 [340]. *Blackwells Island* Now called Roosevelt Island, in the East River, New York City.

358 [342]. *Coffer dam* Part of the Croton aqueduct, which brought the first clean public water to New York City; it was begun in 1837 and completed in 1842. It carried water forty-one miles from the Croton reservoir to reservoirs on the present sites of the Great Lawn in Central Park and the New York Public Library. It was in use until 1955.

359 [343]. *Trinity Church* Built in 1790, it still stands at Broadway and Wall Street.

359 [344]. *Edwin Brown . . . sailed on a whaleing voyge Yesterday—his wife goes with him* Martha Brown kept a diary of the voyage, which is in the OHS archive. See Anne MacKay, *She Went A-Whaling* (Orient, NY: Oysterponds Historical Society, 1994).

361 [348]. *Orient Meeting House* The Congregational Church.

"Mans life is a vapor" Frequently quoted; for example, Rev. Dr. Emerson, "A Call to the Christian Ministry," *The Journal of the American Education Society,* Nov. 1834, p. 164; in *The American Quarterly Register,* VII (Boston: Perkins, Marvin, 1835).

363 [350]. *ellection* Polk was elected President.

363 [351]. *"Shadows we are, and Shadows we persue"* Attributed to Edmund Burke (1729–1797) and widely quoted.

Temperence League The Washingtonian Temperance League was founded in 1840.

1848

366 [356–357]. *Wharf* See above, Vol. II note 349 [326].

372 [368]. *Daugertypes* Daguerrotypes were named for Louis Daguerre, who perfected this photographic process in 1839. Samuel F. B. Morse, who developed a camera for the technique, was instrumental in its rapid spread in the United States. It was mostly utilized by itinerant photographers for portraits.

374 [370]. *Williamsburgh N.Y.* Williamsburg was founded in 1800 and incorporated into the city of Brooklyn in 1852 and into greater New York City in 1898.

375 [373]. *Select Schoolhouse* The schoolhouse was moved to the site on Village Lane, where the Orient post office or the Orient Country Store now stand.

family Record Griffin would have been compiling Racket's genealogy.

1849

377 [376]. *Gold*   The "gold rush" began with the discovery of gold at Coloma, California, in 1848.

377 [377]. *"All, all on Earth Is Shadow"*   Edward Young, op. cit., "Night I."

"This is not the place of your rest"   Quoted, for example, in "A Practical Commentary on the First Epistle of St. Peter, Verse 11," in *The Whole Works of Robert Leighton D.D.* (London: James Duncan, 1825).

382 [386]. *The invaluable Wife of my Youth and old age, departed her Life*   There is an obituary of Lucretia Griffin by J. O. Terry in Griffin's *Journal*, op. cit., Appendix, p. 256.

384 [388]. *She was my guide . . . called to[o] soon*   Isaac Watts, *Reliquae Juvenalis* (London: James Brackstone, 1742); in Griffin's library. See Appendix B.

384 [392]. *Thompsons History of Longisland*   See Vol. II note 318 [270] and Appendix B.

384 [394]. *first white woman*   As opposed to Native Americans.

385 [399]. *the Navy yard, at Brooklin*   The Brooklyn Navy Yard was established by the federal government in 1801.

386 [401]. *dropsy consumption*   Edema; tuberculosis.

387 [403]. *publick fast*   Requested by President Zachary Taylor, to ask God for relief from the scourge of cholera.

390 [413]. *Greenwood Cemetery*   In Brooklyn, near Prospect Park. It was founded in 1838 as part of the rural cemetery movement. It became a popular tourist attraction, as it was attractively landscaped and the burial site of many prominent New Yorkers.

INDEX

Page numbers in *italics* refer to illustration captions. Page numbers followed by *n* refer to notes—both Griffin's marginalia and endnotes.

THE OYSTERPONDS HISTORICAL SOCIETY

THE OYSTERPONDS HISTORICAL SOCIETY is located in Orient, the eastern-most hamlet on the North Fork of Long Island. Until 1836, Orient and the neighboring community of East Marion were a single settlement called Oysterponds. The Society, formed in 1944 by these communities to preserve their shared history, reclaimed the earlier name. Since the Society's founding, residents have donated works of art, textiles, furniture, tools, diaries, letters, and other historic artifacts. In so doing, they have made a significant and continuing contribution to our understanding of the history of Long Island and our national heritage

Today the Society is responsible for the conservation and interpretation of this invaluable collection, and it continues to collect and record the ongoing life of the community. It offers school field trips, workshops, lectures, and exhibitions, as well as providing archival and museum resources to researchers.

On the OHS campus are seven historic structures, including the eighteenth-century Webb House museum; the Hallock Building archive and library; the Old Point School House, which features rotating exhibitions; and the Village House, originally the home of Augustus Griffin and the only preserved nineteenth-century boarding house on Long Island. The Society also maintains Poquatuck Park in Orient for the enjoyment of the public.

None of this would be possible without Oysterponds Historical Society members, whose dues make up a critical portion of the operating budget and whose contributions enable the Society to preserve and celebrate the history of Orient and East Marion for every generation.

For more information:
www.oysterpondshistoricalsociety.org
Oysterponds Historical Society
P.O. Box 70
Orient, New York 11957
631.323.2480

ABOUT THE EDITOR

FREDRICA WACHSBERGER, a native of New York City, taught art history at Brooklyn College for twenty-nine years. A specialist in Greek and Roman art, she participated in excavations in Greece, Italy, and Turkey. She purchased a home in Orient in 1979, retired there in 1994, and became interested in local history. She served as president of the Board of Trustees of the Oysterponds Historical Society and remains a trustee. As president, she oversaw the renovation of the Old Point School House, the Hallock Building, and the installation of the library and archive in the latter. She is presently engaged in the renovation of Village House and is assisting in the preparation of an installation for that building and an exhibition to open in June 2009, entitled "The World of Augustus Griffin." The installation and the exhibition are based on Griffin's diaries.